One Side by Himself

One Side by Himself

The Life and Times of Lewis Barney, 1808–1894

by

Ronald O. Barney

Utah State University Press
Logan, UT

Utah State University Press
Logan, Utah 84322-7800

Manufactured in the United States of America
Printed on acid-free paper

Library of Congress Cataloging-in-Publication Data

Barney, Ronald O., 1949–
One side by himself : the life and times of Lewis Barney, 1808–1894 / Ronald O. Barney.
p.cm. — (Western experience series)
Includes bibliographical references and index.
ISBN 0-87421-428-9 (cloth) — ISBN 0-87421-427-0 (pbk.)
1. Mormon pioneers—West (U.S.)—Biography. 2. Mormon pioneers—Utah—Biography. 3. Frontier and pioneer life—West (U.S.). 4. Frontier and pioneer life—Utah. 5. Mormon Church—History—19th century. 6. West (U.S.)—Biography. 7. Utah—Biography. I. Title. II. Series.
F593 B24 2001
978.02'092—dc21

2001005898

Contents

Illustrations

Photographs

Maps

Acknowledgments

I am grateful to the many who have make this project possible, both individuals and institutions. A number of Barney family members have been very helpful. In particular, I am grateful to Raymond G. Briscoe, who has supported my work on Lewis Barney since its inception nearly twenty-five years ago by providing documents, photographs, and encouragement. Other family members who have been gracious to my solicitations, generous with their materials, and encouraging in my work are the late Rhoda Black Erickson, Nolan Barney, Ruth Mae Barney Harris, Alex and Nellie Barney, Mattie Barney Cornaby, Kathy Erickson, Gwen Barney, and William Clifford (Cliff) Barney, president of the Barney Family Historical Association.

I am especially grateful to Charles S. Peterson, emeritus professor of history at Utah State University and former editor of the *Western Historical Quarterly*, who employed me and encouraged my study of Lewis Barney while I prepared my master's thesis many years ago. More recently he read and critiqued the manuscript of this book, steering me into broader interpretations of Barney and his life. Will Bagley, editor and historian of the West, has encouraged this project and has been very helpful in his careful review of the manuscript. His suggestions make the book much more readable and balanced, and his views of the Mormon experience in Utah and elsewhere have helped me consider a larger context for Barney's place in Mormonism and in the West. Professor Gene A. Sessions of Weber State University also read the manuscript and offered a number of helpful suggestions to strengthen the volume. The late Professor S. George Ellsworth of Utah State University championed my project in its infancy and undoubtedly served as the initial stimulus directing me to this point.

Many other individuals have been supportive of my work and provided me with historical documentation, ideas, and support that have helped me immeasurably. They include my colleagues in the Church Archives and Church History Library, who are generally underappreciated for their expertise and contribution to Mormon studies. In particular, Steven R. Sorensen, William W. Slaughter, Michael N. Landon, Ronald G. Watt, James L. Kimball, Scott R. Christensen, and Jeffery L. Anderson have been most helpful. I express appreciation also to friends and associates, some who have read portions of this book and others who have provided me with material and information which have contributed to it. They include Polly Aird, Lowell C. Bennion, Alfred Bush, Robert Carter, Ruth Dougherty, Bliss Hansen, William G. Hartley, Douglas C.

Hill, Richard N. Holzapfel, J. P. Hughes, Myrtle Hyde, Stanley B. Kimball, E. Leo Lyman, John A. Peterson, Larry C. Porter, Ronald E. Romig, Carmen Smith, and my mother-in-law, Audine Kennington Stafford.

I am also grateful to John R. Alley, executive editor, and the Utah State University Press staff for their assistance in the production of this volume.

The staffs of numerous repositories and institutions whose materials I have used have unfailingly been courteous and helpful to me. They include, in Utah, the Church Archives, Church History Library, and Family History Library in Salt Lake City; the Utah State Historical Society in Salt Lake City; the L. Tom Perry Special Collections at Brigham Young University and Utah County Recorder's Office in Provo; the Merrill Library Special Collections at Utah State University in Logan; and the Sevier County Recorder's Office in Richfield. Outside of Utah the institutions include the Special Collections at the University of Iowa in Iowa City, Iowa; the Henry County Recorder's Office and Mt. Pleasant Public Library in Mt. Pleasant, Iowa; the Church Archives of the Reorganized Church of Jesus Christ of Latter Day Saints (now titled the Community of Christ Archives) in Independence, Missouri; the Illinois State Historical Library, Illinois State Archives, and Springfield Public Library in Springfield, Illinois; the Primitive Baptist Library and Hancock County Recorder's Office in Carthage, Illinois; the Case Western Reserve Historical Society in Cleveland, Ohio; the Ohio Historical Society in Columbus, Ohio; the Fayette County Historical Society in Washington Court House, Ohio; the Knox County Historical Society in Mt. Vernon, Ohio; the Clarence Historical Society in Clarence, New York; the Newstead Historical Society in Akron, New York; the Erie County Historical Society and Erie and Buffalo Public Library in Buffalo, New York; the Kroch Library at Cornell University in Ithaca, New York; the New York State Archives in Albany, New York; the Firestone Library at Princeton University in Princeton, New Jersey; and the National Archives and Library of Congress in Washington, D.C.

Lastly, I am thankful to my immediate family for their patience, forbearance, encouragement, and support. My wife, Marilyn, endured countless nights over several years while I sequestered myself in front of our computer. Of course, there was a toll paid by my family for my distractions from other important family matters because of my preoccupation with my ancestor. My children, Joshua and his wife Colette, Alison and her husband Steve, and my son Christian, have also suffered from the project, though they have tolerated the absence of their father with good humor. My late father and mother, Vernon D. and Kathryn O. Barney, were very supportive in a number of ways during my initial work on the Barneys.

Notwithstanding the contribution to this work by others, the ultimate responsibility for the story rests upon me. This book is not an authorized publication of the Church of Jesus Christ of Latter-day Saints nor of its Family and Church History Department, where I am employed.

Introduction

A frontier preacher in 1831, writing from American civilization's fringe in western Missouri, described to an eastern religious superior a strange characteristic of some who settled in his vicinity, at society's edge. Rather than welcoming the development and civilizing effects of community-building, he said, "To live in the midst of a neighborhood thickly populated is to them very disagreeable." From their youth this type had become "accustomed to live one side by themselves."[1] The preacher, characterizing the hardy lot who shunned everything urban and wrested their livelihoods from pristine landscape, could have been describing the nineteenth-century family of Lewis Barney. Barney's grandfather and father—Luther and Charles—set the pattern in New England, New York, and Ohio, progressively moving westward in search of land compatible to their inclinations. And parroting his father's and grandfather's dispositions, Lewis Barney carried the trait through Illinois, Iowa, and then into the vast western interior. After nearly a half-century in the West, Barney could have claimed, before his death in southwestern Colorado, to have helped establish for settlement ten valleys in Utah, New Mexico, Arizona, and Colorado. Rarely content, generally on the move, or calculating their next option, he and his family shunned the trappings of genteel society for the back edge of progress which marked Lewis Barney's domestic practice throughout his life.

The Barneys' preference for civilization's perimeter does not indicate reclusive dispositions. Instead, this family lived in an age and in a land when boundaries were more abstract in both theory and reality than today. There was a significant draw to a segment of America's populace for this terrestrial territory and landscape of the mind—the frontier. Western historian Ray Allen Billington has stated that there has been in the American past "a geographic region adjacent to the unsettled portions of the continent in which a low man-land ratio" defines the region and the people who live there. Far from being a place of limitations, Billington continues, the frontier had instead "unusually abundant, unexploited, natural resources [providing] an exceptional opportunity for social and economic betterment" to those who followed its siren call.[2] And while there were many on the frontier who found "social and economic betterment" elusive, tens of thousands gambled with that hope. "Like locusts they swarmed, always to the west," summarized Walter Prescott Webb, "and only the Pacific Ocean stopped them."[3]

America's frontier phenomenon lasted from the first of the 1600s to the last of the 1800s, roughly three hundred years. A defining feature of the concept of frontier was the availability of easily acquired land. It was not a stagnant commodity to be surrounded and conquered. It was a moving frontier, elusive to all but those willing to keep pace with its retreat. For three centuries it backed away from being tamed and constricted. Its inherent characteristics of freedom and new life gave America a vibrant personality that had been unavailable in Europe for centuries.[4] Lewis Barney's life-span roughly covered the last third of this period which significantly influenced American culture. His own death in 1894, after a lifetime of chasing civilization's edge, was coincident to the subtle closure of the American frontier. This story is about a man and his family for whom "frontier" and its alluring garb of freedom and independence, despite ever-present hardship, characterized the course of their lives better than any other word with the exception of one.

That other word is "Mormon," an appellation applied to those who followed Joseph Smith and believed in his Book of Mormon (discussed later). With more than one-third of his life behind him, in 1840 Lewis Barney subscribed to an unpopular religious organization whose theological outline overlay his latent religious inclinations to a remarkable degree. For the rest of his life, he adhered—heart and soul—to the Church of Jesus Christ of Latter-day Saints (also referred to in this study as the Church of Jesus Christ), a faith born just seventy miles from where he first drew breath in the hinterlands of western New York. Being a Mormon or a Latter-day Saint (LDS), nicknames for adherents of the church, was no easy life. For the first generation of church members, regular relocation was a requisite for belief. Barney's propensity for westward movement dovetailed into what was required of him subsequent to his affiliation with the Saints. But once in the West, when settling down permanently was much more feasible, Barney ignored the option and melded his ambition to "establish Zion" with building his family kingdom on the American frontier.

Concurrent with Barney's personal and family ambitions, he and his kin found themselves in the swirl of events that shaped early Mormonism and the settlement of the Intermountain West. The establishment and flowering of Nauvoo, Illinois, its demise, the 1846 Iowa crucible, the ordeal and adventure of the Mormon Battalion, the 1847 vanguard to Utah, the California Gold Rush, and tenure in the Mormon settlements on the Missouri River were episodes in which the family was involved prior to their settlement in Utah. Once in the Great Basin they became settlers and community builders in Utah, Arizona, New Mexico, and Colorado. Beyond that they were eyewitnesses and participants in the Walker and Black Hawk Indian Wars, the Mormon Reformation, the Utah War, construction of the transcontinental railroad, the Mormon United Order, and federal efforts to break plural marriage among the Saints. The story of the Barneys on the frontier and within the social milieu of Mormonism portrayed here is at once unique and representative, a story that Barney, himself, once tried to publish.

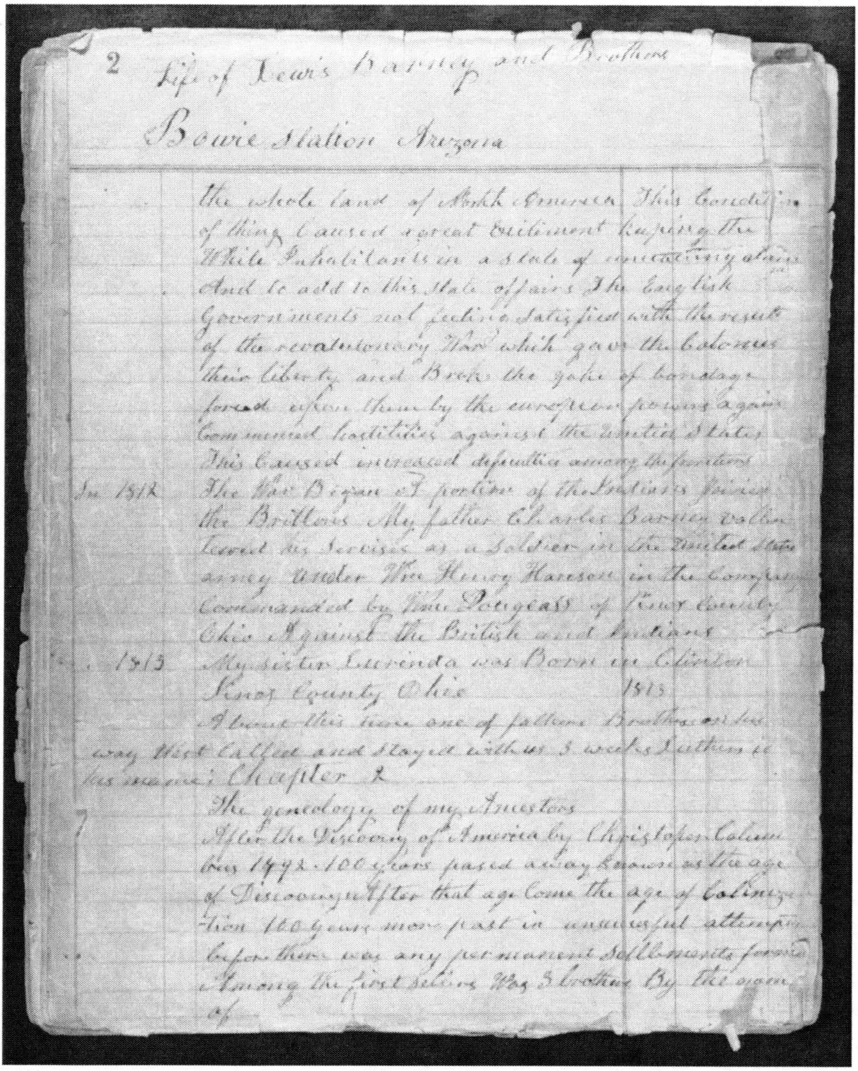

Lewis Barney, Reminiscence, ca. 1886 (Autobiography 2). Photograph by William W. Slaughter. Courtesy Church Archives, the Church of Jesus Christ of Latter-day Saints.

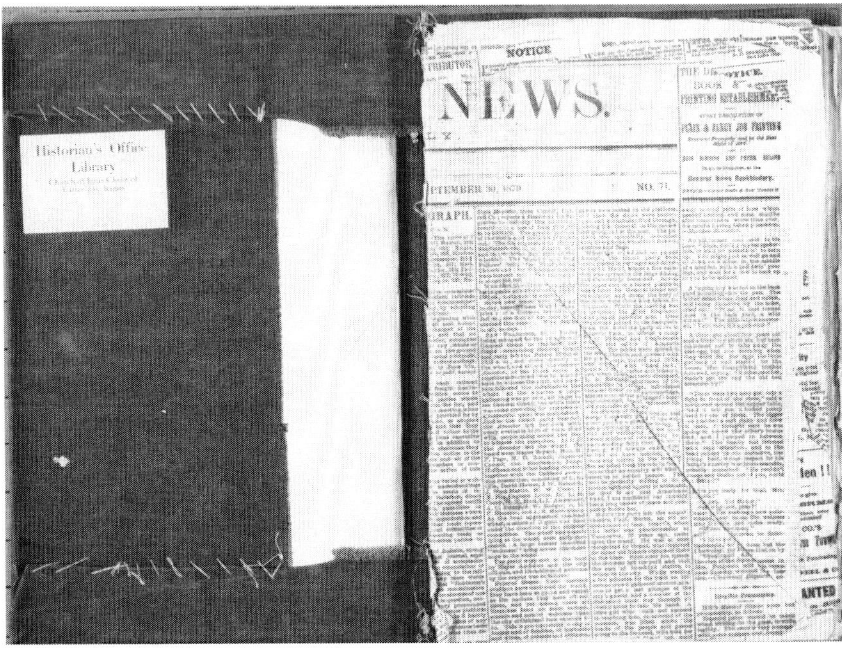

Lewis Barney, Reminiscence and Diary, 1878–1882 (Autobiography 1). Photograph by William W. Slaughter. Courtesy Church Archives, the Church of Jesus Christ of Latter-day Saints.

Lewis Barney's Life Writings

Some time in the late 1880s, Lewis Barney, nearly eighty years old, appealed to an editor, probably in Salt Lake City, stating, "I have wrote a journal of my life and things that I have done and observed since I have been a member of this Church of 300 pages which I never saw in public print which would be useful for the young and rising generation."[5] This story, of which only a forty-page fragment survives (known as Autobiography 2 in this book), was written while he lived in southern Arizona in 1886.[6] Had the account made it into print, the title of his book might have been one of those used later by Juanita Brooks for either Hosea Stout's edited diary, *On the Mormon Frontier*, or *On the Ragged Edge*, her biography of Dudley Leavitt.[7] For it was on the ragged edge of the Mormon frontier that Barney lived his simple but extraordinary life.

The success of a biographer in portraying a subject is often dependent on the quantity and quality of sources available which describe the object of his work. Public figures, the famous and infamous of history, tend to generate sources that are not only numerous but which also provide context and characterizations of the object of the biography. This is, of course, of great assistance to the biographer. While there are notable exceptions, lesser known

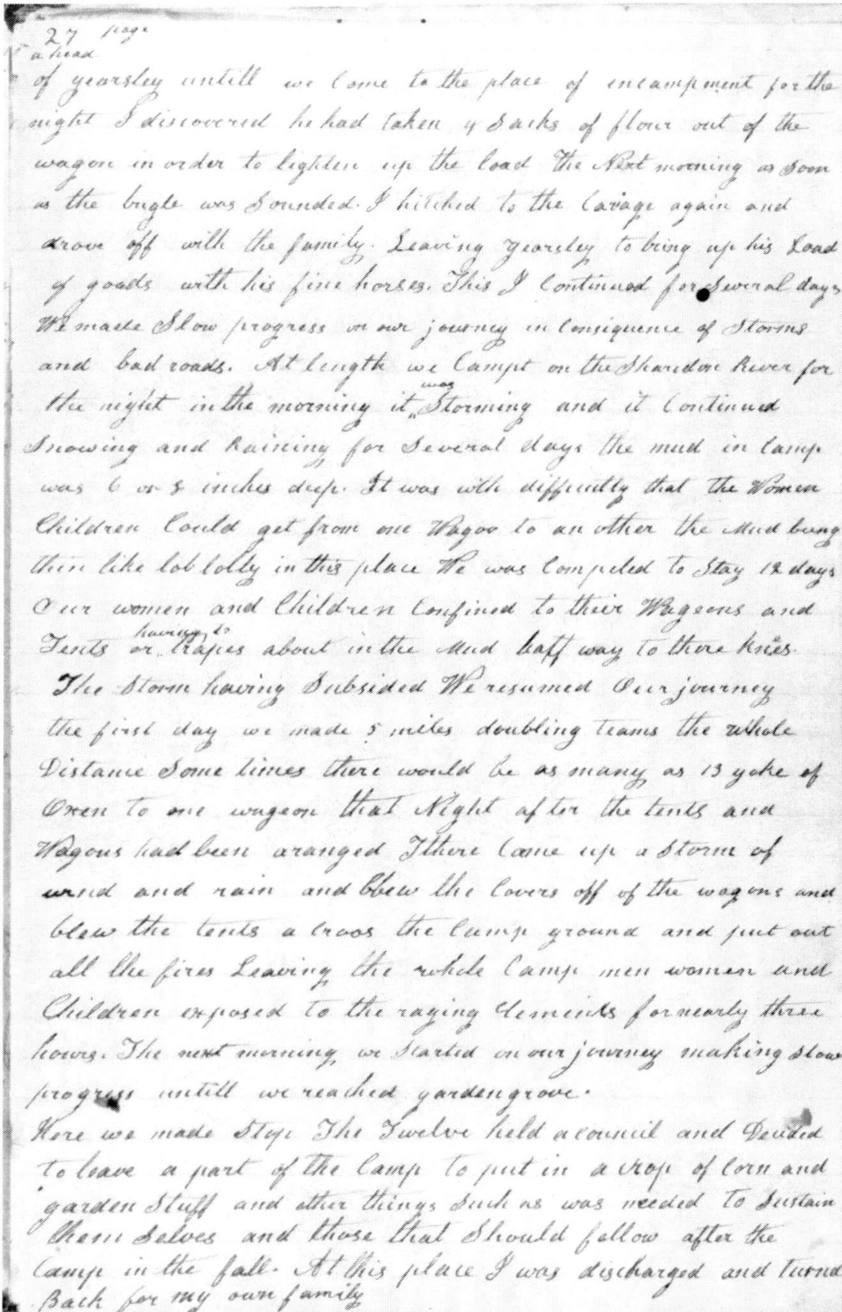

27 page

a head of yearsley untill we Come to the place of incampment for the night I discovered he had taken 4 Sacks of flour out of the wagon in order to lighten up the load The Next morning as Soon as the bugle was Sounded I hitched to the Cariage again and drove off with the family Leaving yearsley to bring up his Load of goods with his fine horses. This I Continued for Several days We made Slow progress on our journey in Consiquence of Storms and bad roads. At length we Campt on the Shardon River for the night in the morning it was Storming and it Continued Snowing and Raining for Several days the mud in Camp was 6 or 8 inches deep. It was with difficulty that the Women Children Could get from one Wagon to an other the Mud being then like lob lolly in this place We was Compeled to Stay 12 days Our women and Children Confined to their Wagons and Tents or having to traipes about in the Mud half way to there knees. The Storm having Subsided We resumed Our journey the first day we made 5 miles doubling teams the whole Distance Some times there would be as many as 13 yoke of Oxen to one wagon that Night after the tents and Wagons had been aranged There Came up a Storm of wind and rain and blew the Covers off of the wagons and blew the tents a croos the Camp ground and put out all the fires Leaving the whole Camp men women and Children exposed to the raging elements for nearly three hours. The next morning we Started on our journey making slow progress untill we reached gardengrove.

Here we made Stop The Twelve held a council and Decided to leave a part of the Camp to put in a crop of Corn and garden Stuff and other things Such as was needed to Sustain them Selves and those that Should fallow after the Camp in the fall. At this place I was discharged and turned Back for my own family

Lewis Barney, Reminiscence and Diary, 1878–1882 (Autobiography 1), 27. Photograph by William W. Slaughter. Courtesy Church Archives, the Church of Jesus Christ of Latter-day Saints.

figures usually generate sources proportional to the level of their invisibility and insignificance in their particular population. Individuals at Barney's level of the pecking order generally become imperceptible to subsequent generations, unless by some anomaly in the normal course of their obscurity their lives are sparked with a touch of immortality. (With the exception of his son Arthur, no one who knew him had interest enough to identify, describe, and characterize Barney or his life.) In his advanced years, Lewis, himself, determined to do something about his likely fate.

In 1878, eight years before beginning the three-hundred-page memoir, Lewis Barney sat down in his Monroe, Utah, home and penned the initial rehearsal of his life's story (known hereafter as Autobiography 1).[8] This volume contains autobiographical narrative, correspondence, a business ledger described in chapter 19, and other miscellaneous items. From 1886 to 1890 Barney also gathered his personal papers created during this time which include correspondence, reflective writings, and a diary account of his journey from southern Arizona to central Utah in 1886. In 1963 librarians at Brigham Young University made an edited 188-page typescript of Barney's narrative and correspondence described above (absent the forty pages of Autobiography 2). The final fourteen pages of the BYU typescript also contain Barney's account of his late 1883–early 1884 journey from Burrville, Utah, to Luna Valley, New Mexico. Regrettably, the whereabouts of the original document from which this latter account was made (known hereafter as the BYU Typescript) are not known to the author.

After settling in 1887 in Wellington, Utah, with his son Arthur Barney, whose own autobiography is a significant source for and is invaluable to this study, Lewis Barney, filled with nostalgia and family pride, initiated yet another account, this time of his father Charles's family.[9] Unfortunately not even the first page of the project was finished. Other life writings of Lewis Barney referred to in this biography include a lecture he wrote in 1888 espousing his belief in Mormonism and a letter he penned to a Washington, D.C., legal firm in 1893 seeking pension assistance for his military service to the United States and loss of property during Indian wars. Barney's writings about frontier life show a passion for living at civilization's edge throughout the four score and six years of his existence, particularly when he was elderly, that gives pause to subsequent generations preoccupied with leisure and pleasure.

There are three chief resources making this study of Barney's life possible. (1) Barney's autobiographical chronicle written in his last sixteen years described above is, of course, the principal source of this account. (2) The Church of Jesus Christ, of which he was a member for nearly two-thirds of his life, has conscientiously preserved its historical records—institutional and private—from its formation in 1830. These records, for the most part, are housed in the Church Archives in Salt Lake City. Other Utah institutions such as Brigham Young University, Utah State University, the University of Utah, and the Utah State Historical Society also maintain significant collections relating to Mormon and Utah history.[10] (3) The Church of Jesus Christ has also aggressively gathered domestic and international records—genealogical, civil, and religious—now housed in the largest genealogical library in the world, the Family History Library, in Salt Lake City, Utah. In the absence of these sources, Barney would be, like hundreds of thousands of his nineteenth-century American countrymen, ignored and largely forgotten.

The Barney Family

The Barneys, in the first decades of the 1800s, were like numerous other American families following the frontier's westward progress. The Barneys' world view transformed after becoming Latter-day Saints in 1840, but joining the Mormons did not alter their frontier lifestyle nor did it restructure their economic and social status. Before and after their Mormon affiliation, the Barneys struggled in the margins of financial solvency. This gnawing aggravation, along with their comfort with rural living, relegated the family to a particular status within Mormon culture. Leonard J. Arrington characterized Salt Lake City bishop and noted businessman Edwin D. Woolley as a "middle wagon" man in contrast to the "first wagon" stratum of Mormon society composed of the church hierarchy and other religious, political, and economic leaders. If Woolley was a "middle wagon" Saint, Lewis Barney was a "last wagon" man, one whom Arrington classified as "followers whose primary prerogative was to demonstrate faith in the policies of those at their head."[11] Most of this last class in rural Mormonism were of rudimentary means and humble circumstances. But juxtaposing his socio-religio-economic backwardness with those of the first wagon, Barney found satisfaction in his simplicity. His contentment was derived away from the motion and noise of centers and people of influence.

Historian Dale L. Morgan described Barney's kind as those who lived "rich and quiet lives outside the boiling currents of their times." And "who shall say," he queries, "whether the thousand existences in quiet do not more nearly express the shape of human experience than the fiercely spotlighted existence that survives as history?"[12] These "existences in quiet" make up a social history that historian James M. McPherson says "has vastly enriched our understanding of the past." McPherson continues, "It has given a voice to ordinary people, whose experiences are as much a part of history as the actions of presidents and generals."[13] Barney's penchant for writing provides an important view of the frontier subculture, both American and Mormon. Indeed, as historian Charles S. Peterson has stated, "Perhaps the restlessness of pioneering Mormons is nowhere better revealed than in the diaries and letters of the family of Lewis Barney." The Barneys were by no means the only Mormon family with a record of struggle and hope, but their perpetual frontier circumstances forced upon them a hardship many of their "last wagon" contemporaries refused to bear. The family's "longings focused upon the church," Peterson continues, "the father and his children anxiously [following] the advances of the frontier, crossing back and forth over most of the vast region lying between Mexico and Wyoming."[14] The Barney chronicle provides a window into the hopes and aspirations of many on society's fringe who struck out for satisfaction in the country's empty corners.

Another reason this story is important is that it comes from the voice of the under-represented, quiet majority of Mormonism. There is a propensity within LDS culture to accentuate examples of the "first wagon" stratum of Mormonism. While in no way does this elevated level within Mormon culture misrepresent an authentic segment of LDS society, the larger view of Mormon life may very well be found among the lesser known but significantly more numerous rank and file. Regrettably, the lives of these worker bees of the kingdom in the nineteenth century remain mostly unavailable to modern observers. Because Barney's common life was representative of the plain folk of Mormonism and because of abundant, though obscure, sources that corroborate and provide context to his witness, the telling of his story expands our understanding of an important segment of American and Mormon history.

I have concluded from my experience as a student of LDS history over many years that the essence and marrow of Mormonism is far better understood through the lives of its participants in the form of edited writings, autobiographies, or biographies than in the narrative generalizations we call history, as valuable as they may be. At a step farther, I also believe, as Cicely Veronica Wedgewood observed, that "the behaviour of men as individuals is more interesting . . . than their behaviour as groups or classes."[15] I am satisfied that through the careful examination of individual Latter-day Saints' lives, we will not only find greater insight into the religion itself but will also have revealed to us the realization that there is a much broader and more diversified assembly of adherents to Mormonism than homogeneous stereotypes. While it is true that "a single biography is more likely to mislead than a history of the period," it is equally true that "several biographies are often more deeply instructive than a single history."[16] This portrayal of Lewis Barney, while not a summary of Mormonism, is meant to serve as both a revelation of his life and as one view of the many required to understand the marrow of the faith.

Lewis Barney's Memoirs as History

As Barney's autobiographical account is the primary source for this summary of his life, the question of the reliability of his memoirs is relevant. Barney commenced his first personal sketch when he was sixty-nine years old. The second, and apparently more complete, account was finished when he was nearly eighty. How accurately did Barney tell his story? Was his memory faulty? Did his advanced age or other factors limit his ability to render a reliable account? Did he deliberately alter events found in his record? Recently Douglas L. Wilson, writing about reminiscences as sources for Abraham Lincoln's early years, wrote: "Reminiscent testimony is admittedly problematical. Not only is it often vague and ambiguous, it is notoriously subject to the aberrations of memory, the prejudices of the informant, the selective character of the reporting, and the subtle transformations that occur when a story is either resurrected from the depths of the past or recalled repeatedly over time."[17] Do these features of memory-as-history disqualify Lewis Barney's memoirs as an accurate review of his life or of the milieu in which he lived? Addressing the issue, Richard M. Ketchum argues, "Usually it is possible to corroborate the verisimilitude, if not all the particulars tossed up from a person's memory, by testing his or her account against those of other witnesses or reports in newspapers, magazines, journals, diaries, memoirs."[18] In the case of Barney's life writings, my methodology has been to do just that: substantiate and verify, to the extent possible, every event and circumstance he described. My conclusion overall, after an endeavor of authentication lasting over two decades, is that Barney is a remarkably reliable witness to the events he describes despite a number of minor difficulties with his narrative which will be noted in the story.

The Biography

Ronald W. Walker, himself a Mormon historian and biographer, in 1982 addressed the issue of writing Mormon biography. Questioning the ability of Mormons to responsibly tell the life stories of other Mormons, he warns that "biography is a demanding art form which rarely surrenders itself to excellence," with "religious biography only [increasing the] odds." Seduced by "hagiographic dangers," most accounts by Mormons suffer from the writers' "selectivity, arrangement, and use of emphasis" to aggrandize the subject, often with an underlying intent "to evangelize." "Fervid passions"—the writer's religious faith—"not only distort personality," he warns, "but often refocus a book into something which is no longer biography."[19]

Fortunately for any who contemplate the daunting task of writing Mormon biography, Walker does allow for acceptable life-writing about Mormon subjects. A volume which appropriately reveals the individual in context has to be written, he says, by someone who knows "their subject personally and intimately," a process available "only [by] interminable digging in the historical trenches." The successful biographer employs "back-breaking research with the impossible aim of comprehensiveness" crafted "without mealymouthing or dissimulation." Giving "the transcendent its proper due," that is, acknowledging a person's interaction with the Divine, the writer about Mormons must also "allow the biographical subject and his peers largely to speak for themselves" concerning their belief and faith. Lastly, the biographer must use "the tools of scholarship—investigation, [skilled writing] technique, and openness" to even hope for a semblance of biographical success.[20] It is a lofty expectation. While the reader will undoubtedly find this a sympathetic sketch of Barney and his religion, I have tried to avoid the pitfalls identified by Walker by providing the larger cultural context, not always favorable to Barney or his Mormon contemporaries.

The difficult task of capturing the essence of a man or woman's life through biography is daunting. But as the prologue to David Attenborough's film, *Gandhi*, states: "No man's life can be encompassed in one telling. There is no way to give each year its allotted weight to include each event, each person who helped to shape a lifetime. What can be done is to be faithful in spirit to the record and try to find one's way to the heart of the man." That has been my purpose.

The intent of this volume is not to retell the story of Mormonism or its major players. My purpose has been to simply provide a physical, social, and religious context to the environments in which Lewis Barney lived. The more visible characters from Mormon history are considered only as the course of their lives intersected Barney's. So it is with the primary events of the Mormon chronicle; only those in which Barney played a part are considered, though they are many. Barney's quiet, simple, labor-dominated, rustic life limited the number of his associates and neighbors. With family relationships primarily defining his universe, the circle of his influence was small. Nevertheless, his story is a remarkable one.

To represent contemporary geographical perspectives, I have used, primarily, period maps to illustrate the locales pertinent to Lewis Barney's life. Because the accuracy of the period maps is not reliable, locations and routes are approximate.

Because a preponderance of Lewis Barney's writing appears in the text, I have modernized and standardized his writing for ease in reading. Capitalization has been standardized and punctuation added.[21] Spelling has also been corrected except where a word, such as "throwed" instead of "threw" or "builded" instead of "built," portrays his manner of speech. Barney's wording and expressions have not been altered. I am familiar with the trend in historical writing and editing to prepare historical texts in facsimile transcription, supposedly to represent a more authentic past. I am not satisfied in every case that it does so. Indeed, in some instances it renders the historic figure obscure and more illusive to the reader because of the difficulty in deciphering and understanding the text. I decided to modernize excerpts from Barney's writing to make him more accessible. Paradoxically, I have reproduced in facsimile transcription quotations from the other figures that appear in the text to satisfy current historical methodology. Also, if a manuscript document has been published, I cite the published account for the reader's ease in accessing my sources. Because I have not changed wording or altered Barney's expressions other than as noted above, I do not believe I have violated Lewis Barney nor his intent.

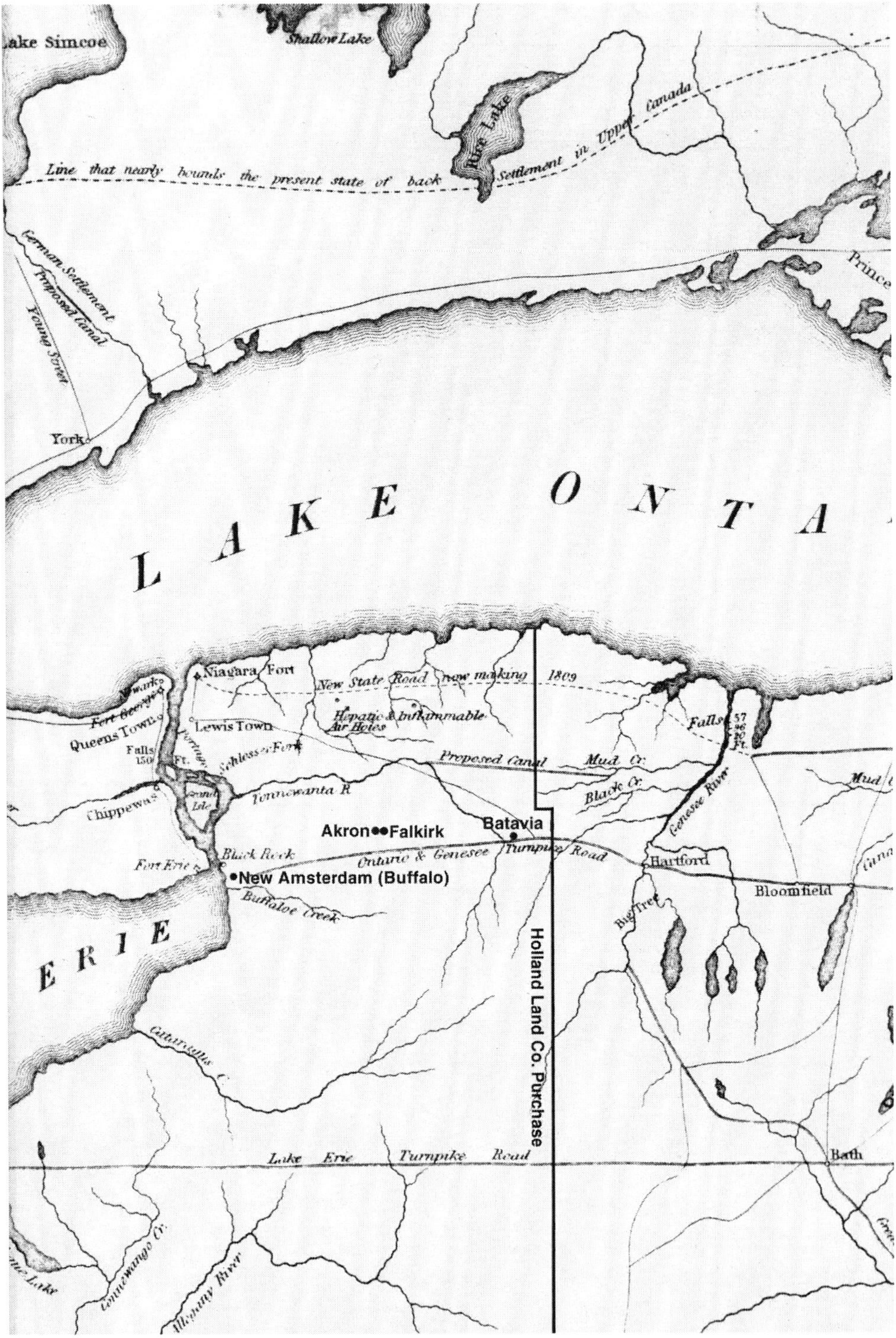

Western New York, 1809, showing Holland Land Purchase. From Thomas Cooper, "A Ride to Niagara," *The Portfolio* (July–October 1810).

Chapter 1

The Barneys on America's Frontier: The Holland Land Purchase, 1800–1811

Lewis Barney's family precedent in America first landed upon Massachusetts's shore about 1630. Jacob Barney, a British Puritan born at the seventeenth century's beginning, arrived in the Massachusetts Bay Colony at its inception, becoming a visible figure in Salem before his death in 1673. From Jacob and his wife Anne descended the bulk of Barney family strains in the New World. Lewis, among the family's eighth American generation, was preceded by New England roots nearly two hundred years deep. For several generations family numbers swelled in Salem, Taunton, Swansea, and other eastern Massachusetts villages before the opportunistic beckon of untouched lands lured family members westward. A noted Puritan clergyman, the Reverend Samuel Danforth Senior, Lewis's fourth great-grandfather, in 1670 characterized the Puritan venture in the Western Hemisphere as an "errand into the wilderness."[1] The phrase embodied to America's first generations both a religious and geographical context. While the religion and geography changed, it was a phrase that applied to Lewis Barney's nineteenth-century errand.

Little had changed in lifestyle for those inhabiting America's frontier at the nineteenth century's dawn from those first venturing onto New World soil nearly two hundred years before. While a change of the country's sovereign power the previous generation altered the political arrangement, wresting a family's livelihood from the hinterlands remained as difficult as ever. Rudimentary technological advances at the time had little effect upon most whose surroundings were rustic, but they did not feel deprived of urban settings. Provincial agrarians were there by choice. The parents of Lewis Barney, numbered with the few on New York's western frontier at the turn of the century, were among those content to live primitively as they labored to establish family farms from the virgin land.

Charles Barney, father of Lewis Barney, a sixteen-year-old six-footer of "fair complexion, dark hair, [and] dark blue eyes" in January 1799 witnessed the passing of his mother incident to the birth of his youngest brother, Abigail (known as Nabby) Barney's tenth child.[2] By the time of his mother's death, which had a devastating impact on the young man, Charles had some notion of his future. Born in the southwestern corner of Vermont in Sandgate, the son of Revolutionary War veteran Luther Barney, Charles had known nothing but frontier life since his birth on 23 March 1783, three weeks before Congress declared the end of the war with Great Britain. Four years later Luther Barney moved his growing family 180 miles southwest to New York's southern tier to the village of Chenango Point, later named Binghamton, in Broome County. There, at the starkly beautiful confluence of the Susquehanna and Chenango Rivers, they stayed another four or five years before in 1792 relocating sixty miles northwest to the young hamlet of Genoa, Cayuga County. A rival to the beauty of Chenango Point, Genoa was part of the famed Genesee country in the Fingerlake region of western New York.[3] The death of his mother after seven years in Genoa hastened Charles Barney's maturation and perhaps his departure from the family hearth.

In 1793, the year after Luther Barney settled in Genoa, Dutch bankers and businessmen purchased from American land speculators over three million acres of western New York wilderness. This small group of wealthy Dutch entrepreneurs temporarily reasserted Dutch influence in North America after having lost their discovery claims the previous century. They capitalized on America's passion to fill western New York's empty spaces, once the domain of the Seneca tribe of the Iroquois Indians. The huge tract, bounded on the north and west by the Great Lakes—Ontario and Erie—and Pennsylvania and the Genesee River on the south and east, was known thereafter as the Holland Land Purchase.[4]

Charles Barney and Mercy Yeoman: New Life on the Holland Purchase

Handbills describing the western New York land opportunity circulated throughout the Atlantic states as well as having wide distribution in England and Holland. Word also spread about the region from war veterans who had tramped the area. Described as being "more eligible, desirous, and advantageous for settlers than any other unsettled tract of inland country of equal magnitude in the United States," the "Holland Land Company Geneseo Lands" promised "black and white oak, hickory, poplar, chestnut, wild cherry, butternut, and dogwood" flora while being "finely watered . . . with never-failing springs and streams, affording sufficiency of water for grist-mills and other waterworks."[5] From every quarter it was considered a beautiful and alluring territory which settlers began to purchase in 1800. Charles Barney, twenty years old in 1803, found the Dutch land promising. Ready to leave the orbit of his father's influence, he located property in what was then a part of Genesee County, New York, and stepped for the first time over that line that finally separates sons from fathers.[6] His brothers Philemon and Joseph, of the same disposition, joined in the move.[7] Most of those attracted to the mammoth tract were from New England, Pennsylvania, Vermont, and central New York state, and the brothers fit within the profile along with others who were discontented, hopeful, and adventurous.[8]

In concert with his move to the Holland Purchase, Charles married. It is likely that Charles Barney previously met Mercy Yeoman, his future wife, at a time when their families were in proximity to each other in Cayuga County. The Yeomans lived near Genoa in the first decade of the nineteenth century.[9] Previously the Yeomans resided in the extreme eastern sector of New York in New Cornwall, Orange County, where Mercy was born in October 1785. Cornwall, the name by which the town was known after 1797, is a picturesque area located on the Hudson River seven miles upstream from West Point—the location of the United States Military Academy. The 1790 federal census shows Mercy's father Stephen, a Revolutionary War veteran captured and tortured by the British during the war, living in New Cornwall Township, Orange County, New York, with his family of eight.[10] Sometime near the turn of the new century, the Yeomans apparently cast their lot for Genesee country where circumstances brought Charles and Mercy together. About 1803 Gilbert Yeoman, either a brother or uncle of Mercy's, moved farther west and purchased property in Newstead Township, New York, the same time that Charles left Genoa for the Holland Purchase.[11] This was the time that Charles left Luther's household in Genoa to establish his own life. Thus, it may be that Charles and Mercy were already a family and the move to the Holland Purchase was an extended family enterprise, though some family genealogical information approximates the date of their marriage at 1805.[12]

There was very little settlement in Genesee County prior to Charles Barney's interest in the area. The vast county held but a dozen families in 1800 and only forty parties purchased land the following year.[13] In the township where Barney's family eventually settled, four purchased property in 1802 and five more in both 1803 and 1804.[14] It is not clear exactly when—perhaps 1803 or 1804—or how Charles Barney obtained his Holland Purchase lot. Land in that part of the purchase was selling for $2.75 per acre, though a cash purchase reduced the price.[15] While it is true that land payment could be delayed for as many as ten years, Barney was likely bereft of means to purchase anything of consequence at the time.[16] Three-fourths of the land applicants were in the same situation. Some even importuned the land agent to accept sweat equity for their land.[17] For the most part, these people "were as poor a class of men, generally, as ever became founders of new settlements . . . whose last dollar was spent when they had arrived at their locations in the forest."[18] Still, there were also lower middle class farmers, semi-skilled artisans, and a few skilled professionals and craftsmen.[19] Despite Barney's lack of capital to make advance purchase, he is later identified as having land in Township 12, Range 5, in what was called Newstead Township. His property adjoined that of Gilbert Yeoman.[20] It is likely the case that Barney was one of those who made a small

"It Is Winter." Drawing by Ebenezer Mix. From Orsamus Turner, *Pioneer History of the Holland Purchase of Western New York* (Buffalo: Jewett, Thomas & Co., 1849).

advance payment with the hope of obtaining future title to the land.[21] It was the expectation of the land officers that new settlers build a cabin and improve four acres of land during the first year. We are left to assume that this was true of Barney's occupation of what his son Lewis would call his father's "farm."[22]

The chief surveyor and later agent for the Dutch employed a crew in 1798 to improve the Seneca trail-turned-road that crossed the Holland Purchase. This improved road coursed through most of western New York including Batavia, headquarters of the land office, and ended in Buffalo on Lake Erie. The road, known thereafter as the Buffalo Road and today as state road 5, became the most important route of transit in the region, central to both settlement and economic development.[23] Land adjacent to the Buffalo Road became prime land for purchase and within a decade had increased in price a dollar per acre.[24] The road became an important military route during the War of 1812 with soldiers, supplies, and prisoners of war traversing the thoroughfare along with the populace of the area.[25] Charles's father Luther followed him a decade later and purchased nearly three hundred acres in two parcels on Buffalo Road in Newstead Township. There he lived for eighteen years and became the township's first postmaster in 1823.[26]

When the Barneys moved to the Holland Purchase, the most western extension of New York was virtually vacant of white habitation. "The country is entirely destitute [of] population," wrote a frontier preacher in 1803 to his superiors.[27] Only two settlements of any substance were located in western New York at the time; Buffalo, founded in 1801, and Batavia, established the following year.[28] Slowly a few villages sprouted in the region, including Akron, located just north of the Buffalo Road in Newstead Township. For many years prior to the arrival of white men, the area around the village, located twenty-four miles east of Buffalo, was a favorite locale for the Seneca Indians and was known as De'-on-gote, the place of hearing.[29] Just a mile east of Akron lay a hamlet known as Falkirk. It was in Falkirk where Charles and Mercy Barney cleared and grubbed the land in "heavy timber" that would become their farm, though they apparently also had a home along the Buffalo Road.[30] In the middle of the woods, Charles Barney worked out the beginnings of his family circle.

Establishing a farm from the raw land was a significant enterprise for a young man. Even if the farmer-to-be was a skilled woodsman, seven to ten days were required to clear an acre of land. To clear, grub, and then plant three or four acres of land in the first year was as much as could be expected. Preparing ten acres would have been a great accomplishment. Constructing a dwelling, outbuildings, a fence, as well as sustaining life by providing food, required a family's full attention. Hence, "it took a lifetime to bring a farm of any size under cultivation."[31] The difficulties of establishing farmsteads, however, were often assuaged by assistance from neighbors. Elijah Knight, one of Barney's neighbors after 1807, wrote that once the logs for his 18' by 22' log home were cut, "the third day the neighbors all along the road to Clarence Hollow turned out readily to raise the house. They made a good shingle roof and pine floor, cut out a door, made a rough pine door. . . . It was ready for the occupants in about two weeks after it was fairly begun."[32] Charles Barney, who probably had a similar dwelling, undoubtedly was one of those who helped the Knights construct their home.

The habitation of the area by the Seneca Indians for scores of years had modified the landscape some. Parcels of virgin forests were cleared for their villages and cornfields. When Holland Purchase surveyors charted the land at the end of the century they found a treeless prairie adjacent to the old Seneca trail and in other parts of the southern sector of the Newstead township.[33] This open space was attractive for white settlement. Newstead settled slowly while the simple trappings of civilization and society were employed by its inhabitants as the population nudged upward. The first improvement was a tavern, often the precursor to all community growth on the frontier, built along Buffalo Road in 1802. (Taverns were combinations of restaurant, hotel, and social centers during the eighteenth and nineteenth centuries.) A store was also built on the Buffalo Road in 1806–1807. The next feature of society was often a church or school, both of which were organized in Newstead in 1807.[34]

The Barneys, already acquainted with religiosity,[35] rather than being preoccupied with spiritual connections, likely concentrated on building a farmstead for themselves. Sufficient numbers of their countrymen followed a pattern so similar that together they created something of a subculture of their own. Defined as being "accustomed to hardships, hard work and dangers" and bereft of any of civilized society's advances, they suffered with "no conveniences of any kind and the bare necessities of shelter, food and clothing." They were "a sturdy lot . . . and not easily discouraged."[36] While it is a generalization, some not being so hardy or so enduring, it appropriately fit enough of the settlers that their frontier persona was considered a lifestyle in the mix of American life. To the Barneys, as will be shown, it applied.

The Birth of Lewis Barney

Two or three years after grubbing and clearing a farm on the New York frontier and the year following their marriage, Charles and Mercy brought their first child into the world. Named after Charles's father, Luther Barney was born in obscurity in Newstead Township, New York.[37] Exactly two years later to the day, 8 September 1808, their second son, Lewis, was born in the same place. The second child's birth came at the beginning of the second generation of post-Revolutionary America. The fourth president of the United States, James Madison, was elected just two months after the baby's birth. Since the Revolution four more states—Vermont, Kentucky, Tennessee, and Ohio—had joined the coastal thirteen. The remainder of the expanse acquired by the Treaty of Paris in 1783, stretching U.S. territory to the Mississippi River, created a diverse land, one formidable to govern. The republic had survived infancy and was now into a precarious adolescence whose outcome—viability or collapse—would not be determined for nearly another decade. Just two years before Lewis Barney's birth Lewis and Clark returned from their epic two-year exploration of the upper reaches of the Louisiana Purchase. President Thomas Jefferson's 1803 bargain with France nearly doubled the sovereign lands of America. The United States in 1808 was, therefore, primarily a vast wilderness pregnant with opportunity but blurred by the uncertainty of its barely calculable perimeters.

At the time of Lewis Barney's birth 95 percent of Americans lived rurally. His grandfathers insured his frontier inheritance by moving the previous generation from the coastal interior past the Alleghenies into regions scarcely settled. The impulse to advance to the cadence of individual prerogative was strong for many of their enterprising countrymen. The frontier culture, born of liberty, land, and labor, despite inherent risk, was infectious. This culture was bred into the young boy from his infancy as surely as if it was biogenetic. There are notable exceptions of others who, like Lewis, were born into unpromising frontier circumstances, but who were drawn away from countrified simplicity to sophisticated urbanism.[38] The Barneys were not only content with living on America's fringe, it is evident that they intended to maintain the arrangement.

While there is no specific information from the Barneys about the nature of their lives in western New York, it is not difficult to ascertain generalities of their existence shared by most of the others who bought land from the Dutch.

Farmsteads were family operations. While the family structure was patriarchal in nature, every person irrespective of gender played important roles in the success of the agricultural enterprise. Animals (cattle, sheep, and hogs), crops (primarily corn), and the production of potash for making soap were the economic lifeblood for most Holland Purchase settlers. After the initial clearing and grubbing of the land the remainder of a family's time in the routine year-long enterprise was associated with planting, cultivating, and harvesting their crops, raising livestock, and making potash.[39] Depending on the size of the family and the farm, several years may have been required to make a farm viable. Concurrent with the essentials was the regular maintenance and repair of their farm. Frontier life was a culture of work, but for children growing up in the backwoods there was a romance to the experience. Levi Jackman, who moved as an eleven-year-old boy to the Holland Purchase in 1810, later reflected,

> Those days of my youth were among the happiest of my life, spent in helping to clear off the dense forest of trees, clothed in their mantle of green leaves and foliage, the ground covered with a profusion of flowers of every description, color and hue, crystal streams wending their way to the larger streams lower down in the valleys, the denizens of the forest—the bear, the deer, wolves, and other animal life—roamed at will around our humble home unsuspecting of danger. Those days were moments of supreme joy and contentment covering my boyhood days.[40]

At the end of the nineteenth century's first decade, immigrants to the Holland Purchase swelled the population of the land tract to about sixteen thousand as "homeseekers came crowding in." In another ten years the number soared to sixty thousand.[41] The land office in Batavia in March 1811 was "thronged each day and week from morning till night with land purchasers, land jobbers, and land speculators." In that month the land agent reported as many sales as in all of 1808.[42] "Congestion" became particularly acute for the frontier folk along the Buffalo Road. One local on an 1811 journey from Buffalo to Batavia complained that "the houses were so thick along the road" that he "was seldom out of sight of one."[43] Another said in 1812 that "aside from the villages, there were more framed tenements upon this road, than upon all the rest of the Purchase."[44] Increasing numbers of new faces and families and the concomitant change of landscape undoubtedly caused the Barneys to rethink their Newstead location. More people meant more stress on an already strained agrarian economy.

Despite the region's lush beauty, fertility varied according to the configuration of the terrain, contrary to advertisements luring people to the area. Parcels of land in proximity to rivers and streams were among the only that proved productive.[45] For anyone interested in something more than subsistence farming, the markets for produce were limited. New York congressman Peter B. Porter reported to his colleagues in 1810 that "the great evil . . . under which the inhabitants of the Western [New York] country labor, arises from the want of a market . . . [which] is already beginning to produce the most disastrous effects not only on the industry but upon the morals of the inhabitants." "The fertility of their lands," he explained, was so poor "that one half of their time is spent in labor . . . for their own consumption, and there is nothing to incite them to produce more. They are, therefore, naturally led to spend the other part of their time in idleness and dissipation."[46] And there was also the factor of New York's taxation upon Holland Purchase residents that proved to be an onerous burden on many already struggling to make their farmsteads productive.[47] Exactly how this slumping economy and rate of taxation affected Charles and Mercy's thinking is not known, but the threat of insolvency likely provoked them to reconsider their future in western New York. After half a dozen years Charles had been unable to secure their land and the outlook looked bleak.

Probably not long after the birth of their third son, Lucien, on 11 October 1811, Charles and Mercy Barney gathered up their three small boys and household essentials and relocated southwest in Ohio, farther into the interior.[48] A pattern for the Barneys was being formed. With seeming unfettered territorial limitations in a land whose western boundary was so far distant it was mythical, the risks of moving westward were far outweighed by opportunity. Labor, backbreaking labor, was the primary requirement. Lewis Barney later wrote that their western New York situation "offered strong inducements to push ahead into the unsettled and unexplored wilderness toward the West."[49] Ohio was worth whatever inconvenience and difficulty was necessary.

Chapter 2

The Silhouette of Ohio: Barneys in America's Interior, 1811–1826

Lewis Barney was but three years old when in late 1811 or early 1812 "his father moved to Ohio on the waters of Owl Creek in Knox County in a little town by [the] name of Clinton near Mount Vernon."[1] The environment of youthful Knox County was visually beautiful. The rich, unadulterated stream-fed bottomlands in the county were accented by lush hills in the north and east.[2] To even the casual observer, the area held great promise. Ohio's attractions for settlement had been noised about the nation for years. The Treaty of Paris (1783), ending the Revolutionary War, opened a vast interior region immediately doubling the size of the newly hatched sovereignty. The western boundary of the United States once defined by the Appalachians now extended west to the Mississippi River, bisecting the North American continent. The territory gained in 1783 altered not only the borders of the United States but also the thinking of many of its citizens. Dreams drifted westward. The land acquisition known as the Northwest Territory wrested political claims of the region from England, but those who really controlled the area took counsel from no capital in Europe or America.

For generations the Delaware, Huron, Miami, Shawnee, and Wyandot Indians possessed the region north of the Ohio River. The Treaty of Paris failed to transfer the Native Americans' allegiance to the new owners. Several Ohio River Valley tribes had allied with the British against the colonial rebellion, the colonialists presenting the greater threat to their dominion, and later continued resistance to the intrusions of white settlers. The ordinances of 1785 and 1787 provided legal context for Americans to plan in earnest for its habitation. In 1788 a party of adventurous settlers departed Pittsburgh, rafted down the Ohio River, and established a settlement on the north bank of the river in what became Ohio. Native American reversals via General Anthony Wayne at Fallen Timbers in 1794 and the subsequent Greenville Treaty in 1795 mitigated the Indian threat to the first permanent white settlers in the Ohio River Valley.[3] But it was not until the demise of the Shawnee chief Tecumseh and his brother, the Prophet, coincident to the Barneys' relocation in Ohio, that the Indian threat largely abated. The Battle of Tippecanoe in November 1811 and Tecumseh's 1813 death in the Battle of Thames, north of Lake Erie,

Eastern Ohio, 1823. From A *Complete . . . American Atlas of North America and South America to the Year 1822* (Philadelphia: H.C. Corey & I. Lea).

doused the ambitions of regional Indians to reclaim their homeland north of the Ohio.[4] These events removed the final barriers of settlement for the optimistic homesteaders in whose eyes the silhouette of Ohio was fixed.

The year before the Barneys arrived in Knox County, the population was 2,149. Ten years later the number of settlers had quadrupled to 8,326.[5] The pioneers to Knox County came, in part, for agricultural purposes, but found after a time that corn and potatoes would have to be their staple as the lands were "too rich for wheat" which when made into bread "had the effect of an emetic and produced feelings similar to seasickness." Yet the Knox County area was fruitful enough that John Chapman, popularly known as Johnny Appleseed, owned property there and planted orchards helping to establish his nineteenth-century reputation.[6]

Unlike their pioneering venture in western New York, the Barneys were not among the first settlers of Ohio's interior. Virginians and their countrymen from New England, Delaware, and Pennsylvania had already poured into the area. By 1810 one quarter-million acres of Ohio land was improved by those who preceded the Barneys. By the end of the next decade, when the Ohio frontier was closing, Buckeye farmers increased that acreage to nearly three million.[7] The Barneys were doubtless aware of this trend toward civilization, they were looking for economic viability. The Owl Creek settlement of Clinton looked good to them.

Clinton, Ohio, on Owl Creek

The young village of Clinton, located a little north of Ohio's center, was surrounded by a fertile region interspersed with hills and their attendant streams and ravines. The Delaware Indians, successors to the ancient Mound Builders, previously lived upon the lands which became Knox County. They once frequented as a "resort" the land later called Clinton, one of three timberless land parcels in the area, and there traded with the earliest settlers. To these white homesteaders, the tract was known as the "Indian fields." Despite the growing white settlement, there was still anxiety about Indians who remained in the vicinity, enough to fix a fearful impression in Lewis Barney's mind during his early childhood.[8]

After Clinton's modest beginning in 1804, it enjoyed a decade of growth while in competition with nearby Mt. Vernon for county dominance. Besides a community plat with 160 lots, a public green, and seven named streets, a general store, tannery, chair manufacturer, Masonic lodge, newspaper, and a brick "house of public entertainment" bolstered Clinton's prospects.[9] Apparently two of Charles Barney's uncles preceded him to the community, perhaps providing an incentive for Charles and Mercy to relocate in Clinton.[10]

Owl Creek, 1998. Photograph by Ronald O. Barney.

While social and economic growth were significant to village residents, something more important concerned the Barneys.

The most important feature of agrarian life in Ohio in the first decades of the nineteenth century was productive land. This fact did not escape Charles Barney. But land records indicate that Charles held no title to property in Knox County.[11] Barney probably either contracted for a farm for which he never obtained title, or perhaps he rented from others, possibly from family members. It is likely that in Clinton he rehearsed again the fundamentals of building a viable farmstead—clearing, grubbing, fencing, home building—to sustain his family. Charles also stepped into community life, joining the Masonic lodge in Clinton about 1812, an indicator of his interest in permanence.[12] The precarious frontier difficulties they encountered in western New York were at this point a stage the Barneys had moved beyond. But while in Clinton they faced a most challenging circumstance, a difficulty which also affected the rest of the country.

The War of 1812

British interests in North America did not abate after the American Revolution. They claimed Canada, had their eye on interior lands on the continent, and still held the loyalties of the Native Americans near the Great Lakes. A number of unresolved and continuing irritants, including manifestations of American expansionism, kept American-British relations sour. After mutual provocation, Congress declared war on Great Britain on 18 June 1812, hoping to rout the English out of North American once and for all, but English forces in the American Northwest coupled with their Indian allies left American success questionable. Despite the threat, the prospect of war with Britain was very unpopular, particularly in New England, and in Ohio as well.[13] Soon vigorous efforts were made to supplement the 10,000 U.S. army regulars with local militias. Ohio provided over 25,000 enlisted men and nearly 2,000 officers to the American cause.[14] One of the enlisted men was twenty-nine-year-old Charles Barney.

Luther Barney, Charles's father, risked person and property for homeland a generation earlier in the Revolutionary War. Once again the note of citizenship, now 182 years old for the Barneys in America, was being called due. Could Charles do less now? Two months after war was declared, Charles left his wife and three small sons, enlisted as a private under Captain William Douglas—a subordinate to future American president William Henry Harrison—and marched off to fight against the British. Harrison's objective was to retake territory lost to the British in the early months of the war. Of his father's departure, Lewis Barney wrote, "Well do I remember standing by mother's side with her cheeks wet with tears in the town of Clinton on the waters of Owl Creek in Knox County, Ohio, seeing my father shoulder his rifle and step into the ranks of his company and march to share the trials and hardships of a campaign in the war of 1812."[15] Samuel Yeoman and John Barney, Charles's brother-in-law and uncle, also signed on with Douglas's company. Charles knew there was hazard in taking up arms against an enemy. Still he went. His initial duty covered but forty-five days, being discharged on 10 October 1812. The following spring the company was recalled for another half month in May 1813.[16] The Ohioans broke the English brawn with the death of the English Indian ally Tecumseh in 1813 and the American naval victory on Lake Erie in September 1813, which effectively removed the British/Indian threat from Ohio. No longer were the British a menace to the eastern sector of America after 1815, though the two nations would nearly declare war three decades later in the boundary dispute over Oregon.

Charles Barney's military service made a deep impression on his four-year-old son, Lewis. In several retrospective accounts of his life, the younger Barney emphasized his father's service against the British and Indians.[17] Thus, the participation of the boy's grandfathers—Luther Barney and Stephen Yeoman—in the Revolutionary War and his father's military service in the War of 1812 endowed him with a sense of ownership in the land of his birth. A fertile seed of nationalism was planted in the youth which, coupled with other factors of his adult life, gave him a personal investment in the providential destiny of America.

Clinton's newspaper, the *Ohio Register*, which operated in the county from 1813 to 1816, was dominated by news of the war. Reports from the field included troop movements accented by successes and disappointments. The burning of Washington by the British in August 1814 was known to Clinton's residents not long after the attack. Along with national and international news items, mostly reprints from other newspapers, Clinton's inhabitants were updated weekly regarding the conflict in the four-page paper. The Barney family was, undoubtedly, particularly thrilled to read in the *Register* about the exploits of Commodore Joshua Barney, a relative who became somewhat of a national hero from his maritime ventures for the country.[18]

Another event which left a significant impression upon Lewis played out during the Barneys' stay in Clinton. One cold Ohio winter, during a substantial rain, an extensive pit excavated for brick clay filled with rainwater. The north part of the pond created by the downpour was frozen during the bitter storm. Lewis recalled that after the weather cleared his little brother Lucien, probably only three or four and thrilled with the nearby pond, was gleefully playing on the ice. The older boy, himself only six or seven, was opposite him on the other side of the pond. Lucien, oblivious to the danger, ventured "too near the edge of the ice, broke through and was in the act of drowning" when, Lewis said, "I was impressed with an overruling and irresistible power." The older brother, seeing the tragedy-in-the-making, "sprang into the water and was led to my little drowning brother." He collared the little boy and "took him to a large rock that was in the middle of the pond and got on the rock holding him out of the water. As soon as we were safe," Lewis stated, "the power left me standing on the rock." Their mother heard their cries and raced to the pond. She waded through the icy water to the rock, secured her babies, and coddled them home. Lewis, considering his fearless feat, and that "the water was up to my mother's arms which was deep enough to be over my head," concluded that his action and the survival of his little brother was "an intervention of Providence."[19] Childish notions of religion during his short life were now supplanted by a profound sense of God's intervention that would serve as a mindset for the rest of his life.

The salvage of Lucien's life was not something considered lightly by the family. None of life's reversals had the impact upon a household like death in the family. And death visited the homes of most frontier families in Ohio. Perhaps as many as 25 percent of newborns died before their first birthday. A similar number failed to reach the twentieth anniversary of their birth.[20] But the Barneys were fortunate. While living in Clinton, to their three sons was added in 1813 their first daughter, Lucinda.[21]

Winchester, Knox County, Ohio

The viability of Clinton waned during the Barneys' stay as did the interest of the Barneys in remaining there.[22] After only three or four years in Clinton, the inconvenience and unpredictability of relocating was less daunting than prospects of struggling on in a dying settlement. Charles's younger brother Luther, in his early twenties "on his way west," visited Charles in Clinton for three weeks before continuing his dream in the wilderness.[23] Charles could have followed his brother, but Charles and Mercy were favorable to the region and upon deciding they had to move, relocated just nine miles south, still within the county.[24] Winchester, a small settlement found within Morgan Township, became their new home.[25] "Here," Lewis wrote, "my father opened a farm in the heavy beech and sugar tree timber."[26] They again cleared, grubbed, planted, and hoped for a prosperous harvest. By this time, the older children were trained in farm habits and labor. Besides the satisfaction of family life and companionship, children were an economic component as they grew older and were able to bear a larger role in the burdens associated with farm maintenance. On 1 June 1816 another child, Henry—their fourth son—was added to the household, increasing the family prospect of making a viable living from the land.[27] Two and a half years later on 7 January 1819 Walter joined the growing family.[28]

The economic progress of most farmers was limited by the size and configuration of their cultivated land, the number of their livestock, and the hands available to work the land. Most were relegated to subsistence farming. These frontier farmers supplemented what they could raise from the soil—primarily corn—with a few animals, what meat they could secure from hunting, and their vegetable gardens. But most did not prosper beyond the subsistence level to surplus agriculture where they could raise a cash crop for local sale. The advanced level of staple crop agriculture, where produce was marketed to areas beyond their locale, was even more elusive.[29] Charles and Mercy were by all indications subsistence farmers.

Already larger by two than most families of the time, the domestic pattern of life for the Barneys was probably similar to their agrarian contemporaries. "Farmyard, garden, house, kitchen and hearth, in diminishing concentric circles, enclosed and bounded women's daily realm." But "the world of men's work circled outward. It began with farmyard, barn and workshop, and went on through gates and across fences to fields, pastures, woodlands, and then to the roads leading off the farm."[30] The course of rural life for parents and small children was predictable, if anything. Their diet consisted primarily of some variation of pork and corn. Indeed, pork was so important and prevalent that "perhaps the hog, not the dog, was man's best friend on the frontier."[31] Clothing was usually homemade; the women made almost all apparel. The odors associated with farm life were frequently unpleasant. The combination of nearby privies and "napkins" (diapers) gave certain moments an acrid redolence, and raising pigs only exacerbated the pungent smells. While the youngsters had a "childhood," duties and demands equipped children to assume more advanced farmstead responsibilities. Very early, they became adults in miniature.[32] Country life was not one of ease for adults or children. Still, the natural world provided a variety of experiences including adventure, science, and beauty. Human intercourse was both simple

Yeoman Mill on Paint Creek, foundation ruins, 1998. Photograph by Ronald O. Barney.

and complex, and dreams and glimpses of betterment were available to family members both individually and collectively.

While the Barneys eluded the most enervating vicissitude of life in losing family members, they could not escape the devastation of losing their investment of labor and resources. In Winchester a fire struck their home during the winter of 1818 or 1819 destroying nearly all their possessions. Lewis Barney remembered their pitiful plight of being "left without a shelter from cold and storms of this inclement season."[33] This reversal may have caused the Barneys to consider, again, another place to subdue the earth.

Paint Creek in Fayette County, Ohio

About the same time that the Barneys made their second move in Knox County, Mercy's brothers in New York packed their belongings in the spring of 1815 and started for new climes. Bidding farewell to their native state, they made their way to the Allegheny River in southwestern New York and secured a raft which they guided downriver through western Pennsylvania to Pittsburgh. After reaching the confluence of the Allegheny and Ohio they floated the latter waterway, following the southern boundary of Ohio, to Cincinnati. That fall they moved eighty miles northeast to Fayette County, Ohio, about eighty miles southwest from Mercy and Charles in Knox County.[34]

Stephen Yeoman followed his sons, and the family soon claimed about fifteen hundred acres of Wayne Township in what was known as the Bibbs survey.[35] There the Yeomans formed a partnership with Paint Creek by building a gristmill and millrace reliant upon the waterway.[36] Paint Creek is the primary watercourse in the area emptying into the Scioto, the Ohio River's largest tributary in Ohio. The elder Yeoman built the first brick home in the frontier settlement, known by the rocky character of the locale: Rock Mills.[37] Here the Yeomans would live for generations.

After nearly a decade in Knox County, Charles and Mercy pulled up stakes, probably in late 1819, and moved their six children and their belongings to Paint Creek in the vicinity of Mercy's family who were well established there at the time the Barneys arrived.[38] While Ohio was still young to settlement, the Barneys moved into a historic region. The "ancient works" of earlier Native American residents were located nearby.[39] And not only were they near the Indian villages on Paint Creek that had been the object of Daniel Boone's retribution against the Shawnee in August 1778,[40] they were also only twenty miles from Chillicothe, one of the oldest inhabited sites in the American interior.

The already stable Yeoman family connection was a boon to the Barneys. Lewis, eleven or twelve years old at the time of their relocation, later wrote, "In this place we had the privilege of again associating with my mother's relatives and enjoying their society, for the term of seven years."[41] Social progress for children on the frontier, including the luxury of education, was rare. "For children, limited schooling, hard labor on the farm, and a work-oriented youth left them tired as adults and painfully shy in social situations," states one historian of the Ohio frontier. "A life in the woods on the early trans-Appalachian frontier conferred few social skills."[42] Still, Lewis later wrote, it was here in Rock Mills that "I commenced my studies at school."[43] In contrast to many children in the hinterland, the Barney children were fortunate to obtain a rudimentary encounter with reading, writing, books, and ideas. Later in Lewis's life, he would capitalize on what little education he acquired in Ohio.

Lewis's exposure to education, however, was probably not the only social tool provoking the intellectual inquiry that eventually formed his adolescent world view. The Barneys had a religious bent. Not only did the elder Luther Barney's family align themselves with the Baptists in Cayuga County, New York, but in all likelihood Charles's family affiliated, in association with his Yeoman in-laws, with the Primitive Baptists at Paint Creek. Nineteenth-century American children often experienced their "intellectual quickening" by way of religion rather than schooling. It was in the climate of home and church that adolescent Americans mulled the place of God, not only in the universe, but in their personal lives. And, of course, the particular brand of religion in which a child was indoctrinated affected the way he or she considered the world. "Public grammar schools in the nineteenth century were becoming important institutions, but they were not the reason that religion mattered to young children."[44]

Religion was for many a vehicle in intellectual and emotional maturation recognized by young and old alike. However, religious teaching at the hearth and from the pulpit was a two-edged blade. Because religious discussion was probably the primary form of intellectual stimulation in the life of a child at this time, as the boy or girl matured and weighed his or her training against the visible world, the possibility of doubt and disbelief was a potential outcome. Religious controversies "set the first intellectual arenas of doubt and uncertainty, the first stimulants to logical reasoning, the first opportunity for youthful rebellion."[45] In Lewis's case, doubts likely planted in his youth regarding organized Christianity played a major role in the manner in which he viewed life.

Fayette County, named to honor the Marquis de Lafayette of Revolutionary War fame, had been settled near the first of the century, becoming formalized as a county in 1810. Washington Court House, the county seat, was located on a fork of Paint Creek forty-three miles south-southwest of Columbus, Ohio, the state capital after 1816. The county is "flat," with "about half the soil [being] a dark vegetable loam on a clayey sub-soil, mixed with limestone gravel, the rest [being] a yellow, clayey loam." The same matters of settlement affecting the early settlers of Knox County also affected Fayette County pioneers, though "the wet lands . . . when drained, proved highly productive." By 1820 the population of the county was 6,336.[46]

One of the first features to temper the wildness of the frontier for new settlers, as mentioned earlier, was religion. A Primitive Baptist Church was organized in 1805 in the county. Not long after the Yeomans arrived on Paint Creek, they, with others, formed the Paint Creek Primitive Baptist Church.[47] The Primitive Baptists were a different stripe than regular Baptists, a notch or two more fundamental in Calvinism, but they shared characteristics described by one historian as being "a plain people, and their capacity to touch the frontier was, accordingly, large. Their churches exercised much independence, as befitted a denomination that struggled so long for freedom from established religion."[48] The Yeomans subscribed to Primitive Baptist ideology for years, and Mercy's brother James became one of the preachers at Rock Mills.[49] The Barneys likely participated with the Yeomans in Primitive Baptist belief and practice.

Fayette County land records do not show Charles Barney owning property there initially.[50] His arrangement was probably not unlike that which he attempted in New York. A man who could not afford to purchase land usually housed his family in a log structure on the ground he was calculating to acquire. It is likely that the loss of the home and possessions in the Winchester fire reduced the Barneys to another prolonged period of subsistence living, though having Mercy's family nearby was undoubtedly a boon in their poverty. Still they struggled their entire tenure in Rock Mills. By 1825, the first year Charles appeared on an Ohio tax roll, he had apparently obtained possession of fifteen acres of land, which included his residence by the "watercourse," Paint Creek. His tax for the property—twenty-two cents. In contrast Mercy's brothers,

Samuel, James, Gilbert, and Walter held and were, respectively, taxed for land: 50 acres, $.75; 232 acres, $3.48; 100 acres, $1.50; 143 acres, $7.57.[51] It is obvious that Charles Barney was not keeping pace with his in-laws. The only visible asset the family acquired in Fayette County was the birth of their sixth son, and seventh child, John, on 23 April 1823.[52]

Neither Knox nor Fayette Counties provided the dividends hoped for by the Barney family. The sum of their Ohio tenure of fourteen years was that they stayed alive, no more. If financial failure was not enough, the Buckeye landscape was changing for the Barneys as well. Towns now existed where only a generation earlier a ragged frontier defined the area. Even the animals that once characterized the wild land were being killed off in staggering numbers.[53] By the spring of 1825 Charles and Mercy, with seven children ranging from eighteen-year-old Luther to two-year-old John, decided on a drastic, even desperate, move which illustrates their extreme circumstances.

Spoon River Dreams

"In the spring of 1825," Lewis Barney wrote, "father bought a soldier's patent right to a quarter section of land laying on the water of Spoon River in the state of Illinois. So we commenced making preparations to move to that land."[54] Veterans of the War of 1812 were compensated for their service, in part, with an opportunity to acquire bounty land in Illinois. For the Barneys, this time they weren't relocating in the next county or even the next state. The Spoon River in Illinois was four hundred miles away. Charles's failure in Ohio had not dulled his instinct for opportunity. Six hundred forty acres in Illinois were worth whatever inconvenience was required to claim it. It is likely that the Yeomans, to whom the Barneys had become attached, were not fond of a separation. But Charles was now over forty years old with little to show for his life of work. After hearing favorable reports and perhaps reading promotional literature about the area, he hoped that the Illinois prairie would embrace him.

Preparations to move consumed the months that followed. How do you transport a large family across the bosom of America? "Moving family and household goods, to say nothing of farm implements and livestock, any great distance was a formidable feat."[55] And to exacerbate the difficulty, Mercy was pregnant for most of the year with their eighth child. As their plans matured she grew proportionally. They anticipated leaving after the baby's birth. But as their preparation climaxed, everything was altered by the most devastating of a family's misfortunes. Mercy had complications in delivering her second daughter. With the baby's birth on 18 October 1825, Mercy expired.[56] She was forty years old. It was widely known that childbirth was an event which took the lives of many mothers, younger and older, in the rural regions of the country.[57] Her death had a profound effect upon her family. "This circumstance was the cause of much trouble and confusion," Lewis wrote. "I was in my seventeenth year. Consequently I felt the shock very sensibly."[58] Charles's mother had died under identical circumstances when he was about Lewis's age and undoubtedly his own experience with grief helped his children cope. One can only mentally stab at the devastation of a husband and father of eight children in losing his life's mate, particularly with the anticipated move. Surely the Yeomans were crushed as well.

With their happiness shattered, Charles might have reconsidered everything for which he had hoped. But a month after his wife's passing, without prospects of local recovery, he decided to complete the plans to move his family to Illinois. Lewis later wrote,

> In consequence of Mother's death we changed our arrangement. And in place of taking the whole family we left the children and our effects with our connections and Father and myself and Lucien fitted up a team of a wagon and three horses and on the 15th day of November 1825 started for Spoon River in the state of Illinois to settle ourselves on the land that Father bought the previous spring.[59]

In this venture they joined "the frontier in motion," when "the mobile societies of the nineteenth century were in the process of replacing the motionless societies of the eighteenth."[60]

The object of the Barneys' hope, the military bounty tract in Illinois, was surveyed in 1815–1816 for the war veterans. The wedge-shaped 3.5 million acres of land were found between the Mississippi and Illinois Rivers in northwestern Illinois. The Spoon River, a 140-mile ribbon through northern Illinois, was one of the main sources watering the tract, though it was navigable for only a short distance. With two-thirds of the land in the area being prairie and the remainder being timbered, it was advertised as a very favorable place for settlement.[61] Still, there was a wariness about settling on the unproven prairie of Illinois. There was a prevailing belief that "any land that did not support a natural growth of trees would not be fertile enough to grow corn or wheat."[62] But the Barneys were optimistic enough, perhaps desperate enough, to believe that their yearnings might be satisfied.

The route of their journey to Illinois is not known, though Charles and his sons had no difficulty crossing the woods and forests of Ohio and Indiana. The time of their travel, late in the year prior to the wet season, avoided the summer heat and accompanying insect annoyance which tormented man and beast. They coursed through country with few white settlers. While there were villages sprinkled across Ohio, Indiana, and Illinois, they were small and distant from one another. "The inhabitants in this quarter are very few," wrote Chester Loomis, another 1825 traveler through the same area. "Many towns[hips] have not as yet a single inhabitant and scarce an instance can be found for 30 miles in any direction of a family who has lived in this country more than three years."[63] Passing through Ohio and Indiana without incident, the Barneys encountered a complication that nearly cost Lewis's life after they entered Illinois.

Nearing the area of the Sangamon River mid-state, their horses were spooked during one night episode followed a couple of days later by another fright when the horses "started full speed down [a] hill. They soon straddled a tree which stripped the horses of every particle of harness and broke the wagon tongue and smashed in the end gate of the wagon." Lewis later mused, "How I passed the tree without being literally mashed to pieces has always been a mystery that I could never solve in any other way than to give Providence the credit for saving my life."[64]

Now at the Sangamon River in Sangamon County, Illinois, their wagon broken, they stopped for repairs. Coming to the first blacksmith they could find, Charles discovered him to be an old acquaintance. While the wagon was being repaired, Barney and his sons listened to the promotion of the region by the old friend, and being taken by the unusual beauty of that section of prairie, Charles Barney altered the family plans. The fact that the area was "thinly settled" also played into their decision.[65] Sangamon River country would be a good place in which to start anew. The Barneys never did eye their Spoon River destination.

The blacksmith friend arranged for Charles to rent some ground at Lake Fork on Salt Creek, a tributary of the Sangamon. James Turley, among Sangamon River country's first settlers, became their landlord and would become a great friend to the Barneys.[66] Located about fourteen miles northeast of the growing regional center of Springfield, Lake Fork sprouted in the middle of the Illinois prairie. The Barneys' first acquaintance with the prairie was a good one. Very different from the physical environment of dense timber, hills, and glens, to which they had been accustomed in Ohio and New York, there was, nevertheless, something compelling about the prairie. Loomis, the 1825 traveler mentioned above, upon encountering the prairie for the first time exulted that the "Grand Prairie" appeared "on three sides as boundless as the ocean." Characteristics such as the "deep rich soil of inexhaustible fertility, covered with great growth of grass and vegetation," "the richest and most beautiful land," and "the best timbered land I have yet seen" spilled from his pen.[67] Another Easterner crossing the Indiana-Illinois border in 1834 wrote that "the beautiful coat of grass wave[d] its head with the gentle breese . . . with an innumerable variety of the most splend[id] flowers purfuming the western gale."[68] The Barneys were undoubtedly no less taken.

Deciding upon Illinois for their future meant a change of culture, if not of lifestyle. Preceding the Barneys by four months, Loomis, the 1825 traveler, noted that the Illinoisans, just seven years after statehood, had acquired an identity for themselves, a characteristic of which was their use of English.

> In their language, they have many peculiar phrases, & make use of the words *sort*, *mighty*, *recken*, *powerful* on all occasions. In answer to

> the question, How do you do? They commonly answer, 'O *a sorter middling*'—If they feel ill or feeble frequently reply—That they are '*mighty weak*' or '*powerful weak*.' The word *allow* is about universally used in lieu of believe or think. The word *heap* is much used—*a heap of folks*, a *heap of horses* & The word '*scarce*' is pronounced '*Skerce*.' and many other peculiar phrases.

Transplants from other regions carried the labels of their geographical origins. "For instance," he said, "The Virginians are *Tuckehoes*, The North Carolinians are *Buckskins*, The South Carolinians, *Brown Backs* & New England, New York, & New Jersey are all Yankees."[69] Thus, the Barney Yankees became part of a collective human organism where everybody was from somewhere else.

Working through the winter of 1825–1826 to sustain themselves and to improve the land, in the spring Charles and his boys "put in forty acres of corn and other grain which produced us two thousand bushels of grain over and above paying the rent of the farm." Now it was time to gather his family. Leaving Lucien, just fifteen years old, to tend their fledgling enterprise, Charles and Lewis hitched up their wagon and started back to Ohio for the rest of the family on 16 July 1826. After a journey severely complicated by "chills and fever," probably malaria, Charles and his son arrived at Paint Creek and reunited with their family.[70]

Making preparations to return to Illinois, Charles stumbled into a fortuitous circumstance that softened the difficulty of carrying on without a wife. A young eighteen-year-old woman, Deborah Riffle, made the acquaintance of the Barneys.[71] Just two weeks younger than Lewis, Deborah was an orphan whose family life prior to her association with the Barneys was fraught with hardship.[72] Stacking and cramming what he could into his wagon, Charles was about to bid the Yeomans goodbye when Deborah appealed to the family. Displaced and having no blood kin around and seeing in the Barneys a means to flee her circumstances, she asked to be taken with them to Illinois. Charles declined. Considering her age, that she was unattached, and given the difficulties that lay ahead of them, she needed someone who would look after her, to be her "protector." Apparently neither Luther or Lewis, her peers in age, were volunteers. Still, she pled with Charles to reconsider and not leave her behind. Acquiescing, but wanting to be proper, Charles "told the girl if she could make up her mind to become his companion he would take her with [them]. To this she readily consented." They stopped their team in the middle of the road and Charles took young Deborah Riffle to the home of Mercy's brother Walter and there another of Mercy's brothers, Samuel—the local justice of the peace—married them on 20 September 1826 after one of the shortest and most uneventful marital engagements on record.[73] A family reconstituted was now on their way to a new life in Illinois where they arrived 8 October 1826.[74]

Chapter 3

These Fertile Prairies: Yankees on the Illinois Frontier, 1826–1832

The year 1826 was a time of endings and beginnings for the Barneys and for the United States. Just two weeks before Charles left the Sangamon country to retrieve his family so they could reinvent their family's circumstances in Illinois, Thomas Jefferson and John Adams, died 4 July 1826, within hours of each other. The eerie coincidence of their passing on the fiftieth anniversary of the adoption by the Second Continental Congress of the Declaration of Independence appeared to fit a providential timetable. The passing of these friends-turned-foes-turned-friends symbolized the end of the revolutionary era—the formative years of American democracy. The United States had wrestled for much of that fifty years with the polemics of republican agrarianism and federalism, with modifications at both ends, to see the emergence of what came to be called Jacksonian democracy—the era of common folks.

The Barneys were common folk. Certainly the Barneys were not of the upper or even middling of society. In the next decade or so they typified the masses of the low in rank who moved into the hollow corners of an expanding America with hopes of land, viability, and an advance in their status. If there was a dream fifty years after American independence, the Barneys optimistically embraced the vision of what had, to them, previously been so illusive. In Illinois, in the wake of Mercy Yeoman Barney's death, the Barney family was starting anew with a reloaded dream.

The place Charles determined to raise his family—Sangamon River country—was popularized sufficiently to insure that the Barneys had company in their new start. Illinois, included in the acquisition of the Northwest Territory in 1787, became a state in 1818. Its lands soon became the object of one of the most successful real estate promotions in American history. The population of Illinois almost trebled during the decade of the 1820s from 55,211 to 157,445.[1] The prairie, vastly different from eastern forests and verdant highlands, provoked a charm used by publicists to entice Americans and others who yearned for new beginnings.

In all of the promotion of Illinois land for settlement, no territory was described more favorably than the central Illinois region around the Sangamon River. "The prairies are . . . the richest and best kinds of prairies, the uplands as

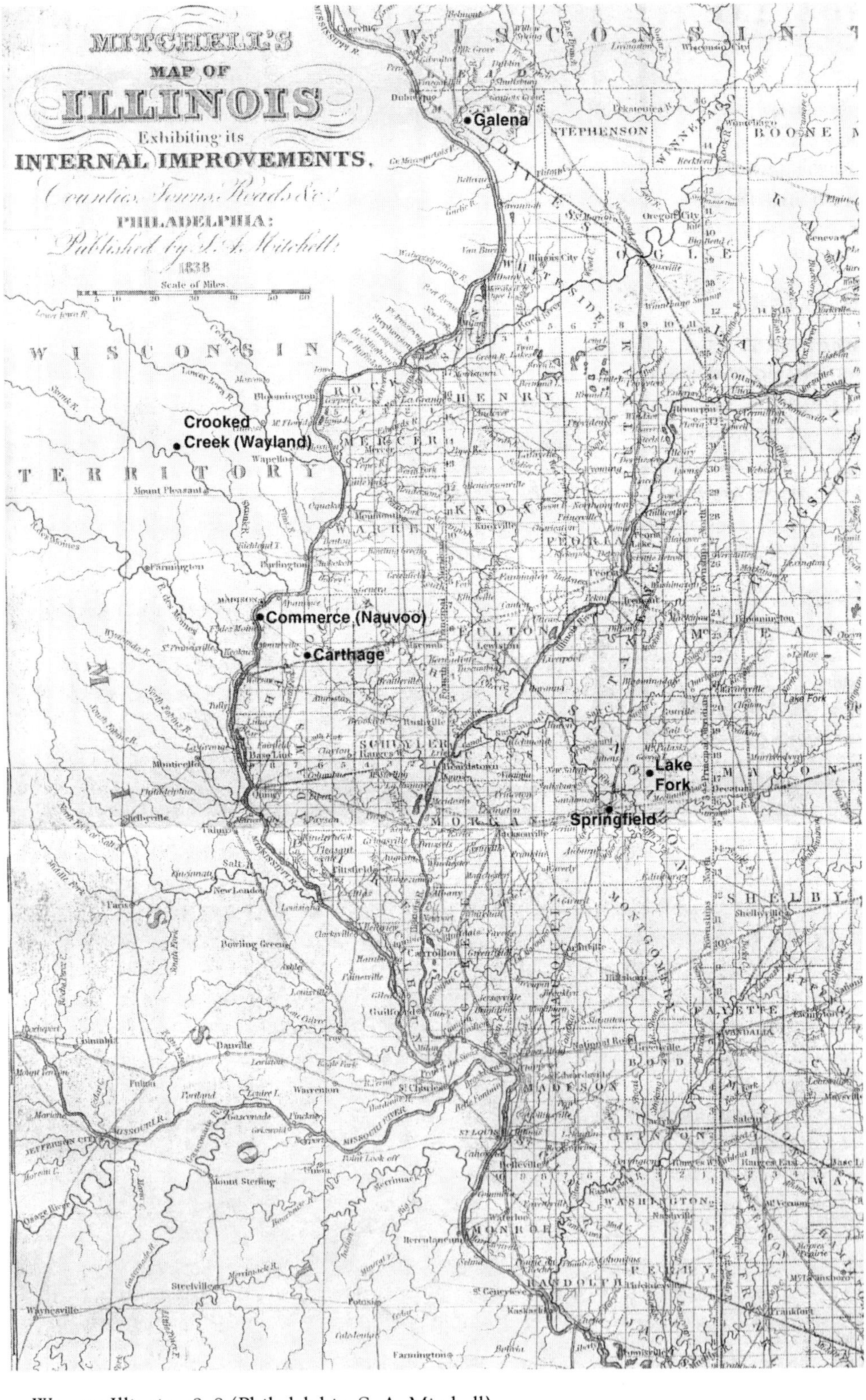

Western Illinois, 1838 (Philadelphia: S. A. Mitchell).

well as the bottoms," wrote an Edwardsville *Spectator* correspondent in 1819. "The timber is very large and lofty. . . . The country is well watered with large and small springs. . . . [T]he springs continue to hold the usual quantity of water during the dry season."[2] A young geologist and ethnologist, floating down the Illinois River in 1821, heard such praise of the area that he dubbed it "a district almost proverbial for its fertility, and fast rising into importance."[3] "The County of Sangamon, since its first settlement, has been justly esteemed the most desirable tract in the state," stated promoter Lewis Beck, "and it consequently has been settled with a rapidity heretofore unequaled. Previous to 1819, not a white inhabitant was to be found on the waters of the Sangamon; at present (1823) the population amounts to near 5,000."[4] An 1826 Springfield correspondent, contrasting Illinois and Indiana, noted, "The emigrant to Indiana must [clear] away the forest before he can p[repare] the earth for a crop; while [the] Illinois [settler] finds the field ready fitted for the plough & scythe. The soil here produces almost spontaneously."[5] The fame of the Illinois prairie, and in particular the Sangamon River region, promised limitless opportunity for large numbers of Americans willing to gamble for life on a prairie. Enough immigrants took note of the regional promotion that the state legislature established Sangamon County in 1821, with Springfield being the largest community in the area.

Those drawn to the region were not of uniform character or manner. The virgin prairie appealed to several settler types. Christian missionaries, prone to appraising society and morals, writing to their associates in eastern cities from the distant prairie, provide insight about the tendencies of frontier folk.[6] One preacher writing from Kaskaskia, Illinois, the first winter the Barneys were in Illinois, stated that, while religious devotion was hard to find, political acuity was rampant among frontier people. There was, he wrote, "little, indeed, if any, [C]hristian influence . . . felt in this place." Instead, "political discutions & disipations is almost all that is heard of here. Wealth & publick offices are the reigning deities of the West."[7] Despite interest in things political, ambition for educational advancement was wanting. "The literary advantages of this region are few," wrote another Springfield preacher in 1826. "At least one half of the children are growing up in ignorance. Many families are without the Bible & some could not read did they possess it."[8] But these were among the least of the settlers' problems. Chances for improvement looked bleak to some. "You can have little hope of seeing a radical *permanent* change in the character of the people, such as you desire, without giving them a taste for reading." Instead, "youthful energies" were expended on "the amusements of the rifle, the billiard table and the dance" in contrast "to the pleasures of intellectual cultivation."[9] Idleness was a significant problem noticed by the clergy. "If citizens were poor on their arrival, they have not in general been the most [ambitious] in improving their conditions," observed a Springfield preacher in 1826. "Indeed, they are more addicted [to] indolence than to any other vice. Hundreds do not labor to the value of two months work [during] the year."[10]

While the preachers did not paint a very flattering image of those who lived in Illinois at this time, before long something redeeming emerged. The need to be socially and civically cooperative to establish permanence and continuity in the settlements nudged the people toward a level of civil behavior that fostered progress and growth. One Scottish visitor stated, after a tour of the United States, "In no part of the world is *good neighbourship* found in greater perfection than in the western country [of America]."[11] While it cannot be demonstrated that the Barneys were a complete contrast to the generalized negatives described above, they clearly were of a mind to cooperate and prosper and found opportunity and satisfaction in their frontier setting. But there was another frontier propensity which typified the Barneys and which eventually affected the length of their stay in Illinois.

The characteristic of unfettered freedom and opportunity passionately held by so many in the western country was and would remain a Barney trademark. Another minister-in-the-wild wrote to his superiors in 1831 to say, "A large portion of the inhabitants of this county [Clay County, Missouri] are frontier folks; that is, they have always lived on the frontier & reared up large families of children." Having previously located in uninhabited tracts of land, "as soon as the inhabitants settled around the[m] . . . they sold out & pushed on fa[r]ther with the forest, & thus they continued to do [so] again & again." "A neighborhood thickly populated is to them very disagreeable, who have from early life been accustomed to live *one side by themselves*."[12] While the Barneys' residence on the Illinois prairie would exceed a decade, this appraisal described the cycle to which the Barneys were becoming accustomed and which would somewhat characterize the course of the remainder of Lewis Barney's life.

Advertisement brings business and the Sangamon River country felt the mixed effect of the widespread publicity. "The fame of these fertile prairies has attracted here a greater variety of character[s] than is to be found in the neighboring states," wrote one of the Springfield ministers in 1826. The winnowing process, where undesirables eventually moved on, had not yet been manifest in Illinois. The state was "not yet purged . . . of those outlaws and apostates from good society who ever linger around the confines of civilization. Illinois has rec[eive]d it[s] immigrants from a greater number of sources than have the adjoining states or probably than even Ohio."[13] This was no surprise to those who were veterans of America's hinterlands, and certainly it was little hindrance to the immigrants in Illinois.

There were other risks to the first wave of settlers in central Illinois. Peter Cartwright, the famed Methodist clergyman, arrived in Sangamon County the year before the Barneys. He described an area where any sod turned was virgin and where Native Americans had not been entirely displaced: "Just north of us was an unbroken Indian country, and the Indians would come in by scores and camp on the Sangamon River bottom, and hunt and live there through the winter. Their frequent visits to our cabins created sometimes great alarm among the women and children."[14] The threat of the Indians' presence would persist after the Barneys' arrival for another half-dozen years. The American record of displacing the indigenous inhabitants of North America was well-known to the Mississippi River Valley tribes and before too many years they would respond.

Clearly Charles Barney went to Illinois to acquire land offered him due to his service in the War of 1812. Side tracked in Sangamon River country, the charm of the landscape and promise of economic recovery, if not prosperity, winked at him, and there he and his family gambled once again with others of a similar bent. The first of the "hardy and enterprising pioneers" to come to the area where Charles Barney located his family was James Turley. "Father Turley," as Lewis fondly referred to him, moved to central Illinois from Kentucky in 1819 with his sons Washington and Jefferson—patriotic namesakes. Turley's Kentucky roots made him one of a substantial body of early Illinois settlers with southern origins, primarily Virginians and Kentuckians. The first six governors of Illinois and most of its legislators for its first twenty-five years were from the South. But an influx of northerners in the 1830s and 1840s diluted their early dominance.[15] Turley was the first to secure a government patent to land in 1824, the year the land office came to the area, in what came to be known as Mount Pulaski township.[16] But not all who followed Turley acquired land in this conventional manner.

Many who migrated to Illinois during this period simply did not have the means to secure government title to the land. "To buy and fully open a farm, a man did best to bring about five hundred dollars in cash with him," one historian of the region wrote. "And many settlers simply never had such financial resources," resulting in "two-thirds of the state's farmers in 1828 [being] squatters on the public domain." Because of their numbers, others acknowledged the improvements made by the squatters upon their untitled properties and defended their claims to the land.[17] It appears that many squatted on or rented their land, planted a crop, and hoped for a harvest that would allow them to purchase their meager enterprise.[18] Had Charles taken the War of 1812 bounty on the Spoon River his situation may have been different. But given the financial circumstances of the Barneys in their removal from Ohio, they were starting again from square one.

A few small villages sprouted up in Mt. Pulaski township in what was then the northwest sector of Sangamon County. Elk-hart, Georgetown, Buffalo-hart, Salt Creek, and Lake Fork represented settlements serving as gathering spots for the first pioneers in the region. Charles and his sons Luther, Lewis, and Lucien have been identified among the three dozen earliest settlers in the township.[19] Within a year after their arrival in Sangamon River country, Charles found a place about five miles farther up Lake Fork from the farm they rented from Turley where they applied what resources they had for permanency. Lake Fork of Salt Creek was "formed by a long [and narrow] lake in the north eastern part of Sangamon County, [which] runs a north course and forms one of the heads of Salt Creek."[20] In the summer of 1827, Lewis wrote, "we built a house and fenced 25 acres of land on our claim. We sold corn and bought cows and hogs so we had enough for the use of the family."[21] Improving the land included building a log home, a typical one of the area being about sixteen foot square,[22] laying out a vegetable garden to provide produce for the family, a small orchard, and then clearing the land for planting corn to sustain their animals and to provide some source of income. "Although the ax and the rifle were the technological means with which settlers . . . swept obstacles from their paths, the household was the basic social and economic institution by which this feat was accomplished."[23] It was no different for the Barneys.

Primitive (Predestinarian) Baptists and the Barneys

Charles Barney and his family, which included his wife Deborah and eight children, had, by all indications, found a place in Sangamon County to their satisfaction. With land and the prospect of economic resources, they now asserted the means to claim their niche in America, so illusive in their previous attempts in New York and Ohio. One of the chief indicators of Charles's satisfaction with the region and his prospect of permanency was shown in his religious inclinations. Before the winter of 1826–1827 was over, Charles Barney joined a few others in the vicinity of Lake Fork to organize "The Baptist Church of Jesus Christ at Lake Fork," also called the Lake Fork Predestinarian Baptist Church.[24] Charles and some of his family's affiliation with this group, organized on 20 January 1827, gives valuable insight into the contemporary attitudes of the Barneys about religion and American society, absent in the reflective writings of Lewis.

This little group of Christians which the Barneys helped organize were part of a larger restless quest within American Christianity that had been festering for decades. There was a religious subculture in America which aimed to recover the purity and perfection of biblical Christianity thought by them to be vacant in traditional forms of contemporary religion. Their spiritual forbears, the seventeenth-century Puritans, manifested this same objective in their separation from the English Anglicans. Most religious groups in America in the eighteenth and nineteenth centuries were affected by this restorationist or primitivist movement whose occupation it was to distill Jesus' religion to its ancient New Testament antecedents in theology, doctrine, and practice.[25] Though there was wide diversity in their particular forms of expression, the primitivists believed that "whatever good the Protestant Reformation had done, it had not reopened the heavens or restored authentic Christianity."[26]

The American version of the Baptist faith is popularly associated with primitivist Roger Williams in the 1630s as he broke from the Puritans.[27] As the

Baptists grew in numbers and influence they found themselves in the same circumstances as the Puritans before them. Both groups, which professed primitivist principles in their formative years, before long became the object of their own reformers who believed that contemporary religions had become what they had originally abhorred. The dissonance was rooted in what was believed to be a cultural metamorphosis which accepted "modern" thinking and methods to the neglect of biblical purity. One manifestation of Baptist reaction came in a form of Calvinist predestinarianism or, as they came to be known, Primitive Baptists.

The Primitive Baptists were reformers. They could not tolerate current practice. "Popular creeds are substituted in the place of the faith once delivered to the saints—the commandments of men instead of the gospel of Jesus Christ—human inventions take the place of divine ordinances—the work of the Holy Ghost, in gathering in and quickening the elect of God, is superceded by human contrivances," wrote Gilbert Beebe, one of their most visible early nineteenth-century leaders.[28] It can also be argued that the success of the Primitive Baptists, as well as other conservative New Testament–oriented denominations, was an outgrowth of a reconfiguration of Christianity in the wake of the American Revolution, though their origins predate the conflict. There were several characteristics of the "democratization of American Christianity" that likely represented the views of the Barneys and ordinary folk like them regarding their religion and place in American society. According to historian Nathan Hatch, the primary features of religious egalitarianism were a rejection of the traditional lofty status given educated clergy and the attendant protocols which subordinated the views and influence of laity. Religious outsiders were verified and popularized thereby promoting an escalation of alternatives to traditional religious norms.[29] This religious populism with hues of primitivism had a particular appeal to those on the frontier.[30] They were substantiated in their rejection of the complications of eastern urban culture and also legitimized in their world view regarding God and man. Of course, these attitudes spilled over into the political and economical activities of the common people, effectively creating a subculture countering the polish and sophistication of the educated elites to the east. It is not a stretch to assign the Barneys to this subculture.

As the settlement of Illinois's interior increased, particularly in Sangamon River country, there was a somewhat proportional establishment of Primitive Baptist congregations which doubled in number the regular Baptist congregations by 1835. By the time the Lake Fork church was organized in 1827 there were nearby Primitive Baptist congregations in Lick Creek, Springfield, Sugar Creek, Spring Creek, Island Grove, and Liberty, all within the bounds of Sangamon County. Three years later there were thirty-nine Primitive Baptist churches comprising the Sangamon Association.[31] The congregations of the Sangamon Association followed a protocol in doctrine and organization that carefully defined their profession of Christianity.[32]

Charles Barney, who likely aligned himself with the Primitive Baptists on Paint Creek in Ohio earlier in the decade, was a charter member of the Predestinarian Baptists along with the Turley family and other founders and builders of the community of Lake Fork. Besides their adherence to Primitive Baptist scriptural imperatives, their religious life included subscription to a dozen "rules of decorum for the church," which included provisions for organizational administration such as the moderator and clerk, with the option of other officers. There were also expectations for attendance and appropriate etiquette at meetings.[33] The church met one Saturday each month for worship and church business and again for worship on the following Sunday. In the first ten years of the Lake Fork church, nearly fifty adherents added their names to the list of believers.

On the church's charter roster for 27 January 1827, Charles was listed third among the men. Deborah was twenty-fourth among the women and may have joined as late as 1830. From the criteria for membership among the Primitive Baptists, it is clear that Charles and Deborah exhibited overt manifestations of belief to the Primitive Baptist gospel of Jesus Christ, and Charles was clearly not just a nominal believer. He was appointed in March 1828 to a committee of three whose objective it was to secure an adequate meetinghouse. This growing group of believers melded together and finally constructed a place for worship in the early 1830s providing a spiritual and material foundation which fostered the Lake Fork church through the end of the century. Charles's oldest son, twenty-five-year-old Luther, also "come forward and joined by experience" in June 1830.[34] No other Barney family members made the profession of faith. Charles's activity and support was strong, including his appointment early in 1831 as moderator, whose duty it was to conduct the services by "open[ing] meeting by singing and prayer to God." He also served as a delegate in April 1831 to the larger Sangamon Association, of which the Lake Fork congregation was a part, and was elected to help establish a satellite congregation in an outlying area in June 1832. Charles's devotion influenced his son Luther, who was appointed moderator in July and August 1832. Charles was reappointed moderator in September. Father and son were obviously active and making a contribution to the small group of believers. But the momentum of the Barneys' church participation ran into a snag the following month over Luther's desire to preach.

Being appointed moderator was one thing; acceptance as a preacher was quite another. In October 1832 a "motion [was] made and seconded that the church take into consideration the gift of brother Lewther Barney to preach the gospel" to the congregation. The "gift" referred to a recognition by the congregation that God had bestowed upon Luther the call to preach. The process likely included scrutiny of personal characteristics and the outward religious attributes of the candidate. Some of the congregation apparently had concerns about Luther. Immediately after the motion to consider Luther's gift, another motion was made and seconded to postpone a decision to the next meeting. The minutes show that Luther's case was considered at the monthly business meetings each month until January 1833 when "the question [of Luther's call] was taken and the church deside[d] that [they] thought Not." Luther's "gift" was rejected. Luther did not take the negative vote well. What the extent of his dissonance was is not known. In a roster of members compiled about November 1836 the word "excluded" appears next to Luther's name; he had been severed from the church. While Luther may have wallowed in his rejection, Charles and Deborah apparently continued their participation with the church while they lived in Lake Fork. Their Primitive Baptist affiliation, initiated at Rock Mills, Ohio, in the early 1820s, spanned nearly two decades and had, no doubt, a profound influence on the world view of the Barney patriarch.

Particulars of Lewis Barney's religious thinking at this time are not known, though he made no profession of faith to the Primitive Baptists or any other religious group in the area. No doubt he watched with interest Luther's involvement with their father's church. Clearly Lewis's general attitude toward organized religion, probably stemming from his youth, was reinforced during this period. "I cared nothing for religion," he later wrote. He saw in organized Christianity a hollow argument, primarily because of what he described as the misbehavior and hypocrisy of those who professed its absoluteness.[35] Lewis shared in a skepticism of religion apparently felt by others in central Illinois at the time.[36] Lewis's attitude was not unlike that of Abraham Lincoln, whose family, similar to the Barneys, embraced the predestinarian beliefs of the Primitive Baptists in Kentucky and later Indiana.[37] Had not Lewis later found the religious faith that would dominate the rest of his life, he would likely have remained unchurched, as was Lincoln. What particular events or experiences contributed to Lewis's jaundiced view of Christian churches are not known, but it is clear that a zest for organized religion was not something held by all members of the Barney family.

The Galena Lead Mines

After a couple of years of land-squatting at Lake Fork, all the while improving their homestead, the Barneys realized they would have to legalize the claim to their land. "The country began to settle up rapidly," Lewis wrote, "and [it] become necessary to secure a government title to our lands. So Luther and myself started for the lead mines on Fever River in the north part of the state of Illinois [in 1828] for the purpose of raising money to secure our lands."[38] The agrarian economy on which they depended was not sufficient to produce a surplus to provide the means to purchase their property.

Lead had been discovered near the Fever River, now the Galena River, in northwestern Illinois and southwestern Wisconsin in the late eighteenth century. The valuable commodity was mined there increasingly until the population warranted a post office which was opened in 1826 in Galena, named for the sulphide of lead identified with the area. One Illinois correspondent in January 1827 wrote to friends in the east to say that, "You have doubtless observed the late accounts of the state of the mines in Illinois. They have not been over rated. Thousands are flocking there for the next summer season."[39] Trail guides were published by Galena promoters inviting others to join the boom in northwestern Illinois. A notice in the *Illinois Intelligencer* in March 1827 identified the route to the lead mines from Sangamon County. The promotion of lead mining was so effective that there was a "rush" into the area in 1828–1829, at the very time Luther and Lewis arrived there. It was a 205-mile trek from Sangamon County and the brothers likely followed the Lewiston Trail.[40] Others, referred to as "Suckers," made their way up the Mississippi River in the spring to the diggings before returning downriver in the fall.[41] The lure was sufficient that any means available was used to get there.

Galena, later the place where U. S. Grant began his Civil War career and where he retired after his presidency, became a boomtown. Within a half dozen years of the Barneys' arrival the population had swelled to nearly 1,000 inhabitants. There were about 250 houses and 42 stores and warehouses. A weekly newspaper kept the populace informed. Fifty steamboats navigated the Fever River every year to dock at Galena transporting goods and people.[42] The social climate associated with gold rush camps later in the century flourished in Galena with its "miners, smelters, merchants, speculators, gamblers, and every description of character" whose "intelligence, enterprise, and virtue, were thrown in the midst of dissipation, gaming, and every species of vice."[43] Missionary societies contemplated strategies to mitigate "the open fronts of vice & impiety" in the booming settlement.[44] The Barney brothers were young, unattached men and found themselves, with many others, thrown into a mix of humanity and excesses unlike anything previously experienced.[45]

Charles Fenno Hoffman, an American literary figure of some note, visited Galena while the mining was at its height. His description of the mines provides some insight into Luther and Lewis's venture. Coming to a "huge mound of earth," Hoffman said he and his guide approached the three-foot square entrance to a mine "over which a windlass was placed." The opening was "lined with split logs crossing each other at the angles down to the original surface of the soil." From there down, though, "the adhesiveness of the earth seemed to be all that kept the sides of the pit together." Now in the dark cavity, he grabbed the rope attached to the crank-controlled windlass and placed his foot in a wooden hook at the end of line. Stepping into the open hole, "in a few moments [he] descended some seventy or eighty feet below the surface." Once in the work area, what awaited them was not for the claustrophobic. In the dim light, Hoffman said, "looking round . . . I found myself in a long horizontal passage or narrow gallery, with a grim-looking miner approaching me with a lantern in one hand and a pickaxe in the other." His guide introduced him to the miner "who proceeded to show us about these subterranean premises." The workplace for the miners "consisted of three or four galleries, generally terminating in a common centre, though one or two short ones, just commenced, appeared to run off at right angles to the rest." In the corridors Hoffmann saw "the lead-ore, which glitters like frosted silver in its native bed [appearing] to lie in thick horizontal strata along their side." The pick-wielding workmen then thrust their tools into the ever-widening walls separating the ore from the clay. Hoffman said he "remained long enough to see several tubsful hauled up by the conveyance which had admitted us into these dusky regions."[46]

It wasn't just the process that fascinated the traveler, Hoffman also observed that the "labour and exposure of these miners is very great." Mining in the Galena mines carried a very real risk to one's life. He noted, however, that "to those who have an interest in the work, [it] is said to be so exciting." Even "the most indolent man, when he has once fairly burrowed under ground, and got a scent of what is called 'a lead,' will vie in devotion to his toil with the most industrious of those who labour in the light of heaven."[47] Something other than adventure was the incentive for the risk and hard work in the mines. "Fortunes were made almost upon a turn of the spade" but were also "lost with equal facility."[48] Hoffman explained that for the lead miner, "His stimulous, indeed, resembles that of the gold-hunter; for the lead, when delivered at Galena, is as good as coin in his pocket; which, if he chances to strike a rich *lead* of mineral, he at once becomes independent."[49]

A shrinking market caused the price of lead to drop nationally in 1829, cooling the passion of the miners.[50] Lead production plunged from eleven million and thirteen million pounds in 1828 and 1829 to eight million in 1830.[51] The Barneys worked through the zenith of the run on the mines. Their exposure to civilization's extremes undoubtedly affected the way they considered society thereafter. Whatever the social cost, they obtained the money they sought. Working into the summer of 1829, they "returned home with money enough to enter 80 acres of land." This secured their father's well-fenced "80 acres of farm" at Lake Fork and plotted out their own futures.[52]

A Foothold in Life

A few months before Lewis and his older brother returned to the family farm in the summer of 1829, Andrew Jackson—War of 1812 hero—was sworn in as president of the United States. The ascension to power by a "westerner" found a White House advocate for folks like the Barneys and their Sangamon neighbors. Though the aura of Washington did not reach much beyond the Potomac for those struggling in subsistence living, common people felt they had a friend in the White House.

After the time of Luther and Lewis's return from the Galena mines and the purchase of the Lake Fork property, they were both eligible to leave the orbit of their father's household. The natural consequence of reaching the age of majority, having property, and the means for family support was marriage, but the two oldest Barney boys remained unattached. In the fall of 1830, when Lewis was twenty-two, he went to work for "Father" James Turley to feed and care for his stock. He later reflected that "while working for him, one of his daughters become very fond and intimate with me. . . . She was considered the most lovely, handsome, and intelligent young lady in the country and had many admirers of high rank and position but her choice of all her attendants fell upon myself. She every way managed to court my favor and attention."[53] Lewis was keen toward her, but something aborted their courtship; they did not marry. Still, he worked the social conventions of the area with satisfaction. He declared that he "enjoyed the society of the young ladies and gentlemen very much."[54] That Barney would, when recounting this experience at the age of seventy, include a description of his early ventures in popularity and romance is an indication that this was a time of happiness and optimism, despite his apparent disappointment in not marrying James Turley's daughter.

As the villages of Sangamon country expanded, the trappings of civilization emerged from the settlers' interests in community, one of which was self-protection. Local militias were raised with the expectation that all able-bodied men participate. There was still a regional threat from Indians. The influx of white immigrants to the area continued to agitate several of the local Indian communities to reconsider their accommodation of the white men. The evidence of Indian activity was sufficient to require some preparation for defense. Lewis was commissioned a first lieutenant in the 25th Regiment of the state militia on 4 March 1830, and apparently later held the office of infantry captain in the company for several years.[55] While the Sangamon militias never amounted to much militarily, even when called upon to engage in combat, the function of the militia was critical to the community. These men, primarily from the more populated villages, augmented in number from outlying Sangamon farmers, found themselves organizing elections, conducting censuses, and taking the lead in other community ventures which fostered fellowship and sociality among them despite their rural condition.[56] Militia musters became social occasions for the participants. The militia was an integral component of the county's civil life.

The involvement of the Barneys in county matters included the desire for internal development, which was a significant issue at the time.[57] The government that touched frontier folk was at the county level, and while county officials wielded a great deal of influence over the quality of life for many, locals interested in economic and social improvement had a say in how they were governed.[58] Six months after Charles Barney purchased another eighty acres of land at Lake Fork,[59] he and his two oldest sons were three of fifty-seven men who petitioned county officials to reconsider plans to build a road circumventing their interests. They wanted the road to pass "through Lake fork Settlemt" or nearby to "promote the public" rather than "private interest" of the influential of Sangamon County.[60] Local residents made the pleas knowing that it was likely that they would have to perform much of the work themselves.[61] Such was the process of improving the territory.

As the acreage of Charles's property grew, so also did his family. Deborah bore three daughters, Emerine (12 August 1828), Elizabeth known as Betsey (7 March 1830), and Louisa (1831), after the Barneys settled at Lake Fork.[62] However, the infant Louisa did not survive. They had previously felt the sting of death in the passing of Charles and Mercy's daughter, whose birth in 1825 caused her mother's death; she did not survive her second birthday. Notwithstanding the presence of other children, Louisa's death must have been a severe blow despite the rate of infant mortality of which they were undoubtedly aware. When Benjamin Franklin Barney, Deborah's first son and Charles's twelfth child, was born on 12 March 1832 it was undoubtedly a time of great rejoicing.[63] Obviously, Charles named this boy for the great founding father. Another son, to be born four years later, would bear the name of the nation's third president, Thomas Jefferson. Clearly, Charles saw himself and his family, eventually to include one more son and two more daughters,[64] as extensions of the American soul, enough so to risk life and happiness for their stock in the national enterprise.

The Black Hawk (or Sac and Fox) War

That same spring of 1832 a "tragicomedy" began its play across the northern Illinois prairie. On April 6, the Sac chief Black Hawk, with about five hundred warriors and their families totaling nearly two thousand people, crossed the Mississippi River eastward from Iowa into Illinois in defiance of U.S. restrictions on their range of movement defined in a treaty signed the previous year. Black Hawk, who sided with the British in the War of 1812 and who was generally antagonistic thereafter to American designs, did not intend to provoke the U.S. authorities; his people needed to be fed. "Their purpose was not to make war, but to join the Winnebagoes and raise enough corn to keep them through the next winter."[65] So they returned to their ancestral lands, now populated with increasing numbers of white settlers. Soon after the Indians returned to Illinois, the state governor demanded military intervention to eradicate what he saw as the threat of Indian aggression.[66]

Lewis Barney's appraisal of Black Hawk's circumstances demonstrates some sympathy toward the Indians in contrast to many of his countrymen who characterized them as subhuman. Though in chronicling his own involvement in the episode he referred to Indians as "savages," he stated, "It would be doing an injustice to the Indian race not to give a statement of the cause of the outbreak." He said, "The white authority, contrived to get the leading chiefs together [and] traded them out of their lands," forcing the Indians to relocate on the west side of the Mississippi and abandon their traditional habitat. But the desperation of his people for food that spring negated the chief's commitment to the treaty. As Black Hawk led his people into their ancestral lands, "the whites raised a small force and drove the Indians off of the land . . . and killed some of them,"[67] provoking what one historian called "the one military engagement in the Northwest after the War of 1812 that was serious enough to warrant the designation 'war.'"[68]

Two weeks after Black Hawk's crossing of the Mississippi, twenty-three-year-old Lewis Barney "volunteered my services . . . and was enrolled in John Dawson's company in the Spy Battalion commanded by James D. Henry" under the overall direction of General Henry Atkinson.[69] Dawson's company consisted of seventy-eight men composed of one captain, two lieutenants, four sergeants, four corporals, and sixty-seven privates of which Lewis was one.[70] Their unit joined with several thousand other militiamen, a third of which were part of the regular United States army, who were called into service against the Indians. Included in the ranks were men whose names would mark the annals of America's military future: Abraham Lincoln, Winfield Scott, Zachary Taylor, Jefferson Davis, and Albert Sidney Johnston.

The soldiers in Lewis's unit marched from Sangamon County to Beardstown on the Illinois River. Other units were assigned duties which took them into both Illinois and Wisconsin. There on the Illinois River, Barney's group awaited the arrival of other troops and boats bringing supplies. Finally organized, they marched north until reaching the Mississippi River where they received more provisions and recruited their animals. They then followed the Rock River northeast to Dixon where they stalled, waiting again for needed supplies to maintain the large army. A military enterprise with these numbers was unprecedented on Illinois soil. As the army marked time at Dixon, poet, editor, and political leader William Cullen Bryant passed through the region and drew an impression of the soldiers: "They were a hard-looking set of men, unkempt and unshaved, wearing shirts of dark calico [plain white cotton fabric heavier than muslin], and sometimes calico capotes [a long hooded cloak or overcoat]."[71] Obviously these Illinois volunteers were something less than military regulars, but little more could be expected of local militiamen.

During the wait, "about midnight three men road into camp," Barney reported, "wounded and bleeding, bringing the word that [Major Isaiah] Stillman's company was defeated and all killed numbering 300 men. The alarm being given, the bugle sounded and all hands ordered on parade."[72] While the rumor of three hundred being killed was only a rumor, Lewis wrote that on arriving at the scene of the battle "we found eleven men all cut to pieces and 18 or 20 horses dead on the ground. We gathered up the dead and buried them.

We then searched the county for 10 or 12 miles round" but only "found 2 Indians hung up in a tree."[73] This patrol took three days after which they returned to Dixon. For Lewis, this was the end of his military service against Black Hawk and his people. He was mustered out on 28 May 1832 after serving for "forty-eight & a half days."[74]

The conflict was "one of the great ironies of American frontier history, for the war was not a planned aggression by either side nor a last-ditch stand of noble natives against Indian-hating frontiersmen." Rather, "misunderstandings were the key to the conflict."[75] The Black Hawk War lasted for about four months with only about seventy settlers and soldiers losing their lives in battle, though over two hundred soldiers died from cholera during the period.[76] The war continued to 2 August 1832 when the Indians were completely subdued.[77] The removal of the Indian threat from the Mississippi River Valley settlers served as another key further widening the gates of white immigration to the vast region.

Chapter 4

On My Farm: Lewis Barney Comes of Age, 1833–1839

Upon his return to the family farm after his military service, Lewis Barney, still unattached, calculated to remedy his detachment. His younger sister, Lucinda, now twenty years old, married a local man, John Daniel Copeland on 7 March 1833, and together they set their new household within Lake Fork. The Copeland family had been in the area for several years and were active Lake Fork Baptists like the Barneys. Lewis was now twenty-three and older than many young men who had already assumed the marital role. The list of essentials for marriage were not extensive, but the items on the list were consequential. Number one was a partner. While not providing information about his courtship, one month after Lucinda's marriage, Lewis married Elizabeth Turner on 4 April 1833.[1] The second essential was some demonstration of ability to provide for a family, the primary component in rural regions being land. Two months before his marriage Barney secured forty more acres in Lake Fork.[2] The ideal for the pioneer farmer in Illinois was settling in timber or on the perimeter of prairie in proximity to wooded lands. Access to timber would give him the advantage of wood for fuel, fencing, and other farm uses.[3] Barney's acquisition fit this situation.

The new bride, known as Betsey, was a month older than her husband. Born in the village of Madison in Greene County, Ohio, her father Walter Turner was one of the early settlers of that region of the Buckeye state.[4] Turner and his wife, Lydia Ballinger, were born North Carolinians, from Guilford, prior to the Revolution. Both found themselves in Jefferson County, Tennessee, likely before their marriage. Their eldest children were born in Tennessee prior to their removal to Greene County, Ohio.[5] From there, apparently, they moved to the Illinois prairie. How Lewis and Betsey became acquainted is not known other than their living in a common locale. The Turners moved to Sangamon River country at least as early as 1826, purchasing eighty acres of land.[6] Turner kin were, with Barney's father Charles, charter members of the Lake Fork Predestinarian Baptist Church in 1827.[7] Betsey's family in Sangamon County in 1830 was composed of her father and mother, herself, a brother and sister, and two other brothers who had established households of their own. Two of Betsey's uncles also lived close by with their families.[8]

Elizabeth Turner Barney (Lewis Barney's first wife). Photographer and date unknown. Collection of Ronald O. Barney.

If there was a time appropriate for Lewis Barney to separate from his father, to move on in his own enterprise, the time was now. While Barney's writings neglect descriptions of family relationships between siblings and the generations, the fact that he chose to stay by his father suggests something affirmative about their association. His siblings appear to have shared in their affinity toward their father. That the Barneys clanned together is a feature of their lives that generally marked their familial behavior for decades. Barney's own ambition for a family dominion later in his life may have been rooted in their father-son connection at this time. While this positive generational relationship was likely not extraordinary, it was also not universal. At about the same time the Barney brothers worked the lead mines of Galena, nineteen-year-old Abraham Lincoln, "seeing no prospect of betterment of his condition, so long as his fortune was interwoven with that of his father, . . . at last endeavored to strike out into the broad world for himself."[9] Not long after, young Lincoln found himself mixing in the frontier life of Sangamon County just a few miles from the Barneys, confident, but alone. That the Barneys stayed connected indicates they employed behavior toward one another that kept their relationships intact.

Another insight into Lewis Barney's thinking at the time of his marriage, also related to family connections, was his choice of lifestyle. Not only could Barney and his new bride have relocated away from their parents, it was also within their prerogative to flee the frontier, the prairie, and gravitate to more urban climes. A consciousness regarding the choice of living simply in contrast to the increasingly pervasive quest for wealth and luxury was an issue that had been stirring in America since colonial times. The opulence found in centers of European culture was thought by many to be the natural consequence of the growing American economy, but voices for restraint and modest living came from several sources of American society including government, religion, and the arts. It is not demonstrable that Lewis's choices were prompted by the voices for "plain living and high thinking"; however, evidence suggests his conscious disdain for the trappings of urban prosperity throughout his life.[10] But living simply was not simple.

The grueling necessities required of every emerging frontier family challenged Barney's energies and resources. First, a home had to be constructed. Then the land had to be cleared, grubbed, and manipulated for production, and domestic animals were required—for labor and food—to sustain life. Like others having seen their parents rough out a living from the land, an optimism surrounded young couples determined to exact their own living from the earth. Forever counting on favorable weather and environmental conditions, their ambitions were satisfied by domestic contentment, a healthy crop, and the addition of children. For Barney's part he later wrote that after his marriage, "I then settled down on my farm and continued making improvements until I had 80 acres of land enclosed with a good substantial fence, a hewed log house

18 by 22 feet, also a frame house. Also suitable stables, cribs, and corrals."[11] Later he "secured a government patent to 200 acres of good land, one-half timber the other half prairie joining father [who] also had the same amount of land and improvements."[12] But he and Betsey were initially disappointed in the integral feature of children in their lives.

The bearing and nurturing of children in the nineteenth century was fraught with a high degree of unpredictability regarding the survival of the little ones. That uncertainty did not escape the newlyweds. The year following their marriage, Betsey bore a much-anticipated daughter on 5 June 1834 in the primitive condition of their modest home in Lake Fork. The little girl they named Sarah Jane, however, did not survive. After the baby's death, in a wake of sorrow, they carried her little body a few miles north where they buried her on a lonely hill rising above the vacant prairie.[13] "Whereas the world beyond the household paid little notice to infant mortality, for mothers the lives and deaths of their infants were matters that took a powerful emotional toll."[14] The infant mortality rate then was significantly more frightening to parents than it is today. Indeed, "during the nineteenth century as much as 40 percent of the total death rate was comprised of the deaths of children under the age of five."[15] So many young children died in infancy that many frontier families "invested less emotionally in their babies until they were a few months old and past the worst risks." Most families experienced the loss of at least one of their young children.[16] A first child's death plagues a couple with lingering doubts about a future family, and it was surely no consolation two months later that little Sarah Jane was joined on the cemetery hill by her grandfather Walter Turner.[17] What a discouraging season it was for Betsey to see her only child and her father leave her association. But the unusually wet summers of the mid-1830s, which fostered disease and sickness, were very hard on many Sangamon families where the "sick frequently outnumbered the well and the dead accumulated so quickly that people had to bury them in blankets, two to a grave."[18] Undoubtedly there was great joy among the Barneys later in the year when Lewis's stepmother Deborah bore Margaret Matilda Barney, though Betsey's emotions were likely mixed.[19]

It was not until two years later that Lewis and Betsey had a child who survived. Named after his grandfather, Walter Turner Barney, born 18 September 1836, found himself the object of great attention and love, completing for his parents the family triangle. Undoubtedly Deborah's new son Thomas Jefferson Barney, born three months later on Christmas day, was not competition for Lewis and Betsey's son, but rather considered an additional gift from God.[20] The providential views of the Barneys held God as the benign, though occasionally chastening, benefactor of the human family.

Deborah and Betsey Barney were the same age. They both approximated the female maternity pattern of having children within the first year of marriage, retaining a cycle of fertility over the next score of years. Women commonly gave birth every twenty-six to thirty months, evidenced by the custom of mothers nursing their children for nearly two years. Before Betsey had her first child, Deborah had delivered four. But Deborah's next four children were born in years comparable to the first five of Betsey's. Because of their close physical proximity and age, Deborah and Betsey were surely more like sisters than mother-in-law and daughter-in-law. Together they shared the struggle of nurturing their offspring through "feeding, teething, weaning, and walking [which] all possessed their peculiar dangers."[21] It also meant encountering the pleasure of similar experiences and commonalities, perhaps occasional jealousies, and more intimate overall familial associations. Lewis's fondness for his stepmother in their later years suggests a favorable relationship during their early decades together.

The Barney women probably became prairie women, typical of the time. Given contemporary societal norms, the role of frontier women was largely domestic. Their contribution to the maintenance of house and hearth was irreplaceable, primarily through their function as mothers. Since the middle of the previous century "mothers [had] emerged as guardians of their [children's] moral and physical well-being," in contrast to the "father-dominated family of early America." A mother's role was comprehensive and mothers became "the most influential force in shaping and preserving a child's life."[22] But women, for the most part, were limited in their influence beyond their property line, even though it is the case that many women of the time co-owned land with their husbands. In Sangamon River country, public life was the life of men.[23] In the few instances where the Barney family was visible at all in county matters, it was via the men.

Lewis Barney later recorded several incidents regarding his life at Lake Fork that indicate satisfaction in his circumstance. But there was one terrifying experience told in a humorous context that had a providential angle to it. Barney, "having business at Springfield, the county seat of Sangamon County about 25 miles from home," made the journey with a friend, John Rodgers, during a midwinter storm that nearly cost them their lives.[24] Finishing their business, during their journey home they encountered a blizzard that paralyzed everything that wasn't moving. Reaching a substantial hundred-yard-wide slough between them and home, the foul weather tricked them into trying to cross on horseback. Not far into the venture Barney's horse reared, dumping him into the freezing water. The "perfect gale" froze his clothing to his body. Remounting, they crossed the slough before spurring their horses full throttle the three miles to Lake Fork where the "waves [were] rolling and the white caps flying in a fearful manner." Finding they could not cross, they weathered the night in the remains of a haystack where they "lay and shook with the cold all night." But the death-bated gale that nearly took their lives during the night now reversed their fortunes by freezing the lake, or so they thought. Without their horses, desperate, and believing they could cross on the ice, they scrambled across the frozen water only to break through time and again.

Rodgers ended up barefoot. But they were too far to turn back. Gathering what internal resources were left, they made it home.

Finally home safe and relieved of the deadly cold, they found the Primitive Baptist preacher visiting. "As Rodgers was a very profane man, the preacher said, 'Well, Rodgers, did you swear any last night?' The shivering man replied, 'No, by G.D. I did not know but [what] I should be in the middle of Hell before morning.'" But their ordeal was not over. Their horses were still on the other side of the lake and losing a horse to the horrid conditions would be an unacceptable economic loss. Their return for the horses was as eventful as their previous ordeal. Crossing this time in a canoe, they found their horses and started toward home on horseback, the horses plodding along on a lower layer of ice. Two-thirds of the way across the horses broke through and Rodgers "plunged in and went under the water out of sight." As Rodgers grabbed desperately for air, Barney reached and grabbed his arm and pulled him onto the ice. Once his friend was out of harm's way, Barney joked about Rodgers's bad luck. Not out of humor and reconsidering his oath to the preacher, Rodgers replied, "Yes and bless your kind self, if it had not have been for your help I would now have been in Hell in a good deal warmer country than this!" The horses swam and kicked their way out and raced home with Barney and Rodgers following. They both "arrived all safe, once more thankful for the good fortune we had."[25]

Along with sustaining life, social exchange, religious worship for some, and raising their children, the Barneys no doubt retained an interest in the affairs affecting the country in which they felt so inextricably entwined. There was not a stereotypical political posture held by those in America's interior. At the same time the Barneys were establishing themselves on the Illinois prairie, Andrew Jackson assumed the White House. And while Jackson's Democratic party ostensibly championed the segment of society who were typically rural, common, and poor, the Whigs were well represented in Illinois. While both parties vied for sectional popularity, the Barneys undoubtedly sided with Jackson's ideology. "Old Hickory," as Jackson was fondly known by his constituents, was the first president not of eastern aristocratic origins and ties. His two-term tenure, 1829–1837, coincided with the Barneys' subdivision as the older of Charles's children established their own households and nurtured their world view into the minds of their own children.

Not all the rural folks in Sangamon County favored Jackson, though he drew more votes than opponent Henry Clay in 1832, garnering 56 percent of the vote.[26] Abraham Lincoln, the tall, awkward Kentuckian, who lived about as far northwest of Springfield as the Barneys lived northeast of the county seat, made a name for himself in the county, preaching the gospel of Henry Clay.[27] Despite his own humble beginnings, Lincoln identified with the Whigs because "it was the party of the better sort of people, and young Lincoln meant to associate with the better sort rather than the Jacksonian masses."[28] Indeed,

Lincoln's influence in the previously Jackson-dominated county left Jackson's Democratic successor, Martin Van Buren, on the short end of the county's vote, where Clay won in 1836 by a margin of 62 to 38 percent.[29] In the state elections the Whigs dominated the entire Sangamon County delegation, with Lincoln himself winning his second election to the state legislature.[30] While the Democrats and Whigs sometimes ran neck and neck for advantage in Illinois, it is likely that the political sentiments of the Barneys were found with the "Jacksonian masses."[31]

Clearly the Barneys had visions of permanency in Sangamon County. Over the next few years in the 1830s they continued to marry, bear children, purchase land, and participate in village and county affairs.[32] That the Barneys purchased several hundred acres of land indicates an economic status above subsistence farming. Life in Sangamon River country, overall, was good for the Barneys. Speaking of the frontier prairie, "I enjoyed myself very much with the rifle," Lewis wrote. "I spent my leisure time in hunting, game being very plenty, such as deer, turkeys, racoons, wolves, prairie hens, geese, ducks, squirrels, and wild pigeons." Besides the leisure and sporting and hunting pleasures he found, he also prospered on his rural farm by "raising an abundance of grain, pork, and stock, and every variety of vegetables, also sugar, honey, and fruits of all kinds in abundance."[33] While the Industrial Revolution was unalterably marking technology's advance east of the Appalachians, the Barneys did not live their lives with regret in the absence of it. For them, for a time, life was good in Sangamon River country.

But in the midst of the prosperity in Sangamon County and elsewhere in America, an economic recession hit. It was not without warning. Debate about the viability of the Bank of the United States during Jackson's tenure, the financial medium Americans would use—specie or paper currency—and whether local banks could issue the latter created a volatile economic climate. A number of other monetary policies, such as the lack of regulation and the tariff, also undermined confidence in the country's economic posture. From this, a fiscal reversal that had devastating repercussions, extending even into America's hinterlands, struck at national institutions and traditions.[34] The recession of 1837 was compounded by a severe drought parching central Illinois in 1838. The lack of water took a great toll on both crops and animals in the region.[35] Together these economic negatives may have caused the Barneys to rethink their situation in Sangamon River country.

Other factors such as increased settlement likely affected the Barneys' outlook at Lake Fork. The population of Illinois soared after 1820. By 1835 Sangamon County had grown to a population of 17,573, a gain of about 25 percent in four years, making it the largest county in Illinois both in population and size.[36] In the same time Springfield, the county seat, had grown from 850 to 1,419. The Barneys, of course, exhibited a pattern of distancing themselves from the effects of urban growth and life. There may have even been some residual cultural differences with their neighbors: the Barneys being Yankees and many Sangamon settlers having southern roots. Then there was Luther's expulsion from the local Primitive Baptist congregation. The sting for Luther was severe enough that he left Sangamon County for McLean County, in 1836 or 1837. For whatever reason or reasons, "In the year of 1838," Lewis wrote, "I, in company with my father, started from our home in Sangamon County, Illinois, west to look for a new home and see the country of Iowa." They focused on Henry County, Iowa, where Charles "bought a claim of 1,000 acres of choice timber and prairie land."[37] They were taken by their introduction to Iowa, intending to make it their final residence.[38]

Over the winter of 1838–1839, the Barneys finalized their departure from Sangamon County. Their tenure on the central Illinois prairie lasted fourteen years, by far the longest Lewis, and even Charles, had stayed in one place. Here Lewis Barney married, became a father, and became a thread in the weave of life in Sangamon River country. Lewis and his family departed Lake Fork in May 1839 with Charles and his family apparently following that summer.[39] The Barneys were not like those who after having once faced the unsettled American domain "were perfectly content to let the frontier, with all its opportunities and difficulties, slip away from them" and who "would no longer shoulder the burden of advancing the frontier." The Barneys joined the "energetic souls . . . [who] kept pace with the advancing wave of pioneer settlement most of their lives," which "required enormous energy and several migrations helping to propel the line of settlement westward."[40]

Henry County, Iowa

The western bank of the Mississippi River prior to the Black Hawk War of 1832 formed a line of demarcation that legally separated the white population from the western regions owned and inhabited by Native Americans. After the war the residual claims of the Sac and Fox Indians to the area of western Iowa were extended to 1837 before they were extinguished. Soon after, Iowa became a territory separating from Wisconsin in July 1838, the same year the federal land office in Iowa opened.[41] Henry County, named for Colonel James D. Henry under whom Lewis Barney served in the Black Hawk War, was initially settled by white Americans in 1835, the first hailing from Sangamon County, Illinois. The county was formed in 1837 and the county seat located at Mt. Pleasant, which for a time vied to become the territorial capital.[42]

Nestled in the southeastern corner of Iowa, Henry County is one county removed from the Mississippi River. Principally watered by the Skunk River, which empties into the Mississippi just below Burlington, Iowa, its tributaries served as millsites for five grist- and eight sawmills. When the Barneys first surveyed the area there were just over three thousand settlers in the county. In the next two years the county population increased by nearly eight hundred. Despite the relative newness of the county, eleven hundred residents were engaged in farming, twenty-six in commerce, about one hundred in manufacturing and trades, and eighteen in the professions. The percentage of farmers in the area at the time was among the highest in any of Iowa's counties. Reputed to have soil of exceptional quality, the proof was in the ample production of wheat, corn, oats, rye, hemp, and potatoes which lured agrarian folks to the region.[43] Henry County had all the appearances of a good place to land.

When the elder Barney moved to his thousand acres of Iowa farmland, several of his children from his first marriage were on their own.[44] While Luther (from McLean County, Illinois) and Lewis and their young families followed Charles to Iowa, Lucinda Barney Copeland remained in Sangamon County.[45] The 1840 census in Henry County indicates that Charles and Deborah lived there with their four sons and three daughters and an unidentified woman between thirty and forty years old, perhaps a boarder. Both Luther and Lewis and their wives were there with their sons, two apiece.[46] The collective move of the family to Iowa illustrates at this time a pattern of familial association, cooperation, and enterprise that was now multigenerational.

Two of the Barney boys do not appear on the 1840 Iowa census. Instead, twenty-eight-year-old Lucien and twenty-three-year-old Henry, both still single, were off in 1839 searching for possible family alternatives in Arkansas. Achieving statehood in 1836, Arkansas was the westernmost of the southern states and still very much dressed in frontier garb. Not unlike Luther and Lewis's family errand a decade earlier to the lead mines in Galena, Illinois, Lucien and Henry were looking for options to aggrandize the family by testing the Arkansas frontier. It is not known exactly how long they stayed in Crawford County in the northwestern sector of the state nor the success or disappointment of their labors there. While the particulars of their stay in Arkansas are not known, the venture was a precursor for another family reconnaissance for Lucien and Henry six years later in the young republic of Texas.[47] The American frontier was still pregnant with opportunity for the Barneys. If their extended effort in Illinois was disappointing, Iowa, or Arkansas, or somewhere else was always an option.

Iowa at first blush looked so promising the family spoke of making it their final destination. Native American rights had been extinguished. The land was virtually untouched. They were at least the social equal of most of their countrymen. They were a family of means from their tenure in Illinois and, like their erstwhile Sangamon County neighbors, everybody in Iowa was from somewhere else. Their purchase of hundreds of acres of land (improved farm land was worth \$3 to \$12 per acre by 1842)[48] and the favorable circumstances of the Iowa prairie held great promise. But their move to Iowa was coincident to their encounter with something that eventually altered the course of their future lives completely.

Chapter 5

An Honest, Industrious People: Conversion to Mormonism, 1839–1840

The Barneys' settling in Iowa had, by all appearances, provided them with the prospects of prosperity and peace. At the same time, events in the state immediately south of Iowa were everything but peaceful. Perhaps as many as ten thousand members of the Church of Jesus Christ of Latter-day Saints were displaced from several northern Missouri counties to western Illinois during the winter of 1838–1839. Publicity about the conflict between the Mormons, as the Latter-day Saints were called, and the "old settlers" of Missouri likely reached the ears of everyone in the Mississippi River valley. It was more than a dispute of ideology and religious differences. Charges, countercharges, death, destruction of homes and property, and the question of law soon caught the attention of people across America. Accounts of civil aggression in Missouri involving warfare and bloodshed, reports the Barneys undoubtedly noticed while in Sangamon County, grabbed their interest as they were building their homes and working their land in western Iowa. Lewis Barney later wrote that he became aware of the "heavy persecution in Missouri raised against the Mormons" and that "the whole country was stirred up against them. And from these reports," he said, "I, in common with the rest of the people, supposed they were the most outrageous and hardened set of criminals that ever graced the earth."[1] The primary reason for the heightened interest of Lewis in the plight of the Saints was that older brother Luther, rejected by the Primitive Baptists a few years earlier, had become a Mormon, probably about the time the Barneys were engaged in moving to Iowa.[2]

The Latter-day Saints first settled in western Missouri at wilderness edge in 1831, when they were called the Church of Christ. Shortly before this time, the moniker "Mormons" was attached to them from their belief in the Book of Mormon, produced by the founding Mormon prophet Joseph Smith in 1830. Jackson County, the western boundary of the American frontier, was a location of destiny which figured into the prophetic vision of the Mormon prophet. Independence, the Jackson County seat, soon grew into a small city as many Latter-day Saint faithful gathered there. Joseph Smith, the leader, told his increasing numbers of followers that a portion of the apocalyptic calendar of the Almighty, the end times, would find expression in Jackson County,

Joseph Smith, ca. 1840s. Artist unknown. Courtesy of Church Archives

including the construction of a temple to God. While this declaration propelled the Saints into vigilant preparation, the "old settlers" of Missouri, as they became informed of Mormon designs, were far less enthusiastic. Indeed, to quell Mormon ambition some county residents became vigilantes who took it upon themselves to rid the area of the unpopular religious group. Before the decade was over, Missouri muskets forced the Mormon retreat to Illinois where they regrouped and, though temporarily interrupted, prepared for the promises made by their prophet-leader.

The Founding Decade of an American Religion

In 1805, three years before Lewis Barney's birth in western New York, Joseph Smith, Jr., was born in Sharon, near the center of Vermont, about sixty miles northeast of the birthplace of Charles Barney. Smith family origins in America were also rooted in Massachusetts, similar to the Barneys, and the Smiths' incremental moves from Massachusetts to Vermont to the western New York frontier also paralleled the Barney experience. About four years after Joseph Smith's father relocated his family in 1816 to Manchester, New York, young Joseph became mixed in an interplay between heaven and earth that would see a new prophetic religion emerge which had a significant impact on America's western progress and future.

Joseph Smith, Jr., his family, and a handful of other believers formed the Church of Christ on 6 April 1830 in Fayette Township, in the Fingerlakes region of western New York.[3] Opposition from outsiders forced Smith and his church to move from New York to the western reserve of Ohio within a year of its organization. There they gathered in a small village known as Kirtland, about twenty miles east of Cleveland, where they first established an organizational structure akin to other Christian churches. The numbers of those drawn to Kirtland swelled. From Kirtland, missionaries were sent in all directions to gather a harvest of those accepting a religion which declared that God was then revealing himself and his plan to mankind from an open heaven. One legation of Mormons trudged west to the western Missouri border where, contemporary with the growth of the church in Kirtland, new converts gathered in Jackson County. The primary tenets proclaimed by the missionaries were a new Christian revelation given to the world in the form of the Book of Mormon and the attendant principles of faith, repentance, baptism, and gifts of the Spirit. The Book of Mormon contained the account of a group of Judeo-Christians who left Palestine about 600 B.C. and sailed to the Western Hemisphere. They lived as orthodox Jews, but knew of the coming of Christ from Old Testament–style prophets who lived among them. After the mortal ministry and crucifixion of Jesus in the Eastern Hemisphere, the Book of

Mormon people were visited by the risen Lord, who revealed anew the singular teachings of Christian life. The missionaries who declared these matters also taught that the ancient biblical authority to baptize, heal, and bless had been restored, offering renewal in a world declared by Joseph Smith to be limited by only "a form of Godliness."

The newly formed church, initially but a frontier curiosity, soon attracted attention that extended beyond its western American origins. It aroused antipathy from the clergymen of its Christian competitors from the outset, but it could not be easily dismissed, despite its heterodox differences with the traditional religious organizations of the day. Somewhat like other churches with primitivist origins in America at the time, Mormonism grew from the belief that Jesus' religion, passing through time from its first century origin, had been diluted in theology, corrupted in practice, and emasculated of authority. But it was different from the other organizations with similar motivations. "If Puritans, Baptists, and 'Christians,' sought simply to emulate the faith and practices of the ancients," according to religious historians Richard Hughes and Leonard Allen, "Mormons embraced a scheme of restoration that was cosmic in its scope, that penetrated space to the ends of the earth and the outer bounds of the universe itself, and that encompassed time from its very beginning to its end."[4] Clearly this new church was not an eroding knoll upon the landscape of American religion.

Cosmic theological difference was only one feature of the Mormons' demarcation from other Christian groups. Historian Jan Shipps states that another significant difference came from Mormon belief "that the Church of Jesus Christ was removed from the earth when direct communication between divinity and humanity ceased at the end of the apostolic age." Only "when direct communication between humanity and divinity was reopened" could the true "restoration" reform the impotent form of Christianity then existent.[5] That link between "humanity and divinity" for the Mormons was in the person of Joseph Smith. Needless to say, such declarations were not well received by most of their countrymen, particularly the denominationally devout. Claims of a prophet who spoke by way of an open canon, the extrabiblical Book of Mormon, and theological differences were only a few of the problems between the Mormons and their neighbors.

The initial Mormon presence in Jackson County was aborted in July 1833 when increasing Mormon numbers and their Yankee attitudes aroused acrimony in the southern-bred old settlers. The Saints packed and moved to the northern counties of Missouri, established by the Missouri legislature to accommodate the displaced Mormons. There they found a more benign climate for a time, but within five years, rumors and threats again characterized interactions between the Mormons and their neighbors. Missourians pushed and shoved. Mormons retaliated. Missouri governor Lilburn W. Boggs, whose patience frayed from the persistent conflict between Missourians and Mormons, issued an expulsion order on 27 October 1838 to rid the state of the religious zealots who seemed to beckon trouble with their swelling presence. The infamous order was preceded three weeks earlier by a report about the Saints to Boggs by one of his chief military commanders stating that should the local state militia encounter "those base and degraded beings" they would "be exterminated from the face of the earth." And should, per chance, one of the "old settlers" be killed by a Mormon, "there will be from 4 to 5 thousand volunteers in the field against the Mormons, & nothing but [Mormon] blood will satisfy them."[6] There was little chance for compromise or conciliation in this atmosphere. Whatever measures were required to expel the Mormons, even the resort to extermination, were within reason. Within days of Boggs's extermination order, a pocket of Mormon settlers at Haun's Mill on Shoal Creek in Caldwell County were attacked by an armed militia-mob of 200-plus who ruthlessly slaughtered seventeen men and boys and wounded another dozen or so at the millsite. Other settlements of Saints were threatened and worse. A Mormon militia encounter with their Missouri equivalents resulted in the death of one of the Mormon apostles at Crooked River in Ray County.[7] Despite desperate actions of defense and retaliation, the Mormons' fate in Missouri was fixed.

While claims and counterclaims still fly, Missouri historian Kenneth Winn's appraisal of the 1838 conflict summarizes the encounter:

> The largely abstract case against the church's intentions paled against the brutal facts of anti-Mormon violence. The looting and burning of Gallatin and Millsport [by Mormons] seemed a trifle compared to the ruthless slaughter at Haun's Mills. During the entire course of the conflict, the old settlers lost only one man; at least forty Saints died. Furthermore, the quick resettlement of Mormon lands by their conquerors suggested that the latter had gone to war only for the spoils. Most shameful of all, Governor Boggs's order to expel or exterminate the Mormons seemed to many Missourians the act of a tyrant.[8]

The tumultuous events, which included the incarceration of Joseph Smith and other church leaders in two Missouri jails in 1838 and 1839, were bewildering to the Saints who anticipated emancipation from oppression in contrast to the very real threat of extermination.[9]

As they dragged themselves and their few belongings east across the Missouri prairie in 1839, fleeing *to* rather than *from* the United States, the plight of the Mormons evoked sympathies in the Mississippi River town of Quincy, Illinois. A godsend, the townspeople in April 1839 offered a respite and refuge to the disoriented lot. Joseph Smith, freshly escaped from a western Missouri prison, joined his followers and soon fostered a phoenix within his flock. Potential demise in the previous three years was replaced by a vigor and revitalization as the church rose out of the ashes.

At the same time the Barneys built their homes and nurtured their land in Henry County, Iowa, Joseph Smith and his followers, stunned by their defeat in Missouri and grasping for any foothold, moved upstream to the latent river town of Commerce, Illinois. Here in the next half-dozen years, industry and theology crystalized the religion into an entity fit to fulfill the divine prospectus outlined by the prophet in the previous decade. Nauvoo, Illinois, as Commerce was renamed, acquired all the signs of a large urban-center-in-the-making as the Hancock County peninsula it anchored expanded in population and influence with a steady influx of converts from the eastern United States and Great Britain. "If we are suffered to remain," Smith wrote in August 1840, "there is every prospect of [Nauvoo] becoming one of the largest cities on the river, if not in the western world."[10] The vitality and strength of the church emerging in Nauvoo attracted the attention of the nation, but not to the benefit of the church. Luther Barney's affiliation with the Saints in 1839, in their darkest hour, awakened his extended family to the religion which had previously been to them but a curiosity.

Illinois became part of Mormon geography beginning in 1830, when traversed first by missionaries and then by church members who migrated between the dual centers of gathering for the Saints—Kirtland and Independence.[11] Missionaries were in the Sangamon River region as early as July 1831. Others in the early 1830s solicited interest in Mormonism near the Spoon River and western Illinois.[12] In May 1834 the body known as Zion's Camp, dispatched from Kirtland to recover Jackson County properties seized from the Saints, passed through Springfield, Illinois, just a few miles from the Barneys. "A great many questions were asked" about the armed corp of 205 which "excited considerable curiosity" in the region's residents.[13] The chance that the Barneys heard about the "curious" expedition at this time is great. Later as many as a dozen and a half Mormon missionaries worked the string of communities in a twelve-county area in western Illinois.[14] But prior to 1839 what the Barneys had heard about the Mormons was composed "of evil reports . . . put in circulation about them."[15]

Conversion

The circumstance of Luther Barney's 1839 conversion and baptism into the Church of Jesus Christ of Latter-day Saints is not known. It is evident though that Luther, now thirty-three years old and married two years, craved spiritual revitalization after his rejection from the Primitive Baptists, an event which could have soured him on all organized religion. Instead, Luther responded to the Mormon missionaries and was constrained to reveal the new light to his family. The transformation from predestinarian Calvinism to Arminian Mormonism indicates a significant transformation in the family's religious thinking, though there are other general features of Calvinistic and Mormon thought that are compatible.[16] After Luther's conversion, according to Lewis, he "commenced talking with Father and the neighbors upon the gifts and blessings of the gospel enjoyed by the former-day saints and contended that it was the privilege of the church now to enjoy the same gifts and blessings. And if the church was not in possession of that power, it was not the true church and was not acknowledged of God as his church."[17]

Lewis Barney's religious views at this time were tainted by his general dismissal of American Christendom. His early dissatisfaction blossomed to an increasing prejudice against organized religion, compounded by the futile efforts of some to save his infidel hide.

> The Methodist and Cumberland Presbyterians had been trying to convert me to their faith, and I had followed their instructions without receiving the promise they made to me. This set me to thinking. And I came to the conclusion that religion of every kind was a hoax and that none was right and that all preachers of religion were hypocrites and were preaching for money and popularity and cared nothing for the salvation or welfare of the human family.[18]

Initially Luther's appeal to his family to consider Mormonism had no effect upon his younger brother.

Lewis Barney's attitude ill equipped him to be a responsive proselyte when first contacted in 1839 by Mormon missionaries who spread the word in the northwestern sector of Henry County, Iowa, near a settlement at the time called Crooked Creek.[19] One day upon observing "two Mormon Elders coming along the road both afoot with their valises in their hands," he was reminded "of the way the Savior sent out his disciples when he was on the earth preaching the gospel." "Curiosity [more] than anything else" pulled him to a Mormon missionary meeting. There he heard their claims about having "the power to heal the sick, cast out devils, and that all the gifts and blessings of the church in former days was again restored to the church in these latter days." They also taught "that God had raised up a prophet and restored the priesthood again to men on the earth and had set his hand again to gather Israel from the four quarters of the earth to prepare for the reign of Christ on the earth a thousand years and that the great millennium was about to usher in."[20] The appeal by the missionaries disarmed some of Barney's prejudice toward the Saints and awakened within him the possibility that perhaps after all God was not an absentee Lord.

Others of the Barney family were also persuaded by the message of the missionaries. Sometime in the course of the family's investigation of Joseph Smith's new faith, they traveled the sixty miles to Nauvoo to witness for themselves the practice of Mormonism. Lewis's younger brother Walter reported they "passed through that city before I had embraced the church and I was greatly pleased to see the youth of that city at the time so well behaved and good mannered as they were."[21] When the Barneys found that Mormonism "embraced principles belonging to the primitive church and organization with prophets, apostles, seventies, elders, priests, teachers, and deacons together with the gifts and blessings enjoyed by the former-day saints," they were compelled that they "could do no better than attach ourselves to the church."[22] In Lewis's case, "after a year and a half's careful investigation," and after "becoming acquainted with Joseph Smith and the Mormon people generally and their principles, finding them an honest, industrious people, and most wickedly misrepresented, I presented myself for baptism" in the spring of 1840. After his baptism in the Mississippi River, he was "confirmed a member of the church under the hands of Joseph Smith the prophet in the first settling of Nauvoo."[23] An enduring affinity for the Mormon prophet was born within Barney from this time.

Joseph Smith, Jr., a tall and substantial man in his mid-thirties, was three years older than Barney. Becoming acquainted with the Mormon prophet, Barney likely learned that Smith shared with him not only a similar pattern in family geography but also of family life and economic disappointment in their early lives. The prophet, who had light brown hair, a prominent nose, little facial hair, and described by many as having a handsome look, was open, common, and affable. There was no apparent affectation, piety, or pomposity in Smith. It was easy for new believers in the Mormon gospel to connect to its prophet. William Clayton, a British convert who arrived in Nauvoo five months after Barney's baptism, described Smith to his countrymen in Britain,

> We have had the privelege of conversing with Joseph Smith Junr. And we are delighted with his company. We have had a privilege of ascertaining in a great measure from whence all the evil reports have arisen and hitherto have every reason to believe him innocent. He is *not* an idiot, but a man of sound judgment, and possessed of abundance of intelligence and whilst you listen to his conversation you receive intelligence which expands your mind and causes your heart to rejoice. He is very familiar, and delights to instruct the poor saints. I can converse with him just as easy as I can with you, and with regard to being willing to communicate instruction he says "I receive it freely and I will give it freely." He is willing to answer any question I have put to him and is pleased when we ask him questions. He seems exceeding well versed in the scriptures, and whilst conversing upon any subject such light and beauty is revealed I never saw before. If I had come from England purposely to converse with him a few days I should have considered myself well paid for my trouble.[24]

While Smith's detractors held him in contempt, Barney, like so many others, was taken by the compelling leader of the Mormons who obviously related well to the widening social spectrum of church membership.

But Smith's charismatic presence was a secondary feature to those who subscribed to the religion he espoused. The relationship between the leader and the follower in Mormonism, notes Mormon historian Richard Bushman, is founded on the premise that "the power of Mormon leaders depends almost entirely on . . . individual spiritual convictions." Further, he continues, Mormons "were not simply weltering Americans infatuated with the Prophet's promises of Utopia. Through Joseph they found God, and it was the measure of divinity in him and his teaching that held them. Nauvoo would never have risen or fallen without that spiritual life. Belief powered the entire enterprise."[25] It is evident that the Barneys and those like them fit this characterization which insured the survival of the faith even through the incredible ordeal that awaited them.

Even with a diversity of backgrounds and circumstances, the checklist, spiritual and mental, employed by the Latter-day Saint converts in considering affiliation with the church was shared by most, including the Barneys. Besides accepting the theological tenet that "the old-line churches were corrupt," there were other shared characteristics of Mormonism's American adherents at this time. Not surprisingly, nearly three-fourths of converts during this period lived in rural settings, neither wilderness nor metropolitan. Most were born in New York or New England. Few were well-educated, but on the other hand, few were illiterate. Most were about thirty years old. The majority of American recruits were "religiously alienated," once affiliated with other churches, primarily Methodist or Baptist, although nearly a third held no previous affiliation. While neither extremes in wealth or poverty were preponderant, the gospel net gathered new believers from a cross section of all classes and backgrounds.[26] The Barneys qualified as typical Latter-day Saint converts.

The Church of Jesus Christ of Latter-day Saints had a decade of experience at the time of the Barneys' conversion. The contemporary legacy of Mormonism, subject to chronic persecution, produced a core of believers whose skin had leathered via their ordeals. Despite its youth, this resilient and determined constituency had demonstrated that Joseph Smith's church endured from a theology and spirit that prospered under extreme conditions. Most other religious-oriented organizations born in America temporarily flourished and then ebbed, but the gauntlet of Kirtland, Independence, and Far West produced a church with a swaggering sanguinity that insured its survivability. The literature produced by the Saints since 1832 reveals an organization with seemingly unsophisticated principles that wrote and spoke with a prophetic confidence characteristic of a group which deeply believed they were modern Israelites.[27] The Saints who welcomed the Barneys into the church were not an ordinary lot. Undoubtedly their stories of sacrifice and valor in the face of fire were inspiring to the Barneys and provided a foundation of belief anxiously acquired by the converted family.

Mormons in Iowa

Within a short period of time after the first missionaries entered Henry County, a branch of the church numbering about thirty was established, probably centering in or near Crooked Creek. Credit for the branch was largely due, according to Lewis Barney, to the efforts of his brother Luther. Nauvoo's satellite settlements in Iowa and Illinois received attention from headquarters, it being the objective of church leaders to build a network of outlying congregations to strengthen the posture of the church in the Mississippi River valley. At this point, a concentration of Mormons exclusively in Nauvoo would subvert church purposes in building the hoped-for strength and extending influence. This posture regarding "the gathering of modern Israel" changed about the time Lewis Barney had been in the church a year.

About the time of Barney's baptism in June 1840, Alva Tippetts, James Carroll, and several Nauvoo elders took a short mission to Henry County, perhaps a return to a place of their earlier missionary service. (The names of the two missionaries who first contacted Barney were not identified by him, though Carroll and Tippetts are likely candidates.) During their missionary enterprise Carroll and Tippetts wrote to the Nauvoo news organ, the *Times and Seasons*, to report that for three weeks in June they labored in Henry County, Iowa, baptizing ten, who likely became part of the small branch organized around the Barneys. After returning to Nauvoo the first week of July, they again visited Henry County three weeks later preaching and teaching until 1 October. Of the latter endeavor they reported that, holding "twenty eight meetings, we felt that the Lord was with us, and the signs truly did fellow [*sic*] them that believe, and it appeared that desolating sickness followed them that railed out against us."[28] Early in 1841 twenty-seven-year-old Amasa Lyman in an official church capacity visited Henry County and stayed with Charles Barney, indicating that the Barneys were known to leaders in Nauvoo.[29] The presence of the Nauvoo emissaries was undoubtedly an optimistic note for the work which appeared to be taking hold in Henry County.

As the branch grew a feeling prevailed among a number of members that there was no reason for them to stay in Iowa. As Nauvoo began to prosper, a growing number wanted to sell out and move to Nauvoo. Some, having moved to Iowa recently, would have little to give up and would gain much by being close to the prophet and the other Saints. Barney was against the mass move. So opposed was he that he went to Nauvoo and asked Joseph Smith's counsel on the matter. The prophet supported the idea of colonizing the area of Henry County and discouraged their transfer to Nauvoo. Upon Barney's return, despite presenting Smith's recommendation to the little congregation, they persisted in their determination to gather to Nauvoo.[30]

Adding to Barney's aggravation, one of the missionaries responsible for raising the little branch of church members stirred the fears of the new members, declaring that the world was coming to an end. James Carroll, a forty-four-year-old former Methodist preacher from England who tended toward excess, and earlier had baptized several Barney family members, got "the whole branch excited in relation to the judgments of God that was to precede the coming of the Messiah." According to Barney, he "made the members of the branch believe that these destructions was to take place almost immediately and that our lands would be of no benefit to us."[31] Carroll's zeal and apocalypticism required the intervention of several, including Barney, to check his heterodoxy. The meeting called to calm branch members, already tense from the controversy, was electrified by a mob of forty breaking into the meeting intent on mischief. Before anyone was injured, Barney jumped to a bench and appealed to the mob's sentiments by describing his grandfather's and father's service in the Revolution and War of 1812. His forbears "laid down their lives to secure to us the privilege we now enjoy of living on our farms and pleasant homes unmolested." Couldn't they just hold their "little prayer meeting" without being disturbed? His appeal to their common origins mollified the mob and they dispersed without doing any damage. Embellished by spiritual manifestations, the meeting temporarily resolved the confusion with the fledgling members. While all difficulties were not resolved, it was a memorable meeting for Barney.[32]

The Iowa Branches, 1841

The four southeasternmost counties of Iowa were those closest in proximity to Nauvoo, separated only by the "father of waters." Enclaves of Latter-day Saints were sporadically situated across the four counties—Lee, Des Moines, Van Buren, and Henry—some organized by colonization and others after missionary efforts. The labors of church leaders Lyman Wight, Amasa Lyman, and George Miller "succeeded, after an untiring effort, to lay the foundation of a great work throughout different parts of Iowa Territory" in the early part of 1841.[33] Despite the "untiring effort" to establish a foothold for the church in Iowa, the difficulty described earlier in the Barneys' branch was but one instance in a longer list of struggles for the church in the area. By this time there were at least a dozen and a half branches in southeastern Iowa.[34] John Smith, the fifty-nine-year-old uncle of Joseph Smith, who had responsibility for church administration in Iowa, wrote at the beginning of 1841 to his son, apostle George A. Smith, a missionary in England, about his consternation regarding his assignment:

> As to the church in Iowa, it increases in numbers as fast as could be expected but scattered over so large a tract of country that it requires the patience of Job and the wisdom of Solomon and the perseverance and faithfulness of an Abraham to keep such order as ought to be in the Church of Christ, which causes me considerable labors. It is difficult for me to write, for brethren are continually coming in to ask council.[35]

Two months later Joseph Smith received a revelation designating two Lee County, Iowa, sites—Zarahemla and Nashville—as gathering places for Latter-day Saints.[36] Later in the year John Smith was appointed president of the newly formed Iowa Stake, headquartered at Zarahemla, composed of 750 church members in the branches mentioned above.[37] The Henry County congregation had by this time apparently disorganized and the members relocated to Illinois.

Barney's tactics of pacification when the branch was in turmoil may have been successful, but the intent of the Saints to migrate was not assuaged. Regional gathering had been narrowed. A call to the "Saints Scattered Abroad" by Smith and his counselors in January 1841 to "dispose of their effects as fast as circumstances will possibly admit . . . and remove to our city and county" sealed the fate of the branch.[38] When the move became inevitable, the Barneys reluctantly made their own preparations to return to Illinois. Later in the year the Saints were instructed that Hancock County in Illinois and Lee County directly across the Mississippi River in Iowa were the primary locales for gathering.[39] With the move to Nauvoo a new era opened to the Barneys: their initiation into Mormon belief and practice.

Chapter 6

Unaccustomed to City Life: Nauvoo and the Hancock Prairie, 1841–1844

The conversion of the Barneys to the Church of Jesus Christ of Latter-day Saints ignited the reformation of their religious world view with life-altering impact. Not only did their spiritual outlook reform, in gathering with the Saints in Nauvoo these villatic folk entertained the prospect of settling within an urban society-in-the-making for the first time. The freedom, independence, and lifestyle options available to those on society's fringe were at the outset supplanted by their adherence to Mormonism. When considering the adjustment required of them to affiliate with the highly organized Latter-day Saints it is remarkable that there was not some type of residual fall-out from their newfound fealty. But the family moved forward with trust and hope in their new faith.

Still on the frontier, Hancock County increased in population not unlike other hinterland communities incident to the country's western Manifest Destiny. The same year the Barneys returned to Illinois, the first large overland company with Oregon in its sights traversed the prairie and plains before climbing into the Rocky Mountains. From there the epic trek took them to Oregon's Willamette Valley and other Pacific slope settings. The westward trickle of the early 1840s gushed before the end of the decade. While America's acquisitive and domineering bravado demanded a western destiny, the quiet seed of a private vision developed within Lewis Barney. At this point he had little or no plan, only an emerging objective: unfettered private space which he could fashion into something of his own making, a family kingdom.

As the Barneys gathered up what was transportable and fixed their plan to move from Iowa, they suffered a poor return on their Iowa investment. "Through the influence of Benjamin Leland," Barney wrote, "Father sold his farm for $2,200 which was worth $10,000."[1] (Though Leland apparently did Charles no favor, within a month he became the elder Barney's son-in-law by marrying Emerine Barney.)[2] It was not a convenient move for Charles and Deborah. Charles, now fifty-eight, relocated his pregnant wife and young children, buying "a house and lot in Nauvoo" in March 1841.[3] Within the month, Deborah delivered a son, William. Lewis also sold out in Iowa, likely in the spring of 1841, "bought a city lot of Brother Hyrum Smith, and built a frame

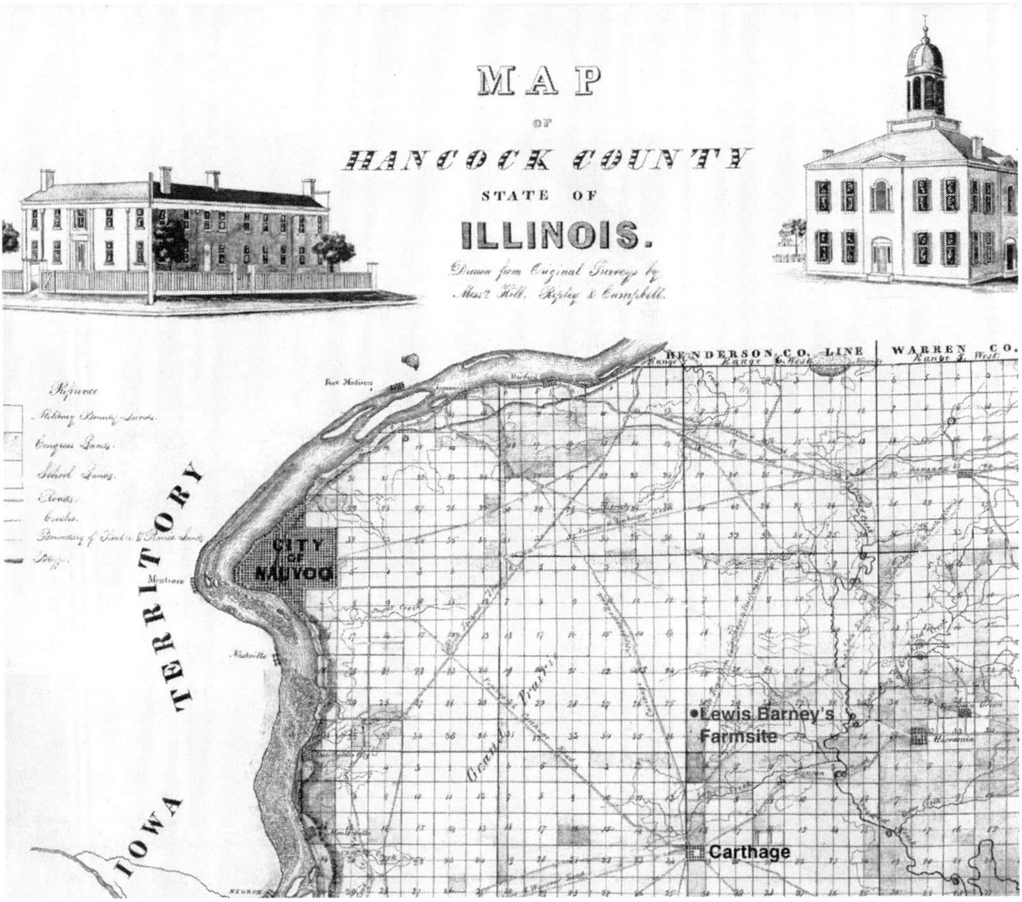

Hancock County, Illinois, ca. 1843 (Hill, Ripley, and Campbell).

house on it."[4] Luther Barney's family likely moved to Nauvoo in concert with his father and brother. There in the bustling Mormon center of gravity, the Barneys spent the rest of 1841.[5]

A little city life, with a population of over three thousand at the time, satisfied Lewis Barney that notwithstanding his devotion to his new religion, the busyness and other distractions of urban living grated against the lifestyle to which he had become familiar. And, in the proclamation that hastened the demise of the little Iowa branch the previous year, church leaders invited members gathering to Hancock County to "purchase and cultivate farms in the county."[6] Therefore, early in 1842, "not being accustomed to a city life," Lewis Barney wrote, "we bought, each of us, a quarter of a section of prairie land about 12 miles from Nauvoo. I paid $750 for my land [adding] 400 dollars more for improvements."[7] Establishing themselves, once again, on the Illinois prairie, they coupled their preference for rural living by spending "part of the time . . . on the farm and part of the time in Nauvoo."[8] With Nauvoo a metropolis-in-the-making, the Barneys' return to the Illinois prairie in central Hancock County had a familiarity that portended a prosperous future, in their own way.

The emerging city of Nauvoo had antecedents that stretched back to the beginning of the century. As early as 1805, the same year in which government explorer Zebulon Pike marched across the site, a farmstead was established in what became Nauvoo. The first permanent white settler moved to this bend in the Mississippi River in 1823. Others followed. Six years later, the same year that Hancock County was organized, the few who inhabited the future Mormon site established a post office with the exotic name of Venus. Five years later the small frontier village became Commerce. Adjoining Commerce a sister settlement creatively called Commerce City was organized three years later. Early in 1839 as the Latter-day Saints fled Missouri, several church members traveled north from Quincy, Illinois, their temporary refuge, searching for something more promising and permanent for the displaced church members. Initially investigating land on the Iowa side of the Mississippi River, they soon entered into negotiations for Commerce on the Illinois side with Isaac Galland, a speculator. Joseph Smith, after escaping Missouri authorities, first cast his eyes on what would become Nauvoo in April 1839. Before the end of that month, the first land purchases by Mormons were transacted, comprising the Hancock County peninsula bordered by the Mississippi River.[9]

Located about 250 miles southwest of Chicago and 150 miles upriver from St. Louis, Nauvoo grew with most of the new settlers purchasing or negotiating homesites on the peninsula flat. This is where church leaders settled, and most who initially came to Nauvoo followed the pattern. Promoting the city as the gathering locus for the Saints, Joseph Smith lauded the site without exaggeration. The splendid setting, he wrote, "is situated on the eastern bank of the Mississippi River, at the head of the Des Moines Rapids, in Hancock County; bounded on the east by an extensive prairie of surpassing beauty, and on the north, west, and south, by the Mississippi."[10] A seventy-foot bluff formed the eastern perimeter of the flat. The city of Kirtland, Ohio, once the heart of the Mormon gathering but abandoned as a church center somewhat coincident to the Missouri exodus, was not much of a precedent for the lofty ambitions of Nauvoo's city fathers. These visionaries, employing many of the techniques of earlier American city builders, incorporated urban benefits such as culture, education, and recreation into the lifestyles of Nauvoo's citizenry.[11] But their mark came from the infusion of religion into the growing center. While it was true that other religious communities arose across the American landscape beginning in colonial times, none acquired the multidimensional scope of Nauvoo. Certainly few rivaled the notoriety of the city of the Saints. "A comparison of the Mormons," states Robert Flanders, "with other religious Utopian societies such as the Amana Church Society, the Harmonists, the Shakers, the Separatists of Zoar, and the Perfectionists of Oneida, suggests that the Mormon endeavors were of an entirely different order of magnitude."[12]

Nauvoo was different from other urban centers in other ways. Where most developing towns in frontier Ohio, Illinois, Missouri, and Iowa were preponderantly male by population, Nauvoo "was attracting families rather than unattached males," making the ratio of men to women in the city nearly even.[13] This portended a level of stability not enjoyed by other frontier communities, but the particulars of Nauvoo society, which made it different from every other antebellum city, eventually cast the municipality and its citizens in a role they did not expect nor want. The very success of this river city proved to be the cause of its downfall.[14]

Two months previous to the Barneys' move to Nauvoo, the first presidency of the church wrote "to the Saints Scattered Abroad" that "the name of our city (Nauvoo) is of Hebrew origin, and signifies a beautiful situation, or place, carrying with it, also, the idea of *rest*; and is truly descriptive of this most delightful situation." The next month the first election for city officials was held in Nauvoo. The month of the Barney's arrival, Nauvoo was divided into four ecclesiastical wards (religious congregations defined by geography), and a city ordinance passed giving all "religious sects, and denominations, whatever, . . . free toleration and equal privileges in this city."[15] Once past the initial season of malaria in 1839–1840 where many were taken ill, the progressive nature of the city was matched by its speedy growth. Having performed missionary work for over two years in England, Wilford Woodruff, upon his return to Mormon headquarters in October 1841, wrote, "When I left their [*sic*] was not more than a dozen houses in the town but now their [*sic*] was several hundred."[16] The same week in which Lewis became a Latter-day Saint, Joseph Smith wrote a memorial to the Nauvoo High Council, an administrative body which helped regulate temporal and religious affairs in the city, asking for relief from some of his nonreligious duties. The growth of the church, and consequently the size of Nauvoo, forced the prophet to "devote himself exclusively to those things which relate to the spiritualities of the church."[17] Despite the building boom, housing in Nauvoo created dilemmas for its citizens. The expansion of the city and the church continued unabated until 1844 when the population peaked at between 12,000 and 17,000.[18]

Despite the appearance of prosperity and opportunity, Nauvoo was plagued by an economy with chronic fatigue. The primary growth industry in Nauvoo was the building business. Nauvoo's focus as the center of the Mormon gathering required housing for immigrants. A thriving economy required more. The Mormon capital, whose fiscal situation was initially very optimistic, soon had to face the economic liability of being far removed from the urban centers of the east. The month after the Barneys' move to Hancock County, Mary Ann Angell Young reported to her apostle husband serving as a missionary in England that the supplies, tools, and other necessary equipment associated with prosperity were "very hard to get . . . here so far west of a Good quality to Supply So many that wants to work." She lamented that those who had just emigrated to Nauvoo from England "have no money to buy things with and nothing to work with and no thread to mend their clothes with." Indeed, clothing was so hard to obtain that she asked him, upon his return later that year, to bring "Calaco & factory Cloath [which] would be very prophetable," for the family.[19] Barney recognized the limitations facing Nauvoo's inhabitants and figured he could prosper doing what he knew best, farming.

For the Barneys, the first year in Nauvoo was an important period of physical and spiritual assimilation into the church. Barney wrote that while living in Nauvoo, his family "attended most of the meetings and received much instruction upon the principles of the gospel."[20] The Church of Jesus Christ operated by a lay priesthood which officiated in Mormon meetings, rituals, and procedures. Charles and his sons Luther and John were ordained as elders in the priesthood of the church in 1841.[21] Lewis was later ordained to the missionary body of the church called the "seventies," another priesthood office.[22] The significance of Mormonism's lay priesthood cannot be overstated. The "hands-on" religious activity of adherents not only enlarged their participation in organizational functions but it also gave them a sense of ownership in the church. The objective was to include as many men in the priesthood organizations as possible. Before the Saints departed Nauvoo, three-fourths of Nauvoo's males were priesthood holders, with four of five being seventies, like Lewis.[23]

While embracing some traditional Christian beliefs and rituals, unique to the Latter-day Saints was the practice of vicarious baptism for the dead. Introduced to the church by Joseph Smith in 1840, Smith taught that the components of salvation offered by Jesus Christ, such as baptism, were not limited to those in the mortal world nor to the small percentage of the earth's inhabitants privileged to hear the gospel of Christ. "Salvation of the dead" became one of the central theological features of Latter-day Saint belief, a fuller explanation of which will be given later. Within the year of the Barneys' gathering to Nauvoo, Charles, Luther and his wife Lurinda, Lewis's wife Elizabeth, and his brother Walter all were vicarious substitutes in baptism for their deceased family members.[24] Participation in rites, rituals, and ordinances melds adherents to the organization of which they are a part. And so it was with the Barneys.

Also in 1841 Lewis Barney obtained a church blessing, a "patriarchal blessing," prophetic in nature and given to believing Latter-day Saints. Bestowed by Joseph Smith's brother Hyrum, officially the church patriarch, Barney was told that he descended from ancient Israelites and that the "holy priesthood [would be] handed down through you upon your posterity to the latest generation" and that his name would "be had in honorable remembrance by [his] posterity forever."[25] If Barney had previously lacked vision of his place in the mortal world, the blessing provided the spiritual superstructure that, thereafter, undoubtedly shaped his purpose for living. Barney and the other recipients of these blessings found themselves abstractly woven into the fabric of God's particular occupation with the Latter-day Saints. The involvement of the family in these Mormon rituals is an indication that their acceptance of Joseph Smith's teachings was not peripheral. The Barneys had embraced Mormonism.

The family's immersion into the Church of Jesus Christ was one thing, but they found that other forces were at work that defined their place within Mormon society. Notwithstanding the egalitarian promise of Mormonism's doctrine of salvation, a multilevel strata measured by the religio-socio-economic status of an individual or family existed within Latter-day Saint society not unlike that of the secular world. While the strata had not matured in the first generation of Mormonism, the antecedents of the cultural parameters were in place in Nauvoo. The ubiquitous poverty of the Saints during this period, with few exceptions, diminished the importance of wealth in Nauvoo's class arrangement. Rather than wealth being the primary qualifier of class differentiation, there were other factors of demarcation that stratified Mormon society.

Beginning in the early 1830s a hierarchical structure imposed by divine appointment shaped Latter-day Saint life. By 1835 a cadre of church leaders had emerged. A church First Presidency composed of Joseph Smith and two counselors presided over other leadership groups and individuals such as the Twelve Apostles, the presidency of the seventies, the standing high council, the church patriarch, and the bishop.[26] (The immediate and extended families of most of these leaders, as acknowledged by the rest of the culture, formed the top stratum of the scale.) Subordinate to these presiding quorums were other priesthood bodies, such as the seventies mentioned earlier, who helped carry on the ministry of the church. As the church expanded, a middle level of leadership also developed in the form of local congregational authorities. While the intention was not necessarily the creation of a religious elite, the inherent differences between those who led and those who were led fostered a societal differentiation within the theocratically oriented church. It did not take long for new initiates, such as the Barneys, to recognize their place in the religious structure of life in Nauvoo.

Lewis Barney's move from the city after a year in Nauvoo also had an impact on the nature of the lives of his family. Not only did he relocate from the motion and cacophony of urban living, he also solidified thereafter his and his family's place in the structure of Mormon culture. It was a matter of the simple difference between city and country existence. The geography of domestic life and where one lived had everything to do with how one lived. Where Nauvoo was the only Mormon city, those who chose not to operate within its perimeter but lived within its extended orbit defined themselves into another stratum of Mormonism.[27] Barney, by his choice of geography, found himself and family in the lower stratum of Mormon society. There is no evidence to suggest family disappointment in their identification within Mormon culture. Indeed, much of it was of their own making.

The Hancock Prairie

Lifestyle preference found Barney's attention predictably focused on his farm in Hancock County, though he retained his familiarity with Nauvoo. The lack of economic opportunity available in Nauvoo also probably played on his decision. Accustomed to life on the prairie, Barney found circumstances on the farm more compatible with his skills and experiences, though he first settled with a negative perception of the area. When Barney and his family left their Lake Fork, Illinois, homes in 1839 to relocate in Iowa, they passed westward through Carthage en route:

> On nearing the town we discovered foot prints of a large band of horses and a few wagon tracks turned off the road to a lone tree about 100 yards from the road. Curiosity led us to visit the spot and on arriving at the tree we discovered a newly dug grave and on examination we saw a piece of rope tied to a limb of the tree. The thought struck me that some one had been hung and buried there. This cast a feeling of gloom over me. On arriving in town we learned there had been a man executed for murder the day before. So ever after the name of Carthage caused a feeling of gloomy sadness to rest on me as being a city of blood.[28]

Barney's new farm in Pilot Grove township was one hundred miles from his Sangamon County home, but just three miles north of Carthage, the county seat of Hancock County.

Settlers arrived in Hancock County, the most westerly extension of Illinois, about a decade later than newcomers to Sangamon County. Most towns and villages in Hancock County were established in the mid-1830s, the earliest in 1832, although some settlers moved on the frontier prairie at the decade's beginning. Two-thirds of the county, running thirty-eight miles north and south and about twenty-four miles wide, is prairie, the remainder is composed of timbered lands, most of which were located along the meandering forty-five-mile bank of the Mississippi River. Surveyors in 1835 platted Carthage, located in the geographic center of the county and the town closest to Barney's farm on the prairie. Sixteen full and eight partial townships comprised the county, one of the former being Pilot Grove.[29] The grove's first settlers arrived about 1830. Their successors hailed primarily from Virginia, Ohio, Kentucky, and New York. Upon arriving they found a "wide expanse of prairie, covered with ducks and deer and waving grass and wild flowers."[30] By 1834 nearly 2,000 called Hancock County home. In the next three years the numbers rose to nearly 5,000. Carthage had grown to nearly 400 with forty or fifty homes by the time the Barneys passed through on their way to Iowa.[31]

The former owners of Barney's farm may have improved the land some but there was still much work to do. "I continued working on my farm," Barney wrote, "building and improving my place until I got eighty acres of land enclosed with a good stake and ridered fence."[32] Barney obtained another eighty-acre plot of farmland located about a mile southwest of his home in the county.[33] Charles Barney also had farmland just south of Lewis's property. While it appears that Charles resided in Nauvoo, perhaps seasonally working his county land, the cycle of Lewis's life revolved around his spring, summer, and fall residence on the farm raising his family's sustenance and relocating to Nauvoo for the winters.[34]

A consequence of Lewis and Betsey Barney's lives on the prairie was mostly missing opportunities for their family only available within the trappings of Nauvoo's urban personality. Nauvoo's several schools operated primarily in the fall, winter, and spring, meaning that their older children, spending most of the year on the prairie, probably had limited educational opportunities, likely not exceeding that obtained by their father. The level of socialization available only in urban settings was also absent in their lives. The family probably never associated in the Nauvoo lyceum or the Nauvoo Library and Literary Institute. Notwithstanding provisions of the Nauvoo Legion, the local militia, which required military service of all male adults, no Barneys can be found in existing legion records. The records and rolls of the roughly 1,300-member female Relief Society of Nauvoo organized in March 1842 do not show that any Barney women were participants. Because many community worship services were held in the city's two or three outdoor groves where hundreds and even a few thousand congregated during favorable weather, the family likely missed many of the spiritual gatherings.[35] Country folks by choice, the level of Barney activity in community life in the Mormon capital during their five-year stay in Hancock County was largely shaped by their rural disposition. Nevertheless, they attached themselves to all that they could that was Mormon.

Nauvoo, Illinois, with temple in background, ca. 1845–1846. Photographer unknown. Courtesy Church Archives, the Church of Jesus Christ of Latter-day Saints.

The Barneys found themselves not only absorbed into the theological and ecclesiastical core of the church, they were also a small factor in the growth and development of the physical kingdom. The Mormon realm required economic resources to sustain its presence. Members in good standing were required to contribute a tithe of their "increase" to the church and during the Nauvoo Temple construction, a tithe of their time.[36] Tithing ledgers from Nauvoo show that the Barneys—who donated such diverse commodities as $5 in gold, produce, "old cast iron," and a "four year old brown steer"—were committed to sustain the church.[37] In early 1841 the Saints were told by Joseph Smith to build a hotel in Nauvoo, "a house for boarding, a house that strangers may come from afar to lodge therein." Barney reported he also "donated liberally . . . for the Nauvoo House."[38] Far more important to the overall master plan of Nauvoo as a religious center was raising the holy temple "for the Most High to dwell therein," after the pattern of Israel's ancient monuments to God. Smith was told by God, in the same revelation announcing the directive for the Nauvoo House, that "there is not a place found on earth that [I] may come to and restore again" ordinances and revelation fundamental to the destiny of modern Israel.[39] Building the Nauvoo Temple became one of the Latter-day Saints' primary objectives during their stay in Nauvoo. Every family, at one time or another, was involved in some way in its erection.[40] Barney "furnished a team and wagon to haul rock for the Nauvoo Temple,"[41] and later "found that provisions was needed much more than work" on the edifice. From his farm production he furnished "grain and other provisions for the temple hands."[42] The Barneys had some measure of satisfaction in 1846, if only briefly, from their contribution to the construction of the temple by participating in the sacred rites for which the temple was built.

As Nauvoo physically prospered, its economy struggled to keep pace. A business district provided commodities and other essentials, as well as some creature comforts, for the growing citizenry. The three Mississippi River docks skirting the city were busied not only by immigrants but by freight trade as well. While nearly 40 percent of city breadwinners were involved in farming, a wide range of other occupations were employed in the community, two-thirds of which would today be classified as blue-collar workers.[43] The town was bustling with activity. A visitor to the area noted,

> Scores of mechanics and laborers are busy as bees . . . and as they are all influenced by a *public spirit* unknown to the most of our communities—they do more work and bring more to pass than people do elsewhere . . . they present the appearance of an enterprising, industrious, sober, and thrifty population indeed, as in the respects just mentioned, have no rivals east, and, we rather guess, not even west of the Mississippi.[44]

City fathers initially hoped to develop a business district on the flat near Joseph Smith's home, below the bluff on which the temple-in-progress reigned. There was even an elaborate design for Main Street, bordering the Smith home, which included plans for a canal stretching north and south the full length of the peninsula.[45] As the city grew, contrary to Smith's intentions, a commercial district developed on the bluff adjacent to the temple. As it turned out, the overwhelming population growth of the city outran the hoped-for simultaneous economic increase. The result was that farmers outside the city, who carried on traditional methods of agrarian increase, often had the economic advantage of many who came to Nauvoo only to be underemployed or worse.[46] Still, economic activity increased even though it could not stay in step with population growth.[47]

The Barneys' agrarian economy benefitted them. After a year and a half in Hancock County, Lewis Barney's tax assessment, indicating that he was licensed to sell goods from his property, showed that he had accumulated personal property about average for county residents, although it exceeded that of Nauvoo's citizens. His brother Luther's holdings were comparable, but their father's wealth was substantially more than either of his sons.[48] This was in 1842, the year when the overall economy of Illinois slumped significantly.[49] Lewis Barney's trade with Smith's store in Nauvoo indicates a regular presence in Nauvoo to conduct personal business.[50] On one occasion, he wrote:

> Being in company with Joseph [Smith] and several other persons, Joseph said he needed a little money and if [he] had it he could put it to a better use than any other person in the world. I said nothing to him about it but went home, got 200 dollars, and went down to Joseph's store. Joseph not being present, I, being acquainted with Lyman Wight, said to him, "I have a little money for Brother Joseph that I wish to let him have." Brother Wight said, "Let me take it and I will hand it to him." I told him to write me a receipt for it. While he was writing the receipt, Brother Joseph stepped in. I said, "Brother Joseph I have some money for you that I was about to let Brother Wight have for you." Joseph said, "I am the man to take it." So I handed him the 200 dollars for which he gave his note, payable 6 months after date.[51]

Despite the maturation and progress of the city, with laws characterizing Nauvoo a city-state, its principal citizen was still vulnerable to the Saints' enemies. Numerous complaints were filed against Smith, including one charging him with conspiracy in the attempted murder of former Missouri governor Lilburn Boggs. Several charges resulted in the prophet's arrest. While he eluded conviction, the harassment with which he was plagued carried over into the domestic tranquility of Nauvoo. Not only were there threats from without, Smith's status was eroding among a small but determined cadre of discontented insiders. The atmosphere in Nauvoo, once tranquil and ebullient, was darkened by suspicion and unpredictability.

In the spring of 1842 Smith built a moat surrounding the Latter-day Saints in the form of a fraternal organization whose reputation for organizational loyalty was singular. A lodge of Freemasons, whose meetings and rituals were secret, was organized in the city on 15 March 1842. While other Illinois lodges opposed Nauvoo's application because of the unpopularity of the Mormons, a number of Latter-day Saints were practicing Masons prior to their conversions, including Charles Barney. Indeed, most church leaders in Nauvoo either were or became Masons.[52] Masonry itself suffered widespread derision in America, roughly equal in time to the existence of the Church of Jesus Christ, including a national opposition political party that held great sway in regional politics. Meeting in buildings such as Smith's store, Nauvoo Masons increased in numbers, requiring the construction of a Masonic Temple which was dedicated in the presence of 550 members from throughout the region in April 1844.[53]

Near the Masonic Temple's completion, Lewis Barney applied for affiliation on 1 February and was admitted to the lodge a month later on 7 March 1844.[54] While he and his family did not participate in other Nauvoo organizations because of their rural living, Barney may have become a Mason as part of the defensive bulwark growing in Nauvoo. He demonstrated some activity in lodge activities initially, but neglected his association thereafter.[55] Barney's father, Charles, a Mason since his Owl Creek (Ohio) days, finally petitioned the Nauvoo lodge for membership in April 1845, at sixty-two one of the oldest to apply.[56] The timing of the elder Barney's reassociation with the Masonic order was ironic. Agitation increased as Illinois Masonic lodges outside Nauvoo became increasingly opposed to the Mormon Masons. In January 1843 non-Mormon Masons in Illinois numbered 227; the Nauvoo lodge totaled 330. Over time as the numerical disparity widened—1,348 Mormons eventually applied for membership in the Nauvoo lodge—so also did the suspicion of the non-Mormon lodges which feared domination by Mormon Masons. In October 1844 the grand lodge of Illinois severed their relationship with the Nauvoo lodge. This, coupled with Brigham Young's 10 April 1845 recommendation to suspend Nauvoo lodge activities, doomed a flourishing Masonic presence just at the time that Charles Barney renewed his Masonic membership.[57]

Opposition toward the Mormons in Nauvoo

Quite predictably, as the influence and visibility of Nauvoo's citizens nudged upward, opposition from Hancock County and other Illinois residents increased comparably. Within eighteen months after the Mormons took refuge in Hancock County, many of their non-Mormon neighbors were firm in their distrust of the Saints. A La Harpe resident living just fourteen miles northeast of Lewis Barney's Hancock County home wrote a relative in August 1840, "If the predictions of Joseph Smith prove true you may expect to hear of two thirds of the [older] inhabitants of our county being swept away in one year." Claiming that Smith would insure the genocide by sending "his followers two by two [to] poison the wells" of the Hancock residents, the correspondent predicted, "the prospect is fair that they will meet with the same difficulty in Ills. that they did in Mo."[58] Misunderstanding and bias from both sides of the matter seemed to insure the inevitability of irreconcilable differences wherever the Saints gathered.

There was also an ideological spin which separated Mormons from their neighbors. The roots of the differences were couched in the American republicanism embraced by the county's earliest residents juxtaposed to the Mormon view of themselves as latter-day Israel. A historian of the conflict has written that

> what Joseph Smith did, while Americans were giving birth to a society marked by pluralism, egalitarianism, and individualism, was establish a new source of authority, a new hierarchy, and a new, highly unified community, based on fresh spiritual experience. . . . But theocratic authoritarianism and popular sovereignty were incompatible, so Smith's extension of his religious ideology into . . . the Jacksonian era placed the Mormons on a collision course with the rest of America.[59]

Few Latter-day Saints failed to realize the significant contrast their theocratic posture represented in light of American thinking at the time. Their leader knew something had to be done.

Recognizing the sorry state of the Saints' public image, Joseph Smith initiated a personal campaign for the U.S. presidency in early 1844 to disabuse his countrymen of their erroneous perception of the Mormons. He believed as the larger American community became enlightened about the church, the litany of violated rights toward his people would arouse the sympathies of the people in their favor. Notwithstanding his hopefulness, the track record of local governments toward the Saints dictated consideration of alternatives.[60] Smith predicted in 1842 that the Saints would find themselves in the mountains of the American West, an obvious indicator he was resigned to remove his people from American polity. In February 1844, the same week a convention of anti-Mormons gathered in Carthage, Illinois, the prophet directed the Quorum of Twelve Apostles to organize a company of men to "explore Oregon and California and select a site for a new city for the Saints."[61] While the expeditionary force never materialized, it was apparent to most that the tenure of the Saints in Illinois was limited. The focus of opposition was primarily aimed at Smith and other church leaders, but increasingly the Saints at large were targeted. Paradoxically, while life in Nauvoo manifested the activities of permanence, inside and outside interference mounted, compelling church leaders to search for alternatives to protect the church and its members.[62]

During this tenuous period, while Lewis Barney focused on his farmstead in Hancock County, Charles Barney's family kept quarters in Nauvoo. The elder Barney's favorable economic position in 1842 may have taken a hit by the end of his tenure in Nauvoo. Now about sixty years old, Charles, with his wife and their five children, lived for a time in an apartment on "Brick Row" in Nauvoo, suggesting the loss of their previous domestic assets.[63] Later it appears that Charles moved his family to Joseph Smith's property in Nauvoo where his last child, Sarah Jane, was born 13 May 1845.[64] With uncertainty hanging over the future of the Saints, as the church contemplated its options, the Barneys plied options of their own on the frontier again.

Near the time of Sarah Jane's birth, Lucien and Henry, two of Charles's older sons, returned to their exploratory ventures for family security. While they reconnoitered Arkansas six years earlier, this time they made their way to Texas. Their venture in Texas came at a particularly exciting time. Texas in mid-1845 was an independent state on the verge of being internationally recognized, even by Mexico from whom it broke in the previous decade. At the same time, newly elected U.S. president James K. Polk in his inaugural speech in March 1845 suggested U.S. intentions to annex Texas. The Mexicans were outraged and tension between the two former enemies mounted. By the end of the year Texas became the twenty-eighth of the United States. Henry and Lucien, apparently in behalf of the extended family, in May 1845 filed on over twelve hundred acres just below the Red River in Lamar County in northeastern Texas.[65] After an unknown length of time the brothers returned to Illinois, apparently disappointed, with nothing but land receipts and a potential opportunity never realized in Texas.[66]

While his younger brothers were hundreds of miles to the south, Lewis Barney's energies were primarily absorbed in maintaining his family and farm. Lewis and Betsey's third son was born there on 5 March 1843.[67] They named him Alma after one of the principal figures of the Book of Mormon. Several miles removed from the center of church activity in Nauvoo, Barney was, nevertheless, quite aware of the predicament in which the Latter-day Saints found themselves. "I was living near Carthage and was frequently in the company of the Carthaginians," he recalled, "and learned their fears in relation to the Mormons, which was that the Prophet Joseph Smith was gaining too much power and that he soon would control the state elections and something must be done to get him out of the way."[68] Provoked by their fear of Smith's motives in the county, real or imagined, the "old settlers" of the area initiated organized resistance to any and all Mormons. "Persecution continued to increase," Barney wrote,

> Brother Joseph was continually harassed by the mob from Missouri with vexatious lawsuits which stirred up the feelings of the people of Illinois . . . and left the inhabitants of Nauvoo exposed to all the

Brick or Widow's Row, Nauvoo, Illinois, 1885. B. H. Roberts Photograph Collection. Courtesy Church Archives, the Church of Jesus Christ of Latter-day Saints.

> insults and abuses that the mob felt disposed to inflict upon them. I became a witness of these things—wicked, unjust abuses—which gave me a more firm belief that all the former reports of their persecutions was true and was heaped upon them without cause or provocation.[69]

The mounting tension within the area could not continue without resolution in one way or another. With all the personal and material resources that had been invested into Nauvoo, it was difficult to imagine it could have been for naught. The balance of the scale was tilting against the Saints.

Chapter 7

A Gloom over the Country: The Final Years in Hancock County, 1844–1846

For the Saints, Illinois had been good for them for only the first two years of their residence on the Hancock County peninsula. Nauvoo flourished, despite the difficulties of the economy. Streams of converts, many being those baptized during the mission of the Twelve Apostles to England beginning in the late 1830s, vitalized Nauvoo and surrounding environs, expanding Mormon influence in the region. By 1842 pressures from outside and inside the church exacted a toll on the Saints collectively and certain church leaders individually that changed the nature of life in the Mormon capital. Joseph Smith was required to hide for days at a time within and without Nauvoo to avoid the legal grasp of Missouri and Illinois officials determined to chain him to the attempted assassination of Missouri's former governor Lilburn Boggs, author of the infamous Mormon extermination order of October 1838. An atmosphere of fear and siege enveloped the Saints in Hancock County.

The Murder of the Smiths

In the early months of 1844, a clandestine conspiracy from within the church brewed against the prophet. Several insiders including his former counselor, William Law, calculated to expose what to them were the prophet's excesses in a series of events culminating in the destruction of Law's opposition newspaper, the *Nauvoo Expositor*. The dissenters were disturbed by the progressive nature of religious doctrine and behavior, most notably polygamy, which was manifest in Nauvoo. They formed their own church claiming allegiance to early Mormon theology, but their word-of-mouth cause stalled. Publishing their grievances, they charged Smith with usurpation of power, false doctrine, and aberrant behavior. The interdiction by the city council against the *Expositor* on 10 June 1844, palpably a violation of the freedom extended to the press in America, led to Smith and his brother Hyrum's incarceration on 24 June in Carthage, Illinois, on charges of treason. The Smiths were now in precarious territory. "Some of the brethren," Barney wrote,

> was in favor of having him go to Carthage and stand his trial and said it would all come out right and he would be acquitted and that would put an end to the trouble. I told them that if Brother Joseph ever went to Carthage he would never get away alive. I lived in the neighborhood of Carthage about 3 miles from town and knew their intense, wicked hatred against Joseph and the Mormons, and that it was their intention to get him there and assassinate him.[1]

The leading proponents of Smith's demise, besides Law and his confederates, were newspaperman Thomas Sharp of Warsaw and other Hancock County non-Mormons primarily from Warsaw and Carthage. They found this circumstance too fortuitous not to act. The local militia, a unit of several dozen called the Carthage Greys, employed by the Illinois governor ostensibly to protect the Smiths, became instead facilitators for their executioners.[2] Scores of militiamen with blackened faces stormed the jail on the hot, sultry afternoon of 27 June and in a few moments dispatched Joseph and Hyrum Smith into eternity. The Mormon prophet was dead.

This was the most dramatic event in the short life of Mormonism. Benjamin F. Johnson remembered the shock: "'Oh God! What will thy orphan church and the people now do?' was the only feeling or thought that now burst out in groans."[3] Not only were the Saints' emotions shattered, a pall was cast over the region. "The whole country was deserted," Barney reported.

> Men, women, and children fled for their lives, not taking time to shut their doors after them. Stores was left standing open and there was a gloom cast over the country so much so that strangers passing through the country spoke of it. As I was out looking for my stock, I met a stranger. He asked me what was the matter, that everything looks so gloomy and lonesome.

After describing the deaths of the Smiths, Barney said, "When the blood of a prophet is shed it has a tendency to cast a gloom over the country."[4] As the lifeless bodies of the Smith brothers were carried by wagons from Carthage to Nauvoo, the virulent opponents of the church anticipated the dissolution of the Mormons. While Mormonism did not melt away, the Saints could not have possibly imagined the dilemma into which they were then thrust regarding the future of church leadership.

No precedent for succession to Joseph Smith's role existed. Rivals for the position and the loyalty of thousands of Saints were centered primarily in four personalities: (1) Sidney Rigdon, first presidency counselor then out of favor with the church, (2) James Jesse Strang, a newcomer who claimed a commission from Smith as his successor, (3) William Smith, representing the Smiths who anticipated a family dynasty, and (4) Brigham Young, president of the

Twelve Apostles.[5] Church members, still in a state of bewilderment, weighed the claims of each, yearning for a viable succession. Later, George Q. Cannon said he remembered "how men's minds were indulged in; the guesses, the anticipations, some thinking one man would be chosen, and others that some one else would be. Many of the people were at an entire loss to know who would take charge of the church affairs."[6] The course of succession was clear to some, but many had questions.

Forty-two days after Joseph's death, 8 August, a meeting held in the east grove in Nauvoo proved to be the point of demarcation for most church members. Sidney Rigdon, erstwhile resident of Nauvoo recently returned from Pittsburgh, made his bid as "guardian" of the church. Barney was present: his interest piqued. After Rigdon's case was made, he said, "President Young then arose and took the stand, his face and countenance having the appearance of Joseph." But to Lewis it was not only Joseph's apparent visage manifest in Brigham Young; "his voice and words were the familiar voice and words of our martyred prophet so much so the whole congregation was fully satisfied that the mantle of the Prophet Joseph had fallen on him and some of the Saints really believed it was in reality the prophet himself." The impression left on the Saints was a distinctive and indelible one.

> I knew it was Brigham Young and being familiar with the countenance, voice and manner of the speech of the Prophet Joseph Smith, I also knew the mantle of the prophet had fallen on Brigham and it was marvelous and a miracle wrought by the power of God in the sight and hearing of the whole multitude that they might never doubt that Brigham was the chosen leader of the church.[7]

The challenge from the other rivals continued for a time, but Brigham Young and the Twelve were fixed clearly in the minds of the majority of Latter-day Saints as the authentic successors to the prophet from this point. Barney lined up behind forty-four-year-old Young, a Vermont native.

Cleansing Hancock County of Mormons

While the death of Joseph Smith was directly the result of internal conflict between Mormon dissidents and church leadership, it was but a scene in a larger play involving the church and its Hancock County neighbors. Common citizens were so inclined against the Saints that organized groups such as the "Anti-Mormon warriors" known as the "Brick-Batters" formed in the county.[8] Robert Flanders, clarifying the conflict between the two sides, has written that:

> In all these places, the gentile [non-Mormon] neighbors were eventually excited to uneasiness, then to hostility toward the sect. To be

> sure, the Mormon religion was unorthodox, but the nation knew and tolerated many unorthodox sects. Contemporary observers did not regard individual Mormons as fanatics or find them, as individuals, very different from thousands of others of Yankee descent who spread across the upper Midwest during the first half of the nineteenth century. But Mormonism, the gentiles observed, was more than the unorthodox doctrine of ardent believers. It was a burgeoning, centralized, corporate sect committed to action upon its beliefs—and those beliefs entailed the reordering of society and the conversion of the world. It was the Mormon Church in action that aroused its neighbors.[9]

While there was an air of passivity exhibited by the Saints after the murder of their leaders, which abated the resolve of their neighbors for a time, within a year the Mormons had regrouped in a formidable way. On the first anniversary of the Smiths' deaths, Brigham Young wrote to a church apostle in England: "There never was a more prosperous time, in general, amongst the saints, since the work commenced. Nauvoo, or, more properly, the 'City of Joseph,' looks like a paradise." The city he described was anything but writhing in despair. Indeed, he said, visitors to Nauvoo expressed "their astonishment and surprise" to see the "beauty and grandeur" of the city.[10] It was not just visitors who took note of conditions in Nauvoo; the activity did not escape their Hancock County neighbors. When it was apparent that the church and its members were not going to fragment and dissolve, the tenuous peace, smoldering for months, threatened to flare in the Saints' faces again.

Not only were differing ideology and jealousy of Mormon prosperity sources of incompatibility, non-Mormons claimed that some Mormons flagrantly violated "old settlers'" property and rights. Charges of Mormon thievery spread through the country bolstering the resolve of most county residents that the Mormons had to go. The *Warsaw Signal* in January 1845 notified its readers that any hope of peaceful coexistence was futile. A hostile correspondent declared that Mormons brought their problems on themselves alleging them guilty "of most of the thieving practices in the county." Prior to their arrival, "it was not considered necessary to place lock or bar on anything," but as Mormon numbers increased in the vicinity, "in the same ratio has thieving increased." And, he asserted, "as [Mormons] have been removed from some of the neighborhoods, [the thievery] has ceased."[11] A Carthage resident later complained that Mormons "murdered many of our best citizens . . . and there was nothing . . . that they would not steal. . . . Our lives and property was at the mercy of the worst set of outlaws that ever congregated together."[12] The prognosis was clear; the immovable object and the irresistible force were now to meet with full measure. Flaming words were finally followed in the late summer of 1845 with flaming torches.

Some county residents, organized as vigilantes, agitated to cleanse the region of Mormons. Beginning in Adams County, just south of Hancock County, LDS communities in early September were assaulted. One contemporary observer, no friend of the Saints, later wrote:

> The houses burnt were mostly log cabins of not much value, though some pretty good dwellings were included. The manner was to go to the house and warn the inmates out—that they were going to burn it. Usually there would be no show of resistance; but all hands, burners and all, would proceed to take out the goods and place them out of danger. When the goods were all securely removed, the torch would be applied, and the house consumed. Then on to another. We are not aware that a correct count was ever made of the number they burned; but our informant states that there were probably 70 or 80. Some accounts have placed it as high as 125.[13]

"About this time," Barney, who still lived north of Carthage in September 1845, wrote, a group of county vigilantes "sent a committee of three men to me to try to get me to give up Mormonism." Barney reported they initially cajoled him saying, "We know you are an honest man and we feel sorry for you and if you will give up Mormonism and that Book of Mormon you are welcome to stay with us and we will protect you." They made no secret of their "determination . . . to drive all the Mormons into Nauvoo, then surround it, and burn the city and drive the Mormons into the river." Barney told the delegation he thought them to be unjust and cruel and he would not comply. Given a temporary reprieve, he was later visited again by "seven armed men" who wanted Barney's gun. Barney replied that he had a "first class rifle," that he "knew how to use it," and he wasn't about to give it up. Barney's stubborn resistance could have left him homeless or lifeless or both. Instead, before riding off the vigilantes matter-of-factly warned him, "We will give you until tomorrow morning to get away and then we will . . . burn your house and if you are here you will have to take what follows."[14]

Word having circulated that Mormon lives and property were in jeopardy, Barney realized resistance was futile. "I then set to work making the necessary preparation for leaving my hard-earned home" which included "an orchard of 100 apple trees and as many peach trees and other shrubbery" which he planted the previous year. While making final arrangements to move to Nauvoo, he said, "I turned my pork hogs into the field of corn of about 35 acres, well fenced, with a good, tight, strong, seven rail, staked and ridered fence so that a three month old pig could not get out or in to the field." After a week retrofitting his Nauvoo home for occupation, he returned to gather what he could from his farm, stopping in Carthage en route. Luther, his brother, was the subject there of a legal entanglement over a debt involving

Lewis's horse. Barney reported that he had "loaned a fine mare to my brother Luther, and as he was owing a man in Carthage two dollars, [the man] attached my brother's wagon and team for the $2." The younger brother's appearance in court allowed him to retrieve his own horse, "but [Luther] lost his horse and wagon."[15] Legal proceedings in Hancock County involving Mormons tended to find them the responsible parties. Returning to his farm about the second week in September 1845, Barney found his hogs absent from their enclosure. Approaching his nearest neighbor, George C. Waggoner, he inquired about the missing hogs. Their encounter typifies the conflict between the Mormons and non-Mormons in the outlying areas of Hancock County.

Waggoner, a Kentuckian, was twenty-eight years old and a resident of Hancock County for about eight years in 1845 making him, despite his youth, one of the region's first residents. He and his neighbors closely observed the wave of Mormons pouring into the county after 1840. Waggoner was one of the Carthage Greys, the local militia which likely served the same function for Hancock settlers as the unit to which Barney previously belonged in Lake Fork did for those living in Sangamon River country. As Mormon numbers escalated, so also did their neighbors' wariness of the Saints' designs. By the time the Latter-day Saints reached their peak, the Carthage Greys, clearly protecting what they perceived to be the best interests of non-Mormon territory in the county, were decidedly anti-Mormon. As the fateful events of 27 June 1844 unfolded, Waggoner was one who carried ammunition for his comrades when they stormed the jail at Carthage to murder the Smith brothers. He was reputed to have been the first person to enter the Smiths' jail cell after their murders, even retrieving the revolver uselessly used by Joseph Smith to counter the assault.[16] Indeed, Waggoner "boasted of having old Joe's pistol that the prophet had in the jail and would shoot any Mormon down like a dog," according to Barney.[17] Neighborly is not a word to describe the relationship between Barney and the man on the adjacent property.

As Barney approached his neighbor, Waggoner coldly complained that Barney's "hogs had got into his cornfield and was tearing down his corn and he had to shut them up to save his corn." Barney replied that Waggoner's claim was rather suspicious as "I left the hogs in my own field of corn when I left." But sensing Waggoner's design and "not wishing to get into a quarrel with him" the Mormon asked Waggoner to what extent he had been damaged. Waggoner figured the cost to be five dollars. Barney replied, "You know you are owing me four dollars. I will give you that if you will let me take the hogs." But the neighbor insisted the damages totaled *five* dollars. Recognizing the futility of his stance, but having no money to satisfy the demand, Barney told him he would later pay him the dollar. Gathering his animals, which were very important for his survival, he herded them to his farm.[18] As Barney approached his farmstead, Archibald Patten, a Mormon friend whose brother, Mormon apostle David W. Patten, was killed by a Missouri militia seven years earlier, warned him that he was in for more trouble if he returned the hogs to his farm. Following Patten's advice, "I immediately hitched up my team and threw what things I could into the wagon," he said, "and started for the doomed city of Nauvoo with my wife and 4 small children, leaving my comfortable home for which I paid 750 dollars in gold and silver besides four hundred dollars spent in improvements in the hands of the mob."[19] But the calculating neighbor was not finished.

Waggoner, living within three miles of Carthage, immediately went to the courthouse and placed a lien on "the loose property" of Barney's farm "amounting to over 100 dollars for that dollar." Barney said that Waggoner further "got out a warrant for me for stealing his pork hogs out of his pen. This he done in order to get me in the Carthage jail, as they had several other Mormons in the same way."[20] Reports of violence to other Mormons in the county tempered any fight Barney had in defending his rights or recovering his property. "As the whole country was in a state of excitement I declined going back to my farm. So Waggoner took what property I left."[21] Cleansing the outlying county of Mormons was but a feature of the objectives of those opposed to the Mormons. Fed in part by the vitriolic assertions of *Warsaw Signal* editor Thomas Sharp, many area non-Mormons—akin to their Missouri neighbors—considered it a patriotic obligation to rid the region of Mormons. Nothing short of purging the county of the remainder of Smith's followers would satisfy them.

The same day the vigilantes threatened they would destroy Barney's farm, one of the primary leaders of Mormon opposition, Frank Worrell, was killed on 16 September by Orrin Porter Rockwell. News of Worrell's death spread quickly, which temporarily curtailed destruction of Mormon property in the county for fear Mormons en mass would retaliate.[22] Already smarting from the 15 September death of Betsey Barney's mother, Lydia Ballinger Turner, in nearby Macedonia, the middle of the month was a time of endings for the Barneys.[23]

Hancock County tension was high. The destruction of Mormon homes spilled over into the adjacent county to the south. The burning of homes and threatening of human lives in the counties mustered the Nauvoo Legion into defensive activity at a level previously unknown. A cohort of the Nauvoo Legion returned to the city on 17 September from an operation trying to protect Saints in outlying county areas and reported "the families which they designed to rescue were all fled" but that "on their entering Carthage they were fired upon by the mob who instantly fled." Rumors circulated that the Nauvoo troops were preparing to march on Carthage again.[24] But county anti-Mormons, outraged by Worrell's death, a man they viewed as a patriot, were undaunted by the Mormon threat of retaliation. A call to arms in the

Warsaw Signal on 17 September for retribution was not unlike the one fifteen months earlier which provoked the murders of the Smiths.[25] This was countered by proclamations of the Hancock County sheriff, a non-Mormon who sympathized with the Saints, warning the self-proclaimed "anti-Mormons" against any more violence.[26] The climate for open conflict was increasing.

Barney's removal to Nauvoo in September was forced at harvest time. Many like him were robbed of the opportunity to gather the return of their hard work the previous spring and summer. Despite threats to life and limb throughout the county, Nauvoo officials, anticipating a winter complicated by refugees, sent over a hundred teams to rescue families and grain from outlying areas of the county.[27] Not willing to concede his hard work fruitless, Barney asked Nauvoo Legion colonel Stephen Markham to arrange for teams to retrieve his grain as a part of this effort.[28] Securing what he thought his family needed, Barney wrote, "I let those that were destitute have the greater part of my grain to help them through the winter."[29]

With tensions at fever pitch, cooler heads moved to avert civil war. Before September was over, a citizen committee in Quincy, Adams County, where the Saints once found refuge in their flight from Missouri, proposed a cease-fire. Their entreaty to Mormon church leaders produced a reply of capitulation from the Saints. Concurrently, Illinois governor Thomas Ford sent the state militia to Carthage to restore order. A treaty was drawn and accepted the first two days of October providing for the evacuation of Nauvoo "when the grass grows and water runs."[30] Brigham Young, in October 1845, wrote to fellow apostle Wilford Woodruff in England: "The prejudice of the people are such that the state cannot posably [*sic*] protect us and that it is therefore advisable for us to remove as the only conditions of peace. We have determined to do so in the Spring."[31] A strategy was even employed to curry the help of the federal government to facilitate the Saints' removal from the United States.[32]

Nauvoo became a flurry of activity hastening its own demise. "All was busy, no loafers lounging around the stores or on the corners of the streets; everything that could be done was pushed ahead with energy and dispatch," said Barney. "Wagon shops was soon erected in every ward of the city," he continued, "and all hands [were] busily engaged in making wagons."[33] Nauvoo became the wagon-making capital of the western world during that fall and winter. Newcomers "were astonished to see the hundreds and thousands of wagons that were turned out in a few months."[34] The "clink of the smith was heard allmost continualy."[35] Substantial and comfortable homes were replaced by wagon boxes on wheels as repositories for family possessions.[36] The pursuit of civic and residential beauty gave way to maintaining the most basic elements of human survival. The work was both personal and communal.[37]

Preparations for Exodus

Institutionally, the primary objective of church members was the completion of the Nauvoo Temple started in 1841. Joseph Smith and now Brigham Young promised the Saints an endowment of spiritual power through the rites available only in the building being completed at the crest of the bluff overlooking the city. As the Saints hastened their activity to complete their temple, the hostility of their Hancock County antagonists increased as they viewed the work on the temple as a sign that the Saints had reneged on their promise to leave. Still, the temple had to be completed. Meetings, public and private, were held in the temple a year before the building's eventual dedication in May 1846. But the sacred rituals associated with the temple—ordinances and endowments—were not introduced to the Saints generally until December 1845. Had the temple been completed sooner, the time of departure to the West would also have been abbreviated. Young stated, "The main and only cause of our tarrying so long was to give the brethren those blessings in the Temple, for which they have labored so diligently and faithfully to build."[38] In the two months that endowments were given in the temple, more than 5,500 Saints acquired the ordinance while consolidating their earthly goods for transit in their wagons.[39] The significance of the effort extended beyond the physical departure of the Saints from Nauvoo. On 7 February, the last day temple endowments were given, George A. Smith, one of the Twelve Apostles, said "upwards of 600 had went through and got their endowments" that day. "Now," said he,

> let the mob work, the Priesthood is secured on the earth and the temple has answered the end for which it was built. The mob thought when they killed the head the body would surely die but they made twelve heads and if they kill the Twelve they would have 70 more [referring to the seventies quorums] and they never can kill the body.[40]

Prior to this last order of business, Barney had, somehow, arranged to sell his county land and improvements, notwithstanding George Waggoner's claim on his portable property. The farmstead he purchased in January 1842, he sold for $320 to John F. Charles, a physician and Hancock County resident since 1834.[41] The transaction, contracted previously, was recorded four days after Lewis crossed the Mississippi. Anticipating the departure of his own family later in the season, the terms of the agreement stated that the animals and equipment were to be delivered to the Barneys prior to 1 April 1846.[42]

Complicating plans was the birth in Nauvoo of Lewis and Betsey's fourth son and fifth child just before Christmas 1845.[43] Named by his parents after the martyred prophet, Joseph Smith Barney would live his infancy on the road. Once he had done all that he could to outfit his family, Lewis was ready to finalize his sojourn in Nauvoo. Luther and Lurinda were the first of the Barneys to participate in the spiritual ordinances of the not-quite-completed Nauvoo Temple in early February 1846. Lewis and Betsey followed at 5:30 on the cold winter morning of 6 February.[44] The other Barneys eligible by age and faith to obtain their temple blessings were endowed the following day, the last day the Saints were given their temple blessings.[45] Sometime on that same February 7, thirty-seven-year-old Lewis Barney waited at river's edge for his turn, no doubt with his wife and four young sons by his side, before ferrying the imposing Mississippi River without them. He would not see his family again for three months.

Chapter 8

Midst Sighs and Lamentations: Iowa—Prelude to the West, 1846

Notwithstanding the initial success of the Saints in Nauvoo, Joseph Smith as early as the summer of 1842 related to close associates that the time would come when the center of the church would be far away from the Mississippi River Valley. Their destiny lay in the West, on the other side of the Rocky Mountains.[1] But in 1842, the Mormon prophet may not have seen that the fate of the Saints would be forced upon them so soon. The Latter-day Saints became a refugee people.

The Iowa Crucible

An anxiousness surrounded the evacuation of Nauvoo. After all, it was the depth of winter and no one could say with certainty just where they were going, though most knew that the Missouri River was the initial objective. The first phase of departees left during that first week of February with others following for several weeks. Most were not as well prepared as hoped. There was a need for assistance to enable as many as could to leave the city. "There being a call for volunteers and teams to assist the poor from Nauvoo," Barney wrote, "I volunteered my services and two wagons and teams to help the Saints out of Nauvoo."[2] Undoubtedly an arrangement was made for his father and brothers to keep watch over Barney's immediate family while he went ahead assisting the poor. However, as circumstances unfolded, the family he assisted was hardly numbered among the poor. Why it fell to Barney's lot to serve as David Yearsley's teamster is not known. But, intending to assist the poor, it undoubtedly grated on him some to escort one of Nauvoo's prosperous merchants while his own family was left behind.

David D. Yearsley, just older than Lewis by a few months and a church member since 1841, was a former Pennsylvania Quaker who became a successful businessman in Nauvoo. For a time, after Joseph Smith retired from his own Red Brick Store mercantile business, Yearsley managed the operation. His high profile found him involved with the influential bodies of the city, including the Nauvoo High Council and the Council of Fifty, the latter being a secretive organization which played a significant role in the evacuation of

Nauvoo and preparation for the journey west.[3] Barney was assigned to serve as teamster for Yearsley's wagon transporting his mercantile goods to the Missouri to reestablish his business, while Yearsley drove his stately carriage carrying his wife and children.[4] The Yearsleys were accustomed to a manner of living unavailable to Barney. They were leaving a new three-story brick home, built so well that it was the only three-story brick structure in Nauvoo to survive into the twentieth century.[5] The fine carriage, certainly less functional than a wagon, was used to transport Yearsley's wife who "was not used to riding in a wagon."[6] The Yearsleys' feelings upon departing their home, despite their social differences, were no doubt very similar to Barney's, who wrote,

> On reaching the summit between the Mississippi and the Des Moines Rivers the company made a halt for the purpose of taking a last and peering look at the Nauvoo Temple, the spire of which was then glittering in the bright, shining sun. This last view of the temple was witnessed in the midst of sighs and lamentations, all faces in gloom and sorrow, bathed in tears at being forced from our homes and temple that had cost so much toil and suffering to complete its erection.[7]

Barney and the Yearsleys were part of what turned out to be the first phase of a three-part evacuation of Nauvoo. This first contingent, referred to as the Pioneer Camp, was composed of about two thousand exiles in five hundred wagons.[8] Departing in February, these forerunners camped in the snow and ice at Sugar Creek, about eight miles west of Nauvoo. Their plight was significant as they braved the inhuman winter weather which drove the thermometer to twelve degrees below zero during their three-week stay at Sugar Creek, the stream where baptisms for the dead had been performed in gentler times.[9] Here it was that the order of the migration was formalized along military lines into subdivisions of ten, fifty, and one hundred.[10] The organizational preparation to move such a group under forbidding circumstances is staggering. One group of ten, for example, was asked to acquire "5 wagons, 9 head of horses, 2 yoke of oxen, 1000 pounds of flour, 12 bushels of corn meal, 2 bushel parch corn meal, 250 pounds of crackers, 150 pounds of meat, 2 bushels seed corn, 1 bushel of spring wheat, 3 bushels Buckwheat, 100 pounds of all wheat and a variety of garden seeds." The foodstuffs would hopefully sustain them across Iowa. Further, to maintain a viable future they were to bring "2 set of plows, 2 spades, 2 hoes, . . . 1 iron wedge, 5 augers, 50 pounds soap, 100 papers of smoking tobacco for Indians, 3 rifles, 3 muskets, 2 kegs powder, and 100 pounds of lead," along with personal effects.[11] The enterprise, even in its initial stages, was an enormous undertaking requiring the limits of human effort.

After three weeks being lined for a mile up and down the creek in the dead of winter, the first of the wagons pulled out of camp. The effectual start of Iowa's crossing for the Saints was 1 March 1846. Stephen Markham, a forty-six-year-old New Yorker, captained the group to which Yearsley was assigned which also carried Eliza R. Snow and, of course, Lewis Barney.[12] Barney's duties for Markham's company multiplied as he not only drove the heavily laden wagon, he also found himself assisting in making "roads, bridges, and looking out for supplies" for his charges. It was not pleasurable labor, but necessary if the mass of exiles were to successfully traverse Iowa. "Well do I remember," Barney stated, "taking my rifle and wading through snow knee deep to hunt squirrels for soup and nourishment for the women in confinement and women traipsing through snow and storm with their dresses wet and frozen up to their knees from tent to tent or wagon to wagon to wait on the sick."[13]

The main route of the Mormons across southern Iowa looked like an undulating financial chart reading from right to left, a chart showing a loss of assets. It covered a known course to the middle of the state and thereafter used traces of old Indian trails to get them to the Missouri River. "We experienced almost unendurable suffering" after Sugar Creek, wrote Barney, "the streams of water almost thick with mud, the whole camp being forced to bring water from a spring more than a mile away for drinking and cooking purposes; horses also [had] to be taken there for water."[14] While battling the elements and difficult traveling conditions, they often had to double the ox teams, occasionally being compelled to hitch thirteen teams of oxen to pull a single wagon.[15]

Finding themselves at the substantial Des Moines River on 3 March, Eliza Snow, traveling with Barney, recorded the extraordinary acumen of the Saints in surviving amid difficult circumstances. "Our encampment this night may truly be recorded by this generation as a miracle. A city rear'd in a few hours, and every thing in operation that *living* required, & many additional things which if not *extravagances*, were in fact *conveniences*." Two days later she wrote that as quickly as the encampment was erected it disappeared: "Our newly constructed city is razed and the inhabitants thereof take up their line of march."[16] They repeated this procedure over and over again. "Our *town* of yesterday has grown to a *city*," Snow wrote on 9 March. "I notic'd but a few rods from our tent, a black-smith's shop in operation, and every thing indicated real life; not a cooking utensil was idle."[17]

The camp slowly crossed Iowa. "The members of the Pioneer Camp," Barney said, "[were] off hunting work amongst the settlers, clearing off land, building houses, making rails, and every kind of work that was required to be done to get provisions which was brought into camp and turned over to the commissary to be rationed out to the families of the Saints according to their necessities."[18] Despite Eliza Snow's report of consistent progress, the pioneers were frequently interrupted by storms—punctuated by freezing temperatures, howling wind, and hail—mud bogs up to the wagon axles, and the inevitable irritations resulting from disappointments in their fellow travelers' behavior. Day after day, week in and week out, the unnatural circumstances of refugee travel took their toll on the exiles.

No doubt harboring some resentment from the outset, Barney groused after a few weeks about Yearsley's criticism of Barney's inefficient team pulling Yearsley's wagon. One day "Yearsley, coming by with a splendid span of fine horses to his carriage, commenced complaining about my horses not being able to take the load up the hill. I told him to try it with his horses and commenced unhitching my team from the wagon." Switching loads, Barney "drove off with the carriage and Yearsley's family and left him to bring up the load." Under this new arrangement, Barney wrote, "I managed to keep 2 or 3 miles ahead of Yearsley until we come to the place of encampment for the night [where] I discovered he had taken 4 sacks of flour out of the wagon in order to lighten up the load." Barney ignored Yearsley the next morning. "As soon as the bugle was sounded I hitched [my team] to the carriage again and drove off with the family leaving Yearsley to bring up his load of goods with his fine horses."[19] Such was the pettiness manifest in the unusually trying circumstances. Coincidentally, about this time the larger Pioneer Camp also fragmented for travel into smaller groups, some for practical reasons. Yearsley's contrariness in other matters of trail travel soon alienated his traveling companions to such an extent that on 5 April, Stephen Markham, whose family had been traveling and culinary companions with the Yearsleys, broke their arrangement and left Yearsley to himself. Predictably, Barney went with the Markhams.[20]

As the weather moderated and the grass greened, the pioneers were confronted with another foe of travel—rattlesnakes. The horses and cattle would have had to hopscotch across the prairie to avoid the reptiles. "Four or five days traveling through this snake district," Barney noted, found "several of our animals would come up snake bit."[21] Sporadic encounters with the rattlers plagued them throughout the spring. And still the storms pounded the pathetic sojourners. Barney and others suffered through a particularly horrid storm the first week of April. One night "after the tents and wagons had been arranged, there came up a storm of wind and rain and blew the covers off of the wagons and blew the tents across the camp ground and put out all the fires leaving the whole camp, men, women, and children, exposed to the raging elements for nearly three hours."[22] After over two months on the trail many were discouraged about their lack of progress. Most knew it was the intent of church leaders to get to the Missouri River early enough that year to send a vanguard expedition to the Rocky Mountains. It became apparent such a venture in 1846 was less and less likely. Untimely delays compelled them to ration their food. Disruptions multiplied, ambushing their yearnings for some respite after so many weeks on the road. Some undoubtedly wondered if this was better than what they had left.

Three weeks into April, the Pioneer Camp reached Iowa's midpoint: 155 miles west of the Mississippi River and 130 from the Missouri. Here in the middle of a beautiful prairie, broken by sections of timber in the ravines and on the hills, church leaders established a way station for the thousands to follow—Garden Grove. The grove was a welcome respite for the impoverished wayfarers

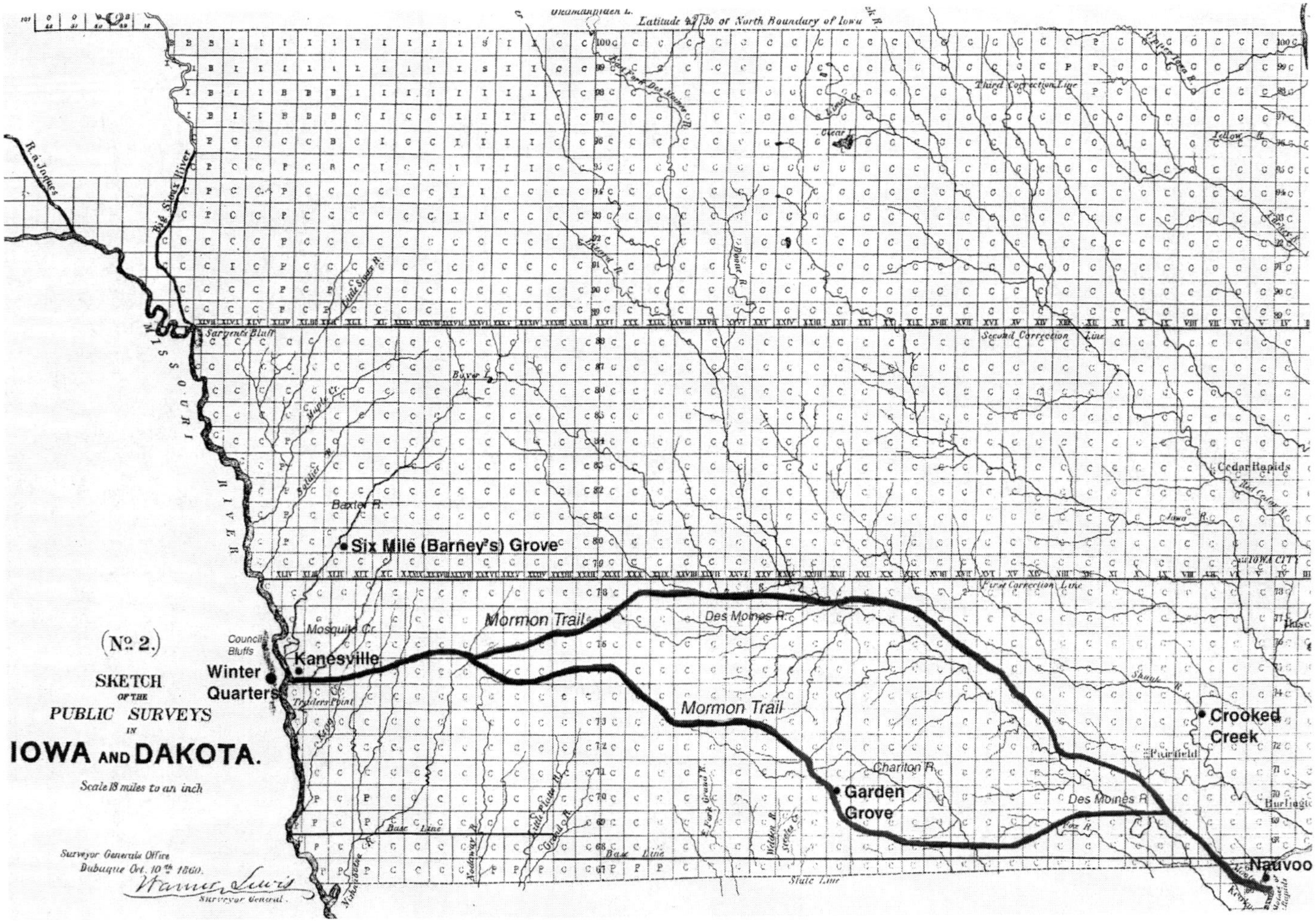

Iowa, 1860, showing Mormon trails to the Missouri River (Dubuque: Surveyor General's Office).

after their difficult two-month crossing of southeastern Iowa. At Garden Grove on 3 May Willard Richards reported that Brigham Young lamented, "I am reduced in flesh so that my coat that would scarce meet around me last winter, now laps over 12 inches. It is with much ado that I can keep from lying down and sleeping to await the resurrection."[23] Applying a penchant for work, Orson Pratt stated, the Saints within a short period built numerous homes, dug wells, and fenced farms giving "the whole place . . . the appearance of having been occupied for years and clearly shows what can be accomplished by union, industry, and perseverance."[24] Assisting with the improvements mentioned by Pratt, Barney remained at Garden Grove for one week. On 2 May, Eliza Snow noted in her diary, "Br. Barney left for N[auvoo] yester[day]."[25]

Barney's return to Nauvoo involved another complication with David Yearsley. Believing naively that Yearsley ought to sponsor his return to Nauvoo after having served as his teamster to Garden Grove, Barney asked Yearsley for assistance who, strapped himself, refused.[26] Yearsley's wife mercifully handed Barney thirty cents. "I told her that I had three rivers—the Chariton, the Des Moines, and the Mississippi—to ferry and must have more money than 30 cents to pay my ferriage," Barney lamented. "But that was all the money she had so I went to Brother [Heber C.] Kimball and laid the case before him." Kimball, a forty-five-year-old church apostle from Vermont, reached into his pocket, extracted a dollar, and handed it to Barney. "I will give you a dollar for him," Kimball said. "Go and you shall be blest." Taking the dollar and a half bushel of crackers given him by Markham, Barney started eastward. Providing assistance to an Iowa settler, Barney transported the man's family and eight hundred pounds of freight to Montrose earning eight dollars for the effort.[27] Kimball was right.

Final Adieu to Nauvoo

Upon his return to his Nauvoo home, Barney found his father's family had already departed for the West. When the elder Barney left is not precisely known, but Luther and his family were still in Nauvoo when Lewis arrived. Together they readied their young families and departed the "City of Joseph" in June 1846 toward the end of the second wave of Saints to leave Nauvoo.[28] This second contingent of nearly ten thousand numbered five times those who composed the initial Pioneer Camp. (A third body, significantly smaller and destitute, fled Nauvoo in the Battle of Nauvoo's aftermath in the late summer of 1846.) Whereas the first pioneers took fourteen weeks to cross Iowa, better weather and better information allowed many of the second contingent to cross in four to five weeks.[29]

The second wave of Nauvoo exiles left with a rush. With the Nauvoo Temple's formal dedication and the removal on 1 May of Governor Ford's troops posted in Nauvoo, the refugee floodgates fully opened. "On the Nauvoo side of the river," one observer noted, "two or three hundred wagons were waiting at one time for the ferry."[30] The third week of May alone saw 1,350 of the Saints leave. At the same time an Illinois newspaper reported that Mississippi River ferries made over seventy trips in one twenty-four-hour period from three docks in and near Nauvoo.[31] The metamorphosis of Nauvoo from a burgeoning frontier metropolis to a mostly hollow townsite was dramatic.

As the lifeblood of the ruptured city drained away, it looked like a sad end to a once thriving organism. But this was much less an end for the Saints than it was a beginning. For through this exodus were the pioneering Mormons forever self-remembered as the children of modern Israel. "A scene of human suffering and endurance for the gospel's sake, on so large a scale, has seldom if ever before been seen on the earth," one participant reported.[32] The exodus was a crucible through which this people was created and unified. For the Saints who followed Brigham Young, this was a shared experience that forged a spiritual superstructure unavailable, probably, in any other way.

Bound for the West

The course west taken by Charles Barney and later by Lewis, Luther, and their families was an alternate to the main Mormon Trail across lower Iowa. Known as both the Des Moines River Valley Trail and the Dragoon Trail, the Barneys probably took the route because of less traffic and the greater likelihood of economic opportunity along the way. The trail, following the Des Moines River in a northwesterly direction to the center of Iowa, was blazed in 1835 by the First U.S. Dragoons under Colonel Stephen W. Kearny from old Fort Des Moines (later Montrose, Iowa) to Des Moines, Iowa. Kearny, who as commander of the Army of the West called up the Mormon Battalion, had been ordered to locate a site for a new fort (Fort Des Moines II) near the confluence of the Raccoon and Des Moines Rivers.[33] At Des Moines, after paralleling the river of the same name, Lewis and Luther caught up with their father and his family. Charles and Deborah had temporarily paused there to replenish their meager supplies. From there the family caravan "traveled a southwest course along a dim trail in order to strike the Mormon Trail."[34] That trail across central Iowa was the one likely used ten years later by the handcart pioneers en route to Utah.[35] The remainder of their journey was hampered by an insidious foe that wreaked havoc on many western travelers.

Any parties traveling west without being touched by "the ague and the fever" were few and most fortunate. Particularly in the spring and summer, malaria, as the ague is called today, flourished where mosquitos bred in a habitat of stagnant water and moist surroundings.[36] The Barneys were attacked. Leaving central Iowa, Barney wrote, "[James] Henry, one of our children, was taken sick with a burning fever and the next day Joseph, another of [the] children, was taken down with sickness." While six-year-old Henry held his own, six-month-old Joseph Smith Barney, the baby named after the prophet, continued to sink. "One day I was walking by the side of my team with Joseph the babe in my arms and all of a sudden he threw himself back and straightened himself out then fell back limber and lifeless in my arms." Consigned to the child's death, Barney matter-of-factly said to his wife, "'Here Betsey, the child is dead,' and handed it to her." But the baby's mother clutched the child, pressing him to her breast crying, "O my God, have mercy on us." "At that moment," Barney exclaimed, "the child opened its eyes and commenced to recover and continued getting better until it was entirely well."[37]

After a few more days on the dim trail they struck the main road, happy to find themselves among "our friends and companions in tribulation" once again, despite the sickness in their camp. "I found the Saints scattered along the route for over 100 miles," Barney wrote, "some of them camped in wagons and tents, sick from exposure and destitute of the comforts of life."[38] As the Barneys approached the eastern bluffs of the Missouri River near the first of August 1846, one of the family's first concerns was to locate Lewis's twenty-seven-year-old brother Walter who had preceded his family across Iowa. Walter was not to be found. The noise stirring among the camps of Israel explained his absence.

Five hundred of the most available Mormon men had been recruited by the United States government to protect American interests in the Southwest against the Mexicans in what came to be called the Mexican War. The 1846 conflict was coincidental to Mormon leaders' effort to secure federal assistance for their move west. Given their numbers and their proximity to the region, the Mormons were candidates, paradoxically, to serve the government from which they fled. The deal benefitted the Saints and government alike. Yet, most of the Saints were outraged at the request. Many, like Lewis Barney, thought the plan was a conspiracy "concocted by the authorities of the states of Missouri, Illinois, and Iowa to complete the destruction of the kingdom of God."[39] What Lewis and most of the Mormon rank and file did not know was that church leaders had been negotiating with Washington through church legates in the East for some time to accomplish an arrangement somewhat akin to the one offered by government agents when the Saints reached the Missouri River. Another compensation for cooperation was the government's agreement allowing the Saints to settle on the Iowa and Nebraska lands on either side of the Missouri, giving them some respite, if only temporarily.[40]

Walter Barney was recruited as a private into the Mormon Battalion's Company C on 16 July 1846 with a promise of new clothing, a government-issue weapon, and pay to assist the Saints now forced to encamp at the Missouri until the following spring.[41] On 20 July the battalion mustered into service and started for Fort Leavenworth, Kansas, where they were equipped before their march to the Southwest. On 1 August the battalion, with camp followers numbering about six hundred souls, arrived at Leavenworth. There was anxiety over the following months in the absence of this significant body of men, not knowing what awaited them in the Southwest.[42]

Ignorance of the precise location and extent of their stay at the Missouri River compounded the affliction which hit the Barneys as they settled down for the fall and winter. They "finally made a halt at Bullock's Grove on Log Creek," but not before both Luther and Lewis contracted cholera.[43] Characterized by severe spasmodic intestinal pain, diarrhea, and vomiting, the bacteria-born cholera was a quick killer. Afflicted for three weeks, there was little Lewis and his brother could do when they were needed most to provide their families with food and shelter, not to mention preparation for the coming winter. So ill that he suffered a "spell of vomiting that nearly took my life," Lewis said, "I turned blind and deaf. I knew if I had another turn it would be the last of me." Nearly having crossed the line, Lewis said that when he was most desperate "Mother Bullock [likely Benjamin Bullock's wife] gave me a little flour and water which turned the sickness and stopped the vomiting and I began to get better." But as Barney began to recover, his young son Alma, intermittently ill for weeks, declined. In three days the little boy expired. They buried him in a hazel thicket at Bullock's Grove.[44] Rather than finding respite after a year of uncertainty and displacement, Barney sighed, "here we had death, sickness, sorrow, and famine in our camp."[45]

Thousands of Nauvoo refugees, by July 1846, formed a "Grand Encampment" which stretched for nine miles along the 200- to 250-foot bluffs on the Iowa side of the Missouri River.[46] The exact location in this mix of exiled humanity where Barney settled his family in Iowa is not known. Having first arrived at the Missouri River on 14 June, most Saints located on the Nebraska side of the Missouri. After a couple of interim attempts, on 11 September 1846 they selected a spot on the west bank afterwards known as Winter Quarters.[47] The first organized community in Nebraska, Winter Quarters was built in what is now a northern suburb of Omaha. But the Mormons were not alone.

This was Indian country. Native Americans had been pushed westward to the Missouri River through a succession of treaties where whites usurped their lands as American settlement displaced them from their lands. When the Mormons arrived at the Missouri there were "about 2,250 Pottawattamie/Ottawa/Chippewa Indians settled in at least five widely scattered villages of southwest Iowa." These were complemented by another 1,300 of the Omaha tribe living in a fortified tepee village across the river in Nebraska.[48] How the Mormons would fare in proximity to the Indians was a concern for all of the refugees.

The extended Barney family situated together in Pottawattamie County, Iowa, near Mosquito Creek which diagonally courses through the western third of the county before emptying into the Missouri.[49] "We were," Barney said, "under the necessity of building houses, cutting hay, and preparing for the coming winter." Despite the residual weakness he felt from the cholera, he said, "Father and myself commenced cutting hay" until "I had become so weak that

I could not cut a swath more than a rod before I would be obliged to lay down and rest. In this way we continued until we cut 25 or 30 tons of hay."[50] But they could not live on hay.

After settling his family, Barney, still not fully recovered from cholera, struck south for the settlements in northwestern Missouri to secure provisions by hiring himself out for day work. Luther accompanied him. Hundreds of other destitute Latter-day Saints also flooded the area. "It was with feelings of regret that I left the [Mormon] Camp," one of the Saints wrote, "but my means was so limited that I was obliged to flee Egypt for Bread."[51] The goods they obtained for their families from their Missouri labor, primarily corn, temporarily relieved their destitution.

The thousands of refugees huddling in makeshift hovels and huts quickly exploited the natural resources of the broad floodplain of the Missouri and much of the prairie adjacent to the bluffs, forcing some, like the Barneys, to find sustenance elsewhere. After replenishing his "pantry," it became apparent this trip to Missouri would not do his family for the winter. "I took my horses and went back to Missouri to winter, working for grain and horse feed and such other things as we needed."[52] It was ironic that Missourians displaced the Saints in the 1830s and then helped save them from starvation in the 1840s. The Barneys on the Missouri were not the only ones of their clan with difficulties that fall and winter. While Walter struggled with the battalion in the southwestern desert, Lucien, thirty-five and unmarried, died in circumstances presently unknown. After his venture with Henry in Texas the previous year, no trace of his existence is extant beyond a family memory that he died in 1846.[53]

Lewis Barney worked through the Missouri winter to resupply his family with food. In the spring of 1847 he returned north to the Pottawattamie settlements, taking "a load of provisions . . . to the bluffs to see my family." The tenuous circumstance of the insecurity of their immediate and foreseeable future was undoubtedly depressing. Upon Barney's return, as with all of the other exiles who wintered on the Missouri, he was also interested "to find out what was going on and what arrangements were being made for the continuance of our journey into the wilderness."[54] After seeing to his family's needs he crossed the river to Winter Quarters, headquarters of the church which had grown over the winter to be a community with 538 log and 83 sod houses.[55]

Church leaders, indeed, were figuring "out what was going on" over the winter and what they would do to move the Saints from their temporary status on the Missouri. While crossing Iowa the previous year, Brigham Young and his lieutenants decided "to send a company of men without families across the mountains [with] seed grain, farming utensils, provisions &c. to make preparations for those who should follow."[56] In their preparations, they became familiar with John C. Frémont and others' writings whose reports helped narrow their interest to the Great Basin.[57] Engineering the expedition was now undertaken in earnest.

In the middle of January 1847 at Winter Quarters, Brigham Young, having assumed the prophetic mantle for modern Israel, received "The Word and Will of the Lord concerning the Camp of Israel in their journeyings to the West."[58] This communication, believed by the Saints to be inspired, served as the outline to transport tens of thousands of Latter-day Saints to the uninhabited region of the Great Basin eventually earning Young the appellation of "American Moses." Instructions were given confirming the structure of travel employed the previous year in crossing Iowa. But the revelation was not a divine treatise on the rudiments of transportation en mass. Rather, as much as anything else, it was a reminder to the Saints that the parallel of their journey to ancient Israel's exodus from Egypt had divine imprimatur, and as such, they must behave as the children of God, for "my people must be tried in all things, that they may be prepared to receive the glory that I have for them, even the glory of Zion." Indeed, they were promised by the Lord that, if faithful, "Zion shall be redeemed in mine own due time."[59] Their first order of business was to organize a vanguard company to establish a colony of Saints in the far reaches of the West.

When Barney crossed the Missouri in March 1847, he found two of the principals with whom he crossed Iowa the previous year as a teamster for Yearsley: Stephen Markham and Heber C. Kimball, the former his immediate leader and the latter the commander of the hundred with whom he traveled. Fortuitously for Barney, they were just then in the process of recruiting the vanguard.[60] Barney's timely inquiry of his old friends resulted in an invitation to join the group. "They told me there was going to be a company raised to go and find a home for the Saints. They asked me if I could go with them. I told them I could." While others who constituted the advance company were selected for skills and attributes needed for the success of the expedition, Barney was obviously chosen because of his willingness to participate, even at the expense of his family, demonstrated the previous year in the Iowa crossing. He was told to be ready in two weeks, giving him "time to go to Missouri and get a load of provisions to leave with my family."[61] While the two week grocery run to Missouri was one thing, his acceptance of the invitation to go to the West was surrounded with enormous risk, not to mention his absence for who knew how long from a family of wife and children still wounded by the death of little Alma the previous year. Still, he was ready.

Chapter 9

A Story Makes a People: The Exodus to Zion, 1847

In the popular image of Mormonism, the removal of the Saints from the Midwest to the valleys of the Great Basin, beginning in 1847, remains one of the defining events of the religion. The previous pivot points of Latter-day Saint history to 1847 had been witnessed or experienced by only a minority of church members. The trek to Zion in the mountains over the next half-century by tens of thousands of Saints of high and low station alike, Americans and Europeans, provided a common context that welds the seams of disparate entities into a people. "Although [Mormonism is] called 'the Church of Jesus Christ of Latter-day Saints' and may very well be in theological definition a church," argues religious historian Martin Marty, "I perceive it more as a people. . . . What's interesting about the Mormons is that they are from a mixed ethnic stock not much different from the rest of the majority and yet they are a distinct people. A story makes a people."[1] The "story" provided by the western exodus from Nauvoo was the catalyst for people-making for most of those who struggled through the wilderness expedition.

Because the vanguard expedition of 1847 is one of the best documented epics of Mormon history, with most of the fine published accounts accessible, and because Barney's account is reminiscent rather than contemporary, I have chosen not to retell the story from Barney's perspective, though his reflection from hindsight is, overall, a significant viewpoint.[2] The events of April–October 1847 constitute nearly one-fourth of Barney's first autobiography, giving some indication of its importance to him. Though unknown at this time, his role in the trek became to him the meridian of his life. The vanguard trek set him apart in the laudable posture of one of the "original pioneers" of modern Israel. Thereafter, at every annual local celebration of the Saints' arrival in the Great Basin, Barney was identified as one of the few who discovered Zion's homeland. While the highly organized and efficient vangaurd trek is hardly comparable to other episodes of Mormon hardship, its symbolic place in history gilded its participants ever after.

After a general summary of the constitution of the vanguard company, the significant particulars of the journey identified by Barney, which illustrate not only the charm of the trek but also illuminate his personality, will be recounted

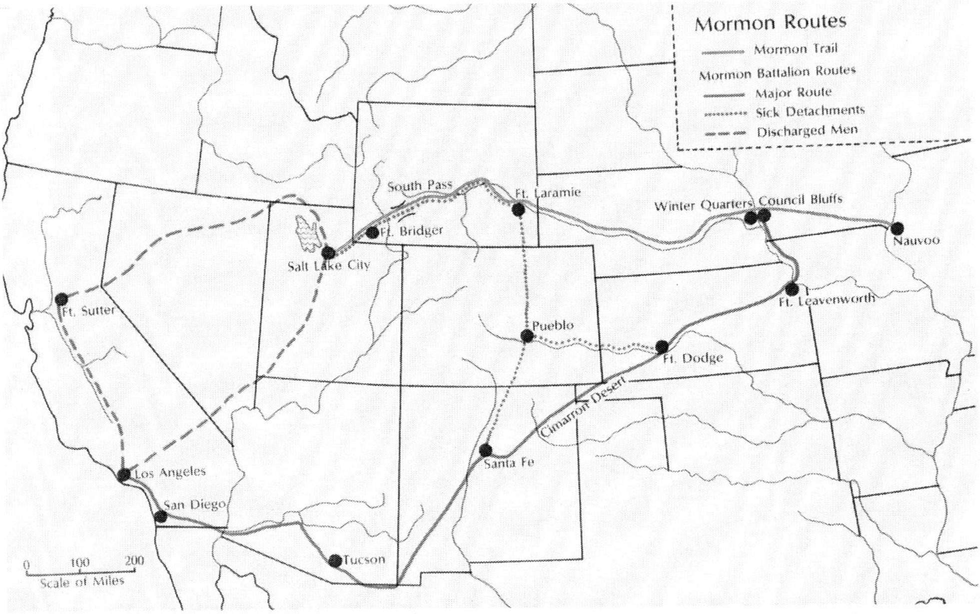

From Richard D. Poll, et al., *Utah's History* (Logan: Utah State University Press, 1989).

here. Of note is the return of the pioneers to Winter Quarters in the late summer and fall of 1847. Barney's view of this component of the pioneer venture is important and when coupled with contemporary accounts gives the weighty attention merited by the events of the 1847 vanguard's second half.

The Trek

Upon Barney's early spring return from Missouri with what he hoped would be adequate provisions for his family, he bid them farewell. With "one wagon and a span of horses," Barney "started for Winter Quarters." Upon his arrival at headquarters, he found his recruiter Stephen Markham, who assigned Barney his role for the journey. "Brother Markham furnished the provisions for the journey and I furnished the wagon and team,"[3] Barney said upon becoming Markham's teamster. Already over a month late from their intended departure the first of March 1847, the camp assembled, trickling west from Winter Quarters to the Elkhorn River, their first formidable hurdle. Hauling the wagons across on rafts, there they waited for their leader who was tying up loose ends at headquarters. The expedition, outfitted as best they could, numbered 148 souls.[4] These were led by five major companies headed by apostles, with forty-six-year-old Brigham Young as the last word. Subdivisions of hundreds, fifties, and tens (fourteen) were organized on 16 April when they were about fifty miles west of Winter Quarters.[5] "I was," Barney stated, "with Colonel Markham in the same wagon under Norton Jacob, he being captain of the ten I belonged to."[6]

Thirty-four of the company, almost one-fourth, were New Yorkers, of whom Barney was one. Forty-five were New Englanders. Fourteen were Ohioans, sixteen from the American South, a dozen from Great Britain, ten Pennsylvanians, five Canadians, two each from New Jersey, Illinois (the children), and Indiana, and one each from Denmark, Bavaria, and Norway. (The birthplace of three is unknown.) The group also included three African Americans, three women, and two children. The average age of the company was thirty-one, seven years junior to Barney.[7] William Clayton, one of the careful chroniclers of the trek, recorded that the camp was accompanied by "72 wagons, 93 horses, 52 mules, 66 oxen, 19 cows, and 17 dogs, and chickens."[8] The animals were just slightly less important to the success of the journey than the men.[9]

The Mormons were not the only hopeful sojourners that spring. Since 1841 a steady current of emigrants departed the western boundary of American civilization with Oregon or California in their eyes. Over a thousand crossed the country in 1843. The year of the Mormon pioneer vanguard, about 4,500 traveled the Oregon Trail for Oregon and California, twice the number of Saints who would descend into the Great Basin that year.[10] Cognizant of the immigration to Oregon and California, Mormon leaders intended to leave Winter Quarters early in the season, primarily to travel without non-Mormon competition.[11] But pressing matters postponed departure for a month. While the emigrant roads from Independence and St. Joseph began a considerable distance from the projected route of Mormon travel, they converged near the southern most dip of the Platte River about 185 miles west of Winter Quarters. The well-known Oregon Trail then paralleled the Platte on the south. The projected western route of Mormon emigration was the north side of that water source of the plains.[12] This arrangement eliminated difficulties potentially arising from competition over animal feed, not to mention the suspicion of the Saints and the Oregon and California settlers toward each other.

Ten days after the first of the Saints put reins to their animals at the Missouri, the fragments came together near modern Fremont, Nebraska, on 16 April. At 2:00 that Friday afternoon whips could be heard snapping over the oxen amid the yells for the company to move on.[13] A pattern for travel was set early: "As soon as morning light appeared all hands was busy getting breakfast, harnessing horses, yoking oxen, ready for a start."[14] The body, optimistic to a man, "took up the line of march westward penetrating the unexplored regions of the far west, singing the songs of Zion, telling stories and anecdotes, passing away the time very agreeably around the campfires at nights."[15] A hundred peach and orange sunsets splashed with hues of blue and white framed their journey. This was the heroic final stretch of the difficult exodus into the wilderness initiated a year earlier. Adequately equipped and highly organized, there were few surprises and interruptions to their military-like travel. The disciplined, focused collection of Saints—representative of those who stayed behind awaiting their opportunity to gather to Zion—stepped to a cadence and rhythm that further refined and coalesced the group into a people. Caution and care made their neophyte venture one befitting veterans.

Barney noted the near-confrontation with Pawnee Indians the first week after leaving the Elkhorn and the accidental killing of his horse a week later, forcing him to accept charity in the loan of a horse to reconstitute his team.[16] But it was the designation of the company's hunters on 25 April that initially aroused his attention. He was not one of them. So "that there might be an end to every man's running ahead with his gun to scare away the game," twenty-five were "organized and set apart to hunt game for the benefit of the whole camp."[17] To say that Barney was disappointed in being overlooked as a hunter is an understatement. With the exception of the Twelve Apostles, only the hunters were allowed to supply meat to the camp. Barney had no ambition to lead, command, or otherwise influence the expedition, but considering himself an expert marksman, he wanted to be a hunter. Driving a wagon day in and day out was no substitute for the freedom and pleasure he knew the hunters enjoyed. This disparity became particularly acute when they entered buffalo country.

On 1 May the company encountered for the first time the mighty resident of the plains—the buffalo. Awed by the sight of the large, hairy beasts, the hunters were giddy with anticipation. "Of all the sights of buffalo that our eyes beheld," Wilford Woodruff reported,

> this was enough to astonish man. Thousands upon thousands would crowd together as they came from the bluffs to the bottom land to go to the rivers and sloughs to drink until the river & land upon both sides of it was one dark spectacle of moving objects. It looked as though the face of the earth was alive & moving like the waves of the sea.[18]

The abundance of fresh meat harvested by the hunters was a welcomed reprieve from salt pork and their otherwise mundane foodstuffs, though some suffered "bowel complaint" from the new meat-rich diet. Dried buffalo dung also served the travelers on the treeless plain as the only accessible fuel. Buffalo country also applied a severe hardship on their animals because the plains grass was denuded from the roving behemoths. The trail had "the appearance of a pasture that had been overstock with cattle," wrote Levi Jackman. Jackman also reported another problem: "The Buffalo are so plenty at this time that it required a strict watch to keep them and our cows from running together."[19]

Struck by the enormity of the numbers of buffalo, where they were "as thick as sheep in a pasture on both sides of the river," on 3 May leaders allowed everyone in camp hunting privileges.[20] Barney, to say the least, was excited, but just as he departed camp he and the others were recalled by Wilford

Woodruff who, galloping after them, yelled that a large body of Indians was threatening the camp.[21] Woodruff couldn't have come at a more inopportune time for Barney, who groused in his disappointment, but the cry of Indian trouble quickly grabbed the attention of everyone. The would-be hunters scrambled back to camp anxious about the Indians' designs.

The threat of Indian depredations on the overland trail was real. Eight emigrants were killed during the 1845–1846 emigrations. In 1847, of the 6,650 people estimated to have traveled the Mormon and Oregon or California Trails, the number killed by Native Americans trebled over the previous two years.[22] While none of the Mormons were numbered in the statistics that year, the visibility of the Plains Indians, of which little firsthand knowledge was known, chilled them into caution. To bolster their precarious presence on the plains, the Mormons carried a small cannon with them, the "Old Sow" as it was called, which they limbered up for "an occasional salute." That evening and again early the next morning the "Old Sow" belched loudly to "frighten the Indians and to let them know that we had big guns in camp." The ploy worked and the next morning they were on their way, but "seeing fresh signs of the Indians" they traveled "five teams abreast with a line of rifle men on each side of the wagons and teams."[23]

The tedium of crossing the dry, dusty Nebraska plain during the month of May was accented first by Young's praise of the camp on 23 May for their cooperation and conformity only to be countered by Young the next week near Scott's Bluff. Thundering his aggravation at their indulgence in idleness, card playing, practical jokes, and swearing, he demanded each man to "repent of his weaknesses, of his follies, of his meanness, and every kind of wickedness." Young would have none of such nonsense in the camp of Israel.[24] Young's ponderous tactics may have seemed harsh to the men, but the success and efficiency of the westbound vanguard must be credited to his influence.

By the time the camp moved into eastern Wyoming where the Rocky Mountains first came into view, Barney's discontent from being denied hunting privileges provoked him to act. One day seeing "5 or 6 antelope passing by" he grabbed his rifle and started after them.[25] But Porter Rockwell, eccentric, intimidating, and one of the hunters, yelled at him demanding he return: "You are not one of the hunters and no man is allowed to hunt game but those that are chosen to hunt." Barney, disgusted but not willing to counter the long-haired legend-in-the-making, "came back a good deal out of humor as I thought I could kill game as well as some of the hunters."[26] To further gall Barney, as they moved out of buffalo country, the hunters had been reproved by Young for inefficiency.[27] The time between abundance and scarcity of game was short. "Our meat is getting scarce," wrote Barney's captain Norton Jacob, forcing his men to a diet of "mush and milk" every night.[28] After May, having become accustomed to abundant buffalo flesh, the absence of game as the pioneer camp moved beyond the plains gave Barney his chance for vindication.

With "fresh meat becoming a rarity," Stephen Markham, Barney's division commander and the man for whom he served as teamster, came to his driver about 9 June complaining the "strong bacon," the only meat then available, was not palatable. "I wish you would take your gun and go and kill some meat for I am nearly starved." Barney complained that as Markham had been one who appointed the hunters, "If you wanted me to hunt, why did you not choose me?" Markham patiently explained that because of his responsibility "for the whole division," he needed Barney to "take care of the wagon and team." Indulging in a little self-pity, Barney whined, "Then to take care of the wagon and team is my business and I will do it." Besides, "Do you think I can kill game where there is none?"[29]

The following day Markham approached Barney again. Desperate or just trying to mollify Barney's pouting, he complained, "I shall starve for I cannot eat anything we have in our wagon." Would Barney "go and try to kill something?" Barney, playing on Markham's apparent need, muttered, "When the game was all round us I had not the privilege to take my gun and go after some antelope that was passing by when we was stopped for noon without being called back by Porter Rockwell . . . and you stood by and said nothing to him about it." "My feelings was hurt at that time," he grumbled. "However," realizing the moment, "if you will find a man to take care of the team and let me choose a man to go with me I will go and see if I can find anything." Markham, no doubt humoring Barney, while at the same time in real need, conceded. Before long Barney and John Norton, an Indianan twelve years younger than Barney, managed to bring down "a nice fat buck" antelope. Markham "soon noised it through the camp that Barney had killed an antelope, the first that has been killed for the last 10 days [an exaggeration]." The kill drew much attention and "the antelope soon disappeared," Barney boasted, "without my getting a smell at it." The antelope was his validation. "This was the very thing I wanted, for that gave me notoriety among the officers and chagrined the hunters." Thereafter, "I had full liberty," he said, "to hunt when and where I pleased and no one dare say a word against it." He reveled that "the eyes of the whole camp was on me as being as good a hunter if not the best in camp."[30]

Soon "Brother Heber C. Kimball came to me," Barney exulted, "and asked me if I would be his hunter and furnish him with meat. I told him I would. I then was numbered with the hunters for the camp of pioneers." Joseph Hancock, one of the hunters, adopted Barney as his partner and together they hunted "the balance of the time furnishing the camp with more meat than any other two in the camp."[31] Thereafter, Barney's pioneering experience changed considerably. Confined to a wagon and the monotonous and incessant daily routine of rising early, hitching the animals to his rig for repeated dust-eating, day-long plodding sapped his ambition and enthusiasm in the endeavor. His new vocation as a hunter gave him the freedom enjoyed only by the hunters.

While this was the high point of Barney's experience in the pioneer vanguard, there was another associated with hunting much more humorous and satisfying to Barney.

Coincident to Barney's assignment as a hunter, he also managed to measure up to the famed Orrin Porter Rockwell. Rockwell, seven years younger than Barney and the devoted if notorious bodyguard of Joseph Smith, was the hunter who shut down Barney's hunting enterprise earlier in the trek. Successful hunting still at a premium, "One day at noon one of the officers said to Porter Rockwell, 'Port, what is the matter? You don't kill anything. Here is Barney. He brings in something every day.'" Defensively, Rockwell countered, "Oh, he kills does and all. I could kill more than twenty does a day if I would, but I don't want to kill old suckling does." "Better does than nothing," was the retort. "'Well,' says Port, 'I don't want to kill anything but nice fat bucks.'" Barney's moment came the following evening when "Port came in with an antelope, skinned and dressed up in nice order, saying, 'See here, what a nice buck I have got.'" Needling Rockwell, someone spoke up and said, "Barney has brought in a buck and a doe." Irritated, Rockwell snapped, "I could have killed half a dozen does if I wanted to." Barney, undoubtedly smiling as he wrote, continued, "I came to see Porter's nice, fat buck. I looked. I thought that it was rather poor for a buck. So I took up the skin and examined it and found it was an old suckling doe skin. I called out, 'See here boys, what nice tits Port's buck has. It must have gave a good mess of milk.'" Capitalizing on Rockwell's embarrassment, those around the campfire "hooted Port for his nice buck while Port scratched around for a while in a terrible rage."[32]

Crossing the North Platte River near present-day Casper mid-June, two weeks west of Fort Laramie, another episode involving Barney merited attention in his memoir. There in Wyoming's highlands the Saints established a ferry to facilitate not only Mormon emigrants but other travelers willing to pay for ferry service. Finding the most accommodating site and constructing the proper equipment to operate the ferry employed the efforts of many. One detail involving Jacob, Markham, George Mills, and Barney, after foraging upriver two miles, made a raft from dry cottonwood.[33] Even though they ferried three wagons over on the raft, with wind gusts and a strong river current, the craft was not large enough for safety. The next day another detail of sixteen or eighteen including Barney, searching a few miles downriver, found a stand of timber from which they "selected two large trees, 3 feet through" from which they "made two large canoes, 30 feet long."[34] After felling the substantial trees, they "then cut two other trees and hewed them down to 2 inches thick and straightened the edges making planks of them, 14 inches wide and 30 feet long. We then loaded them on our wagons and drove back to camp." Once in camp they "lashed the two canoes together and fastened the 2 planks on the canoes length-wise." Launching them in the river, they "ran a wagon on the plank that was far enough apart to be under the wheels of the wagon," making the ferry feasible.[35] The operation held such promise that church leaders left a cohort of men at the site to man the ferry and take advantage of the Oregon Trail traffic.[36] The North Platte ferry proved to be a great asset for the fledgling pioneers.[37] In less than a month the ferry garnered nearly six hundred dollars in ferry fees from nearly five hundred wagons carrying two thousand non-Mormon travelers.[38]

The remainder of Lewis Barney's account of the westbound pioneer trek of 1847, with six more weeks on the road, was covered in a few sentences. Significantly, on the last lap of the journey near the Green River at the end of June, disease infiltrated the camp. "At this place several of the men was sick with the Mountain Fever," Barney wrote, "I being one of the number."[39] Because tick fever incapacitates its victims physically and often causes delirium, this was especially disconcerting to the sojourners, as they were so close to their objective. But on they trudged. Once across the substantial Green which later converges with the Colorado River, they continued westward to the Bear River. Near the Bear, an important watercourse to the mountain men of earlier times, originating in the high Uinta Mountains of Utah before emptying into the Great Salt Lake, Barney happened upon what became a landmark of western travel. While hunting a couple of miles south of the wagon train, he "discovered the tar or oil springs," which he found "would burn like a lamp," and served as a fine remedy for the sore shoulders of livestock.[40] From the Bear River the camp descended from the high Wyoming plains into the final stretch for the Great Basin.

Here at the gateway into what became Utah, the momentum of travel and the leader who led them to the West slowed. Brigham Young was grounded with the mountain fever which afflicted so many others the previous week. The nature of the vanguard reformed at this time. Young, needing rest and recovery, sent Orson Pratt ahead with forty-two men and twenty-three wagons to "look out and make a road" into the Salt Lake Valley.[41] Barney, not part of this advance group, remained engaged in the duties of a hunter.[42] But Markham's section, to which Barney was assigned, soon "crossed over the mountain, struck on Big Canyon Creek working our way up the creek, cutting willows, making fords, and bridges for a passage for the train." From there they passed over Big Mountain, crossed Little Mountain, and followed Emigration Creek down the canyon, "making the road as we went."[43] Hunting in advance of his company and anxious to see their destination, Barney said, "I . . . worked my way down the creek through the brush and entered the valley. I went on a little rise of ground, cast my eyes over the valley, saw the Great Salt Lake glittering in the sun in the distance." Before long all of the company "reached the summit and cast a cheerful look over the future home for the exiled Saints."[44] The first division of the pioneer camp entered the basin on July 22. Young, still weak from fever, entered two days later. The Saints were finally home, a place they had never been.

The Great Salt Lake Valley

It was apparent to many of the Mormon vanguard that what they were doing was of note.[45] Arriving at the point of their destination embossed their sacrifice and faith in their own minds. As remarkable as their feat was in an immediate way, their legacy of being the first permanent settlers into the Great Basin, the forerunners of scores of thousands, etched their names in the memory monuments of all who followed them. An exultant, almost euphoric, spirit possessed them. "I am happily disappointed in the appearance of the Valley of the Salt Lake," a journey diarist wrote on the day of Young's arrival, "& if the land be as rich as it has the appearance of being, I have no fears but the Saints can live here, & *do well*, while we will *do right*."[46] For most, anticipation was great as they gazed over the valley imagining fields, roads, homes, and a city. Theirs was a unique opportunity almost unparalleled in the annals of American history. Completely isolated from their former countrymen, and knowing the apparent sterility of the region would discourage non-Mormon settlement, their own determination and initiative would establish the pace and agenda in civilizing this wild, forlorn place. Young established, at this time, the cooperative strategy upon which the mountain kingdom was to be founded: a mechanism of land distribution which would foster societal destratification that undoubtedly rung true to Barney's ears.[47] Individual initiative coupled with cooperative expectations provided a context for the Mormons which proved proverbial.

Had they arrived in June, their plan at the outset, it would have allowed them a near-normal growing season. But their late July entrance into the valley made the fall harvest uncertain. The only remedy was toil, sweat, and providence. A flurry of activity consumed the pioneers. Before the afternoon of 23 July was over, Barney was involved, like so many others, in cultivating the ground. "All seemed to partake of the unity of the Spirit and separated each to his respective part of the labor," wrote Norton Jacob. "I went to work with Lewis Barney and made two harrows by four o'clock p.m."[48] Barney remembered "plowing and putting in corn, potatoes, and all kinds of garden seeds . . . until we got in 100 acres." To their good fortune, "the seed put in the ground come up and looked well and grew very satisfactorily."[49] What little was harvested weeks later was crucial for those who wintered in the valley.

Young, feeling better and heartened by the exhibition of industry before him, "called the camp together and asked the pioneers if they were satisfied with this place or whether they wished to explore the country still further to find a better place for a location for the church as a home and center spot for the gathering of Israel."[50] The camp responded that they were "satisfied and believed this was a good place to make a stand and locate the Latter-day Saints, with the exception [of] two who thought we might perhaps find some place better to make a beginning."[51] Young replied:

> You may explore the whole region of these mountains and you will not find a better place. This is the place for us to make a beginning. I know this place as well as I know my old home and farm in the states. I have seen this place many times and right here will be the Temple and up yonder is Ensign Peak where the ensign to all nations will be raised."[52]

Besides the vanguard, nearly three hundred others coincidentally converged on the valley the last week of July. Fragments of Latter-day Saints representing the Mormon Battalion's sick detail, who had wintered on the Arkansas River with a group of Mississippi converts and a handful of others, now stirred about the dusty landscape. They had to be fed. Provisions were low. Once crops were planted, sustenance became a priority. "The ten I was in was entirely out of provisions," Barney said, "the 5 wagons belonging to the ten having been searched the evening previous to get something for supper which consisted of a few dry beans and some old crusts of bread." "Under this extreme circumstance," Barney continued, "I applied to Lorenzo [Dow] Young for a piece of bread." Somehow stocked with a surprising reserve, Young, Brigham's younger brother, replied that he would accommodate Lewis's request if he would go to work for him as others did in the same condition. But Barney wanted charity rather than employment and said he told Young that "before I will consent to such terms I will take my rifle and lay around the saleratus swamps and shoot snipes for a living."[53] Glib replies, however, would not provide them with food.

On 26 July, the same day that Brigham Young symbolically identified the valley as their terminal destination by a ceremony on Ensign Peak, Barney reported, "Joseph Hancock and myself took our rifles and started up the mountain on the east side of City Creek." Other parties at the same time went off in all directions to ascertain just what it was they had providentially inherited. Unwittingly, Barney and forty-seven-year-old Hancock joined the reconnaissance becoming the explorers of the upper reaches of what came to be called City Creek Canyon. Tracking "several large grizzly bear tracks" they found themselves at "the summit among the pine forest visible from Salt Lake City." Crossing the ridge and descending the mountain westward, they finally killed "a large black-tailed deer." Without food for two days they built a fire, gutted the animal, roasted the flesh and ate "as long as we dared to for fear of hurting ourselves." They then divided the meat and continued their course down the mountain. Soon they found themselves at the entrance of the canyon as it opened into the valley, several miles north of the camp of pioneers. Following the contour of the mountainside southward, they came upon a stream of water. Being very thirsty they bent to drink only to find the water hot and not potable. By this time it was late in the evening and they camped for the night amid the hot springs and smell of sulphur. At ten the next morning, 28 July, they were back in the pioneer camp.[54]

As Barney and Hancock, hefting their kill from the previous day, approached their comrades, busy clearing and preparing the land, the first person they encountered was Lorenzo Dow Young. Blandishing Barney, Young greeted them saying, "Brother Barney, won't you let me have a piece of your venison?" Barney replied, "Brother Lorenzo, we have had a hard time to get this venison, climbing mountains and starving for over two days and nights. However, I will exchange a little of it for bread." Young promptly went to his wagon, secured a large loaf of light bread, and traded it for a favorable piece of venison. "We were both well pleased with our bargain," Lewis said. Most importantly Jacob's ten were provided with dinner and had a "fine time making jokes over the venison and loaf of bread."[55]

The vanguard's days after their arrival into the valley were consumed with diverse activities to benefit both those who were to stay in the valley for the winter and those to follow. Another of the events, in which Barney found himself involved, affected every one of the sojourners. At the end of the first week of August, the Saints dammed what came to be called City Creek and renewed their commitment to God by submitting to rebaptism and reconfirmation. On 6 August church leaders were themselves baptized and confirmed followed over the next two days by the rank and file.[56] On 8 August Barney was immersed in City Creek by Charles Shumway before having the baptism confirmed "under the hands of President Brigham Young, Heber C. Kimball, and Willard Richards," with Kimball being voice.[57]

Two days later on 10 August, the same day in which the pioneers commenced building the fort where many would live who stayed for the winter, Barney visited the ancient Great Salt Lake, the most significant landmark in the Great Basin. Its notoriety had circulated in European and American conversation for decades, even before its first circumnavigation by white men in 1824 when Jim Bridger, James Clyman, and others explored the lake. With Norton Jacob, John Norton, and John Wheeler, Barney and his companions rode to the southern shore of the lake to find Black Rock, "a large rock standing out 40 or 50 rods into the water." They stripped down and "bathed in the most beautiful water I ever saw—so clear that you can see the bottom where it is 10 feet deep and can float or walk in it at pleasure as it is impossible to sink." On their return to camp after an hour at the lake, they "fell in with some 150 Indians—Utahs, mostly naked—going to our camp."[58] While these native neighbors were friendly, ignorance of the basin's Indians left Barney and most of his fellow pioneers suspicious of the native residents.[59] Barney had no idea at the time how much his life over the next three decades would be affected, for good and ill, by Utah's Indians. For Barney—after planting, hunting, exploring, building—the next day would be his final day in the valley for five years.

Chapter 10

A Band of Brethren: The Return to Winter Quarters, 1847

It was the design of church leaders to establish the Saints' foothold in the Great Basin in time to accommodate not only a fraction of the pioneer company who would winter there but also to assist the companies following the vanguard. As it turned out, about 1,700 of the roughly 2,100 who converged that year upon the Salt Lake Valley would winter there.[1] The plan also called for church leaders to return to the Missouri River to sustain their families, among them 95 of the 143 original westbound pioneers.[2] The return of the major portion of the vanguard, accompanied by Mormon Battalion veterans and others, was drafted in four parts. (1) Ezra T. Benson was to head an express composed of Porter Rockwell and three ex-battalion men leaving 2 August to hurry eastward to inform others on the trail of the Salt Lake Valley destination.[3] (2) A small group of hunters were to precede and provide meat for (3) a substantial contingent of, ox teams which would, in turn, be followed by (4) a yet larger body of returnees with horse teams, led by Brigham Young, all of whose objective it was to winter in Winter Quarters.[4] This four-part eastward reverse of the western expedition is a notable feature of the 1847 migration, somewhat neglected by historians and never described at length. Lewis Barney's account of the venture provides a slant to the story emphasizing the struggle of the return.

The return to Winter Quarters was designed to be as efficient and trouble-free as the trek west. Each segment of the return had its own agenda. "Arrangements was made to start back, the ox teams in advance of the horse and mule teams. Also a company of 12 men," of which Barney was one, was chosen "to precede the ox teams as hunters to go as far as the buffalo country and there stop and kill and dry meat for those that followed."[5] Half the hunters were chosen 11 August, largely, it appears, based on their hunting prowess during their westward journey. The other half were Mormon Battalion veterans who joined the pioneer camp in the valley. Word circulated soliciting donations to sustain the men until they could forage for themselves on the trail. But only sixty pounds of flour could be raised for Barney's group. Heber Kimball apologized to Barney for the lack of resources and asked, "Do you think you can go through to the Missouri River with that without starving to death?" "I can go through myself," Barney replied, "and feed 20 other men and not go hungry either."[6] Barney's optimistic, "can-do" attitude in coping with the natural world, while bordering on braggadocio, reveals a confident personality strain that helps explain much of his behavior in the future.

Jacob, captain of the hunting company, was given Young's instructions for the hunters. Young, a proven master of organization, cautioned the group to work in concert, to take care of their animals, and to "be prudent in all things." In particular, "do not give way to a hurrying spirit, not letting your spirits run away to Winter Quarters before your bodies can arrive there." Young implored the men to "be humble; be patient; be prayerful" and by so doing they would "be blest."[7] The direction was reasonable but, as Wallace Stegner observed, "they never were humble, rarely patient, seldom prayerful, nor did they listen to counsel. Neither were they blest."[8] Barely into the Wasatch Mountains on their eastbound return, Jacob on 16 August wrote, "Joseph Hancock and John Norton grumbled and murmured" over the site of the night's camp, even though it was agreed upon by everyone in the morning. That "evening John Norton threatened to cowhide John Wheeler" over the distribution of flour. This was followed the next day by "Hancock and Norton . . . murmuring that we were delaying too much and would get caught in the mountains by the snow as the gentiles did last winter [a reference to the ill-fated Donner-Reed party]."[9] Thus, from the start, the return seemed a lot longer than it really was.

The contrast between Brigham Young's larger-than-life presence for the westward journey and Norton Jacob's finite leadership on the return partially explains the irascibility of the hunters. A dozen men, some of whom had not seen their families for over a year, commissioned to hunt for those who followed only after they arrived at a "good hunting country" (meaning several hundred miles to the east) operated without many restraints despite Young's counsel. Their boorish behavior toward one another hobbled them most of the way east. A week after the hunters set out, the ox teams composed of seventy-one men with thirty-three wagons and led by Shadrach Roundy and Tunis Rappleye, left the Salt Lake Valley.[10] Twenty-four of the men were part of the vanguard and almost double the number, forty-six, were battalion veterans. With them they drove ninety-two yoke of oxen, eighteen horses, and fourteen mules.[11] They, too, were subject to the same pettiness afflicting the hunters before they reached Winter Quarters.

In the last week of August after crossing the Green River, out hunting as usual, Barney found himself alone and potentially in a lot of trouble. He was delayed in returning to the group and fell behind "eight or ten miles" besides "being two or three miles from the road on a smooth open plain." Before he knew it, "a band of Indians [probably Snakes] about 15 in number" came charging at full speed over the hill toward him on their horses. Too late to do anything defensive, he "walked along towards them." Surrounded, completely vulnerable, and undoubtedly unnerved, he said, "I made signs that my feet was very sore and that I was very hungry and wanted to buy a pair of moccasins and some buffalo beef." To his surprise:

> The chief talked to his men and they seemed to sympathize with me. One of the squaws handed me a pair of moccasins. I asked the price. The chief said 20 loads of powder and balls. I showed him that I would give him 10. He studied a little and finally accepted my offer. I then handed him my rifle to hold while I measured the 10 charges of powder and balls. They then gave me a buffalo tongue and my gun and went on their way.

Out of that fix, he continued, he "had not proceeded but a short distance until I met another band of Indians about the same number." Again he was surrounded and several made attempts to take his rifle and powder. Not as confident with the stoic bravery manifest previously, he "made a rush and broke from them and went on my way." Luckily the Indians "stood and watched me till I got 4 or 5 hundred yards from them" before "they went on their way." It was his good fortune that the Snake tribe at the time was not threatened by white travelers. Still, his encounters left him with a ten-mile walk before he reached camp that evening.[12]

The farther the hunters traveled from the Salt Lake Valley, the less inclined they were to follow counsel. Instead, rather than stepping to a common cadence, they were guided by individual pulse. Jacob, in charge, was disappointed at the lack of deference paid him by several of the hunters, though Barney was never one of those he noted as opposing his lead. Jacob found most of his difficulty with the Mormon Battalion veterans. Several of them treated him with complete indifference, if not disdain. Frustrated, he wrote that prior to reaching Fort Bridger, three of them went off toward the fort "without my counsel." Complaining to his diary, he related that John Norton, one of the pioneer vanguard, "commenced abusing me in the most vulgar manner, threatening to whip me," and the battalion veterans, except David M. Perkins, "were all full of cursing and swearing." "Thomas Brown [was] as profane as any of them, swearing they would leave the company and with their horses go ahead to Winter Quarters when we get to the Sweetwater."[13] Progressing twenty miles a day was not fast enough for some of those with visions of Winter Quarters swirling in their heads.

The hunters met Parley P. Pratt's company of 360, the second westward pioneer company of 1847, on 29 August. Benson's eastbound express had met Pratt's company two weeks previously and gave them a very favorable report about the valley. Jacob became particularly perturbed at John Norton's impertinence in front of Pratt's company when he countered Benson's report which caused "uneasiness in the minds of some of the brethren."[14] At about the same time that the hunters were parleying with Parley, the fourth and largest group of returnees from Salt Lake Valley left two and a half weeks behind Jacob's group. Led by Young, this group of 108 men, with thirty-six wagons, seventy-one horses, and forty-nine mules, had little of the discord of those who preceded them, Young's commanding presence insuring compatibility.[15]

The distance between the Jacob and Young parties gave liberties to Jacob's group unallowable in Young's company. For example, a few weeks into the journey, just past Independence Rock, Joseph Hancock, Barney's forty-seven-year-old former hunting partner, vented his latent feelings concerning Young's leadership and the destiny of the church. "He did not know [that] he should ever go back to the Valley," Jacob quoted Hancock as stating, "for Joseph Smith had promised that he should have *his* inheritance in Jackson County." It made no sense to Hancock in "building so many temples and then sell[ing] them to the gentiles." He was particularly pointed when he said, "I do not believe that Brigham Young is a prophet or that he ever received any revelations but what he [had] got from Joseph Smith."[16] Hancock's outburst of mutiny and apostasy indicates the extreme mental ordeal plaguing some who found no respite in perpetual exile. Three days after Hancock's flare-up the ox teams, on 8 September, finally caught up with the hunters, but it would be some time before they joined together as brethren.

The ox teamsters believed the hunters irresponsible and callous by sprinting ahead when they should have been laying aside meat for their brethren's arrival. But Pratt's and the subsequent emigration companies inadvertently complicated the union of the ox teams and the hunters. "[We] soon began to meet other companies which gave us much satisfaction," Barney wrote. But these companies had driven "the buffalo and other game from the road making it scarce and hard to get hold of. Consequently we were under the necessity of going much farther than we anticipated before we could make a halt to kill and dry meat for the company with the ox teams."[17] The ox teams arrived with their own difficulties, having fragmented themselves, and as if God was trying to tell them they needed to pull together, snow fell on them the previous day as they passed near Wyoming's Black Hills. Summer was drawing to a close and they had a long way to go.

Perturbed by the hunter's delay in rendezvousing with the ox teamsters, the advance fragment of teamsters ignored those in the hunter's camp as they passed. While Barney and the other hunters were out stalking buffalo, "the ox teams had passed about the middle of the afternoon and had gone on down the river never stopping to say, 'How do you do?' 'Good bye,' or anything else." The hunters "felt themselves slighted and insulted."[18] The next morning, Jacob's group, starting before sunrise, traveled six or seven miles when they caught up with the ox teams. "We called a halt," Barney explained, "and asked them why they did not stop at our camp, that we had killed a large quantity of meat for them and as they did not stop we left it where it was killed for the wolves." The teamsters replied with contempt; they could obtain their own meat and wanted none of their help. The insult then turned to inconvenience for Barney. Having lost his horse to accident in April on their westward journey, Barney had borrowed a horse to form a team to pull his wagon for the return journey. "Lyman Curtis [a former hunter on the westward trek and one of the ox teamsters] came to me and demanded his horse he had agreed to let me have until we got home."[19] Bad feelings had obviously been simmering for some time. (Later the ox teamsters found themselves the object of derision from Young's group for the same reason they excoriated the hunters.)[20]

As the fragmented camps moved on, Barney took a little perverse pleasure in the same manner he did the previous year in the aftermath of David Yearsley's insult. The morning of 10 September, "we discovered a large band of [Sioux] Indians traveling down the river on the opposite side with a large band of horses," Barney reported. "I said to the company, 'there is a horse in that band [that] looks like Lyman's horse.'"[21] When Curtis and two other ox teamsters came to their camp the next day searching for eighteen head of lost horses, Barney related what they had seen and told them that among the horses was "a large grey horse with them that looked very much like Lyman Curtis's white horse that he took from me when we passed their camp."[22] Curtis never recovered his animal.

Barney and his companions arrived at Fort Laramie on 14 September. Still the feuding camps ignored each other, and to complicate the mix, internal discord within the ox teamsters' camp was mounting. "In consequence of some things which have passed and some which at present exist," wrote forty-year-old William Clayton, "I have concluded to go on as fast as circumstances will permit to Winter Quarters." Knowing that by doing so he would later suffer the reprimand of church leaders, he declared to his diary, "I will bear the censure in preference to what I now bear."[23] While Clayton later softened his resolve and remained with his division, others struck out on 17 September for the Missouri River ahead of their cohorts.[24] That day, recognizing they had to close the breach, the advance ox teamsters and hunters "called a council among ourselves."[25] But even in the attempt at reconciliation, they managed to etch deeper cuts in their relationships.

Reconciliation?

At a time when the fragmented components of pioneers ought to have been at full attention cooperatively, Jacob and Clayton, respective leaders of their divisions—and both diarists—found themselves pitted against each other. On 18 September Jacob wrote, "Last night at 12 o'clock John Pack's gray mare, a valuable animal was stolen, being tied to the fore wheel of his [wagon] within 10 feet of the dog and 20 or 30 [feet] from two men on guard." Rather than laying the theft to the Sioux, Jacob asserted "that it was done by some man acquainted with the manner pursued every night in fastening that mare, and also with the dog, who is very cross." He concluded the blame lay with the ox teamsters.[26] Clayton, defending his camp, cried foul and was, in turn, collectively castigated by Jacob and other hunters whom Clayton said "heaped a pretty long string of severe [and] abusive language" against the ox teamsters whom they assumed stole the horse. Though Jacob proved to be partially correct (they tracked the mare five miles to the camp of the maverick ox teamsters who had moved on ahead), no apologies were extended.[27]

Still, for protection from the Sioux, both groups stayed close as they "traveled down the [Platte] river as far as the Chimney Rock" where they stayed for five days "killing buffalo and antelope" while they waited for the rest of the teamsters.[28] "Here," at the well-known trail site, Barney said, "we packed our wagons with dried meat, also beef that was not dried."[29] Not only did the delay prove to be a salve for the divided camp, when the trailing ox teams caught up to the advance teamsters and hunters on 23 September the hunters were able finally to fill their responsibility to the ox teamsters. At "about 10 o'clock in the evening," Barney said, "the camp of ox teams came up and called a halt. Brother John Gleason and [William H.] Carpenter came to my wagon and said, 'Barney, have you anything to eat? . . . We have not had a morsel to eat for the last three days and the whole camp is nearly starved.'" To the twenty-eight-year-old fellow New Yorker, Barney replied, "Well John, what will you have? I have aplenty of dried and green meat fresh from the plains," giving them "a quarter of antelope and piece of buffalo beef." Joseph Hancock also contributed an elk hindquarter to the hungry men. Also providing utensils and pots, Barney said, "'Now boys, help yourselves,' which they readily did, keeping up a fire and roasting, boiling, and frying meat until daylight, the whole camp following suit." The night-long repast proved to reforge the broken weld and return them to their sacred objectives, at least for a while. "During the night all past feelings were dropped and many hearty jokes passed. To say the least it was a night long to be remembered for the good feeling and social that [we] enjoyed in a wilderness." The next day, Barney continued, "we resumed our journey and traveled together as a band of brethren should do."[30]

Still in the middle of the Great Plains and over a month from their destination, notwithstanding their reconciliation, personalities managed to manufacture difficulties which nipped at their progress across Nebraska. Barney, while not malicious, played into the discord borne of monotony. He glibly recounted an incident that occurred not long after the feast when his

> wagon broke down and my mare lost her foal leaving me in a crippled condition. Father [James] Dunn came to me and proffered to haul 100 lbs. of tallow for me if I would kill him a buffalo. To this I agreed. So we loaded the 100 lbs. of tallow on his wagon and continued our journey. I, being worn out with excessive hunting, concluded to rest that day. So I got in the wagon and rode during the day.

But Dunn, fifteen years Barney's senior, wanted satisfaction, now! Barney's casual response to their agreement provoked Dunn the next morning when, Barney said, he "harangued me for not killing his buffalo." Putting Dunn off again, even after Dunn's display of frustration, Barney said, "I thought I would let him sweat over it another day." This was just the kind of attitude and behavior that exacerbated already difficult circumstances. But the following morning, Barney "started out for the old gentleman's buffalo" and before long he found "a small herd feeding." Firing his rifle, he dropped one of the mammoth beasts. Two more shots brought down two more animals. The wagon train pulled out about this time and after a mile-and-a-half run, Barney chased down Dunn to tell him he had his buffalo. "So," said Barney, "he and I went and brought it to camp leaving the other two for the wolves."[31]

The dreariness of travel, often revealing the ill temperament of the pioneers, also occasionally provoked them to humor. Barney and young Eric Glines paired, probably on 27 September, to retrieve buffalo meat for the ox teams at the request of Clayton. Glines, an American raised in Canada and not yet twenty-five years old, and his older companion tracked a group of the huge beasts and between the two of them they downed five. After the slaughter, "the company then came up [and] there being five buffaloes laying dead on the ground . . . I thought I would have a little fun with Eric." "Eric, which of these buffalo did you kill?" Barney asked. Pointing to the ones he shot, the young man said, "I killed this one and that one and that one." But, to unsettle Glines, Barney protested and, pointing to one of those his hunting partner had killed, said, "I know I killed this one." Glines, standing next to the animal, mildly retorted, "I know I killed that one myself." Barney appealed to William Clayton complaining, "Captain, didn't you see me kill three buffalo?" Clayton, having caught on to the gag, confirmed the assertion: "Yes, I know you killed three for I seen them fall." After having stuck the knife to Glines, Barney, much older than his younger hunting companion, then started to turn it: "Now Eric, I have proved that I killed three buffalos and as there are but five here you could not have killed but two." "By this time Eric was getting pretty warm." Barney then stiffened, pointed at the animal, and stated again, "Now see here, Eric, I believe I killed this one." With that, Barney kicked the buffalo, and as if on cue "it sprang to its feet and off it went at full speed as though nothing had been the matter with it." Barney then shrugged and matter-of-factly said, "Well Eric, I must have been mistaken. That must have been your buffalo for I don't kill buffalo like that so they come to life in half an hour after they have been killed." After having "some sport about Eric's buffalo" they "went to work and dressed the [other] buffalos, loaded them into the wagons, and started on."[32]

Despite the shared humor and good will between the hunters and the teamsters since their union the previous week, differences between personalities within the groups erupted again the first week of October.

> A debate arose in camp about remaining in camp the next day to dry our beef. The camp was divided on the subject; about two thirds voted to stop, the other third, not being satisfied, said they would not stop. I told the company that we were hurrying on too fast, that we should wait here until the Twelve [Brigham Young's company] came up. But few seemed willing [to] wait for them. Here then was another split in camp.[33]

With another fissure in the ranks, "Those that wanted to go on was determined to do so and those that wanted to stop was equally as determined." Those inclined to proceed "gathered up their teams and started on." Resigned that he could not influence them otherwise and anxious himself, Barney "harnessed up and joined the advance company, leaving about two thirds of the camp behind."[34] But their zeal to move on was soon checked by their own independence and by the Pawnee.

The first morning after their departure from the ox teams, Barney reported, "Every man seemed to be his own captain and apparently tried to see who should be off first. Accordingly the first that could get breakfast and harness up was the first to start." When grouped in large numbers, the white travelers discouraged Indian interference, but this maverick body of twelve wagons was now in number insufficient to thwart Indian mischief. Moving on, the little caravan drew the attention of a band of Pawnee warriors who jumped "out of the grass and came running as fast as their legs could carry them."[35]

The Indians with great confidence surrounded the company, even striking at the heads of their horses with their weapons. Seeing Clayton in his carriage off by itself with a horse in tow, a dozen Indians went after him and tried to relieve Clayton of the trailing horse. At this,

> Lisbon Lamb, who was in the carriage with Brother Clayton, sprang out of the carriage, ran up to the horse, grabbed hold of the lariat, and tried to get it away from the Indian. Not being able to do this, he drew his knife and cut the lariat and sprang upon the horse. At this the Indians caught the horse by the bridle reins and surrounded him and pitched Lamb off the horse [before one jumped on the animal and galloped away] leaving Clayton, Lamb, and the carriage to take care of themselves.

With "whooping, yelling, and flourishing Bowie knives and guns in the air," the Indians planned to leave the entire group on foot.[36]

Not the least hesitant to confront the travelers, another warrior grabbed for Clayton's carriage reins, attempting to drive off the horse and carriage. Clayton had had enough. He "cocked his rifle and raised it to a shooting position and shouted, 'Be ready boys!' This command being given, the click of the gunlocks was heard along the whole line and every gun was in readiness." The

Indians sensing the white's resolve drew their own arms, Barney reported, "ready for the word for action."

> Their line was about 15 feet from us. It so happened the chief stood in front of me not more than 15 feet off, his gun in his hands nearly in a shooting position. I also had my rifle cocked and elevated a little above his head with my eye fixed on his. He also had his eye on me. In this position we stood about two minutes. Not a word was spoken on either side. I was determined; if the chief made the least move to shoot, I would put a ball through his breast. He seeing the position and danger he was in made a quick turn on his heel and gave a shout to his men. They all whirled round and started off full speed. They went as fast as they come and was soon out of sight.

Shaking as the Indians ran off, Barney said, "I moved that we go back to the other company, repeating it perhaps fifty times."[37]

The Indian threat broke the overanxious overlanders' resolve to go on by themselves without the protection of the larger numbers of ox teamsters. On 8 October they retraced their steps and, eating humble pie, found themselves amid their erstwhile comrades. "We was more willing to meet and join them than we was to leave them the previous morning," Barney observed.[38] Clayton's account was more telling: "After traveling back about six miles, we met the company, told the story and bore their slang and insults without saying much, but not without thinking a great deal." As they regrouped, "Many hard speeches . . . passed among the brethren, such as 'damned hypocrites,' 'damned liars,' 'mutineers,' etc., and most of those who started ahead are [now] ordered to travel in the rear all the time."[39] All the good feeling once retrieved was gone. "This savage tyrannical conduct was one thing which induced some to leave and undertake to go through alone and more peaceably," Clayton wrote that night, "and it will still leave feelings of revenge and hatred which will require some time to cover up." "For my part," Clayton closed, "I shall be glad when I get in more peaceable society, and I think I shall not easily be caught in such a scrape again."[40] After absorbing the insults with everything being placed in the open, "We again resolved to travel together as brethren and no more separate until we reached Winter Quarters," Barney wrote. "All former feelings and difficulties was again laid aside."[41]

Brigham Young, the Twelve, and their company, no less anxious to reunite with their families than the brethren in advance, moved along as fast as they could though the distance between them and the teamsters and hunters lengthened. While they were amply supplied with meat traveling through buffalo country, they were short of other required provisions. "If the ox teams do not stop," wrote Horace K. Whitney on 11 October, "the brethren, weak & faint from living entirely on meat, must, necessarily give up the chase."[42] But the ox teamsters and hunters were ignorant of, if not indifferent to, their needs.

About ten days away from Winter Quarters, the teamsters and hunters on 10 October were again confronted with a decision about travel. The itch to get home still festered. The camp came together and a vote was taken regarding the final leg of their return to Winter Quarters. A vote of thirty to seventeen favored moving on instead of waiting, though the remainder of the group abstained from the poll. "The majority having voted to go on," Clayton said, "we started and traveled very slowly,"[43] but not slow enough for their trailing brethren. Having heard a report about the substantial distance between them and the hunters and ox teams, Young and his associates were aggravated at the impatient men for abandoning their agreement. Thomas Bullock, with Young's camp, called them rebellious and wrote, "If they did not think they were, they had only to look at their instructions, which they had in their pockets." Later he called them "perfectly reckless of their promises."[44] It was clear by this time that all strategies planned in the Salt Lake Valley had been abandoned. The tedium of travel and lure of home on the Missouri River erased all promises.

The haste of the hunters and teamsters outweighed the caution that circumstances required. Believing, after the last confrontation, that they were out of Indian danger, "William Clayton, Captain Redden, William Empey, Joseph Hancock, and myself started ahead of the train [on 16 October] not however with the intention of leaving for good but for the purpose of looking for game, being two or three miles ahead of the camp."[45] Reaching the summit of a hill overlooking the Pawnee Missionary Farm, they were discovered by the Indians.[46] Immediately, "5 of them mounted their horses and came dashing toward us at full speed. They dashed up to our wagons with long spears in their hands in a state of great excitement." But instead of doing harm, "they inquired if we had seen anything of the Sioux Indians." Quick thinking and lying tongues drove them to say they had seen the Sioux and they "would be here in two sleeps. As they were at war with them this stratagem had the desired effect." Soon, "the whole [Indian] camp was in motion gathering up their horses and in fifteen or twenty minutes there was a line of them stringing out a mile or more long leaving the way clear."[47]

Pushing on eastward toward the Missouri River, on 14 October the ox teams and hunters were visited by an express rider from Winter Quarters, led by Hosea Stout, sent to meet Young to provide information and provisions to the travelers. "Not finding Brigham Young with us," Barney said, "he went on not leaving a morsel of provisions with us."[48] Only a week away from Winter Quarters, the slight could be overlooked. While the ox teamsters and hunters found themselves almost in sight of their destination, the company attached to Brigham Young and the Twelve did not overlook the breach of protocol displayed by their advance brethren. Their transit had been complicated by the abrogation of duty of the ox teamsters and hunters. When the express rider from Winter Quarters reached him on 18 October, Young was told of the location and designs of the ox teamsters and hunters. His entourage was not happy.

Not only had the teamsters and hunters shirked their duty, they also proved a hindrance to Young's company in another way. Bullock, the official clerk traveling with the Twelve, wrote, "At this place there was beautiful feed when our [advance] brethren passed, but the ox team company appears to be determined we should not have any of it for what they did not eat, they set fire to, leaving us a prairie of burnt ashes."[49]

The vanguard, designed for efficiency and speed, traversed the land westbound from the Missouri River to the Great Basin in about fifteen weeks. Barney and his cohorts, despite all of their interruptions, made the eastward return in about ten weeks and arrived in Winter Quarters on 21 October; Brigham's company reached their destination at the end of the month. After their ordeal recrossing the Rocky Mountains and the Great Plains, Barney reported that he and his companions "arrived all safe in Winter Quarters where we had the happy privilege of once more meeting the smiles and pleasant countenances of our wives, children, and friends after a hard and hazardous journey of 1200 miles amongst Indians, blood-thirsty, and uncivilized."[50] Despite the return's disappointing circumstances, the 1847 pioneer trek was a glorious venture fixing Barney's place in his religion's foundation monuments.

While the pioneers no doubt mused over the importance of their "errand into the wilderness," they were immediately returned to the regular fare of life—survival. For Lewis Barney it was no different. Casting his eyes on the bustling Mormon community at Winter Quarters, he had more important matters to consider now than how his reputation and place in the Mormon legacy would survive. Crossing the Missouri River to Iowa, "I found my wife and 3 children without provisions and nearly without clothing."[51] With the wolf at the door, yet again, Barney returned to that with which he was most familiar: working his immediate circumstances to keep his family in the mortal world.

When Lewis Barney sat down at the table in his Monroe, Utah, home in 1878 and began committing his life story to paper, the account of his venture as a vanguard member of Utah's pioneers became the memoir's preeminent event. Though his life's experience and geographical exposure were diverse and filled with significance, the remainder of his tale paled in contrast to his role in this epic journey. It is clear that in his later years he considered it so; history has proven it so. This heralded group became the substance of a story, a story that would be forever remembered and oft repeated, a story now transformed to history and legend. This tale which they created served and gave definition to all Saints who followed them, blood kin or not. It is difficult to overstate the significance of the Mormon exodus to the modern children of Israel and subsequent generations. The odyssey of planting the "ensign to the nations" in the mountain valley is a rival for the most important story in Latter-day Saint memory.

Chapter 11

Barney's Grove: Iowa and the Last Trek to Zion, 1847–1852

The satellite of Mormonism planted in the western desert was now more than a dream. Its transformation from colony to headquarters in 1848 excited all who dreamed of gathering to Zion. The focus for most Winter Quarters Saints was preparation for a spring emigration, but concurrent with the planning was the hard reality of sustaining life. The heroic aura surrounding the vanguard company did not eliminate the survival concerns for some of the venturer's families. Finding his family in very difficult straits, Barney was, upon his return to the Missouri River, still "thankful to find them alive."[1] The circumstances of Barney's family during his hiatus to the West is not known. Betsey and her three sons, thirteen-year-old Walter, Henry who was seven, and Joseph the baby, nearly two, likely passed Lewis's absence in close proximity to his father's family located on Mosquito Creek in Pottawattamie County. Despite the probable extended family support, dire situations among the exiles were ubiquitous, though, most families acquired the resources to survive. Gathering his wife and children around him upon his return, Barney reported, "I had not the privilege of enjoying their society long as I was under the necessity of going to Missouri, a distance of 150 miles, for supplies which I had to procure by my labor." Undoubtedly revisiting the locality where he had three times previously labored in northwestern Missouri to sustain his family, this time flour, cornmeal, and bacon were the returns he obtained for his work. The foodstuffs were welcomed as he rejoined his family at the end of November 1847. Because access to Iowa resources only decreased, this venture was followed by another Missouri winter trip "for provisions and clothing" to keep his family viable.[2]

Walter Barney and the Battalion

While Lewis Barney crisscrossed the Great Plains and Rockies and his father's family worked to survive in Pottawattamie County, his younger brother Walter, as a recruit in the Mormon Battalion, was making his own mark in the Mormon legacy. But there was little heroic about the makeshift army as they began their

The Salt Lake Tribune.

SALT LAKE CITY, UTAH, SATURDAY MORNING, JUNE 12, 1897.

FIFTY YEARS AGO TODAY,

SATURDAY, JUNE 12, 1847.

Saturday, June 12th, the pioneers arrived at the last crossing of the Platte. They camped on the west banks, having made 11¼ miles during the day. The week's record was 98¾ miles, and the distance from Winter Quarters 667¼ miles.

Several days before, as has been related, a party of the pioneers had been sent on to make ready for the ferrying of the train across the river. This party had arrived some hours before the Missourians, and the latter, seeing the boat which was owned by the pioneers, made a bargain whereby the latter would ferry their goods over the river and float the empty wagons.

They paid the pioneer party $1.50 for each wagon and load, in flour, at $2.50 per hundred.

As flour was readily worth $10 at that point, it was a good bargain.

The party was engaged in this work when the main body of the pioneers came up and formed the encampment.

The payment was made also in some meal, bacon and other stores. The flour, however, was the greatest blessing to the camp, as many had been entirely out of breadstuffs for weeks, and the stores secured at the Platte were supposed to have saved the lives of some of the pioneers.

The hunters killed three buffaloes, six antelope, one bear and three cubs on Saturday, the variety of meat greatly and agreeably adding to the provisions of the camp.

It was decided to lie over at this camp on Saturday, and commence the work of ferrying on Monday morning.

Lewis Barney of the pioneer company was born in Niagara county, New York, September 8, 1808, and died in Mancos, Colo., November 5, 1894. He was distinguished as one of the best hunters in the camp. He returned to the States in 1847, but came back to the valley in 1852, and settled in Provo, where he engaged in the lumber business.

He moved to Spanish Fork, and in 1861 he went to Spring City. From there he migrated to South Bend, now Monroe, which he helped to settle in 1864. Monroe town was abandoned in 1866, on account of Indian troubles, and he, with others, returned to Spring City, but they settled in Monroe again when peace was restored.

He was a resident of Grass Valley, Sevier county, Utah, for three years, and then went to Arizona on foot, staying there one year. His last home was in Colorado, where his widow and children still live.

LEWIS BARNEY.

[From a photograph loaned by his brother, Walter Barney of Monroe.]

Walter Barney (Lewis Barney's brother). *Salt Lake Tribune*, 12 June 1897, which misidentified the image as of Lewis Barney.

march. Ill-prepared for what they would encounter, almost a third of the force had to winter in Pueblo, Colorado, due to sickness and disease. Those who carried on exhibited human endurance in the extreme. Walter, at just over five and a half feet tall and slightly built, was one of the exhibitors. His service took him and his companions into the desolate American Southwest, through their own tribulation of starvation, and finally to San Luis Rey in southern California where they cast their eyes on the Pacific Ocean on 27 January 1847. Just two weeks previously General Kearny established U.S. control in Los Angeles.[3]

The ordeal for the battalion was complicated by the non-Mormon officers, some of whom were hostile to the Saints, assigned to lead them.[4] One incident involving Walter illustrates the conflict between the volunteers and the army officers. At the point of starvation, battalion members "had taken the lining out of their saddles and boiled it up to make soup to eat or drink." Desperate, Walter recalled that Ephraim Hanks, his mess mate, "slipped into an officer's tent and stole a slab of bacon and when the officers missed it they searched every tent in the camp." Observing the officers on their way to search their tent, Walter "put a blanket over his shoulders and took the slab of bacon and put it under the blanket and while the officers came in the front door he met them in the door and went out while they come in." While his tent was being searched Walter carefully buried the slab in the sand to await a more opportune moment for he and Eph to capitalize on their booty.[5]

Spared combat with the Mexican enemy, the battalion nevertheless played an important role in protecting American interests in the Southwest. But just 335 of the original 500 dragged themselves into San Diego County at the end of January 1847. "Upon reaching California, there was little resemblance to an army."[6] The ordeal was extreme and it is remarkable that the numbers who reached San Diego were not totally debilitated.

Near the end of the battalion's enlistment, Walter was seriously injured. In Los Angeles, in late May or early June "while driving U.S. stock to water, he was thrown from a horse and crippled in the Spinal column and right hip and leg." He also "contracted an attack of Malarial fever, and palpatation of the heart" placing his life in peril.[7] His injuries and illness required a military doctor's attention and hospitalization during May and June before he was finally discharged from the hospital and military duty the following month on 16 July 1847 at "Ciudad de Los Angeles, Cal.," one year after enlistment.[8] Three hundred seventeen of the battalion gathered for their official release, each receiving $31.50 for their service. Eighty-one men, about one-fourth of those at the ceremony, reenlisted for eight more months. Another 223 traveled north on El Camino Real to Monterey or up the central valley to Sutter's Fort. Twenty-eight-year-old Walter remained in southern California with five comrades until year's end, working forty miles east of Los Angeles for Isaac Williams.[9] Williams tended to Walter's condition while the latter recuperated at Williams's Rancho del Chino.[10] Convalescing, Walter helped build a mill and helped to slaughter

1,800 head of cattle for his employer. He then traveled north with three others to Monterey, California, and worked there until July 1848.[11]

About two dozen former Mormon soldiers who marched to Monterey later moved north to the American River to work for John A. Sutter in September 1847 where they met up with other battalion veterans. Five were working at Sutter's millrace near Sacramento on 24 January 1848 when gold was discovered by John Marshall. Battalion diarists Henry Bigler and Azariah Smith provide the only contemporary record of the discovery which inaugurated the California gold rush the following year. Soon two hundred veterans and men from the Mormon ship *Brooklyn* were panning for gold in the area.[12] Word of the find spread internationally. Walter, after his stay at Monterey, was apparently one of the two hundred who went to the diggings. The scope of his goldfields involvement is not known, but he later told his nephew that when he and his companions "couldn't wash out $50.00 per day they quit that place and hunted new diggings." Walter claimed to have obtained several thousand dollars worth of gold dust before leaving for the Great Basin.[13] How long he stayed in California is not known. A few dozen battalion veterans left the Sacramento area in July 1848 arriving in the Salt Lake Valley the first of October. Walter probably stayed longer, strengthening his economic condition. The earliest indication of his presence in Great Salt Lake City is shown in a 1 March 1849 deposit of fifty dollars in gold dust to church coffers.[14] Before the year was over, Walter Barney settled in Utah Valley, just south of the Salt Lake Valley.[15]

Six Mile (Barney's) Grove

Lewis Barney returned from Missouri to his family in Iowa, probably about the end of 1847 after his fifth trip for provisions.[16] Upon his return the reality of his family's situation was evident. There was no way he could return to the Great Basin in 1848. "Finding I could do but little more than support myself and family," he explained, "I concluded to make a farm and try farming for a fit out." With another home-seeker, Barney investigated northern Pottawattamie County and "made a location in the Six Mile Grove on the waters of the Boyer River about 40 miles north of Kanesville."[17] Coincident to Barney's search, Apostle George A. Smith at the April 1848 church conference "proposed raising a company for a settlement on Boyer [River] as there was a good country there."[18] It was good country. The Boyer River (pronounced "Boo-yea" by some, as in French) is a substantial stream flowing southwesterly, diagonally bisecting what is now Harrison County, Iowa, before emptying into the Missouri River. At the time the region comprised the northern sector of Pottawattamie County (later separated and organized as Harrison County in 1853). The area eventually supported about fifteen of the ninety-eight Mormon communities in the Missouri River Valley.[19]

Henry Barney (Lewis Barney's brother). Photographer and date unknown. Courtesy of Kathy Erickson.

Contemporary descriptions of this Iowa county whose western border was the Missouri River seem remarkable. One nineteenth-century observer of the Boyer River region wrote, "For the person who would like a wild, romantic life beyond the bounds of real civilization, there could have been no more fitting spot. In the very midst of wild game and wild fruits, with plenty of grass, timber and water, unrestrained by the tight reins of society, he could here let loose his fancy and live with but little labor."[20] What appears an idealistic exaggeration of the county is confirmed by early settlers. "We located in this county in 1850," an early resident stated, "and here found, as we thought, the garden of Eden, a vast prairie of beautiful flowers and a great abundance of wild fruits. . . . [W]e had a large supply of meat, including venison, prairie hens, wild turkeys, etc."[21] The parcel where Barney settled was the only part of the county having a native stand of timber complementing the rich agricultural region.[22] The territory opened for settlement coincident to the Mormons' expulsion from Nauvoo. Prior to that time it was part of the Pottawattamie Reservation granted by treaty to the tribe in 1830. In June 1846 the Indians relinquished the reservation to the federal government and moved west of the Missouri River. Thus, in the same year of Iowa's statehood, the state's western perimeter was a virgin wilderness to white prospects. The first settlers in Pottawattamie County's upper sector were Mormons, Daniel Brown and Uriah Hawkins, the former exploring the area in late 1846 before settling there the following summer.[23]

In Cass Township where Hawkins first settled, among the first to break prairie sod was Lewis Barney. With his brothers, probably John and Henry, he lived in a tent while, once again, creating a farm from pristine land.[24] After identifying a promising location, Lewis "commenced clearing a place and planting corn and potatoes on the 15th day of May [1848]. I put in 5 acres of corn and [a] half acre of potatoes. From this I raised 75 bushels of corn to the acre and enough potatoes for family use."[25] As the Barneys prospered in the area, the hamlet acquired for a time the name of Lewis and his brothers: Barney's Grove.[26] This was not enough to draw the rest of the family, however. The family patriarch, Charles, remained with others of the family, including Luther, Benjamin, and their families, on Mosquito Creek in the lower portion of the county.[27] For Lewis, the bucolic landscape and land's richness portended a fine life. He particularly noted the "great amount of wild game such as deer, turkeys, geese, ducks, chickens, and squirrels" in the Boyer River valley.[28] Still, the Mormon villagers sparsely sprinkled over the county's northern sector were reliant upon the lower, more populated county settlements for their milling and some grocery needs.[29] The Barneys with all others who settled in the county also shared another commonality: they held no legal title to the land—they were squatters.[30]

Not long after the Barneys established themselves in Six Mile (Barney's) Grove, designated for being six miles north of Harris Grove, other Latter-day Saints moved to the hamlet, including Tunis Rappleye, a New Yorker who was a year older than Lewis and who was one of the captains of the ox teams with whom Barney was involved the previous year. Bryant Jolley, who would later play the role of nemesis in Barney's final journey to Utah, also settled in the grove.[31] Barney's prowess at harvesting the abundant game and his farming success helped sustain the newcomers until they established themselves. He had also learned the skills of carpentry which he no doubt used in general construction in the area.[32] Most of the small Latter-day Saints settlements had their own ecclesiastical organizations regionally directed from Kanesville. Even with all this, there was an air of temporariness.

Lewis Barney likely relocated to northern Pottawattamie County to prepare for the 1849 immigration to Utah. But their positive situation in Barney's Grove forestalled any perceived need to gather to the Great Basin. Instead of a one-year pause, it became five years of tenure on the Iowa prairie. However, Lewis's brother Henry, exhibiting independence from family cohesiveness that marked the remainder of his life, did not share his brother's exuberance for western Iowa. Gathering his small recently formed family, Henry left the Missouri River Valley for Utah, likely arriving in 1849.[33] The stay in the grove for the Barneys provided a respite from the tenuous pattern of being a driven people. For the first time in three years the threats of violence, disease, starvation, and separation were exchanged for an atmosphere of tranquility and sustenance, if not frontier prosperity.

The Latter-day Saint settlements on the Missouri River continued to be an object, if only temporarily, of the gathering Saints. But by December 1847 it was clear to church leaders from government pressure regarding their residence on Indian lands, they would have to abandon Winter Quarters. In July 1848 the center of the church on the Missouri was transferred east across the river.[34] Kanesville, on the bank opposite Winter Quarters, thereafter absorbed the influx of the displaced Saints heading westward. Formerly Miller's Hollow and now Council Bluffs, Kanesville became headquarters for the Saints in the Midwest. After a winter at the Missouri River where he was formally accepted as church president in December 1847, Brigham Young left for the Salt Lake Valley on 26 May 1848. Hundreds of anxious Saints followed him in the second year of a twenty-two-year cycle of wagon and handcart transit to Zion. Others, like the Barneys, elected to stay for the time among the Mormons in western Iowa. The 1850 census indicates there were 7,828 residents of Pottawattamie County and of these over 7,000 were Latter-day Saints.[35]

Orson Hyde, one of the church's Twelve Apostles, was assigned to direct the Mormon settlements on the Missouri. After 1848, Kanesville became the chief staging site for church members with Zion on their minds and also served as a major point of departure for forty-niners crossing the country for California's goldfields. A Plainfield, Illinois, minister, on his way to the goldfields, described the area on 8 May 1849:

> I was much surprised and disappointed, in the view of the country around the bluffs; it appears for some 50 or 60 miles on up the river, up and down, as though the table land had been scouped out by an enormous large spoon, and turned over, by the side of the hole in a pile one or two hundred feet high, presenting one of the grandest of landscapes in nature; here in all these deep and intricate windings are located herds of Mormons, who bring forth their young in the most prolific manner; they show their weakness of intellect by their location, and manner of living; there are thousands of them lodged in these hills.[36]

The negative characterization of the Saints' physical condition resulted from the transitory nature of many who viewed their stay at the Missouri River as a temporary hindrance to their Salt Lake Valley objective. Having put away their traveling trunks, Lewis Barney and his family were enjoying their good fortune in Barney's Grove when a life-altering situation arose in their household.

Elizabeth Beard Tippetts and Polygamy

Three days after Barney returned to his family after his Rocky Mountain venture, Alva Tippetts, his friend and Latter-day Saint mentor, died. The pause at the Missouri had not been kind to the Tippetts family. Three months prior, Alva's one-year-old namesake, Alva, Jr., died of what was reported as "summer complaint."[37] The deaths left Alva's wife Caroline with a world fallen apart. The Tippetts deaths were two of hundreds of Latter-day Saint deaths during their stay at the Missouri, 1846–1852. But the effect of Alva's demise was that he left two women mourning. Tippetts was a polygamist.

Alva Tippetts's religious fervor and ardent belief in the Mormon gospel of Jesus Christ had not only influenced the Barneys in 1840, he ministered a few years later as a missionary in Indiana, particularly in Clinton County. There in Middlefork he contacted the family of Christian and Margaret Beard. Family tradition holds that Christian Beard was something of an aristocrat coming from a line of slaveholders in Virginia, holding slaves himself before moving west to Indiana.[38] The Beards were compelled by the missionary message and became Latter-day Saints in 1842 or 1843. The Beard household thereafter became a hub of Mormon activity in the area, including being instrumental in a small Mormon congregation's organization about forty miles north of Indianapolis. Perhaps some of the interest of Mormon missionaries in the Beards was Christian Beard's four pretty daughters of, or soon to be of, marriage age. Alva was attracted to nineteen-year-old Caroline, whom he married on 19 September 1843. Two other daughters of the Beards married missionaries about this time. After the family migrated to Nauvoo, Alva also married the Beards' then sixteen-year-old daughter Elizabeth in 1845 or 1846.[39] Tippetts became a part of the practice that characterized Mormons in the nation's minds throughout the nineteenth century: plural marriage or, as it is more popularly known, polygamy.

Among a number of singular elements of Joseph Smith's revelatory religion was a restoration of the ancient biblical practice of polygamy, technically polygyny: a man having more than one wife. Mormonism was not, like many of its contemporary Christian organizations, bound by New Testament models. The prophets and patriarchs, some of whom were polygamists, held great relevance to their Latter-day Saint equivalent, modern Israel. As the practice of plural marriage emerged among church members, their initial shock and disinclination was followed by resolution. The "restitution of all things, which God hath spoken by the mouth of all his holy prophets since the world began" (Acts 3:21) portended a revival of ancient antecedents. Plural marriage was part of a much larger package.

The particulars of polygamy's practice may have been revealed to the Prophet Joseph as early as 1831. Smith himself may have initiated the new form of marriage in the mid-1830s. It was not until the Mormons settled in Nauvoo with its initial stability and prosperity that the new marriage arrangement was introduced to the Saints, first to a very limited and selected segment of church members. Rumors circulated in the early 1840s that some church leaders were involved in polygamy. Its introduction by innuendo was not well received. A defector, John C. Bennett, once very visible and influential in Nauvoo civic and religious circles, scandalized the Saints with his 1842 exaggeration and expose of Mormon practices, in particular plural marriage.[40] Other dissidents, including Smith's former counselor William Law, exposed Smith's polygamy through a rival paper, the *Nauvoo Expositor*, in June 1844. The Nauvoo City Council's destruction of the *Expositor* was a major factor in Smith's arrest which led to his death in Carthage, Illinois. By and by the Saints were generally informed about what came to be called the "new and everlasting covenant of marriage."[41]

With Tippetts's death, the Barneys became benefactors to his relicts. On 27 April 1849 Charles and Deborah's oldest son, Benjamin Franklin, then just seventeen, married twenty-three-year-old Caroline Beard Tippetts. Caroline was mother to three children, with but one living at the time of her marriage to Benjamin.[42] They lived close to Charles in Pottawattamie County.[43] Caroline's sister, Elizabeth, herself a teenage widow with a young child, was taken into Charles and Deborah Barney's family. Nothing is known of their circumstances until Elizabeth became ill. Lewis wrote that during a visit to his father's family on Mosquito Creek, probably in 1850, he found Elizabeth there, that she had been sick for some time, and was not expected to live. "As Alva Tippetts, her husband, was dead and had been one of my old chums," Lewis wrote, "I was moved with compassion for the poor sick woman."[44] That Elizabeth's little girl, Rachel, was deaf obviously intensified their pitiable status.[45] Lewis noted "that [Elizabeth] had no home nor anyone but strangers or friends to take care of her." Willing to take the young widow into his own home, her health was so tenuous she could not be moved to Barney's Grove. "So," he wrote, "I told my father and brother Luther to do the best they could for her and when she got able if they would bring her up to my place I would take care of her and her child." A month later Benjamin took Elizabeth to Lewis's, though "she was still weak and unable to do any work." She stayed with Lewis and Betsey for about a year.[46]

It is not known how Elizabeth Beard Tippetts fit into the Barney household. She was a Virginian, born 7 June 1830.[47] One would think that, being twenty-one years younger than Lewis and Betsey, both twice her age, she would be nurtured as one of their children, but circumstances proved otherwise. As her health improved, Barney said that "she become somewhat attached to me and I also become attached to her. We, knowing the Lord had commanded his people to take to themselves a plurality of wives, I proposed to her that she become my wife to which she consented." He said that as they were living "among Gentiles," non-Mormons, they were secretly "sealed on the 12th day of March 1851."[48] Notwithstanding the general knowledge of polygamy among

Elizabeth Beard Barney (Lewis Barney's second wife). Photographer and date unknown. Courtesy of Raymond G. Briscoe.

the Saints, the entrance of a new woman in a monogamist home may have been difficult though Lewis wrote nothing about it.[49] It is likely that Elizabeth's new role as wife rather than boarder was a greater adjustment for Betsey than it was for her. As there were few plural marriage role models among the Saints open to public scrutiny at this time, it is probable that the new domestic relationship of the Barneys was experimental as well as experiential.

Evacuation of the Missouri River Valley Mormons

Later that year, 21 September 1851, the church First Presidency—Brigham Young, Heber C. Kimball, and Willard Richards—from Great Salt Lake City published an epistle to the Saints in Iowa, counseling them to close the Missouri Valley settlements and come west.[50] Barney and his now-expanded family never trifled with the general instructions and counsel of church leaders. The wisdom of an inspired leadership had become something in which Lewis had developed confidence. He had witnessed firsthand the fragmentation from Mormonism of those disappointed in church leadership and counsel. Thus, when counsel was given to abandon the settlements at the Missouri River, at least for the Barneys, there was no question about compliance, despite their favorable experience at Six Mile (Barney's) Grove.

Once the call to gather was issued, the Barney clan began preparations for their trek to the valley. Lewis "got out timber for a few wagons and made two wagons for the journey."[51] Their preparation was complicated by the pregnancy and later birth on 8 February 1852 of Betsey's fourth living son and last child, William Orson Barney. Elizabeth was also now pregnant with her first child by Lewis. After carefully calculating what they could carry with them and preparing their family for the journey, which included four boys ranging from Walter at seventeen to the infant, their biggest obstacle was selling their farmstead which, while not palatial, was significant. As Lewis's family prepared for departure, their improvements at Six Mile (Barney's) Grove in Cass Township included three log cabins and 160 acres, 40 of which had been cultivated.[52] Church leaders counseled those departing to "give not your heritage to reproach, neither sell your improvements in Pottawatamie to strangers for nothing. No! rather sell your improvements for their value."[53] By mid-May 1852 it was reported that "The Saints are selling a goodly number of their farms, improvements &c &c. and some is getting pretty good prices."[54] They wanted no repeat of the Nauvoo debacle.

As it was generally known that the Mormons were leaving the Missouri River Valley, their land and improvements became the objective of newcomers into the region. "About this time," Lewis Barney wrote, "there came a man and his nephew from New York to look at the country. He, hearing of my place,

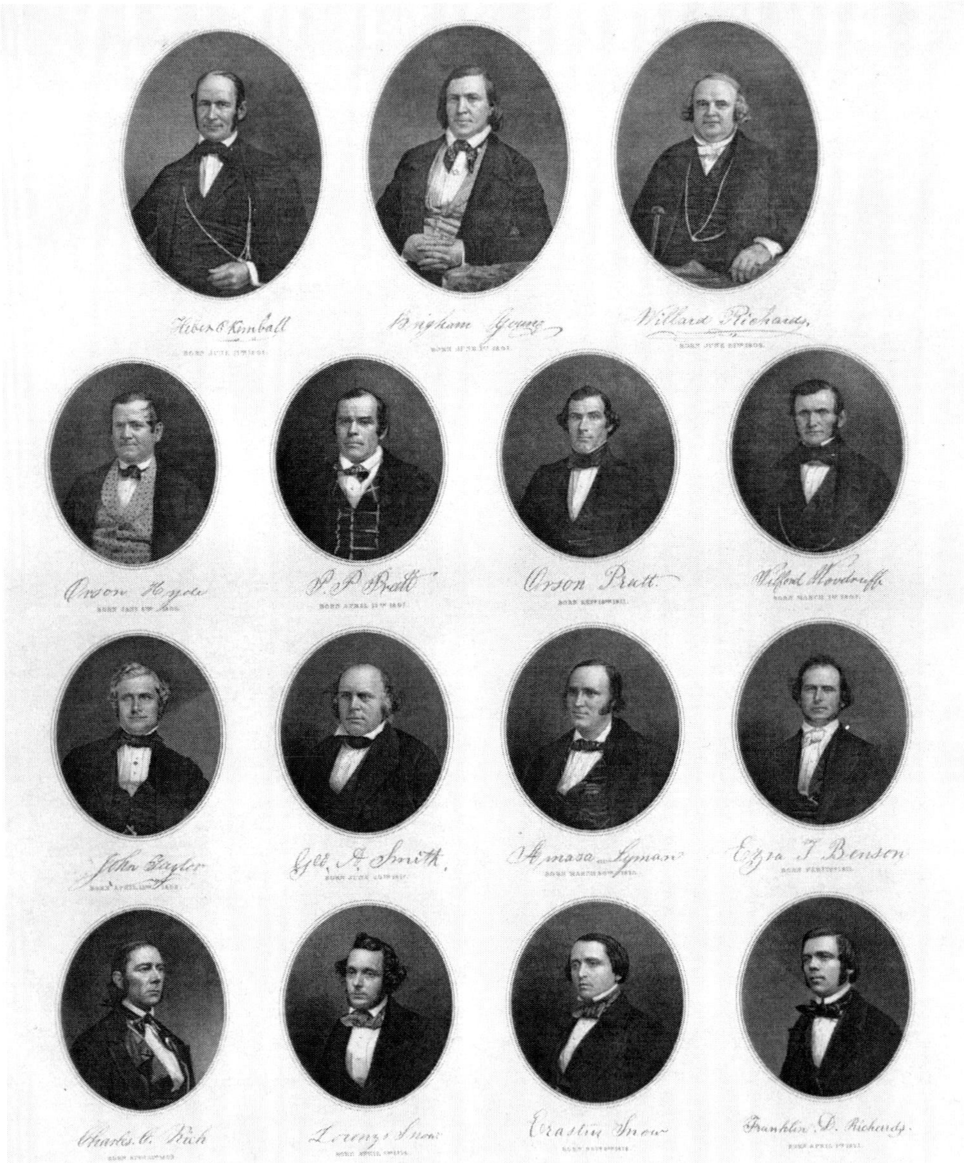

First Presidency and Twelve Apostles, the Church of Jesus Christ of Latter-day Saints. Engraving from the Marsena Cannon Daguerrotypes, by Frederick C. Piercy, 1853. Courtesy Church Archives, the Church of Jesus Christ of Latter-day Saints.

came to see it."[55] The New Yorker interested in his land was thirty-one-year-old Stephen King who had just moved to Iowa. He later became one of the county's most prominent citizens, serving as an educational, religious, and civic leader. When Harrison County was organized as a county in 1853, Stephen King was elected county judge and was thereafter widely known as Judge Stephen King.[56] Barney reported that "after looking at the place he [King] asked the price, to which I replied, 'The place is well worth $1000. But I will let you have it for $300.'" King said he would consider the proposal, though he exhibited no anxiousness to obtain Barney's property. After a few weeks King inquired if Barney had lowered his price. Despite being told that Barney was holding firm, King shortly approached Barney again only to receive the same answer. By this time, however, Barney realized the weakness of his own position. First of all, he held no legal title to the land; most of the Mormons were squatters in western Iowa. Second, there was a certain window of time for emigration which was quickly approaching. When King showed interest again, Barney "replied that if he would give me $100 in cash down he could have the farm." Again, King walked away.[57]

The time to prepare was over and the call to assemble with the emigrant company arrived in early June 1852. As Barney loaded his wagons, ready to start the following morning, King "came again and pulled out 2 $20 gold pieces and said, 'I will give you that for your place.'" Barney told him "to put $60 more to [it] and he could have my possessions. This he refused to do." Considering the circumstances, Barney had nothing to control the situation. He was faced with abandoning his assets. At that late hour he and his family had already joined the emigrant company which had moved three miles out onto the prairie where they would spend the night before departure the next morning. Still unsettled, that night his traveling companions heard his plight and advised him to return and take King's offer. Recrossing the river he found King and said he had concluded "to take the forty dollars he had offered for my place." King laughed at him "and said he would not give five cents for it," and turned away. Considering his situation, and desperate for some return on his property, Barney found King's brother-in-law while searching for King. Barney said to him, "I know what you and King is after. You intend, as soon as I am gone, to jump my place." Barney, with a stern look, then positioned himself to negotiate. "Now I will tell you the terms. If you will give me 50 dollars I will go off peaceably. If not, tonight I will burn every house, rail, and pole there is on the place and you may think yourself well off if I stop at that." His posturing worked. The brother-in-law ran to find King to explain the new situation. When King arrived, Barney said, "Now, Mr. King, if you hand me out 50 dollars, it will all be right. If not, there will not be a house, rail, or pole on the farm." Sensing Barney's determination, King said, "Mr. Barney, don't be in a passion. I have not got any more than forty dollars in money but I have a pair of boots and a coat I will let you have to make up the 50 dollars." "Finding that was the best I could do," Barney conceded, "I accepted it and returned to camp ready for a start for the mountains the next morning."[58] So ended the Barneys' tenure in the Midwest.

Though this was another displacement from home and property, the Barneys were off to Zion with hope in their hearts. The comfortable life for which Lewis Barney and his family had labored for so long, by cultivating and building, would be only a sad memory for the family. Never again would they reach the level of prosperity they had won in the Midwest. While the western frontier was a land born of hope and dreams, forever after rural prosperity was illusive to the Barneys.

After being relieved of his property, Barney rejoined his traveling companions, a number of them from Six Mile (Barney's) Grove. When "morning came, the company in readiness moved forward and made camp on the bottoms near the crossing of the Missouri River. Here we remained several days awaiting the rendezvous of the Saints."[59] Lewis and his wives were joined by his father's family for the 1852 emigrating season including brothers John and Benjamin and their families. The summary of Barneys and their assets emigrating from Iowa reads: Charles (three males, three females, one wagon, six oxen, and six cows); Lewis (five males, two females, two wagons, two oxen, four cows, two horses, and one young stock); John (two males, one female, one wagon, four cows); and Benjamin (three males, two females, one wagon, four oxen, two cows, four young stock).[60] Henry and Walter were already in Utah, but something happened to Luther Barney's and Elizabeth Barney Leland's families.

For unknown reasons, Luther, the first of the Barneys to embrace Mormonism, chose an alternative to gathering to Utah. Whether Luther found disagreement with his family or with his religion or just took another direction in life, Charles's oldest son would never be seen by his father or siblings again. Perhaps remembering reports of his younger brothers' venture in Arkansas in the late 1830s, Luther apparently took his family south to Benton County, in northwestern Arkansas, some time after the Mormon evacuation of the Missouri River Valley. Working away from home to sustain his family, Luther apparently died during the winter of 1859–1860 in Oklahoma.[61]

Elizabeth Barney Leland, known as Betsey, and her husband Benjamin also took another direction. Benjamin Leland, known to the Barneys at the time they became Mormons, married Charles's daughter Emerine in April 1841.[62] The following 22 February, Emerine died "near Carthage [Illinois] . . . strong in the faith of the new covenant" at the age of "14 years and 8 months."[63] Two years later on 13 April 1844 Leland married another of Charles's daughters, Elizabeth, known as Betsey, and together they embraced the outward expressions of Mormonism.[64] But at the time the rest of the family moved across Iowa to the Missouri River settlements, the Lelands moved back to central Illinois where Betsey had been born.[65] Later they moved to Shelby County, Iowa, to what became known as Leland's Grove, and

Benjamin became the townships' first justice of the peace. Having become "disgusted . . . with the evils that crept into the [Mormon] church," they later joined with the Reorganized Church of Jesus Christ of Latter Day Saints (RLDS), later led by Joseph Smith's son Joseph III.[66] In Leland's Grove, Betsey lived until June 1878 when she died "in full faith" in the RLDS Church.[67] The Lelands apparently never reconnected to the Barney clan.

The 1852 Trek to the Great Basin

The Mormon emigrants of 1852 were joined by the largest migration of West Coast–bound travelers in American history. The fifty thousand on their way to California and ten thousand with sights on Oregon more than doubled the first year travel of the gold rush.[68] Three weeks before the departure of the Barneys, Orson Hyde wrote to Brigham Young from Kanesville: "The Oregon and California emigration is beyond calculation. The like was never known before. The tens of thousands of heads of loose cattle, aside from the teams, that are swarming on the plains, are truly alarming when considered in connection with scarcity of grass above Laramie." Reports of little grass for the emigrants' animals even provoked Hyde to recommend that church leaders in Salt Lake City consider finding a more southerly route than the Oregon/California/Mormon Trail for cross-country travel because he feared "the trip may be disastrously ruinous to many for lack of grass." He warned, "The plains are literally covered and crowded with Emigrants and their wagons and stock."[69] The following day the *Frontier Guardian* reported, "Our streets are still thronged with emigrants bound westward, and from the news from all portions of the country below us, we are led to believe that the emigration will far exceed in numbers that of any former year."[70]

Many of the non-Mormon overlanders funneled through Kanesville before embarking on the Great Plains, as Kanesville was the last place to replenish emigration essentials before reaching Fort Laramie, seven hundred miles and weeks away. The *Frontier Guardian* reported at the end of May 1852, "There has been five or six thousand teams crossed the Missouri River, at different ferries near here, already this season, and there are many thousands more around this vicinity, aiming to cross."[71] Not only were the 1852 West Coast–bound emigrants the most ever, the abandonment of Mormon settlements on the Missouri River consequentially made the Latter-day Saints emigration of ten thousand the largest since 1847 by four times.[72] One-seventh of the entire pre-railroad migration to Utah occurred in 1852. The enormous numbers of travelers, Mormons and non-Mormons alike, made careful execution of procedures of transit a necessity.

The great journey westward, particularly for neophytes, was risk-filled. Mormon emigrants in 1852 were warned, based on the huge numbers projected to be emigrating that year, "that their suffering will be unparalleled in the annals of history of any previous year."[73] The lack of adequate animal feed was of grave concern, but the travelers did what they could. A woman in a Mormon emigrant group just ten days behind the Barneys' company wrote, "We crossed the Platt River 13 times[,] more times than would have been nesesary [*sic*] if it had not been for the Purpose of finding feed for our animals."[74] Two other foes of overland travel clouded the optimism of every emigrant train: Indian depredation and disease.

The emigrants did not have access to statistics which would have allayed their fears of Indian attacks some. Overall, only about 4 percent of emigrant deaths before the completion of the transcontinental railroad were attributed to assault by Indians. In 1852 only 45 of the 70,000 who crossed the Great Plains were killed by Indians, who themselves suffered about 70 deaths at the hands of emigrants.[75] A company which left the Missouri River just a week before the Barneys was attacked one day into their journey by Indians determined to relieve them of their cattle. While the Mormon company drove them off, the Indians "then swooped down on a camp of gold diggers on the creek, killed three of them and drove off some of their mules."[76] Disease and trail accidents were the real threats to emigrant survival. One report that year stated, "The Small Pox has already crossed the Missouri River, and is among the emigrant trains for the West."[77] And worse, about 2,000 emigrants in 1852 died from cholera. The Mormons, who were better organized than the California or Oregon overlanders and who traveled on the north side of the Platte River, suffered fewer deaths proportionally than their counterparts on the south side of the Platte. Twenty-two emigrant companies of Saints, to which were attached the unprecedented numbers of Mormon travelers, crossed the Missouri River during the 1852 travel season.[78] One Saint returning to the Missouri River from the Salt Lake Valley encountered the entire Mormon migration that year. It was astonishing. He reported "about fourteen hundred (1400) 'Mormon' teams and not less than ten thousand (10,000) Saints on their way to the Valley."[79]

Bryant Jolley's Emigrant Company, Seventh of the Season

The Barneys and their traveling companions were a fraction of this remarkable move to evacuate the Midwest. "Our camp was organized under Bryant Jolley as capt. of fifty families," Lewis Barney wrote. "I was also chosen as capt. of the first ten families."[80] Henry Bryant Manning Jolley, known as Bryant and H. B. M., was a former associate of the Barneys from their years in Pottawattamie County. Appointed company captain by church leaders in Kanesville, Jolley called his caravan of over three hundred emigrants to move out on 15 June 1852. The company was comprised of the Barneys and others from Six Mile (Barney's) Grove, members of the Macedonia (Illinois and Iowa) Branch, a Mormon congregation who opted to travel together, and others. There was nothing at the outset to suggest that this company's journey west would be unusual, but the usual included the predictable litany of difficulties afflicting a summer's overland journey.

Very little came easy for the travelers. The routine features of transit, to which even frontier folk were unaccustomed, were difficult to endure. Shortly after leaving the Missouri River they came to the Elkhorn where they "swam all the cattle across and rafted the wagons across on logs." On another occasion, "the cattle ran away with the wagons and tipped one over." The farther they traveled the common features of plains travel were encountered. For the women, their work expanded beyond culinary requirements. Caroline, Benjamin Barney's wife, said that "when we were crossing the plains I had to yoke up the cattle and take care of them."[81] While some no doubt considered the excursion an adventure, travel for families with small children was tough, at best.

Disease was a companion to most who embarked on the westward trails. Caroline Barney said that during their 1852 journey, "I had three small children and two of them had measles, which I had to care for." Fortunately, the children recovered, but not all in the company were so fortunate. George M. Brown, a young member of the Jolley company, remembered, "Sarah Forbush, wife to Rufus Forbush," was taken ill. The camp halted for a day for her benefit but she slipped quickly and died. "As soon as the corpse was stiff," Brown said, "we dug a grave and began preparing to inter it."[82] A certain callousness was required to carry on after family and friends expired in the difficult circumstances of overland travel. The sojourner had to move on, mourning in transit. One Oregon-bound traveler in 1852 recorded the locations of 401 new graves, surmising the number was only a fraction of the fresh digging. Another 1852 emigrant noted fifty-two final resting sites at one encampment.[83] Most of these deaths were caused by the number one killer on the trail, disease.

Jolley's company traveled, with him in the lead, and the rest followed in single file; "the train reached a considerable distance along the road," Brown remembered. Security being a concern, Brown continued, "Our mode of encamping both for noon and night was to form the wagons into two half circles, which formed a corral or circle with a gap at each end" guarded "by two armed men, who stood half the night, when they were released and others took their place and stood till morning." The guards were "placed on each side of the corral and they walked each half-way around so as to keep a look out over the entire camp and be able in case of attack from Indians to instantly give the alarm."[84] Not every feature of trail travel was couched in caution and concern. Caroline Barney remembered that "the folks danced every night. There were fiddles and the people would dance on the prairie grass barefooted."[85] Without such diversions, the human spirit would be stretched beyond elasticity. The seemingly incessant day-by-day routine rigors for neophyte travelers were hard enough as it was.

Crossing the nearly treeless plain in western Nebraska, the only fuel available for cooking was "Nebraska Wood"—buffalo chips—which was ubiquitous.

Once in buffalo country the large, hairy behemoths were critical in providing both meat and the means to prepare it for consumption. And in the early days of the overland migration, the buffalo on the plains were everywhere. Indeed, Elizabeth, Lewis's new wife, later told her granddaughter that one time "the buffalo were so thick . . . that it took four days to drive through one herd." Elizabeth was pregnant with her first child with Lewis. While the fuel was efficient, the noxious smell destroyed Elizabeth's appetite for food cooked over the buffalo droppings "until she got so hungry it began to taste good."[86] For Lewis's part, they traveled "quietly," "all feeling lively and cheerful" until they approached Fort Laramie in modern Wyoming.[87] What happened there entirely changed the rest of their journey.

A generalization regarding the Mormon emigration to Utah is that, because of organization and an inclination to submit to authority, the human difficulties which beset other overlanders had a lesser effect upon the Saints. The generalization is accurate, but the multiplicity of challenges in trail travel did not exempt the highly organized and efficient Mormons from difficulties, including personality clashes, after weeks on the dusty trail.[88] The conflict between Lewis Barney and Bryant Jolley illustrates an extreme expression which ambushed the tranquility of a number of overland companies.

Two months into the trek before arriving at Fort Laramie, Barney and "about one half" of the camp decided that Jolley exercised too much "authority over the camp." Despite his feelings, Barney stayed with Jolley's command while the others moved on.[89] Before long, though, Barney said, Jolley "seemed to center all his malice on me and discharged me as being capt. of the first ten." Barney's ten refused to follow Jolley, which just raised the level of Jolley's rancor.[90] A point of contention between the two may have been that Barney, five years older than the North Carolinian, was probably vocal about already having been to the valley. It may have been difficult for Jolley to lead when others had more experience. This situation probably only served to accelerate a confrontation between the two. "Finally one day there chanced to be a small herd of buffalo crossing the road ahead of us. He [Jolley] called the camp to a halt and sent three or four men to try and kill one of them. I told him there was no use of their going for they could not get near them."[91] Of course, few things frustrate a leader like someone on the sidelines gainsaying his instructions. But Barney, probably aware he was undermining Jolley, went about his own business while foiling Jolley's.

As the hunters chased after the buffalo, Barney attended to his own animals which he said were "nearly starved" and in need of feed. Barney's independence and apparent indifference to Jolley's lead provoked Jolley to scream, "Lewis, what are you doing? There you are, never in your place!" For Jolley, Barney's recalcitrance was the last straw. "Jolley then gathered a singletree from a wagon and came running toward me, yelling as he come, 'I'll mash you to the ground!'" Seeing the rage in Jolley's eyes and knowing "he was bent on hurting me,"

Barney quickly grabbed his rifle and boldly demanded: "Jolley, stop or I will blow your damned heart out of you!" Seeing the rifle and Barney's determination, Jolley stopped in his tracks. Sensing his advantage, Jolley yelled, "Run here everybody. Barney is going to shoot me." Of course, the camp came running to see the cause of the commotion. As the people gathered on the dusty trail, surrounding the two defiant belligerents, an impromptu counsel brought the conflict before the whole camp. When the "pow-wow" degenerated, "nigh ending in a general war," Barney stood on his wagon tongue and raising his voice said,

> Listen to me one minute. You all know all about the trouble between Jolley and myself and there is no use of multiplying words about it. It will make it no better. All I want to say is this, that I will not travel another inch with Jolley, if I have to go from here to Salt Lake alone. Now brethren, if any of you want to go with me you are welcome to do so and we will do the best we can.[92]

With that, Barney hitched his team, gathered his family, and started on. Eighteen wagons and their occupants followed him.

After dinner that afternoon, Jolley's company approached and stopped about a hundred yards away. Before long Jolley was in Barney's group "threatening to report every one of our camp to the authorities at Salt Lake." Barney retorted, "We will take care of our selves and all the favors we ask of you is to mind your own business and let ours alone." Jolley ignored the rejoinder and to the mutineers demanded, "I order you to get up your teams and start on!" There was a pause. When no one moved he turned around and walked back to his company, had them put leather to their animals and continued on. Late the next day Barney's division passed Jolley's train. No words were spoken between the two groups. Camping for the night Barney said that it wasn't long before Jolley passed, his group camping about half a mile away. After the families were settled "two or three of Jolley's men came to our camp and spent the evening with us. They said they would like to join our crowd but was afraid to disobey Jolley's orders." The next morning, those who sided with Barney waited for Jolley to move on, "traveling slow to let Jolley keep head." Managing to avoid contact for several days, when they got to the upper crossing of the Sweetwater River, the two camps eyed each other again. But with the passage of time cooling their ardor, nothing happened between the company leaders or the camps. That was their last contact before reaching the Salt Lake Valley.[93] From the accounts of all of the pilgrim companies who gathered to Zion, this certainly had to be one of the more unusual ones.

For the Barneys, a highlight of the trek greeted them on the Pacific side of the Continental Divide which they had just crossed. As Barney and his string of eighteen wagons, camped at Black's Fork of the Green River near Fort Bridger in what was later southwestern Wyoming, Lewis's wife Elizabeth, pregnant all year including nearly three months on the trail, had her baby. It was 3

September. The infant boy was named Arthur, Lewis and Elizabeth's first child together.[94] Their circumstances were replicated hundreds of times by other Mormon sojourners. Something as major as a pregnancy or having a nursing newborn generally did not alter schedules. For Elizabeth, there was not even a period of recuperation for the new mother. On they trudged. It is useful to be reminded at this point, as John Mack Faragher does, that "despite the overwhelming masculine prejudice of our backward glances at the American West, in the day-to-day experience of wagon travel the emigration was not a he-man but a family experience."[95]

Barney wrote that less than two weeks later "on the 12th of September we rolled into Salt Lake City which had by this time become quite a settlement."[96] Entering the valley, some "burst forth in an ecstasy of admiration." Viewing the bustling young city, "some shed tears, some shout, some dance and skip for joy" to be among "the industrious, the free, the intelligent, and the good."[97] Now, having endured a summer of trail dust and other more formidable obstacles, the three-month adventure and ordeal had placed the family once and for all in the West; they were now among the gathered.

Chapter 12

We Managed to Live: The Palmyra Plain, 1852–1856

Quite remarkably, on their way to Utah the Barneys had traversed one-third of the continent without the loss of or serious injury to any of their family. Now, after three months on the trail as they rolled into the valley from Emigration Canyon, the eastern gate to and from the Mormon settlements, they were within the perimeter of a religious sanctuary of which they had vividly dreamed for months, if not years. The sanctuary, with the innocuous title of the Territory of Utah, was established by the U.S. Congress in 1850 to provide a federal context to the growing population. Government distrust of Latter-day Saint motives had not abated despite their flight to the wilderness. The Saints were disappointed in the outcome of their first negotiation for statehood with its inherent provisions of self-government in contrast to federal domination under territorial status. But isolation from things American allowed them, for a time, their own hand in creating a religious empire which they dubbed Deseret. Named after the industrial symbol of honeybee found in the Saints' Book of Mormon, the designation of Deseret was part of the biblical Zion now renewed in America's western wilderness. Here, isolated by distance from those who rejected and rebuffed them for two decades, the Latter-day Saints could apply the framework and principles of their restored gospel of Jesus Christ without restraint. That framework they called Zion, the place where the people of God dwell in peace and righteousness.

Despite their zeal for Zion, some who endured the cross-country journey were disappointed in the barren contrast to the more lush and fertile river valleys of the Missouri and Mississippi and elsewhere. Indeed, the dry and arid West was a contrast to every place a Mormon previously called home. But the extended Barney family was prepared emotionally and spiritually for Mormon culture and physically for the land and climate of the Great Basin due to Lewis Barney's earlier transcontinental journey. They were grateful for their good fortune in transit to Utah, which the family considered providential. For years the Saints had been reminded by church leaders of their part in a story much larger than themselves. The Old Testament seer Isaiah issued the prophetic promise that "it shall come to pass in the last days, that the mountain of the Lord's house shall be established in the top of the mountains, and shall be exalted above the hills; and all nations shall flow unto it" (Isaiah 2:2). The

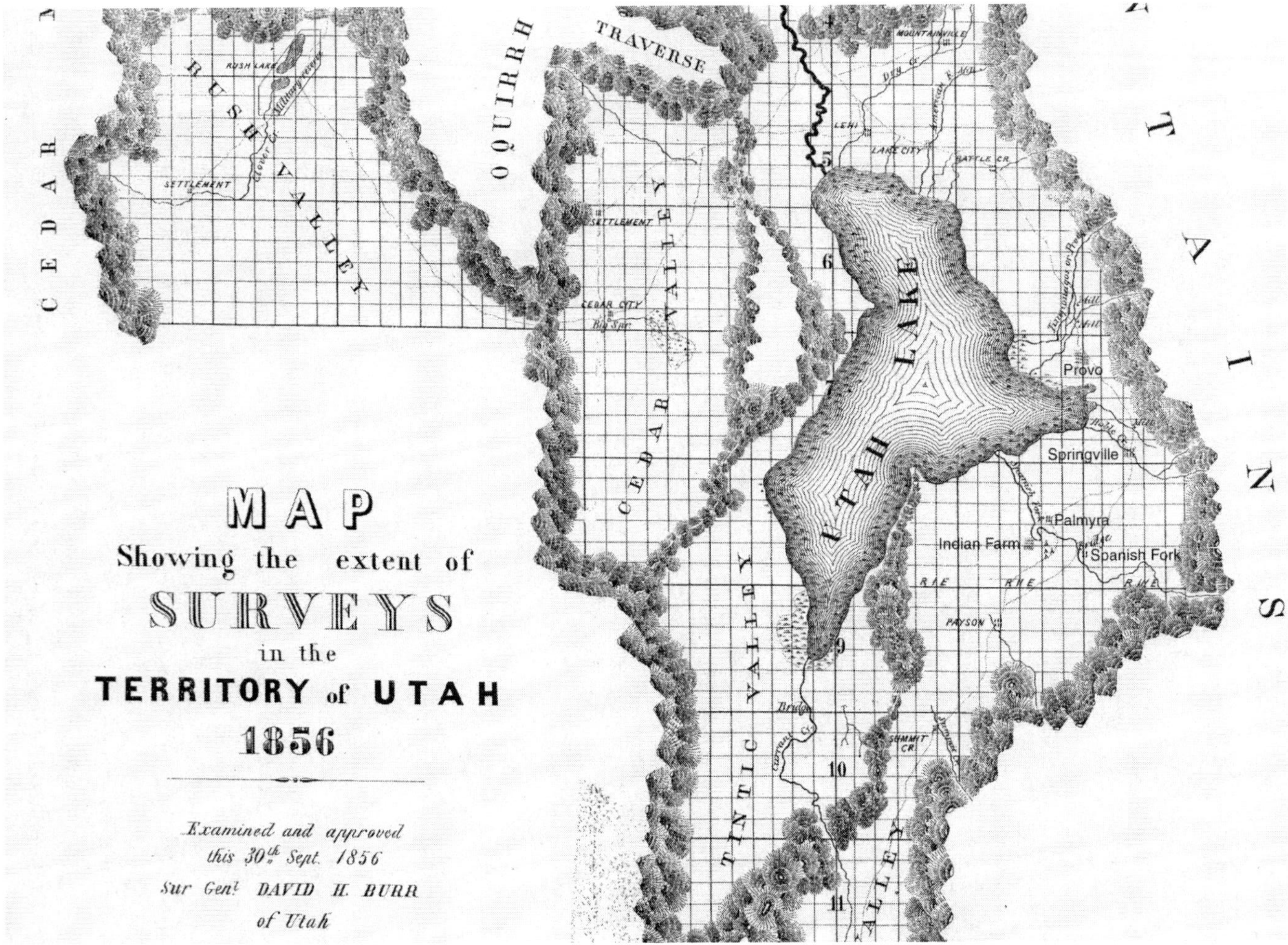

Utah Lake and neighboring valleys, 1856 (Philadelphia: P. S. Duval and Son).

Latter-day Saints viewed their presence in the Rocky Mountains as the divine fulfillment of Isaiah's apocalyptic vision. While the Barney family was mindful of the mercy extended them in transit, they were also perplexed by questions about their present and enduring survival. This required, at least for a time, their reconnection to the larger organism of the Mormon community.

The entry into Utah of Lewis Barney and his family, nuclear and extended, was the beginning of their involvement in a socio-geographical phenomenon called the Mormon village.[1] The assignment of the Barneys to a settlement after their arrival in Utah initiated them into a process later to include repeated ventures of exploration, settlement, and community development. The Saints had built communities before, but Kirtland, Independence, Far West, Nauvoo, and Winter Quarters/Kanesville were generally localized spots for gathering. Once the Saints were firmly rooted in Utah the gathering metamorphosed with an ever-expanding perimeter. Lewis Barney's family found themselves near the boundaries of this perimeter most of the next forty years.

Charles Peterson has argued that the formula of Mormon farm-village development in Utah, "the Kingdom in small," after eight years of refinement finally came together about 1855.[2] After the mid-1850s the components of physiography, topography, and hydrography in the establishment and perpetuation of villages were more systematic and predictable. While some attempts failed, the majority survived. Most villages had characteristics somewhat peculiar to Mormon settlements: "wide streets, irrigation ditches, large blocks divided into building lots which were in turn occupied by houses, flowers, trees, gardens, orchards, and barnyards." Indeed, "a town lot, twenty acres of outlying farm land, common grazing, a stake in the irrigation ditch, and timber from the hills were every resident's inheritance."[3] Diverging from some rural settlement patterns outside Utah where isolated farmsteads or spread-out line villages occupied the landscape, Mormon communities were established with a residential center surrounded by adjacent fields where the farmer spent his days, returning to his home within the settlement at night.[4] For the next generation the Barneys carried on within this structure.

Utah Valley

After their immediate needs were met upon arrival, the Barneys inquired about their "inheritance," a plot of land in Zion promised to Lewis from his part in the vanguard five years earlier. Whether Bryant Jolley made good on his threat to report Barney as a mutineer is not known, but Barney wrote that after their arrival,

> I then went to Brother [Heber C.] Kimball and enquired about my lot and farming land.[5] He informed [me] that it [had] been given to another party . . . [and] that my brother Walter was sent out south to

> help build a new settlement on the Provo River and [I] was advised to go there. So we continued our journey to Provo, arriving there on the eighteenth of September.[6]

In the thick of the sixth year of immigration to Utah, the Barneys arrived in Salt Lake City where nearly 1,200 families lived already. Another 350 homes were found in other parts of the valley. In contrast, Utah Valley to the south had roughly half the larger county's population. Where the Mormon capital had nineteen organized church congregations, each unit averaging sixty families, Provo had five congregations of Saints, averaging sixty-five households each.[7] That fall, a survey of Latter-day Saints in the territory indicated the Salt Lake Valley had more than twice the population (5,873) of Utah Valley (2,751) to the south, which more than doubled Davis County numbers (1,119) to the north. (The other six inhabited valleys stretching south to the Little Salt Lake Valley in Iron County totaled just over 2,000 Mormon settlers.) The focus of early settlement centered in the Wasatch Front valleys close to church headquarters.[8] While Utah Valley was one of the most densely inhabited, the population centers were clustered leaving much unsettled land in the valley. At first blush, Utah Valley looked to be a place where Lewis could establish his family.

Lewis, with his brothers and their father, Charles, found Walter in "a farming district lying north of the Provo city survey . . . extending eastward to the mountains and westward to the Provo River."[9] It had been six years since the battalion veteran had seen his father and brothers. Henry, who bid his father's family adieu three years earlier, was close by. Most of the clan settled near Walter. Benjamin's daughter-in-law later recounted that after Benjamin's arrival in Utah his family moved to "the old Fort in Provo where they lived for some time."[10] In Lewis's case, that fall of 1852, "I took up a lot [near Walter] and built a small doby [adobe] house on it and worked and got a few bushels of wheat and potatoes and some beef for my family."[11] The winter of 1852–1853 found Barney family members once again in proximity. This time they carried on with a looming mountain range forming the eastern boundary of Utah Valley, a reminder that in gathering to "the top of the mountains" they figured into a chosen people's divine destiny.

While Utah is mostly an arid, desert-like region, a narrow strip of land bisecting the state and stretching from the northern boundary to almost the center of Utah has environmental characteristics unlike the rest of the state. It is in this corridor that most of Utah's population resided. Designated a "humid continental-hot summer" climatic zone and comprising only 3 percent of Utah's land mass, the primary geologic factor is the Wasatch Mountains, running north to south, which stalls and cools moist western clouds and winds forcing moisture to the ground, thereby creating mountain valleys conducive to farming and habitation. The cold winters and hot summers are separated by distinct springs and autumns making for a favorable place to reside.[12] Utah County exhibited these characteristics.

The stately Wasatch Range forms the ponderous eastern and southern mountain perimeter to Utah Valley, which is bordered to the west by Utah Lake, backed by the Lake Mountains. In the nineteenth century it was a setting for poets. Because of its proximity to the Salt Lake Valley, the fertile former bottom of ancient Lake Bonneville quickly drew Mormon pioneers. Provo, located forty miles south of Salt Lake City, is 300 feet higher than the Mormon capital at about 4,500 feet above sea level. Located toward the southern extension of the favorable climatic zone, thirty families first settled Provo in March of 1849, establishing their crude domiciles on the Provo River.[13] The community was near Utah Lake, the region's largest freshwater body, and longtime habitation of the Timpanogos Ute tribe. The twenty-five-mile-long lake, fed by substantial streams (the Provo, Spanish Fork, and American Fork rivers and smaller creeks), served as a fertile and fruitful habitation of the Timpanogos Utes.

Catholic Franciscans Dominguez and Escalante in late September 1776 were the first white Europeans to visit the Ute homeland on Utah Lake's shore. Befriended by the Native Americans, the friars were taken by the valley's beauty and potential including "good farm land quality for all kinds of crops."[14] Preceding the Mormons to the valley by seven decades, their stay among the Indians, whom they described as "very simple, docile, gentle, and affectionate," was short lived.[15] Though they planned to return, they never did, but the importance of their visit is remembered by, among other features, the stream they followed into the valley—the Spanish Fork River. Thereafter only periodic visits from trappers and explorers constituted Caucasian contacts with the Utes. One of the Santa Fe trappers, Etienne Provost, is memorialized by the largest settlement of the valley.[16]

As the Mormon settlers entered Utah Valley in 1849, the Timpanogos Utes recognized the white presence as a grave threat to their residence and tradition. Mormon entreaties to the Indians pacified them temporarily, and though hostilities were initially averted, early in 1850 the Utes laid siege to the fort built by the settlers of Provo. White response was quick and severe.[17] Still other encounters through 1853 between Native Americans and new settlers, resulting in the loss of both Indian and settler lives, demonstrates the Indians' reluctance to relinquish their regional claims. But the resistance failed to dissuade Mormon objectives for the valley.[18] Indeed, by decade's end over two thousand Provo settlers portended what became the valley's most substantial community.[19] Indian rights were largely ignored. Further, unwittingly, the settlers' domestic animals carried microbes, from which they had formed an immunity, that adversely affected the native wild game, reducing a traditional source of Ute sustenance. Thus, the settlers' livestock became a means of Indian survival in the valley, which only forecasted future conflict.[20] This, coupled with continuing white encroachment upon land which the Utes seasonally occupied, remained a significant problem for decades.

The Mormons, before their arrival in Utah, regarded the Indians more benignly than did their American counterparts. Called Lamanites in the Book of Mormon, the Indians were therein promised a future ultimately elevating their primitive status. Indeed, the Saints were to be the catalyst to raise the benighted Indians.[21] But this positive view of Native American destiny did not preclude Mormon immigrants from intruding into the valleys traditionally possessed by the Indians.[22] Manifest Destiny's spirit, driving Americans westward in the previous decade, naturally motivated Mormon designs on Deseret's habitable valleys. Moreover, the divine imprimatur on Utah's mountain valleys for Mormon settlement in fulfillment of Isaiah's prophecy presented a paradox for the Saints. Efforts to establish "Indian farms" in Utah, designed to assist and educate the natives in domestic horticultural skills, had but temporary effect. Rather they played into the incongruity of Mormon ideology and practice concerning Native American lands.[23]

With Lewis Barney's family settled in Provo, if only temporarily, providing for them became preeminent in Barney's mind.[24] "The country being new and no lumber or mills to make it, I together with [three other men] went into Peteetneet [Payson] Canyon and put up a sawmill," where he worked through the winter and spring of 1852–1853.[25] The mill was probably "an upright saw, run by water," and was one of several in the vicinity.[26] This new venture as a sawyer proved to be one of Barney's primary occupations for much of the next quarter century. It was a labor-intensive operation subject to seasonal extremes. There in the wide-mouthed canyon which served as the southern boundary of Utah Valley, he wrote, "I worked in the snow and storm all winter getting out timber for the mill. The snow being about 3 feet deep, I suffered very much with cold and for the common comforts of life."[27] By July 1853 the mill was in operation and he and his partners were producing commercial lumber for valley residents.

Palmyra, Utah Territory, 1853–1856

The settlement of Utah towns was concomitant with the establishment of Mormon ecclesiastical congregations, the larger units called wards and the smaller ones called branches. The Barneys, upon their arrival in Utah Valley, found themselves part of the Mormon ward's superstructure, an organism designed to satisfy human needs both sacred and secular.[28] By the end of 1852 over three hundred families were located in the five Provo wards and it was obvious that more settlers were destined for the growing settlement. Sometime in the late winter or early spring of 1853 Lewis decided to move his family to a new settlement about ten miles south of Provo. In the summer of 1852 a town site was surveyed and a house built by the first settlers near the Spanish Fork River, a watercourse flowing eastward from the canyon of the same name in the valley's southwestern quarter. As other settlers gravitated to the area Mormon apostle George A. Smith on 5 August 1852 officially designated the site Palmyra, in memory of the boyhood home of his cousin, Joseph Smith.[29] A sister settlement called Spanish Fork was at the same time growing to the east. (Palmyra was located about a mile and a half westnorthwest from the center of present-day Spanish Fork City.) The apostle was optimistic about Palmyra's future, lying just east of Utah Lake.[30]

Some of those with whom the Barneys traveled to Utah the previous year found themselves part of the Palmyra community, including Bryant Jolley. By October 1852 as many as seventy-five families claimed Palmyra as their home.[31] At year's end George A. Smith wrote to a correspondent in England, "I have sought out the location for the City of Palmyra, on the Spanish Fork River in Utah County, and procured a survey of 360 lots containing one hundred rods each, a Temple Square of thirteen acres, and four school squares of two and one-half acres each. . . . A good adobe school house thirty-five feet by twenty two feet inside has been erected."[32] The report indicated a progressive settlement. The reality was a rudimentary enterprise with a scattered populace, some surviving in dugouts along the bluff above the river with log and adobe homes speckled about the area. Considering that a year earlier the area was an untouched grassy plain, the new residents and their leaders had cause to rejoice. Zion was spreading.

The larger Barney clan did not find satisfaction in Provo. After about six months northeast of Provo, Charles, Lewis, John, Benjamin, and their families, after hearing favorable reports of the new settlement of Palmyra relocated yet another time. Three-quarters of a century earlier Dominguez and Escalante described the Palmyra area as a "plain" with "spreading meadows" and pasture lands.[33] To a farmer's eyes it was pregnant with potential. Besides the favorable area reports, that Palmyra was closer to Peteetneet Canyon, where the Barneys continued milling lumber, likely played into their decision.

Writing contemporarily about one's intimate family associations is difficult. Lewis Barney's neglect in describing family relationships and domestic arrangements is the most disappointing and frustrating feature of his personal writings. However, soon after settling in Palmyra, we get a glimpse of how he and his family viewed their familial ties in light of Mormon theology. Traveling from Palmyra to Salt Lake City on 12 March 1853, Barney and his wives, by appointment, paid a visit to Brigham Young.[34] The rite of eternal marriage, with its attendant socio-familial implications, with no temple available was executed in the president's office. There Barney was "sealed" to his wife of twenty years, Elizabeth Turner Barney, by Heber C. Kimball, witnessed by the church president and his clerk.[35] This sacred ceremony, according to Mormon theology, coupled Lewis and Betsey in an eternal bond for mortality and beyond the grave. Elizabeth Beard Barney was also made part of an eternal union. Mormon doctrine stipulated that a woman could be sealed to but one man, while a man, in light of the doctrine of plural marriage, could be mortally and eternally attached to one or more women. Between the three—Lewis, Betsey, and Elizabeth—it was determined that Elizabeth would be vicariously united to her first husband, Alva Tippetts. After the Old Testament pattern requiring a deceased man's brother to wed the widow to raise their subsequent children to the memory of the deceased man, Lewis and Elizabeth's arrangement tied their children to Tippetts's eternal posterity.[36] Other Latter-day Saints in comparable circumstances were similarly connected. While particulars of the Barneys' domestic arrangement thereafter are absent, their relationships were sufficiently visible that the family was one of seven remembered as composing plural households in early Palmyra.[37]

Establishing an economic base for the maintenance and preservation of their families most occupied the attention of Palmyra's residents. Agriculture and horticulture was in Palmyra, as it was in all rural communities in Utah, the primary occupation. While farmlands required no clearing of timber, the cyclical agrarian life in Utah was one of demanding physical labor. Crops and animals needed regular attention, but the early Palmyra settlers also had other things in mind. The importance of the village's expanded economy was discussed early in March 1853, when in a church priesthood meeting a "manufacturing and agricultural committee" considered other means to enhance the community.[38] The multidimensional committee also nominated "the city officers which were to be elected on the 4th of April next." Discussions regarding community use of a "big field," a land tract east of town where citizens could augment their home horticultural production, were held. All who needed land within the field were to give their names and quantity of land they wanted to community leaders for equitable distribution.[39]

In these deliberations, nothing was decided without consideration of the religious protocols expected within the community. The hub of community life was the Church of Jesus Christ, manifest through the local ward. In this instance, Palmyra was no different than any of the nearly seven dozen other Mormon communities established before 1853.[40] By definition a community is a cooperative arrangement of individuals with common objectives, and Mormon culture, emphasizing unity and collaboration, fostered ventures that accelerated community development. Consequently, there was a melding of the religious and secular functions in most LDS settlements. Matters such as the education of youngsters, for example, had both religious and secular overtones.[41] There was, at the time, no alternative, and at the outset, it worked. One early Palmyran wrote, "We were all common people, all socially equal, all striving for the same end, and that was to get all the pleasure out of our condition there was in it."[42]

The geographical layout of the community into "upper" (Spanish Fork) and "lower" (Palmyra) settlements soon after its organization seemed a logical consequence of the topographic features near the Spanish Fork River flood plain. The Catholic fathers in 1776, appraising the area watered by the Spanish Fork, proved prophetic when they wrote that there was "sufficient irrigable land for two good settlements."[43] The single "community" of two settlements was inevitably affected by geography, one of several irritants agitating Palmyra and Spanish Fork in the formative years of the 1850s.

Growth of the two entities and squabbles over land usage, such as utilization of the "big field," required adjustment. George A. Smith returned to the twin communities on 22 March 1853 and divided the single ward serving the settlements into two congregations configured by their "upper" and "lower" designations.[44] It was a good move. With a new start for the Palmyra folks, many within the Palmyra congregation were rebaptized as a renewal of their religious commitment. Most of the Barneys living in Palmyra were rebaptized on 27 May 1853. Other family members submitted on 29 May 1853. While Lewis waited until 9 June 1853, the collective submission of the Barneys at this time to the ritual indicates, again, their acceptance of Mormonism.[45]

Palmyra was not a monolithic enterprise of religious singularity. Despite or because of the dominating influence of the Church of Jesus Christ, some Palmyrans did not uniformly subscribe to Mormon ideology. Some of the Saints, after their difficult transit to and settlement in Utah, found the Mormon mountain kingdom something other than what they anticipated. While the majority adhered to Mormon theology and goals, private and public rebellion concerning belief and conformity served as periodic obstacles to community cohesiveness. For example, Bushrod Wilson, a Mormon veteran of nearly twenty years, who had been a missionary, a policeman in Nauvoo, president of a seventies quorum, and an immigrant to Utah and Spanish Fork the previous fall, after being pressured to move his home to Palmyra and having his horses confiscated by the militia "with no redress," finally had enough. "I have Been mobbed by the Gentiles for being a mormon and at last I have been mobbed By the Mormons Because I was not willing to do all that thay told me to do. So," he lamented, "I left for California" in December 1853.[46] Also within two weeks of Smith's reorganization of the community, Palmyrans had to deal with a rift by some over disbelief in several tenets of the Mormon faith.[47] Difficulties in the settlement were such that a month after George A. Smith's visit to Palmyra, Brigham Young, Heber C. Kimball, and several of the Twelve Apostles visited the community, in part because of reports of friction within the town.[48]

Perhaps caught up in the dissonance afflicting the village, one of the Barney family left the family orbit. One of Charles and Deborah's daughters, Margaret Matilda, born in 1834, went off on her own. While she had been rebaptized in 1853, indicating some allegiance to Mormonism, the following year she made two significant alterations in her life. She married Joseph D. Gilbert and later that year the two of them departed Utah for California in a train of thirty-two wagons led by a U.S. military command.[49] The Gilberts settled in San Bernardino,

California, location of a substantial Mormon colony prior to 1857.[50] Never enthused about the growing settlement in California, Brigham Young called for its evacuation coincident to the U.S. Army's march to Utah in 1857–1858. However, for a variety of reasons, about one-third of the Mormon settlers ignored the beckon to Utah.[51] The Gilberts, who had likely disaffiliated from the church by that time, were among those who chose to stay in San Bernardino.

The Barneys in the Walker War

A feature of Brigham Young's concern for the community was the proximity of the settlement to the valley's Indians and rumors of the latter's discontent. During his visit Young, along with giving counsel about unity and conformity, recommended "the people to build a fort for protection against the Indians." Sensing uneasiness among the local natives, while there he sent two from Palmyra to warn the southern settlements about a possible Indian uprising. Palmyra residents pledged their support for a fort, but upon the return of the emissaries from southern Utah on 15 May 1853, the settlers were found working in their fields as usual. Their recalcitrance to heed Young's warning would later exact a sharp toll on the community.[52]

Utah Territory's part of the American domain is accompanied by a list of peculiarities marking the territory's history as unique from all other United States entities. One unusual feature is the relationship between the white settlers and Native Americans in the nineteenth century. In other instances during America's westward movement, the U.S. government quickly employed means to extinguish Indian rights to lands desired by whites. In Utah's case, because of antipathy between the federal government and the Church of Jesus Christ, the government made no effort—by hook, crook, or treaty—to obtain title to tribal territory. Instead, Utah's pioneering generation was left to handle the matter internally. The problem took two decades and a number of white and Indian lives for resolution, of course, in favor of the whites.[53]

Simultaneously as Barney moved his family to Palmyra, he continued working at the Peteetneet Canyon sawmill. About the time the mill was ready for production the early summer of 1853, James R. Ivie, a Utah Valley resident in Springville, confronted a Ute resulting in the Indian's death on 17 July. The local Utes, initially susceptible to appeasement for the "trifle sum of $50.00," were instead outraged by the killing and retaliated the next day. Alexander Keel, a few miles south of Springville near Payson, was the victim.[54] The settlers in Utah Valley's fledgling communities were frightened by the anticipated retaliation despite the recent organization of local militias.[55] They had no idea the events of 17–18 July 1853 would define a war's beginning.

The Indian leader taking the offensive was the notable Ute chief after whom the war was named, Wakara or Walker. After three years of tenuous peace since the 1850 Fort Utah confrontation, Ivie's regrettable act brought to a head the mounting hostility felt by Native Americans toward their subtle conquerors. Ironically, Wakara and other Ute leaders had accepted Mormon baptism in 1850 before the larger designs of the Mormon kingdom were clear.[56] Little by little, the most favorable sites in the valleys just south of Great Salt Lake City had been claimed by the continuing flow of Mormon immigrants into Utah, numbering about eighteen thousand in 1852–1853 alone. Unrest was in the air. To the Indians, it appeared that the only recourse to stem the infestation of white intruders was violence.

The killing of Keel occurred near Peteetneet Canyon's mouth, the broad gorge in which Barney, his family, and business associates worked on their sawmill. One of Wakara's chief lieutenants was his brother Arapeen, whose band coincidentally camped near the canyon that July. The night previous to Keel's death, Arapeen, baptized in 1850, had attended a Mormon worship service and had partaken "of the sacrament" with his white brethren.[57] The dead Indian was one of his tribesmen. Wakara and Arapeen, their outrage shown by heated forays against the whites, intended at the outset to conduct their initiatives in Sanpete Valley, far flung enough from other Mormon communities to increase their chance of success.[58] Wakara ordered Arapeen's band to break camp and temporarily regroup in Peteetneet Canyon before heading south into Sanpete. They were undoubtedly aware of the milling activity of the settlers in the broad canyon and knew the sawyers had cattle with them. Consequent to Keel's death, Barney said, the Indians "come up Peteetneet Canyon and camped a mile-and-a-half below our sawmill."[59] There on 19 July the Indians took step number two of Wakara's revenge.

With Barney at his mill were several immediate family members, including his brothers Walter and Jeff and his son Walter T.

> I was up very early in the morning and had just started the mill to sawing. My [sixteen year-old] son Walter was out with me on the mill to work. As soon as it was light enough to see, two Indians came galloping up the canyon and rode up to the mill and motioned to us to come down. Accordingly we went down to see what they wanted. They said, "You kill one Utah and we kill you," pointing to me and my son Walter.

The sawyers were terrified as they broke for cover. The Indians, primarily interested in relieving the settlers of their livestock, were momentarily distracted while trying to free a mule chained to a nearby post, allowing the Barneys to escape what appeared to be their certain fate. "I ran into the cabin," Lewis said, "and roused up the men and told [them] to get up for the Indians was mad and was upon us." As the men scrambled through the brush the Utes went after them. With the cracks of gunfire echoing through the trees in the canyon and "bullets . . . whistling around us tearing up the ground and cutting the brush at a rapid rate in every direction" the Barneys scattered. Warning neighboring camps as they ran, they scurried out of harm's way, searching for any position to hide. Not knowing of the Indian's killing which ignited the raid, the Barneys were wholly unprepared, "without firearms or anything to defend ourselves with." That none of them were killed in the raid was remarkable.[60]

With other family members in hiding, Lewis and his brother Walter ran for help at Pondtown (now Salem), near the mouth of the canyon. Crossing over into adjacent Loafer Canyon, Lewis and Walter made it into Pondtown where they found the townsfolk "in a state of great excitement, expecting every minute to see the Indians coming to take their lives. They also supposed that the whole camp in the canyon was massacred," but no more lives were lost. The extent of physical injury to the Barneys was limited to Walter limping into the settlement with sore feet.[61] It was surprising that the potential slaughter had been averted, but the war was just beginning.

Wakara's trouble with the Mormons continued for most of the next year. In May 1854, after ten more settlers were killed and an unknown number of Utes, Brigham Young and Wakara made peace.[62] Once the "prince of the mountains," with a formidable reputation that circulated throughout the West, Wakara was now weakened and ill. His violent response had only a temporary effect. While Indian futures diminished, the continuing influx of Mormon settlers portended the inevitable white occupation of Utah's best human habitat. Though the Barneys escaped death in Peteetneet Canyon, the attack's residual effect impacted their lives for some time. "We were forced to abandon the mill," Barney lamented, "our only source for supplies for our families. I was then under the necessity of working by day's work for my provisions and clothing to support my family."[63] Not only was Barney forced to return to his farm, obviously providing only a subsistence existence, many of the settlers in both Palmyra and Spanish Fork had to alter their manner of living as well.

With hostile Indians in proximity, those in the upper settlement were compelled to move to Palmyra, some relocating into the hastily finished fort. Others abandoned their homes altogether and moved into Salt Lake City where there was little threat of Indian violence.[64] Every able-bodied Palmyran male was enlisted in the local militia. Lewis was in July 1853 mustered into the "Regiment of Minute Men" ranks, a division of the revived Nauvoo Legion. His teenage sons Walter T. and Henry joined in 1854 and 1855, respectively. Circumstances required that the community acquire a military hue.[65]

After the initial flurry of hostilities, Indian activity remained lively near the mouth of Spanish Fork Canyon, leaving Palmyra residents on the valley's opposite side somewhat removed from the threat of impending attack. Their energies were applied to returning to some semblance of normalcy. The tensions with the Indians, however, took an adverse toll on the village's populace. In the fall of 1853 Palmyra counted 404 residents including 112 children under the age of eight. By the following spring Palmyra residents had decreased by 65, despite 12 births, a decrease of 16 percent.[66]

As the fiery climate abated after the May 1854 treaty ended the "Walker War," a handful of families who spent the winter in Palmyra's fort moved to the mouth of Spanish Fork Canyon where they built another fort nicknamed Fort St. Luke.[67] By the end of 1854 sixteen houses were under construction in the fort. Because of the strategic location of the fort, in light of Indian movement, George A. Smith, not particularly pleased the Palmyra settlement had been diluted, suggested the new residents build a fifteen-foot-high wall surrounding the fort.[68] While the fort ended up only a temporary locale for living, its construction signaled a return to the upper-settlement thinking of a number of Palmyrans. Others, like Lewis Barney, were content to work what they had in the lower settlement. The spring of 1854, Barney wrote, "I put in 5 acres of wheat and 6 acres of corn and a patch of potatoes and other garden stuff from which I gathered 162 1/2 bushels of wheat, 150 bushels of corn, and potatoes enough to supply the wants of my family." But he recognized he could not prosper on such fare. Despite a lingering fear of Indian mischief, "through necessity we were obliged to venture into the [Peteetneet] Canyon for lumber at the risk of our lives and through the winter we run the mill, got logs, and made considerable lumber."[69]

Grasshopper Plague

The following spring Lewis Barney initiated again the routine of seasonal planting, tending, and harvest to keep his family viable. But the Palmyrans and most other Utah residents encountered an enemy which depleted their resources, if possible, even more effectively than did the Indians. "The next spring [1855] I put in 18 acres of wheat and several acres of corn," Barney wrote. "But the grasshoppers took it as fast as it made its appearance through the ground. This they continued to do until the ground was entirely destitute of every green thing." There were no seagulls to repeat the miracle of 1848 to save the harvest. Once the grasshoppers had their way, devastating the settlements over a period of several weeks, they departed. After all their effort the plague "had cleaned the settlements of every vestige of vegetation."[70] Despite the infestation and its devastation, people had to eat. Sometimes extreme circumstances produce extreme results.

In Barney's case he carefully nurtured "a few spears of corn" left by the marauders with the hope of some return. His care netted him seventy-five bushels of corn. From a neighbor he borrowed two bushels of wheat (with the promise of returning four in the fall) and planted his town property in wheat. Despite the late season planting, his effort produced 105 bushels of wheat. Many of his neighbors were not as fortunate, and having been the recipient of others' kindness, he in turn became a benefactor and distributed his harvest.

> This would have been all the grain I needed if I could have kept it. But as the country was destitute of breadstuff I could not keep my grain and see my neighbors go hungry. I accordingly rationed myself and family and put them on ⅔ rations and gave out my provisions to those that needed. I continued to do so until my supply was all gone. This was 2 weeks before the next harvest.[71]

His carefully nurtured barley crop also aggrandized his neighbors that year.[72]

Agricultural cycles, insect infestation, weather reverses, etc., which have minimal impact upon the modern observer, were the ebb and flow of life for these Utah agrarians. Adversity fostered cooperation which expanded individual humanity. One of the settlers, for example, was struck by the compassion exhibited by Palmyra bishop Stephen Markham whom he said "deserves special mention for his fatherly care over the people, in supplying them with seed grain. He took all the money he could raise of his own, and all he could borrow and bought seed for us, and loaned it to us till after harvest."[73] Seeing their neighbors in need, altruistic outreach characterized many within the settlement. The dependency upon each other provided the catalyst for community progress and cohesiveness that times of plenty did not provide. Much good came from their poverty and destitution.

The spring of 1855 was a time of new beginnings for Spanish Fork. Whereas the "upper" settlement had been abandoned during the conflict with the Utes in 1853–1854, settlers' interest in the fort near the mouth of Spanish Fork Canyon renewed Spanish Fork as a viable community site. While life in Palmyra carried on, Spanish Fork was surveyed and chartered as a city in January 1855. Those at Fort St. Luke moved out and located homesites in the nine surveyed blocks. Even though Palmyra had a better location than Spanish Fork during Indian difficulties, the ground around the former tended to be lower and wetter for farming causing some in Palmyra to consider the higher Spanish Fork location more suitable for both living and farming. The communities shared the fields that lay between them.[74] Before long all the Spanish Fork lots were taken up, requiring an extension of the survey in 1856. Barney was one of those who "took up a lot and a piece of farming land in Spanish Fork and moved onto it." He also kept one foot in Palmyra maintaining his previous property.[75]

A look at community demographics after the split is worth noting. A Palmyra Ward report, including Spanish Fork, for September 1855 shows 371 in the Palmyra Ward. Children under eight numbered 122.[76] Primarily from the same ethnic background, three-fourths of the ward were American born. Almost 10 percent were native Utahns. One-fifth of the community were from Great Britain, most from England. Three percent were Canadians. By age, one-third of the community were thirty-five to fifty-five years of age. Another one-fifth were between twenty-five and thirty-five. Only ten people, 2 percent of the townspeople, were born in the eighteenth century. The population of the community was seasoned with mature adults and with children sufficient to warrant an optimistic future.

Church records indicate that 1855, despite the grasshopper setback, was a good year for Lewis Barney. Besides the sawmill, which produced 4,600 board feet of lumber that year, Lewis farmed sixteen acres of land with four oxen and a few other domestic stock. His younger brothers, except Walter who still benefitted from his days in the gold fields, did not do as well. Overall, Lewis's assets were two-thirds more than the average of the other sixty-seven Palmyra households, where 94 percent were farmers. But Palmyrans, like the others in Utah settlements, did not always control their own destiny.

While the Mormon influx into Utah predictably insured expanded settlement, the Ute Indians were not content with the pattern. White encroachment was all that could be seen from the Native American point of view. By 1856 more than a dozen new Mormon communities appeared after the close of previous hostilities in May 1854. Two years of relative peaceful coexistence were broken when several Indians raided Mormon horse and cattle herds in Utah and Cedar Valleys resulting in the deaths of two white herders west of Utah Lake on 21 February 1856. A posse tracked the renegades resulting in the death of an Indian man and woman and a member of the posse. The little fray, subsequently called the "Tintic War," provoked Utah territorial governor Brigham Young on 23 February 1856 to order the Nauvoo Legion to restore order to the region.

The same day President Young, considering Palmyra in harm's way, also wrote to Palmyra bishop Stephen Markham to say the church's First Presidency had determined it "would be best for you to remove to the bluffs [where Spanish Fork was located] and use your present city flat [Palmyra] for farming purposes."[77] With that move John Lowe Butler, a Kentuckian of Lewis's age, was called to lead the newly conjoined settlement as bishop. Meeting with Young, Butler was reminded "that the people of Palmyra was to leave their places and come and build in Spanish Fork." One can imagine that after three or four years of improvements to their farmsteads, a portion of Palmyra's populace would be unhappy with the direction. "There were some," Butler reported, "that always had a bitter feeling against the folks at the Upper settlement and they did not like the idea of having to move up and live with them." Because it was Brigham Young's counsel though, "they were willing to obey."[78] The result: "Palmyra was entirely vacated in the spring of 1856, and the site was included in the Spanish Fork field."[79] The Lewis Barney family was no exception. "I, together with the rest of the residents of Palmyra," Barney wrote, "broke up [and] left our houses and improvements in Palmyra and moved into Spanish Fork City."[80] While it was not the end of Barney's involvement in Palmyra, his family for the time became residents of Spanish Fork.

That spring the Barneys lost another child. Lewis and Elizabeth's second child, Margaret Mariah, born in March 1854, had just passed her second birthday when she died in April 1856. She was the third of Lewis's children not to survive childhood. Without question her death enervated her parents. Betsey had already witnessed the deaths of two of her children before arriving in Utah and would see one more child die before adulthood. Elizabeth would suffer the passing of three more of her own over the next twenty years. Only half of her children would live to become adults.[81] The most debilitating of life's vicissitudes visited the Barneys with regularity in Utah.

Butler's appointment as bishop of Spanish Fork in the spring of 1856 marked the amalgamation of two communities. While there was overt compliance to consolidate Palmyra into Spanish Fork, some still groused about the arrangement. Brigham Young, contrary to his reputation for unyielding inflexibility and strong-handed demagoguery with which he has been unfairly tagged, after hearing of community concerns, wrote to Butler at the end of May 1856 to say, "Owing to your dissensions and divisions you are suffering in common in your feeling loss of confidence in each other, also loss of property in labor, crops, etc. . . . I have no objection to the brethren who desire to do so, to live in the *old* Palmyra Fort if they can do so and *not* endanger the destruction of their crops by their livestock." But above all, Young pled for the people to "be united and work together."[82] While every matter of dissonance could not be resolved, the tenuous circumstances were handled without significant casualty.

Chapter 13

He Would Not Forsake His People: Spanish Fork and the Utah War, 1856–1858

The newly minted settlement of Spanish Fork enjoyed significant growth in 1856 after a year's stagnation in the former twin communities. This village, at 4,565 feet in elevation and built upon three alluvial fans from the course of the Spanish Fork River as ancient Lake Bonneville receded, witnessed its population bounding to 439, a jump of nearly 20 percent from the previous year.[1] Its attraction was noted widely. "Spanish Fork is the most favorably situated settlement in Utah County for the purposes of agriculture and stock-raising," wrote one nineteenth-century historian. Covering a tract of nearly forty thousand acres, it had the "advantage of being located immediately south of and contiguous to the Utah Lake, occupying the broadest part of the valley not covered by water."[2]

While the populace of Spanish Fork increased, the people still struggled for the most basic physical human needs. Benjamin Barney's daughter-in-law recounted that after her in-laws' relocation from Palmyra to Spanish Fork in 1856, "times were very hard and food very scarce. While the men and boys would work tilling the soil, digging ditches, fencing and guarding against the Indians, the women would dig roots and other greens to go with the fish and bran diet."[3] Though the circumstance modified in the next decade, Spanish Fork at this time, despite being within a few miles of the growing city of Provo, still exhibited characteristics consistent with frontier life where subsistence living was the primary occupation.

Adequate housing was also a struggle. Living arrangements were not taken for granted. Many, some who were veterans of the first settlement of Palmyra and Spanish Fork, still lived in dugouts along the bluff above the river, including Stephen Markham, among the town's most visible leaders.[4] While the Barneys' mill in Peteetneet Canyon was a source for building material, Lewis Barney chose to construct an adobe home for his family. This was the second and last adobe home Barney built in the West. Thereafter, his homes were built of local materials found in adjacent canyons—logs. It has been said that you can tell a lot about a man by the home in which he resides. Indeed, "those who construct their own shelter replicate themselves, at their deepest and most significant level, in their houses," one biographer has written. "They are what they build."[5] Barney's choice of dwelling in log homes contributes to our overall view of this man of the frontier. Descriptive terms such as simple, rudimentary, modest, without polish, even primitive could be applied to his manner of living and the style to which his family became accustomed. Log homes were usually composed of:

> A floor of rough boards, curtains at a solitary window, and a huge fireplace flanked by high-backed wooden settees which more than likely took up one end entirely; into its built-in side oven went the once-a-week baking. Pots swung on their hooks from a crane over the hearth. Candles, made by dipping cotton strings in hot, melted tallow, stood on the mantel. A spinning wheel, a dash churn, a hand loom, a big board table scrubbed clean every day, a corner cupboard holding all the family dishes, a box of wool in one corner and a box of linsey-woolsey from the loom in another—these were the furnishings, relieved perhaps by a string of dried apples or peaches hung along the wall.[6]

At the same time when frame and rock homes were being constructed in Utah's more urban areas, Barney was content to live in a dwelling typifying his frontier life.

Spanish Fork Indian Farm

Given the continuing Indian-white tensions, it became apparent to territorial leaders and settlers alike that something had to be done about the area's Indian presence. In an effort to both help the Native Americans and to protect the tentative peace, the federal Indian agent, Garland Hurt, a thirty-year-old Virginian, commissioned the construction of three farms for the Indians. Mormons collaborated on the concept. From the whites, the Indians were to learn horticultural and domestic skills. "Self-sufficiency for the Indians, not assimilation, was the basis of his philosophy."[7] One of the three, the Spanish Fork Indian Farm, was established in the spring of 1856 with the assistance of local settlers employed to build a large farmhouse, two corrals, a dam, an irrigation canal, and later a Spanish wall fence to encircle the tract.[8] Bounded on the north by the Spanish Fork River and on the west by West Mountain and Utah Lake, the farm was located about two miles west of Spanish Fork and just south of Palmyra. Originally composed of 640 acres, the reservation eventually expanded to 12,380 acres.[9] At the outset relations with the surrounding settlers were amiable. The farm served as an asset for locals; some supplied materials, others helped build the reserve, and others found the Indian farm a place of commerce, including Priscilla Evans who, at the end of 1856 "walked down to the Indian farm, and exchanged a gold pen for four yards of Calico" from which she made dresses.[10]

The proximity of the Indians, despite pledges of peace from both the natives and the whites, warranted attention by the settlers for defense and security. The local militia, trained to handle any Indian threat, was part of the fabric of community life.

> When the Militia was organized in Spanish Fork, the R[elief] S[ociety] made their tents for them by hand. On training days they looked like an army. . . . In Spanish Fork when the visitors would come they would pitch their tents south of town across the river and camp. They would train and have sham battles and all kinds of interesting skirmishes. There would be hundreds of people there to view them.[11]

Despite the locals' overall goodwill toward the Native Americans, something that did not escape Garland Hurt,[12] suspicions remained high between the two sides and their close proximity did not allay the anxiety of either. Barney described a confrontation about this time illustrating the difficulties resulting from coexisting on land once the exclusive domain of the Northern Utes. With the Indians of Utah Valley "continually annoying the settlers by stealing and killing stock and by begging, the brethren gave them the privilege of gleaning grain in the fields in harvest." But for hungry Indians, this was not enough. Some, he claimed, "took advantage and would steal grain from the shocks. As grain was scarce and very high [in price] and the only means we had to pay for our clothing and every thing else that was used, some of the brethren refused to let the squaws glean on their land." One day a settler found several squaws in the field outside the settlement having already "gleaned and thrashed about [a] half bushel" before they were discovered. The Mormon confronted them, "took their wheat, and scattered it over the ground and ordered the squaws off" the land. They, of course, ran to their camp complaining of the mistreatment. Barney "happened to be in the field" when Grosepeen, one of the Ute subchiefs, came rushing toward him with fight in his eyes.[13]

Grosepeen was a brother to both Arapeen and the late Wakara and thus an important figure among the Northern Utes. "I knew something was wrong with him" by his hasty approach, Barney said. Having "a little [understanding] of the Indian's tongue," he understood Grosepeen when he demanded, "this is our land and this is our water, our grass, our valleys, and this is our wheat. I will have this field and this wheat." Despite being known as having a less demanding and aggressive disposition than his warrior brothers, Grosepeen yelled, "Mormon whip my squaw. Mormons want to do like Mericats [Americans]: whip, kill, and take Utah [Ute] land, Utah water, and Utah grass. You rob our squaws and throw away their wheat. Me kill you!" To underscore his threat, Barney said, "he cocked his rifle." As the chief stepped back to level the gun, Barney "sprung forward and caught his rifle by the

Benjamin Franklin Barney (Lewis Barney's brother). Photographer and date unknown. Courtesy of Mattie Barney Cornaby.

breech and had as good [a] hold of the rifle as the Indian." They jerked one another around for several minutes. Neither could get the upper hand until Grosepeen "got out of wind and found I had the best of the scuffle. He gave up [and] stood a minute eyeing me. Finally he said, 'let us be ticaboo [friends],' and began to laugh." With the heat turned down, Barney was relieved when "we then agreed to be friends," though each continued his grip on the gun. In the aftermath, Barney "told him to send the squaws into the fields and glean all they wanted to and they should not be molested." As the momentary tension eased, he said, "I then let go [of] the rifle and he went off to his wickiup satisfied and sent the squaws to the field again to glean." Reporting "what I had done to the Bishop," Barney said he "requested him to use his influence with the brethren to let the squaws [more liberally] have the privilege of gleaning in the fields."[14]

Another incident showing Lewis and the Barneys' compassion for the Indians is related by Benjamin Barney's wife Caroline.

> Lewis Barney gave me a little Indian baby girl; he seen the Indians killed some of their children because the white settlers wouldn't give them cattle or other things they wanted. And they were going to kill it, so . . . Lewis gave them a yearling steer for her, and then his wife would not have her, so he said he would give her to me if I would take her.

"I had many mouths to feed but I took her anyway," Caroline continued, "and raised her as I would one of my own."[15] Such were the encounters between the settlers and those they nudged off the land.

But no matter how many kindly gestures were made between the two camps, anxiety always colored the atmosphere. Benjamin Barney, who like Lewis lived near the Indian farm, wrote that "many a night we have taken our family and went to the [Utah] lake and got in boats and went way out on the water and spent the night where we would be safe from the Indians."[16] Until the 1870s, underlying all associations, there was an incessant suspicion of Indian farm residents by the local settlers.

The settlers maintained a military posture for good reason. Despite professions of support for coexistence, within two years of the establishment of the Indian farm, Utah Valley settlers began to dispute tribal land claims to the farm. Of course, the Indians were angered and the Indian agent became increasingly hostile to the Mormon settlers around Spanish Fork and to what he viewed as Mormon initiatives. Relations between the locals and government appointees, which apparently started positively, increasingly fragmented. In the early 1860s the federal agents complained to their Washington superiors about settlers' ambitions for Indian lands in Utah Valley. The federal government during the Lincoln administration seemingly resolved the Indian-settler problem by establishing a reservation in 1861 in the Uinta Basin to permanently displace the Indians from traditional Utah Valley lands. For once the Saints concurred with federal designs. But from the Indian angle, frustration over the government objectives regarding the Spanish Fork Indian Farm eventually played into the uprising of the Ute tribe later in the decade in what came to be called the Black Hawk War.[17]

The Mormon Reformation

At the time the Saints first entered the Salt Lake Valley in July 1847, Brigham Young told the weary pioneers, "If the people of the United States will let us alone for ten years, we will ask no odds of them."[18] Left unmolested and isolated for ten years, the Mormon leader believed the Saints would employ the divinely revealed principles given through Joseph Smith and himself which, previous to their Utah isolation, had limited application due to the oppressive conditions in previous locales. Yet nine years into their seclusion, the church First Presidency expressed disappointment with the Saints' lack of spiritual progress. In September 1856 President Young spoke to church members in Salt Lake City declaring, "We need a reformation in the midst of this people; we need a thorough reform, for I know that very many are in a dozy condition with regard to their religion. . . . You are losing the spirit of the Gospel."[19] Thus was initiated the period of 1856–1857 known among the Saints as "the Reformation."

Historically, one of the primary features of the Mormon gospel had been a call for personal righteousness among the Saints. A reformation of sorts was instigated in Nauvoo with this in mind in 1842.[20] Historian Richard Bennett has recently argued that the Mormon exodus to the Great Basin in 1847 was a conscious exercise in reformation.[21] Anticipating the Second Coming of Jesus, the objective was a repentant and holy people. Ten years after the initial exodus from the United States, the purpose remained the same. Notwithstanding charges that Brigham Young's focus was empire building, the evidence is preponderant that his primary objective was nurturing the acquisition of Christian virtues by church members.[22]

The spirit of reformation in Utah pervaded every aspect of Mormon living. Effort was applied at both the general and local levels to ensure that the lethargy and recalcitrance perceived by church leaders were eradicated. One technique introduced was the call of a select body of men in each local branch and ward to serve as "home missionaries." These agents of change were charged by church leaders to echo the call to holiness and renewal among the Saints by means of home visits, indoctrination, and the rhetoric of reform. The design was, in Barney's words, to "cultivate the feeling of love and friendship one with another and deal honestly and uprightly with all men as the law of gospel requires and also the laws of the land."[23] Overall, the benign objective was successful. But in the zeal to reform, there were occasional excesses among the locals.[24] Barney complained that, despite instruction to the contrary:

> Many of these elders transcended their bounds, and in place of cultivating a feeling of love one for another, they cast a gloom over the Saints and it become necessary to send more experienced elders to reverse the preaching of the first elders. Under these circumstances I was chosen by Bishop Butler as a home missionary to preach peace and quiet the feelings of the Saints.[25]

Those chosen for this assignment were selected with care; they "were generally the most capable and devoted . . . men in the kingdom."[26] Barney took his role seriously. Strategically organized into four districts, he and the other

Spanish Fork Ward home missionaries successfully nurtured the spirit of reform within the community. Upwards of four hundred were soon rebaptized in Spanish Fork demonstrating their commitment to renewal.[27] After serving as a home missionary for about a year, Barney characterized his service as meeting "the satisfaction of the Bishop and the Saints in the vicinity where I labored."[28] Coincident to the Reformation was the enactment of another feature to refine church members which required the most serious reflection.

Consecration

Soon after the Church of Jesus Christ, the original name of the Mormon Church, was organized, an economic component of discipleship was invoked upon believers. The law of consecration revealed to Joseph Smith was established among the Saints. Hearkening to the Old Testament prophet Malachi's charge to the faithful not to neglect their "tithes and offerings" (Malachi 4:8–12), church leaders since Independence, Missouri, days regularly echoed the principle to provide an operating budget for the church.[29] A revival of the concept was instituted in Utah in the mid-1850s. In Spanish Fork, as throughout Utah Territory, the faithful tallied their properties and other goods and "consecrated" the sum to the church. One of the chief goals of consecration was to foster a spirit of altruism in church members with the objective of eliminating poverty among the Saints. Thus, the concern for public improvements and community development became secondary; the spiritual component of unity through giving became primary.[30] "How," the First Presidency asked, "can [the Saints] become united in spiritual matters, and see eye to eye, which they can only partly understand, until they become united in regard to temporal things, which they do comprehend?"[31] The willingness of church members to jettison the natural inclination toward societal stratification for the sake of unity was the ideal.

The revival of consecration was invoked by church leaders in the church general conference in Salt Lake City in April 1854. Generally carried out at the local level, the first deeds of consecration were recorded in Millard County in January 1855.[32] The Spanish Fork Saints consecrated their assets mostly in 1856 and 1857. While the expectation seemed extreme to outsiders, most Saints in Utah County conformed, including the Lewis Barney family.[33] Barney's family had already been regular contributors to the Palmyra and Spanish Fork Wards' tithing accounts.[34] On 27 February 1857 Lewis Barney consecrated to Brigham Young, as church trustee in trust, property and goods valued at $742 which included his adobe house in Spanish Fork, about three acres in Palmyra and Spanish Fork, two yoke of oxen and a wagon, four cows, a gun, and household goods, among other things.[35] The church never took possession of the consecrations, but the Saints' willingness to offer their all to the building of the Kingdom of God had benefits measured only in private spiritual advancement and satisfaction.[36]

Amid the fervor of reform and consecration and the formidable distraction of potential Native American uprising, the daily routine of providing sustenance for the families of the settlers demanded their incessant attention. The routine was fraught with complication. The episode with grasshoppers the previous year, barely out of mind, was revisited upon the territory in 1856. The fall harvest in Spanish Fork was again sparse. Discouragement after a second year of insect infestation was pervasive. Yet in the difficult time of scarcity, many who otherwise would have been involved in the annual harvest for their families were able to spend substantial time on public works embellishing the community.[37] Again, a paucity of abundance proved to benefit the settlement. The full expression of human compassion and empathy was felt among Spanish Fork's citizens. Yet, often it is only in the tragic, the dramatic, the notable, even the bizarre, that we investigate the human spirit and heart. The day-to-day, commonplace intercourse between humans, mostly benign and kindly, is overlooked because it is so regular, so common.

With Spanish Fork expanding, due in part to the first of many Scandinavian converts settling there in 1856, community government served as a means of drawing together two former friends turned foes. The reader will remember the confrontation Barney had with H. B. M. Jolley, the company captain in transit to Utah in 1852. In the second municipal election in Spanish Fork held 4 May 1857, Barney and Jolley were two of the nine city councilors elected.[38] Three months previous Jolley, as a witness, signed the document of transmission of Barney's consecration just discussed. The old hostility that almost brought the two to bloodshed was apparently supplanted by the neighborly relations characterizing their association the previous decade in Six Mile (Barney's) Grove, Iowa.[39] Good things were happening in Spanish Fork. But as the community expanded and the rest of the territory matured, events in the eastern United States, which would unalterably effect the Mormons, were being hatched behind closed government doors in Washington. The isolation and detachment from America, enjoyed for a decade by the Saints, was soon to expire.

The Utah Expedition and the Mormon War

It was not by accident that Latter-day Saints settled over a thousand miles from the western fringe of American civilization. Disgusted in their previous experience with how both state and federal laws were administered denying them rights and property, a system of self-government based upon U.S. constitutional principles was their intent. Utah, being Mexican territory when the Saints arrived, looked to be a promising place for such a religious society. After the U.S. government acquired "upper California," which included Utah, in the aftermath of the Mexican War, their hope for self-government was available only through statehood. After appealing for sovereignty as one of the states, the Saints were disappointed when Utah became part of the mix in the Compromise of 1850 which designated New Mexico and Utah as U.S. territories at the same time that California became a state. Territorial status provided that Utah be governed from the District of Columbia and not Great Salt Lake City; territorial government officials were appointed at the pleasure of the U.S. president. Fortunately for the Saints, a successful lobby facilitated appointment of Brigham Young as governor over the vast territory which was still two thousand miles from the eastern seat of government. For most of the remaining government posts a handful of non-Mormons were appointed.

The "gentile" appointees (gentile being the Mormon designation for non-Mormons) came to Utah with reform on their minds. Mormon practice and doctrine were a self-evident affront to American culture and the new officials intended to administer the Saints into conformity, but Utah's citizens were noncooperative and contumacious. Their vivid memories of Missouri and Illinois were not easily forgotten. Consequently, an open hostility to anything federal characterized jeremiads from Latter-day Saint pulpits. To the ears of government officials Mormon sermons could be interpreted in only one way: treason and rebellion. By the mid-1850s government legates had witnessed several years of resistance to government intentions by the Saints. During their brief tenures, several of the appointees, persisting in their efforts to create an unmistakable federal presence in Utah, managed to insult and provoke the territory's residents. Not surprisingly, the Saints reacted with contempt. Outraged at Mormon defiance, feeling impotent and their lives in peril, one by one the officials fled Utah. Their reports to Washington of the situation in Utah were everything but favorable toward the Saints. The Mormons were in rebellion. Brigham Young, their leader, was seditious and a traitor.[40]

Responding to negative reports of territorial officials and countering Republican momentum which coupled Mormon polygamy with southern slavery, Democratic president James Buchanan took action. At the very time when the fabric of American polity was unraveling between the North and South, the newly inaugurated president sent a significant component of the U.S. military force to squash the "rebellion in Utah" by installing a new governor and establishing a military district in the territory. In May 1857, the old army hero, General Winfield Scott, ordered 2,500 U.S. troops to prepare for departure for the West. Two months later, the Tenth Infantry, the advance of the larger government force, marched out of Fort Leavenworth, Kansas. They were followed shortly by the Fifth Infantry and two batteries of artillery. The last army unit to head west, the 2nd Dragoons, departed Leavenworth for Utah on 16 September. With the strength of the U.S. military on its way to corral the Saints, Mormon isolation was at an end.

In President Buchanan's State of the Union address to the 35th Congress in December 1857 he declared that "all the officers of the United States [in Utah], judicial and executive, with the single exception of two Indian agents, have found it necessary for their own personal safety, to withdraw from the Territory, and there no longer remains any government in Utah but the despotism of Brigham Young." Therefore, he continued, "I was bound to restore the supremacy of the Constitution and laws within its limits." Considering "the religious opinions of the Mormons . . . deplorable in themselves and revolting to the moral and religious sentiments of all Christendom," the "path of duty" demanded that he appoint "a new Governor and other federal officers for Utah." They were to be escorted by "a military force for their protection, and to aid as a *posse comitatus*, in case of need, in the execution of the laws" of the federal government.[41] If the Mormons would not respond to federal ideology, a substantial army would get their attention.

As the Saints gathered for their tenth anniversary in the mountains, 24 July 1857, word was officially delivered of the movement of U.S. government troops, though rumors of government designs had circulated for weeks. Brigham Young reacted with a bravado born of contempt for the standing government and confidence that the children of Israel could not be driven into the wilderness again. The church mobilized in a remarkable fashion which included the evacuation of outlying Mormon communities on the perimeter of the Great Basin to consolidate resources near headquarters. Local authorities throughout northern Utah were warned of the intrusion and assigned to ascertain points of vulnerability in the otherwise formidable barrier of the Wasatch Mountains. Militia units in the communities, the reconstituted Nauvoo Legion, were alerted and called to duty to resist with force, if necessary, any effort by government troops to enter the Great Basin.

The action of the government and the reaction of the Mormons portended a bloodbath in the mountain canyons. The contest between Buchanan and Young pitted the right of the federal government to suppress a territory in rebellion versus U.S. citizens claiming to have been violated by a prostitute government. The "incompatible personalities [Young's and Buchanan's], even more than incompatible policies," brought the two sides to the brink of field battle.[42] Propaganda, both accurate and skewed, forced the postures of the government and the Saints, creating overreaction on both sides due to the lack of timely communication.[43] Had efficient communication lines been available the differences bringing the belligerents to war may have been averted. That was not the situation in the summer and fall of 1857.

A major military reorganization of the Utah militia by the territorial legislature had been effected on 14 January 1857, weeks before the Utah expedition was even contemplated. One of the purposes of the reorganization was to increase participation by Utah's rank and file citizens. A section of the "Act for the further organization of the Militia of the Territory of Utah" provided that "All able-bodied white male persons, between the ages of eighteen and forty-five years, residents of the Territory, are liable to military duty," similar to that enacted in Nauvoo, Illinois, seventeen years earlier. The result of the act was an increase in representation in the militia from Utah's communities. Many of the county military organizations were reconfigured. The single district in Utah County was expanded to three: the north (Lehi), the Provo, and the south (Peteetneet) districts. Spanish Fork was in the southern district which was composed of a brigade commander, Brigadier General Aaron Johnson; a regiment commander, Colonel John S. Fullmer; and seven battalion commanders, including Major Albert K. Thurber who with Major John L. Butler, the local bishop, represented Spanish Fork. One of the companies from Spanish Fork, captained by Svend Larsen, had a unique twist: it was composed almost entirely with recently immigrated Scandinavian personnel.[44] With a hostile armed force marching against them, a variety of maneuvers were required by the militia to protect the Utah settlements and settlers from the government troops. By 1 August the Utah militia, including many citizens of Spanish Fork City, had developed strategies for resistance, which did not preclude combat.[45]

The federal military expedition thundered on. Rather than being a seasoned collection of troops, they were, as a military leader described them, composed primarily of "raw recruits."[46] However, they were led by military veteran Albert Sidney Johnston, a fifty-four-year-old Kentucky native. Johnston's anti-Mormon posture did not preclude any means in subduing and humbling the Saints.[47] Still, it was the hope on the part of the government that this sizeable military presence would give the Mormon "rebels" reason to reconsider their errant ways without bloodshed. But the Mormons knew nothing of the soldiers' inexperience or of any government intentions other than to finish what was started in Missouri and Illinois. To them, the government had one intention and it struck fear and resolve in the hearts of every settler.

Captain Stewart Van Vliet, advance U.S. Army representative, entered the Salt Lake Valley on 8 September 1857 far in advance of his comrades to arrange for winter quarters and gauge Mormon intentions and strength. He met with Brigham Young and other officials before returning to the westbound army on 14 September.[48] Amiable as Van Vliet's meeting was with Young, he left having witnessed Young's resolve manifest the following day by Young's declaration of martial law in Utah Territory. The call to action aroused the loyalties of the Mormon faithful, particularly those who had previously given up homes and suffered otherwise in the Midwest. Barney's initial participation in Mormonism's defense came about the same time. Though military obligation was required only of those between eighteen and forty-five, forty-eight-year-old Lewis Barney enlisted his service. "I, together with my Mormon associates threw our lives into his [Brigham Young's] hands and the God that had delivered us out of every trouble," he wrote. "We was certain he would not forsake his people at this time."[49]

A requisite to prepare for the oncoming army was the reconnaissance of canyons and valleys east of the Wasatch Front to ascertain vulnerable avenues of access by the intruders. Barney "was chosen as one of these men to go into the mountains to explore the mountains east of Spanish Fork City and also south." Assigned on 18 August to a detail under the command of forty-six-year-old Captain James Pace, a Tennessean now of Payson, "we set out on our mountain expedition," he reported. They climbed "up Peteetneet Canyon, passed over the divide, and the second night camped on Sanpitch above where the settlement of North Bend [present day Fairview] is now situated. The next day we passed over the mountain and camped on the head waters of Spanish Fork [near present-day Soldier Summit]."[50] After scouring the drainage of the Spanish Fork River in inclement mountain weather, they followed Indian trails and broke northeast toward the towering Uinta Mountains. They soon found themselves at the Duchesne River where they stopped for a few days, the "men scattering out in different directions" searching for possible routes of entrance into the Great Basin. Barney and a companion "went up the mountain, got on the divide, and followed it until we supposed we was opposite the head of the Provo River. Being satisfied that there was no pass through the mountains anywhere in that section of the country, we returned to camp the following day." The reconnaissance had taken about two weeks and they returned to Spanish Fork confident that the army could not surprise the Saints via the Spanish Fork River area.[51] Barney's participation was not all that was asked of him in the defense of the territory and his people.

Coincident to Governor Young's declaration of martial law in Utah, two months after the first detachment of army regulars marched west, more troops were dispatched from Fort Leavenworth to Utah under the direction of Colonel Philip St. George Cooke, who once commanded Mormon troops in the Mormon Battalion. Despite the orders originally directed to the army's commander on 29 June 1857 which read, "In no case will you, your officers or men, attack any body of citizens, whatever, except upon such requisition or summons, or in sheer self-defense," conflict between the army and the Utah militia appeared inevitable. As the army caravan stretched for hundreds of miles across Kansas, Nebraska, and Wyoming, the window of opportunity to muscle their way into the Great Basin diminished. Winter was fast closing in. Thirteen hundred Mormons under the overall command of Lieutenant General Daniel H. Wells had been dispatched to reinforce those already in Echo Canyon in northeastern Utah, the most logical route of entry of the army into the Great Basin. Their strategy included building defensive bastions from which they could assault the intruders should they dare to march on Salt Lake City. Fortunately for both sides, the winter of 1857 hit the high

Wyoming plains early with a fury forcing the troops to establish winter quarters about the middle of November on Black's Fork near Fort Bridger at what became Camp Scott. By the time the U.S. troops were preparing for hibernation, they numbered 1,807—far below the requisitioned number of 2,500. (The 1,807 made up only 11 percent of the national force totaling 15,764.)[52] Mormon numbers in Echo Canyon alone almost matched the government strength. Barney was one of the 1,300 called to reinforce the several hundred already in the canyon whose purpose it was to turn Echo Canyon into a gauntlet of war for the soldiers. In all, about eighty men from Spanish Fork City served, probably about two-thirds of the adult male population of the community.[53]

Men of Spanish Fork were not the only ones involved in defense. It became a community project. The women of the Relief Society "made quilts and all kinds of clothing." Priscilla Evans reported in February 1858 that "Luretia Gay worked 10 days carding and spinning wool for shirts. She furnished half lb. of wool. Worked four days carding & spinning 'hair' for lariets, for the brethren she worked one day, and donated cloth for one pr. of garments $2.40. She also helped to make a pr. of pants and she made one pr. of mittens." Others made their contributions: "Armelia Berry worked six days knitting and donated one wool shirt $5.00. Ruth Davis worked one and one-half days carding hair, one day quilting, one and half day making garments. She also donated one wool blanket $7.50." The men who could not participate due to disability "sent their clothes."[54] The locals were confident their preparation was not in vain.

The Saints felt assured that if provoked to action they would dictate the course of victory. At the height of the war rhetoric, one Spanish Fork resident wrote with verbal swagger to his friends in the east that the troops

> have come here for the purpose of using up the mormons, but they are disappointed. they found we was to much for them and could use them up and it would not be but a breakfast spell. they said our mode of warfare was not a fair way of fighting but when we fight, we fight to whip. . . . we care not how many comes; the more the better. we have all the advantage of them in the mountains and canyons. they are as good a shield as we want. there is places they have to pass through that ten men can whip five hundred by rolling rocks off the mountains on to them and secrete themselves at the same time that their cannons and bumshells can not have any effect on us. this you may think is a big story, but it is so. we are not afraid of all that can come.[55]

Notwithstanding the heroic optimism of the volunteers, willing to give their all in defense of their homes and religion, they were woefully ill-prepared to contend with the well-equipped U.S. infantry. A third of the local militia was without arms, complemented by the rest whose armaments were primitive to the side of the army. Mormon tactics against the troops, once calculated to include hand-to-hand combat, were modified. Now bloodless measures meant to irritate and thwart every design of the army became the strategy. The first contact by the Mormon militia with the advance column of government troops occurred on 26 August at Pacific Springs, near South Pass in Wyoming. A month later the Mormons initiated their tactics of mischief against the army by stampeding federal cattle near South Pass on 24 September. Lot Smith's famous raid on the government trains at what is now Simpson Hollow was executed on 5 October. Still, the army had ample resources to subdue and humble the Saints.[56]

The orders called for extreme defensive efforts to hinder the army from even approaching Salt Lake City. The battlements planned for Echo Canyon were constructed with the intent to pester and torment rather than to entrap or massacre. By mid-October about seven hundred minutemen from Utah and Tooele Counties camped on the public square in Salt Lake City ready to march at a moment's notice. Lewis Barney may have been one of the seven hundred. One regiment of Utah County militia was called up to leave for "East or Echo canon" on the fifteenth. Barney, perhaps a part of this unit, stated,

> Our orders from our commanding officers was to harass the Army, keep them awake, and not let them sleep night nor day, stampede their stock, burn every patch of grass that would burn, but not fire a gun, only in self-defense. Under these trying circumstances I volunteered my services in the defense of our homes, our wives and children, and our religion and marched to Echo Canyon.[57]

Barney's rush to defend his people and his faith can only be described as a strain on his family. War is always inconvenient. Betsey and Elizabeth were both in the thick of mothering. Betsey's youngest was five and did not require a mother's incessant watchfulness. But Elizabeth, just a year away from the death of her daughter Margaret Mariah, was nursing little Martha Ann, born 24 January 1857, and she was three months pregnant with her second son, the namesake of his father, Lewis, Jr., to be born the next spring on 21 April 1858.[58] In the mix of the energy and clamor of war mothers bore and raised children, and their men left for the battle.

Upon his arrival in the canyon Barney reported that he was "stationed as a guard." There, he said,

> We built a heavy breast work across the canyon [and] also built a dam across the creek leaving a narrow space in which we placed a gate. In case the army made its approach the gate could be shut down and stop the water and thereby form a lake in the narrow pass.

> We also went on top of the cliff of rock that overhung the road, perhaps a thousand feet above, and piled up cords of rocks that could be hurled on the trains if they attempted to pass. Our express [mail] bringing tidings every few days kept us posted in relation to the moves of the army.[59]

In their ventures of roguery against the federals, fortifying the mountain passages into the Great Basin, Barney said, "We enjoyed ourselves in songs, dances, and other amusing recreations. The companies that was sent to harass the army and stampede stock would bring by our camp every few days small herds of cattle, horses, and mules. By this means we weakened the camp of our enemies so they could not move their supply trains."[60]

The tedium of surveillance without action in the canyon, enshrouded by an early winter of severe storms which hit the middle of October, became discouraging to many of the militia. By this time perhaps as many as 2,500 of the Saints were posted throughout the lengthy canyon.[61] The bitter weather was compounded by inadequate winter clothing for the Utah forces. For some, after weeks in the canyon, their defensive work reduced their apparel to rags; some were barefoot. A severe shortage of food also afflicted those on watch.[62] But their objective subordinated their ordeal.

Still they yearned for respite from their vigilance. By 26 November 1857 Mormon leaders received word that the U.S. troops were digging in for the winter in Wyoming. Three days later Brigham Young suggested to Daniel H. Wells that "the boys return home."[63] Within the week, one of Barney's comrades wrote, "The Lord has accepted our offering, has confused & stopped our enemies & we have not had to kill them or even fire against them but we have showed them that we would stand for our rights, & would not submit to such unlawful & unjust demands as they were determined to force upon us."[64] As the government expedition was establishing winter quarters near Fort Bridger, most of the militia dispersed. "I arrived at my home in Spanish Fork City in good health and spirits after a hard tour of 72 days in snow, mud, and storm," Barney wrote, "guarding my family my friends and our rights and our religion from our persecutors."[65]

Barney's return to his family, probably the early part of December 1857, found them "all well, but destitute of the comforts of life," particularly clothing. "I was under the necessity of selling one of my cows," he said, "for which I got a blanket and enough cloth to make a woman a dress and a few other little articles, cows at the time being worth $50 a head." His compatriots shared his need but "there was nothing in the country to be had in the shape of clothing."[66] Oddly, in the absence of most of the community's men for the winter, food was not scarce. Apostle George A. Smith reported on 6 January 1858 that "Bishop Butler of Spanish fork just comes in and says the Threshers report 25,000 bushels of wheat threshed in Spanish fork settlement."[67]

Conversely opposite the common ratio between food and clothing in times of want, the presence of abundant food and the optimism of a coming spring stemmed discouragement considering that just over the mountains the federal army was, as soon as weather permitted, perhaps preparing for an assault upon the Mormons.

But as spring replaced the forbidding winter, the potential bloodbath was mitigated by men of good will determined to detour any course of conflict. The intervention of Thomas L. Kane, a moderate peace commission, the appointment of a reasonable replacement for Brigham Young as Utah governor, and a winter that cooled the ardor of both sides combined to douse the smouldering embers of conflict. The arrangement allowed the U.S. Army to establish a federal presence far enough away from Salt Lake City to satisfy the Saints' concerns about being imposed upon by the federal government. Still wary of government intentions, most living in Salt Lake packed up in May 1858 and moved south. The city was evacuated. It is estimated that thirty thousand people—twenty thousand from the city and another ten thousand from areas outside the city—fled southward, most to Utah County, to wait until federal designs became apparent. (A guard was left behind to torch all improvements should the army attempt to occupy the city.)

The Provo population soared from four thousand to as many as fifteen thousand Saints in the "move south." The other Utah Valley settlements swelled significantly as well. The Centerville Ward from Davis County temporarily settled on the Spanish Fork Indian Farm. Most of the West Jordan Ward from Salt Lake County located on Utah Lake's shore between the Spanish Fork River and Peteetneet Creek.[68] The population of Spanish Fork in 1858 temporarily exploded; four hundred families moved to Spanish Fork, most being housed with village residents.[69]

The army broke camp at Camp Scott in Wyoming on 14 June and marched through the abandoned canyons into Salt Lake City where they passed unmolested on 26 June 1858. Mormon colonel Robert T. Burton reported six hundred wagons, six thousand head of cattle, and three thousand troops passed through the city.[70] Despite the "move south," sanguinity among the Saints was high. On the day the troops entered the valley, a Spanish Fork woman wrote to her brother in the east, "the troops of the united States, could have been all used up, and not a man left to tell the tale in 3 hours had not the Mormons Extended the arm of mercy."[71] Clearly the peace commission mollified what could have been a violent confrontation. With Salt Lake Valley residents returning home two months after "the move south," relations between the government troops and the Mormons remained strained, particularly through the next year.

The events of the years 1856–1858 have had an inordinate impact on the Church of Jesus Christ and on what became the state of Utah. The Mormons' image cast before the rest of the country during this extraordinary period was, by most measures, negative, though the Buchanan administration was severely criticized for the expedition's folly.[72] The sour impression of Mormonism formed during this period was one which not only endured but escalated during the remainder of the nineteenth century. Perhaps no increment of Utah's history has had the impact upon the Utah or Mormon image as has this three-year episode. From this period came the local excesses of the Mormon Reformation from which emerged tales of clandestine Danite murders at the whim of Brigham Young and his associates. Also coincident to this came the slaughter of innocents by locals at Mountain Meadows, the evidence against the Mormons of which was demonstrable. From this period came the plethora of dangling, poisonous tentacles waving in the aftermath of the "Utah expedition" which produced the actions of the carpetbagger-style reconstruction of Utah Territory for the rest of the century. And for the short term, while "the Mormon community won some media sympathy, . . . the war's costs were more extensive and enduring than any gain."[73] The impact was enormous.

Lewis Barney. Photographer unknown, ca. 1850s. Courtesy Church Archives, the Church of Jesus Christ of Latter-day Saints.

Chapter 14

We Left Them Crying: Spanish Fork and Springville, 1858–1861

Sometime in the 1850s, likely during his tenure in Utah County, Lewis Barney posed for a photographer. It is the only known likeness of him extant. Probably about fifty years old at the time, the portrait of Barney somewhat belies our image of the hardworking, weatherworn frontiersman. Rather we see his lean and sober, clean-shaven, square-jawed countenance decorated by fashionable attire. (The time required for a subject to sit still while the image adhered to the plate precluded many smiling faces in the nineteenth century.) His hair, long and parted on one side according to Mormon fashion of the day, nearly reaches his collar. He is dressed in a coat, vest, and dress shirt with a small turn-down collar. His necktie is horizontally tied in a half-bow with one end expanded, typical of the time.[1] His attire demonstrates that, notwithstanding his residence in frontier settings, refinement in manner, demeanor, and looks were important to him. (His later experience as a frontier educator, illustrating his interest in the advancement of culture, is no surprise.) Still, Barney was no dandy; he was a frontiersman whose life reflected the rural existence in which he flourished. This rural tradition and preoccupation with family things defined his interests and ambitions in Utah County.

It is important to remember that everything affecting individual Barney family members mentioned in this story was shared by other kin at one generational level or another. (Regrettably, consistent with their contemporaries regarding silence about family matters, the Barneys hid for posterity particulars about their interpersonal associations.) Not only were Barney's wives and children subject to periodic relocation, they also had to contend with the unusual arrangement of two families living as one. His two wives, Betsey and Elizabeth, cohabited together for about fifteen years after arriving in Utah. Where Betsey bore seven children, Elizabeth had eight; still, half of Barney's children did not survive to the age of majority. What the impact of living in a two-layered polygamist home was on his wives and children is not known. Indeed, we know nothing of their domestic lives. What was Lewis's temperament and disposition at his fireside? A conclusion is guesswork, at best, but an event in 1858 gives a hint at the course of Barney family home life. In October, twenty-two-year-old Walter Turner Barney, Lewis and Betsey's oldest son,

Walter Turner Barney (Lewis Barney's son) and wife. Photographer and date unknown. Courtesy of Ruth Mae Barney Harris.

married. His bride, Sarah Matilda Farr, was a seventeen-year-old from Ohio. She would be Walter's only bride.

The culture of plural marriage, gaining momentum among the Saints since its 1852 public announcement, was rejected by Lewis Barney's children.[2] While his children were exposed to only one generation of polygamous practice, it is unusual that not one of them entered into a plural relationship. Plural marriage in territorial Utah became an acknowledged tenet, and not a minor one, of Latter-day Saint belief. Thereafter, the preaching and teaching of the "principle" by church leaders from the pulpits and otherwise accelerated. That the Barney children were practicing Latter-day Saints yet shied from the precept says something about their perception of the practice. One should not necessarily conclude that his children's uniform monogamy indicates a poor or conflictive domestic life under Lewis's roof while they were growing up, but that is a possibility not to be overlooked. There were also around them plenty of other plural marriages sufficiently visible from which to fix an attitude. The Barneys were not unlike many other Mormon plural families who witnessed an ebbing of orthodoxy in the next generation's marital practices. For the Barneys, plural marriage within Lewis's family ended with the first generation.

The 1850s, a time for Barney family maturation, was also for the Latter-day Saints a period wherein the Church of Jesus Christ of Latter-day Saints moved from adolescence to nascent adulthood. The isolation of the Great Basin served to affix an internal esteem previously unavailable to the Saints. Literally making "the desert blossom as the rose" demonstrated to every believer that the confidence they consigned to Mormonism's ideology was more than a fleeting wisp of the divine on earth. They reshaped the land at the same time the rhetoric of personal reform resounded from the pulpits. Subduing the environment and humbling the human spirit were two of Utah pioneers' unofficial articles of faith. Their successful stare-down of the federal government confirmed to them the nature of the power to which they looked for strength. Like the ever lengthening shoots of an aspen grove, the expansion of the Mormon kingdom into every habitable Great Basin vale positively portended that the network of belief and ambition would survive difficulties from within and without.

There *were* problems from within and without. Despite the concerted effort by Brigham Young and the Latter-day Saints to engage in a benign and equitable presence among those not of their kind, first the Indians and then later the gentiles, there was an inevitable fallout from the cultural clash. The displacement in the 1850s of the Native Americans from Utah valleys, punctuated by the Walker and Tintic Wars and culminating in the establishment of the Uintah Basin Reservation in 1861, tainted the Mormon settlement of the Great Basin.[3] The California gold rush, the federal expedition and residual presence, and other factors which brought non-Mormons into Utah's mountain valleys created tensions that were not resolved by amalgamation. As outside influences became more widespread, the less committed of the Saints were affected.

A number of those who braved the cross-country ordeal of getting to Zion arrived only to find disappointment in the arid, desert environment or the theocratic manner of business in Utah. Some of the disgruntled quietly turned around after a year or two in the valley and returned to civilization across the mountains, the plains, and the Missouri River, while others hitched up their wagons for the West Coast. Others who chose to stay among their erstwhile associates in the faith were sometimes vocal in their objections. Dissent became more visible from within. While much intended good designed for church members came from the Mormon Reformation, the isolated excesses offended some adherents and tended to exacerbate the dissonance of those already estranged. And the horrific Mountain Meadows Massacre forever stained the image and reputations of the Saints in the minds of those whose fixed bias gave no slack to Mormons no matter the issue. In all of this Lewis Barney remained resolved and committed to the faith which had undergirded his life for the previous eighteen years.[4] The Barneys were not spectators of the emerging kingdom; they were and always had been frontline participants. While some in the 1850s found themselves distanced from their previous loyalties to the faith, the practical involvement of the Barneys in the physical growth of the kingdom further fixed the dye of the restored gospel of Jesus Christ into their bones.

Return to the Palmyra Plain

Soon after Barney's return from his winter defense in Echo Canyon, he and his brothers decided to relocate once again. Without explanation as to his discontent east of the Spanish Fork bluff, upon his return he "located a ranch at the mouth of Spanish Fork River and opened a farm which I cultivated a few years."[5] This farm was located in the westernmost part of Palmyra on the river's north side near where it poured into Utah Lake. The record after the Indian farm's establishment on the river's south side two years earlier had apparently diluted fears that living on the community's outskirts was dangerous. Not long after the Barneys' move Henry Hamilton also located there. "I & George, my Father-in-law, went & staked off 40 acres of land down towards the lake," Hamilton wrote on 4 March 1858, "close upon where L[ewis] Barney, J[oh]n Barney, J[effer]son Barney has gone to settle."[6]

Given the strictures regarding land associated with Palmyra just two years earlier, it is interesting to note that the Barneys and the Hamiltons returned to the outlying parcel of ground, apparently without restriction. However, even with an influx of settlers to Spanish Fork, the means of land acquisition at this time was still somewhat precarious.[7] The possession of land was the most critical feature of survival outside the Salt Lake Valley. The Barneys' movement at this time to the farthest reaches of the community, several miles from the heart of Spanish Fork, illustrates, yet again, their discontent in settings where the accouterments of city living dominated life. They preferred the edge of society, even proximity to the Indians.

The threat of Native American discontent was ubiquitous, even in otherwise tranquil times. About the first of June 1858, not long after the Barneys settled near Utah Lake, a band of nearly three hundred agitated Utes came into the valley creating mischief in Springville, Pondtown, and Spanish Fork. Twelve hundred pounds of flour and six beeves given them upon the order of Brigham Young allayed their "verry saucy & ugly" behavior until they moved on.[8] Still, the fear of Native American disturbance was minimal when considering the potential catastrophe of a war with the government. Barney reported that at his new home, "I was brought into the society of Lamanites [Indians], there being 20 or 30 lodges almost continuously camped nearby."[9] His continued associations with the Native Americans on the Spanish Fork Indian Farm, like those previously, proved amicable. All his former encounters with Indians since his infancy in western New York were based on suspicion and fear. Here, at the Spanish Fork's mouth, the Barneys had friendly relations with Utah's natives. At the time, the Indians were much less threatening than the military juggernaut in the next valley. In spite of the threat and suspicion of the army by Barney, he capitalized on the military presence.

Camp Floyd

The motives of Lewis Barney in moving to the Palmyra plain likely included the realization that life in Spanish Fork limited the means to adequately support his family. For Barney and most others in the valley, farming was the primary vocation. While forced out of the lumber business by his Echo Canyon service, the military's presence in adjacent Cedar Valley sparked Barney's revival of his lumber enterprise. Recognizing the potentially lucrative opportunities with a military base-in-the-making he found himself back in Utah Valley's canyons. Before long he related his "principal business was to work in the canyon getting out lumber for Camp Floyd."[10] The army established their federal post in Cedar Valley, thirty miles northwest of Peteetneet Canyon. Cedar Valley being mostly uninhabited required a military establishment built from scratch. Lumber was a critical commodity and Barney became one of their suppliers.[11] To Barney and the rest of the Mormon population, the presence of the troops ironically proved that "the Lord over ruled what they intended for the destruction of the Latter-day Saints [and turned it] into a blessing to them."[12]

The construction of a U.S. military installation had a profound effect upon the territory. What had been an empty valley west of Utah Lake very quickly became the third largest city in Utah, after Salt Lake City and Provo. Camp Floyd was the largest military base in the American West. While the psyche of Mormon settlers tightened with the army so close (to their disadvantage), the economy of Utah was significantly altered (to their favor).[13] To take advantage of the potential windfall, Barney wrote, "I went into Loafer Canyon [adjacent to Peteetneet Canyon] to work getting out lumber and hauling it to the Army at Camp Floyd, taking about 1500 feet each load bringing over $100 a trip." With the army paying "7 dollars a hundred for lumber . . . by this means I fitted myself up with wagons and teams and clothing so we was well supplied with such things as we needed."[14]

While Lewis Barney made money from the federal army, his relations and attitudes toward them were comparable to others who had to work in proximity to the troops. "Father had business at Salt Lake City," wrote Barney's son Arthur.

> He went there and took me with him and when we got to . . . where there was a long dugway around the point of the mountain [near present Bluffdale, Utah] just above [the] Jordan River . . . we met Johnston's army. As father had an old yoke of bulls working on a wagon, a soldier said, pointing to this bull team, "That's old Brigham." Then another one would say, "that one is old Heber C. Kimball." As the road was very narrow, Father got to one side of the road. While Johnston's army passed the above remarks was hurled at us until they all got passed. They were playing the band all the time we were waiting for them to pass. And as it was a long string or train of soldiers, it took them about an hour to pass us.[15]

The aggravation of the army presence was not limited to nasty remarks to the Mormons.

The Powder Keg That Needed Only a Spark

Following a year of mutual toleration between Mormon and government troops, a series of incidents in early 1859 brought the parties toe to toe, the closest to open conflict since the troops entered Cedar Valley. Several factors played into the mix which nearly exploded into violence. In March 1859 the federal boys executed a strategy to round up both local and general church leaders in the suspicious and unresolved March 1857 Parrish-Potter murders perpetrated in Springville and the equally clandestine Aiken murders committed between the towns of Payson and Nephi.[16] John Cradlebaugh, a forty-year-old federally appointed judge from Ohio, set up court in Provo to break through the crust of Mormon resistance regarding the murders. He also tried to line up evidence to breach the silence of locals about those culpable for the September 1857 Mountain Meadows Massacre.[17] The judge and other federal officials intended to implicate the church for the dastardly deeds with the objective of reaching all the way to Brigham Young.[18]

When Cradlebaugh on 8 March 1859 addressed the Mormon grand jury, he lectured them: "You are the tools, the dupes, the instruments of a tyrannical church despotism. The heads of your church order and direct you. You are taught to obey their orders and commit these horrid murders. Deprived of your liberty you have lost your manhood and become the willing instruments of bad men."[19] The judge's arrogance was countered by the locals' defiance. To reinforce the judge who issued the warrants and the federal marshal who executed them, Colonel-made-General Johnston sent troops from Camp Floyd to Provo. Utah County locals were outraged. Signed petitions were sent in March 1859 to territorial leaders pleading for relief from the prospect of federal troops camped in their backyards. Lewis Barney was one of fifty-seven from the "Spanish Fork precinct" who petitioned Cradlebaugh to send the soldiers back to Camp Floyd.[20] The new governor, Alfred Cumming, a fifty-six-year-old Georgian, recognizing the volatile situation, ordered Johnston to withdraw his troops. Johnston refused. Cumming, in a surprising move, then ordered Mormon militia commander General Daniel W. Wells to hold the Mormon militia in readiness to counter federal resistance. With rumors flying, "A critical moment had been reached in the relations between Gentiles and Mormons in Utah. . . . Only in the heated days of 1857 had the possibility of an engagement between the Saints and the army been greater."[21] Fortunately, deft negotiations facilitated the troops' removal from Provo early in April which momentarily pacified matters. The residue of hostility only accelerated the impasse in subsequent matters of disagreement; and innuendo, due to lack of efficient communication, exacerbated the already tense situation.

Another smouldering problem was a charge of counterfeiting against Brigham Young, the result of the dishonesty of a "young Mormon engraver" which Johnston believed they could attach to the Mormon leader. Rumors circulated that a battery of artillery and two regiments of infantry were soon to march on Salt Lake City to arrest Young for counterfeiting.[22] Another point of contention that incensed the Mormons was that the federally appointed judges were releasing without trials criminals who perpetrated crimes on Mormons including two men who ravished a woman and her daughter without consequence.[23] Other rumors reported another thousand troops on their way to Utah from California to reinforce the Camp Floyd army. And as the murders of the emigrant train at Mountain Meadows in September 1857 had never been resolved, Judge Cradlebaugh and several hundred infantry and dragoons were headed for Iron County, Utah, to arrest alleged conspirators—Mormons. These were only several of many concerns blowing in the wind of rumor and intrigue.

The Latter-day Saints were more convinced than ever that the federal government's express purpose was the destruction and overthrow of their church. Even some soldiers posted at Camp Floyd were mystified at the overt aggression against the Saints, who, overall, to this time had exhibited restraint. One of the government troops who had some interaction with the Saints reported, "If the Mormons are not the most consummate hypocrites beneath the sun, Uncle Sam has not a more faithful, loyal, liberty-loving people within his proud domains than they; and from my association with them I am convinced that they are not liable to the charge of false pretence."[24] But the government record, exhibited by every legal entity they had encountered, created an understandable paranoia in the Saints regarding government leaders and designs. The federal rhetoric threatening the church and its leaders provoked the Mormons to both defensive and offensive measures.

As the rumors circulated throughout the northern Utah valleys, church leaders took the threat seriously and began packing vital books and papers for removal should Johnston attack the city.[25] As word spread to outlying communities, Latter-day Saints were ready, as they had been in the fall of 1857, to protect the territory from the agents of the federal conspiracy against them. Brigham Young met with Governor Cumming on 24 April 1859 encouraging him to stand up to General Johnston and declare that the military had no jurisdiction in territorial and civic affairs. "The course pursued," Young told Cumming, "was driving hundreds of men into the mountains" to await the call to engage the army in guerilla warfare.[26] Barney's attitude represented the views of many Saints: "We had witnessed the slaughter and a robbery of our people for nearly 30 years and we did not intend to stand still and let them cut our throats and shoot down our best men without resistance. Consequently," he continued, "there was many companies secreted in the mountains ready to make a dash into Salt Lake City with a sufficient force to repel the force sent by them for the capture of President Young and at the same time rush into Camp Floyd and capture it and take possession of their stores."[27] Local residents met clandestinely to plot their resistance to thwart federal designs. In Utah County they were particularly active and Lewis Barney was in the thick of it.

On 1 May 1859, Indian farm superintendent Garland Hurt wrote to a federal authority in Salt Lake City of a conspiracy afoot by Spanish Fork locals, in cahoots with other community militias, to assault federally appointed officials. Hurt suggested that there might be "another *dreadful massacre by the Southern Indians*," referring, of course, to the killings at Mountains Meadows in 1857, which he correctly believed was committed by Mormons who blamed the awful deed on Indians. Hurt obtained the information from sources in Spanish Fork who covertly undermined their Mormon neighbors, though it was no secret that dissent from within Utah was increasing. The spies reported to Hurt that "another party headed by A. K. Thurber left Spanish Fork last night and they have heard that another party is to start to night," whose design likely was to do just as Barney outlined. Of the thirteen local conspirators Hurt named, two were Lewis and his brother John Barney.[28]

The following day Hurt wrote again to underscore his warning of the previous day and reiterated his informants affirm "that there is a secret military movement on foot among the mormons. They think that 100 persons or more have left Spanish Fork after night under arms."[29] Indeed, there was among the Saints a paramilitary operation ready to move to action: an operation believed by the desperate participants to be a patriotic mission to preserve their liberty. "I was called on as one of these minute men," Barney said, "and left my home in the night with Bishop Butler and hid ourselves in a canyon waiting the arrival of an express with orders to march."[30] Other units from Spanish Fork also anticipated orders to counterpunch the federals.[31] And adjoining Utah County residents rallied to perform like service.[32]

When Governor Alfred Cumming finally waded through the rumors and reports of both the army and Mormons, he issued a proclamation on 9 May 1859 dispersing all local militia units. The Mormons, trusting Cumming who had treated them fairly during his short tenure, complied. A week later, territorial marshal John Kay, after investigating the proclamation's effect, reported to Governor Cumming that no militia groups were then "concealed in the mountains, with a view to military organization or service," and that any claim to the contrary "is entirely a mistake and without any substantial foundation."[33] The near confrontation evaporated and both sides returned to detente.

Not only was 1859 a notable time in federal-Mormon relations, once again Lewis Barney began to think about relocating his family. This time it is quite obvious that economics was the root of his thinking. Once Camp Floyd was built, the need for Barney's service to supply lumber was eliminated, and his farmlands in Spanish Fork likely could not provide for his family. Circumstances in Spanish Fork were difficult for other residents as well. A report about the town in late 1859 gives some dimension to their situation:

> Spanish Fork, up to the present season, was considered one of our best grain districts. But this year the irrigating water has washed up the saleratus from beneath, until scarcely fifty acres of their fine rich bottom fields remain clear of the white alkaline crust. The vegetation turned yellow and finally disappeared, so that many of the farmers of that settlement have not raised enough to cover the seed they put in the ground. The consequence is that a number of them have determined to leave that vicinity, to try their fortune elsewhere.[34]

Despite the reversals, at decade's end Spanish Fork had grown into a substantial community by Utah standards. Over a thousand residents now called the village home.[35] The settlement's demographics had dramatically changed in less than five years. The population more than doubled since the mid-1850s with foreigners, most from Great Britain, composing 40 percent of the community. The agricultural reversal had a significant impact on the townsfolk. A large portion of the Danes were still living in dugouts in 1859.[36] The 1860 census accounted for 282 dwellings in Spanish Fork, but indicated that 95 of those homes were unoccupied.[37] The reasons for Lewis Barney to stay in Spanish Fork were few, if any, by the end of the decade.

Not giving up on Utah County, Barney eyed Springville, a ten-year-old community just east across the valley, as a possible place of removal. Now believing he could reverse his misfortune nearer the mountains, Barney ignored the mood of many to leave the valley. His departure from Spanish Fork included a tender incident concerning the Native Americans among whom he had lived in close proximity for nearly two years. By this time there were about four hundred of the Ute tribe living on the Spanish Fork Indian Farm and, as stated, he lived with his family near a number of their lodges. Over time he befriended his Indian neighbors.

> I had several cows that we milked having a surplus of milk. I gave the squaws this surplus [and] also helped them otherwise. By this means I gained their friendship and good feelings so that when I was about to leave they gathered around me and begged me not to leave them. I told them I was obliged to go. They then commenced crying, saying, "This land is our land and you can have all you want if you will stay here with us." The squaws clung to my wife weeping and crying, saying, "You must not go for our children will starve as they did before you come here." We told them we could not stay so we bid them goodbye and left them crying.[38]

The circumstances and timing of Barney's move to Springville are not known. There is evidence that not all of Lewis's immediate family made the move, his first family apparently staying in Spanish Fork into the early 1860s.[39] Thus, it is likely his two wives' families temporarily separated at this time and maintained households in separate communities, Betsey in Spanish Fork and Elizabeth in Springville. Some plural households in Utah remained together. Barney's did not.

Springville

First settled in October 1850, Springville grew to require a Mormon ward the following February, which portended steady growth through the 1850s. As Mormon immigrants looking for a favorable spot of land spilled into Utah Valley, Springville, after Provo, attracted the most attention. The settlement, founded just below the mouth of Hobble Creek, gained a reputation as being one of the finest locations in Utah Valley measuring just five miles southeast from Provo and about three miles east of Utah Lake. By the end of 1853 nearly eight hundred were numbered in the Springville Ward. The primary events impacting Spanish Fork through the middle of the decade also affected Springville, including the Walker War in 1853–1854. They later built a fort and city wall, eventually enveloping eight blocks. A school was built in 1853 as well. Despite Indian concerns and the grasshopper invasions of 1855–1856, the community and church continued to flourish.[40]

But the bucolic, optimistic atmosphere in Springville broke. The killings in March 1857 of two Parrish family members, a father and son about to depart Utah after having given up on Mormonism, and Duff Potter, one of the elder Parrishes' enemies, sent chills through the town. That the murders were never fully explained nor were the responsible parties brought to justice served as a festering wound throughout the nineteenth century in Mormon/non-Mormon relations.[41] The killings occurred in the midst of the Mormon Reformation which in Springville ironically provoked unrest when the intent of the movement was to foster cooperation and brotherly love. Suspicion crept through the streets and to the farms. Even some town leaders suffered the glare of an overzealous portion of the citizenry.

These extremists in Springville set one former church and community official on edge. Noah Packard, veteran church member of many years and formerly of the Springville bishopric, wrote, "I acted as an Alderman in the City Council of Springville, when I told the people I did not wish to act in that office any longer." His resignation aroused the suspicions of "wicked men" who stalked him trying to catch him doing or saying something "to make me an offender for a word." Their intent, he said, was to "cut [him] off from the Church." Packard lamented, "I have hardly had the liberty of conscience or speech since I have been living in Springville."[42] The fanatical, twisted zeal of some community leaders and others provoked a few lukewarm Saints to abandon ship which further aggravated efforts of amelioration and goodwill. As late as 1859 the problem "of blending the [church block] teacher's calling with that of the policeman, thereby bringing continual clashing between the civil and ecclesiastical authorities" still plagued the settlement.[43] George W. Bean, one of Springville's principal citizens, wrote to Brigham Young in April 1859 describing the condition of the area. "There are many persons in Utah County who are uneasy. Some had openly apostatized, others wished to move to other parts of the Territory."[44] The unchecked atmosphere of distrust severely hampered community relationships for the last few years of the 1850s.

Into this cauldron Barney moved in 1859 or 1860. Likely lured to Springville by reports that year that "town property can be bought cheap, especially at Springville,"[45] Barney was surely aware of the fissures within the settlement from the negative publicity surrounding the oppressive climate. Unusual for a Mormon community, the atmosphere among Springville's 1,300 residents was primarily the residual of reformation excesses. The federal presence in the territory and its attendant cultural pluralism, which loosened the structure of Mormon society in many of the territory's communities, also contributed to the tenuous setting. Strict orthodoxy and unanimity, if they ever existed, decreased.

Just as the garment appeared ready to unravel, Springville experienced a reversal in about 1859 that appears to have had both a religious and civic cause. Cyrus H. Wheelock, longtime veteran of church affairs, asserted a remarkable phase of spiritual leadership and healing within the community. "A most eloquent preacher and a great favorite of the people," Wheelock's beneficent influence prompted one to say the satisfactory nature of his administration "will be remembered to this day [1900]." Other religious leaders, who fled town earlier to avoid Judge Cradlebaugh's claw, returned from their "summer vacation" which helped to stabilize the town as well. One observer of the time wrote, "During the turbulent times of 1859 some bad feelings had arisen between the brethren in regard to church matters, but after the old regime was again inaugurated, an era of good feeling had been ushered in."[46] The following February, church apostles Charles C. Rich and Erastus Snow visited Springville and reported that "Springville is becoming quiet and settled; and under the mild policy and teachings of Elder Cyrus H. Wheelock, will, we trust, pursue the even tenor of her way, despite the efforts of a few misguided spirits to the contrary."[47] The "era of good feelings" fostered improvement within the town civically, economically, socially, and even militarily.[48]

Regrettably, Barney's view of this interesting period within Springville is not known, nor is there any information regarding his participation in activities within the community. There is a gap in extant Springville Ward records for this time resulting in no mention of the Barneys during the "year or two" in which he lived in the community.[49] Something else not chronicled by Barney or the Springville and Spanish Fork wards was the passing in 1860 of Lewis and Elizabeth's son, the namesake of his father, Lewis Junior. The little boy would have been about two in 1860.[50] The wounds in family hearts were still far too fresh from little Margaret Mariah's death two years earlier for consolation in what appeared to be the fate of Elizabeth's children. Her joy the next year at the birth of another son, David, was probably tempered some as she cautiously watched the child's first weeks and months, for Elizabeth's small children did not fare well in Utah.[51] Now at the very time Springville was emerging from its malaise, Barney decided, probably late in 1861, to move on once again. We are again left without explanation for the move beyond the apparent call of new land.

Chapter 15

Busted Up: Utah's Sanpete and Sevier Valleys, 1861–1865

With new beginnings for the Barneys in the 1860s, the mother country from which they and their Mormon brethren withdrew years before was fraught with a malady capable of dissolving the Union. In 1860, the same year of the Pony Express's inaugural, meant to draw the country together, Abraham Lincoln became president, provoking South Carolina to leave the family. Within months Mississippi, Florida, Alabama, Georgia, and Louisiana, five other southern siblings, severed their familial ties and formed the provisional Confederate States of America. The primary effects upon Utah's citizens from the brewing fratricide were the withdrawal of U.S. troops from Camp Floyd, the preoccupation of Washington with surviving the divorce, and the satisfaction that the federal government was now schizophrenic and suicidal. There was no love lost on the part of the Saints toward the United States government.

Before Confederate troops had even fired upon Fort Sumter, Utahns prognosticated a bitter wind stinging the United States. Sermonizing to his brethren, one Spanish Fork Mormon noted, "The rebellion in South Carolina [was] in fulfillment of the prophecy delivered by our martyred Prophet Joseph Smith" in 1832 when the prophet declared the time would soon come when "the Southern States shall be divided against the Northern States" and "with the sword and by bloodshed the inhabitants of the earth shall mourn."[1] The war's course from 1861 to 1865 satisfactorily fulfilled the prophet's prophesy and more. While matters of national survival enveloped the federal government, Lewis Barney calculated the factors of his family's survivability.

Springtown

When Barney moved to Springville in 1859 or 1860, his father Charles moved his family south to a central Utah valley, Sanpete, named after one of the area's principal Indian chiefs. The move required that Charles's family drive their heavily laden wagon south from Spanish Fork to Payson, to Santaquin, to Clover Creek, then on to Nephi. From Nephi they climbed east through Salt Creek Canyon to Fountain Green, southeast to Moroni, and then south to

Fort Ephraim. Upon their arrival at Ephraim they turned northeast before arriving in Springtown (later Spring City).[2] By the time of the 1860 census the family patriarch's sons Walter and Benjamin had joined their elderly father in Springtown. Charles in 1861, now seventy-eight and deaf, and his fifty-three-year-old wife Deborah had only their youngest son, nineteen-year-old William, living with them.[3] After a year or two in Springville, Lewis Barney found nothing compelling to keep him there and he, too, migrated south to Springtown.

Sanpete Valley, the terrain varying from 5,000 to 6,000 feet above sea level, is elevated higher than both Utah and Salt Lake Valleys. It is couched where "the Wasatch mountains [plateau] form a perfect natural watershed and eastern boundary line, dividing the snow reservoirs on the summit, and supplying numerous streams for irrigating the cultivated area in the valley. A similar boundary is formed on the west by the Sanpitch mountains [Gunnison Plateau], thus enclosing one of the most delightful valleys of Utah."[4] Manti was the first and most prominent village in the county, settled in 1849. Sanpete County was organized in 1852 followed by the establishment of Mt. Pleasant, Springtown, and Ephraim in 1852–1853. Springtown, at almost 5,700 feet in elevation, was laid out on the east side of the valley in the shadow of a horseshoe-shaped formation of the Wasatch Plateau. Three creeks fed the community—Canal, Oak, and Cedar. The part of town closest to the foothills is rocky and gravelly with the lower part of the community built upon clay. The plain is fertile and agriculturally compatible for habitation. The family of James Allred, southerners from North Carolina and Tennessee, initially claimed Springtown, whose dominance denominated the village Allred's Settlement. Later Danish immigrants who gathered there came in such numbers that "Little Denmark" nicknamed the site.[5] But the Danish namesake did not last. As it was, the valley was so remote from population centers along the Wasatch Front that it became a target for Native Americans who saw the Mormon settlement pattern again preempt their traditional lands.[6]

The 1853 Walker War affected the settlers in Sanpete Valley profoundly. Several settlements, including Springtown, were evacuated and consolidated with Manti's residents as the Indians destroyed property, stole cattle, and threatened the settlers' lives. Notwithstanding the recent completion of a fort, the day after Springtown folks were attacked in July 1853 they fled the town for Manti. The refugees swelled to 765 the total county population which had crowded into Manti. Premature attempts at resettlement preceded the eventual abandonment of other Sanpete communities while Walker's warriors marauded through the valley. Almost the entire count of Springtown livestock were appropriated during Indian raids. In January 1854 the Indians obliterated the vacant settlement, apparently out of spite. With the war's conclusion in May 1854 and Walker's passing, his brother Arapeen acknowledged the inevitable and deeded all of Sanpete County to the Mormon settlers.

In the aftermath of the Walker War Springtown mostly lay fallow until late June 1859. An Irish clan named Black led the reestablishment of Springtown. William Black, among the first Latter-day Saint missionaries to Ireland and patriarch of the family, wrote from Ephraim, Utah, to Brigham Young on 4 July 1859 asking, "If it would meet your approbation we would like that you would allow us to go to Little Denmark." Receiving an affirmative response, Black wrote again on 1 August saying, "I have gone to Little Denmark and has got it surveyed and is now waiting for your instructions. We expect about 30 families to go their this fall."[7] The site was surveyed into a 640-acre plat. While no farming was pursued that first year, the survey provided for five- and ten-acre lots with no more than fifteen acres going to any family head.[8] Soon others came to the townsite, some of them Allred family members returning to their former habitation. After some dispute over leadership between the Blacks and Allreds, church leaders Ezra T. Benson and Erastus Snow visited the settlement and in January 1860 chose C. G. Larson for bishop, with Reddick (sometimes spelled Redick) N. Allred and Joseph Smith Black as counselors.[9] Black, the second counselor, may have figured in Lewis Barney's decision to locate in Springtown.

The reason for the Barneys' move from Utah Valley to Springtown is likely tied to hope for better opportunity.[10] A seemingly limitless frontier made such moves viable. With Charles was his youngest daughter, a fifteen-year-old named Sarah Jane. In 1860 she was "tall and slim, light complexioned, with light hair and blue eyes." Catching the attention of the bishopric's second counselor Joseph Smith Black, he noticed "she was a beautiful figure, quite gay and considerable coquettish." In November of that year she became the second wife of twenty-four-year-old Black, who, by this time, had also been elected selectman for Sanpete County as well as justice of the peace for Springtown.[11] In 1860 there were 220 Springtowners. The Blacks, because of their numbers and obvious interest in making Springtown viable, exerted inordinate influence in the community initially, and William Black was not about to let the momentum stall.

The month after the bishopric was organized, the elder Black complained to Brigham Young that there were influential persons in Manti "underworking against us."[12] Earlier Reddick Allred had written Young that Ephraimites had appropriated one of the primary water sources for Springtown.[13] Before the Springtown folks could be viable, they would need help. Soon fifty-six-year-old Mormon apostle and Connecticut native Orson Hyde set his home in Springtown while he administered church affairs in Sanpete Valley. His choice of Springtown for a residence cast a new light on the village. A year later Black wrote back to Young expressing appreciation for Hyde's advent in the valley. "When he came here we were all in turmoil and confusion," Black wrote. "Neither life nor property was safe. Since he came, he has been a blessing to the upright and faithful brethren and sisters, but a terror to evil doers."[14] For over a decade Hyde's influence significantly affected matters in Sanpete and the soon-to-be settled valley of Sevier to the south.

The ethnic components of the settlement made for interesting community relationships. Many of the Scandinavians who settled in Springtown in the first phase returned during resettlement. Other Danes were then drawn to the village. Their natural commonalities tended to draw them to a residential district in the settlement's northern part. The cultural distinctions and language differences that separated those fresh from Denmark from their American neighbors established boundaries both real and imagined between the groups. The particulars of Danish life found their way into practice within Springtown, including distinctive architectural forms and manner of livelihood. Instead of the agrarian bent of most Americans, the Danish tended toward trades and craftsmanship. Their contributions marked the community for good in many ways unavailable to other Utah towns. The Danes who firmly embraced Mormonism, though there were some who did not, found that worshiping in their own tongue with their countrymen made their lives more satisfying and meaningful. They built a one-room adobe meetinghouse where they held a weekly service while they melded into the larger community by participation with the others in Springtown in regular worship services.[15]

Lewis Barney's family members living in Springtown had been there nearly two years by the time he joined them, probably in 1861. He likely ventured into Sanpete Valley on his own, leaving his wives and children to follow later.[16] The reason for Barney's new enterprise in Springtown was, like his extended family, probably economically motivated. He found the new community had need of a commodity he could provide—lumber. Soon he "put up a saw mill in Oak Creek Canyon for the benefit of the Saints of Sanpete County. This I accomplished by much trouble at the cost [of] $1500."[17] His was the first mill in Oak Creek Canyon, east of town.[18] Despite local competition, he discovered a market that extended beyond Springtown. Barney's son Arthur remembered,

> The lumber that he made at this mill in Oak Creek canyon, about 5 miles above Spring Town, some of it was shipped to Salt Lake City, a distance of 120 miles. . . . With [the] oxen which we used in them days, it took 12 or 13 days to make the round trip. If I remember right we got from $60.00 to $80.00 per thousand feet of lumber and with two yoke of oxen we would haul about 2,000 feet per load.[19]

Barney had hopes he could return to a level of business he enjoyed in supplying the army a few years earlier.

But the return on Barney's investment was not satisfactory. The survival of his family was in jeopardy. He reported:

> The following season was a hard winter [probably 1862–1863] and many of my cattle died and even through the summer [1863] they

> continued dying. Cows fat enough for beef would take sick and in a few hours lay down and die. Thus in this way I lost 6 cows and one ox through the summer. My stock continued dying until the last animal I had was gone leaving me in debt for the building of my mill.

This coupled with an infestation of grasshoppers nearly subdued him. "The grasshoppers come and cut off the crops, and wheat raised in price to 5 dollars per bushel causing me to pay $750 dollars instead of 150 dollars."[20] It seemed no matter how favorable the circumstances initially, his pursuit of economic stability was continually rebuffed. If there was consolation, he was not the only one disappointed; his brethren on the edge of the Mormon frontier suffered equally.

The Murder of Thomas Jefferson Barney

While Lewis struggled economically in Springtown, one of his brothers was in real trouble. When the bulk of the Barney clan moved on to Sanpete, Thomas Jefferson Barney, Lewis's younger half-brother, stayed in Utah County. Jeff Barney, as he was known, had been raised in the church, and was not much more than a toddler when his father Charles became a Mormon. But Jeff chose another orbit as he matured on the outskirts of Spanish Fork. Once a member of a grand jury in Provo in 1854 and having married in 1856, after his family moved on to Sanpete Valley, he flaunted the law and found himself one of Isaac (Ike) Potter's cattle rustling gang. Potter was a twenty-nine-year-old Ohioan who had also been raised a Mormon. He became one of the most notorious outlaws in the territory, apparently turning to rustling in the aftermath of the Potter-Parrish Springville murders in 1857 which involved his kin.[21] It may have been the poor economy in Utah County that drove Jeff into Potter's pack, composed of both whites and Indians. But near the time of his twenty-sixth birthday, Jeff had had enough of life outside the law and the church and at the urging of his brother Benjamin determined to retrack his life. Jeff soon had a falling out with the thieves and Potter did not take it lightly.[22] In early September 1862, the repentant young man went to the Spanish Fork bishop A. K. Thurber and confessed his shady activities.[23] Thereafter, Jeff Barney tried to distance himself from his erstwhile associates, but on the evening of 9 December 1862 his past caught up with him.

Prior to retiring for the night, with a babe in arms, Jeff settled into a chair about 7 or 8 P.M. in his dwelling (described in court as a hut) near the Spanish Fork River. While sitting in the chair several "Indians . . . blacked up" snuck up to the dwelling and fired two shotgun rounds through the window. One blast hit him in the left side of his neck, throwing his body forward so that the second shot slammed into the left side of his back. In all, the rounds punctured his body with eleven wounds. Benjamin, his older brother who still maintained a home nearby, was called immediately, as was a doctor. The prognosis was gloomy. During the waning hours of his life, with Benjamin at his side, Jeff bore his soul. Declaring his guilt, he also implicated his accomplices. He knew who it was who shot him. With his life ebbing away, he was bent on revenge, but it was not to be. Two days after the attack, he died.[24] He left a young wife and three children, the babe-in-arms apparently surviving the shooting.

While Indians working for Potter were the likely killers, Potter, the notorious desperado, was arrested for the murder. The trial, held in Provo mid-March 1863, came the same week Potter was also indicted for grand larceny for another crime. Caught in the judicial battlefield where federal judges punished the Saints by exonerating those who committed atrocities upon the Mormons, Potter was acquitted of masterminding Jeff Barney's death. While he was later found guilty for the crime of grand larceny and sentenced to a five-year prison term, the judge released him. His criminal career gaining momentum after Jeff's death, Potter was finally killed in 1867, the result of leading Indian raids on white settlers near Coalville, Utah, during the Black Hawk War.[25]

Lewis Barney had always taken a fatherly interest in the religious training of his family which continued to grow.[26] While the record is circumstantial, it is certain that his family was nurtured in the values and world view of the Mormon gospel. Latter-day Saint practice in the nineteenth century, however, was somewhat dissimilar to today's outward expressions of faithfulness in the Church of Jesus Christ. To the first generations of Mormons, "whether it be to plough and sow the fields, to buy and sell goods wares and merchandize, houses or lands; to go to the polls and vote, to the prayer meeting or to the sacrament of the Lord's supper," these diverse activities were "ordinances of religion." To them "the kingdom of God includes every thing necessary for man's present and future well being." Combining the temporal and the spiritual, they claimed, "whatsoever we do, we wish to do all to the glory of God."[27] Consequently, "the Sunday sermon dealt as often with potatoes as with prayer, for the practice of religion was a matter of everyday survival in a community where things big and little had to be shared."[28]

Meeting attendance for the Saints, a present gauge of faithfulness, was less emphasized in Barney's day, especially in frontier communities. Meetinghouses in the rural settings were generally small and uncomfortable structures incapable of holding a large percentage of the church's local membership.[29] A much smaller percentage of Saints gathered weekly than the level of meeting attendance which presently characterizes the faith.[30] Faithfulness in the Church of Jesus Christ was more behaviorally oriented than measured by visible activity. Building the kingdom of God for Mormons in the nineteenth century had as much to do with turning the waste places into the blossoming rose of Zion as it did in attending meetings.[31] Still, in most of Utah's rural communities, a group of believers came together regularly where church members were encouraged, reproved, and challenged by sermon and instruction. Connecting the rising generation to the warp and woof of Mormonism was of singular importance.

Indeed, the spiritual belief a Latter-day Saint father wished to see in his children was demonstrated in Springtown for Lewis. On 30 March 1863 seventeen-year-old Joseph Smith Barney was one in a priesthood meeting describing themselves "as feeling well & striving to do what they could towards building up the kingdom, sustaining the [church] authorities and living their religion." Later in the year in another priesthood meeting Joseph "expressed satisfaction in being in the kingdom of God [and] promised to do [his] best in the same." Six months later in October 1863 twenty-three-year-old James Henry Barney "said he felt well in the work of God and liked to do what he could to build up the kingdom." He had matured sufficiently to candidly state that "he felt to realize his weakness and liability to do wrong, but he wished to sustain his brethren and do what he could to roll forth the work."[32] This kind of commitment to Mormonism was the kind of language a father yearned to hear from his children. Perhaps satisfaction from the spiritual circumstances of his family compensated for his poor economic showing.

Exploration and Settlement of Alma (Monroe) and Circleville

Many Mormon colonies in the Intermountain West were populated by families who had responded to a "call" from church leaders. Families were called to relocate to destinations, often forbidding, designated by the hierarchy to expand the geographical Mormon kingdom. The "Cotton" and "Iron" missions in southern Utah and the "Little Colorado" mission in Arizona are representative of the phenomenon. However, as often as the Barneys relocated, their moves were always at their own initiative.[33] Their continued presence on the expanding Mormon frontier's edge precluded the need to "call" them to such locales. After just a couple of years in Sanpete, Lewis Barney exercised this initiative again.

In the spring of 1863, Brigham Young and his counselor Heber C. Kimball made a tour of settlements south of Salt Lake City. They arrived in Springtown in late April. Here they found Orson Hyde, the apostle in charge of the Sanpete settlements, in a house "of hewn logs, one and a half stories, with a stone kitchen . . . [and whose] corrals, yards and sheds are substantial, neat and orderly."[34] Barney's status in Springtown was not nearly as encouraging. Not one to accept the fate of poverty and deprivation, he dreamed of something better. "Being broken up in Sanpete," he lamented, "and having no land or at least very little land in Sanpete I thought best to hunt a home elsewhere."[35] Coincident with Barney's economic struggle, Orson Hyde "introduced [to the Springtown Saints] the idea of the necessity of moving out and hunting for new places where homes might be built." Hyde announced that "the settlements of Sanpete were overcrowded. That the water was not sufficient to sustain the people."[36] The summer of 1863, George A. Smith sent a small reconnaissance party into Sevier Valley, just south of the Sanpete settlements. Returning with a favorable report, a few families then moved into the region, initially near what is present-day Glenwood.[37]

Later that year, when other Mormon frontier families pushed the northern perimeter of Mormonism into Bear Lake Valley, James T. S. Allred and a half-dozen others from Ephraim organized in December 1863 a party to search for a favorable community site in the unsettled regions of a more southerly valley. Traveling south they exited Sanpete Valley into the Sevier River Valley and followed the river as far as present-day Marysvale, seventy-five miles from Ephraim. While acknowledging some possibility for habitation, the distance from other villages was the primary objection to endorsing the enterprise of settling Sevier Valley.[38] Their report was noised about the Sanpete villages. What Barney heard piqued his interest.

A larger exploration venture was organized for February 1864. Barney joined. "There was a company of about 60 men gathered up to explore the Sevier country to ascertain for themselves the particulars in relation to making a settlement at Marysvale." The expedition left on 4 February with Allred as captain, beginning their venture "up the river."[39] Paralleling the Sevier River's east side, they concluded the location where Richfield now stands not close enough to the river "to get the water out of the river to mature crops that year." They pushed on several miles arriving at the site of present-day Monroe. Here they found "four or five families on a little creek which [some of the group] considered too small for a settlement."[40] The little place, called at the time South Bend, was the southeasternmost reach of the Sevier Valley. The handful of adventurous settlers arrived just before the exploring company.[41]

Pressing on, the explorers crossed mountainous terrain by "hitching several yoke of oxen to one wagon at a time" before negotiating "a rough, steep canyon to pass down before reaching the bottom of the valley." The Sevier River led them into what became Marysvale, "a lovely little valley with beautiful green meadows where the Indians were sporting and tumbling in all their glory."[42] While the Indians appeared friendly, their presence gave pause. "When we arrived at Marysvale," Barney wrote, "we found there was not a sufficient amount of land to make a settlement sufficiently strong to protect [ourselves] against the Indians." And, "I being one of a committee of three to examine the country and ascertain what amount of farming land there was suitable for cultivation, upon careful examination it was found that there was not more than 300 acres of land suitable for cultivation."[43] While Marysvale was at the time rejected for settlement, another option opened to them.

The group learned from the Indians "that by going farther south we would find a place that would be more suitable." The going was not easy. They had "to cross and recross the river, cutting our way through willows and bushes, filling gullies, etc., so we could get our wagons along." After struggling another twenty miles upriver they arrived in a "large valley in a circular shape surrounded by high mountains, with the river flowing down through the center." Circle Valley, at just over 6,000 feet above sea level, seemed an appropriate name for the mountain vale. They "found the hills abounded in cedar wood [with] fence posts easily reached [and] a good supply of timber growing in the mountains for building and fencing." They also found they "could easily tap the Sevier River with a reasonable amount of work."[44] Circle Valley was a location with promise.

After an extensive exploration of the upper Sevier River Valley, they retraced their trek toward home. Despite some optimism for Circle Valley, arriving back in Sevier Valley about thirty miles downstream, Barney said that as they came upon "Alma Creek," at the base of the towering mountains to the east, Moses Gifford, Walter Jones, and others said, "This will be my home." Not one of those who thought the site had limited potential, Barney was one of the enthusiasts. With his sons Walter T. and Henry, they "moved down the creek and struck camp by the willows" in the place called at the time South Bend.[45] Obviously, the decision to start over yet another time was not made lightly for any of those who decided upon South Bend as their future. It stretches our present understanding to consider that Barney, clearly on the declining side of life, was willing to drag his family into yet another episode of starting life anew. This time, they were confronting a wilderness which but few white men had even glimpsed.

"The next day," Barney reported, "we commenced surveying the city plot," due to the good fortune of having the Sanpete County surveyor in the party.[46] As the new neighbors drew lots for their homesteads and prepared to build their rudimentary housing, Wiley P. Allred, forty-six-year-old brother of the exploring expedition's leader, volunteered, "If nobody else will be captain, I will be captain." No one particularly objected, after which the new settlement was renamed Alma, for the Book of Mormon figure. (Alma became Monroe within a decade.) Allred's assumption of authority was accepted that spring by Orson Hyde, now also in charge of the villages sprouting up on the Sevier River, who formalized the arrangement by ordaining Allred bishop of the settlement.[47]

The little village began to take shape. While they used dead timber along the creek and elsewhere for much of the construction taking place, they also had to rely upon green wood to assemble their Spartan dwellings. The sound of axes chopping, hewing, and shaping logs echoed against the mountains just to the east. The settlers worked together "opening farms, making water sects, [and] taking the water from the creek and also from the Sevier River." After creating the semblance of a community out of nothing, most of the men returned to the communities of Sanpete Valley to retrieve their families. "As my family was in Springtown," Lewis said, "it became necessary that I should go and see after them."[48]

About three dozen hopeful families with Alma as their objective entered the valley later in 1864 from several Sanpete communities including Springtown, Fountain Green, Moroni, Wales, Ephraim, and Gunnison.[49]

Lewis's younger brother Walter and his family started south before joining other families in "Nephi and further additions through Sanpete County" before arriving in Alma.[50] Lewis had too much to do in Springtown to join his brother. "I found it necessary to remain with [both wives and their six children] through the summer in order to provide means for their support."[51]

Working for provisions to carry them through the fall and winter, Lewis was involved in an incident giving dimension to the struggle to provide for one's family. Barney and his son Arthur, a thirteen-year-old at the time, went into the mountains near Springtown to hunt for food. Climbing through the brush and over the boulders in the canyon "a big buck deer" presently appeared. The father aimed and shot but his old "Kentucky rifle" misfired. Their dinner ran off. Fumbling around with a waterproof cap to replace the damp cap that failed, they encountered wildlife of another sort. A "big grizzley bear" crossed their path. Arthur was petrified, so much so he begged his father *not* to shoot, but Lewis, poised, leveled his weapon, squeezed the trigger, and a ball exploded from the long barrel. The shot, however, "turned crooked and shot thin." Aiming to "hit the bear in the but of the ear," Barney "must of shot too low, for it got up and went back as it had come." As the bear bounded into the brush "it left such a perfume that the old dog wouldn't follow it, so we did not get anything that day."[52]

Preparing his family for transit to Sevier Valley, Barney became a man of two minds. Despite the work and preparation he made in Alma, his memory of the favorable prospects of Circle Valley recaptured his fancy, forcing him to reconsider. Others remembered Circle Valley favorably as well. With "a company called for to make a settlement further up the [Sevier] river," Barney said, "I, as usual, volunteered . . . and started up the river again to make another location." Once in Sevier Valley, they skirted the fledgling settlement of Alma on their way up the Sevier. What was Lewis thinking? Passing Marysvale and what later became Junction, they soon entered Circle Valley. Three from the group, including Barney, were chosen to select a site for a new settlement. Investigating possibilities, they eventually decided upon "a town site west of the river" which they named Circleville.[53] About fifty families, including Barney and his sons Walter T. and Henry, decided to give the place a chance.[54]

At first blush, Barney was optimistic about Circleville. "Believing this location the most suitable for a home, I had lots and land surveyed for myself, and Walter, and Henry. We then put in a crop of wheat, potatoes, and other stuff. [We] took the water out of the river for the field on the east side and for the city lots on the west side of the river." Not long into the project Barney's enthusiasm for the place dropped. The "farming land was very sandy and the wind was almost continuously blowing so that every morning our water sects was level full of sand causing us to have to clean them out nearly every day." The repetition and tedium of clearing the water sects was but one difficulty. "The wheat come up and looked well for a short time," he complained, but then "there came a heavy wind that was called a poison wind and killed everything. The wheat looked like a fire had ran over it." After a summer of hard work away from his wives, his dream was for naught. "These things so discouraged me I concluded to leave the place," and he was not alone.[55]

Compounding his disappointment was the response he received from his sons when he explained to them that they had "better leave and try and find some more suitable location." His hardy and youthful sons, Walter T. and Henry, undoubtedly sympathetic to their father, retained their original optimism and wanted to make it on their own. They told their father they preferred to stay. He appealed to them with fatherly authority: "my feelings was that we would do no good here and we would not be prospered in this valley and that I had made up my mind to go back." They would not budge. It was a significant moment considering the traditional course of Barney familial relationships and patrilocal gathering. After two emotional appeals, "Finding I could not persuade them to go with me," Barney lamented, "I hitched up my team and started down the river. . . . I left them with a heavy heart, bowed down with sorrow." Trudging back to Springtown "to see after the other part of my family that had been left there," one can only imagine his pain, and perhaps his anger, as Betsey asked why their sons were not with him.[56]

Circumstances in Sanpete Valley were such that despite Barney's disappointment in Circle Valley, Springtown simply was not a place upon which to build his future. So "making arrangements" for his family in Springtown, and having given up on Circleville, Barney "returned to Alma and the next spring [1865] put in 18 acres of wheat."[57] Clearly the little townsite he had previously abandoned became the object of his ambition.

While Lewis was gone, eighty-one-year-old Charles, visiting his son Benjamin who still had a wife living in Spanish Fork, died on 26 February 1865.[58] Having lost his hearing several years previously, the Vermonter frontiersman had finally worn out. His widow Deborah was fifty-six and became the charge of her youngest son William in Springtown. Charles had married twice and fathered sixteen children, ten of whom were still living. His posterity had become a clan of sorts. They had grown numerically and, for the most part, had grouped together. Lewis left no description of the relationship he had with his father, but the fact that he had stayed in proximity to the elder Barney through the younger's entire life is an indication that the sire-son bond was very strong. The Church of Jesus Christ of Latter-day Saints had changed the course of Charles's life for twenty-five years. His life was a study in pioneering. The Barney family patriarch was buried in the original Spanish Fork cemetery on the bluff overlooking the fertile Spanish Fork River floodplain.

The year after the initial reconnaissance of Sevier Valley for settlement, word spread through Sanpete Valley of the favorable conditions for living along the Sevier. At the time Barney worked his Alma property, a company of settlers from Manti arrived in Alma planning to establish their own homesteads, but to

Wiley Allred, the bishop, they were too late. Allred, a Kentuckian, claimed that the settlement could hold only forty families and the Manti group could not be accommodated. Rebuffed, the disappointed group turned around and returned to the Sanpete Valley. Soon a caravan of twenty-five families from Moroni, twenty miles north of Manti, also came looking for homes in Alma. Allred took his stand with them as he had with the Manti folks, but the Moroni people would not be dissuaded. They stayed despite Allred. Over time Allred's aggravation swelled to dissonance with Orson Hyde and other church leaders who encouraged colonization and eventually a corrective was implemented. "There being some complaint raised against Wiley Allred as bishop," Barney reported, "he was released by Orson Hyde and Frederick Olson [a forty-year-old Dane] put in his place."[59] The Sevier Valley was too promising to limit settlement for those willing to start over, and the Mormon kingdom could not be curtailed.

Chapter 16

Beginning to Be Old: The Indian War and the Railway, 1865–1869

A constant throughout most of Lewis Barney's life was his proximity to Native Americans. The pattern began in his infancy near the Tonawanda Reservation in western New York. In Ohio he encountered Indians while the family lived on Owl Creek. Within a half-dozen years of settlement in Illinois, Barney was enlisted against the Sac and Fox in the Black Hawk War in 1832. His plunge into and return from the western wilderness in 1847 brought him into precarious contact with the Plains Indians. Once in Utah's Utah County, he spent most of his time with Indians nearly at his back door. Ever mindful of their presence near Springtown, Indians influenced Barney's domestic life. There was irony to this pattern. Despite several life-threatening encounters with Native Americans, his personal writings suggest he possessed a benign view of Indians. Indeed, at a time when many contemporaries plotted for Indian eradication from the ever-expanding white domain, Barney exhibited sympathy and compassion to the former landholders, but he soon found himself in the thick of the most significant white-Indian confrontation in Utah history. Given the toll exacted on him, one would think his previous disposition toward Indians would reverse. His writings indicate it did not.

Utah's Black Hawk War

At the same time Alma acquired the trappings of a viable settlement, the relationship between the settlers in Sanpete and the Native Americans went sour. The day after Confederate general Robert E. Lee surrendered to the Union's General U. S. Grant at Appomatox Courthouse, Virginia, on 8 April 1865, effectively finalizing the American Civil War, a scuffle in Manti, Utah, brought war to Utah. A scrape between Ute subchief Arapeen and resident John Lowry instigated an ethnic conflict that eventually kicked most Utah settlers into a state of fear for a half-dozen years. The Arapeen-Lowry encounter ignited the dry tinder piling up since the Walker War almost a dozen years before.

Not surprisingly, the continuing encroachment of white settlers into traditional Indian habitat served as the underlying factor of discontent. The

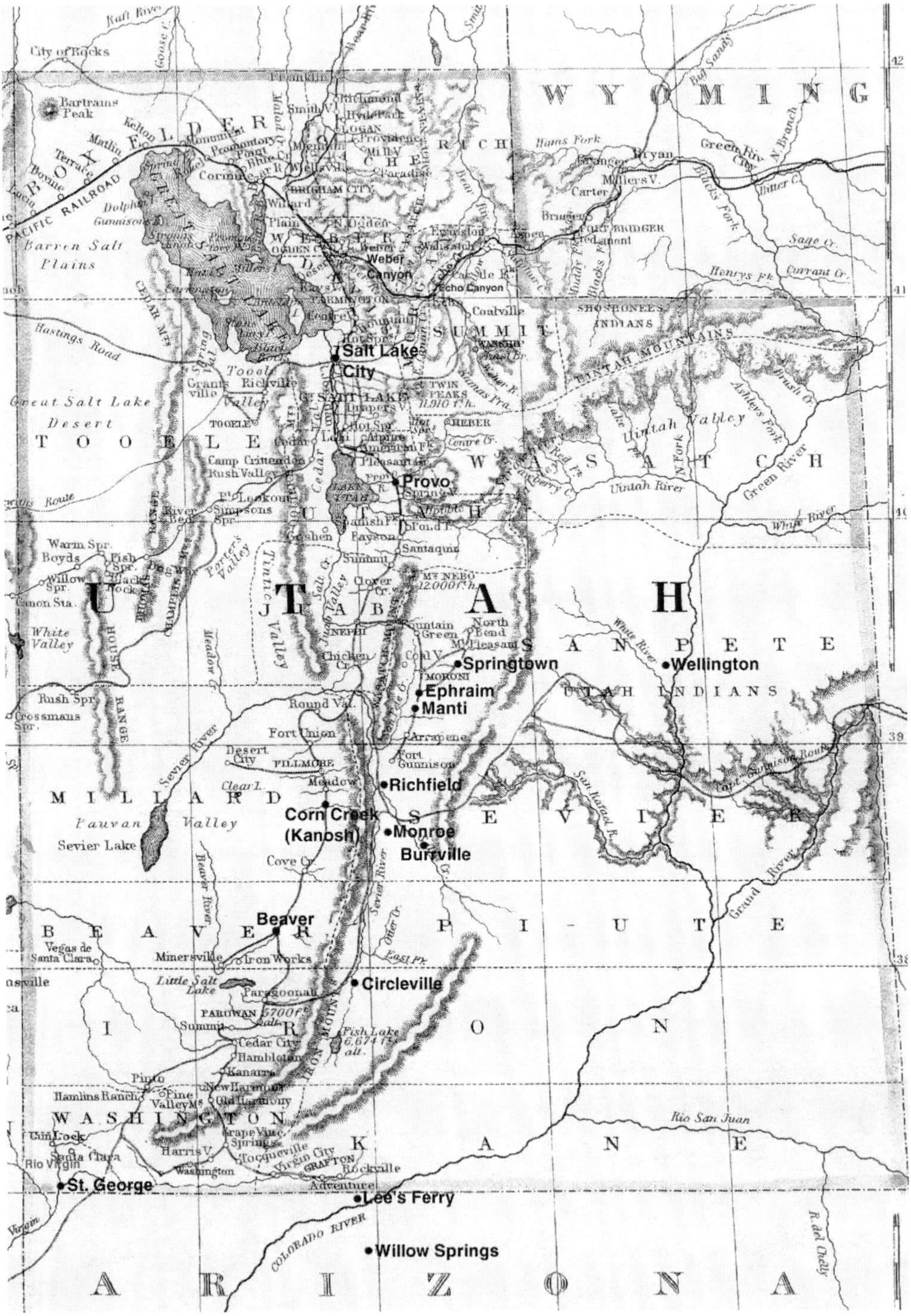

Utah, 1879. From *County Map of Utah and Nevada*, drawn by W. H. Gamble (Philadelphia: S. A. Mitchell).

approximately fifteen thousand Native Americans in Utah were intimidated by the numbers of whites that kept pouring into Utah, despite the partial integration of some influential Ute leaders into the Church of Jesus Christ.[1] The Indians eventually conceded that with proper compensation they would accommodate Mormon settlers in the unsettled mountain valleys. When compensation was withheld or other diversionary tactics untracked Native American prerogatives, they cried foul in the traditional manner; they struck at their oppressors. The displacement in 1861 of the Utes from their traditional Wasatch mountain lands to the Uintah Reservation in northeastern Utah was a particularly aggravating issue to the Indians.

Hostilities beginning that April Sunday in Manti continued for seven years, though the primary period of conflict lasted only through 1867. It was the most destructive confrontation between whites and Native Americans in Utah history both monetarily and in human lives lost.[2] In 1865 Lewis Barney's search for and range of habitation happened to place him in the very center of his second encounter in a Black Hawk War. The Indian conflict would cripple his family, not only in terms of aborting his ambitions to relocate, but also upon the very corpus of his household.

Of course the Native Americans and their white neighbors had lived in close proximity since the 1850s. John Peterson, historian of the war, asserts that as "intertwined as the two societies had become, the Black Hawk War, unlike most Indian wars of the era, was a war fought between acquaintances."[3] Barney himself was an example of this peculiar situation given his tenure near the Spanish Fork Indian Farm. Despite their familiarity, the war aroused fear and hatred within both camps. With scores of stock raids aimed at the settlers' animals and nearly six dozen white deaths over the course of the hostilities, Utah's white population abandoned most of their settlements in the central valleys of the Mormon domain. In turn, the Saints in these most volatile sectors retaliated against the natives in defensive and offensive maneuvers that eventually took about 140 Indian lives.[4]

The day following the Manti scuffle, the first blood of the conflict was shed; a Manti settler was not only killed but desecrated when a long strip of flesh was carved from his back and eaten by the Indians "as some sort of ceremonial opening of hostilities." The same evening two other white settlers were killed in Sevier County's Salina Canyon, including Barney Ward, the veteran Mormon mountain man who had been tromping the area for three decades.[5] That the Indians, with whom he had been interacting for so long, would kill and mutilate Ward, who had an Indian wife, struck horror into the residents of Sanpete and Sevier Valleys. Before the killings got out of hand the Utah militia sent patrols to quell Indian depredations, but the Indian raids did not stop. Tensions and confrontations continued through April and May. When, on 8 June at the Spanish Fork Indian Farm, a treaty was signed between several Ute chiefs and Brigham Young, the settlers gave a collective sigh of relief. Their reprieve was premature.

The Indian assaults continued indiscriminately in Sanpete and Sevier Valleys. The valleys were the field of conflict and the settlers increasingly took defensive measures. "We was under the necessity of building a fort for our protection," wrote Barney, "and also of herding our stock by day and corralling them by night, having to place 10 men on guard of days around our herd for their safety and also a strong guard around the fort and corral of nights." The attention to village security curtailed internal improvements both privately or civically. Preoccupied with protecting life, "forces in making [community] improvements was greatly reduced."[6]

After the initial trouble in Alma, Barney, knowing his family in Springtown was proximate to harm's way, soon returned to the Sanpete settlement to look after his kin. Stress was ubiquitous. "The Indians [in Sanpete Valley] broke out and commenced driving off stock and killing our people where ever they could come across them alone on the roads or in the canyons," he wrote, and "I was obliged to abandon my mill and do the best I could for a living." His primary means of family support was gone with no equivalent substitute available. "Being broken up" by the Indian threat, the effect was, he said, that "I was forced to work for my support by day's work," and, "with the ravages of grasshoppers and continuous depredations of hostile Indians, we was subjected to many privations and almost unendurable trouble."[7]

By July the Indian raids on settlers' stock in Sanpete Valley forced the local defenders into action. Warren S. Snow, Manti's forty-seven-year-old militia general from New Hampshire, ordered Springtown colonel Reddick Allred to organize five or six dozen men to retrieve stolen cattle east of the Sanpete Valley mountains where the Indians fled after their raids. The body left 20 July 1865. "I was selected by our colonel to go as a pilot for this company," Barney wrote, and "although I was by this time beginning to be old, yet I cheerfully complied with the call."[8] A detachment of what was later called the "Green River Expedition," Allred's posse planned to search the Wasatch Plateau's eastern canyons and meet Snow's men on the Price River in Castle Valley.

Scouring the canyons, following "fresh pony tracks," after a few days of monotonous tracking the military expedition rendezvoused with General Snow's force, together now numbering 175 men. They followed the Price River across the barren and desolate valley to Gunnison Ford on the Green River, near the present town of the same name. At the Green they found the Indians had just beaten them there and forded the stolen cattle across the river. A number of eager men were hot to continue the pursuit, but Snow and his officers, considering their poor condition, wisely stopped the chase. Had they continued, they learned later, several dozen Indians with rifles awaited them hidden in the willows and would have decimated the posse while they were in the river.[9] The pursuers turned homeward angered and disappointed.[10] Their failure anticipated other Indian successes that increasingly augmented their confidence against the settlers.

Anxious to get his family and property out of harm's way in Sanpete, Barney ignorantly thought Alma, forty miles south, a safer location than Springtown. In Alma he joined others who simultaneously continued domestic and infrastructure development in the village. That September church apostle Franklin D. Richards, during a lull in Indian hostilities, visited Alma and reported the settlement had "seventy families on town lots, who cultivate twelve hundred acres of land." He said most of the people lived "in dugouts [with] but a few houses above ground." The creek from the eastern mountains watered the farmland, supplemented by "water from the Sevier, which runs two and a half miles west of town, in a ditch ten feet by two feet deep and three and one half miles in length." What a project that was for the villagers! He also described a sixteen by twenty-four foot log meetinghouse, also serving as a schoolhouse.[11] Despite the difficult circumstances created by Indian threat, the town engaged survival tactics.

The Circleville Attack

While Barney buttressed his Alma investment, his sons Walter T. and Henry tried to do the same in Circleville. Leaving Alma, Apostle Richards continued that summer up the Sevier until reaching Circleville which he described being "some two miles above the junction of the east and west forks of the Sevier on the west bank." Richards reported a hundred families lived in the circular valley with fifteen hundred acres of cultivated land. They, too, had a log meetinghouse, twenty by thirty feet. Though his appraisal of the village was optimistic overall, he pointed to two liabilities facing the Saints: (1) they had no flour mill, meaning travel of over a hundred miles to Manti or west over the mountain to Beaver, and (2) because of the valley's lofty elevation frost had destroyed about one-fourth of their crops that season.[12] Part of the optimism that September 1865 came from what was thought at the time to be the end of Indian hostilities. Those in Circleville were soon jolted into the reality of the conflict.

That fall increasingly brash and aggressive Indians became more visible to the Circle Valley settlers. Some villagers, frightened by escalating signs of Indian provocation and isolated from other settlements, decided in November to return to Sanpete. The Barney boys and other resilient ones called the "weak hearted . . . not only cowardly, but wicked, to leave at such a critical time when every man was needed for community protection."[13] Their neighbor's censure and threat of church discipline for abandoning the settlement pricked some to turn around.[14] As subsequent events played out, the justification for their departure was warranted.

The returnees trailed back into Circle Valley, when any passivity formerly displayed by the Indians was discarded. The vulnerability of the returning teams, with their attendant cattle, did not escape the Ute's attention. As the caravan reentered the valley, a dozen or more Indians led by Tamaritz (Shiberetch), an important Ute tribal figure also known by whites as the White Horse Chief, descended from the eastern foothills to the outlying fields driving away the settlers' animals. The cattle raid got out of hand and turned into a small massacre. Two men in the fields were "riddled with bullets and stripped." The body of one of the men killed was brutally mutilated. Two boys out tending cattle were chased and shot, both killed. One of the two, a thirteen-year-old hunting stock about two miles northeast of the settlement, as he tried to outrun the raiders, had part of his head blown away by an Indian's bullet. The thirteen-year-old was Lewis and Betsey's youngest son Orson. The raid was over within an hour. The townsfolk, stunned by the attack, mounted a feeble posse to recapture their cattle only to be repelled in the canyon to the east by Tamaritz, who held them off with a Henry repeating rifle. The day after the attack, the villagers recovered the dead only to find them "stiff and naked" and "filled full of arrows." The village was in shock and rage.[15]

Another of Lewis's children was taken in his youth. "During these days of trouble and sorrow," Barney wrote, "the Indians made a raid on the settlers and killed two men and two boys, one of them being my son Wm. Orson. This gave me much sorrow and grief and also was the cause of much grief to his mother and brothers as also to the entire settlement."[16] One woman who tended to the preparation of the dead boy's body said that to make him look better before his mother saw him, "we stuffed cotton in his hair" where part of his skull had been blown away.[17] The funerals were held on 27 November and "there was mourning and weeping in the settlement for many days afterwards."[18] In the eight months of 1865 since the fighting began, twenty-five settlers had been killed and eight wounded.[19] The hope to contain the outbreak was dashed, the pace of violence and fear only seemed to accelerate.

Despite the death of his son, Barney continued in the vulnerable location of Alma hoping with the others for the war's atmosphere to subside, but it did not. "One morning," probably in early 1866,

> an express arrived in Alma with instructions to raise men to forward it on up to Circleville. Bishop Olsen called on several young men wishing them to take the express letters up to the company stationed at Circleville. They all refused to go saying they would be liable to be scalped at any moment. Besides the [Sevier] River was swimming and they might be drowned.

Their reasoning was sound. Despite their argument Frederick Olson, now the church authority in Alma, stated the communication had to be sent. "I know of a man that would go," the bishop said, "but I do not want to call on him for he has been in the front enough already." "I suspected he had his mind on me," Barney surmised. Asking who it was, the bishop responded to him,

"Well, it is yourself." "Bishop, if you will give me the privilege of selecting three men to go with me and let me ride your mule," Barney replied, "I will deliver the express safe to . . . Circleville." The bishop agreed; Barney selected his companions and he was off.[20]

While they encountered no Indians, the raging Sevier River in the canyon between the valleys was a formidable obstacle. Arriving at the river, Barney said, "It looked fearful, it being up level with the banks, being very rapid and muddy. The appearance rather dampened the courage of my men." Appealing to God, Barney challenged his associates "to give the horses a loose rein and not try to check them while they were swimming and we will throw our lives in the hands of the Lord for safety." It worked. Drenched to their arms, once out of the canyon, they carried on to Circleville arriving at midnight. There Barney reunited with his sons and, finding them well, he stayed for two nights and a day. After his visit, the four from Alma, accompanied by three others from Circleville, retraced their steps to Sevier Valley. Those in Alma, excited to see them, thought them victims of violence due to their delay.[21]

The hostilities continued. Alma stood in a strategic but vulnerable position. George A. Smith, returning to Salt Lake City after a late winter mission to southern Utah to organize the Saints there militarily, visited Alma on 25 March 1866. He found a settlement of thirty-six families "scattered all over the town plot." Most of them, he reported, lived "in holes in the ground with dirt roofs, as the Indian war has prevented them from getting timber in the mountains." He saw they were ill-prepared for what awaited them. With just "23 guns and several revolvers" among them, their naivete was all too apparent. He said that when he suggested "they would be safer in a fort than in that scattered situation," his audience met the recommendation with "wonder." Smith said, "they are almost wholly defenceless and perfectly unconscious" of their precarious situation.[22]

Barney was called upon in April 1866 by Alma's leaders to undertake another express mission, similarly risky, to the Circleville venture, to inform Orson Hyde in Sanpete Valley of Alma's situation. Notwithstanding "it was considered unsafe to travel that road with less than 25 men," Barney and two others, including the bishop, dashed their way to Springtown without incident. On their return from Sanpete, "three or four miles above Richfield," Barney wrote, "we saw two persons [on] horse back. We supposed them to be Indians." But studying carefully the men's mannerisms, they concluded them to be white men. Feeling more confident as they rode toward them, "we then put our hats on our ramrods and waived them over our heads and motioned to them to come to us." As they got closer, "who should it be but brother Walter Barney and George Robinson." Relieved, both parties shared information, but Walter was anxious. Walter told his brother that while he was on the express to Sanpete, Alma had been attacked.[23]

At about midnight on 21 April 1866, while taking his turn at guard duty, Walter "was walking around the corral [and] discovered something in the shade close to the corral." "All at once," he reported, "there sprung up 15 or 20 Indians and started off as fast as they could run." He shot at them three times, but they raced "to Andrew Rasmussen's corral where he had some stock and killed his cattle and some sheep, then made for the mountains."[24] The attack changed things for the Sevier Valley settlers. "Soon after this," Barney said, "we received orders to take the women and children to Richfield and let the men stay and take care of their crops and stock and keep a strong guard at the fort."[25] Their exposure and the very real danger they faced finally countered their nescience.

The Circleville Massacre

A day or two after Barney and his companions returned to Alma from their Sanpete mission, a related incident—"the greatest single tragedy of the Black Hawk War"—occurred in Circleville, showing the scope of terror and extreme measures taken by the settlers during the Black Hawk uprising.[26] An express making it to Springtown described simultaneous attacks on Alma and Circleville occurring about 23 or 24 April 1866. Reddick Allred relaying the report stated that when "men from Richfield and Glenwood pursued the Indians . . . at the corner of Marysvale field" they "were fired upon by the Indians killing Alfred Lewis and wounding three others." In the attack upon Circleville, the raiders took "twenty-five head of cattle, two mules and two horses." While they were chased into a canyon by the settlers, the whites "could do nothing as the Indians had secured positions" making it suicidal to pursue them. Further Allred reported "the Indians had fired upon two of our men at Pear Creek around Circleville, wounding one slightly in the neck."[27]

Given the deadly Indian raid the previous fall and the most recent attack, the isolated Circleville settlers that spring were more than anxious. Nearby, a band of Piede Indians who had no record of belligerence aroused the suspicion of the settlers who thought them in collusion with the Ute raiders. The Circleville militia surrounded the camp numbering about twenty, including women and children, and hauled them into the settlement until a decision could be made about their futures.[28] Allred reported the captive Indians were tied "hand and foot," and imprisoned.[29] Oluf Christian Larsen, a thirty-year-old Norwegian Circlevillian watching over the Indians, wrote, "we marched the men into the meetinghouse and placed them under guard. Later we moved the squaws and children and belongings into a vacant cellar with guards watching them. The Indians," Larsen continued, "were seated with sticks across the small of their backs and their elbows back of the sticks were tied to the sticks. While close together with blankets across their shoulders they untied each other and were loose, ready to make their escape as soon as it was dark." Making "a bold break for their liberty," all at once, they "pulled the sticks from their arms, sprang for the guards and tried to knock them down." To protect themselves, the guards "were forced to shoot." Nine male Piedes died, but the killing did not stop in the so-called "escape." Later five women and two older children were dispatched as well. Only four children were spared. It was an awful scene.[30] The townspeople having recently endured raids on their animals, the killing of their neighbors, and mounting fear felt justified in what was done. Others, including Brigham Young, thought the action extreme and unwarranted.[31] Despite the war conditions surrounding the killings, the "Circleville Massacre" remains a controversial part of Utah history.[32]

Alma, partially evacuated, maintained a tenuous existence. Barney's tenure there in 1865–1866, "in consequence of the trouble with the Indians," had been without his family's company. "I was on guard most of the time for near four months being exposed to danger and hard ships of every kind; my clothing worn out, no shoes on my feet, no provisions to eat."[33] Black Hawk's war, now over a year in duration, had accomplished a number of the Indians' objectives. White settlement in the interior valleys of Utah was stemmed. Indeed, a number of communities were completely abandoned. Richfield, the principal Sevier Valley community, became the refugee camp for Alma and Glenwood residents during the summer of 1866.[34] Circleville finally emptied in June 1866. Some from the community returned to Sanpete. Others moved west over the Tushar Mountains to the town of Beaver. Barney lamented the effect this measure had upon his own family. "The Saints at Circleville divided; part coming down the [Sevier] River, the other part going over the mountain to Beaver, my folks at Circleville going with the company over the mountain to Beaver."[35] The residual effect of this move changed the structure of Barney's family ever after. "By this move my family become separated and have not been located together up to this day—May 1880," the time when he recorded the account.[36] With Betsey's boys moving to their own impulses, thereafter, Barney focused his energy and resources on Elizabeth's family. Having Betsey's sons physically distanced from him served as Barney's chronic lament throughout the remainder of his life.

As aggressive Indian raids intensified in Sevier Valley, even Alma's guard, of which Barney was one, terminated. Continuing Indian hostilities created a situation requiring Brigham Young to dissolve the Sevier River settlements, including the Richfield refugee camp, in the spring of 1867. "It was a very sad, yet a very colorful caravan which left Alma, to be joined by other settlers until the company totalled more than 200 wagons."[37] When Barney arrived in Springtown, he said,

> I found the settlement of Springtown had been broken up and the people moved into Fort Ephraim where I also found my folks. They

> was destitute of clothing and provisions and 25 dollars in debt. They had sold a set of shingle mill irons to help themselves with. I got a load of freight off a merchant to take to Salt Lake City which payed the 25 dollars and left me 50 dollars with which I bought clothing and provisions.

After securing means to reestablish himself and family, he said, "We soon returned to Springtown."[38]

Despite the difficulties the Indian war created for Lewis Barney, including relocation and more significantly the death of his son, his long-term pattern of goodwill toward the local Indians may have saved his life during this period. Barney's son Arthur recounts the story of his encountering a band of Indians who, when they noticed the lone traveler driving his oxen, appeared bent on mischief. The oxen were distinctive in their appearance and coloration, "one being amuley, and the other a red spotted one." Closing to a distance where they recognized Barney or his oxen, the Utes soon disappeared and let him continue unmolested. The younger Barney said his father believed that because he "was well known by all the Utes on account of his kindness to them, and feeding all that came around, and by being on friendly terms with them in times of peace," that his earlier friendship "kept the Utes from killing him."[39]

With many of the Sevier refugees returning to their former residences, the conditions causing Orson Hyde to encourage new settlements in 1863 were now exacerbated in Springtown. The omnipresent poverty, lack of provisions and clothing in the Sanpete settlements clouded the future. Because of Barney's earlier designs on the Sevier River Valley, he previously liquidated his Springtown improvements, meaning upon his return to the Sanpete Valley he "had no house nor land in the settlement." But, he said, still having "my sawmill and house . . . in Oak Creek Canyon, I went to work getting my house out of the canyon." Fear of Indian menace was so great that "the Colonel [probably Reddick Allred] on learning that I was going into the canyon every day forbid me doing so saying, 'you are liable to be killed with the Indians,' and if I did not stop it he would place a guard over me." Under the circumstances, Barney could not submit to such a demand. "I had no house, but the wagon, and no material to make one," but, he said, "I was bound to have one, even at the risk of my life." The clandestine manner in which he removed his house from the canyon was on this wise: "I would be at work with the men all day. Then about sun[set], two hours high in the evening, start for the canyon, coming home [at] 10 or 11 o'clock in the night. By this means I got a house for my family. In the same way I managed to get timber for my portion of the fort that had to be built around the town."[40]

The killing in August 1867 of two Springtown men kept local citizens tense and fearful. A yoke of Barney's oxen turned up missing, leaving Barney believing Indians had rustled them, but a village patrol spotted the animals in the canyon and informed Barney about their find. While recovering his oxen, he encountered several barking dogs. From the dogs, Barney "could smell the Indians," which hastened his return to the village. Neglecting to immediately report the incident, he received censure from townsfolk, in particular an "Englishman by the name of Ellis." Barney explained with "so many false reports" circulating he didn't think an encounter with dogs merited exciting the villagers. Joseph T. Ellis, thirty-nine and influential in Springtown, screamed, "You orto have your ass kicked." Barney, even though twenty years Ellis's senior, snorted, "Maby you would like to have the job of kicking it." While Ellis backed down, the incident illustrates the anxiety among the settlers created by the Indian threat.[41]

Just at the time, it seemed, that Barney and his family recreated their niche in Springtown, Indian depredations decreased in the Sanpete-Sevier area by the end of 1867. Erstwhile Sevier Valley residents noised their plans of relocating to their Sevier Valley homes. As early as March 1868, some from Alma cautiously plotted their return. Soon a company of twenty-three, including Lewis and Walter Barney, with a dozen teams and wagons, pulled out of Springtown to resettle Alma. As they approached Cedar Ridge, near present-day Vermillion in Sevier Valley, thirty Indians intercepted them. Walter took a ball in the shin, penetrating his pants and boot. The incident cooled their enthusiasm to resettle Alma at the time and they hurried back to Sanpete.[42]

Forced to wrest a living out of Springtown's reluctant environment, under the difficult circumstances of war, the villagers' problems multiplied in the harvest of 1868. "The grasshoppers put in their appearance and destroyed our crops."[43] The plague spared no one in the region and reminded many of the hard hit taken by the settlers in the mid-1850s. Springtown's infestation was particularly dreadful. "It seemed," Barney lamented, "that every avenue was closed and the Saints cut off from supplies." With little recourse now but faith, Barney said that despite their dilemma, "the Lord who had brought them safe through all their troubles had not forsaken them."[44] The manner in which this product of faith was manifest could never have been guessed by the Sanpete settlers.

The Transcontinental Railroad

Toward the end of May 1868, Orson Hyde, still church supervisor in Sanpete, wrote to Brigham Young stating, "Much of our wheat in this settlement is eaten off by the grasshoppers; consequently, several are ready to go to work on the rail road."[45] The railroad he spoke of was, of course, the road of iron rails then being built to connect the country. Its importance that spring was significant to not only the desert Saints: "next to winning the Civil War and abolishing slavery, building the first transcontinental railroad, from Omaha, Nebraska, to Sacramento, California, was the greatest achievement of the

American people in the nineteenth century."[46] Its construction became a national priority. Just before Abraham Lincoln's election, he told Grenville Dodge, one of the Union Pacific promoters, "There was nothing more important before the nation than the building of the railroad to the Pacific."[47] As early as 1853 government surveyors traversed the mountains and deserts of Utah to plot the best route across the intermountain area for a railway that would unite the coasts. Brigham Young, from the outset, welcomed a rail connection joining America's disparate geography.[48] An ancillary reason for constructing the road played into an ironic twist for the Mormons. General William Tecumseh Sherman, Civil War hero and promoter of the Union Pacific project, stated: "I regard this road as the solution of the Indian affairs and the Mormon question."[49] Eastern influentials planned a feature of the railway to be the subjugation of the Saints.

Slowly the operation took shape and by the mid-1860s the machinery to join the vast continent was engaged in earnest. The well-known race by teams from the east and west to grade and lay track pushed toward Utah in 1868. By this time it was clear to Union Pacific executives that to make a good showing in their contest with the Central Pacific, they required Mormon assistance. Brigham Young's help was first solicited by Union Pacific officials on 6 May 1868, by telegraph, offering a contract to the Mormons. Young affirmatively answered within the hour.[50] The plan called for the the Saints to grade fifty-four miles of road from the Wasatch Mountains into the Great Basin. (A gentile contractor graded Utah's first fifty miles, preceding the Mormon contract.) The contract for the Saints provided a summer and fall of work. For this they would receive beside wages, "powder, shovels, picks, sledges, wheelbarrows, scrapers, crowbars, and other necessary tools at cost plus freight charges."[51]

It did not escape Young that eastern interests used the railway as a tool to influence the center of Mormonism. He had long been interested in its completion. The economic windfall from the Saints' participation loomed very attractive at the time and the Mormon contract precluded most non-Mormon workers from interloping into the heart of Zion.[52] Moreover, John W. Young, the prophet's son and one of the primary Mormon labor contractors, believed "that the building of this Railroad is one of the greatest achievements ever accomplished by Latter Day Saints and will realy do more good in giveing us influence with the World than anything we have ever done."[53] Like the arrival of the U.S. Army ten years earlier, the railway ironically reinforced the objectives of the Saints despite the ostensible negatives of its construction.

The railroad's arrival in Utah provoked and was coincident with other significant territorial events. Formal treaties were signed in August 1868 between Ute leaders and the territory Indian superintendent settling the three-year Black Hawk War, though sporadic raids in central Utah valleys continued for several years.[54] The last year of Mormon overland immigration travel by wagon and team was 1868. Over seventy thousand had endured the ordeal of dust, disease, and death since 1847. Those who came thereafter could crowd their belongings into railcars and travel in the comparative comfort of railway passenger cars from the East to the mountain valleys. Anticipating an infusion of non-Mormon influence into northern Utah valleys, potentially diluting latter-day Israel's objectives, church leaders inaugurated among the Saints several features of retrenchment and fortification. These included the churchwide reinstitution of women's Relief Society and an auxiliary effort to bolster and retain the loyalty of Mormon youth. To provide a market for local and eastern goods and to build a spirit of community cooperation, Zion's Cooperative Mercantile Institution (ZCMI) and its local branches were established throughout the territory beginning in 1868. Most communities had one of these general stores to service Mormon customers. The railroad was a significant milestone in Utah and the Church of Jesus Christ's history because the central barrier of assimilation into American culture—limited access—was removed for Mormons and non-Mormons alike.

At the height of grasshopper infestation of 1868, Orson Hyde's 27 May letter to Brigham Young asked for particulars regarding the railroad contract currently being noised about the settlements. The contract's announcement, appearing in Salt Lake City's *Deseret News* the same day that Hyde wrote Young, indicated that caution was required in supplying manpower to the railroad project. Bishops were responsible to see that sufficient numbers within the settlements stay to "preserve that which . . . has [been] sown and planted" not already destroyed by the grasshoppers. Hyde informed Young that the "more responsible men" in the communities would likely stay at home to take care of harvest and civic matters. Those not required to sustain the settlements would go "to the Railroad and work for money." These men, before signing up wanted "to know where they are to work, when to begin, and the wages they are to receive per day."[55] Barney, apparently not among "the more responsible men" of the community, "together with Brother Walter [Barney], Moses Gifford, George Robison, John Zabriskie, and my son Arthur started for the railroad to find work for our support in these times of famine and trouble."[56]

This was a significant undertaking for the Sanpete Saints, as well as those from other Utah valleys. The rail route was nearly two hundred miles north of Sanpete Valley. It required another relocation for Barney family members. With little advance planning, the Mormon work force deployment was somewhat chaotic. Four thousand of the Saints initially responded to the opportunity.[57] On 8 June 1868, three of Brigham Young's sons, serving as their father's agents, left Salt Lake City for the head of Echo Canyon to coordinate the contract and distribution of work. Two days later the Union Pacific engineers completed their survey of the canyon and that morning broke ground for the Echo Canyon project.[58] The Saints began to fill the canyon with workers, successors to the ten thousand Orientals, Irishmen, and others who had pushed the line from the East and from the West.

As Mormons clamored for work, many were initially disappointed. For Barney and those who accompanied him, they found upon meeting with two of Young's sons "that there was not sufficient work to accommodate all that had applied." Brigham, Jr., and Joseph A. Young advised them "to go down the [Weber] river to [John] Reedhead's camp and they [the Youngs] would see Reedhead and get work for us for a few days until there would be work laid off so we could get a job of our own." With Reedhead they worked for $1.50 a day plus board.[59] Reedhead's crew was one of forty-five camps in Echo Canyon that summer.

Reedhead's project neared completion by August.[60] The Barneys had to find other employment. Now sixty years old, Barney found he had to scavenge work himself. After their work for Reedhead, "in a few days Moses Gifford and myself went down to Croydon to try and get a timber contract that we had heard of but we failed to get it. But as they wanted to hire a man to hew a lot of timber I engaged with them to hew that lot for three dollars a day and board." But, "after I had been to work a few days they wanted me to take the contract myself so I took the contract and employed John Zabriskie, Brother Walter, and his son Walter to help finish up the job which lasted about three weeks."[61] Thereafter, Barney's railroad work became a series of contracts. With the three-week task complete, "we then fell in with a company that was making a road up the canyon to get into a heavy body of timber 4 or 5 miles above." Joining in partnership with four others, they did $2,500 worth of road work. "After completion of the road," he wrote, "we went to work getting out ties and bridge timber for the railroad on our own responsibility, which we disposed of to good advantage, clearing from 5 to 7 dollars per day. But provisions being high, as also clothing, our wages was principally consumed in the support of ourselves and families."[62]

Not having accumulated money sufficient to sustain his family, Barney planned to spend the winter in the canyon doing what he had been doing since summer, but Arthur became ill and needed more attention than his father could give him under the circumstances. Returning with Arthur to Spanish Fork where Elizabeth was temporarily living at the time, he found her "in great trouble in consequence of one of the children being very sick." The sick child was their youngest child, thirteen-month-old daughter, little Harriet Viola. The little girl, reaching for a cup on a table, fell into a large kettle of hot water just removed from the fire that her mother had placed under the table. The scalding was so severe, she "continued to grow worse and in a few days [23 October 1868]," Barney lamented, "we had the mortification of seeing her breathe her last."[63]

The pathetic situation inclined him to stay with his heartbroken wife after he laid his child to rest, but his family's meager circumstances forced him to return to the railroad with Elizabeth and her children in tow. The expedition north was an ordeal in itself and after their arrival he set up some semblance of home life in Dry Creek Canyon. The north–south draw, which opened on the north side of the Weber River a half-mile from Devil's Slide, was just a few miles west of Henefer where the Mormon vanguard turned south on the final and most difficult leg of their journey into the Salt Lake Valley in 1847. The area was rugged. "I continued all winter working in the canyon getting out timbers," complained Barney, "working every day up to my knees and frequently up to my hips in the snow coming to my cabin dripping wet in the evenings." Despite the difficulty, he "was making high wages which induced me to expose my health to provide means for my support in these times of Utah's famine."[64]

By the middle of January 1869, the track had been completed to Echo, a little railroad boomtown at the canyon's mouth. A week later, in the Weber Canyon narrows, the milestone of a continuous stretch of iron totaling a thousand miles from Omaha, Nebraska, was reached. By 8 March 1869, Mormon work on the track was completed to Ogden, Utah, forty miles north of Salt Lake City.[65] Brigham Young's understanding at the Echo Canyon project's outset was that the railway would cross south of the Great Salt Lake thereby insuring a station in the capital city, which, of course, was important to the Saints. As the project continued westward, the Union Pacific's engineers had other ideas. They concluded a northern route would cut the distance by sixty or seventy miles by grading north of the lake rather than going through Salt Lake City. Their course would take them through Ogden and over Promontory Summit. Young, angry at first, quickly determined a southern spur would rectify the wrong and accepted the decision. Within eight months, the Mormon-owned Utah Central Railroad made Salt Lake City the primary station in Utah.[66]

While the railway's completion finalized the competition on 10 May 1869, maintenance on the hastily finished project was required. After a cold, wet winter Barney said, "In the spring of 1869 I moved out of Dry Creek Canyon and around by Mountain Green and went up Cottonwood Canyon [in a northeasterly direction] about 10 miles and entered into partnership with Edward Rumsey to get out bridge timber and ties for the railroad company. Here I cleared about 500 dollars through the summer."[67] Dissolving his partnership with Rumsey at summer's end, apparently believing he had accumulated enough to reestablish himself and family, Barney gathered up his family and returned to Springtown.

Upon his arrival in Sanpete, "I found the country full of grasshoppers and everything devoured by them and not a morsel of bread or anything else to be had to sustain life." While others in Springtown, present to nurture their crops, were probably not as adversely affected as was Barney, his personal prospect for a successful harvest was dismal. "Consequently," he said, "we were under the necessity of going back to work on the railroad." Upon returning to Weber Canyon, he teamed with another man "getting out and hauling spikes and ties. At this I made 500 dollars." It was time to go home again, finally.[68]

Barney's venture in the most significant transportation project of modern man, a project that impacted the nation as well as Utah, was finished. After the significant personal and economic reversals of the mid-1860s, the godsend of railroad construction provided the means for Barney to refurbish his family economically. The Mormon workers replenished not only their personal coffers, their skill and work ethic helped the railroad company and consequently the nation. The noted nineteenth-century western American historian Hubert Howe Bancroft wrote two decades after the project's completion that "it was acknowledged by all railroad men that nowhere on the line could the grading compare in completeness and finish with the work done by the people of Utah."[69] Barney then returned to what he knew best, coaxing life out of the Mormon frontier.

Upon his return to Sanpete Valley the autumn of 1869, he "got a city lot and 10 acres of farming land," and "went into [Oak Creek] Canyon in the winter, cut, scored, and hewed a set of house logs and put me up a house and moved my house out of the fort on the lot."[70] No one could predict the pacification of the Native Americans and, while he still had designs on Alma, he poured his family's energy into a Springtown future.

And his family was still growing. Now in his early sixties, Barney fathered his last child before his final winter in Weber Canyon. Late the next spring, Elizabeth bore William Edward Barney on 7 June 1870 in Springtown. That year's census showed Lewis's family in Springtown consisted of himself; his wives Betsey, 61 (who had rejoined her husband after his return from Weber Canyon), and Elizabeth, 40; along with Elizabeth's five children, Arthur (18), Martha (13), David (8), Sarah Emeline (6), and William Edward (one month). His assets were $400 in real estate and $200 in personal estate, not much to show for sixty-two years.[71] His two younger brothers Walter and William also lived with their families nearby. The brothers had comparable assets to their older brother. Lewis's stepmother Deborah Barney was also there, still living with her son William after Charles's death five years earlier.[72]

Just as Lewis recreated his Springtown niche, some of Alma's former settlers, restless to return, decided to venture again to the abandoned community. Since 1868 there had been only isolated confrontations with Native Americans who became more resigned to their fate.[73] In November 1870 six men reentered the settlement which had been switched on and off several times since its beginning in 1863. They stirred around and made some improvements. Some decided to stay the winter in Alma. It was a gutsy, determined measure but the potential held by Alma for a prosperous settlement was a compelling lure. The stop and start pattern of the vacated community was about to end.

Chapter 17

A Frontier Village: Monroe, Utah, 1871–1874

Utah, at the beginning of the 1870s, was significantly dissimilar from the Utah two decades earlier. The population had increased by nearly eight times and was approaching 87,000. Almost 250 Mormon settlements and cities dotted Utah, southern Idaho, southern Nevada, and northern Arizona. Technological advances in communication and transportation accounted for much of the change. In 1850 Utahns viewed the outside world primarily through the weekly *Deseret News.* With the short-lived Pony Express in 1860 followed by the telegraph in 1861, Mormon settlements within Utah's valleys had timely access to information previously delayed for weeks or months. The contemporary world became more relevant. The advent of the railroad had a dramatic impact on immigration, but, maybe as importantly, a consumer market in Utah formed that altered attitudes and forced issues which were of much less consequence before 1869. The word *modern* was packed with more meaning for Utah's citizens than just a decade earlier. Of course technological progress was more acute on the urban populace in Salt Lake City, Ogden, and Provo than the arteries of rural colonies stretching north and south from the Wasatch Front. Before the 1870s passed, many of the outlying villages and hamlets of Mormondom accessed the world through new eyes.

Kanosh

Lewis and Betsey's three sons Walter T., Henry, and Joseph, who followed their father to Circleville in the early 1860s, separated from the family in the mid-1860s to make their own way in Circleville. James Henry, at twenty-six, and Joseph, twenty, both married in 1866.[1] The time when every son must distinguish himself from his father, usually by venturing on his own, was a collective experience for Barney's older sons. The boys severed, no doubt reluctantly, their proximate continuity with their father. Try as they might to coddle their farms in Circleville into production, it was not their ignorance of horticulture nor lack of work ethic that drove them from Circleville. The continued threat of Black Hawk's raiders finally forced Lewis's sons out of

Joseph Smith Barney (Lewis Barney's son) and family. Photographer unknown, ca. 1885. Collection of Ronald O. Barney.

Circle Valley. From Circleville they relocated over the mountain, twenty-plus miles northwest to Beaver.[2]

The southern Utah village of Beaver, first settled in 1856, grew from veterans of Little Salt Lake Valley's Iron Mission in southern Utah. With the refugee influx from the Indian war, the community incorporated in 1867 and connected to the Deseret Telegraph line that same year. Adobe homes dotted the valley. The comparatively large number of new residents severely taxed the already enervated community. Despite the "rich range land, soil, and growing conditions for pasture grasses" and the "temperate climate," Beaver struggled during this period.[3] The less-than-encouraging situation probably made a poor first impression on the Barney brothers. Their stay was short.

Not giving Beaver much of a chance, the Barney boys moved fifty miles northeast to Pahvant Valley's southern end, site of the Corn Creek Indian Farm established in 1856. The Tushar range drainage, then the domain of Chief Kanosh's Pahvant tribe, had been inhabited by the Fremont Indian culture as many as eight hundred years earlier.[4] Father Escalante reported the valley in 1776 to be "a vast plain surrounded by sierras . . . [where,] although two rivers enter it . . . we saw no place whatever suitable for settlement."[5] Geographically, the valley served as the western base of the Pahvant Plateau, "a platform aver-

James Henry Barney (Lewis Barney's son). Photographer and date unknown. Courtesy of Merlene Olsen.

aging between 8,000 and 8,500 feet in elevation [with] higher ridges reaching a little above 10,000 feet," lording over the plain below.[6] Once under Lake Bonneville's waters, the valley soil left when the lake receded was fertile for those who first saw promise in the area. The Mormons, not as picky as their Catholic predecessors, thought the Pahvant region suitable for settlement. Passing through the Pahvant Valley in early 1850 with a band of exploring brethren, Parley P. Pratt reported the valley "sufficient to sustain the present population of Rhode Island."[7]

While Pratt exaggerated, by the mid-1860s the townsite of Kanosh, seventeen miles south of Fillmore, appealed as a settlement to several families. (Fillmore was once designed to be the territorial capital of Utah because of its central location to Utah settlements.) The village named after the Pahvant chief whose band still inhabited the area, Kanosh was first colonized by white settlers in 1867. Kanosh first attracted thirty or forty families from the Panguitch, Circleville, and Petersburg areas and another dozen households relocated from elsewhere. By March 1869 a Latter-day Saint ward functioned in the community. Among the earliest settlers, who located homesites by lottery, were the Barneys. Kanosh's tribe's displacement in 1869 to the Uintah Basin Indian Reservation portended white permanence in the area.[8]

Kanosh became home for Betsey Barney in the late 1860s, coincident to the time her sons Walter T., James Henry, and Joseph moved there. If Lewis had a purpose in Kanosh beyond relocating his wife, it is not known. Though he obtained land, he apparently never worked it, his preoccupation centering in Sevier Valley. Thereafter, though they could not know it at the time, Betsey and Lewis were separated physically for most of the rest of their lives. The separation, broken only by brief and infrequent interludes, continued over the next quarter century.[9] Later Walter T. and Joseph themselves moved on from Kanosh, but James Henry, apparently after a short try at Monroe in the early 1870s, remained in Kanosh until his death in 1911.[10]

Sevier River Valley

Brigham Young, in the summer of 1870, gave permission to settlers to resettle Sevier Valley.[11] Some of Alma's former residents returned to their homes the following spring. Barney, undoubtedly monitoring progress in the village, arranged to reclaim his farm "in the fall of 1871."[12] "As times were very hard and money scarce," nineteen-year-old Arthur wrote, "Father took me and started for Monroe [Alma], Sevier County, with a span of old roan horses and a span of mules—one mule we called Jack and the other Hunchback."[13] Returning to his property, quiet for four years, Lewis said, "I made another start for a home, making water sects, grubbing, and clearing of 14 acres of land."[14] His claim required much work.

Monroe, Utah, 1999. Photograph by Ronald O. Barney.

The valley of the Sevier held great potential for human habitation. Had the conflict between the settlers and the Native Americans been quickly resolved, the valley in the 1860s would have been quickly populated. In 1848 Orville C. Pratt, an Illinois attorney commissioned by the U.S. government to handle a western military matter, while on his way to California and Oregon from New Mexico, passed through Sevier Valley and left an early glimpse of the valley's surpassing charm. Following the Old Spanish Trail through eastern Utah, in late September 1848 he and his party camped at the Sevier River. Bounded on the east by the Sevier Plateau within which are found Signal and Monroe peaks both over 11,200 feet in elevation, the valley was formed by the Pahvant Plateau providing the western horizon. The uninhabited valley was visionarily idyllic.[15] "The valley of the Sevier, where we struck it," Pratt wrote on 26 September, "is the finest I have seen since leaving the United States. Many thousand of acres of the best of bottom land all lie in a body." The next day he exulted, "This valley of the Sevier is truly the loveliest spot, all things considered, my eyes ever looked upon!" He followed with this prediction: "Some day or other, & that not *distant*, it will swarm with hundreds of our enterprising countrymen and be regarded, as in truth it is, the garden of the great basin of the California mountains."[16]

Pratt's prophecy was confirmed the following year by another Pratt, Parley Parker. Interested in just what it was that the Saints had inherited in 1847, Brigham Young sent Mormon apostle Parley P. Pratt in 1849 through Utah's central and southern valleys on an expedition of discovery. Pratt, heading the "Southern Exploring Company" took his company of forty-seven men into the Sevier Valley early in December and followed the river upstream into Circle Valley. The apostle's report to Young regarding the valley encouraged settlement,[17] but establishing a northern Utah foothold postponed settlement efforts along the Sevier River until the mid-1860s. Varying from just under a mile high in the northern part of the valley to just over a mile in elevation in the southern sector, early reports of the valley during settlement were encouraging:

> Timber in the kanyons at the head of Sevier and also on the hills on the lower Sevier is abundant and of fair quality. Grass is also plentiful on the upper Sevier, but not so much in the valley, although in that vicinity there is excellent range on the hills. . . . The Sevier country is a splendid locality for raising garden produce of every kind. Vegetables seemed to be more abundant and of a better quality than in much older settlements.[18]

As word spread, Sevier's erstwhile settlers were joined by new immigrants hopeful for permanence on the Mormon frontier.

Many of Alma's returnees made their temporary homes in the abandoned fort, but as the weather allowed for working the land, those in the fort moved to their former lots and the process of community building started anew. A post office was applied for and named after America's fifth president. The name Monroe soon identified the hamlet. As if the settlement had something of a history, the old names of South Bend and Alma were no more. In addition to the work of refurbishing housing and farms, the municipal infrastructure, through water and land distribution and regulation, roads, and community buildings, required work and more work. It was an enterprise of sweat. Life in the growing settlement was also leavened by distractions, like baseball, introduced in 1871 by a Scandinavian immigrant who had learned the game in Chicago en route to Utah. A gardener's club was also organized in Monroe and "one night each week [was] devoted to the delivering of lectures and entertaining subjects."[19]

Monroe's reconstitution coincided with the replenishing of other Sevier Valley communities. Richfield, Salina, Glenwood, Joseph, and Monroe all functioned in the 1860s. Annabella, Vermillion, Central, Venice, Elsinore, Aurora, and Redmond emerged in the 1870s once the valley reopened to settlement. Richfield, the county seat, sparked by a few returning families in November 1870, remained the valley's dominant and largest community.[20] Of course, consistent with the territory's Mormon pattern, a structured church organization began simultaneous with village development. Tied as units of the Sevier Stake, Monroe and other valley settlements were governed religiously and civically from Richfield, located ten miles north of Monroe. Brigham Young's talented eldest son Joseph A. Young, just thirty-seven years old, was appointed by his father as the valley's presiding authority.[21]

In Monroe, second largest of Sevier's settlements, the dual leadership of church and community centered in Lewis Barney's railroad partner Moses Gifford. As more and more settlers, preponderantly Mormon, expanded the townsite, a Sunday School organization was instituted early in 1872 with forty-five officers and teachers (including Barney's son Joseph) and 126 students. The schoolhouse, used for all public purposes, held church services until 1875. For the women, a Relief Society was organized in 1872, a relatively new feature for the church's sisters in Utah.[22] These significant facets of religious practice opened participation to the Mormon laity previously unavailable.

By 1872 eighty families called Monroe home, in contrast to the 150 families in Richfield, 75 households in Glenwood, and 33 in Salina. Twenty-three other families also lived in other parts of the valley.[23] That same year the telegraph line linked Monroe to the northern Utah valleys. Monroe correspondents to the *Deseret News* regularly reported community development, lauding the quality of life and inviting prospective settlers with statements like, "There is still a large quantity of good land that could be brought under cultivation upon which good people are invited to settle."[24] The reluctance for growth held by Alma's leader in the 1860s was not retained by village leaders refurbishing the settlement.

Upon their arrival in Monroe that fall of 1871, the Barneys made quarters in the old fort while reinvigorating their land. After borrowing five dollars from "an old miner" near Marysvale, Barney bought four bushels of wheat to restart his venture. Together Lewis and Arthur "cleared off a patch of land by grubbing up greasewoods with a grubbing hoe," and after burning the brush "sowed the 4 bushels of wheat on 11 acres of land." The land, "very loose and mellow . . . did not need plowing." Remarkably, according to Arthur, "you could kick your foot into the soil clear to your shoe tops."[25] Besides the wheat, they planted potatoes and other subsistence vegetables to sustain them when harvested. Once the planting was completed Lewis left Arthur to watch their investment and improvements and returned to Springtown to retrieve Elizabeth and her children.[26] Upon his return to Sanpete, Barney found his "folks out of provisions." Reduced to exiguous living yet again, a recurrent cycle broken only occasionally since the 1840s, and with no capital or assets to build upon, Barney "took a job of getting out timber" in Oak Creek Canyon, once his domain. He netted "120 dollars. This job took me till harvest [1872] to finish it up."[27]

Monroe did not wait for Barney's return to capitalize on the momentum rebuilding their village. The optimistic and industrious settlers provided for infrastructure development by building saw- and gristmills and advertised for more settlers. Regular news reports from Monroe appeared in the *Deseret News* in 1872 touting the locale and its progress. In January readers learned about the village's cultural advances. May's installment boasted, "There is neither profanity nor drunkedness in [the] locality and the people are all engaged in minding their own business." Utahns were notified in July, "Our cooperative store is in a good condition and doing considerable business." Each of the reports contained a similar appeal for "good people" to settle the "large quantity of good land." One community leader in late summer claimed "a better or more united people he has never been acquainted with" and "that a few years of assiduous labor will transform it into the richest and most [prosperous] locality in the territory, south of Salt Lake City."[28] While their initial expectations were overly optimistic, it was not unrealistic to hope for a settlement where a family could sink a deep root.

Not yet ready to transport Elizabeth and her children to Sevier Valley, Lewis returned to Monroe to find that "from the 4 bushels of seed we had over 300 bushels of nice, clean wheat," with "a good crop of corn and potatoes and garden stuff sufficient for our supply until the next harvest."[29] When Lewis's family moved to Monroe, later joined by brothers Walter and Benjamin, his stepmother and her thirty-one-year-old son William Street Barney's family decided to stay in Springtown. In short order William became an important figure in Springtown affairs. On 5 August 1872 he was elected one of two justices of the peace and on 26 December became city assessor and collector for Springtown.[30] For Lewis and his family, "We moved every thing we had from Spring Town to Monroe," Arthur wrote, which "took about 4 days to go from Spring Town to our new home, which we diden't have, as we was to make a home after we landed in Monroe."[31] The best they could immediately do upon their arrival was to build a log structure for habitation, crude by Utah's urban standards in the 1870s.

Despite the promise of growth and development during resettlement, Monroe remained a frontier colony, a village. In contrast, Salt Lake City, in the early 1870s, had become a commercial, mining, and transportation center. Cultural and municipal refinements had been available for a quarter century. Fine homes, the new tabernacle, a theater, a streetcar system, hotels, institutions of higher learning, several banks, and stores with eastern finery characterized the growing city. Street lights in Salt Lake City were gasified in the 1870s and electrified at the beginning of the next decade. Salt Lake City's population soared from 12,854 in 1870 to 20,768 in 1880. Monroe in 1880 claimed only 744 souls.[32] Information showing the contrast between Monroe, a fledgling village, and the growing metropolis of Salt Lake City was known to Lewis Barney through the *Deseret News*, but he was not tempted by urban prosperity. The frontier and villatic living was his way.

While Monroe lacked urban polish, there was promise for her residents and for the community they hoped would flourish. The Barneys' stay in Monroe started modestly. After a year and a half, Lewis's property in March 1873 totaled $50 in land, two cattle valued at $40, two horses at $70, one swine at $10, and $25 in other taxable property, together worth $195. His brothers Walter and Benjamin and Lewis's son James Henry were assessed for property worth $354, $255, and $276, respectively; Monroe residents averaged $330.[33] If Sevier Valley's resources were to be harnessed, something more than individual enterprise was required. In mid-March 1873 the Monroe Cooperative Mercantile Institution (MCMI) incorporated with Moses Gifford as president.[34] A branch of Salt Lake City–based Zion's Cooperative Mercantile Institution then spreading territory-wide, the cooperative organization found a sympathetic component in Monroe's citizens. But community ideals and objectives were individually interpreted to such an extent that an unforeseeable future of friction and fracture awaited Sevier Valley's runner-up village.

The Educator

Sometime after Monroe's resettlement Lewis Barney made an unusual addition to his resumé. Taking up pencil and slate, he became a frontier schoolteacher, preceding the formalized educational system which later emerged in Utah.[35] While it is not known how long Barney taught at this time or of the circumstances of his teaching, he became noted as Monroe's first teacher and conducted his first class in the old Monroe fort.[36] About thirty students attended the Monroe "day school" by March 1873. A year later fifty scholars enrolled.[37] Just four months later in 1874 the number jumped to eighty, requiring several teachers to meet educational needs.[38] While there was ready interest by townspeople to increase Monroe's education level, the circumstances and exigencies of resettlement rendered education Spartan and primitive for the children. Frontier parents had minimal educational expectations for their children. The best they could hope for was literacy at a time when most focused on subsistence living. Criteria for teachers had been established by Sevier Stake leaders in July 1875: "School teachers [are] to be of ourselves, not outsiders."[39] Later that year Sevier Valley Mormons were told by stake leaders to "Patronize Mormon school teachers and not infidels. Don't employ Gentile school teachers, but a well-tried Mormon Elder."[40] Barney qualified. In his role as teacher he could claim he was literate and within the perimeters of Mormonism.

Monroe's primitive educational situation was not lost on those trying to elevate the cultural level in territorial Utah. In March 1875 James Dwyer, Utah Education Bureau business manager, visited the Sevier settlements and reported: "At the school at Monroe we found a large attendance . . . and the [eighty to ninety] students were getting along tolerably well under their present teacher [probably not Barney]." But as a result of his Sevier visit Dwyer lamented the educational circumstances to which the children were subjected:

> Shall [the children] be allowed to grow up in ignorance in those settlements for the want of good teachers? Shall they be crammed into poor miserable school houses, without ventilation and good comfortable seats, and be presided over by a teacher or teachers who do not understand their physical, mental, and moral composition? The remedy for this is the establishment of a normal school.[41]

Notwithstanding the good intentions of territorial officials and parents alike, "Primitive schools [in Utah], were built in pioneer times and children sometimes attended; but schooling was a hit or miss affair that had only fleeting influence on the lives of many."[42] Normal schools in rural Utah communities had to wait for decades. Still, literacy, the most important door through which a child had to pass to enter the modern world, was attentively pursued.

As the settlement's citizens organized for permanence, there were several personalities central to community matters. Barney was a background player. Because of his experience and age, being one of Monroe's older citizens, he had a role in the course taken by the community. When determining the village's ecclesiastical leader, "I used my influence," he wrote, to see that Moses Gifford was chosen. Gifford, nearly forty years old and one of Alma's most energetic settlers, was "voted . . . in to be bishop."[43] A Welshman, Walter Jones, and a Dane, John (Johan) B. Hesse, were Gifford's counselors.[44] Unlike the modern method of selecting local Mormon leaders by way of appointment from their superiors, in many nineteenth-century Mormon communities the bishop was selected by majority vote. Gifford, a leader with great promise, was a second generation Mormon born in Jackson County, Missouri, in 1833, having witnessed from his infancy the difficulties experienced by the Saints. Though a quarter century separated them in age, Barney, having known Gifford for about a decade, had confidence in him. They shared experiences in Springtown, in the initial founding of Alma, and together they worked on the transcontinental railroad.

One feature of electing a bishop was a hoped-for loyalty due to popular selection, but in Gifford's case, surprisingly, the favorable feelings quickly eroded. "We soon found we made a mistake," Barney wrote.[45] Gifford's views in some things were extreme. In August 1872, for example, with the Black Hawk War experience behind the Sevier settlers, Gifford was reported as being "pretty rabid" in demanding the region be cleared of Indians. "Tired of acting the squaw," he demanded action to settle the Indian question once and for all, meaning, of course, their entire expulsion or extermination.[46] Another of Gifford's problems was his deferral to "Michael Johnson who had but little faith in the Gospel," and who "controlled . . . all [Gifford's] moves."[47] After settling in Monroe, Johnson, naturally disposed to leadership, initially curried favor enough to be elected justice of the peace in March 1872 as well as postmaster.[48] When Monroe's Cooperative Mercantile Institution incorporated in Monroe, Johnson became Gifford's secretary in the organization. Later that year he was appointed to be on a county-wide cooperative herd committee representing Monroe.[49] As the community's future course developed, Johnson and, consequently, Gifford dissented.

Planning for the village's infrastructure was the initiation of difficulties. A late December 1873 report to the *Deseret News*, probably by Gifford's counselor Walter Jones, described the prospects for community growth: "Could the people unite on a good plan for irrigation it could be made in a few years the second or third size city in Utah territory, as we have the water and the land."[50] The matter of harnessing the water forced the community fracture. Barney detailed his part in the problem: "Bishop Gifford, through the influence of

M[ichael] Johnson, was made to believe that there must be a canal cut from the Sevier River to [be] taken out 6 or 7 [miles] above where the old river canal [from the 1860s] was taken out of the river." "As I was one of the irrigation trustees," Barney reported, "the bishop asked me my opinion about the contemplated canal. I told him under existing circumstances it was altogether impracticable; that the people was not able to complete such a job." The project simply required too much at the time, Barney argued, when many in the village were "without a house to shelter their families . . . and not a month's provisions on hand and no means to buy more, having to depend entirely on the labor of their hands for their supplies." And, Barney claimed, "the old . . . canal [built in Alma's initial settlement] with a little work was all sufficient for the supply of water . . . for several years." Barney's reasoning held no sway with Gifford and Johnson. "So," Barney said, "they rejected my counsel and me with it." Thereafter Barney and Gifford disassociated.[51]

Three years after resettlement, Monroe's citizens faced the realities of maintaining momentum under adverse circumstances. A Monroe correspondent complained, "We are having a bitter cold winter." With deep, hardened snow and infrequent days of sunshine, "[our] out door work has ceased and everybody and his wife feel contrary-wise because they are confined to the house." While "many private dwellings have been erected," he continued, "some of them quite tasty . . . the public works are backward." Housing and public works were secondary and tertiary to the primary concern, "bread is the first necessity in a new settlement."[52] Just as spring dawned, with hope anew, an answer to their difficulties was laid upon them.

Chapter 18

A Division with the People: The Monroe United Order of Enoch, 1874–1878

Population changes in the 1870s involved increased immigration of non-Latter-day Saints into Utah, fostering pluralism and diversity in the mountain valleys. To Mormon leaders it was apparent there was a demonstrable lack of progress for church members toward the ideals expected of modern Israel, something akin to their Mormon Reformation concerns in 1856. Other factors contributed to this unsettling condition, such as the nationwide economic depression of 1873 and an increase in federal pressure manifest by the arrest and hounding of the now elderly Brigham Young. A course correction circulated through Mormondom. "To consolidate the interests of all Latter-day Saints, [Brigham Young] inaugurated in 1874 the United Order, a system that from one perspective may be regarded as his supreme effort to check disintegrating forces developing within and without the church, forces that threatened the economic and political independence of the Mormon people."[1] The idea had been, to the Mormon leader, simmering on the back burner for several years. The time for implementation was at hand.

To understand the impact of Barney's involvement in the United Order, a description of the enterprise and its purpose is warranted. Beginning in February 1874 the Mormon president announced the introduction of one of the most thorough revisions of Latter-day Saint society found among the Saints to that time. Most every Utah community as well as several in Arizona and Idaho, over two hundred in all, were affected to some degree by the innovation.[2] Cooperative endeavors were operating in most Mormon communities already. These included collaborative enterprises in irrigation, horticulture, and animal husbandry. Young in 1869 said, "This co-operative movement is only a stepping stone to what is called the Order of Enoch, but which is in reality the order of Heaven."[3] The cooperative level in Mormon communities was then on a level quite different from that soon to be expected of the Saints.

The visionary objective was modeled somewhat on the biblical New Testament precedent described in Acts 2:44–45, "And all that believed were together, and had all things common; And sold their possessions and goods, and parted them to all men, as every man had need."[4] Having "all things common" would affect the Saints both spiritually and economically, retracking Mormon society as a whole. From St. George, where the innovation was announced, the president and several of the Twelve systematically moved north community by community introducing the order to the Saints. Reaching Nephi in Juab County on 18 April 1874, Young declared,

> We have gone just as far as we can be permitted to go in the road on which we are now traveling. . . . Babylon is here, and we are following in the footsteps of the inhabitants of the earth, who are in a perfect sea of confusion. . . . We now want to organize the Latter-day Saints, every man, woman and child among them, who has a desire to be organized, into this holy order. You may call it the Order of Enoch, you may call it co-partnership, or just what you please. It is the United Order of the Kingdom of God on the earth.[5]

There had been seasons of this type of consecration during Joseph Smith's tenure as church prophet, but what came from Young's direction approached a scope never before attempted.[6]

While the present proposal was a cooperative economic endeavor, the emphasis on individual righteousness and regeneration was primary. A list of objectives to that end were formulated, becoming the standard for all Mormons in all Latter-day Saint settlements. Stressing personal purity and devotion to God by reemphasizing the rudimentary religious practices of personal and family prayer, adhering to the Ten Commandments and other Christian principles, the intent was to foster a holy people, but the standards extended beyond religious devotion. Maintenance of the Mormon cultural peculiarities of economic isolation from gentiles and non-order businesses, self-reliance, and simple living were also objectives. The expectation was given to the Saints not as suggestion but as injunction. Church leaders rallied the Mormon faithful not only in cooperation's direction, but also in the added feature of consecration of personal resources.[7] While there were regional modifications in the order, in general "each person in the community was asked to contribute his economic property to the order in return for equivalent capital stock. The order would thus be provided with the enterprises and the capital with which to commence its operations."[8] One who chose to participate "pledged all of his 'time, labor, energy, and ability'" to the enterprise. Together, the property and personal resources of labor and energy "became subject to the direction of an elected Board of Management" for each organized order.[9] This surely was a step beyond the rudiments of cooperation.

Brigham Young's eldest son, Joseph A. Young, directing the church in the Sevier Valley from Richfield, gathered the Sevier bishops to Richfield on 18 April 1874 and generalized to them the objectives and purpose of the order. In explaining the enterprise he drew lines: "The time has come when we may enter into that order or we may not, but if we do not, with few exceptions we will reject all."[10] A week later, on 26 April, Joseph A. Young visited the Monroe

Saints gathered in the town bowery and organized a United Order branch in the settlement.[11] Monroe's United Order was introduced coincident to the Gifford-Johnson fissure in Monroe. The time to draw the community together was just right. While Joseph A. Young's intent was to pave the way for acceptance of the order, his counsel cooled some in Monroe toward the venture. As he had instructed the valley bishops the previous week, he told the Monroe folks, "It will be made a test of fellowship to oppose the Order."[12] Many were enthused, but some questioned the order's communal expectations.

At the Monroe organizational meeting, Barney wrote, "the Constitution of the United Order was presented to the Saints and read and explained by Joseph A. Young," after which "names then was called for as members for the order, a large majority of the settlers giving their names to become members of the order." "But," Barney added, "after some reflection quite a number refused to put there names to the list. So there was not over half the settlement that become members of the order."[13] While Barney initially pledged support for the proposal, he was not officially accepted into the order until about three weeks later on 17 May when it was "moved and adopted that we receive Bro Lewis Barney into the Order with his crops."[14]

One of the Monroe order's casualties was the leader of the community, Moses Gifford. When Young briefed Bishop Gifford on the plan and expectations for ward members, he resigned. While it was not required that the ward bishop also be the order president, though the dual roles were shared in some settlements, Gifford could not continue as bishop under the circumstances. He told the Monroe Saints, "It is well known that I was born in this church & I wish to die in the church, but [I] cannot see this 'order.'" Obviously chagrined at having to make this personal stance, he appealed to his former flock, "I don't want you to judge me harshly. I do not wish to preside over a people who are in an 'order' that I cannot understand."[15] Gifford's stance "was a source of trouble both to those in the order and those that did not join the order," Barney stated.[16] Thus from the start, the United Order exacerbated the already mounting division in the community, and Monroe was not alone.

Of the eight other Sevier settlements which organized United Orders, most also wrestled with its introduction. Though 80 percent in Richfield joined the order, in Salina only sixteen of thirty-seven enlisted. Just half joined in Annabella. George Wilson, the presiding elder in the Sevier Valley village of Joseph, like Gifford, told his congregation that though he, too, expected to die in the church, he could not accept the order. Wilson, like Gifford, was immediately released and replaced.[17] Gifford's replacement, a relative newcomer to Monroe and Alabama native, James Thompson Lisonbee, was appointed by church leaders as president of the order and acting ward bishop. Later, having proven himself to the Richfield authorities over the summer months, he was ordained Monroe Ward bishop in September. John B. Hesse and William A. Warnock were his counselors.[18]

In appraising Monroe and its constituents during this period, the heterogeneous nature of the settlement is important to consider. There were probably about five hundred living in Monroe in 1874, and eight or nine of every ten were practicing Mormons. About one-third of the community was Scandinavian, just over one-fifth were American born, and just under one-fifth were English. The remaining quarter was a mixture of the three.[19] Danish numbers were sufficient that when United Order matters were introduced to stake leaders on 19 April 1874 they had to be translated into Danish.[20] This complexity of ethnic background, notwithstanding the mostly successful integration of northern European peoples into the corpus of Mormonism, may have portended an uncertain future in economic considerations.[21]

The protocols established for the orders called for a body of leadership to direct and manage the enterprise's operation. Each community order became a business corporation—a company—with a president, vice presidents, and a board of directors. The initial Monroe board was headed by president James T. Lisonbee, 45. Dennison L. Harris, 49, was vice-president. Other officers included a secretary, assistant secretary, treasurer, and three directors who also doubled as appraisers of the materials consecrated to the order.[22] By October, after an early defection from the board of directors, a new election was held and the board restructured. Lisonbee was again chosen president. The other officers elected by the order's subscribers were Thomas Hunt, 47, and Dennison L. Harris, vice-presidents. William A. Warnock, 37, and John B. Hesse, 46, served as secretary and treasurer, respectively. Each of the presidency and secretary and treasurer was also a director. The remaining board was composed of Bent Larson, 28, Thomas Cooper, 39, Jens Jensen, 45, Andrew Larsen, 30, and the old man of the board, Lewis Barney, 66. "My name was placed on the list as a candidate as one of the first directors," Barney said, "and was voted in to that office by the unanimous votes of the order."[23] Barney, considered elderly by most standards, was the senior by seventeen years of any on the board dominated by middle-aged and younger men. He was honored. Forty-eight other men subscribed to the order at this time by contributing property and goods counted as individual shares (capital stock) varying from three to sixty-nine, the average being twenty-four shares. Lewis obtained forty-two shares. His son James Henry and brother Benjamin took twenty-seven shares each.[24]

Other than the order's constitution, which is best described as a generalization of principles and objectives, there was no policy and procedures manual and little precedent for operating the community corporations.[25] This gave each order flexibility in making adjustments to fit their particular circumstances. The United Order in Salt Lake City's urban wards, for example, operated differently than the congregations in the more rural settlements, a few of which adopted the communalism noted in Orderville, Utah, thought by some to be extreme.[26] While the lack of an operational handbook allowed flexibility, it also eliminated the practical bearing walls necessary to support a business in infancy. In Monroe's case, the board of directors—business executives by this new standard—was composed of men with little or no business experience. These men were farmers, mainly. The expectations for success were reliant upon the exhibition of Christian behavior and principles coupled with common sense and a cooperative spirit which it was hoped would compensate for any lack of business acumen. This higher road of conduct envisioned by leaders, therefore, made the commitment expected of United Order subscribers in Monroe not only feasible but reasonable to most because those who constituted the order were folks of faith. They had in the past demonstrated numerous times their willingness to submit to authority and to sacrifice individualism for the good of the whole.

Optimism was high at the order's instigation. Individual families maintained a degree of autonomy by producing their own garden vegetables and fruit, but the cultivation of grain and distribution of flour, because of the extensive outlay of resources required to produce the commodity, was an operation of the order. The features of community life to which the townsfolk had become accustomed were to be maintained and expanded. Each of the village needs, such as irrigation and education, was to be satisfied by coordination and assignment by the order's board of directors. The initial success of the cooperation is evidenced by the project of finishing a community building on the public square, thirty-eight feet by seventy feet, which served both church and civic purposes. Even those who chose not to join the order were hopeful that the spirit of cooperation, essential for a young community, would pervade the personal and community life of each citizen of Monroe, despite the differences in philosophy.

Initially, if a person did not join the order, it did not preclude their participation in church affairs, though there was obviously some strain. Joseph A. Young, recognizing what a polarized community would do to civic order and progress, warned the order's members to be "wise, prayerful, cautious, mild, and not to take notice of rumors, to keep our mouths shut on points that would create a bitter feeling among those either in or out of the Order."[27] And Moses Gifford, still the Monroe Cooperative Mercantile Institution president which continued operation in the community, spoke in church in August 1874 enjoining the Saints: "Let us be united, there is nothing [that] will build up a place like union and nothing retard the progress of a place as much as disunion."[28] But once the inevitable line was drawn dividing order subscribers and those not joining, each camp seemed to defend their particular postures with vigor. Monroe Ward worship services regularly served as forums to advance purposes of the order, which, of course, were endorsed by church leaders in Richfield and Salt Lake City. Because order participants viewed themselves as faithful and their nonparticipating counterparts as less devoted, there was a distinct gap between the two camps.

Having the imprimatur of the Salt Lake City brethren upon the order made the difference in how matters—religious and civil—were conducted in the community. From the start, the order's effect on everyday life in Monroe was a point of ubiquitous discussion. One participant stated, "The 'Order of Enoch' seems to be the every day topic, even the boys on the street discuss [it]."[29] The discussion came from two perspectives. Barney's son Arthur, now twenty-two years old, described the "division with the people. That put them in two parties, the Enochites and the outsiders." The separation created a situation where "the orderites would have their dances in one building, and the outsiders would have their dances in another hall." From this tension they "had some lively times."[30]

As for Lewis Barney, early in August 1874 at a church service he "addressed the meeting saying that we should be on hand at all times for any call that may be made upon us believing that the fulfillment of all things is about to take place," and stated, "It is necessary for us to live our religion that we may escape the judgments that are coming upon the nations." Explaining "how the Spirit of God had worked with him until he could not refrain from joining the United Order," it was his "desire to live his religion all the days of his life." In the same meeting his brother Walter bore witness of the "power of God in his own behalf by deliverance from evils seen and unseen."[31] The following month Lewis reiterated his view, "There is no other place for us but in the United Order and to push it ahead and accomplish the object of God."[32] His age and experience no doubt underscored to the congregation his own commitment and endorsement of the order's objectives and of his religious belief. It was no surprise that the week after this latter sermon, he was voted in as one of five appraisers of property consecrated to the order which preceded his appointment as treasurer the following month when he was also elected a director.[33] The Barneys, and in particular Lewis, wholly endorsed the plan.

The regular verbal reinforcement from the pulpit and recruiting appeals to those who for one reason or another chose to refrain from joining continued. Before long the leaders' rhetoric made compliance a matter of belief. In December 1874 Joseph A. Young declared, "The Order is a test of faith—those who comply have it, those who don't lack the faith necessary and should cultivate the principle."[34] Some who were initially reluctant later joined. Others who were original subscribers chose to leave. This latter action caused consternation on the part of church leaders. A mechanism for separating from the order had not been included in the bylaws. Thus, the lack of clear direction for such circumstances emerged as a serious problem in the order's cooperative spirit.

Three months after the inauguration of the order, Bishop Lisonbee on 18 July 1874 reported to Sevier Stake president Young that "Albert Thompson [one of the directors] had fallen back from the order and wished to be released."[35] Thompson had reported to the Monroe board "that he could not do justice under his present feelings" and asked to be released from his obligations to the order.[36] Of course, this posed a threat that could affect the entire enterprise. If significant numbers of the subscribers withdrew, for good reasons or otherwise, the organization would collapse. Thus, a week after Bishop Lisonbee's report, Young visited Monroe and at the community schoolhouse spoke to the townsfolk describing the problem. President Young described Thompson as being a good man whom he liked from their first acquaintance. But, he said, "he has signed his name by his own free will and he has no right to withdraw. A man who has not signed his name can go along as he has done heretofore. But you cannot withdraw after signing your name without being dealt with."[37] Toward the end of September two more in Monroe objected to the twenty-five-year obligation, which was apparently added after the initiation of the order, and declared their participation null and void. In November another withdrew, but could a man who withdrew be sent away empty-handed? President Lisonbee offered a compromise. He determined after the latter withdrawal that "in any case where a person wanted to draw out of the Order [taking with them their consecration], they were to be charged their q[u]ota of Public improvements."[38] It seemed an equitable way to handle the circumstance.

The erosion of hoped-for unanimity concerned not only the Monroe executives but was so common in the valley villages that it also caught the attention of the Richfield leaders. Joseph A. Young recognized the strain and in November 1874 counseled his charges, "The United Order will try men as plurality [plural marriage] has tried women."[39] A greater exhibition of faith was required to pass the test, but it was not just the order's general membership who would be tried. In Monroe's case, even those who managed the operation were subjected to trial that strained and stretched the community fabric.

As the months rolled by, the order's leaders in Monroe, lacking precedent and adequate guidelines, struggled to maintain the momentum needed for unanimity among order subscribers. Barney said that as matters proceeded during the summer, "there was considerable enthusiasm [excessive zeal] among the officers of the order which was a cause of much trouble." He laid blame at James T. Lisonbee's authoritarian approach to management. He was not the only one to feel this way. The situation was complicated by what Barney said was a dissatisfaction by some with Lisonbee's appointment as bishop earlier in the year. Thus from the outset, in the aftermath of the Gifford-Johnson difficulty, Lisonbee's acquisition of authority in the community was, according to Barney, "the means of widening the breach among the people of the settlement."[40] The evidence is clear that Lisonbee tried to do what he was charged with doing. While his style grated some, his intentions appeared above reproach.

Mormons have a tradition of giving their appointed leaders deference and allegiance. One of the central explanations for Latter-day Saint success in community building and successfully configuring their local environments is their practice of "following the brethren," the loyal support of those called for a season to lead. There is not a professional nor trained clergy in local church administration. Lisonbee, like most other community bishops, likely did not lobby for the job of pastoring the congregation. Unlike Gifford, Lisonbee was appointed by his ecclesiastical superior, not elected by popular vote. The Saints understood that their appointed lay leaders were nonprofessionals, usually good men possessing laudable characteristics who gave the assignment their best effort, despite whatever personality quirks they might have. In the majority of cases, the local bishops proved capable and won the people's hearts. Even for those who did not quickly endear themselves to their congregations, there was generally a great deal of tolerance manifest on the settlers' part regarding the style and views espoused by their leaders. They believed these men had access to the inspiration of heaven in shepherding the local flock.

Trying to work out the personality and policy difficulties within Monroe United Order leadership, "the directors of the order had several meetings to make arrangements for carrying on business but they could not agree fully on every point."[41] The internal polarity of good men with contrary points of view regarding procedural matters made Monroe United Order administration inefficient. Probably the primary point of contention was over individual enterprise needed by those in the order. The order's purpose was to employ individuals and their resources full-time for the good of the order and its members. Despite the worthy intention, the reality of order operation failed to temper the chronic poverty found in most Mormon frontier settlements and in Monroe in particular. Subscribers were not guaranteed economic relief. There were those in the order finding themselves in dire economic hardship and, not wanting to withdraw from the order, wished a temporary furlough from order obligations to pursue personal economic recovery.[42]

In the Barneys' case, within a month of the order's beginning Lewis's brother, Benjamin, then supporting three wives and their children in Monroe and Spanish Fork, appealed to the board to be allowed to work on his own for two weeks to reduce his debt. In November 1874 another brother, Walter, made the same appeal for the same reason. Benjamin asked again for a reprieve in January 1875.[43] Of course, this meant that for whatever period they were away from their cooperative endeavors for the order, the organization was reduced in capital and resource. But individual enterprise was a necessity because, despite the capital stock acquired through contributed shares, the Monroe United Order did not have provisions to sustain life for some of its members. This was Lewis's situation. His son Arthur wrote, "My father's family all joined the order but me, and if I had of joined the order, I don't know what we would have done for a living, as father only got a little flour and some potatoes out of the order." Arthur's father "put in all his time in the order and got credit for his work, but credit wouldn't buy clothing and groceries and things we had to have to live on."[44] Lewis's situation requiring his private enterprise soon mushroomed in a way that challenged his very allegiance to the order.

Lewis Barney, like his brothers, suffered from indigence. The result was a period of great difficulty for him not only temporally but also spiritually. Despite over three decades of fealty to Mormon leadership, he was now caught in a situation where he was pitted against his file leader, the bishop and order president. For so many others in Mormonism's previous forty-five years, this type of personal estrangement often ended in his or her separation from the church. Barney found himself in the ambiguous position of maintaining loyalty to the church while faced with practicing heterodox economic pragmatism. While not alone in his contrary views about operational procedures, being the eldest and one of the men of lengthiest church and community tenure, Barney felt that some deference should be paid to his perspective by the board leaders. His view being rejected by most of the board, he came to the realization the order was heading into chaos and crisis. Some provision had to be made for those who couldn't exist on United Order support. A board meeting held 27 November 1874 brought his dissonance to a head.

At that meeting board president James T. Lisonbee, after a half-year's experience, complained that some within the order were doing work for those outside the order and pocketing the profit; they contributed only part of their time to order work. How could the order operate if its participants gave half-heartedly? After the president's statement Barney responded, arguing "he had considered all these points and concluded that every class and all the labor done for those in or out of the order should be done through the order." He admitted that "in his own workings he found that he had worked out of the order and only turned part of his earnings in." Relying solely upon order provisions simply did not provide a reasonable standard of living for his family. Abraham Washburn offered another objection: "he did not like to be tied up so closely, as he thought it would cripple the enterprising." To him, "if a man works late and early, he considered it but right for him to use the overplus." Lisonbee responded by saying that it was not right that "a mechanic was using the tools that belong to the order [for his personal enterprise], and had no more right to do so than the man who turned in his team and wagon [to the order and then] had a right to run around with them at night." Several other board members at the meeting then admitted that they, like Barney, were also out of harmony in the same way, but pledged that they would comply. Lisonbee's position seemed reasonable given the nature of their individual consecrations and the intent of the order. At that time his view was "unanimously sustained,"[45] but by no means was the matter closed. Because the hope for cooperation and unity was great, compliance was pledged despite mounting discontent. Yet there remained a glaring incongruity in the standard of living expected by order members and what the order could provide.

Despite Barney's apparent agreement with Lisonbee's rationale, his consternation over the impracticable posture demanded by Lisonbee drove him to act. "Seeing the situation [and] knowing the course that was adopted would end in a failure and be the means of breaking up the order" and, recognizing that "my counsel together with several others [was] being disregarded and not noticed by the president and three of his favorites," he had to act. Privately appealing to board member Dennison L. Harris who shared a similar philosophy regarding operational procedures, he said, "You know the course that is taken will end in failure and will ruin the settlement and [that] our counsel is entirely disregarded. Under this circumstance," Barney continued, "I cannot take upon my shoulders the responsibility of this failure and ruin that this system of business will bring upon the settlement." Therefore, "my intention is to withdraw from the board of directors and let them enjoy the fruits of their own counsels." Harris advised him to be patient and not to act in haste. Barney replied, "If my counsel would be listened to I would stick to it. But you know," he reasoned, "that neither you nor I can do anything to change the thing for the better." Barney, hardened by his years and the circumstances, declared, "My mind [is] made up. I will never meet with that council again."[46] He resigned. The meeting of 27 November 1874, just over a month after being elected to the board, was the last Barney attended as a board member. While he broke with the board he still believed in the divine purpose of the order and remained one of the consecrators.

Coincident with his decision and discussion with Harris, Barney found an opportunity to take him out of the fray temporarily and unite him, once again, with his sons. Walter T., James Henry, and Joseph, who had rejected their father's plea to stay close to him eight years earlier, had by this time tried Beaver, Utah, and now lived in Kanosh, in Pahvant Valley, just over the western mountain from Sevier Valley. James Henry called on his father that fall explaining that he and his brothers were building a sawmill in the canyon east of Kanosh and desired their father's expertise in their venture. Would he come and help them? Barney was thrilled with the invitation which came at just the right time. "So," with his son Arthur, "I left Monroe and went to work with my boys in the canyon to build a saw mill."[47] Their work on the mill construction continued into the new year.

In January 1875 a new United Order board in Monroe was elected with Lisonbee still at the helm.[48] Three weeks later the board manifest its new look by cutting off rations to Barney's family in Monroe while he was gone.[49] Barney found out about the action near the time the mill was ready for production. "The president of the order sent for me to come home and take care of my family for they would not furnish them any more flour." Perplexed about the action which appeared to be capricious and meanspirited, he reasoned that because he had donated to the order "property amounting [to] over $1500 and 122 dollars worth of lumber," the generous consecration should carry his family while he was away for a few months.[50] Upon his return about the third week of February 1875 he found his independence was only one point of contention with his erstwhile peers.

On 26 February he met with the board to discuss his situation. In the course of the evening he was told that his family's subsidy had been cut off because they were sharing the flour with Charles Robinson, husband of

Barney's daughter Martha Ann. Robinson carried a reputation in Monroe of being "an enemy to the order" and supplying him with foodstuffs while he thumbed his nose at the order galled the board members. Barney apparently acknowledged the reasoning, and when reminded by the board that "as he was a member of the Old Board . . . he would have done the same in such a case," he offered no objection. When questioned about his action of leaving Monroe to help his sons, he rehearsed his reasoning claiming he "did not like to be tied down." The board all spoke against his view but were otherwise charitable in their feelings toward Barney. Even Lisonbee, who "spoke to bro Barney and told him that his rations were stoped [*sic*] for the purpose of finding out the truth of the flying Reports," felt that it was only "right to honor the Veterans of the Church and Bro Barney was one of them." After listening to his superiors admonish him, Barney, their senior by as many as three decades, humbly submitted stating, "I came into the order not for flour but for salvation. The way you brethren talk it seems you have lost confidence in me. I do not intend in the future to do anything but what will help the order and the cause generally." In closing, the board agreed "that Bro Barney complete the mill he has under construction and then be subject to the board." They even reinstated his foodstuff subsidy "as Charles Robinson had [now] left his (Bro Barney's) house."[51]

What happened next is an important indicator of Lewis Barney's personality and attitudes—stubborn and conciliatory, independent and cooperative—toward his leaders and the community overall. The next day mulling over the previous night's meeting, Barney wanted something clarified by the order's board. That evening, 27 February 1875, he stood before them and "said that after reflecting on what had been said last night, he thought there [was] a lack of brotherly freedom that to him was not quite reconciliatory and wished to know of the Board if there were any disagreeable feelings existing towards him." The board "after a few explanations agreed to extend the hand of fellowship to him [Barney] which was kindly accepted."[52] It is very clear from Barney's reflective writings about this incident that, notwithstanding the apparent reconciliation, he harbored some resentment against those who governed the order. Acknowledgment as being loyal was important to him, which is why he did not want to "come out in open rebellion against the authorities."[53] And he did not.

As per the agreement Barney went back to the sawmill with his sons, where they worked together through the spring and summer of 1875 making lumber "which," he said, "proved a blessing to my family and also to the settlement of Kanosh and also to Monroe."[54] In May 1875 he checked in with the board, explained that the mill was up and ready to go, and asked permission of the board "whether he could run it or not." The board clerk reported Barney as "willing to act as the Board dictated," and that the board, "thought it would be better for the order for him to work there [at the mill] as he would turn in his profits to the Order."[55] Barney's expectation was, of course, that with that endorsement his wife Elizabeth and her children were to be subsidized during his absence.

While Barney worked the mill with his sons, Monroe's citizens continued to deal with the polarity affecting their community. At the same time in March 1875 that Monroe church leaders described to stake leaders in Richfield "an increase of faith, [a] good day and Sunday school & Theological class" in the ward, they also reported that the Liberal Party had been organized in the settlement. Two Monrovians, they said, had been corresponding with the *Salt Lake Tribune*, church nemesis in Salt Lake City, and had asked to sever their relationship with the church.[56] A counter to the Mormons' pervasive influence had been hatched in Salt Lake City in the 1860s. Dubbed the "Godbeite Movement" after one of its principal organizers, William S. Godbe, the group lobbied for a more pluralistic and less church-dominated climate in Utah for several years. Composed of several of the leading literary lights within the Mormon community, men who had at one time been counted among the most devoted and effective advocates of the faith, their defection caused quite a stir throughout the territory. The economic isolation and insulation espoused by Young during the 1860s was anathema to them. Religiously, they advocated a mix of Mormonism with spiritualism, involving seances and mediums, which, of course, did not play well in Mormon circles. Politically, they charged, the monolithic loyalty expected of the Latter-day Saint faithful was undemocratic. After being cut off from the church in late 1869 they inaugurated a three-pronged counter to Mormonism which trickled out to surrounding communities in the 1870s and influenced attitudes for decades thereafter. They organized a new church, initiated a political rivalry to the Saints—the Liberal Party—and their organ, the *Mormon Tribune*, popularized their opposition to the Mormon church.[57] While the number of those influenced by Godbe in Monroe was comparatively small, their attitudes were widely known. The influence tended to add to the atmosphere of division found within Monroe.

Over the ensuing months a number of Monroe Saints who considered themselves devout found themselves, like Barney, out of sorts with their leaders. Early in the spring of 1875 Curtis E. Bolton, instrumental two decades previously in opening Mormon missionary work in France, wrote to the *Deseret News* from Monroe acknowledging that "a few have been cut off for apostacy," and if not for a "wise and merciful" bishop (Lisonbee) more would have been cut off. Still, he said, "Everybody [is] busy. U[nited] Order working well. . . . The workers of darkness are doing what they can, but the Saints only draw closer." The following month he similarly lauded church and order activity to territory readers.[58] Before the year was over, Bolton, himself, was "disfellowshipped" from the Monroe United Order as he, according to the order board, misrepresented his allegiance to the order, vilified its leaders including Lisonbee, and failed to place all his goods into the order.[59] Clearly the order and its board had become a scythe rather than a tiller in the community.

Despite some attempt by the board to solve order problems, even after a year there was no standardization of prices for goods and labor expended for order purposes. Lisonbee, responding to criticism at a 19 May 1875 meeting, stated, "We have not as yet set any prices on labor or provisions but if the secretary keeps the books in proper order we can see at a glance how a man stands and let him have according to his labors." The secretary shot back complaining "of the difficulty of keeping books when there are no prices settled upon the articles received or the labor performed."[60] Monroe was not alone. Even the Sevier County flagship, the Richfield United Order, was also afflicted by a "failure to work out a schedule of prices." Yet, ironically, at least one other order wrote to the Richfield order for advice on how to manage their organization more effectively.[61] Board members' efforts to find a solution to their difficult situation found little help from Richfield. One board officer asked Joseph A. Young at a board meeting on 24 May 1875 "if it [is] acceptable with God and Brigham Young for each board to adopt plans of there own, as thereby there be different plans." Young replied with advice characterizing local church administration then and now: "God has through all past and present history gave the general rules of guidance and left the people to do the filling up."[62] As board officers implemented their own initiatives, the decisions and results did not become any easier.

Lack of satisfaction within order ranks provoked four men and their families to withdraw from the order the first week of June. Differences within the board soon came to a head. The rift had become so enervating that board members Dennison L. Harris and two Larsen brothers, Andrew and Bent, resigned from the board as well as severing their ties to the United Order itself.[63] The garment was unraveling. Something had to be done. Reaching for anything in July 1875 to soften the harsh feelings, 142 in Monroe were rebaptized renewing their commitment and covenant to the order. Between September 1875 and September 1876 another thirty-seven submitted to the ordinance. Of note, not a Barney was among them.[64]

As church leaders tried to mend fences over the summer of 1875, rather than repairing the breeches, matters continued to decline. At one particularly pointed meeting, former order vice-president Dennison Harris met with the board and when asked his status, Harris stated, "He left [the board] because he differed in the managment [*sic*] of Bussiness [*sic*] and thought from an expression of the President's [Lisonbee], that his council was not wanted in the Board." He also resented the fact that at a recent meeting of the priesthood in Richfield, "President Joseph A. Young stated that parties had been got up there and elsewhere for the purpose of breaking up the Order and that there were some of them present at that meeting." Harris said that when Young said this, "I looked him square in the Eye and he stoped [*sic*] it." Harris adamantly declared to the board: "I have not tried to draw any one away from the Order." When Lisonbee countered Harris's story, Harris, exasperated at Lisonbee's inflexible myopia, complained "it was no use discussing these points [any longer]" and entirely closed his association with the order.[65] Similar defections like Harris's took place in the Richfield United Order by some of its former leaders and formerly strongest supporters.[66] After the summer of 1875 the future of Sevier Valley's United Orders, like a number of others throughout the territory, looked precarious.

Then on 5 August, Joseph A. Young, the stake president and resident authority of the valley, died at just forty-one years of age. His death broke an important cable of continuity for the Sevier orders. Within two months of Young's death, his successors in the Sevier Stake leadership, recognizing the need to accommodate the type of individualism expressed by Barney and others, wrote to Brigham Young asking permission to modify the manner of doing order business in their stake. Young required the Sevier leaders to stay the course: "For you to change your method of doing business to that of stewardships [individualism] would be to take a step backward and would not be in accordance with our feelings. so far as we know of your operations, you have been doing well and the prospects before you are encouraging. What can you possibly gain by changing your system?"[67] The Mormon leader's vision of Saints' unity had not abated, despite the difficulties afflicting orders throughout the territory. He recognized the rigor required but believed that through continued diligent effort and the Spirit of the Lord, the Saints could find themselves a unified, consecrated people.

Midsummer 1875 with the sawmill up and running, Barney returned to Monroe, but he returned to conditions further aggravating his previous estrangement from the order's leaders. Several more months of parrying with the board followed.[68] Then the complete fracture of the order came in the board meetings of January 1876. "President Lisonbee," on 3 January, "stated that he thought it time for the lines to be drawn a little tighter than they have been." At a time when flexibility was required, rigidity was employed which loosened all the footings. On 17 January when new board officers were to be elected, a "turbulent spirit was strongly manifested by many withdrawing from the order" who "urgently [demanded] an immediate settlement" from the board. The flare-up and contention forced the board to adjourn without new elections. When the order reconvened for new elections the following month, Lisonbee was voted out. Hans O. Magleby, a forty-year-old Dane, was elected president. Lisonbee's removal was thought necessary to move the order forward. Despite the difficulty of his personality for some, Lisonbee tried to remain true to the vision of the order held by Brigham Young.[69] But by this time devotees like Lisonbee were becoming rare in United Order organizations. Even Brigham Young became discouraged. The elderly church president said "he had been inspired by the Gift and power of god to call upon the saints to enter into the united order, or order of Enoch, and that now was the time, but he could not get the people to enter it. He had cleared his skirts if he never said another word about it."[70]

Lisonbee's release as bishop and rejection as president of the United Order did not assuage Barney's thinking about the order, but appears to have affected his relationship with the board. On 7 March 1876 he reported to them that he had met earlier with Daniel H. Wells of the church First Presidency and asked Wells if it was feasible and reasonable for him to gather his family together and organize their own family order.[71] "Yes," Wells told him, "and the Lord will bless you and you will accomplish more than you can in any other way." Explaining that he had "talked to my boys on this subject and they are anxious to join together," Barney laid the matter before the board. Given the inordinate attention the board had given to the Barneys' problems over the past two years, it is perhaps not surprising that most of them thought his proposal good.[72] Now, all he had to do was settle with the board and initiate his new enterprise.

While Barney thought his troubles over, the board saw things differently. A week later the "case of Lewis Barney who is withdrawing from the Order was discussed at some length." They "resolved that if he wishes to withdraw from the Order that we settle up with him as with all other brethren and that if he wishes to remain he shall renew [his] covenants and labors as all other of the brethren." Barney had already made up his mind; he was quitting. Rehashing his determination to leave the order only complicated the situation. Still the board ruled on 2 April 1876 that Barney had two weeks to make up his mind about aligning himself with the board or not. If not, "his rations [would] be stoped [*sic*]." On 24 April, Barney reminded the board of his new family arrangement approved by a member of the First Presidency and appealed for flour from the board so he could get started. For the flour he "was willing to assist the order in furnishing or building the shingle machine which is started or any other kind of work they would require of him and not do anything that is derogatory to the Spirit of the Gospel." Either still not comprehending Barney's intention or not willing to let him go without exacting some penalty, he was asked whether his work would be as a member of the Monroe order or as an independent contractor. Barney, recognizing he could not antagonize them because he needed the flour, simply replied that it would be "outside of the order." While a couple of board members seemingly expressed sympathy, they voted against Barney's plan. But Hans Magleby, the new president, said he was willing to *loan* Barney two sacks of flour with the provision that it be returned if they ran short.[73] Finally he could get on with his business.

Three weeks later, Barney had to grovel one more time before the board. On 15 May he asked if it was possible for him to "get out a mule that he turned in to the order," which was required for the success of his new enterprise. If his request was granted, he said, "he would ask for nothing else." After consulting the order ledger where it was shown that he had a credit of $94, it was agreed by the board that he could have his mule.[74] In Barney's final transaction and association with the board, he told them "he was well satisfied with the actions of the board towards him, considering that they had done justice." In turn, "a

Similar expression was made by the Board towards Bro Barney."[75] Lewis's shoulders were rounded during his two-year struggle with the Monroe United Order, but the foundation of his underlying commitment to Mormonism held.

The order survived in Monroe another two years until mid-1878.[76] By the year following Barney's departure from Monroe's order, the Sevier Stake United Orders were in real trouble. Due primarily to the death of Brigham Young on 29 August 1877, the momentum for the survival and perpetuation of the orders slowed to nothing. The primary impetus for its existence was no longer at the helm. At a Sevier Stake conference in Richfield in November 1877, apostle Orson Hyde sermonized, "I am not going to speak against it [the United Order], nor do I feel against it and although you are being disorganized here, be not discouraged. Here is evidence that you have tried to do the will of the Lord and it will be a record in your favor. I am sorry that you failed to carry it out."[77] Brigham Young's successors recognized the futility of trying to keep the dying organism alive and by 1880 all but a handful of orders were dissolved.

Lewis Barney's involvement in the Monroe United Order was among the most telling experiences of his life. His initial enthusiasm for the enterprise gave way to what he viewed were practical considerations that faith and hope could not propitiate. The personality conflict he encountered with his file leader tested his faith. For many, under similar circumstances, it was easier to exit the church than to live with the dissonance and try to remain faithful, which Barney did.[78] Perhaps it is the case that had Monroe's citizens, including Barney, more fully embraced Brigham Young's idyllic vision for cooperation and unity, it may have had a better chance of success. Barney's behavior during this test of the people showed a stubborn, pragmatic strain though he also exhibited a willingness to reconcile. He would not have looked at this as a conflict with his religion but with the human condition of imperfection found in those who have to administer it. His own dissonance, which could have easily led to an uncoupling from Mormonism, was, fortunately for him, smaller than his overall commitment to the faith. His behavior demonstrated his religious belief was larger than the human difficulties of which he was a part.

Chapter 19

The Salvation of Thy Relatives and Friends: The Last Years in Sevier Valley, 1877–1882

The end of August 1877 was a milestone in the history of the Church of Jesus Christ of Latter-day Saints and Utah Territory, as well. President Brigham Young, the leader and guide for the Saints for thirty-three years, passed away in Salt Lake City on 29 August. Surviving the bitter winds of oppression and antagonism for the forty-five years of his association with the church, the summary of his church leadership is of incredible proportion. During his tenure as Mormon prophet the church progressed from adolescence to majority. His last remarkable act was the reorganization of the male priesthood structure and function which configured and platted the Church of Jesus Christ largely as it is known today.[1] His death also proved to be the knell of the United Order which he initiated three years previously. With his absence, "the reins of church government passed into the hands of John Taylor and others whose views on cooperation and practicable means of attaining a unity of the Saints, if previously in accord with those of their departed leader, had been modified with experience and adjusted to changing circumstances."[2] Within a month of Young's death, the Richfield United Order was formally dissolved with similar effect on the other Sevier communities, though the anemic Monroe United Order held on until 1878.[3] The grand consecration, with the exception of a handful of lingering residuals, was over.

Lewis Barney's focus was also redirected in the aftermath of his experience in the United Order. Remaining in Monroe for a half-dozen more years, he was thereafter a man scouting for the means to initiate his vision of his family kingdom. There is little evidence that the larger events which mixed Mormon or Utah with national interests at this time affected him directly. The federal effort in the reconstruction of Mormon Utah paralleled similar government objectives in the former Southern Confederacy. Legislation meant to humble the church and modify its heterodox American subculture mounted during this period. National momentum to alter Utah's religious and political climate increased after Young's death. Far removed from the cauldron in which the Mormon and federal antagonism boiled, Barney's thinking focused on his family's future, the theme which characterized the last years of his life.

Monroe Reconstituted

James T. Lisonbee's missionary call left a void in Monroe's ecclesiastical leadership. The task of his successor was significant. There was much healing and repair necessary within the community. Brigham Young wrote to fifty-year-old Albert K. Thurber, pro tem president of the Sevier Stake headquartered in Richfield, incident to Lisonbee's release which read, in part, "as presiding officer for Monroe, find as good a man as you can there and let him take charge for the present."[4] John B. Hesse, a forty-nine-year-old Dane and one of Lisonbee's counselors, received the appointment. Later that spring four members of the Mormon Twelve Apostles visited Monroe to shake things up.[5] One of the four, Erastus Snow, "commenced by inquiring into the business of the [United] Order and the settlement, in general," Barney wrote, "which was represented as it was, showing the settlement to be split up and formed into several rings, each ring striving for their own system of things." After listening patiently, Snow "arose and chastised the Board of Directors severely, then gave the settlement a warm going over" and "encouraged them in their participation in the United Order," which, as mentioned, survived through mid-1878.[6]

Snow returned to Monroe three months later. This time he came to consider permanent spiritual leadership for the settlement. Knowing the contention prevalent in the past, the apostle solicited views of ward members desiring to know whom they would support. One brother, referring to his problems with Lisonbee's regime, animatedly "spoke about the men who had led with a iron rod and was not fit to lead."[7] After the general discussion, Barney "arose and nominated Dennison L. Harris [for bishop]." While others were suggested, Barney reported, "I pressed my nomination." After a discussion of the candidates Elder Snow called for a vote. Harris, a Pennsylvanian, nephew of Book of Mormon witness Martin Harris, and one of the wealthier Monrovians, was elected by the ward and then ordained by Snow as Monroe's bishop. Andrew Larsen and James Farmer were appointed Harris's counselors.[8]

The reconstituted leadership of Monroe proved to be a balm with ameliorating effect. Harris and Larsen, of course, were formerly members of the United Order leadership who broke with the board and the order over disagreements with Lisonbee and his associates. To Barney, Harris's ordination as bishop vindicated his own differences and dissent from the order. The fissures of the previous years were addressed by the new leadership and, according to Lewis, "from this time things took a turn and gradually improved."[9]

The new bishopric represented the ethnic diversity characterizing Sevier Valley at this time. Harris was a fifty-two-year-old American, Larsen was Norwegian and thirty-three, and James Farmer a fifty-two-year-old Englishman. In mid-1877, of fifty-five principal Sevier stake and ward leaders about a third were American natives, the same percentage were Danish, 15 percent were of English derivation, and the remainder were Scottish, Swedish,

Canadian, Norwegian, Swiss, and German.[10] The cultural and generational diversity of Sevier Valley's Mormon leaders, understandably lacking in cohesion at first, over time proved to be one of the enduring assets of the region's religious climate.

Newly ordained Bishop Dennison Harris used a feature emphasized in the recently enacted priesthood reorganization to foster healing among his new charges. Brigham Young's initiative, issued by missive on 11 July 1877, included a provision that church members "should be visited by the teachers of the Ward in which they reside, and their wrongs be pointed out to them in the spirit of meekness and brotherly kindness, and they be exhorted to repent."[11] The "teachers of the Ward" would serve as the bishop's eyes and ears in ministering to the Saints' needs. The month following his appointment Harris selected eight men to perform the roles of Monroe's ward teachers. "The bishop moved slowly and cautiously selecting for his teachers, the most responsible men in the settlement," Barney wrote, and "after some time I was chosen as one of the ward teachers."[12] Performing a role akin to the one he accomplished in Spanish Fork's reformation days, Barney again felt validated. He was no longer veering near the perimeter of Mormonism where he struggled under the previous regime in Monroe; he was back at the core. Brigham Young died ten days later.

As the settlement wound up business toward year's end, the Monroe Ward numbered 565 members composed of 112 families. Monroe remained the second largest ward in the Sevier Stake next to Richfield with 893 members.[13] While these two Sevier Stake entities were comparatively large for local church units, they showed a rural cast in the manner they did business in contrast to the Wasatch Front's urban wards. Their folksy ways and characteristic neighborliness were still hampered by the divisiveness created by the United Orders. Bishop Harris's report to the stake at year's end stated, "We begin to improve but our progress is slow."[14] Much work to reunite the community remained.

While the church in Monroe was inextricably tied to the United Order for four years, the order's demise did not doom the religious atmosphere of the community. Human beings, social creatures that they are, gather for meetings. Participation in meetings, religious rituals, and sacraments were extremely important to practicing Latter-day Saints. Worship services held on the Sunday Sabbath and gatherings held on other nights of the week fostered community spirit.[15] The nonprofessional local leaders of Mormonism lessened the distance between the laity and the clergy in the church. While bishops of nineteenth-century wards often served the dual roles of a community's civic and religious leaders, their primary responsibility focused on attending to the congregation's spiritual needs. Altogether, the organizational structure of Mormonism worked very well. The integral part the Mormon religion played in the lives of its committed members cannot be overstated.

Barney the Educator, Revisited

Despite Lewis Barney's economic difficulties while a participant in the United Order, the year following his separation from the order his financial status was the best he had known in Monroe. While it was nothing resembling affluence, his taxable status shows him in a state of recovery.[16] As noted previously, Barney had given up farming as his primary means to support his family after leaving Utah County in the early 1860s. The several episodes of working as a sawyer also eventually gave way to his increased age. After his sons put their sawmill in operation in Kanosh's mountains in the year that Barney turned seventy, he returned to Monroe and took up again the role of frontier schoolteacher. While his teaching hardly elevated his economic status, it was a meaningful expenditure of his time. He wrote that in the first week of January 1878 "I engaged to teach a day school in the [nearby] settlement called Brooklyn which I conducted to the satisfaction of all concerned."[17]

Schools in 1878 in Utah were of several varieties. The more urbanized areas had a common school program influenced and supported by the Church of Jesus Christ. The smaller communities, like Monroe, sponsored their own educational forums, but increasingly they faced competition from Protestant mission schools which blossomed in communities large and small. As the Protestants came to the Sevier Valley, Mormons were warned, "Episcopal & sectarian schools are seeking our children."[18] With or without the Protestant presence, Mormon children were taught the *four* Rs: reading, writing, arithmetic, and religion. The proximity of religious competition heightened the concern about the proper indoctrination of Latter-day Saint students. Monroe Mormons, overall, made efforts to upgrade the educational level offered to their children.[19]

Generally, the smaller the community, the smaller the school; the smaller the school, the more primitive the instruction. In such environments the teachers generally lacked training and taught seasonally. This was the case with Lewis Barney. Brooklyn was a small Sevier County settlement just outside of Monroe, first settled in 1873. Lewis's brothers Benjamin and Walter both purchased land and settled there.[20] Lewis ran something equivalent to a private school with children supplied by farm families living nearby. While he was not trained, he was literate and likely conveyed the rudiments of learning to those in his care. "I engaged in teaching a school in Monroe in my own house for the accommodation of my own and Brother Benjamin's children and some other families."[21] In other seasons he conducted classwork in a more formal school setting, and though he taught just seasonally, his teaching career stretched into the late 1880s. He took his duties seriously. During the deep snow and bitter cold in February 1882, for example, he said, "I had a hard time during the winter, as the distance I had to travel to school was two miles and a half."[22] Undoubtedly he had some vision of the value of education and learning for the young generation of Saints.

One of Barney's primary motives in teaching was likely the reality that his own little boy William Edward needed an education. William, Barney's youngest child, was eight years old in 1878, but before the year ended Lewis and Elizabeth suffered the awful tragedy of having their young son die. William expired on 23 December 1878, the eighth of Lewis's fifteen children to die before reaching the age of majority.[23] Despite the trauma of losing his most important student, Barney continued to teach at his school.

The optimism displayed by Monroe citizens in the new era did not envelope the community. While one county resident, via the *Deseret News* in March 1878, touted the area, claiming the "people will compare very favorably with other stakes," and that "a much better feeling exists than a few months ago,"[24] discord still afflicted the folks in Monroe. One resident that summer, thirty-year-old Nephi James Bates, the village's telegraph operator, lamented, "Some of our enemies got up an opposition to our [Sunday School] celebration [complaining that] 'The Sunday School had prohibited anyone but members of the [Sunday] school from taking part in the exercises.'" The rift was so stark that to stem the continuing division many residents were again rebaptized to show their support for community revival.[25] Reliance on traditional community gatherings, such as the celebration of American independence on 4 July 1878, were included in efforts to revitalize the town.[26]

The following year some still complained of a pessimism pervading the village. Bates in April 1879 wrote that it "seems as though everything in town is dying a natural death." "The Choir (once the life of the settlement)," he continued, "has almost become extinct, figuratively speaking." Bates's lament that "at times [the] little patience and forbearance I have, is on the point of giving way," was doubtless shared by many others within the community. Still, he said, "These reflections make me desirous of continuing the struggle to the end. With the help of the Lord I will try and do it."[27] Bates laid blame on the "enemies" of the church, former members now estranged.[28] The Monroe People's Store was incorporated for five years in February 1880 as somewhat of a replacement for the collective endeavor of the United Order. Its subscribers were the Mormon mainstream, but two months after opening for business fire destroyed the store. Rumors swirled that it was arson, purposely set by the so-called "opposition."[29] Whether it was accidental or intentional, the effect was the same. Suspicion and bitterness remained. As late as November 1881, church president John Taylor visited the village hoping to pacify the population in the still-lingering aftermath of the order's demise.[30]

A Decade of Monroe, Utah

The year 1880 was Mormonism's jubilee throughout Utah territory, the fiftieth anniversary of the establishment of the Church of Jesus Christ of Latter-day Saints. It was a time of celebration.[31] At the time of the jubilee and the new decade's beginning, despite a half-dozen years of difficulty, Monroe was residence to 744 people.[32] The 80 families of 1872 nearly doubled to 149 by 1880. Mormons made up 115 of the families (593 people), including polygamist families numbering just over 18 percent of the total. These numbers indicate that about 80 percent of the community claimed a Latter-day Saint identity which replicated Utah's overall Mormon population.[33] While most in Monroe were Mormons, in November 1878 the Presbyterian Church established a school in Monroe and built a log meetinghouse in 1880 which served both as a church and schoolhouse educating Presbyterians and Mormons alike.[34]

Monroe and the rest of Utah at this time were in the middle of a remarkable transformation agriculturally, which had been building momentum since the 1850s. A number of factors fostered the growth, including advances in the science and application of horticulture and the technological development of transportation.[35] Even the Church of Jesus Christ played a significant role in the "practical and ideological" progress of Utah's agriculture. In this climate 58 percent of Monroe's breadwinners were involved in agriculture at a time when "the percentage of those employed in Utah agriculture began to slip below the national average."[36] In the same year that electricity was first introduced in Salt Lake City, Monroe's agrarian character was supplemented by nine businesses including a gristmill (with two millers), two blacksmith shops (with three blacksmiths), two general stores and two cooperative stores (with six storekeepers and clerks), two hotels, a furniture store, and the telegraph operator who also sold stationery and musical equipment. There were also seven carpenters, three schoolteachers, two sawyers, two brickmasons, and one each of cooper, tinsmith, tailor, wheelwright, and cabinet maker. Artisans and other skilled people were required to make a village work. The rest of Monroe's population was lumped into the designation of laborers, which described Barney and his three children in Monroe.[37] As Barney's son Arthur grew older, he often worked for wages outside Monroe, which apparently had little work for laborers.[38] The lack of local work soon affected Lewis as well. Despite the need to muster resources, Barney took a temporary hiatus at this time from the troubles of the world to build upon a postmortal family enterprise.

Personal Religious Revival

Barney was now over seventy. While he had for decades fully subscribed to things Mormon, his religious activity in his twilight years took on an even more devout cast. The first sign of this acceleration of devotion came from the renewal of his Mormon temple experience. It had been thirty-three years since his brief episode in the Nauvoo Temple. Not until 1877 with the completion of the St. George Temple were the full range of temple ordinances made available to Mormon believers. Prior to this time, only select rituals were performed in the Endowment House adjacent to the temple being constructed in Salt

Lake City. Anxious to expand the sacred work to his extended family, "In the spring of 1879, I with my family went to St. George to attend to the ordinances of the gospel for ourselves and some of our friends that had passed behind the veil."[39] The significance of temple rituals for Mormons is based on a concept introduced by Joseph Smith in Nauvoo that included the prospect of salvation for those who had never heard of the Mormon gospel, including the deceased. The mechanism for this practice, as mentioned earlier, was through proxies substituting vicariously for their departed family members. The rituals included baptism, ordinations, and marriages.[40] Thus, to Mormons salvation was possible for people to whom the fullness of Jesus' gospel was not available in mortality. The venue for these ordinances of salvation was Mormon temples, first in Nauvoo and then later in Utah. The consequence for mortals concerning their forebears was described by Joseph Smith in September 1842: "Let me assure you that these are principles in relation to the dead and the living that cannot be lightly passed over, as pertaining to our salvation. For their salvation is necessary and essential to our salvation."[41]

The arousal of Barney's familial passion was part of an overall vision he held regarding the temporal and eternal destiny of his family. Coincident to Barney's acceptance of the Mormon faith in 1839–1840, Joseph Smith taught his followers of a family structure that transcended the mortal world. Parley P. Pratt, a church apostle, wrote that while meeting with Smith in Philadelphia in December 1839 and January 1840, the prophet taught him about an "eternal family organization, and [that] the eternal union of the sexes in those inexpressibly endearing relationships . . . are at the very foundation of everything worthy to be called happiness." Pratt was taught it was a part of God's eternal plan for his children to "prize the endearing relationships of father and mother, husband and wife; of brother and sister, son and daughter," with the promise that "the wife of my bosom might be secured to me for time and eternity."[42] As these teachings were popularized in the Church of Jesus Christ, the faithful calculated to insure that their households embraced their own family kingdom opportunities.

With these objectives in mind, Barney, both of his wives, his son David, his daughters Emeline and Martha Ann, and Martha Ann's husband Thomas Briscoe journeyed 150 miles south from Monroe, arriving in St. George, Utah, 1 June 1879. Beginning 3 June they attended the St. George Temple to stand as proxies for their dead. That first day Lewis was baptized for seventeen of his departed family members, including his son William Edward, who had died just six months earlier, his grandfather Luther, the family's old Sangamon, Illinois, friend James Turley, and other Barney, Turner, Yeoman, and Beard relatives. Betsey was immersed in behalf of Lewis's grandmother Abigail Fountain Barney and Lewis's female Yeoman and Turner kin. Elizabeth was baptized for her mother and several friends. Their children participated as proxies for other family connections.[43] The very process of identifying departed kin requires one

St. George, Utah, with temple in background, ca. 1890. Photographer unknown. Courtesy Church Archives, the Church of Jesus Christ of Latter-day Saints.

to consider his or her own place in the larger family structure. For the Barneys, they were providing the means of celestial opportunity to their family and loved ones. It was a satisfying start for Barney regarding what he viewed to be very sacred work.

A patriarchal blessing he received from Patriarch William McBride in February 1880, somewhat similar to blessings he received in 1841 and 1856, indelibly impressed upon Barney the importance of performing temple work for his family: "Go to [the Lord's] house to do a work that will secure unto thee thy salvation and the salvation of thy relatives and friends."[44] With such weighty consequences to his temple efforts, thereafter Barney became passionate for the remainder of his life about fulfilling this expectation. It interplayed with everything he tried to accomplish over the next fifteen years.

The temple trip and business in St. George took three weeks. Upon their return to Monroe, Barney faced again the routine of providing for Elizabeth and her children; Betsey presumably returned to Kanosh. With Lewis's teaching endeavor providing little support, Arthur's employment outside Monroe provided a chance for the elder Barney to supplement the family with work through the summer of 1879. Castle Valley in Emery County, Utah, was the place. Located about seventy-five miles northeast of Monroe where Lewis chased Indian cattle raiders fourteen years earlier, Lewis and his sons Arthur and David "spent the summer in fencing and dairying." Just before finishing their work, while branding some cattle Arthur "had his collar bone broken and his upper lip split by a cow throwing her head around striking him with her horns in the face and on the shoulder." David's summer of work also had a negative slant. "David was to have a span of horses for his work but in catching them, [Samuel] Gilson [for whom they worked] choked one to death and would not let him have any other. So David got but one horse for his summer's work."[45] But the work was more than they could get in Monroe.

Returning to Monroe for the winter, Barney reopened his small school for six months over the winter of 1879–1880. The school closed in time for the students to assist in their family agricultural requirements. With classwork completed, Barney gathered his portable personal necessities and hiked over the Pahvant Range to the west to rally his family for another trip to the St. George Temple. Much remained to be done. "But," he wrote, "the boys was in the canyon at the sawmill getting out lumber and did not get home for two weeks after my arrival."[46] "By this time," with the St. George trip aborted, "the corn and lucern had to be cut, the potatoes dug, and the apples gathered, [so] I assisted in gathering the fruit and done the chores about the house."[47]

Barney's preoccupation with things religious was also manifest in the more mundane settings of regular Mormon worship. While in Kanosh, a place he had helped settle previously, he "attended the meetings and preached 3 sermons on the privileges of the gospel and the ushering in of the dispensation of the fulness of times, setting forth the first principles of the gospel in a plain and simple manner to the full satisfaction of the entire congregation."[48] Several features of Mormon religious thought dominated his thinking for the rest of his life, two of which were establishing his family kingdom and the pending apocalypse or millennium prior to the Second Coming of Jesus.[49] Both tenets were central to the Mormon gospel and illustrate the beliefs that animated his world view at this time.[50]

Mormonism's practical application of Christianity, though labor intensive, was meant through ecclesiastical structure to assist those in need spiritually and temporally. Barney's commitment to the faith extended beyond just philosophy and ideology as he embraced the requirements necessary to make his religion work. In 1881 he reported,

> [I had] to attend to the ward teachers of Monroe and see that the families of the Saints were regularly visited once a month and see that there was no iniquity in the branch and also to see that the sacrament was administered regularly every Sabbath. Also having a theological class to attend to every Sunday and to see often the poor and those that were sick employed all my time.[51]

And, "about this time [February 1882] I was chosen and unanimously sustained by vote as clerk of the mass quorum of the Seventies of Monroe. This

Arthur Barney (Lewis Barney's son) and family. Photographer and date unknown. Courtesy of Alex and Nellie Barney.

also added to the duties required of me to fill the offices placed upon me."[52] The previous fall Barney reported, "The house where the Saints held their meetings was in a poor condition. It was considered advisable to have it repaired. So there was a committee appointed. I being one of them, I visited the ward for the purpose of raising means for repairing the house. We succeeded in raising the means and the brethren repaired the house."[53] Barney's involvement in the belief and practice of Mormonism was exacting upon him, but he insisted, "I do not wish to have it understood that I am complaining but rather that I rejoice that I am considered worthy to have all this honor and responsibility placed upon me. And I hope I shall be able to discharge the duties of this responsibilities honorably."[54]

The kingdom Barney envisioned for his family, undergirded by religious practice, had a temporal component to it that could not be overlooked. The economics of survival persistently hounded Lewis. In Monroe, "teaching school through the winter of 1880 and 1881," he also calculated for other ways to strengthen his economic status.[55] Lewis's son Arthur, ambitious and desiring to contribute to the family welfare, said "in the spring of 1881 I went down to Salina canyon [located about thirty miles northeast of Monroe] where I worked on the D[enver] & R[io] G[rande Western] railroad grade [for Hyrum Strong] hauling dirt onto a big fill."[56] The foreman's daughter caught Arthur's eye during his employment and he and Mary Strong, his first cousin once removed, were married in May 1881. The family returned to Monroe for the marriage, after which "the party repaired to W[alter] Jones's hall where they joined the lively citizens of Monroe that had been previously invited to join in a free and sociable dance for the purpose of recreation and amusement to finish up the festivities of marriage."[57]

With Arthur returning to Salina Canyon, Lewis, also requiring work outside Monroe, took his son David to nearby Clear Creek Canyon with the hope of obtaining work grading for a railway line in the canyon narrows. But there was no work for them on the project connecting the Sevier and Pahvant Valleys.[58] Hearing of his father's disappointment, Arthur made arrangements for Lewis to work with him in Salina Canyon.[59] Barney again added to his résumé, becoming bookkeeper for the D&RGW crew of James Robbins, the contractor. Their work lasted from the end of May into September 1881.[60] But through discrepancies in Barney's and Robbins's books and from Robbins's charges for supplies, the Strong-Barney connection that summer netted them very little. Lewis believed they had been cheated.[61]

In the fall Barney returned to his school in Monroe which he maintained until February 1882. He returned to a town still unsteady. Dennison L. Harris's appointment as ward bishop had ameliorated tensions within the community to a degree, but polarity continued. In July 1882, Nephi J. Bates, intolerant of pluralism in the village, wrote that in the course of a school trustee election:

> The most remarkable feature of this election is the absence of the "liberal" element of the community; not one of their number came near; making it one of the most pleasant meetings of the kind ever held in this place. After the opposition we have had of late, (about one third of the town being outsiders and apostates) a rest is appreciated.[62]

This was an uncommon pause from several years of tension. Still, dissonance continued to plague the town into the next decade. For Barney, personally, he had his own disappointment to consider.

Arthur Barney and his young bride departed Monroe to make their own way in Castle Valley. Arthur, now thirty, had been a significant asset to the family and his absence was a blow to his father. The recurrent vision of a patrilocal clan of Barneys gnawed at Lewis. The old pioneer's appeal to Arthur in March 1882 summarized his dream, in part: "I have been satisfied for a long time that we would have no luck in the way we have been doing. It is our duty as a family to keep together and if we wish to prosper we must cultivate a feeling of affection for each other and stay together. . . . If we have to make new homes let us all go to some good place and settle together as the Lord requires of us to do." The practical nature of Lewis's dream is evident: "I cannot bear the thought of being deprived of your society. I am getting old and need some comforting words to cheer me up in my troubles and to whom shall I look for consolation but my children and if they are scattered hundreds of miles away how can they say anything for my consolation."[63] With no success or hope at rallying his children around him in Monroe, Barney had to actuate his objective. Much of Utah's hinterlands remained untamed and Barney got wind of a place that just might satisfy his vision: Grass Valley.

Chapter 20

Better Situated: *Farther into the Frontier, 1882–1886*

The United States Senate passed the Edmunds anti-polygamy bill on 16 February 1882, focusing the scrutiny of the American public upon the Mormons once again. A month later the bill passed the House and was signed days later by President Chester A. Arthur. The bill and succeeding legislation created havoc in Utah and within Mormonism in no small way during the remainder of the decade. Polygamists took the government barrage directly. Whether Lewis Barney, whose plural families lived apart, felt threatened by federal marshals worming their way through Utah's settlements is not known. With time ticking away, the machinery of government reprisals against the Saints served as evidence to Barney that the end was drawing near and he had only a short time to be about the business of establishing a family kingdom.

Barney's decision to leave Monroe nearly twenty years after first eyeing the site was probably some time in the making. Monroe's economy had never reached the level hoped by its residents. While he made some advance, certainly it was not satisfactory for Barney. Despite efforts of many residents to recover Monroe's cohesive and progressive potential, Barney, now nearly seventy-four years old, gave up on the village as a geographical destiny. Barney's immediate household was shrinking. While Betsey lived near her three sons in Kanosh, only Elizabeth and two children, sixteen-year-old Emeline and nineteen-year-old David, remained in Lewis's immediate care, though David probably carried most of his father's load. Arthur had moved with his new wife and her family to Castle Valley in the vicinity that later became Emery County's Emery.[1] In Barney's mind, before his family got away from him totally, it was time to act. With winter's cold retreating in the early spring of 1882, Lewis and David "started [on 28 March] for Grass Valley [on] good roads."[2]

This was not a casual move; it was the perpetuation of a lifetime quest. Far less mercurial in his intellectual or spiritual odysseys, Lewis Barney and, indeed, the Barneys generally were quintessential frontiersmen. They exploited the singular token universally offered by America to its citizenry in its first three centuries: the promise of liberty and opportunity. The unfenced frontier, whose primary boundary was the amount of effort required to improve it into production, appeared to the Barneys to have limitless options. And Barney had enough left in him to advance once again, a new start in a new place.

Elizabeth Beard, David, and Martha Ann Barney Briscoe (Lewis Barney's wife, son, and daughter). Photographer and date unknown. Courtesy of Raymond G. Briscoe.

During Barney's Monroe years, he observed the independent and tangential enterprises taken by family members wedging his offspring farther from the family nest. To stem this disappointing movement, into his mind during this period coalesced the outline of a familial domain on the Mormon frontier. There were three components to Barney's ambition. (1) Land. The family had employed patrilocal inclinations (children locating in proximity to the father) from the 1830s, though this trait early on was absent the grander design Barney envisioned in the early 1880s. The move to Grass Valley in 1882 illustrates his more-focused vision. (2) Economy. A financial mechanism was needed to provide material means to support the growing family with food, shelter, and other necessities. Barney's separation from Monroe's United Order in 1875 to initiate his own economic system was his first step in forging this essential to sustain his family. (3) Connection. The family necessarily required something beyond the hope of familial cooperation to bind them together, something transcendent, with implications affecting both mortal and postmortal relationships. Latter-day Saint conceptions of the eternal, extended family unit, implemented through Mormon temple rites and ceremonies, supplied this vital feature of the family's dreams and preoccupations. For an elderly man whose candle continued to burn, perhaps it was too much to consider feasible.

This model of kinship yearnings was not unique to Lewis Barney. Others with similar aspirations and theological constructs manipulated their surroundings on the Mormon frontier to fuse their visions of family kingdom. The Johnson family is perhaps the most notable example. In January 1871 Joel Hills Johnson, nearly seventy years old and the oldest of five brothers, discussed with Brigham Young the idea of establishing a family settlement in southern Utah. Young, while wintering in St. George, suggested Johnson consider Spring Canyon Ranch. By the end of the month Johnson wrote he had "made arrangements to meet my brothers and some others at Virgin City on our way out to look at Spring Canyon Ranch," located fourteen miles northeast of Kanab, Utah. Upon their arrival they "found a beautiful canyon from half to a mile wide several miles long." With water, building rock, fencing timber and firewood, and grass for stock, the Johnson brothers could not have been more excited about the prospect. Within two months the extended family began their gravitation to Spring Canyon. Before long the location acquired the family name; Spring Canyon became Johnson.[3]

With his brothers in proximity, Joel H. Johnson took the next step in 1875. At a family gathering in March, as the family patriarch, he organized his children as the "Sons of Joel." Their stated intent, besides familial consanguinity, was to create "an organized system" to foster affinity among his kinfolk for proper "habits, fashions, customs" and "to observe strictly the laws, rules and customs" of the Mormon faith which inspired their endeavor. Already having employed temple theology and rituals to connect the clan, the Johnson enterprise appeared at the threshold of success. But despite significant strides,

Johnson's family vision broke down. A life-altering drought in 1879 forced them to rethink their Spring Canyon objectives. But undeterred in holding his family together, by year's end Johnson exchanged geography. This time his plan called for them to colonize "some place in Arizona, and organize them in the united order." Neither did this work as Johnson designed. At the age of eighty in 1882, the old family head sat down pining over the status of his family and of his plan for them. "My heart is often pained with sorrow," he lamented, "while tears run down my cheeks by day and wet my couch by night" over the failure to "colonize my family . . . somewhere in Arizona or New Mexico and organize them in the holy order of the sons of Joel." Instead, he wrote, "my sons have scattered to the four winds which causes my present grief."[4] Johnson's family vision was compelling but illusive. Coincident to the demise of the Johnson domain, it was Barney's intent to furbish the setting for his own family's gathering.

Barney's designs were not shared by all of his family. After what appeared to be a tenure of permanency in Monroe, Barney's compulsion to pull up stakes and move created a lingering tension within his family. Thereafter his kinfolk, misunderstanding his objectives, classified him a "wanderer." One granddaughter, speaking about the difficulty experienced by her grandmother Elizabeth, later said, "Grandma lived everywhere [because] Grandpa was a wanderer. . . . He was [a wanderer] before he ever saw the Mormons. His father [Charles] and him was everywhere."[5] Family members misinterpreted Lewis's actions. Post-nineteenth-century moderns misperceive the frontier's opportunity of freedom. Where was it written, where was the statute demanding that as humans mature they immobilize? Barney was never limited by such conventions. With his personal visions of family kingdom, he tested the limits of his family's patience and understanding of their own life's objectives. While his immediate plans for nearby Grass Valley do not seem drastic, other endeavors through the decade of the 1880s, though discountenanced by some family members, are remarkable if seemingly desperate.

Burrville in Grass Valley

Lewis Barney gambled his next move on Grass Valley. Out of the way from most Utah territorial traffic, John C. Frémont likely traveled through the high mountain valley during the fall and winter of 1853–1854 on his last Rocky Mountain venture. The valley to the east of Sevier Valley, parts of which were in Sevier and Piute Counties, was first used for livestock grazing by Sanpete residents. For its proximity to other central Utah settlements, the valley probably would have been settled earlier but for two reasons: the elevation, 7,000 feet at the upper end, and the Indian activity known to exist there. It had its share of commotion during Black Hawk's rampage throughout central Utah in the late 1860s.[6] In June 1873, after the resettlement of Sevier Valley as sites for expansion were considered, Grass Valley was cautiously explored by a party whose objective was to locate possible townsites and ascertain the status of the Ute Indians living there. Hostilities between the Indians and settlers in the aftermath of the Black Hawk War were still vivid in the minds of many. A favorable report from the exploring party resulted in the call of several by Brigham Young to "settle in Grass Valley and assist the Indians." The Ute chief Tabioonah proffered friendship to those on reconnaissance in the valley. On 12 August 1873 several, temporarily including the famed Orrin Porter Rockwell, initiated settlement in Grass Valley.[7]

Difficulties with the valley natives were not extinguished. A few days before Christmas in 1873 the non-Mormon McCarty brothers, living in the valley's northern region, killed three of four Navajo Indians passing through Grass Valley to trade with Utes. The Navajos had slain a beef belonging to the McCartys while waiting out a four-day storm. The fourth Indian, wounded, limped back to his tribe and reported the killings. His tribesmen, of course, were outraged. The resulting tensions took several months to assuage through noted Mormon diplomat to the Indians Jacob Hamblin's intercession.[8] Still, the valley was surveyed for settlement. By April 1874, feeling the threat of Indian aggression was over, Brigham Young encouraged twenty-five families to move to Grass Valley where they arrived in July 1874. Despite the Navajo deaths, good relations with the native Utes were successful for a time. Forty-eight area Indians were baptized as Mormons by July 1875. But even as late as February 1879, threats of violence between Utes and whites still existed.[9]

The lofty mountain valley is several miles wide at points and about forty miles in length. The major stream through the valley is Otter Creek which runs in a south-southwest direction until it empties into a Sevier River branch at the valley's south end.[10] Barney set his eye that spring of 1882 on a site in the valley's northern sector at 7,000 feet, a place called Burrville. A former Monrovian, Albert Thompson, Sr., with whom Barney had served on Monroe's United Order board of directors, had settled there and likely reported Grass Valley favorably to Barney. The townsite was located on Burr Creek, named in honor of the Burr clan who homesteaded the area in the 1870s. The little hamlet was platted, as the crow flies, fifteen miles to the southeast over Monroe's eastern mountains and seven miles north of Koosharem, later the principal valley village. Fourteen miles due east of Burrville is Fish Lake, the beautiful and traditional habitat of the area's Native Americans. Advertisements to lure settlers to Burrville stated it had "a very fine summer range for stock, the vallies [*sic*], hills and almost every nook and corner being covered with luxuriant grass." Though "the nights were generally cool and frosty," it was reported there was "an abundance of wood and some timber in the mountains a few miles distant."[11] A Mormon church organization existed in Grass Valley from 1875, though it was not until July 1877 that the Grass Valley Ward was created, also

David Barney (Lewis Barney's son) and family. Photographer unknown, ca. 1899. Courtesy of Raymond G. Briscoe.

serving those in the valley's northern sector. Burrville was finally organized as a separate church branch in September 1878.[12] Seven years after the initial settlement, 203 people lived in Burrville.[13]

It is almost astonishing that Barney, in 1882 an old man by every definition, had the ambition to not only relocate but to start over from scratch. At a time when most his age conjured strategies for rest, he could not. His primary objectives remained undone. This remarkable drive warrants a review of his labor to create his family's physical domain. It took a day for Lewis and David Barney to get through the mountain pass to Burrville from Monroe. The following day, finding "there was a vacant 40 acres of pasture land I could get by filing on it," Barney said he also, "went to the new sawmill to see about getting lumber for the house [where I] learned by hauling in logs we could get our lumber." Spending three days scouting a homesite and also looking into "getting a school," he found he "could get a 5 acre lot and other land" besides "the school." As there was a vacancy to school the community's children, his teaching experience conveniently fit the settlement's need for a teacher in the small but inadequate log building erected in 1878.[14] Heartened, he returned to Monroe to prepare for his family's relocation to Burrville.

Preparing Elizabeth and Emeline in Monroe for the move in April 1882, he wrote after returning to Burrville, "I bought 5 acres of land of John Burr for which I gave one cow and calf and 5 dollars." David "then grubbed it and put it in oats, lucern, and potatoes."[15] The arrangements made in his reconnaissance of Burrville allowed him to begin teaching soon after his arrival. His school opened on 17 April. His son David returned on 5 May to Burrville from Monroe "with 2 wagon loads of household goods" and Elizabeth and Emeline in tow. A tent likely served as their living quarters after their arrival. David then "finished plowing and putting in his crop consisting of oats, lucern, peas, and potatoes" before returning to Monroe to sell their "house and lot" for a "wagon and span of horses." (They fared worse than when leaving Nauvoo nearly forty years earlier.) David then shuttled back and forth between Burrville and Monroe freighting the Barneys' goods and equipment. By May's end, while Barney taught, they began their home, getting house logs out of the canyon.[16] David's loyalty and service to his father spirited Lewis's dreams.

On the first weekend of June 1882, two of the Twelve Apostles came from Salt Lake City to reorganize the Grass Valley Saints. Two wards thereafter divided the valley: the Grass Valley Ward in the south part and the Burrville Ward to serve the northern Saints.[17] Twenty-two Mormon families comprised of eighty-four persons made up Burrville's ward.[18] Barney's schoolhouse provided seating for the reorganization meeting in the grove, preempting his teaching for a week during which time he "assisted David in watering the grain, laying the foundation of the house," and going into the canyon for more house logs.[19] Once his school closed in mid-June for the summer, he concentrated his energy on finishing the house.

Filing on forty acres of Burrville land on 1 July 1882, Barney traveled the twenty-eight miles to Richfield two weeks later to finalize the arrangement after discovery of a discrepancy in the original transaction.[20] The last log on the home was laid 11 July. Only the roof remained. On 18 July Lewis, David, and Arthur, who had returned for a visit, went to the mountains for more lumber. Finding only corral-quality timber, they loaded their wagon and returned from the canyon after a hard day's work, apparently too hard for the aging senior Barney.[21]

Early the following morning, 19 July 1882, Barney awakened "with a pain near the heart," suffering "severely for 3 hours." The attack so weakened him he was confined to bed for three days. The exact nature of this cardiac difficulty is not known. But on 22 July he was back up and working. Without medical counsel, his hasty return proved unwise for he suffered a relapse on 25 July enervating him into the second week of August.[22] Having been relatively free of serious physical debility, the confinement, while establishing himself in Burrville, was most difficult. Still, when he could, he continued work on his house. It took till nearly year's end before he moved his family into their new home.

His initial experiences in Burrville encouraged permanency. Establishing a school was only part of the welcome and recognition extended him. Three months after settling in the village, on 9 July 1882, he was appointed superintendent of the Burrville Ward Sunday School.[23] He was honored on the Pioneer Day celebration that summer as well. In Burrville's red cedar grove on 24 July he "delivered an oration on the causes of the kingdom of God being located in the valleys of these mountains." In his speech he contrasted the "the entrance of the pioneers into the valley of the Great Salt Lake and the present time showing the advancement that had been made from that time to the present."[24] He was asked to speak at other church meetings as well and was absorbed in local church affairs. Burrville's circumstances felt good to him. Perhaps this was the place he had been yearning for all his life.

Arthur was the first to submit to the patriarch's appeal to gather as a family. Barney's plea to his son in March apparently took effect. Arriving on 10 June 1882 for a visit, Arthur, undoubtedly lobbied by his father and seeing the area's potential, was convinced after two days he could make a go of it there. For three mares, he bought eighty acres of land and meadow. A month later Arthur moved his wife and household goods to their new homesite. Lewis and Elizabeth were elated, but their pleasure was short-lived. "Arthur lost his best mare and colt" in August. After a fruitless two-week search, the loss of a mare and colt was too much for Arthur. Discouraged, with any previous enthusiasm for Burrville gone, Arthur started back to Muddy Creek in Castle Valley on 20 August causing his parents much sorrow.[25] If there was any consolation, their daughter Martha Ann and her husband Thomas Briscoe, the second to respond to Barney's appeal, pledged to give Burrville a try.

Once Barney started feeling better, the veteran, now three-quarters of a century old, resumed work on his home and outbuildings as well as harvesting what had been planted in the spring. He found time on 25 September 1882 to attend "a caucus meeting in the evening to elect a delegate to attend the Sevier Co. convention to elect a representative to Congress."[26] At September's end he laid the chimney's rock foundation, finished the rafters on 17 October, and two days later began shingling his house. Over the next month, he continued "work on the house making doors and window frames, chinking and daubing the house and laying the floors." Finally on 28 November, they moved into their house, though the finishing work continued. A month later he reported he "got a load of wood for John A. Burr to finish paying for the 5 acres of land we builded our house and corral on."[27] His family's homestead, built within the year, was clear of debt.

Another Venture to the St. George Temple

With his home built and Martha Ann's family nearby, as temperatures warmed after a frigid winter, Barney set sights on the temple again. Since his St. George trip in 1879 he had been planning another expedition to continue his family's sacred business. The highlight this time, though, was the marriage of his daughter Emeline to Albert Thompson, Jr. Their temple venture, beginning 25 March 1883, took a week. Traveling south they passed through Joseph, west through Clear Creek Canyon, on to Beaver, Parowan, Kanarraville, and Harrisburg, arriving in St. George on 2 April. They found after their arrival, however, that church president John Taylor's required temple marriage endorsement had not been secured. The wait for Taylor's approval was no problem for Barney, however. Renting a room for a dollar a week, he dove back into performing his family's vicarious temple work started four years earlier. Also, discovering his brother Henry lived in nearby Santa Clara, Lewis soon embraced his brother whom he had not seen for years. "We were pleased to see each other," he said, "and enjoyed the evening in conversation pertaining to father's work and our own salvation."[28]

On 3 April the Barneys, including brother Henry, were involved again in baptisms and endowments for their deceased ancestors.[29] On 6 April President Taylor's dispatch arrived and Sarah Emeline Barney and Albert Thompson, Jr., were married at the temple. While there Lewis and Elizabeth participated in other sacred rituals also requiring John Taylor's approval, receiving on 9 April "our anointings for ourselves and for my father and mother."[30] As part of the Mormon doctrine of connecting the human family, Barney also had his father's family vicariously "adopted to Hyrum Smith the Patriarch." Linking the generations to prominent church leaders, this was, at the time, an important ordinance to the Saints.[31] Having his family participate with him in temple ordinances which undergird Mormon theology about life's purpose and the hope of eternal reward was a great satisfaction to Barney. En route homeward, the party, accompanied by Henry, went by way of Panguitch where Henry presumably visited his son Alma. Lewis's family arrived in Burrville on 18 April 1883.[32]

From all appearances, Barney showed happiness in his Burrville life. On 23 May 1883 he reported to his brother Benjamin's wife, Caroline, Elizabeth's sister, "We have sold out in Monroe and have moved to Grass Valley. We have as good a house as we had in Monroe if not better. And in other respects we are better situated than we have been since we have been in Utah."[33] After all he had done the previous thirty years it looked like there may finally be the return on his investment for which he had yearned, but something significant happened later in the year about which he did not report.

It had to have been life-altering to reorient Barney's thinking after such a favorable start in Burrville. A possible motive for the change may have been that Mormon polygamists were threatened with prison time in the wake of the Edmunds Act passed by Congress in 1882 to curtail both Mormon polygamy and theocratic power in Utah, though the active pursuit of polygamists by government officials did not start in earnest until the spring of 1884. Still there is a possibility that Barney feared, in his old age, that his polygamous circumstances might make him vulnerable to prosecution. Whatever the motive, he decided after so much work to again move on. Released as Sunday School superintendent at September's end, in November he, his wife Elizabeth, his son David, and daughters Martha Ann and Emeline and their husbands were off on another adventure.[34] But this time the objective was not just over the mountain.

The Journey South

Barney's itinerary and intentions were not apparent at the journey's outset, but clearly the Mormon settlements on Arizona's Little Colorado River were a possible destination.[35] A western New Mexico opportunity, just beyond the Little Colorado settlements, also held promise. Mormons had penetrated into the Arizona desert with the object of colonization as early as 1854, but it was not until Mormon missionaries to the Indians became well acquainted with northern Arizona and its native inhabitants that settlement efforts were seriously implemented. In the 1870s, sites conducive to habitation were carefully scrutinized, a number emerging as Mormon villages before decade's end.[36] Traveling south from Burrville that fall, Barney and his family probably followed the Sevier River south to Panguitch, through Long Valley, and east over some of the same terrain covered in 1776 by Dominguez and Escalante to Lee's Ferry on the Colorado River where they entered the desert domain of the Navajos. From there, "after passing over the desert of 250 miles with very little feed or water, we struck the Little Colorado River, a stream of low water, affording about the

Lewis Barney inscription, 29 November 1883, at Willow Springs, Arizona. Photograph by Carmen Smith, ca. 1993.

same as the Spanish Fork River in Utah. The bottoms along the river," Barney wrote, "is from one to four miles wide, mostly sand. The 100 miles are covered with a dense forest of cottonwood trees from one to two miles wide up to the [village of] Sunset [near modern Winslow, Arizona]." His appraisal of the area was not glowing: "This part of the river is of little use as a farming country, but many places is good for grazing. It is a dangerous stream for stock as it is almost a bed of quicksand. . . . After passing Sunset the sands diminished, but the cottonwood is large and covers the bottoms for seventy-five miles."[37] It was not only a journey of difficult physical hardship, there is evidence in Barney's nearly daily account that the family experienced some tension during the desert passage. Under the circumstances, who could expect otherwise?

En route the family rested at Willow Springs "at the head of Hamblin Wash where the Echo Cliffs began flattening out at the south end of the Kaibito Plateau" just north of what became Tuba City, Arizona.[38] This popular rest stop of voyagers in transit between Utah and Arizona was a place to recruit themselves and their animals in the midst of a forbidding environment. There on 28–29 November 1883, Lewis, David, and Tom Briscoe scratched their names in the huge boulders of soft red rock at the mouth of the wash, similarly to scores of other travelers in the 1870s and 1880s. Their graffiti remains visible today.

On 8 December 1883 they reached the Little Colorado River settlement of "Old Fort Brigham," also called Brigham City and Sunset. On the 13th they had the misfortune of losing one of their animals. "One of Tom's [Briscoe] horses balked and Tom struck him with a shovel and, making an accidental blow, . . . killed him and we left him dead on the ground."[39] Passing through Joseph City and Holbrook, they reached St. Johns, Arizona, on 17 December where they stayed for nearly a month. There David and Albert took jobs freighting grain seventy-five miles to Fort Apache while the others pitched tents waiting for their return. While at St. Johns, Barney "had a good visit" with Andrew Gibbons, "my old mess mate and cook," with whom he had traveled in the 1847 pioneer vanguard. Gibbons, now fifty-eight, had also accompanied Lewis's brother Henry down the Colorado River in 1868.[40] During the wait, Tom Briscoe augmented their meager circumstances by gathering wood which he sold to local villagers.[41]

Barney became uneasy and anxious when David and Albert did not return by the first of the year. As their absence stretched to nearly three weeks, his concern led him out on the road to meet them, sometimes miles and miles out of town, before returning only to repeat the procedure the next day. David and Albert returned, finally, on 6 January 1884, their "horses badly used up." The caravan reconstituted, they made preparations to continue. He found nothing along the Little Colorado to stir his imagination. Emeline and Albert Thompson liked St. Johns and decided to stay, not exactly according to her father's plan. Clearly their departure from the party chipped away at the old pioneer's objectives, but Barney would not be deterred. Bidding the Thompsons farewell, they started on 13 January for what now became their destination—Luna Valley, New Mexico. Journeying southeasterly during the winter, they encountered bad weather with cold and snow and, the region being sparsely settled, they got lost and had to backtrack several miles. Passing the little settlement of Nutrioso, Arizona, on 18 January 1884, three days later they sighted their objective. Rolling into Luna Valley that afternoon, they were "very tired and worn out but glad to get to the end of the journey of fifty days over eight hundred miles of sand and desert country."[42]

Luna Valley, New Mexico

Luna Valley, near the western border of New Mexico, is located about halfway between the territory's northern and southern boundaries. The mountain valley, sixty-five miles from St. Johns, Arizona, is about six miles long and two and a half miles wide. Lying forty miles west of the Continental Divide which serpentines through western New Mexico, it is surrounded by timber-covered hills and mountains and is halved by the San Francisco River which waters the area. Two Swapp brothers, Mormons, traveled through the valley in 1882 driving a

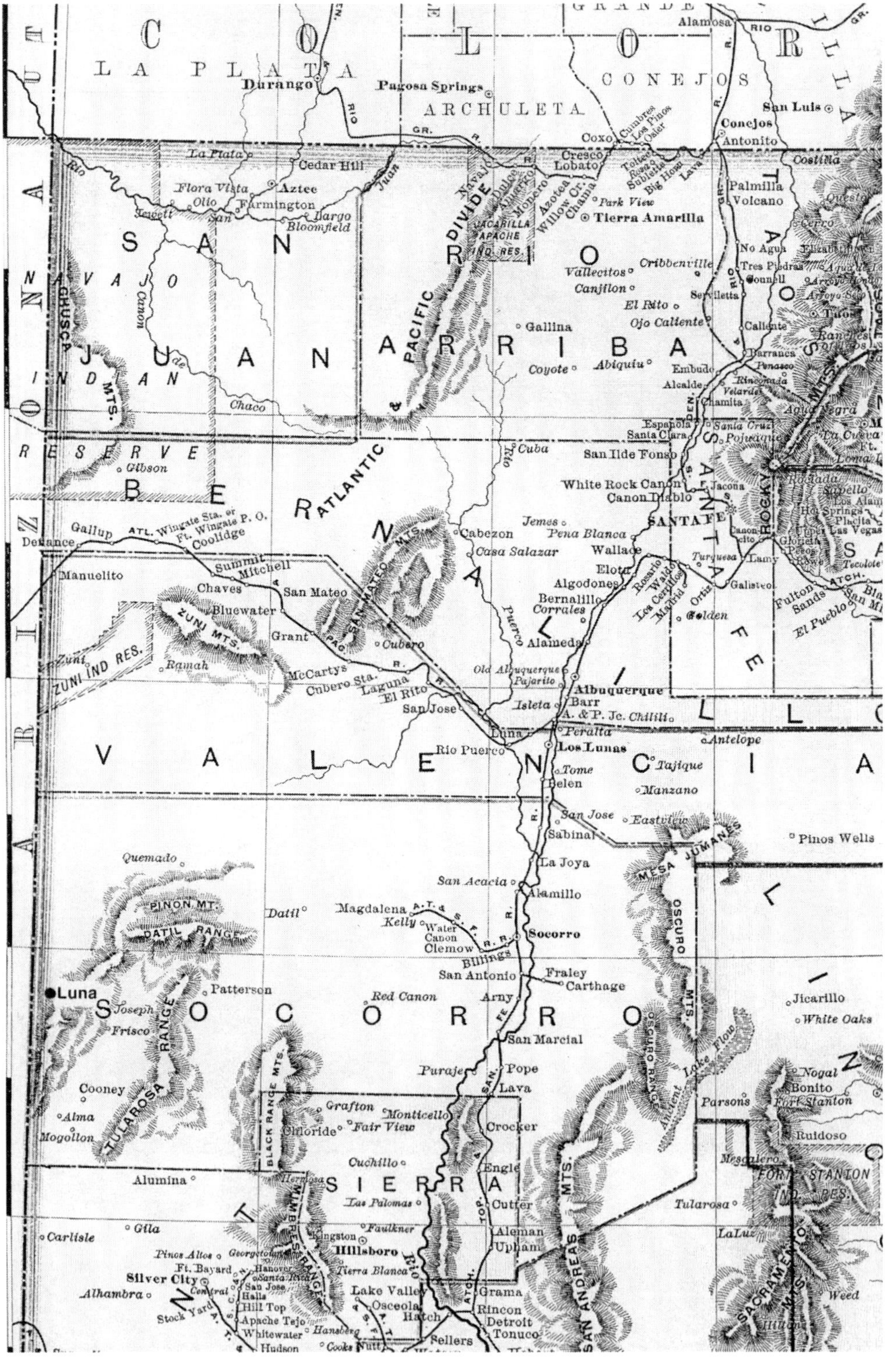

New Mexico, 1894. From *Universal Atlas Map of New Mexico* (Rand McNally & Co.).

herd of cattle from Utah to New Mexico. They recognized the area's potential and determined to settle there the following year. Three Swapp families and a family of Watsons traveled from Utah to Luna Valley during the winter of 1882–1883 arriving there on 23 February 1883. Other Swapps followed. They bought the claims of two trappers and declared the valley as theirs. Soon there were six men, six women, and twenty-two children trying to make a go of it in the unsettled vale.

Shortly after arriving they were visited by the Luna brothers who explained the new settlers were trespassing. The valley was their herd ground, had been for ten years, and the squatters would have to leave. Despite the Lunas' threat of having fifty men to back up their claim, the new settlers decided to stay. Later that year the Lunas ran their sheep into the valley as threatened, but the fledgling homesteaders resisted, driving the sheep from their land. While both sides pressed their claims, fortunately no violence erupted. For protection the settlers built a twenty-foot-square "fort" as a signal to both the Lunas and area Indians who also posed a threat. Deciding the squatters were there to stay, the Lunas figured their sheep business not worth the trouble and sold the herd the following year.[43] When the Barney family arrived in Luna, only four other Mormon communities existed in New Mexico: Ramah, settled in 1876 by former Little Colorado River settlers; Fruitland, settled in 1880; Pleasanton, an entity since 1882; and Gila, founded in 1881.[44]

The week of the Barneys' arrival in January 1884, the Swapps helped them find land compatible for their designs. Checking out several locations, they finally "went over a little hill and found some good claims and located on it." The Barneys planned for three homes: one for Lewis, one for David, and one for the Briscoes. Starting anew yet another time, cutting house logs and digging a ten-foot well soon occupied their time. While Barney had been involved in the process a dozen times before, it had not become any easier. Creating a homestead from nothing was a significant endeavor, no matter the previous experience. Finding the well water plentiful they moved to their claims on 29 January, pitching their tents while improving the land and building their homes. Bad weather and having to secure food through hunting made progress very slow. Feed for their stock was scarce and on 5 February Barney wrote, "My best mare died." A week later he nearly lost another one, but obtaining "a sack of oats" he "saved her." One home was sufficiently finished on 20 February to be habitable. The next month they started on the next one. Limited resources required that David return "to Arizona to work for seed grain to plant and for flour." Tom Briscoe followed suit in March. Despite the interruptions and difficulties, they progressed to where, Barney said, they "commenced cutting logs for my house having finished the others' first."[45]

Lorenzo Watson, a thirty-four-year-old English emigrant and one of the first settlers of the valley, summarized the settlement's status in March 1884: "The six families who entered the valley a year ago have been added to, to the number of forty-five. . . . Twenty-six log houses have been built in the town and one frame house. The latter, with two of the log houses, are covered with shingles. The rest of the people are still living in tents and wagons. Three of the lots are fenced."[46] Emeline and Albert Thompson were apparently among those who later bolstered the hamlet. The settlers, dependent on one another, rendered aid to their neighbors in many circumstances. One episode of such help came in the birth of Tom and Martha Ann Briscoe's child on 2 April 1884 when several families assisted in needed services.[47]

Life in the new settlement was everything but easy. In mid-May 1884 "Thomas Briscoe arrived home from St. Johns without anything for his family and David had nothing but what he pawned his rifle for, not enough for seed and flour to last until we could raise a crop." To complicate things, Barney said, "there is growing trouble between the Saints and Mexicans at St. Johns and Tom went back again as a guard," for which he got "thirty dollars a month and board." Needing resources himself, Barney heard of someone who needed a home built nearby and traveled two days hoping for the employment. Being unable to find "the party that wanted the house built," he wrote, "I started back for my home in Luna Valley and Albert went on to Round Valley to see if he could get any work." That evening Barney arrived home at dusk and lay down to rest for the night sick, tired, and hungry. The disappointment sapped his strength, rendering him unfit for several days. The month had been a continuing exercise of clearing land, building fences, planting crops, and hoping the frost would delay its arrival. The middle of June "heavy frost killed the corn, beans, and all the vines. We are all very discouraged," Barney lamented.[48]

Through the summer of 1884 Barney tended what crops survived while improving his family's circumstance as best he could. In concert with incessant work, he found time to attend church meetings, Mormonism still the pulse of his environment. When the village celebrated the Mormon pioneers' entrance into the Salt Lake Valley on 24 July, Barney was called upon to deliver the address being one of the old pilgrims himself. After a summer's work, despite the report near harvest time that "the melons weigh about fifty pounds and the other crops are in proportion," and "the corn is ten feet high and the grain to my arm pits," he still complained that "we are very discouraged with the country."[49] The record of Barney's stay in Luna Valley after 1884's summer is silent. It is not known when he decided that New Mexico was not the answer to his search, but sometime in 1884 or 1885, he left Luna Valley disappointed and discouraged.

At the same time he struggled in Luna Valley, his oldest son Walter T. Barney received the call of church authorities to leave Kanosh, Utah, and move his family to southeastern Arizona's Gila River Valley. Settling in Graham County near Solomonville (present Solomon), he homesteaded a quarter section of land and later established a mercantile business in Matthewsville (Glenbar), Arizona. He remained in the area to the end of his life in 1914.[50] Solomonville is, straight-line, about ninety miles from Luna

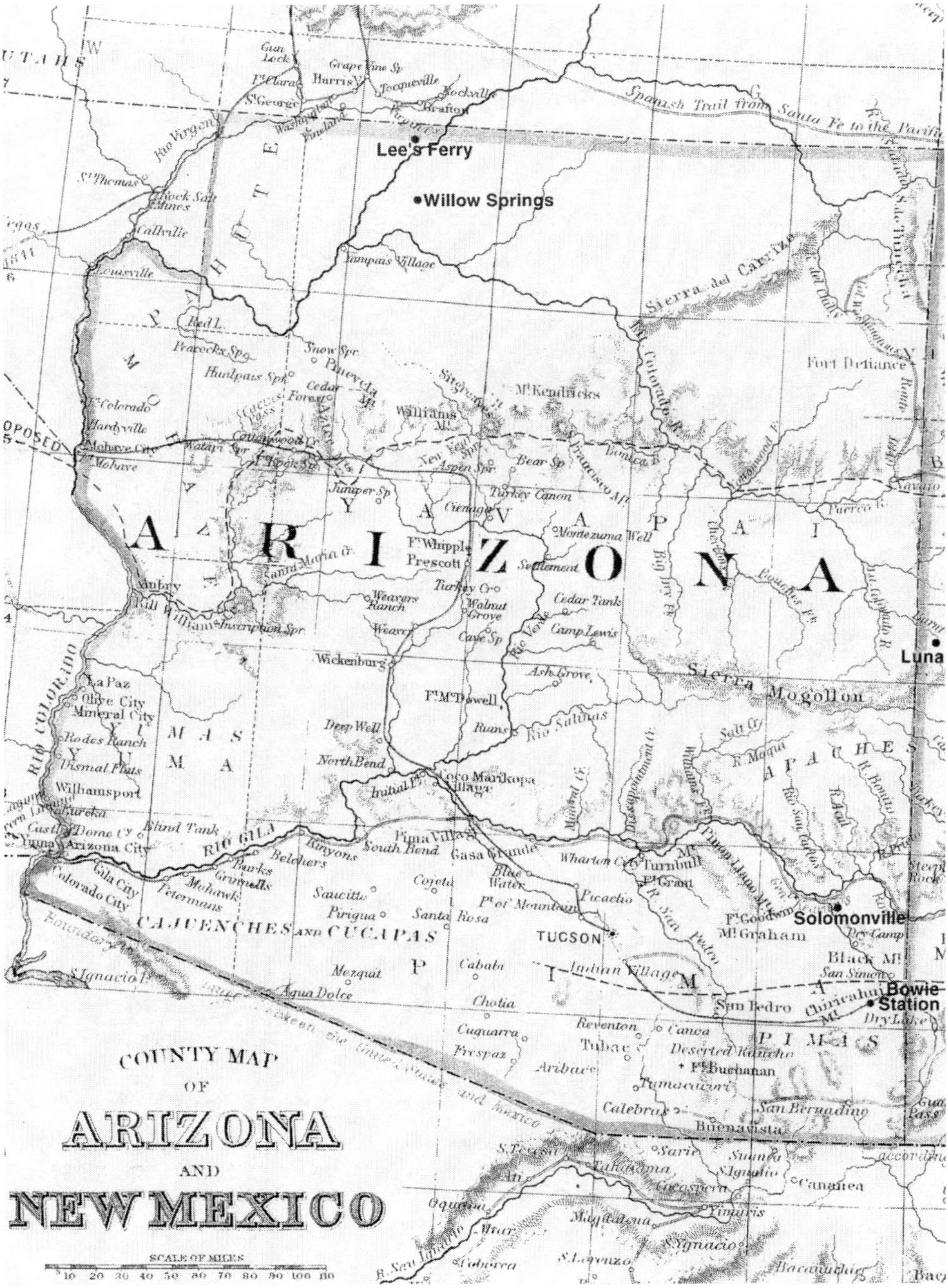

Arizona, 1879. Drawn by W. H. Gamble (Philadelphia: S. A. Mitchell).

Valley. Lewis likely visited Walter T. in the Gila River Valley after his New Mexico disappointment, and sometime in 1885 or 1886 Lewis Barney, his wife Elizabeth, their son David, and daughter Martha Ann and her husband Tom could be found in Arizona themselves.

Bowie Station, Arizona

No information is available to explain why, but early in 1886 the family members resided in Bowie Station, Cochise County, Arizona. The county, located in Arizona's southeasternmost corner, already had a notoriety steeped in fable. Drawn to the area to work the newly discovered mines, the new immigrants were a rowdy bunch. Indeed, Cochise County acquired the reputation for being "the last refuge of a scoundrel."[51] Also found within county lines was what had become the famous town of Tombstone. Located about fifty miles southwest of Bowie Station, by the early 1880s Tombstone had a few thousand residents and already had the distinction of lawlessness and frontier violence. During 1881–1882 Wyatt Earp and his brothers tangled with the Clanton and McLaury clans resulting in several killings, fixing Tombstone's association with the Wild West thereafter.[52] The Barneys arrived in Bowie Station as the smoke cleared.

To the side of Tombstone, Bowie Station was almost tepid. Also called Teviston at the time, Bowie was a stop on the Southern Pacific railway crossing southern Arizona's desert. Located in the county's northeastern part, Bowie was about fifty miles south of Solomonville and seventy miles north of the Mexican border. The old Gila Trail and Butterfield Stage route passing through the region had been used since the 1850s. The station constructed at the time the railway was built in 1881 was named after nearby Fort Bowie, built in 1862 to protect the overland stage from Indian attacks in southern Arizona. Mining developed in the area and in 1881 a hotel graced Bowie Station making the place a strategic stop on the railroad, but 1885–1886 was a particularly precarious time to locate there. The U.S. government, from their Fort Bowie headquarters, had been for several years applying great force to eradicate the area's Apache Indian presence.[53] The Indians were at war simply to protect what had once been their traditional domain from the encroaching presence of the whites. Bowie Station's momentary period of fame came in 1885–1886 when the U.S. military finally stamped out Apache resistance in southeastern Arizona, culminating in the capture of Geronimo. In September 1886, along with nearly seven dozen other Apache captives, Geronimo was forced into a railroad car at Bowie Station and shipped to exile aboard a Southern Pacific train bound for Florida.[54]

Why the Barneys were there and precisely when and under what circumstances they arrived in Bowie Station are not known. Lewis Barney's activities in southeastern Arizona and what he hoped to accomplish there are also obscure. Sometime in 1886 during his stay he again took up the pen to recount his life, first attempted in 1878. Preoccupied with preserving his identity, while in the desolate climate of the American Southwest, he sketched another autobiography, this one of three hundred pages. He also began to accumulate and preserve his personal papers.[55] His days were filled with introspection and nostalgia. His life had not been easy, and there was little, in a material way, to show for it. Still, absent an estate and the accumulation associated with prosperity, the hardness of nearly eighty years of frontier living had conferred on him a mantle of experience he was anxious to preserve. The extent of the vision he wished passed to his posterity and others is not known, although as stated previously he applied to have the second autobiography printed. Barney's personal nineteenth-century saga of the American and Mormon hinterlands was to him worth the telling.

While Barney's occupation in Bowie is not known, to help sustain the family, his wife Elizabeth and their daughter Martha Ann established a restaurant to serve railway passengers at the rail stop. They prospered some, and while in Bowie, Tom Briscoe, became involved in freighting.[56] Whatever Barney's designs were on Bowie, his dream dominated his thinking. While visiting Walter T. in April 1886, Lewis wrote to Betsey in Kanosh, lamenting his search "to find a place where I could have my family all located around by so I could see my children and visit them at any time." For the old veteran, "this has been my desire all the time and I still hope this will be our happy lot some time not far in the future."[57] Besides being a difficult climate whose searing heat debilitated Tom Briscoe, Barney had discovered that Arizona was not the place to satisfy his dream. In June 1886 he packed up once again and set out for a return to Utah. The New Mexico/Arizona experiment ended in failure for the Barneys.

The Return to Utah

Barney did not disclose the reason, but Elizabeth and David did not leave Bowie with him. Some type of disagreement preceded his departure. Separating from his family he traveled north, pausing to visit with Walter T. on 11 July. There in Solomonville he met up with the Briscoes who awaited Barney's arrival to accompany his return to Utah. To Martha, her father explained that "David and his mother had backed out and would not join them in the company to Utah." Later that evening, to Barney's surprise, "David and his mother drove up to camp and gave their reasons for not going on with them."[58] While Barney did not reveal the discussion, it is not a stretch to imagine that some of Elizabeth's reticence was tied to her reservoir of patience being nearly dry, akin to Betsey's years before. Twenty years younger than her husband, but now nearly sixty herself, Elizabeth was likely disillusioned with Barney's ambition and evanescent dream. He had in the previous four years, dragging her in tow, relocated three times, built two homes, and traversed over a thousand miles without satisfaction. Elizabeth's granddaughter, with whom she lived prior to her death, later complained that her grandmother had a countenance of sadness because she was not happy with Barney's singlemindedness. To illustrate Lewis's occasional indifference to his wife's needs, she said, "Grandpa didn't care if there was food in the house."[59] Nevertheless on 14 July 1886 Barney and the Briscoes, including their son Willie, "rolled out, leaving David and his mother going back to Bowie Station."[60] What Elizabeth and her son David returned to or how long they would stay is unknown.

Barney's return with his family to Utah was in the middle of a hot Arizona summer. The journey's terrain varied from sandy desert to steep mountain passes where they had to double-team their animals. The return, itself, was a significant ordeal, and more, Barney walked most of the way. The difficult journey was tempered by expressions of human kindness to the sojourners along the way. Traveling north on an established road to Utah, for example, after two weeks they visited the little Mormon settlement of Pine Creek located in Arizona's center. "Here," Barney wrote, "we laid over on the 31st [July] and was treated with the greatest kindness by the settlers." He was so impressed with the atmosphere of "peace and harmony," he identified the hamlet as "a settlement of God." "We was almost tempted to remain there," he said, "the love for each other was the most wonderful spirit that I ever felt." On they moved. On 13 August, after a month of travel, they arrived in Flagstaff where they stayed "for seventeen days to work for provisions." There they were "furnished a large house to live in rent free and some other accommodations."[61] The exhausting heat and rough landscape were broken by their stay in Flagstaff's mountain setting. Once resupplied they continued northward.

Arriving at the Colorado River on 8 September 1886, for the weary travelers it had been two months traveling the length of Arizona. Already an ordeal, crossing the Colorado, with its sheer canyon walls hundreds of feet above the river, added to their difficulty. On the bank opposite Lee's Ferry, the site established by John D. Lee in 1872 to service travelers, Barney wrote, "Here we examined the road over Lee's Backbone."[62] The backbone was a notorious "one and one-half mile route through tortuous rock gullies of the Shinarump ledge which rises sharply from the river on the left bank." Over this impossible terrain "a road of sorts was dug, picked and blasted into what still looks like a giant rock stairs," from which the backbone derived its name.[63] After trying every alternative they could to circumvent the difficult, jagged spine without success, Barney said, "We went back to try and see if we could get over the backbone." After an already difficult day he said, "We finally succeeded in getting the things all to the top of the hill after dark," where they had to sleep that night. He closed the day with this entry: "This is the roughest birthday I ever experienced." He was seventy-eight years old that 8 September 1886.[64]

Finally crossing the Colorado, they "drove on two miles to the ferry man's [Warren Marshall Johnson] house." Stopping for noon, "we bought a lot of nice ripe peaches, the first we had had for three years." But their difficulty was not over. Besides their travel difficulties, Barney became sick with "the most severe shake and ague I ever felt in my life." The effects grounded him for several days. After having passed House Rock Valley, Johnson (the Johnson brothers' settlement mentioned earlier), and Panguitch, they followed the Sevier River to Circle Valley before finally arriving in Burrville on 24 September 1886. The trip had taken two and a half months.[65] Even his experience with the 1847 pioneer vanguard forty years earlier was significantly less difficult than his Arizona journey that summer.

In Burrville for about a month, the Barneys and Briscoes recovered from their ordeal and worked for provisions while they considered their next step. Returning to the village from which he departed three years earlier, once his most favorable locale, Burrville apparently held no attraction to the erstwhile resident now. Whether he still felt anxious about federal prosecution in returning to Utah is not known, but two days after arriving in Burrville he wrote his son Arthur, who had that fall acquired forty acres of land and built a house in Wellington, Utah. After rehearsing his Arizona trip, Barney, looking for some place to temporarily land, stated if Arthur desired to see his father he would have to retrieve him because Martha Ann and Tom had had enough of life on the road and would stay in Burrville. Having no animals for transit, only "bedding, clothing, and provision," a paltry collection of possessions after seventy-eight years, it required someone else to take the old traveler to his next destination.[66]

Barney's three-year sojourn in New Mexico and Arizona ended. Seemingly his ambition for family refuge was now erased. He was a man without a home. One would think the pattern of his disappointment would have deflated whatever imagination remained, but despite his lack of visible success, the fervor burned. Extraordinarily, nearly eighty years old and somewhat enfeebled, Lewis Barney had not given up. The pulse of his family vision continued to rhythmically beat.

Chapter 21

If It Takes the Rest of My Life: The Quixotical Family Kingdom, 1886–1894

Historian Frederick Jackson Turner, influenced by the 1890 census report, popularized in 1893 the watershed conclusion that the American frontier was closed. Determined in part from the ratio of persons to land, Turner argued the open spaces and wildness of America that characterized the country since its beginnings were now closed, rendering the opportunity offered by the frontier no longer applicable. The concept, as well as the milestone, was significant. The frontier, he stated, had been the underlying tool in the creation of Americanism: "The existence of an area of free land, its continuous recession, and the advance of American settlement westward, explain American development." The westward movement, he claimed, had shaped the American character through the development of the vast expanse of the American West as wave after wave of emigrants filled the landscape. "The true view in the history of this nation," he declared, "is not the Atlantic coast, it is the Great West."[1] The importance of the frontier to the corpus of the American character was foundational.

Subsequent generations of historians have dismantled Turner's concepts arguing he ignored, among other matters, issues of race, gender, and imperialism that played so much into America's "conquest" of the frontier. Of course, the revisionism of Turner's "thesis" itself has been revised.[2] The points of controversy concerning Turner's postulations, however, were outside Lewis Barney's experience with the receding frontier. He and his kin were among the enterprising Americans identified by Turner who filled the frontier's empty corners. While there were a few episodes within Barney's life wherein he temporarily left the frontier's frayed edge, the last dozen years of his life in particular were a reversion to the Barney family quest for new land characterizing the first decades of his life. Turner's claim that "the most significant thing about the American frontier is that it lies at the hither edge of free land" would have meant something to the Barneys,[3] for the perimeter of civilization was their primary domain throughout the nineteenth century. But as the frontier disappeared so also did Barney's chance to fulfill his ambition of establishing a family kingdom in an unfettered spot in the West.

Wellington on Price River

The whereabouts of Barney over the winter of 1886–1887 is not known. The written exchange between him and Arthur upon the former's return from Arizona drew the elder toward his son then living in Wellington, Utah. While he may have relocated to Arthur's prior to the end of March 1887, it was then that Barney reconnected to a Mormon congregation by being accepted into Emery County's Price Ward, of which Wellington was a part until 1890. Upon his acceptance, he submitted to the common nineteenth-century Latter-day Saint ritual of rebaptism that day to demonstrate his unwavering faith in his church. He was the oldest person in the ward.[4]

Barney was not in unfamiliar territory. A detail of the "Green River Expedition" in 1865 chasing Black Hawk's raiders from Sanpete into Castle Valley, the militia, of which Barney was a part, had traversed what was now called Wellington. Located on the Price River in upper Castle Valley, Wellington was first considered for habitation by Mormons in 1877. Castle Valley, named after the unusual physiographic formations characterizing parts of the area, was first used by settlers as summer range for cattle. Though much of the region is desolate and barren, Ute Indians had inhabited the valley for decades, and it also served as their refuge during the Black Hawk War after making raiding forays into Sevier and Sanpete Valleys. The Wellington town site at nearly 6,000 feet in elevation, upstream six miles from Price and 127 miles southeast from Salt Lake City, was located on a bench between hills to the north and the Price River on the south. The first land claim in Wellington came in 1879 followed by enough Latter-day Saint settlers, after irrigation water was drawn from the Price River, that a Mormon congregation was established in 1884. Jefferson Tidwell, the man who reconnoitered the area in the 1870s, was appointed presiding elder. A meetinghouse was built the next year and following further growth the branch became a ward in 1890. It was Tidwell's brother-in-law, J. Wellington Seely, after whom the town was named.[5]

Wellington's first years were very difficult for the settlers. Those who first arrived lived in dugouts while trying to manage water from the river, the success of which would determine whether or not they would stay. Dam building was followed by several events of dam failure, and the resultant flooding made enduring prospects uncertain. Food had to be imported from Sanpete Valley. The meat from successful hunting ventures, which could be significant, in the proximate canyons often sustained life for the early settlers. "One time they brought home one hundred and twenty deer, which they hung in the granary of Jefferson Tidwell. When anyone in the community needed meat, he could go and help himself." A cooperative spirit was the primary resource which made this settlement habitable, a village so small it did not appear on an 1888 Rand McNally map of Utah. While the communities in the west part of what became Carbon County focused primarily on coal mining, Wellington emerged primarily as a farming settlement fostering a community different than a mining town.[6] Finally, after the railroad connected the valley to the Great Basin communities in the mid-1880s, the question of Wellington's survival was considerably lessened.[7]

Wellington, when Barney arrived, was, besides Arthur's family, also home to Lewis's brother Walter's son, Walter, Jr., and his wife. Arthur and young Walter's families were remembered as being among sixteen families settling Wellington prior to 1883.[8] The rest of Lewis's family remained scattered, including his stepmother Deborah. Supported by her daughter-in-law Hannah Stoddard Barney in Spring City, after William's death in 1875, Deborah, nearly eighty herself, would live for one more year, passing away on Lewis's eightieth birthday in 1888.[9] Lewis's brothers Walter and Benjamin remained in Monroe, John in Spanish Fork, and Henry in southern Utah. Betsey remained in Kanosh where in January 1887 the minutes of a Relief Society meeting stated that she "felt weak in attempting to speak [but] said she could see where she had missed [having the gospel as a part of her life] in her young days [and] knew this was the work of God and desired to do right."[10] Lewis and Betsey's son James Henry wrote his father in Wellington from Kanosh in March 1887, describing his mother as "well at present," and said as much about his brother Joseph's family. He encouraged his father, stating he wanted to visit him and would even consider moving "out there."[11] Two months later he reported, "I hardly think that Mother could stand it to [go to Wellington] as she is getting quite feeble and can't stand hardships like she used to do."[12]

Elizabeth, who stayed behind when Barney left Bowie Station the previous year, wrote to Lewis in March 1887 to say that she remained in Bowie where she had lived all winter in a tent and that she was tired of her circumstances. Their daughter Emeline Thompson now lived with her, she said, but David was working in a New Mexico mining camp fifty miles away. Another concern of Elizabeth's was the aftermath of the Indian difficulties surrounding the removal of Apache belligerents run off their land the previous fall. Emeline wrote to her father the same day and while declaring, "We are all well at present," also stated, "I don't know when we will get back but hope it won't be long." Finally in late November 1887, David informed his father that he, his mother, and Albert and Emeline had, after a month in Volcano, New Mexico, landed in Mancos, Colorado.[13] Martha Ann and Tom Briscoe in 1887, after a short episode in Burrville, were in Miller Creek, about fifteen miles from Wellington. Despite the verbal pleas of Lewis, not to mention the energy expended on his part, the old man's dream of a family kingdom, like Joel Hills Johnson previously, ebbed. His children scattered hither and yon were trying to hold to any prospect of prosperity where they were located, but as Barney had consistently demonstrated over time, he was not deflated by disappointment.

Probably not planning for it, Barney found opportunity in Wellington, though he did not prosper. Besides teaching school in 1888–1889, similar to his

Sevier County experiences, he found east-central Utah to his liking.[14] Though the trifling income from teaching hardly tempered his chronic poverty, still, his outlook was surprisingly upbeat. "I acknowledge that I am poor in this world's goods," he wrote in April 1888, "but rich in the faith of the gospel and health of body which I consider the greatest wealth any person can enjoy in this life."[15] This serenity was expressed by Arthur writing to David in mid-1888 to explain their father was then "more contented . . . than he has been."[16] Despite Wellington being five miles from Price, Barney participated in Price Ward church affairs, including affiliating with a new group of priesthood seventies.[17] But the favorable health he reported in 1888 declined. Now at age eighty, his health waned.[18] Having lived a vigorous life where he minimized the boundaries of his physical abilities, as an elderly man, the reality of his limitations discouraged him. At this point it is apparent that striking out for another gathering place for his family was out of the question, or so one would think.

Manti, in the Temple

As Barney's health diminished, his anxiousness concerning the Mormon temple rituals in behalf of deceased family members increased. Already having performed the vicarious ordinance work of baptisms and sealings for certain principal deceased ancestors, he knew there were still many relatives and friends for whom the rituals had not been completed. Despite his grinding poverty, in the late 1880s he hired a man to research his family tree for unknown genealogical connections. Barney tried to gather as much information as possible to accomplish the sacred work.[19] Regarding the actual performance of the Mormon temple rituals, he was again about the business of urging family support for another temple visit. In March 1888 David, responding to his father's solicitation, wrote, "I intend to try and assist you with your temple work as soon as I can," and with what must have warmed his father's heart, also stated, "I am beginning to get my eyes open in regards to these things."[20] The following month Elizabeth, living with David, wrote again to say that she, David, and Emeline were willing to do all that they could regarding temple work.[21] Betsey, herself now eighty years old, had her son James Henry write twice in early 1889 to say she also was willing to perform the temple labor and only waited for her husband to come get her so they could work in the temple together.[22] It appeared like the momentum of family temple participation for which Barney hoped would blossom.

After all the talk, Barney left Wellington the spring of 1889 for Kanosh en route to the newly completed Manti Temple in Sanpete Valley. He had been away from and had not seen Betsey for over five years. It is difficult to understand today the apparent low level of maintenance required in the nineteenth century to keep a family together. By modern standards Betsey may

Manti, Utah, with temple in background, ca. 1895. Photograph by George Edward Anderson. Courtesy Utah State Historical Society.

have considered herself abandoned and made efforts to conclude the marriage. Others in comparable circumstances had done as much. Despite the extreme situation and having witnessed Barney's undimmed quest for years, Betsey apparently felt content to wait, and wait some more, for her husband to satisfy his yearnings. Once in Kanosh he gathered up Betsey and relocated to Manti, Utah, where they presented themselves at the temple beginning their temple work on 2 July 1889. There, in the shadow of the temple, they lived for most of a year while Barney worked to sustain them when he could not be in the temple.[23]

Manti was quite unlike any other place where Barney lived after coming to the West. Rather than being of recent vintage, like most of his residences, Manti was the oldest settlement in Sanpete Valley. The town, initially settled just two years after the coming of Utah's first pioneers, was one of Utah's earliest settlements after Salt Lake City, Ogden, and Provo. Some of Manti's charter settlers found the winter's cold at 5,500 feet above sea level too severe for their liking and left after a season or two for warmer climes. But when Utah's Scandinavian immigration swelled, Sanpete, not as harsh as climates of their homelands, became a logical place to send Utah's new residents. They provided the numbers for permanence insuring the continuation of village life in Sanpete Valley. Despite the interludes of Indian upheaval during the Walker and Black Hawk Wars, the settlers worked hard and soon gained a reputation for having created the "granary of Utah." By the time Barney moved to Manti in 1889, the town required two wards to serve the religious needs of its

Mormon residents. Chosen as the site of Utah's third Mormon temple, Manti residents rejoiced on 21 May 1888 when the temple was dedicated for sacred Latter-day Saint rituals.[24]

If the importance of vicarious work for the Barney dead primarily occupied Barney's attention, his secondary focus, even as he eyed the edge of mortality, was the undiminished hope for a family sanctuary around which to gather his family. In April 1888 Elizabeth, now two years herself without seeing her husband, wrote to him from Mancos in southwestern Colorado calling him to come to her. Making the plea practical, she said the local bishop "wants settlers to come here," promising to provide them "20 acres and a city lot." Elizabeth's endorsement, confirming that "it is a good country and climate," triggered again Barney's yearnings.[25] Arthur, with whom Lewis was then living, received in July 1888 a letter from David in Mancos reporting the area had "some of the finest stock ranches for the summer up here in the mountains that I ever saw to be taken up yet." He also described a satisfactory religious situation, "We have got a very good bishop and have Sunday School and meetings and [he] always gives good instructions."[26] These communications about Mancos's favorable circumstances had not been lost on Barney. With several family members already established there, perhaps Mancos held hope as a family domain. Even James Henry encouraged him from Kanosh in June 1888, "You think of going to Colorado and . . . it may be that Joseph and I will come out there to that country. I would like it if we could live together in some good place."[27] Southwestern Colorado was looking more and more like the geographical destination to finally satisfy Barney's family vision.

Ironically, amid this zeal to unite his family, Barney allowed himself to become estranged from his daughter Emeline and her husband Albert Thompson. The particulars of the division are not available, but David wrote to his father in June 1889 encouraging the old man to reconsider his stance: "You seem to have hard feelings toward Albert and Emeline, but we must forgive each other [and] in as much as we repent and do better, kind words will do more than harsh tones and words." David encouraged his father to "write to Albert and Emeline a good, kind letter and try to persuade them to come back and settle with the saints, for he [Albert] has had nothing but a stream of bad luck where he is."[28] What action, if any, Barney took toward reconciliation is unknown. The estrangement apparently lingered during his final years.[29]

Other influences afoot may have influenced Barney toward Colorado. The federal roundup of polygamists had perhaps prompted him to relocate to New Mexico and then to Arizona, and while his wives were separated by long distance, other family members felt the sting of federal vigilance. His brother Benjamin and brother-in-law Joseph S. Black were arrested and prosecuted. On 20 September 1889 Benjamin, with three wives in Sevier and Utah Valleys, was sentenced to eighty-five days in the territorial prison and court costs after being found guilty in Utah's First District Court of unlawful cohabitation—polygamy.

Sarah Emeline Barney Thompson (Lewis Barney's daughter) with children. Photographer and date unknown.

Three weeks later Joseph S. Black, living at Deseret, Utah, with his three wives including Barney's sister Sarah Jane, was convicted in the same court for the same offense and sentenced to seventy-five days behind bars.[30] In all, about a thousand Mormon men were convicted of bigamy or unlawful cohabitation (polygamy) as national opinion against Mormon infractions of traditional American marriage customs increased.[31] Whether Barney's motive for yet another relocation was influenced by the imprisonment of his brother and brother-in-law is not known.

Sometime over 1889–1890's winter, Barney returned to Kanosh with Betsey after their Manti stay. His Kanosh stop was brief; soon he was on the road again with Mancos on his mind. Visiting Benjamin in Monroe en route, Barney learned his younger brother was interested in assisting with family temple work. Postponing his Mancos trip, Barney returned to Sanpete's temple. There in Manti alone, musing over his hopes, his living arrangements and material world consisted of a small wagon and what he could house within it. This work was of singular importance. "This thing rests on my shoulders and mind heavier than anything else because our salvation depends on its accomplishments," he wrote to a granddaughter.[32] But the work required more than his limited capacity. Appealing to his brother John, still living in Utah County, he said, "If you have faith in this work come right away and join me in the redemption of the dead." Otherwise, "I cannot stay here alone without a cent to live on," and "it is uncertain if the work will ever get done or that I shall ever be able to get back in this life and may never see you again."[33] While the temple closed mid-July into September due to hot weather, he "engaged a house for this summer, fall, and winter" and planned to stay there "until I see it finished up if it takes the rest of my life."[34]

Barney's anxiousness about his family's salvation had awakened in some of them a sense of its importance as well. Writing from Mancos in September 1890, David wrote that his siblings would try to join their father the following year at the temple, as "we have delayed too long already."[35] Barney, thrilled with the prospect, replied "it would be a great help and blessing, if you and Martha Ann and your mother could come and be here also," for there were "seventy-five names of the Beards that haven't been touched yet . . . [and] four hundred names of the Barneys yet to attend to." Barney's brother John and some of his family also responded to Lewis's plea and joined him in Manti. Betsey arrived as well, but with health so poor she could do little. If nothing else was accomplished by this work for the afterlife, his reconnection to his mortal family—wives, siblings, and children—provided a satisfaction he otherwise would have missed. With "more on my hands than I am able to do," Barney appealed to David, "Send me a little money [which] would be a great help for I want to stay here till you can come next summer." Once the sacred work was completed, he said, "then I will go home with you."[36]

At the time Barney prepared for the reopening of Manti Temple in September 1890, he, along with the rest of the church, heard news that church

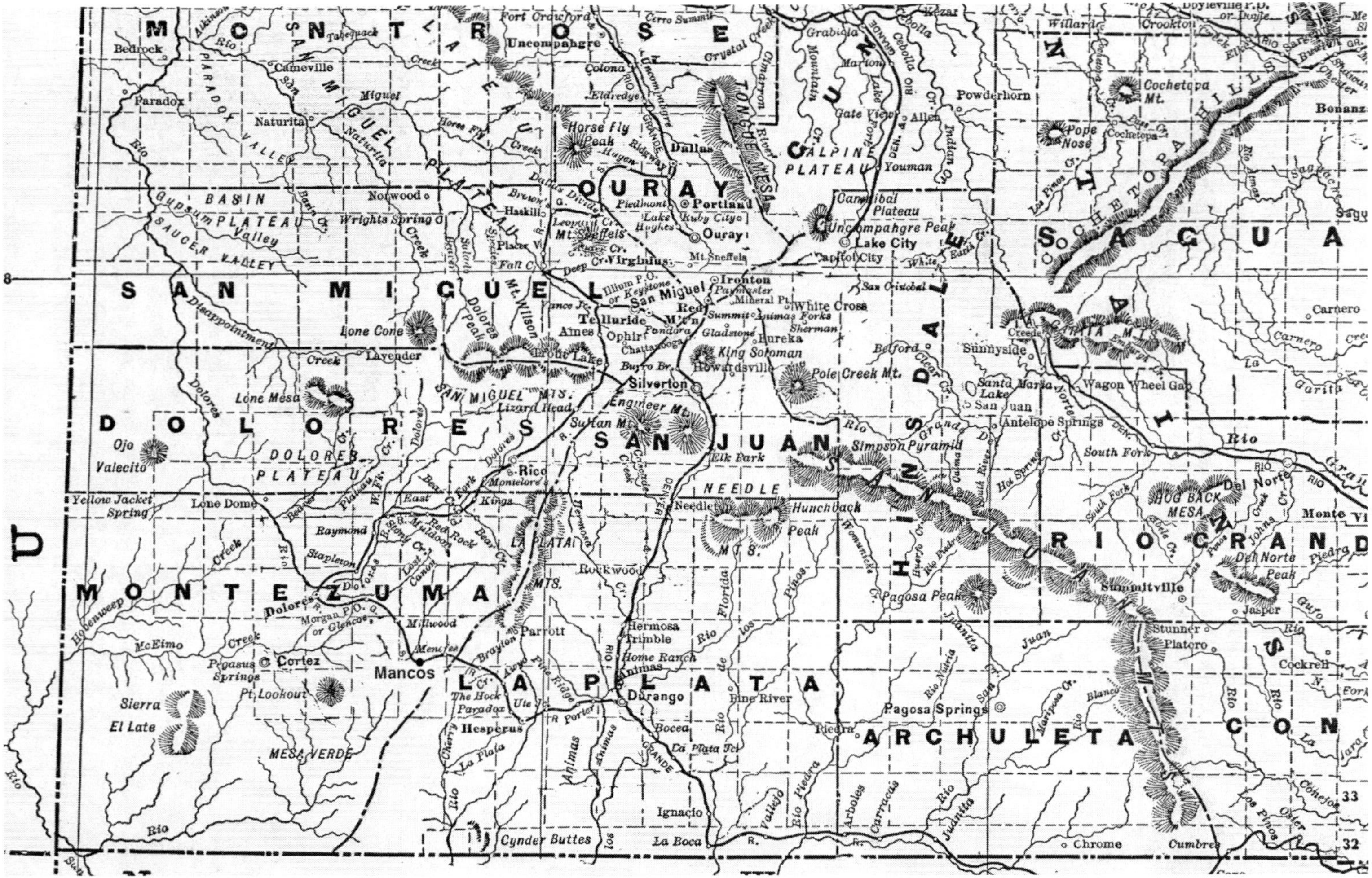

Southwestern Colorado, 1894. From *Potter-Bradley Atlas of the World* (John E. Potter & Co.).

president Wilford Woodruff had announced the cessation of plural marriage as a practice of the Latter-day Saint faith. The announcement, known as the Manifesto, was confirmed at the church general conference in October 1890. The change was the result, said Woodruff, of prayerful inquiry as to what the course of the Latter-day Saints ought to be, given the extreme measures taken by federal authorities to suppress plural marriage. Primarily directed at the Saints' marital excesses in contrast to American monogamy, the federal and territorial governments had also calculated to strip the church of its political power and influence. The pragmatic and courageous stance by Woodruff was the beginning of a new niche carved by the Latter-day Saints in American culture. It was evidence of Mormonism's subtle transition toward the American mainstream given the inevitability of accommodation to Americanism starkly painted on the future's horizon.

The subtlety of the shift became more pronounced in the following two decades when the polemics which had shaped Mormon-federal relations over the previous fifty years abated. Indeed, in the early twentieth century, the church, which in the nineteenth century was viewed by other Americans as traitorous, profligate, and heterodox, became a conservative bastion of so-called American ideals.[37] Lewis Barney never witnessed the assimilation of the Latter-day Saints into the American mainstream. While he held the apocalyptic view shared by most nineteenth-century Mormons, the swirling of world and national machinations were so far removed from him that the extent of his being touched by the change in progress was only by the reports he heard or read.

What mattered to Barney was limited to what he viewed as important and what he could influence. When the Manti Temple opened on 23 September 1890, Barney performed baptisms for 100 deceased Barney ancestors, most of them Massachusetts and Vermont-born during the eighteenth century. Because Betsey's health flagged, rendering her nearly invalid, on 4 November, 109 Barney female ancestors were proxy baptized by John Barney's daughter-in-law Caroline Holm.[38] Barney's temple devotions that fall, though he could not know it, were the last he would perform. Thereafter, the uncompleted temple work weighed on his mind but was beyond his control. His family remained scattered geographically and their general poverty precluded them from doing anything to satisfy the patriarch's desires for a mortal or immortal family kingdom.

Manti also closed Barney's association with his first family. Betsey returned to Kanosh where she took up residence with her son James Henry. At a time when Lewis saw glimpses of his family's gathering, some were actually scattering. Joseph, with whom Betsey had been living previously, finally gave up on Kanosh's chronic economic lethargy and lack of opportunity and in August 1890 directed his attention toward the village of Ferron in Castle Valley, Emery County, eighty miles northeast of Kanosh. There he eventually lived out his days.[39] Sometime in 1890 Arthur bid farewell to Wellington and relocated to Smith's Fork near Fort Bridger in southwestern Wyoming where he leased a ranch.[40] Perhaps this was the time when Lewis Barney finally realized his mortal family kingdom would not materialize.

Mancos, Colorado

When Barney set out for Mancos, Colorado, in 1891, not only did his wife Elizabeth and son David live their, Martha Ann and Tom Briscoe had also relocated there. With his family scattered widely and none thriving, he had few choices about his future. Southwestern Colorado looked to be the most promising, if not the only, option for Barney at this late stage in his life. The mountain valley served by the Mancos River, a tributary of the San Juan River born in the LaPlata Mountains northeast of Mancos, like so many of the other places where Barney once lived, had been carved out of the frontier. While it was settled by Americans only in the 1870s, it was in a historic area. The valley, at just over 7,000 feet in elevation, was familiar to the Spanish traversing the area between the New Mexican settlements and Alta California (which included Utah) during the late eighteenth and early nineteenth centuries.[41] The Spaniards named the valley Mancos, the crippled one, after an eighteenth-century explorer who injured his knee there. Dominguez and Escalante entered the region in 1776. White Americans apparently visited in 1859 and a geological survey party mapped the area in 1874. Miners and ranchers, among others, drawn to the valley in the mid-1870s, numbered enough that a post office was established in Mancos in 1878. The town was laid out in 1881. Four years later one could find a shoemaker, blacksmith, grocery, bank, log hotel, and two saloons in the community. Montezuma County, which served Mancos, was established in 1889. A railroad was built through the valley in 1891, the year Lewis Barney arrived.[42]

The first Mormon settlers laid claim in the area in September 1880. As in most other experimental satellites extending Mormonism in the West, others followed when reports of the area proved favorable. Most of the Saints settled together "in a little valley of their own." The non-Mormons, who moved into the area prior to the Saints, were located in the "main Mancos valley, which extends in a sort of crescent shape" following the main course of the Mancos River.[43] As the population of Saints increased in the "little valley . . . known as the Webber," two Mormon apostles visited on 9 September 1884 and formally organized a church branch there. A thirty-five by twenty-six foot log building served as church, theater, social hall, and school beginning in 1885. The branch grew into a ward on 21 March 1887.[44] Most of the early Mormon settlers came from the San Juan region of southeastern Utah. While internal dissension shut down the branch for a time in 1884, thirty-five Mormon families were part of the ward in 1888, living on four thousand acres of land, five hundred of which were under cultivation.[45] The year Barney moved to Mancos, the Mormon ward membership included thirty-six families numbering 247 individuals, making it the San

Juan Stake's largest congregation.[46] Far removed from any Mormon population centers in Utah, Mancos in the 1880s became a village of refuge for polygamists evading federal officers scouring the Utah valleys for Edmunds Act violators.[47]

There was something familiar to Barney about the Mancos area. A Salt Lake City visitor in November 1893 wrote that the "whole valley and surrounding hills and mountains are covered with almost endless forests of cedar and pine." For the settlers to make farms they had to "cut down the timber and wood almost the same as the people in the eastern states and Canada have to clear farms in the timber." That laborious activity was something with which Barney had familiarity. With the timber cleared, the area was planted in "extensive wheat fields" as well as fruit orchards and most of the settlers sustained themselves raising "grain and hardy vegetables."[48]

Rancher Alfred Wetherill, sometime in late 1887 or early 1888, searching for cattle, wandered into a canyon not far from Mancos when he "looked up and through an opening in the thick growth . . . saw towers and the tops of buildings" that he immediately recognized were of great antiquity. "In the blue dusk and the silence, it had all the appearance of a mirage. The solemn grandeur of those outlines was breathtaking," Wetherill remembered. "I stood looking at the ruins in awe," the discovery surpassing "my wildest dreams."[49] The rancher stumbled into the ancient ruins of the cliff-dwelling Native Americans who inhabited the area centuries before. When Barney moved to Mancos near the ruins, information about the area was sparse, but Mesa Verde National Park now protects the remarkable evidence of the once extensive and sophisticated Indian civilization.

Barney, now eighty-three, had not seen his second family, excepting Arthur and Martha Ann, since leaving them in southern Arizona in 1886. Soon after their separation, David established himself in Mancos trying to foster a life and livelihood. Barney's arrival in Mancos the spring of 1891 after a five-year separation was a time of great rejoicing for the family.[50] There he joined with his wife then living with David, still unmarried. The reality of Betsey's poor health and her children living in the Pahvant, Castle, and Gila Valleys undoubtedly portended in Barney's mind the final separation from Betsey's family. And so it was. Elizabeth Turner Barney, living with James Henry, died at age eighty-four in Kanosh on 11 December 1892.[51] There she was buried near the obelisk marking the final resting place of Kanosh, the Pahvant Indian chief whose name identified the community. Interestingly, it may be that Betsey was buried on land once owned by her husband,[52] but that was her last mortal connection to him.

Now an octogenarian, Barney slowed physically, and with such limitations he still hoped the compensation for Indian depredations he investigated in the summer of 1890 would bear fruit. On 24 April 1893 he wrote to Clark and Johns, a Washington, D.C., law firm, regarding the uncompensated claim he made previously with the federal government desiring them to execute the petition for him. To the attorneys he rehearsed his family background, his experience defending American land and institutions, while complaining about the "marvelous salaries" of senators, representatives, and the U.S. president as being "a little extravagant." Believing his past sacrifice qualified him for compensation, to mollify any doubts the attorneys might have regarding their supplicant, he stated, "I do not want money to spend for any kind of intoxicant drinks, tobacco, or coffee. I never [in] all my life of 85 years took a chew of tobacco, smoked a cigar or pipe, or took a pinch of snuff and if all the whiskey, alcohol, and brandy that ever went into my stomach could be measured I do not think it would amount to five gallons." And, he asserted, "I am never seen lounging around saloons or leaning on the counter hindering the clerk from attending to their business." Closing, he said, "My place is at home with my wife and children attending to the farm. My word is as good as my bond, my verity is never doubted by my neighbors."[53] The letter was of no effect, but this summary of his outward deportment indicates a lifestyle conditioned by principles of conduct, despite his frontier poverty, of disciplined personal behavior.

Barney maintained his practice of Mormonism in Mancos. Invited to speak about his religious experience to the Mancos congregation on 5 August 1894, he summarized his belief of the gospel as the means of "salvation and the final judgement of all men." He looked longingly for "the glorious millennial reign" of the Lord Jesus Christ.[54] The following month a Mancos correspondent to the *Deseret News* in Salt Lake City described a joyous celebration to honor Barney: "On the 8th inst. [September 1894] we had a very pleasant gathering at the home of Brother Lewis Barney, one of the Utah Pioneers. . . . Brother Barney has been living here for about three years. The occasion for the aforesaid gathering was the eighty-eighth [eighty-sixth] anniversary of Brother Barney's birth." In attendance were San Juan Stake president Francis A. Hammond and one of his counselors. "After a very nice dinner . . . Brother Barney related some of the incidents connected with the early days of the Church and the wonderful pioneer journey which were very interesting." After recollection of his life's high point and profession of faith, "all felt to congratulate the veteran on having attained to such a ripe old age and still being quite hale and hearty; being able to walk a distance of five or six miles without any inconvenience." What is more, Barney indicated he had not given up on completing the temple work for his deceased ancestors. "He has quite a lengthy Temple Record to his credit and expects to do a work for about four hundred more of his dead kindred in the near future if his life is spared."[55] Despite his hearty disposition, his life was not spared.

The following month he fell ill. About 2 November he took a turn for the worse. A grandson living nearby reported "he had a cerebral hemorrhage." The ward bishop blessed him, but he did not survive. On 5 November 1894 Lewis Barney departed mortality for the better world of which he had professed so much in his life. His grandson, nearly five years old at the time of the patriarch's death, remembered his grandmother Elizabeth being away from Mancos at the time and did not return until about three weeks after her husband's burial.[56]

Funeral services in Mancos were held on 7 November 1894 at the "Ward Meeting house" over the remains of Lewis Barney. Three speakers, including Mancos Ward bishop George Halls, spoke about the deceased. "Their remarks . . . bore strong testimonies to the Faith and integrity of Father Barney who died as he lived, a faithful Latter-day Saint." Two hours later "Bro. Lewis Barney was layed to rest in the Latter-day Saints Cemetery," where "Prest. William Halls offered the dedicatory prayer" over the grave.[57] Two weeks after Barney's death, his obituary appeared in the *Deseret News*: "Another of Utah's Pioneers has passed away; on the 5th inst. Brother Lewis Barney breathed his last." The *News* reported, "He has been ailing for about a month, but was not taken seriously ill until a few days before his death, the cause of which was old age." The obituary continued, "Brother Barney embraced the Gospel when a young man, was personally acquainted with the Prophet Joseph Smith, and passed through many of the trying ordeals connected with the early days of the Church, among others the expulsion from Nauvoo." Lauding his "anxious" desire "to finish his temple work before he died," the *News* summarized, "Brother Barney was always true to the principles of the Gospel and has now gone to reap the reward of a well spent life."[58] Lewis Barney, a son of the American frontier, passed from the scene at the same time that the frontier itself metamorphosed into another form of existence.

Conclusion

Information about the immediate reaction to Lewis Barney's death by his family has not survived. But upon his demise, his family was clearly left without the figure who had shaped their lives more than any other. While it is true that there were episodes of independence, contrariness, and dissension within the family, Barney's influence and love for his family were generally sufficient to maintain enduring tethers to his children. During his lifetime, his children's ambitions and aspirations matched those of their father. He was understandably closer to some than to others, particularly to those of his second family in the later years of his life. Notwithstanding his extended absences from each of them at times, his single purpose focused on gathering them into a patriarchal setting where his extended family could build lives in peace and prosperity. It was the children from his second family who most closely followed their elderly father when his designs were extreme. It may have been the case that the youth of his second family, a generation younger than his first family, inspired him to do the extraordinary things he did in his life's later years. Several of them, even after their marriages, trailed him with belief their father could lead them to stability and fulfillment. The children from his first marriage, mostly separated from their father for the last third of his life, maintained attachment to the family patriarch and remained subject to his influences once they found themselves in financial reversal. Barney's hope for a family kingdom was apparently held by most of his children at one time or the other.

His wives, of whom we have very little perspective, were mostly tolerant of his ambitions rooted in Mormon objectives and principles. One feature of family life for modern observers to consider in viewing nineteenth-century families is the factor of time. Present concerns about quality and quantity family time were much less relevant for most nineteenth-century Utah families, urban or rural. Mormon husbands and fathers were often away from their families for lengthy periods of times even while younger children were at home. Economic demands often precluded regular gatherings around the hearth. It was not uncommon for husbands and fathers, having to make their living as laborers, to be away from their wife (or wives) and little ones for lengthy periods at a time. Other married men, though they were comparatively few, were called to foreign or domestic proselytizing missions far away from home for two or more years. Thus it was common for females to be both emotionally and physically equipped to handle matters under periods of isolation from their husbands. Both Betsey and Elizabeth lived under such circumstances. It was never easy.

Barney's story is the account of a family. Each of his wives, in the last decades of his life, was left in the care of her children during his absences. Yet after the separations he resumed familial association with his loved ones. His wives exhibited extraordinary patience. One of Barney's descendants, describing his numerous relocations, said that "Elizabeth Beard was the one who took the brunt of the traveling." She "would have to go with him because Elizabeth [Betsey] Turner refused to leave. Once she [Betsey] got a home, she would not go with him."[59] While this is a generalization, it is probably close to the truth. His wives, his companions, underrepresented in this book from lack of information, played into every enterprise of his life. His children also felt the effect of their father's ambition. At the time of his death, some, following the example of their father, pushed farther into the Intermountain West. Thereafter, their movement was according to their own designs. The mastermind of the Barney family kingdom was gone.

Betsey Turner preceded Lewis in death by two years. Elizabeth Beard, a score of years younger than Lewis and Betsey, lived another nineteen years before her demise in 1915 in Pocatello, Idaho. Her last years were difficult, with physical ailments making her uncomfortable and limited in what she could do. Edna Briscoe Perkins, a granddaughter who helped care for her in her final years, said when her grandmother had to use the outdoor toilet "I'd just pick her up and carry her out. It was easier to carry her out and carry her back than it was to lead her out because she was blind. . . . She was helpless." Still, "she was very patient." At the end of her life Elizabeth suffered from edema, called dropsy at the time, a disease where fluids are retained in the body's tissue. Elizabeth "was just swollen up with bed sores all over. She was so sick she could hardly breathe."[60] After suffering for some time she finally died on 15 August 1915.

The life of Lewis Barney, one of the eighth generation of Barneys in America, spanned the first to the last decades of the nineteenth century. From the time that the flesh of adolescent America was still soft until his demise just before the turn of the new century, Barney witnessed both America and

Mormonism from the geographical periphery. Having chosen rural living, much that occupied the attention of other Americans almost entirely eluded Lewis. He is said to have been in Salt Lake City on 24 July 1880 to participate in the celebration of Mormonism's fiftieth jubilee. Two months later electricity first lighted Utah's capital city. It is unlikely Barney ever saw the effect of harnessing this wondrous power. Technological innovations as diverse as the automobile and motion picture camera were made just prior to his death, but he never witnessed the curious machines. Even the transportation and communication advancements of the railroad and telegraph, which he did witness, were virtually unused by this unreconstructed frontiersman.[61] He never felt the need to meld his life with advancement of the times. Social status meant little to him. If he ever did aspire for such things, they were secondary to his indefatigable ambition for family domain. As he moved throughout the physical Mormon dominion in the West, he was content to live in it "one side by himself." Even over a century later most of the climes to which Barney gravitated remain rural, isolated, and sparsely populated. Living life in its simplest form, with its rudimentary tools and rewards, was enough for him.

The Mormon gospel of salvation and providential living suited Barney entirely. He had acquired very little materially. There was no home. There were no barns and stables. There was no estate. There was not even a will. The nature of his dreams precluded accumulation, although that was undoubtedly a part of what he had once envisioned. By present standards the success of his life is, perhaps, questionable. Even the two major objectives driving him through his final years—his physical and spiritual family kingdom—remained unfulfilled at his passing. But his devotion to the foundational doctrine and practice of Mormonism found expression in the extraordinary energy and ambition he exhibited in his last decades.

The world at the time of Barney's death was changing. America was changing, and consequently, so were the Latter-day Saints. Not only were advances of technology and transportation altering the manner of life for most of those who lived near the church's urban centers, the decades-old antagonism between the Church of Jesus Christ and the federal government was now mostly a thing of the past. In 1893 U.S. President Benjamin Harrison gave amnesty to polygamists who subscribed to the church's Manifesto of 1890, and in 1894 Harrison's successor Grover Cleveland pardoned the rest who pledged to abide by the law. Cleveland also signed the Enabling Act in July 1894 legally preparing for Utah's statehood which came in 1896. The political arena in Utah now conformed to national party rivalries in contrast to the old Mormon versus anti-Mormon contests. Many within Mormondom saw a promising future on the horizon.

Coincident with the new political climate in Utah and surrounding states, the Church of Jesus Christ initiated other steps redirecting their objectives. Within a year of Barney's death, Latter-day Saint stakes were created in Canada and Mexico, the first entities of this nature outside the states, inaugurating a move to internationalization that blossomed in the next century. The church's public image had a decidedly different cast which only matured. The Chicago World's Fair in 1893 welcomed the Mormon Tabernacle Choir and two members of the church's First Presidency who gave speeches at Utah's Day at the Fair, something unthinkable just a decade before. Barney witnessed these advances only in newspaper print and through pulpit sermons. Had he been any closer to it, he may have experienced some discomfort. Out on the frontier, where fashionable technology was rudimentary or absent, where the mode and requirements for living were essentially what they had been in the previous two centuries, Lewis Barney's physical world remained static. His urban coreligionists in the north moved to a different rhythm. It was a pulse unfamiliar to him. Perhaps Barney had a sensibility about the conflict between spirituality and materialism more starkly manifest in modernism and urbanism than in frontier simplicity.

Once the Barneys became Latter-day Saints, the immediate family of Lewis Barney participated in just about every major episode affecting Mormons through the end of the nineteenth century. In contrast to his more influential, visible, and urbanized contemporaries, Barney's experience may appear soporific. But it was this stripe of followership that characterized the majority of those who called themselves Latter-day Saints. The role of follower in Mormonism is measured by the collective expansion of the kingdom of God in the earth. Barney was content with his secondary role as a follower within Mormonism. Latter-day Saints believe their leaders to be designated by God through inspiration or revelation, not self-appointment. While the human condition played into church affairs through church leaders, Barney's confidence in God's prevailing direction over the Church of Jesus Christ of Latter-day Saints never abated. To Barney, Mormon leaders—the prophets and apostles—merited his allegiance to them. Challenged by disagreements and misunderstandings with local leaders, primarily during the Monroe United Order episode, Barney could have indulged his independent inclinations and broke from the faith. Many others did, but he did not.

Lewis Barney could have tried to be someone or something else, but his disposition was for the fringe of civilization, for the freedom and opportunity of renewal which only the frontier could bestow. He was unflagging in his devotion to his religion which shaped his life. This is how he lived and how he should be remembered. Thirteen years previous to his death, Wilford Woodruff, then a Latter-day Saint apostle, said at the passing of his associate Orson Pratt, "There are a great many things Concerning Br. Pratt that have not been written and never will be On this side of the veil. They are however recorded on the other side of the veil. He will meet his history there."[62] While Lewis Barney never sought for nor ever achieved the stature of Orson Pratt, he, too, had a life "recorded on the other side of the veil," and he and his progeny, too, will meet that history.

Barney Family Relationships

Charles Barney (1783-1865)

with **Mercy Yeoman (1785–1825)**

Luther Barney (1806–1860)
Lewis Barney (1808–1894)
Lucien Barney (1811–1846)
Lucinda Barney Copeland (1813–?)
Henry Barney (1816–?)
Walter Barney (1819–1917)
John Barney (1823–?)
Daughter Barney (1825–1827)

with **Deborah Riffle (1808–1888)**

Emerine Barney Leland (Leyland) (1828–1842)
Elizabeth Barney Leland (Leyland) (1830–1878)
Louisa Barney (1831–1831)
Benjamin Franklin Barney (1832–1904)
Margaret Matilda Barney Gilbert (1834–1915)
Thomas Jefferson Barney (1836–1862)
William Street Barney (1840–1875)
Sarah Jane Barney Black (1845–1934)

Lewis Barney (1808–1894)

with **Elizabeth Turner (1808–1892)**

Sarah Jane Barney (1834–1834)
Walter Turner Barney (1836–1922)
James Henry Barney (1840–1911)
Alma Barney (1843–1846)
Joseph Smith Barney (1845–1917)
William Orson Barney (1852–1865)

with **Elizabeth Beard (1830–1915)**

Rachael Tippetts (daughter of Alva Tippetts)
Arthur Barney (1852–1946)
Margaret Mariah Barney (1854–1856)
Martha Ann Barney Briscoe (1857–1953)
Lewis Barney (1858–1860)
David Barney (1861–1958)
Sarah Emeline Barney Thompson (ca. 1864–1924)
Harriet Viola Barney (1867–1868)
William Edward Barney (1870–1878)

Notes

Introduction

1. Joel Goodell to Rev. Mr. [Horace] Hooker, 12 May 1831, Liberty, Missouri, Missionary Society of Connecticut, Papers, microfilm, Western Reserve Historical Society, Cleveland, Ohio.
2. Ray Allen Billington, *America's Frontier Heritage* (New York: Holt, Rinehart and Winston, 1966), 25.
3. Walter Prescott Webb, *The Great Frontier* (Austin, Texas: University of Texas Press, 1964), 5.
4. Webb, *The Great Frontier*, 1–8.
5. Lewis Barney, letter fragment to unknown editor, Church Archives, Family and Church History Department, the Church of Jesus Christ of Latter-day Saints, Salt Lake City, Utah, hereafter referred to as Church Archives.
6. The unbound, extant leaves of Autobiography 2 (26 cm. x 19 cm.) are lined, embossed with the manufacturer's mark, and written in blue and black ink. This document was donated to the Church Archives by a family member in 1974.
7. Hosea Stout, *On the Mormon Frontier: The Diary of Hosea Stout, 1844–1861*, Juanita Brooks, ed., 2 vols. (Salt Lake City: University of Utah Press, 1964); Juanita Brooks, *On the Ragged Edge: The Life and Times of Dudley Leavitt* (Salt Lake City: Utah State Historical Society, 1973).
8. Autobiography 1 is just over 120 nearly legal-sized pages of narrative with leaves of the *Deseret News* from 1879 forming the end papers of the compilation. It is bound in a homemade cover of brown canvas sewn around cardboard. The hand-sewn leaves (from at least two paper manufacturers) vary from lightly to heavily lined pages and are written in black, purple, and blue ink. The leaves measure 31.5 cm. x 20 cm. This document was donated by a family member in 1943 to the Church Archives.
9. Arthur Barney wrote his life story in 1933 while living in Leota, Utah. Like the writings of his father, Arthur's story was also transcribed by librarians at Brigham Young University in 1963.
10. For an overview of other repositories in the United States holding materials pertinent to Mormonism, see David J. Whittaker, ed., *Mormon Americana: A Guide to Sources and Collections in the United States* (Provo, Utah: BYU Studies, 1995).
11. Leonard J. Arrington, *From Quaker to Latter-day Saint: Bishop Edwin D. Woolley* (Salt Lake City: Deseret Book Company, 1976), ix.
12. Dale L. Morgan, *The Great Salt Lake* (Albuquerque, New Mexico: University of New Mexico Press, 1973), 325.
13. James M. McPherson, ed., *"To the Best of My Ability": The American Presidents* (New York: Dorling Kindersley Publishing, Inc., 2000), 9.
14. Charles S. Peterson, *Take Up Your Mission: Mormon Colonizing along the Little Colorado River, 1870–1900* (Tucson, Arizona: University of Arizona Press, 1973), 268.
15. Quoted in Edward Hallett Carr, *What Is History* (New York: Vintage Books, 1961), 56.

16. George Macaulay Trevelyan, "Clio, a Muse," in Stephen Vaughn, ed., *The Vital Past: Writings on the Uses of History* (Athens, Georgia: University of Georgia Press, 1985), 197ff.
17. Douglas L. Wilson, *Honor's Voice: The Transformation of Abraham Lincoln* (New York: Alfred A. Knopf, 1998), 6. Another Lincoln scholar considering the same question warned, "Memory fades and, as everyone knows, is subject to tricks: of vanity and conceit, of partiality, error, and displacement." Merrill D. Peterson, *Lincoln in American Memory* (New York: Oxford University Press, 1995), 83.
18. Richard M. Ketchum, "Memory as History," *American Heritage* 42, no. 7 (November 1991): 143–144.
19. Ronald W. Walker, "The Challenge and Craft of Mormon Biography," *BYU Studies* 22, no. 2 (spring 1982): 179, 182, 190–191.
20. Ibid., 180, 186, 188, 191–192.
21. Barney exhibited several idiosyncratic writing characteristics, such as capitalizing the letter C no matter its use and applying punctuation, if at all, unpredictably. The latter was common in nineteenth-century writing.

Chapter 1

1. Perry Miller, "Errand into the Wilderness," in Jon Butler and Harry S. Stout, eds., *Religion in America: A Reader* (New York: Oxford University Press, 1998): 31.

   An extensive overview of Lewis Barney's ancestry is found in Eugene Dimon Preston, *Genealogy of the Barney Family in America*, ed. William Clifford Barney (n.p.: The Barney Family Historical Association, 1990). This extensive work is largely the effort of the editor. Eugene Preston, a Barney descendant, gathered Barney family information for decades. Intending to published the family genealogy and nearly ready to go to print, Preston died in 1926, his dream left undone. The 1,500-page handwritten manuscript Preston created laid mostly unknown in the New England Historic Genealogical Society in Boston, Massachusetts, until 1983 when Cliff Barney, editor of the volume, found the document. The manuscript's discoverer then edited the lengthy document which is a watershed in terms of Barney family genealogy. This author's work simply could not have been accomplished without the work of Cliff Barney, who continues to publish a substantive newsletter for the family organization.

   For a historical overview of Lewis Barney's lineal ancestry from their Puritan origins in 1630 to Lewis Barney's birth, see Ronald O. Barney, "Barney Origins in America: Puritans and Yankees in the New World, 1630–1800," typescript in possession of the author.
2. Abigail Winship Barney died on her forty-fourth birthday, 20 January 1799, the day her son Samuel Chase Barney was born. Page from the Barney family Bible filed in 1832 with Luther Barney, Revolutionary War Pension and Bounty Land Warrant Application Files, National Archives, Washington, D.C., hereafter known as Luther Barney, Revolutionary War Pension Application; Deborah Barney, widow of Charles Barney, Application for Service Pension, War of 1812, 19 November 1878, National Archives, Washington, D.C.
3. The sojourn of Luther Barney's family during and after the Revolutionary War, including an account of his military service on land and sea (1775–1781) and their successive movement west from Connecticut to Massachusetts, Vermont, and New York, is recounted in Luther Barney, Revolutionary War Pension Application. See also Frederick Ward Kates, comp., *Patriots-Soldiers of 1775–1783: The Veterans of the War for American Independence of Chautauqua County, New York* (n.p.: Jamestown

Chapter, National Society, Daughters of the American Revolution, 1981), 3–5, 10–13, 18–19, 26, 92–94.

4. An overview of the land purchase and distribution is found in Paul Demund Evans, *The Holland Land Company* (Buffalo, New York: Buffalo Historical Society, 1924). See also William Chazanof, *Joseph Ellicott and the Holland Land Company: The Opening of Western New York* (Syracuse, New York: Syracuse University Press, 1970).
5. Quoted in E. W. Vanderhoof, *Historical Sketches of Western New York* (Buffalo, New York: The Mathews-Northrup Works, 1907, AMS reprint in 1972), 49–50.
6. The Newstead Township, in which Charles settled, would later become a part of Niagara County in 1808 and still later Erie County in 1821. Lewis Barney, born while his father lived on the Holland Purchase property, most often referred to the place of his birth as being in Niagara County.
7. Rhoda Black Erickson, "Sixth Generation: Continuation of the Descendants of Jacob Barney, 1634," 15, typescript in possession of the author; Elijah Knight, "Early Recollections of Western New York," typescript, 9, Newstead Historical Society, Akron, New York, photocopy in possession of the author. My thanks to John Eckerson, town historian of Akron, New York, for providing me with Knight's recollection.
8. Charles E. Brooks, *Frontier Settlement and Market Revolution: The Holland Land Purchase* (Ithaca, New York: Cornell University Press, 1996), 4, 46; William Wyckoff, *The Developer's Frontier: The Making of the Western New York Landscape* (New Haven: Yale University Press, 1988), 105–106, 109–110, 115.
9. Stephen Yeoman, Mercy's father, is found in the 1810 census in Dryden, a small village not far from Genoa. Erickson, "Sixth Generation," 15.
10. Lewis Barney to Clark and Johns, 24 April 1893, Mancos, Colorado, typescript in possession of author; *History of Fayette County, Ohio 1984* (Washington Court House, Ohio: Fayette County Genealogical Society, 1984), 269; Walter Yeoman, "Sketch of Elder Yeoman," *Messenger of Peace* 51, no. 10 (15 May 1925): 190; *Heads of Families at the First Census of the United States Taken in the Year 1790, New York* (Washington: Government Printing Office, 1908), 145.
11. Karen E. Livsey, *Western New York Land Transactions, 1804–1824: Extracted from the Archives of the Holland Land Company* (Baltimore: Genealogical Publishing Company, 1991); Erickson, "Sixth Generation," 15. It is not known exactly when Charles's younger brothers, Philemon, born in 1786, and Joseph, born in 1787, settled on the Holland Purchase.
12. If Charles and Mercy were married in Newstead, a record of the event is probably not extant. The records of Newstead Township were destroyed by fire in the nineteenth century. H. Perry Smith, ed., *History of the City of Buffalo and Erie County* (Syracuse, New York: D. Mason & Co., 1894), 368.
13. Lockwood R. Doty, *History of the Genesee Country (Western New York)*, 2 vols. (Chicago: S. J. Clarke Publishing Company, 1925), 1:1150–1151. To see the area's growth by year see O[rsamus] Turner, *Pioneer History of the Holland Purchase of Western New York* (Buffalo, New York: Jewett, Thomas & Co., 1849), 531.
14. Smith, *History of the City of Buffalo and Erie County*, 362; Truman C. White, *Our County and Its People: A Descriptive Work on Erie County, New York*, 2 vols. (n.p.: The Boston History Company, 1898), 1:581.
15. In the interest of stimulating the land market, some of the less desirable areas of the tract sold for as little as seventy-five cents an acre. After the first decade of sales with three-quarters of a million acres purchased, the average price was $2.30. As interest in the region grew so did the price of Holland land. In 1817 land was selling for over $5 an acre. Evans, *Holland Land Company*, 228–230.
16. A search of the deed indexes of the Holland Land Purchase records, a part of over two hundred reels of microfilm records at the Family History Library in Salt Lake City,

found no record of Charles purchasing land. Another multivolume nineteenth-century compilation of Holland Purchase records at the New York State Archives in Albany, New York, also fails to show Charles purchasing land from the Dutch. Karen E. Livsey's comprehensive index of those who purchased Newstead Township land during the time of Charles Barney's residence in Newstead, New York, also fails to show any land transaction by Charles Barney. Livsey, *Western New York Land Transactions, 1804–1824*. See also Evans, *Holland Land Company*, 238.

17. Evans, *Holland Land Company*, 234–235.
18. Turner, *Holland Purchase*, 514.
19. Wyckoff, *The Developer's Frontier*, 104–105, 108, 123.
20. Turner, *Holland Purchase*, 454–456; White, *Our Country and Its People*, 1:581; *Illustrated Historical Atlas of Erie Co. New York from Actual Surveys and Records* (New York: F. W. Beers & Co., 1880), 24. The first land in what became Newstead Township was sold in November 1801 for $2.75 per acre. Smith, *History of . . . Erie County*, 360–362.

    Livsey's *Western New York Land Transactions* identifies Gilbert Yeoman's property purchased on 19 May 1803 as lot 6 in Section 12, Township 12, Range 5, in the Holland Land Purchase.
21. Evans, *Holland Land Company*, 234.
22. Brooks, *Frontier Settlement*, 25; Lewis Barney, Autobiography 2, 1. While Charles may have farmed on this property, as noted below, it is possible the family home was located along the Buffalo Road.
23. Brooks, *Frontier Settlement*, 34–35; E. B. O'Callaghan, *The Documentary History of the State of New York*, 4 vols. (Albany: Weed, Parsons & Co., 1850), 2:691. The road was also known as the Ontario & Genesee Turnpike. See Map 1.
24. Smith, *History of . . . Erie County*, 360–362; Brooks, *Frontier Settlement*, 55.
25. Smith, *History of . . . Erie County*, 364.
26. *Town of Newstead, founded 1823: Septquicentennial, 1832–1998* (n.p.: n.p., [1998]), 15; Peter Emslie, A Deed Atlas of the County of Erie, N. Y., showing the Dimensions of Lots and Subdivisions of lots as they were originally conveyed by the Holland Land Company . . . compiled from the Holland Land Company's Deed Books &c., Buffalo and Erie County Historical Society, Buffalo, New York. Luther's brother Nathan L. Barney also moved to Newstead, New York. See Smith, *History of . . . Erie County*, 366. Elijah Knight, whose family moved to the Holland Purchase about 1807, wrote that "Luther Barney bought the farm of Robert Durham on the north side of Buffalo Road ½ mile east of Vandeventer's tavern. Philemon Barney and his bro. Joseph Barney settled on the farm next east of Johnson's tavern afterward known as Canfield tavern." Knight, Early Recollections.
27. Quoted in Charles Wells Hayes, *The Diocese of Western New York: History and Recollections* (Rochester, New York: Scrantom, Wetmore & Co., 1904), 26.
28. John W. Barber and Henry Howe, *Historical Collections of the State of New York* (New York: S. Tuttle, 1841), 75. An 1804 map of New York, drawn by state surveyor general Simeon Dewitt, shows only five settlements west of the Fingerlakes in western New York in what was then called Genesee County. Simeon Dewitt, A *Map of the State of New York* (n.p.: n.p., 1804).
29. Ethelyn Weller, *A History of the Town of Newstead* (n.p.: Buffalo and Erie County Historical Society, 1971), 2; Julia Boyer-Reinstein, comp., *Town of Cheektowaga Historical Atlas*, 1953, Buffalo & Erie County Public Library, Special Collections, Buffalo, New York.
30. Lewis Barney, Autobiography 2, 1; J. H. French, *Gazetteer of the State of New York* (Syracuse, New York: R. Pearsall Smith, 1860), 292. Elijah Knight, Akron's first mayor and a resident from about 1807 to 1856, indicated that Charles Barney lived on the Buffalo Road: "The names of all the inhabitants of what is now the town of

Newstead in 1807 I will give, commencing on the road and at the county line east side of town following the road west to the east line of Clarence. They were all on the road with a single exception. Will give them in rotation as they lived." Charles was the thirteenth of seventeen names listed. Knight, Early Recollections. It is likely that Charles Barney held land in Falkirk which he farmed, just north of Buffalo Road, while also having a home along the thoroughfare.

31. David M. Ellis, James A. Frost, Harold C. Syrett, and Harry J. Carman, *A History of New York State* (Ithaca: Cornell University Press, 1967), 164–165.
32. Knight, Early Recollections.
33. Brooks, *Frontier Settlement*, 17; Smith, *History of . . . Erie County*, 361.
34. Smith, *History of . . . Erie County*, 362–363; *Illustrated Historical Atlas of Erie Co. New York*, 24.
35. Charles Barney's parents, Luther and Mercy, were charter members of a Baptist church in Cayuga County, New York, in 1795. Elliot G. Storke, *History of Cayuga County, New York 1789–1879* (Syracuse, New York: D. Mason & Co., 1879), 440–441.
36. *Town of Newstead, Founded 1823*, 26.
37. Lewis Barney, Autobiography 2, 1; Preston, *Genealogy of the Barney Family*, 188; Ancestral File, Family History Library.
38. In contrast to the Barneys' contentment with social obscurity in light of the pursuit of class and social advancement in New York at the turn of the nineteenth century, see Alan Taylor, *William Cooper's Town: Power and Persuasion on the Frontier of the Early American Republic* (New York: Alfred A. Knopf, 1995).
39. Brooks, *Frontier Settlement*, 2–3. Potash, used at the time for the making of soap and later as fertilizer, is the potassium carbonate produced from the ashes of burned wood. Settlers ran water over the ashes and boiled the residue in large pots to produce potash.
40. Levi Jackman, Sketch of Life, 1851, Church Archives.
41. John H. Thompson, ed., *Geography of New York State* (Syracuse, New York: Syracuse University Press, 1966), 152; Wyckoff, *The Developer's Frontier*, 123; and Jackman, Sketch of Life.
42. Wyckoff, *The Developer's Frontier*, 123.
43. Quoted in Turner, *Holland Purchase*, 584.
44. Turner, *Holland Purchase*, 584–585.
45. Brooks, *Frontier Settlement*, 15.
46. Quoted in Brooks, *Frontier Settlement*, 27–28.
47. Janet Dorothy Baglier, "The Niagara Frontier: Society and Economy in Western New York and Upper Canada, 1794–1854" (Ph.D. diss., State University of New York, Buffalo, 1993), 33–34.
48. Another evidence that Charles Barney likely did not complete the land purchase in Falkirk, New York, is that his name does not appear in the Holland Purchase records as a seller at the time of his removal from the state.
49. Lewis Barney, Autobiography 2, 1.

Chapter 2

1. Lewis Barney, Autobiography 1, 1. The town of Clinton declined within a decade of its founding before eventually disappearing. The location of the community is near where the northern reaches of present Mt. Vernon abut Owl Creek (now called Kokosing River), adjacent to State Highway 13.
2. Henry Howe, *Historical Collections of Ohio in Two Volumes* (Norwalk, Ohio: State of Ohio, 1898), 1:981.

3. Malcolm R. Rohrbough, *The Trans-Appalachian Frontier* (New York: Oxford University Press, 1978), 64–66, 90–91.
4. R. Douglas Hurt, *The Ohio Frontier: Crucible of the Old Northwest, 1720–1830* (Bloomington, Indiana: Indiana University Press, 1996), 324, 341.
5. *Inventory of the County Archives of Ohio, No. 42, Knox County (Mt. Vernon)* (Columbus, Ohio: Historical Records Survey—Works Progress Administration, 1939), 8.
6. *Inventory of . . . Knox County*, 9.
7. Hurt, *Ohio Frontier*, 246–249, 373.
8. A. Banning Norton, *History of Knox County, Ohio: From 1779 to 1862 Inclusive* (Columbus, Ohio: Richard Nevins, 1862), 136; Lewis Barney, Autobiography 2, 1.
9. Norton, *History of Knox County, Ohio*, 27–28; *Inventory of . . . Knox County*, 8; Richard M. Helwig and Richard N. Helwig, eds., *Ohio Ghost Towns, No. 35, Knox County* (Sunbury, Ohio: The Center for Ghost Town Research in Ohio, 1995), 47–48; *The Ohio Register*, 27 July 1813. For an overview of county development in land, government, and society, see N. N. Hill, Jr., comp., *History of Knox County, Ohio: Its Past and Present* (Mt. Vernon, Ohio: A. A. Graham & Co., Publishers, 1881).
10. Deed Book B, 1809–1814, 42, 112, 216, 308–309, Records of Knox County, Mt. Vernon, Ohio, Family History Library; *Ohio Register*, 29 June 1813, 5 November 1814, 24 October 1815; Helwig and Helwig, *Ohio Ghost Towns*, 48; Norton, *History of Knox County, Ohio*, 112–113, 216.
11. Record of Deeds A–F, B, Knox County [Ohio] 1809–1817, Family History Library; Ellen T. Berry and David A. Berry, *Early Ohio Settlers: Purchasers of Land in Southeastern Ohio, 1800–1840* (Baltimore: Genealogical Publishing Co., 1984, 1989) contains entries for Knox County, Ohio, land purchases during this period. Charles Barney's name does not appear.
12. Norton, *History of Knox County*, 156–157. John Barney, Charles's uncle, also joined the Clinton Masons at the same time.
13. See Mark Pitcavage, "'Burthened in Defense of Our Rights': Opposition to Military Service in Ohio during the War of 1812," *Ohio History* 104 (summer–autumn 1995): 142–162.
14. Carol Willsey Bell, *Ohio Genealogical Guide* (Youngstown, Ohio: Bell Books, 1990), 63.
15. Barney to Clark and Johns, 24 April 1893.
16. Index to War of 1812 Pension Application Files, National Archives, Washington, D.C.; Deborah Barney, 19 November 1878, Application for Service Pension, War of 1812; *Roster of Ohio Soldiers in the War of 1812* (Baltimore: Genealogical Publishing Company, 1968), 97, 104; Norton, *History of Knox County*, 143.

    Anticipating further action, Douglas's troops were notified from Clinton, Ohio, on 10 September 1813 that they would be expected to equip themselves as a regular militia. The uniform they were to wear was to

    > consist of a coat, vest and pantaloons of blue cloth; the coat to be double breasted with button holes on the right breast trimmed with white tape; the length of the skirts to be equal to the length of the arm when suspended by the side; the form trimmings, and finishing of the coat, to be in all other respects conformable to the uniform coat worn by the U.S. Regulars, with boots or black gaitors.

    They were told if they were not so equipped by the second Saturday in November they would be fined. See *Ohio Register*, 21 September 1813.
17. Lewis Barney, Autobiography 1, 1; Autobiography 2, 1–2; Barney to Clark and Johns, 24 April 1893.

18. *Ohio Register*, 10 September 1814, 24 September 1814, 22 October 1814.
Several volumes have been written about Joshua Barney. See Mary Barney, ed., *A Biographical Memoir of the Late Commodore Barney from Autobiographical Notes and Journals* (Boston: Gray and Bowen, 1832), ed. Joshua Barney's daughter-in-law; William Frederick Adams, comp., *Commodore Joshua Barney* (Springfield, Massachusetts: privately printed, 1912); Ralph D. Paine, *Joshua Barney: A Forgotten Hero of Blue Water* (New York: The Century Co., 1924); Hulbert Footner, *Sailor of Fortune: The Life and Adventures of Commodore Barney, U.S.N.* (New York: Harper & Brothers, 1940); and James Bertlinski, "Commodore Joshua Barney: Joshua Barney's Naval Career during the American Revolution, 1775–1784" *The Barney Family News* 84, 85 (winter 1999–2000, spring 2000): 27–50, 56–81.
Lewis Barney later identified Joshua Barney as an uncle and once apparently confused the latter's ventures with his grandfather Luther Barney's whom he identified as a commodore, though Luther, both in the infantry and navy during the Revolutionary War, served as an enlisted man only. Lewis Barney, Autobiography 1, 19. In another place, Lewis correctly summarized Luther's military experience. Barney to Clark and Johns, 24 April 1893.
19. Lewis Barney, Autobiography 1, 1–2. For one description of the role of Providence in early America, see Lewis O. Saum, "Providence in the Popular Mind of Pre-Civil War America," *Indiana Magazine of History* 72 (December 1976): 315–346.
20. Hurt, *Ohio Frontier*, 272.
21. Lewis Barney, Autobiography 2, 2; Preston, *Genealogy of the Barney Family*, 189. Some family sources, including Lewis, refer to Lucinda as Lurinda.
22. In April 1818 seven of Clinton's leading citizens petitioned the county court "for a vacation of part of the town of Clinton. Shortly thereafter, the post office at Clinton was closed and the town rapidly declined" into a ghost town. Helwig and Helwig, *Ohio Ghost Towns*, 48.
23. Lewis Barney, Autobiography 2, 2.
24. Ibid., 2.
25. Little is known of Winchester, Ohio. Sometime after the Barneys left, Winchester followed Clinton's demise and sunk to ghost town status. H. C. Carey's map of Ohio shows Knox County with Clinton platted just north of Mt. Vernon. Winchester is the only town shown in the southern part of the county on a road leading due south from Mt. Vernon. *A Complete . . . American Atlas of North America and South America, etc., to the Year 1822* (Philadelphia: H. C. Carey & I. Lea, 1823).
26. Lewis Barney, Autobiography 1, 2. This is likely the same property identified in the 1817 tax record for Knox County, Ohio, which states that Charles Barney lived in Range 15, Township 8, Section 4, Lot 26 in the county. He was assessed $1.50 in taxes. See Knox County, Ohio, Tax Record, vol. 712, Family History Library.
27. Record of Members, St. Thomas Ward, St. George Stake, Miscellaneous Records, 1865–1882, Church Archives. Three patriarchal (church) blessings received by Henry Barney, which include personal information supplied by him, indicate he was born in Winchester, Knox County, Ohio. Patriarchal Blessings, Index, Church Archives, 28 November 1853, 10 March 1854, 4 July 1877.
28. There is some discrepancy regarding the place of Walter's birth. There are no contemporary records of the birth and subsequent nineteenth-century documentation is ambiguous. One church record in the Church Archives from the 32nd Quorum of Seventy, from information likely supplied by Walter, shows him born on 7 January 1819 in Washington, Knox County, Ohio. (He likely meant Winchester, as there was no Washington in Knox County, though Washington Court House was the county seat of Fayette County, Ohio.) Seventies Record, 32nd Quorum of

Seventy. Another church record, also based on information supplied by Walter, indicates he was born "near Greenfield, Ohio," Greenfield being just south of where the Barneys located in Fayette County, Ohio. Walter Barney, Patriarchal Blessing, Index, 26 April 1849, 30 July 1854.

29. Rohrbough, *The Trans-Appalachian Frontier*, 85, 94.
30. Jack Larkin, *The Reshaping of Everyday Life, 1790–1840* (New York: Harper & Row Publishers, 1988), 12, 17.
31. James E. Davis, *Frontier America, 1800–1840: A Comparative Demographic Analysis of the Settlement Process* (Glendale, California: The Arthur H. Clark Company, 1977), 41. Historian Allen G. Bogue has written, "the hog was as important on the farms of the prairie . . . as the steer or milk cow . . . . None of the American farm animals can convert grain into meat of high quality with greater speed or efficiency than can the hog. . . . One litter of pigs will produce as much or more meat than a steer in half the time." Bogue, *From Prairie to Corn Belt: Farming on the Illinois and Iowa Prairies in the Nineteenth Century* (Chicago: Quadrangle Books, 1968), 102, 104.
32. Larkin, *Reshaping of Everyday Life*, 27, 171.
33. Lewis Barney, Autobiography 1, 2.
34. R. S. Dills, *History of Fayette County . . . Ohio* (Dayton, Ohio: Odell & Mayer, 1881), 874–875.
35. *History of Fayette County, Ohio 1984*, 269–270; Dills, *History of Fayette County*, 840– 841; Rufus Putnam, *Pioneer Record and Reminiscences of the Early Settlers and Settlement of Fayette County, Ohio* (Cincinnati: Applegate, Pounsford & Co., 1872), 26; and *Illustrated Historical Atlas of Fayette County, Ohio* (Philadelphia: L. H. Everts & Co., 1875), 11.
36. The stone foundation and part of the mill's wall along the bank of Paint Creek are extant today. See photo, p. ———.
37. Putnam, *Pioneer Record*, 26; Dills, *History of Fayette County*, 874–875.
38. Tax Record, Fayette County, Ohio, vol. 424, 1819, Family History Library, shows James, Walter, Stephen, and Gilbert (Mercy's father and brothers) all paying taxes on land located on the "water course" called Paint Creek. While Charles Barney does not appear on deed or tax lists immediately after their arrival in Fayette County, he is identified in the 1820 census for Wayne Township, Fayette County, as living adjacent to Samuel Yeoman who, in turn, lived next to Stephen Yeoman and other Yeoman in-laws. Fourth Census of the United States, 1820, National Archives, Washington, D.C.
39. Marcius Willson, *American History: Comprising Historical Sketches of the Indian Tribes* (New York: Ivison & Phinney, 1857), 68–69.
40. John Mack Faragher, *Daniel Boone: The Life and Legend of an American Pioneer* (New York: Henry Holt and Company, 1992), 181–182.
41. Lewis Barney, Autobiography 1, 2.
42. Rohrbough, *Trans-Appalachian Frontier*, 85.
43. Lewis Barney, Autobiography 1, 2.
44. R. Laurence Moore, "What Children Did Not Learn in School: The Intellectual Quickening of Young Americans in the Nineteenth Century," *Church History: Studies in Christianity & Culture* 68, no. 1 (March 1999): 60. My thanks to Steven R. Sorensen for directing me to this reference.
45. Moore, "What Children Did Not Learn in School," 43.
46. Howe, *Historical Collection of Ohio*, 1:602.
47. Dills, *History of Fayette County*, 837; *History of Fayette County, Ohio 1984*, 269.
48. Rohrbough, *Trans-Appalachian Frontier*, 148.
49. *Illustrated Historical Atlas of Fayette County, Ohio*, 11. Walter Yeoman, one generation younger than Mercy, also became a prominent Primitive Baptist pastor in

several Ohio congregations and ministered into the twentieth century. Yeoman, "Sketch of Elder Yeoman," 190–192; *Scioto Predestinarian Baptist Association, Minutes of the Seventy-Sixth Annual Session, Paint Creek Church, Fayette County, Ohio, August 13, 14, and 15, 1880* (Mt. Sterling, Ohio: M. W. Schryver, 1880). My thanks to Elder Robert Webb of the Primitive Baptist Library in Carthage, Illinois, for this information.

50. Fayette County, Ohio, Series 1, Grantee Index to Deeds, A–D, 1810–1913, Family History Library, which appears to be a comprehensive index of land transactions, lists none for Charles Barney. See also "A Complete Record of the Sales of Lands within the County of Fayette and State of Ohio," 1820–1828, Ohio Historical Society, Columbus, Ohio.
51. Tax Record, Fayette County, Ohio, vol. 430, 1825, Family History Library.
52. John Barney, Patriarchal Blessing, Index, 25 February 1842, 25 February 1855.
53. Francis P. Weisenburger, "The Passing of the Frontier, 1825–1850," in Carl Wittke, ed., *The History of the State of Ohio*, 6 vols. (Columbus, Ohio: Ohio State Archaeological and Historical Society, 1941), 3:6.
54. Lewis Barney, Autobiography 1, 3.
55. Larkin, *Reshaping of Everyday Life*, 206–207.
56. Mercy Barney was preceded in death earlier that year by her brother James, making the year most traumatic for the Yeomans, as well as the Barneys. James was buried near the highest rise in the Rock Mills cemetery where his gravestone is still extant. While no headstone survives, Mercy's is likely in the same little cemetery. Mercy's father, Stephen, died four years later in May 1829 and was buried adjacent to his son James where his gravestone still stands. Mercy's infant daughter is referred to in family records variously as Lorinda, Melinda, and Lucinda. Preston, *Genealogy of the Barney Family*, 189; and Family Group Sheets, Family History Library.
57. Larkin, *The Reshaping of Everyday Life*, 78.
58. Lewis Barney, Autobiography 1, 3.
59. Ibid., 3. This circumstance followed a modified pattern of others where "one or two adult males . . . blazed the trail into the back country, [and] selected a promising site for settlement, [spending] months or even a year or two clearing the land, planting a crop, and building shelter" before returning east to escort "the rest of the household . . . to the west." Davis, *Frontier America*, 48.
60. Rohrbough, *Trans-Appalachian Frontier*, 158–159.
61. *Illinois in 1837: a Sketch* (Philadelphia: S. Augustus Mitchell, 1837), 19–21, 34.
62. Kay J. Carr, *Belleville, Ottawa, and Galesburg: Community and Democracy on the Illinois Frontier* (Carbondale, Illinois: Southern Illinois University Press, 1996), 33.
63. Chester Loomis, 28 June 1825, 1825 Journey for the Western States, Charles A. Loomis Correspondence, 1821–1839, Rare and Manuscript Collections, Carl A. Kroch Library, Cornell University, Ithaca, New York. My thanks to Steven R. Sorensen for showing this item to me.
64. Lewis Barney, Autobiography 1, 4.
65. Ibid., 5.
66. *History of Logan County, Illinois: Its Past and Present* (Chicago: Donnelly, Loyd & Co., 1878), 240.
67. Loomis, 26 June 1825, 1825 Journey.
68. Moses Martin, Journals, 1834, 26 May 1834, 6, Church Archives.
69. Loomis, ca. 15 July 1825, 1825 Journey.
70. Lewis Barney, Autobiography 1, 5–7.
71. Deborah Riffle was born 22 September 1808, in Miami County, Ohio. Deborah Riffle, Patriarchal Blessing, Index, 25 February 1842.
72. Nolan Barney deals with Deborah's complicated youth in "Deborah Riffle Street Barney," 1992, typescript in possession of author.

73. Lewis Barney, Autobiography 1, 6–7; Fayette County, Ohio, Marriages, Book A, 1810–1830, Family History Library.
74. Lewis Barney, Autobiography 1, 7.

Chapter 3

1. Rohrbough, *Trans-Appalachian Frontier*, 163.
2. Quoted in Rohrbough, *Trans-Appalachian Frontier*, 171–172.
3. Henry Rowe Schoolcraft quoted in John Mack Faragher, *Sugar Creek: Life on the Illinois Prairie* (New Haven: Yale University Press, 1986), 45.
4. Lewis C. Beck, *A Gazetteer of the States of Illinois and Missouri* (Albany, New York: Charles R. and George Webster, 1823), 83.
5. Eldridge G. Howe to Absalom Peters, 23 May 1826, Springfield, Illinois, American Home Missionary Society Papers, Amistad Research Center, Tulane University, New Orleans, Louisiana, microfilm copy, Church Archives.
6. It should be remembered that one of the primary objectives of the ministers' correspondence with their urban peers was to solicit money for their personal and congregational maintenance. The worse the conditions, the better the chance of loosening the purse strings of the missionary societies they represented.
7. John M. Ellis to Matthias Bruen, 29 December 1825, Kaskaskia, Illinois, American Home Missionary Society Papers.
8. Eldridge G. Howe to Matthias Bruen, 11 February 1826, Springfield, Illinois, American Home Missionary Society Papers.
9. John M. Ellis to Absalom Peters, 7 August 1826, Kaskaskia, Illinois, American Home Missionary Society Papers.
10. Eldridge G. Howe to Absalom Peters, 23 May 1826.
11. Quoted in Faragher, *Sugar Creek*, 131.
12. Joel Goodell to Rev. Mr. [Horace] Hooker, 12 May 1831, Liberty, Missouri, my emphasis.
13. Eldridge G. Howe to Absalom Peters, 23 May 1826.
14. Peter Cartwright, *Autobiography of Peter Cartwright: The Backwoods Preacher*, ed. W. P. Strickland (New York: Carlton & Porter, 1856), 249.
15. Robert Bruce Flanders, *Nauvoo: Kingdom on the Mississippi* (Urbana, Illinois: University of Illinois Press, 1975), 15.
16. *History of Logan County, Illinois*, 240, 246; Lawrence B. Stringer, *History of Logan County, Illinois*, 2 vols. (Chicago: Pioneer Publishing Co., 1911), 1:587.
17. Faragher, *Sugar Creek*, 54–55.
18. Bogue, *From Prairie to Corn Belt*, 56.
19. Stringer, *History of Logan County, Illinois*, 1:82, 84, 120, 587. The part of Sangamon County where the Barneys moved in 1825/1826 became a part of newly created Logan County, Illinois, in 1839.
20. John Mason Peck, *A Gazetteer of Illinois, in Three Parts* (Jacksonville, Illinois: R. Goudy, 1834), 272.
21. Lewis Barney, Autobiography 1, 7.
22. Faragher, *Sugar Creek*, 72.
23. Davis, *Frontier America*, 36.
24. Minutes of the Baptist Church of Jesus Christ at Lake Fork, 20 January 1827, photocopy of the mss., Primitive Baptist Library, Carthage, Illinois. I express my appreciation to Elder Robert Webb, director of the library, for providing me with a photocopy of the minutes for the period of the Barneys' association with the church in Sangamon County. See also Emagene Veech Green, *And She Held Forth Her Hand: History and Genealogy of Mt. Pulaski, Illinois* (Lincoln, Illinois: n.p., 1961), 51.

25. For an overview of Christian primitivism in America see Richard T. Hughes, ed., *The American Quest for the Primitive Church* (Urbana, Illinois: University of Illinois Press, 1988) and Richard T. Hughes and C. Leonard Allen, *Illusions of Innocence: Protestant Primitivism in America, 1630–1875* (Chicago: University of Chicago Press, 1988).
26. Nathan O. Hatch, *The Democratization of American Christianity* (New Haven, Connecticut: Yale University Press, 1989), 167.
27. The effort of Dr. John Clarke in the establishment of the Baptist faith in America was contemporaneous with the better known Roger Williams. For a treatment of Roger Williams as a primitivist see Hughes and Allen, *Illusions of Innocence*, 53–78. For an overview of Baptist beginnings in the United States see H. Leon McBeth, *The Baptist Heritage* (Nashville, Tennessee: Broadman Press, 1987), 123–150.
28. Gilbert Beebe quoted in Hughes and Allen, *Illusions of Innocence*, 91.
29. Hatch, *Democratization of American Christianity*, 9–10.
30. See Hughes and Allen's chapter "From Freedom to Constraint: The Transformation of the 'Christians in the West,'" in *Illusions of Innocence*, 102–132.
31. Robert Webb, "The Baptist Church at Lincoln's New Salem," *The Primitive Baptist Library Quarterly* 7, no. 3 (January–March 1995).
32. The Primitive Baptists, for example, rejected a schismatic primitivist movement in Illinois spawned by Daniel Parker who popularized, between 1820 and 1826, "an exaggerated and eccentric form of predestinarianism." Parker pushed a doctrinal innovation dubbed "two-seed-in-the-spirit" which argued that two seeds were planted in Eve, one by God and the other by Satan, and that the election of individuals was determined by their particular seed. Sydney E. Ahlstrom, *A Religious History of the American People*, 2 vols. (Garden City, New York: Image Books, 1975), 2:176–177; William Warren Sweet, *Religion on the American Frontier: The Baptists 1783–1830* (New York: Cooper Square Publishers, Inc., 1964), 74–75. Parker, who preached in Illinois, 1817–1833, was never accepted by most Primitive Baptists although his influence was felt through the end of the century.

    For brief overviews of the Primitive Baptists in America see McBeth, *Baptist Heritage*, 717–724, and Robert T. Handy, "Biblical Primitivism in the American Baptist Tradition," in Hughes, *American Quest for the Primitive Church*, 148–151.
33. Information about the Lake Fork Predestinarian Baptist Church, including quotations below, is found in minutes of the organization, photocopies of which can be found in the Primitive Baptist Library in Carthage, Illinois, and in possession of the author.
34. Luther's profession was somewhat unusual. "Young unmarried people seldom joined the frontier churches. Church membership was a too serious responsibility for young people to assume. It was [generally] not undertaken until they were married and settled in life." Louis A. Warren, *Lincoln's Youth: Indiana Years, Seven to Twenty-one, 1816–1830* (New York: Appleton-Century-Crofts, Inc., 1959), 213.
35. Lewis Barney, Autobiography 1, 16.
36. Eldridge G. Howe to Absalom Peters, 23 May 1826; Flanders, *Nauvoo*, 21, n. 37.
37. Warren, *Lincoln's Youth*, 13, 114, 116–117, 206; Allen C. Guelzo, *Abraham Lincoln: Redeemer President* (Grand Rapids, Michigan: William B. Eerdman's Publishing Company, 1999), 18–21, 36–38.
38. Lewis Barney, Autobiography 1, 7.
39. John M. Ellis to Absalom Peters, 10 January 1827, Kaskaskia, Illinois, American Home Missionary Society Papers.
40. *Illinois: A Descriptive and Historical Guide* (Chicago: A. C. McClurg & Co., 1939), 334, 336; *Brevet's Illinois Historical Markers and Sites* (Sioux Falls, South Dakota: Brevet Press Inc., 1976), 184.
41. J. W. Spencer, *Reminiscences of Pioneer Life in the Mississippi Valley* (Davenport, Iowa: Griggs, Watson, and Day, 1872) reprinted in Milo Milton Quaife, ed., *The*

Early Days of Rock Island and Davenport: The Narratives of J. W. Spencer and J. M. Burrows (Chicago: The Lakeside Press, 1942), 14. Quaife's note indicates that the reason they were called "Suckers" was "Because of the habit of the sucker of ascending rivers in the spring and descending them in the autumn."

42. Timothy Flint, *The History and Geography of the Mississippi Valley* (Cincinnati: E. H. Flint and L. R. Linden, 1832), 327.
43. Peck, *A Gazetteer of Illinois*, 20–21.
44. John M. Ellis to Absalom Peters, 10 January 1827.
45. The Barneys eluded one of Galena's temptations. At a time when the use of liquor in America's hinterlands was ubiquitous, the Barneys were apparently constrained from the immoderate use of "frontier lubrication." Whether they were motivated by religious principles, temperance rhetoric, or other reasons, Luther and Lewis were not unduly affected by the use of alcohol. The year prior to his death, Lewis boasted that through his entire life he had not consumed more than five gallons of liquor. Lewis Barney to Clark and Johns, 24 April 1893, Mancos, Colorado.
46. Charles Fenno Hoffman, "Galena" quoted in Paul M. Angle, comp. and ed., *Prairie State: Impressions of Illinois, 1673–1967, by Travelers and Other Observers* (Chicago: University of Chicago Press, 1968), 150–151.
47. Ibid., 150–151.
48. Peck, *Gazetteer of Illinois*, 20–21.
49. Hoffman in Angle, *Prairie State*, 150–151.
50. Rohrbough, *Trans-Appalachian Frontier*, 336.
51. Peck, *Gazetteer of Illinois*, 20–21.
52. Lewis Barney, Autobiography 1, 7; Sangamon County, Illinois, land and tax records state that Lewis and Luther Barney purchased for $1.25 per acre eighty acres of land, forty each in what was then Sangamon County (now Logan County), Illinois, on 22 June 1829. The exact location is the east half of the southeast half of section 2, township 17 north, range 2 west, meridian 3. Between 1829 and 1836 Charles, Luther, Lewis, and Lucien Barney purchased a total of just under four hundred acres of land in the area south-southeast of present-day Mt. Pulaski, Illinois, just north of the southern border of what is now Logan County, Illinois. Public Domain Land Tract Record Listing, vol. 68, 53, State of Illinois, Archives Division, Springfield, Illinois; and, Lists of Land Subject to Taxation in Various Counties, 1823–1838, 8 vols., State of Illinois, Archives Division, Springfield, Illinois.
53. Lewis Barney, Autobiography 1, 7–8.
54. Ibid., 8.
55. Executive Record, 1818–1832, 1:229, Index, State of Illinois, Archives Division, Springfield, Illinois; Lewis Barney, Autobiography 1, 8.
56. Faragher, *Sugar Creek*, 139–140.
57. The development of Illinois's infrastructure was one of the primary political issues espoused by Abraham Lincoln, who campaigned in Sangamon County beginning in 1832. Stephen B. Oates, *With Malice toward None: A Life of Abraham Lincoln* (New York: HarperPerennial, 1994), 34–35.
58. Rohrbough, *Trans-Appalachian Frontier*, 119, 127.
59. Lists of Land . . . 1823–1838, Illinois State Archives, Springfield, Illinois.
60. Sangamon/Logan County Documents, 81-68, Illinois State Historical Library, Springfield, Illinois. This 1831 petition is the earliest document I have found with the handwriting of Lewis Barney, who signed the document.
61. Faragher, *Sugar Creek*, 137. For an overview of the efforts at internal developments within Illinois at this time see Theodore Calvin Pease, *The Frontier State, 1818–1848* (Urbana, Illinois: University of Illinois Press, 1987), 194–235. Peases's work was first published for Illinois's centennial in 1918.
62. Preston, *Genealogy of the Barney Family*, 188–189.

63. Fiftieth Quorum, Genealogies, Seventies Quorum Records, Church Archives; Preston, *Genealogy of the Barney Family*, 189.
64. The other children were Margaret Matilda b. 8 November 1834, Thomas Jefferson b. 25 December 1836, William Street b. 30 March 1841, and Sarah Jane b. 13 May 1845. Preston, *Genealogy of the Barney Family*, 189. Information on the birth dates of Emerine, Elizabeth, and Louisa are found in genealogical records on file in the Family History Library.
65. Paul M. Angle in William H. Herndon, *Herndon's Life of Lincoln: The History and Personal Recollections of Abraham Lincoln as Originally Written by William H. Herndon and Jesse W. Weik*, ed. Paul M. Angle (New York: De Capo Press, Inc., 1983), 76.
66. For a summary of the Black Hawk War see Francis Paul Prucha, *The Sword of the Republic: The United States Army on the Frontier, 1783–1846* (New York: The MacMillan Company, 1969), 211–231.
67. Lewis Barney, Autobiography 1, 13. Barney was in error when he said that the U.S. negotiators got Black Hawk drunk and then forced the treaty upon him. Black Hawk signed the 30 June 1831 treaty reluctantly, however. Prucha, *Sword of the Republic*, 217.
68. Ibid., 211.
69. Lewis Barney to [?], fragment of letter found in Autobiography 1. There were three brigades of mounted troops mustered with each brigade having a spy battalion. Prucha, *Sword of the Republic*, 225.
70. Ellen M. Whitney, comp. and ed., *The Black Hawk War, 1831–1832* (Springfield, Illinois: Illinois State Historical Library, 1970), 1:204–206; *History of Sangamon County, Illinois* (Chicago: Inter-state Publishing Company, 1881), 163. See also Isaac H. Elliott, *Record of the Services of Illinois Soldiers in the Black Hawk War, 1831–1832 and in the Mexican War, 1846–1848* (Springfield, Illinois: Journal Company, 1902), 106–107.
71. Quoted in Angle, *Prairie State*, 108.
72. Lewis Barney, Autobiography 1, 13–14.
73. Ibid., 14; Prucha, *Sword of the Republic*, 223.
74. Whitney, *Black Hawk War*, 204–206.
75. Prucha, *Sword of the Republic*, 211.
76. Leland L. Sage, *A History of Iowa* (Ames, Iowa: Iowa State University Press, 1974), 50; and Prucha, *Sword of the Republic*, 226. See also Robert P. Howard, *Illinois: A History of the Prairie State* (Grand Rapids, Michigan: William B. Eerdmans Publishing Company, 1972), 145–154.
77. About 150 of Black Hawk's warriors were killed in the final confrontation. Prucha, *Sword of the Republic*, 229.

Chapter 4

1. In Autobiography 1, 8, Lewis states that he married on 11 April 1832. Marriage records of Sangamon County indicate that he married on 4 April 1833. See *Marriage Records, Sangamon County, Illinois, 1821–1840* (Springfield, Illinois: Sangamon County Genealogical Society of Illinois, n.d.).
2. Lists of Land . . . 1823–1838.
3. Bogue, *From Prairie to Corn Belt*, 169.
4. Endowment House [Salt Lake City] Sealings and Endowments, Book A & A1, 1851–1854, Special Collections, Family History Library; George F. Robinson, *History of Greene County, Ohio* (Chicago: S. J. Clarke Publishing Co., 1902), 392.
5. Information found in the Ancestral File, Family History Library. That the Turners lived in Greene County, Ohio, for roughly two decades is indicated in Arthur R.

Kilner's *Greene County, Ohio: Births Prior to 1869* (Bowie, Maryland: Heritage Books, Inc., 1988), 191, which states that Harmon Turner, a son of Walter and Lydia Ballinger Turner, was born in 1802 in Greene County in what was then the Northwest Territory. Another Walter Turner, no doubt Walter and Lydia's son, is listed in the same publication (p. 192) as having been born 23 October 1820 in Greene County.

6. "1835 Tax List, Sangamon County, Illinois," by Marilyn Wright Thomas and Hazelmae Taylor-Temple, Family History Library.
7. Green, *And She Held Forth Her Hand*, 51.
8. Fifth Census of the United States, 1830, National Archives, Washington, D.C.
9. Herndon, *Herndon's Life of Lincoln*, 53. See also Oates, *With Malice toward None*, 16–17; Guelzo, *Abraham Lincoln*, 32–33, 36.
10. For a discussion of the rhetoric in antebellum America for simple living in contrast to the quest for affluence see two volumes by David E. Shi, *The Simple Life: Plain Living and High Thinking in American Culture* (New York: Oxford University Press, 1986), 8–153, and *In Search of the Simple Life: American Voices, Past and Present* (Layton, Utah: Gibbs M. Smith, Inc., 1986), 15–175.
11. Lewis Barney, Autobiography 1, 8.
12. Ibid. Barney had 80 acres adjoining his father's 80 acres in section 1, Township 17 North, Range 2 West, Mt. Pulaski Township, Sangamon County. Land records indicate that Lewis Barney had 120 acres, Charles Barney 160 acres, Luther Barney 80 acres, and Lucien Barney 40 acres of Sangamon County land. See the Public Domain Land Tract Record Listing, State of Illinois, Archives Division, Springfield, Illinois; Lists of Land Subject to Taxation in Various Counties, 1823–1838, State of Illinois, Archives Division, Springfield, Illinois.
13. Ancestral File, Family History Library. A Barney child was the first person buried in what became the Steenbergen Cemetery in Mt. Pulaski Township. Given the date of Sarah Jane's birth and death, it is likely that she was the child, though either of Charles's two daughters who died prior to 1834 could have been this particular Barney child. See Logan County, Illinois Cemetery Inscriptions, 1:25, Family History Library.
14. Nancy Schrom Dye and Daniel Blake Smith, "Mother Love and Infant Death, 1750–1920," *Journal of American History* 73, no. 2 (September 1986): 346.
15. Ibid., 330.
16. Larkin, *Reshaping of Everyday Life*, 75, 78–79.
17. Walter Turner's gravestone showing his death on 17 August 1834 is still extant on the top of the Steenburgen Cemetery hill.
18. Faragher, *Sugar Creek*, 89.
19. Margaret Matilda Barney was born 8 November 1834 in Sangamon County, Illinois. Preston, *Genealogy of Barney Family*, 189.
20. Preston, *Genealogy of the Barney Family*, 347, 189.
21. Dye and Smith, "Mother Love and Infant Death," 341.
22. Ibid., 330, 332, 337–338.
23. Faragher, *Sugar Creek*, 151.
24. John Rodgers served in the same military unit with Barney during the Black Hawk War.
25. Lewis Barney, Autobiography 1, 9–12.
26. Theodore Calvin Pease, ed., *Illinois Election Returns, 1818–1848* (Springfield, Illinois: Illinois State Historical Library, 1923), 80–81.
27. David Herbert Donald, *Lincoln* (London: Jonathon Cape, 1995), 50.
28. Peterson, *Lincoln in American Memory*, 121.
29. Pease, *Illinois Election Returns*, 104–105.
30. Oates, *With Malice toward None*, 31.

31. Luther Barney, Charles's son, voted for Jackson's protégé and vice-president, Martin Van Buren, who won the presidency in 1836. Index, Election Returns, vol. 28, State of Illinois, Archives Division, Springfield, Illinois.

    For an overview of local and national political views in Illinois during this period see Pease, *The Frontier State*, 114–149, 236–277. For Lincoln's influence on Sangamon County politics during this period see Guelzo, *Abraham Lincoln*, 64–101.

32. Charles's son Luther married Lurinda Rhoads (or Brown) in McLean County, Illinois, on 4 December 1837. See Preston, *Genealogy of Barney Family*, 188; *McLean County [Illinois] Marriage Records, 1831–1855* (n.p.: Bloomington-Normal Genealogical Society, n.d.), 5. Charles's son Henry also likely married in Sangamon County. Preston, *Genealogy of the Barney Family*, 189, 348–349.

    For other Barney land acquisitions see the Public Domain Land Tract, Record Listing, vols. 68–69, State of Illinois, Archives Division, Springfield, Illinois.

    The Barneys were involved in civic matters as evidenced by their signatures on petitions concerning land regulation and sales and involvement in committees assigned to select political delegates. See Stringer, *History of Logan County, Illinois*, 1:396; Sangamon/Logan County Documents, 81-68; *Sangamo (Springfield, Illinois) Journal*, 30 March 1839.

33. Lewis Barney, Autobiography 1, 15.
34. For an overview of the economic difficulties of the period see volume three of Robert V. Remini's biography of the seventh president, *Andrew Jackson and the Course of American Democracy, 1833–1845* (New York: Harper & Row, Publishers, 1984); and Arthur M. Schlesinger, Jr., *The Age of Jackson* (Boston: Little, Brown and Company, 1945), 74–131.
35. John Smith, Papers, 1832–1854, Journals, 27, 31 May, 3 June 1838, Church Archives.
36. *Illinois in 1837: a Sketch*, 48–50.
37. Lewis Barney, Lecture on the Exodus of the Latter-day Saints from the United States to the Rocky Mountains, 14 July 1888, hereafter cited as Lewis Barney, Lecture, 1888. Copy in possession of the author. A fragment of the lecture can be found in Autobiography 1.
38. Lewis Barney, Lecture, 1888.
39. Lewis Barney's notice while on their way to Iowa of the aftermath of a hanging near Carthage, Illinois, parallels Thomas Gregg's description of Hancock County's first hanging which occurred on 18 May 1839 placing the Barneys there at that time. Lewis Barney, Lecture, 1888; Thomas Gregg's *A Descriptive, Statistical and Historical Chart of the County of Hancock* (Warsaw, Illinois: Thomas Gregg, 1 January 1846). Charles Barney remained in Lake Fork until at least June 1839. *Sangamo Journal*, 30 March 1839. See also the Minutes of Lake Fork Predestinarian Baptist Church which states that Charles and Deborah Barney were dismissed by their own request after having been in good standing in June 1839.
40. Davis, *Frontier America*, 165.
41. Sage, *A History of Iowa*, 58–60, 68.
42. Charles R. Tuttle and Daniel S. Durrie, *An Illustrated History of the State of Iowa* (Chicago: Richard S. Peale and Company, 1876), 537; Sage, *History of Iowa*, 62; Peter H. Jaynes, ed., *Highlights of Henry County, Iowa History, 1833–1976* (Burlington, Iowa: Doran & Ward Lithographing Co., 1976), 1–3.
43. *Iowa Territorial Gazette and Advertizer*, October 1, 1842.
44. While Lewis Barney indicates in Autobiography 1 and his 1888 lecture that Charles filed for 1,000 acres, a search of the earliest land records in the Henry County, Iowa, show Charles purchased 600 acres which were recorded in January, March, and June of 1840. Lewis Barney, Autobiography 1, 15. He bought land in

sections 14 (240 acres), 15 (120 acres), 20 (80 acres), and 23 (160 acres) of Township 73, Range 7 in Henry County, Iowa. The purchase price for this land was $550 or $650. Charles may have made arrangements to pay for the other 400 acres at a future date. See Original Entries Record [Patents], 409–410, Henry County Courthouse, Mt. Pleasant, Iowa.

45. Lucinda and John D. Copeland had four children while living in Sangamon/Logan County, Illinois. John's remarriage in 1854 suggests that Lucinda apparently died prior to that date.
46. Sixth Census of the United States, 1840, National Archives, Washington, D.C. It appears from this census that several of Mercy Yeoman Barney's brothers—Gilbert, Samuel, and Stephen—may have relocated to Henry County by this time as well, perhaps indicating another reason why the Barneys moved to Henry County, Iowa.
47. Arkansas, State Auditor, County Tax Records, 1829–1869, Crawford County, 2, Family History Library. The record indicates that both Lucien and Henry were "liable to pay poll tax" in 1839 and that Lucien had one horse or mare valued at $50. Conditions in Crawford County at the time were still in the developmental stage with the county seat being established just the year before. Van Buren, the county seat, was still noted as a center for trade with Native Americans during this period. *The History of Crawford County, Arkansas: Press-Argus Centennial Edition* (n.p.: n.p., ca. 1959).
48. *Iowa Territorial Gazette and Advertizer*, 1 October 1842.

Chapter 5

1. Lewis Barney, Autobiography 1, 15. The Barneys while living in Lake Fork, no doubt, were privy to the situation in Missouri from the weekly *Sangamo Journal* published in nearby Springfield, Illinois. Mormon difficulties were regularly considered in the newspaper during the fall, winter, and spring of 1838–1839. See *Sangamo Journal* vol. 7, numbers 43, 51–52 and vol. 8, numbers 3–5, 13, 22, 28, and 36, covering August 1838–June 1839.
2. Luther Barney and his small family may have been living in McLean County, Illinois, where he married and voted in 1837, though there is no record of when and where he was baptized a Latter-day Saint.

   Luther Barney was not the first with that surname to become a Mormon. Royal Barney and his family joined with the Mormons in 1831. Royal, like Charles Barney, was a Vermonter born in 1783. They shared a great-great-great-grandfather, Jacob. Royal's family, in particular Edson and Royal, Jr., was very involved with the Church of Jesus Christ in Kirtland, Ohio, in the 1830s before emigrating to Nauvoo, and then to Utah. Royal, Jr.'s daughter, Harriet, became a plural wife of Brigham Young in 1856. Seventies Quorum, Records, Second Quorum, Biographies, 1, Church Archives; Andrew Jenson, *Latter-day Saints' Biographical Encyclopedia*. 4 vols. (Salt Lake City: Andrew Jenson History Company/Andrew Jenson Memorial Association, 1901–1936), 4:687; Preston, *Barney Family in America*, 282–283, 467–470.
3. Officially named the Church of Christ when organized in 1830, by 1834 the church was known as the Church of the Latter Day Saints to distinguish it from other Christian denominations. Within two years the church was sometimes known as the Church of Christ of Latter Day Saints. The official name by which the church is presently known was adopted in 1838. However, because of widespread identification of church members as "Mormons" the appellation soon became accepted by church members.
4. Hughes and Allen, *Illusions of Innocence*, 138.

5. Jan Shipps, "The Reality of the Restoration and the Restoration Ideal in the Mormon Tradition," in Hughes, ed., *American Quest for the Primitive Church*, 182–183.
6. Samuel D. Lucas to Gov. Lilburn Boggs, 4 October 1838, Boonville, Missouri, State Historical Society of Missouri, photocopy in Church Archives.
7. Stephen C. LeSueur, *The 1838 Mormon War in Missouri* (Columbia, Missouri: University of Missouri Press, 1987), 137–142, 162–168.
8. Kenneth H. Winn, *Exiles in a Land of Liberty: Mormons in America, 1830–1846* (Chapel Hill, North Carolina: The University of North Carolina Press, 1989), 144–145.
9. For a summary of the expulsion of the Mormons from Missouri in 1838–1839 see William G. Hartley, "'Almost Too Intolerable a Burthen': The Winter Exodus from Missouri," *Journal of Mormon History* 18, no. 2 (fall 1992): 6–40.
10. Joseph Smith to John C. Bennett, 8 August 1840, in Smith, *History of the Church*, 4:178.
11. See, e.g., Parley P. Pratt, *Autobiography of Parley P. Pratt*, ed. Parley P. Pratt, Jr. (Salt Lake City: Deseret Book Company, 1972), 51–52, 68, 75–76.
12. John Murdock, Autobiography [ca. 1859–1867], Church Archives; Zebedee Coltrin, Journal, January 1832, vol. 1, 3, Church Archives; Pratt, *Autobiography of Parley P. Pratt*, 82–92; William E. McLellin, *The Journals of William E. McLellin, 1831–1836*, Jan Shipps and John W. Welch, eds. (Provo, Utah: Brigham Young University Studies and University of Illinois Press, 1994), 102–123; Edward Partridge, Diary, typescript, 9, Church Archives.
13. 30 May 1834, Smith, *History of the Church*, 2:76.
14. S. George Ellsworth, "A History of Mormon Missions in the United States and Canada, 1830–1860" (Ph.D. diss., University of California, 1951), 185. Later in the 1830s a number of Mormons lived in Springfield and Mt. Pulaski, Illinois, both of which were in close proximity to the Barneys in Lake Fork. There were "agents" for the *Times and Seasons*, the church organ published in Nauvoo, in each of these cities by February 1840. *Times and Seasons* 1, no. 4 (February 1840): 64. Also a small collection of Saints wintered with Wilford Woodruff near Rochester in Sangamon County in 1838–1839.
15. Lewis Barney, Autobiography 1, 15.
16. Early Mormon periodicals differentiated Calvinism from their theology. See "Faith of the Church of Christ in these Last Days," *The Evening and the Morning Star* 2, no. 23 (August 1834): 179; and *Messenger and Advocate* 2, no. 12 (September 1836): 380–381. See also Marvin S. Hill, "The Shaping of the Mormon Mind in New England and New York," *BYU Studies* 9, no. 3 (spring 1969): 363–364; and Davis Bitton, "The Sovereignty of God in John Calvin and Brigham Young," *Sunstone* 5, no. 5 (September–October 1980): 26–30.
17. Lewis Barney, Autobiography 1, 17. This occurred near the birth of Barney's son James Henry Barney, 30 January 1840.
18. Ibid., 16. The Predestinarian Baptists, embraced by Lewis's family, were but one of a number of denominational organizations in Illinois while the Barneys were in Sangamon County, Illinois. Other faiths represented were Methodists, largest of the Christian churches in Illinois, mainstream Baptists, Presbyterians, Congregationalists, Campbellites, United Brethren, Lutherans, Episcopalians, Friends (Quakers), and a few Roman Catholics. *Illinois in 1837: a Sketch*, 62–63.
19. Crooked Creek, surveyed in 1837 and designated a voting district in October 1840, was successively renamed Marshall and Wayland in later years. *The History of Henry County, Iowa* (Dallas, Texas: n.p., 1982), 54–55.
20. Lewis Barney, Autobiography 1, 16. John Lowe Butler, having a Primitive Baptist background himself, wrote that in 1835 he also encountered Mormon missionaries

whose teaching "astonished" him. "I knew every word they said to be truth. . . . It was just the thing that I had been hankering after." William G. Hartley, *My Best for the Kingdom: History and Autobiography of John Lowe Butler, A Mormon Frontiersman* (Salt Lake City: Aspen Books, 1993), 383–384.

For an indication of the manner and teaching of Latter-day Saint missionaries in the 1830s, one of the best sources is Orson Pratt, Journals, 1833–1836, Church Archives. Some of the more distinctive particulars of LDS doctrine and thought today were not taught by Joseph Smith to the Saints until they were settled in Nauvoo.

21. Record for the Seventies of Monroe Ward in the Sevier Stake of Zion, in Seventies Quorum Records, 1844–1975, 17 January 1883 [1884], Church Archives.
22. Lewis Barney, Lecture, 1888.
23. Lewis Barney, Autobiography 1, 17; Lewis Barney to Andrew Jenson, 21 April 1890, Kanosh, Utah, copy in possession of the author. Barney wrote that he was baptized in May 1840 by his friend Alva Tippetts. However, an entry in an official church record in 1845 indicates that Barney was baptized by James Gough on 15 June 1840. Records of the 18th Quorum, Seventies Quorums, Records, 1844–1975, Church Archives. There are no other records to reconcile the disparity.

    Barney reported that his father's immediate family became Mormons, perhaps including some of his mother's family, some of whom, as mentioned earlier, were also in Henry County. While no information about the dates of Charles and Deborah Barney's baptisms are known, membership information about the rest of the family come from noncontemporary church records. Several, including Elizabeth Turner Barney, Walter and Benjamin F., were baptized by James Carroll. Church records that give information about Barney family memberships are (1) Walter (Provo Utah Central Stake, General Minutes, Series 11, v. 9, 64–65; Record for the Seventies of Monroe Ward, Church Archives), (2) Elizabeth Turner Barney (Kanosh [Utah] Ward, Record of Members, Church Archives), (3) Benjamin Franklin Barney (Seventies Quorum Records, Fifth Quorum, Church Archives), and (4) Henry Barney, who was baptized 15 January 1845 by his brother John, indicating, of course, John's earlier baptism (Seventies Record, 32nd Quorum, Book B, Church Archives).

    Elsy Yeoman, Mercy Yeoman's brother Gilbert's daughter, was married by one of the Mormon missionaries in Henry County, the marriage of which was reported in the Nauvoo *Times and Seasons* 2, no. 10 (15 March 1841): 357, suggesting that she was also a church member.
24. William Clayton to Beloved brethren and sisters, 10 December 1840, Church Archives, published as James B. Allen, "To the Saints in England: Impressions of a Mormon Immigrant," *BYU Studies* 18, no. 3 (spring 1978): 478–479. See also Ronald O. Barney, "'A Man You Could Not Help Likeing': Joseph Smith and Nauvoo, Illinois, Portrayed in a Letter by Susannah and George W. Taggart," *BYU Studies* 40, no. 2 (2001): 165–179.
25. Richard L. Bushman, "The Historians and Mormon Nauvoo," *Dialogue: A Journal of Mormon Thought* 5, no. 1 (spring 1970): 60–61.
26. Marvin S. Hill, "Quest for Refuge: An Hypothesis as to the Social Origins and Nature of the Mormon Political Kingdom," *Journal of Mormon History* 2 (1975): 13; Laurence M. Yorgason, "Preview on a Study of the Social and Geographical Origins of Early Mormon Converts, 1830–1845," *BYU Studies* 10, no. 3 (spring 1970): 279–282; and Ellsworth, "History of Mormon Missions," 332–342. In the 1840s, of course, converts to Mormonism from Great Britain were primarily from the lower echelons of society.
27. See Peter Crawley, *A Descriptive Bibliography of the Mormon Church: Volume One, 1830–1847* (Provo, Utah: Religious Studies Center, Brigham Young University, 1997), 1–144.

28. *Times and Seasons* 1, no. 12 (October 1840): 182.
29. Amasa Lyman, Journal, 23 February 1841, Church Archives. Lyman and Barney shared a common Barney ancestor six generations earlier.
30. Lewis Barney, Autobiography 1, 17–18. For an overview of the fluctuating views of the Nauvoo, Illinois, gathering in 1840–1841, see Flanders, *Nauvoo*, 46–50, 54.
31. Lewis Barney, Autobiography 1, 18. Carroll's errant enthusiasm and doctrine continued after this incident. To a Salt Lake City congregation in 1857, Brigham Young recalled Carroll's problematic disposition of apocalyptic fervor during Carroll's later missionary service in Indiana about 1843. President Young said that Carroll, after accepting the invitation of a Baptist congregation to preach to them, "rose, and began to preach 'Mormonism,' as he called it; and . . . instead of preaching the restoration and first principles of the Gospel, almost the first remark that he made was, 'You have a pretty meeting-house, and good buildings and farms; but do you know that the "Mormons" are coming here to possess the whole of them? . . . By the time he got through with so short a sermon, the congregation was ready to kick him out of the neighbourhood, and he ought to have been kicked out of the pulpit at the first dash." Brigham Young, 6 April 1857, Great Salt Lake City, Utah Territory, *Journal of Discourses* 26 vols. (Liverpool: S. W. Richards, 1857), 4:306. Carroll's excesses later found him severed from the church in Nauvoo, Illinois.
32. Lewis Barney, Autobiography 1, 19–20.
33. *Times and Seasons* 2, no. 10 (15 March 1841): 350.
34. Ten of this number are the Iowa branches represented at the Zarahemla, Iowa, conference on 9 August 1841. Journal History of the Church of Jesus Christ of Latter-day Saints, 18 November 1840, 9 August 1841, Church History Library. See also the August 1841 Zarahemla conference minutes published in the *Times and Seasons* 2, no. 22 (15 September 1841): 547–548. There were other branches in the area, like that where the Barneys lived, that were apparently never formalized as church units. See also Stanley B. Kimball, "Nauvoo West: The Mormons of the Iowa Shore," *BYU Studies* 18, no. 2 (winter 1978): 135–141. See also William G. Hartley, "Mormons and Early Iowa History (1838–1858): Eight Distinct Connections" *Annals of Iowa* 59, no. 3 (summer 2000): 217–260.
35. John Smith to George A. Smith, 7 January 1841, Ambrosia, Iowa Territory, George A. Smith, Papers, Incoming Correspondence, Church Archives.
36. Doctrine and Covenants, Section 125. Nashville was also designated to have a temple built within the community. John Smith, Papers, Journal, 23 August 1840, 3 September 1840.
37. Journal History, 9 August 1841.
38. "A Proclamation to the Saints Scattered Abroad," *Times and Seasons* 2, no. 6 (15 January 1841): 273.
39. *Times and Seasons* 2, no. 15 (1 June 1841): 434.

Chapter 6

1. Charles Barney apparently began to sell off his land in January 1841 when he sold a parcel for $165. Land Deed, Book A, 415–416, Henry County Courthouse, Mt. Pleasant, Iowa. On 6 November 1841 Charles and Deborah Barney sold 440 acres of land for $2,600. Land Deed, Book B, 288–289, Henry County Courthouse, Mt. Pleasant, Iowa.
2. Nauvoo Restoration Incorporated records indicate the marriage was performed by James Carroll on 8 April 1841.
3. Lewis Barney, Autobiography 1, 21. Considering that Amasa Lyman visited the Barneys in Henry County, Iowa, toward the end of February 1841 and Charles and

Deborah Barney's youngest son, William Street Barney, was born in Nauvoo on 30 March 1841, it is probable their move occurred during the month of March.

4. The lot "bought" by Lewis was probably within the 120 acres of Hyrum Smith's farm located in the southwest corner of Section 31 found in the northeast sector of Nauvoo. Because there are no records of the transaction, it is likely that Lewis never fully paid for the land to receive title to it, a common circumstance in Nauvoo. While Hyrum Smith, older brother of the Prophet Joseph, also had land located in the northwest part of Nauvoo, nine blocks directly north of the Nauvoo temple block, it is probable that Lewis located on what had been the elder Smith's farm. Smith's land in both the northeast and northwest sectors of Nauvoo is shown in Gustavus Hills, 1842 *Map of the City of Nauvoo* (New York: J. Childs, lithographer), reprinted by Nauvoo Restoration Inc. in 1971. Of Smith's land in Nauvoo, Flanders has written: "Hyrum Smith bought forty acres on the northeast edge of Nauvoo from Robert Thompson in January, 1840, for $3,100 which he platted and offered for sale. He purchased additional property for an unspecified sum, and platted a second addition of seven lots. Nauvoo did not develop in the direction of his location, however, and he seems to have sold only a few lots averaging $105 apiece." Flanders, *Nauvoo*, 124–125. Flanders's description of land acquisition and distribution in Nauvoo is found on pages 115–143. I am grateful to James L. Kimball, Jr., now retired, of the Family and Church History Department for information about land transactions in Nauvoo.
5. Lewis Barney, Autobiography 1, 21. The location of Charles and Luther Barney's Nauvoo homesites are not known.
6. "Proclamation," *Times and Seasons* 2 (15 January 1841): 274.
7. Lewis Barney, Autobiography 1, 21. Records in the Hancock County (Illinois) Courthouse indicate that on 25 January 1842 Lewis Barney obtained title to the "South half of the South east quarter of Section Thirty 30 in Township Six (6) North of the Base line and Range Six (6) west of the Fourth principal Meridian" (S/2 of SE/4, Section 30, Township 6 North, Range 6 West) for $275 from William O. and Hannah Carrothers [*sic*]. Hancock County, Illinois, Deed Book, Book K, 60–61, Hancock County, Recorder's Office, Carthage, Illinois. The same day Lewis obtained title to the adjacent "North half of the South East Quarter of Section Thirty (30) in Township Six (6) North of the Base line and Range Six (6) west of the fourth principal Meridian" (N/2 Se/4, Section 30, Township 6 North, Range 6 West) for $275 from James H. and Margaret Carothers [*sic*]. Hancock County, Illinois, Deed Book, Book K, 61–62. Barney's memory exaggerated the sale price. Rather than paying the $750 he remembered, Barney paid $550 for his property. He apparently paid $225 at the time of the transaction and mortgaged the rest, which mortgage was satisfied in December 1844. Hancock County, Bond and Mortgage, Book 1, 102, Hancock County, Recorder's Office, Carthage, Illinois.

   Hancock County records also indicate that Charles Barney obtained a quit claim deed on 9 November 1841 to "Twenty Acres East part of the North half of Section Eleven of Township Five North in range Seven West of the Fourth principal Meridian" for $25 from David W. Mathews. Hancock County, Deed Book, Book K, 130.
8. Lewis Barney, Autobiography 1, 21. Joseph Smith's original intention for Nauvoo was to create a community plan "in direct contrast to the typical western American settlement." Mormon "farms were to be located on the perimeter of the city so that after tilling, planting, and harvesting, farmers could return to the city at the close of each day. There they could, with their families, enjoy the cultural and religious refinements which a rural life could not provide." T. Edgar Lyon, "The Current Restoration in Nauvoo, Illinois," *Dialogue: A Journal of Mormon Thought* 5, no. 1 (spring 1970): 15.

9. David E. Miller and Della S. Miller, *Nauvoo: The City of Joseph* (Santa Barbara, California: Peregrine Smith, Inc., 1974), 1.
10. *Times and Seasons* 2, no. 6 (15 January 1841): 273–274; Lyon, "The Current Restoration in Nauvoo, Illinois," 13.
11. Kenneth W. Godfrey, "The Nauvoo Neighborhood: A Little Philadelphia or a Unique City Set upon a Hill," *Journal of Mormon History* 11 (1984): 79–97.
12. Robert Bruce Flanders, "The Kingdom of God in Illinois: Politics in Utopia," *Dialogue: A Journal of Mormon Thought of the Church of Jesus Christ of Latter-day Saints* 5, no. 1 (spring 1970): 26.
13. James E. Smith, "Frontier Nauvoo: Building a Picture from Statistics," *The Ensign* 9, no. 9 (September 1979): 18.
14. For in-depth overviews of the course of the Latter-day Saint habitation of Nauvoo see Smith, *History of the Church*, volumes 3–7; B. H. Roberts, A *Comprehensive History of the Church of Jesus Christ of Latter-day Saints, Century I*, 6 vols. (Provo, Utah: Brigham Young University Press, 1965), vol. 3, and *The Rise and Fall of Nauvoo* (Salt Lake City: Bookcraft, 1965); Flanders, *Nauvoo*; Miller and Miller, *Nauvoo*; and Richard Neitzel Holzapfel and T. Jeffery Cottle, *Old Mormon Nauvoo and Southeastern Iowa* (Santa Ana, California: Fieldbrook Productions, Inc., 1991).
15. *Times and Seasons* 2, no. 9 (1 March 1841): 336–337.
16. Woodruff, *Journal*, 2:131, 6 October 1841. In June 1840 it was reported that there were 250 dwellings in Nauvoo. Smith, *History of the Church*, 4:133. The extant homes in Nauvoo are mostly brick, perhaps giving a faulty impression of the physical look of the city in the 1840s. At Nauvoo's population peak in 1844–1845, a contemporary observer wrote that the types of building structures in Nauvoo may have been 1200 log or timber homes, 300–500 frame homes, and 200–300 brick homes. George W. Givens, *In Old Nauvoo: Everyday Life in the City of Joseph* (Salt Lake City: Deseret Book Company, 1990), 11, while being limited due to its reliance on secondary literature only, offers some insight into Nauvoo social life.
17. 18 June 1840, Smith, *History of the Church*, 4:136–137. Despite Joseph Smith's plea for relief, the city council denied the appeal. Flanders, *Nauvoo*, 121–122.
18. Historian Dean May places the highest Nauvoo population figure at just less than 15,000. Dean L. May, "A Demographic Portrait of Mormons, 1830–1980," in Thomas G. Alexander and Jessie L. Embry, eds., *After 150 Years: The Latter-day Saints in Sesquicentennial Perspective* (Midvale, Utah: Charles Redd Center for Western History, 1983), 43–44. Richard Bennett suggests there may have been as many as 17,000 in Nauvoo during the winter of 1845–1846 given the influx of refugees and other factors. Richard E. Bennett, *Mormons at the Missouri, 1846–1852* (Norman, Oklahoma: University of Oklahoma Press, 1987), 15. Susan Easton Black in "How Large Was the Population of Nauvoo?" *BYU Studies* 35, no. 2 (1995): 91–94, suggests the population of Nauvoo fluctuated from 100 in 1839, to 4,000 in 1842, to 12,000 in 1844, to 11,000 in 1845. See also Smith, "Frontier Nauvoo," 17, and Givens, *In Old Nauvoo*, 7–9, 14.
19. Mary Ann Angell Young to Brigham Young, 15 April 1841, Nauvoo, Illinois, Brigham Young, Papers, Family Correspondence, Church Archives.
20. Lewis Barney, Autobiography 1, 21.
21. The dates of their ordinations were 6 September 1841 for Charles and 19 July 1841 for both Luther and John. Elders Licences, Nauvoo, Illinois, Church Archives. While there is no record of Lewis Barney's ordination as an elder, it is certain he was also ordained to that office.
22. Lewis Barney was ordained a seventy on 2 February 1845 by Joseph Young. The record of this ordination is the one which also lists his baptism as having been performed on 15 June 1840 by James Gough. Seventies Quorum Records, 18th Quorum of Seventy, 2–5.

23. Milton V. Backman, Jr., "The Keys Are Right Here," in Susan Easton Black and Larry C. Porter, eds., *Lion of the Lord: Essays on the Life and Service of Brigham Young* (Salt Lake City: Deseret Book Company, 1995), 121.
24. Nauvoo Temple, Baptisms for the Dead, Book A, Family History Library. Prompted by the Apostle Paul's declaration on the resurrection found in his first epistle to the Corinthians 15:29, Joseph Smith preached a funeral sermon on 15 August 1840 wherein he described the ancient Christian practice of baptism for the dead and inaugurated its restoration as an ordinance for the Latter-day Saints. The Saints explain this doctrine as being the logical extension of Jesus' teaching to Nicodemus: "Except a man be born of water [baptism] and of the Spirit [obtaining the gift of the Holy Ghost], he cannot enter into the kingdom of God" (John 3:5). Considering that most of the world's populace had not and would not have access to the teachings of Jesus Christ, and desiring to extend the blessing of salvation as widely as possible, the Mormons believed the early-day Saints vicariously baptized the deceased as if they had accepted Jesus and his gospel. The biblical references to this doctrine, in part, are found in John 3:5; I Cor. 15:29; and I Peter 3:18–19, and 4:6. Almost seven thousand of these vicarious ordinances were performed in 1841. For an overview of the practice in Nauvoo see, M. Guy Bishop, "'What Has Become of Our Fathers?' Baptism for the Dead at Nauvoo," *Dialogue: A Journal of Mormon Thought* 23, no. 2 (summer 1990): 88–89.
25. Patriarchal Blessings, 6 September 1841, vol. 4, 3, Church Archives. Charles Barney received his patriarchal blessing the same day as Lewis. Other Barney family members also received blessings on 25 February 1842 including Lewis's wife, Elizabeth, his brother John, his stepmother Deborah, and his half-sister Elizabeth. Over 2 million patriarchal blessings of church members from 1833 to the present are on file in the Church Archives.
26. The roles of these groups and individuals fluctuated some before the end of the decade.
27. Of this contrast between city and country, Richard Bushman has written,

> More than an objective measure of reality, city and country were a cultural and social polarity in a mental geography. The words were categories of a simple but useful vernacular sociology. Fashion, refinement, and excitement were at one pole, and simplicity, rudeness, and torpor at the other. City and country represented the extremes of two contrasting ways of life. The words organized the social world spatially, attributing levels of culture to place, even while people recognized the far more complex boundaries of cultural differences in the real world.

Richard L. Bushman, *The Refinement of America: Persons, Houses, Cities* (New York: Vintage Books, 1993), 353–354.

28. Lewis Barney, Lecture, 1888. Thomas Gregg's 1846 broadside advertising Hancock County states, "The first and only execution that ever took place in Hancock County, was that of Benjamin Frame, who was hung on Saturday, the 18th of May, 1839,—for a murder committed in Schuyler county,—and who was tried and convicted in this county, under a change of venue." Gregg, *A Descriptive, Statistical and Historical Chart of the County of Hancock.*
29. Ibid.
30. Gregg, *History of Hancock County, Illinois*, 841–842; Newton Bateman, et al., eds., *Historical Encyclopedia of Illinois and History of Hancock County*, 2 vols. (Chicago: Munsell Publishing Company, 1921), 2:1091–1092.
31. *Illinois in 1837; a Sketch*, 80.
32. Lewis Barney, Autobiography 1, 22. A stake and ridered fence was a way for rural folk with limited resources to fence their property. The fence was formed by driving

a Y shaped branch or "crotch stake" into the ground. Long poles were then laid horizontally in the crotches of the Y shaped stakes. Shorter poles, with one end in the ground, were then placed over the long pole parallel to the direction of the branches of the crotch stake forming another crotch in which to horizontally lay another long pole. This was repeated until the fence was of sufficient height to contain one's stock. George A. Martin, ed., *Fences, Gates and Bridges: A Practical Manual* (New York: O. Judd Co., 1887), 11–12.

33. Nauvoo Restoration Incorporated, Land Records, compiled by Rowena Miller.
34. Jenson, *Latter-day Saints' Biographical Encyclopedia*, 3:594.
35. Godfrey, "The Nauvoo Neighborhood," 85–92. The Barneys may have held religious services in their homes, like other Nauvoo Saints, and gathered with their extended family for worship. No female relatives of Charles Barney are found as members of the Nauvoo Relief Society listed in the *Handbook of the Relief Society of the Church of Jesus Christ of Latter-day Saints* ([Salt Lake City]: General Board of Relief Society, 1931), 80–89.
36. Hartley, *My Best for the Kingdom*, 112.
37. Nauvoo Temple Recorders Ledger, Book A; Tithing Daybooks B, C, Nauvoo, Illinois, Church Archives.
38. 19 January 1841, Doctrine and Covenants, Section 124:23; Jenson, *Latter-day Saints' Biographical Encyclopedia*, 3:594.
39. 19 January 1841, Doctrine and Covenants, Section 124:27–28.
40. Givens, *In Old Nauvoo*, 20.
41. Lewis Barney, Autobiography 2, 2; Jenson, *Latter-day Saints' Biographical Encyclopedia*, 3:594. On 1 March 1842, to the citizens of Nauvoo concerning the building of the temple Smith declared "that an equal distribution of labor should be made, in relation to time [spent on temple construction]." Stating that there was "a superabundance of hands one week, and none the next," he said that the wards would schedule time for men to systematically attend to the work. For those not working directly on the temple, he also appealed to "those who have teams [to] bring them also" to hasten the work. *Times and Seasons* 3, no. 9 (1 March 1842): 715.
42. Lewis Barney, Autobiography 2, 5; and Lewis Barney, Lecture, 1888. The Nauvoo Temple Recorder's Ledger reports show other contributions of the Barneys to the construction of the Nauvoo Temple.
43. Godfrey, "The Nauvoo Neighborhood," 81–83.
44. "The Latter-day Saints," *Latter-day Saints' Millennial Star* 2, no. 8 (December 1841): 123. This item is a reprint from the *St. Louis Atlas* which begins, "An intelligent friend, who called upon us this morning, has just returned from a visit to Nauvoo and the Latter-day Saints."
45. Years later, Robert Ripley of "Ripley's Believe It or Not" featured the trivia that Nauvoo had the only straight Main Street in the world having the same river at both ends. Lyon, "Current Restoration in Nauvoo," 13.
46. Some of Nauvoo's poorer citizens were later forced to purchase and farm communal lots to keep from starving. Godfrey, "The Nauvoo Neighborhood," 82.
47. Flanders, *Nauvoo*, 144, 151.
48. The August 20, 1842, assessment states that for his residence in Section 6 of Range 6 North, from which he was licensed to sell "stock in trade," Lewis had $20 in cattle (probably two or three), $50 in horses (probably one or two, which was unusual as most people didn't have horses), $20 in wagons, $5 in clocks, $5 in watches, $50 loaned, $40 in other property, $120 in personal property (the median in Nauvoo being $55 and $140 for the rest of Hancock County).

    Luther, also licensed to sell "stock in trade," was taxed for $20 in cattle, $80 in horses, $20 in wagons, $5 in clocks, $50 loaned, $15 in other property, and $115 in personal property on land located in the same section as Lewis.

Charles, with residence in Section 5 of Range 7 North and licensed to sell "stock in trade," was taxed for 960 acres, $45 in cattle, $120 in horses, $40 in wagons, $5 in clocks, $50 in other property, and $260 in personal property. Hancock County, Assessor's Office, Books of Assessment, 1840, 1842, and 1850, Church Archives. James L. Kimball, Jr., has been very helpful to me in appraising the economy of the Barneys in Nauvoo and Hancock County, Illinois.

49. Flanders, *Nauvoo*, 167.
50. Joseph Smith, Daybook B, Church Archives; Joseph Smith's store, Daybook C, Iowa Masonic Library, microfilm copy in Church Archives.
51. Lewis Barney, Autobiography 1, 21. There is no extant record of this transaction in the financial records associated with Joseph Smith and no indication as to whether or not the debt was paid.
52. Hartley, *My Best for the Kingdom*, 114.
53. Miller and Miller, *Nauvoo*, 101–107. For an overview of Masonic activity in Nauvoo see Mervin B. Hogan, *Mormon Involvement with Freemasonry on the Illinois and Iowa Frontier between 1840 and 1846* (Salt Lake City: n.p., 1983) and Mervin B. Hogan, *The Two Joseph Smith's Masonic Experiences* (Salt Lake City: n.p., 1987).
54. Mervin Hogan, comp., Record of Nauvoo Lodge Petitions.
55. Nauvoo Masonic Lodge, Account Book, 28, Church Archives.
56. Hogan, Record of Nauvoo Lodge Petitions; Godfrey, "The Nauvoo Neighborhood," 82.
57. Kenneth W. Godfrey, "Joseph Smith and the Masons," *Journal of the Illinois State Historical Society* 64, no. 1 (spring 1971): 89–90.
58. Linus L. Wilcox to Ellsworth Burr, 2 August 1840, La Harpe, Illinois, Western Illinois University, Macomb, Illinois, typescript in Church Archives.
59. John E. Hallwas, "Mormon Nauvoo from a Non-Mormon Perspective," in Roger D. Launius and Hallwas, eds., *Kingdom on the Mississippi Revisited: Nauvoo in Mormon History* (Urbana, Illinois: University of Illinois Press, 1996), 161–162.
60. "Mormon leaders had learned from bitter practical experience that protection of property and personal liberties could not be expected from the federal government which (under the American constitutional system) could not intercede inside state boundaries. (Not until the 1868 adoption of the 14th Amendment to the United States Constitution did the government gain that right.)" Miller and Miller, *Nauvoo*, 10.
61. Smith, *History of the Church*, 6:223.
62. Givens, *In Old Nauvoo*, 13–16,
63. Louisa Black Pratt, "Historical notes on Charles Barney, her grandfather," typescript in possession of the author. Ebenezer Robinson, onetime owner of the *Times and Seasons* building, built "a brick row of eleven tenements for rentals" in Nauvoo from the proceeds of his sale of the printing building. Flanders, *Nauvoo*, 157. "Brick Row" was located on block 125, near the northwest corner of Main and Kimball Street in Nauvoo.
64. Family sources state that the Barneys were residents in a small structure adjacent to the Mansion House. "Diary of Joseph Smith Black," comp. by Kate B. Carter, 20 vols. *Our Pioneer Heritage* (Salt Lake City: Daughters of Utah Pioneers, 1958–1977), 10:316. Outbuildings and shelters on the Joseph Smith property in Nauvoo, apparently in the yards of both the Homestead and Mansion House, were used to temporarily house some Nauvoo residents. Linda King Newell and Valeen Tippetts Avery, *Mormon Enigma: Emma Hale Smith, Prophet's Wife, "Elect Lady," Polygamy's Foe, 1804–1879* (Garden City, New York: Doubleday & Company, 1984), 83–84.
65. Barnes Parker to Lewis and Henry Barney, 8 May 1876, Austin, Texas, photocopy of MS in possession of the author. Lucien and Henry's venture had nothing to do

with Lyman Wight's defection from Brigham Young's control when he took a colony of Latter-day Saints into Texas later in 1845.

66. In 1876 Lewis Barney entered into correspondence with Barnes Parker, an Austin, Texas, attorney, at the latter's instigation concerning the Texas land purchased by Lucien and Henry for the family. Parker ended up trading 850 acres in the Texas panhandle to the Barneys for their 1,280 acres in August 1878. The 850 acres were divided between Lewis, Walter, and Henry Barney. In 1879 Lewis Barney offered to serve as an LDS missionary in the East, with the hope he could personally survey the land en route, though he never filled the mission. On the family's behalf, Lewis offered the land to the Church of Jesus Christ in 1883 but the transaction was apparently never consummated. The final disposition of the land is not known to the author. Lewis Barney and Barnes Parker correspondence, 1876–1877, copy provided to the author by the family of Edna Briscoe Perkins; Lewis Barney to John Taylor, 19 October 1879, Monroe, Utah, John Taylor, Papers, Incoming Correspondence, Church Archives; L. John Nuttall, Diary, 23, 29 October 1879, typescript, Special Collections, Harold B. Lee Library, Brigham Young University; Joseph F. Smith to Lewis Barney, 2 June 1883, Salt Lake City, Utah, copy in Lewis Barney, Autobiography 1.
67. Preston, *Genealogy of the Barney Family*, 347.
68. Lewis Barney, Autobiography 2, 7–8.
69. Lewis Barney, Autobiography 1, 22.

Chapter 7

1. Lewis Barney, Autobiography 1, 22.
2. Dallin H. Oaks and Marvin S. Hill, *Carthage Conspiracy: The Trials of the Accused Assassins of Joseph Smith* (Urbana, Illinois: University of Illinois Press, 1979), 18–20; 29 June 1844, Journal History. While the Carthage Greys were no doubt involved in the conspiracy, Warsaw, Illinois, citizens were tagged as the primary perpetrators.
3. Benjamin Franklin Johnson, *My Life's Review* (Independence, Missouri: Zion's Printing & Publishing Co., 1947), 102.
4. Lewis Barney, Autobiography 1, 23.
5. See D. Michael Quinn's "The Mormon Succession Crisis of 1844," *BYU Studies* 16, no. 2 (winter 1976): 187–233, for a consideration of the avenues of succession possibilities.
6. 8 October 1877, *Journal of Discourses*, 19:231.
7. Lewis Barney, Autobiography 2, 15–16. For a discussion of and a list of eyewitness accounts of the event, see Lynn Watkins Jorgensen, et al., "The Mantle of the Prophet Joseph Passes to Brother Brigham: A Collective Spiritual Witness," *BYU Studies* 36, no. 4 (1996–1997). Deborah Barney later told her daughter Sarah Jane that she, too, witnessed Young's transfiguration. Erickson, "Life Sketch of Charles Barney," 5. Also, Lewis's future wife Elizabeth Beard Barney later reported to her granddaughter that she was also a witness, "when Brigham Young made that speech and he looked like Joseph Smith." Edna Briscoe Perkins and Elda Barney Gillen, interview, interviewed by Raymond G. Briscoe, ca. 1978, typescript, 9, in possession of the author, hereafter referred to as Perkins and Gillen, Interview.
8. Gregg, *History of Hancock County*, 841–842.
9. Flanders, *Nauvoo*, 3.
10. Brigham Young to Wilford Woodruff, 27 June 1845, Nauvoo, Illinois, in Smith, *History of the Church*, 7:431.
11. Zeno, "Origin of the Mormon Difficulties," *Warsaw Signal*, 29 January 1845.
12. Thomas Barnes quoted in Flanders, "Kingdom of God in Illinois," 27–28.

13. Gregg, *History of Hancock County*, 374.
14. Lewis Barney, Autobiography 1, 23–24; Autobiography 2, 18–20.
15. Lewis Barney, Autobiography 1, 24; Autobiography 2, 21–22.
16. *The 1850 Census of Illinois: Hancock County* (Richland, Washington: Locust Grove Press, 1977), 34; J. B. Backenstos's list of Carthage Greys and Warsaw independents involved in Joseph's and Hyrum Smith's murders, Church Archives.

    Thomas Gregg, himself a contemporary Mormon antagonist, in his *History of Hancock County, Illinois*, 858, described George Waggoner's (sometimes spelled Wagoner) role in the deaths of Joseph and Hyrum Smith. In contrast, Thomas Bullock identified Frank Worrell as the first to scale the stairs and to mutilate Joseph Smith's body. See Marvin S. Hill, *Quest for Refuge: The Mormon Flight from American Pluralism* (Salt Lake City: Signature Books, 1989), 174.

    An Illustrated Historical Atlas of Hancock County, Illinois (Chicago: A. T. Andreas, 1874), 66, shows the Waggoner property in Section 29 of the Pilot Grove Township, adjacent to Section 30 where Barney had his farmstead. Barney, in his memoirs, referred to Waggoner as John.
17. Lewis Barney, Autobiography 2, 21.
18. Lewis Barney, Autobiography 1, 24–25.
19. Lewis Barney, Autobiography 2, 20.
20. Lewis Barney, Autobiography 1, 25. For example, Hosea Stout was involved in one of these trivial lawsuits which came to trial on 24 September 1845 with charges eventually being dismissed. Stout, *On the Mormon Frontier*, 1:72.
21. Lewis Barney, Autobiography 1, 25.
22. Franklin Worrell, a lieutenant in the Carthage Greys and a leader of the violent opposition to the Mormons, was killed by Rockwell, adding to Rockwell's notorious reputation. Worrell and others were pursuing Sheriff Jacob Backenstos, an ally of the Mormons, when the sheriff happened upon Rockwell and Return Redden Jackson. The sheriff yelled his plight to Rockwell who sighted his rifle on Worrell's belt buckle. Rockwell's shot slammed into Worrell's abdomen, lurching him out of the saddle. Oaks and Hill, *Carthage Conspiracy*, 195; and Harold Schindler, *Orrin Porter Rockwell: Man of God, Son of Thunder* (Salt Lake City: University of Utah Press, 1966), 145–146.
23. *Nauvoo Neighbor*, 17 September 1845; Lewis Barney, Autobiography 1, 22, indicates Lydia Turner was buried in Nauvoo. There is no record of Barney's mother-in-law being a Mormon. Macedonia Branch records in the Church Archives include no information about her. She may have died in transit to Nauvoo.
24. Hosea Stout's diary entries of 14–19 September 1845 in Stout, *On the Mormon Frontier*, 1:63–66.
25. Marshall Hamilton, "From Assassination to Expulsion: Two Years of Distrust, Hostility, and Violence," in Launius and Hallwas, *Kingdom on the Mississippi Revisited*, 222.
26. John E. Hallwas and Roger D. Launius, eds., *Cultures in Conflict: A Documentary History of the Mormon War in Illinois* (Logan, Utah: Utah State University Press, 1995), 280–288.
27. Journal History, 24–26 September 1845.
28. Markham was one of sixty committee members assigned on 24 September 1845 to assist Saints evacuating the outlying communities of Hancock County. Names of Committee Selected by Council to Move Families, Goods, [etc.,] into Nauvoo, Brigham Young, Papers, Administrative Papers, Church Archives.
29. Lewis Barney, Autobiography 1, 25.
30. Hamilton, "From Assassination to Expulsion," 223.
31. Quoted in Bennett, *Mormons at the Missouri*, 14. By summertime in 1845, church leaders had narrowed the western destination to "the neighborhood of Lake Tampanagos," and the "Great Salt Lake Valley." Lewis Clark Christian, "Mormon

Foreknowledge of the West," in James B. Allen and John W. Welch, eds., *Coming to Zion* (Provo, Utah: Brigham Young University Studies, 1997), 18–19.

32. Bennett, *Mormons at the Missouri*, 21–22.
33. Lewis Barney, Autobiography 2, 25.
34. Benjamin Brown in "Testimonies for the Truth," *Gems for the Young Folks: Fourth Book of the Faith-Promoting Series* (Salt Lake City: Juvenile Instructor Office, 1881; reprint Bookcraft, 1968), 83.
35. James Palmer, Reminiscences, ca. 1884–1898, Church Archives.
36. Bennett, *Mormons at the Missouri*, 15.
37. For an overview of the Mormon abandonment of Nauvoo see Flanders, *Nauvoo*, 306–341. A list of commodities to be packed by each family "of five adults" for the removal from Nauvoo is found in Smith, *History of the Church*, 7:454–455.
38. Quoted in Bennett, *Mormons at the Missouri*, 17.
39. Backman, "The Keys Are Right Here," 120.
40. Henry W. Bigler, Journal 1846 Feb.–1899 Oct., 34, Church Archives.
41. Nauvoo Restoration Incorporated, Land Records, compiled by Rowena Miller, Church Archives, which states the transaction is found in Hancock County, Deed Book O, 183. *The 1850 Census of Illinois: Hancock County*, 78; Gregg, *History of Hancock County*, 522–523, 688.
42. Hancock County, Illinois, Bond and Mortgage, Book 2, 180; Nauvoo Restoration Incorporation, Land Records. John F. Charles, who had been a candidate for the Illinois Legislature in 1840, apparently paid Barney $70 at the time of the deal, and to cover the remaining $250, Charles mortgaged the remainder of the compensation in the form of "4 yoke of good fair work cattle not less than 4 years old the present spring, nor more than 8; with yokes, staples & rings and four ox chains." Charles made good on his agreement according to a release of mortgage included in the document previously cited. "Sketches of the Mormon Era," *Gregg's Dollar Monthly and Old Settlers' Memorial* 1, no. 6 (October 1873), reprinted in *Annals of Iowa* 12, no. 8 (April 1921): 566.

    In comparison, Orson Pratt described the compensation he received for his prime Nauvoo house and lot located adjacent to the Nauvoo Temple and valued at $2,000: "four yoke of oxen with yokes and three chains, one wagon and eight bbls. of superfine flour" plus $15. Orson Pratt, *The Orson Pratt Journals*, Elden J. Watson, ed. (Salt Lake City: Elden J. Watson, 1975), 321–322.
43. Joseph Smith Barney was born in Nauvoo, Illinois, 22 December 1845, the day before what would have been Joseph Smith's fortieth birthday. Preston, *Genealogy of the Barney Family*, 347.
44. *Nauvoo Temple Endowment Register, 10 December 1845 to 8 February 1846* (Salt Lake City: n.p., 1974), 268, 289.
45. Ibid., 322, 350, 352. The other family members included Charles and Deborah, Lucien, Walter, and probably Henry, as well as Elizabeth and Benjamin Leland. Those who received their endowments had to have contributed to the construction and maintenance of the temple. Flanders, *Nauvoo*, 335.

Chapter 8

1. Christian, "Mormon Foreknowledge of the West," 14–16.
2. Lewis Barney, Autobiography 1, 25; Jenson, *Latter-day Saints' Biographical Encyclopedia*, 3:594.
3. Sheryl Smith White, comp., *David Dutton Yearsley and Mary Ann Hoopes* (n.p.: n.p., 1982), 237–258. For information on the Council of Fifty's role in the Nauvoo exodus

see Andrew F. Ehat, "'It Seems Like Heaven Began on Earth': Joseph Smith and the Constitution of the Kingdom of God," *BYU Studies* 20, no. 3 (spring 1980): 272–273.

4. Florence C. Youngberg, "A Heritage of Strength, Love and Endurance," *Pioneer* 35, no. 6 (November–December 1988): 15.
5. Lyon, "The Current Restoration in Nauvoo," 22.
6. White, *David Dutton Yearsley*, 249.
7. Lewis Barney, Autobiography 1, 26. Similar observations can be found in Priddy Meeks, Autobiography and Reminiscence, typescript, 7, Church Archives; James Van Nostrand Williams, Reminiscences and diary [ca. 1894]–1905 May, 8 May 1846, Church Archives; and Thomas L. Kane, *The Mormons: A Discourse* (Philadelphia: King & Baird, 1850), 21.
8. William G. Hartley, "The Pioneer Trek: Nauvoo to Winter Quarters," *Ensign* 27, no. 6 (June 1997): 32–34. Stanley B. Kimball, *Heber C. Kimball: Mormon Patriarch and Pioneer* (Urbana: University of Illinois Press, 1981), 130, suggests 3,000 émigrés. Richard Bennett estimates the total at Sugar Creek to be about 1,800. Richard E. Bennett, *We'll Find the Place: The Mormon Exodus, 1846–1848* (Salt Lake City: Deseret Book Company, 1997), 32.
9. John Smith, Diary, 15 October 1840.
10. Stanley B. Kimball, "The Iowa Trek of 1846," *Ensign* 2, no. 6 (June 1972): 37, 39; Bennett, *Mormons at the Missouri*, 31.
11. Bigler, Journal, 34.
12. Eliza Roxcy Snow, *Personal Writings of Eliza Roxcy Snow*, Maureen Ursenbach Beecher, ed. (Salt Lake City: University of Utah Press, 1995), 114–115. Snow identifies her travel with Yearsley and Markham on 5 March 1846, page 118.
13. Lewis Barney, Autobiography 2, 27.
14. Ibid., 29.
15. Lewis Barney, Autobiography 1, 27.
16. Snow, *Eliza Roxcy Snow*, 116–118.
17. Ibid., 119.
18. Lewis Barney, Autobiography 2, 29.
19. Lewis Barney, Autobiography 1, 26–27.
20. Snow, *Eliza Roxcy Snow*, 126.
21. Lewis Barney, Autobiography 2, 31. Henry W. Bigler wrote on 14 April 1846, "We moved to Locus[t] Creek. Here the pioneers had made a good bridge over the creek where we have good camping, plenty of timber[,] mostly hickory and locus[t]. the young grass begins to show[.] the days are warm, Snakes plentiful and 2 oxen belong to Brothers [Heber C.] Kimball and [David] Yearsley were bitten by them." Bigler, Journal, 37.
22. Lewis Barney, Autobiography 1, 27. Barney likely referred to events which occurred 6 April 1846. See also William Clayton, *An Intimate Chronicle: The Journals of William Clayton*, George D. Smith, ed. (Salt Lake City: Signature Books, 1995), 268–269. A little over a week later Clayton penned his famous Latter-day Saint hymn, "All Is Well" (Come, Come, Ye Saints). Clayton, *An Intimate Chronicle*, 271.
23. Quoted in Dean C. Jessee, "Brigham Young's Family," *BYU Studies* 18, no. 3 (spring 1978): 312.
24. Orson Pratt, quoted in Leland H. Gentry, "The Mormon Way Stations: Garden Grove and Mt. Pisgah," *BYU Studies* 21, no. 4 (fall 1981): 449.
25. Snow, *Eliza Roxcy Snow*, 131.
26. Despite Yearsley's difficulties with Barney and Markham, his talent and skills were needed as the Saints settled on the Missouri River. There he was chosen one of twenty-two bishops at Winter Quarters. Upon Barney's later arrival with his family at the Missouri River settlements he "learned that David Yearsley's fine horses

were both dead by being over loaded while they had my wagon and load to pull." Lewis Barney, Autobiography 1, 30. Yearsley became ill in 1849 and died before reaching the Rocky Mountains.

27. Lewis Barney, Autobiography 1, 28.
28. Ibid., 28. Lewis's family consisted of his wife and four sons age nine years to six months.
29. Hartley, "The Pioneer Trek," 36–39.
30. Brown, "Testimonies for the Truth," 83–84.
31. "The Mormons and Their Temple at Nauvoo," *Deseret Evening News*, 7 March 1876, reprint from the *Cincinnati Times*.
32. Brown, "Testimonies for the Truth," 84.
33. Stanley B. Kimball, "The Mormon Trail Network in Iowa 1838–1863: A New Look," *BYU Studies* 21, no. 4 (fall 1981): 425–426; Stanley B. Kimball, *Historic Sites and Markers along the Mormon and Other Great Western Trails* (Urbana: University of Illinois Press, 1988), 45–46; and Robert W. Frazer, *Forts of the West: Military Forts and Presidios and Posts Commonly Called Forts West of the Mississippi River to 1898* (Norman: University of Oklahoma Press, 1972), 49.
34. Lewis Barney, Autobiography 1, 29.
35. The route they took from Des Moines to the Missouri is one of two possibilities identified by trail historian Stanley B. Kimball. See map 2 in Kimball, *Historic Sites and Markers*, 4.
36. Hartley, "The Pioneer Trek," 39.
37. Lewis Barney, Autobiography 1, 29.
38. Lewis Barney, Autobiography 2, 33–34.
39. Lewis Barney, Autobiography 1, 29–30. Rumors among the Saints had been flying since December 1845 that the federal government was mounting a campaign to crush the Mormons and prevent them from fleeing to the West. Lawrence G. Coates, "Refugees, Friends, and Foes: Mormons and Indians in Iowa and Nebraska," in Allen and Welch, eds., *Coming to Zion*, 64.
40. Bennett, *We'll Find the Place*, 43.
41. Compiled Service Records of Volunteer Soldiers who Served during the Mexican War in Mormon Organizations, National Archives, Washington, D.C.; Walter Barney, General Affidavit, Application for Reimbursement by John Barney, Selected Pension Application Files Relating to the Mormon Battalion, National Archives, Washington, D.C.

    In August 1846 Walter forwarded $10 of his battalion pay to his father whom he identified as being "between the [Council] Bluffs and Nauvoo." Mormon Battalion Subscription Lists, 1846 Aug., Brigham Young, Papers, Administrative Papers, Church Archives.
42. Bennett, *Mormons at the Missouri*, 20.
43. Lewis Barney, Autobiography 1, 30. Bullock's Grove, named after its primary resident Benjamin Bullock, was a small Mormon settlement located near present-day Dumphries, Iowa, in Pottawattamie County.
44. Lewis Barney, Autobiography 1, 30. Alma Barney, born 5 March 1843 in Nauvoo, was three at the time of his death. Richard Bennett estimates that about 150 died on the Iowa side of the Missouri River the first year the Saints lived there. Bennett, *Mormons on the Missouri*, 140. Susan Black estimates that between three and four hundred Saints died in 1846 from the time of the exodus through the end of the year. Susan Easton Black, "Do We Know How Many Latter-day Saints Died between 1846 and 1860 in the Migration to the Salt Lake Valley?" *Ensign* 28, no. 7 (July 1998): 41.

    Bullock's Grove was first identified as Hyde's Park. Orson Hyde inhabited the area prior to his thirteen mile move to Kanesville in 1848 to direct the operations of the church on the Missouri River. Myrtle S. Hyde, "Kanesville Places: A

Preliminary Study," September 1990, 30, copy in possession of the author. See also Myrtle Stevens Hyde, *Orson Hyde: The Olive Branch of Israel* (Salt Lake City: Agreka Books, 2000), 492–493.

45. Lewis Barney, Autobiography 1, 30.
46. Gail Geo. Holmes, "A Prophet Who Followed, Fulfilled, Magnified," in Black and Porter, *Lion of the Lord*, 130, 137.
47. The original intent was for the Saints to winter at the Platte River's Grand Island in Nebraska. Bennett, *Mormons at the Missouri*, 64–67.

    The first center of Mormon settlement in Nebraska had been at Cold Springs. They then moved fourteen miles north to Culter Park and then a few miles to Winter Quarters. The winter of 1846–1847 found approximately 3,500 Mormons on the Nebraska side of the Missouri and another 2,500 on the Iowa side, where the Barneys were located. The rest of the Nauvoo refugees were scattered across Iowa and northern Missouri. Bennett, *Mormons at the Missouri*, 81.
48. Holmes, "A Prophet Who Followed, Fulfilled, and Magnified," 128. For an overview of Mormon negotiations with Native Americans and the U.S. government for temporary settlement and travel in both Iowa and Nebraska, see Coates, "Refugees, Friends, and Foes," 49–97.
49. When the Barneys located in Iowa they were likely unaware that church leaders generally perceived that those who initially settled there were less faithful in following church leaders than were those who settled at Winter Quarters. Richard E. Bennett, "Finalizing Plans for the Trek West: Deliberations at Winter Quarters, 1846–1847," in Allen and Welch, eds., *Coming to Zion*, 114.
50. Lewis Barney, Autobiography 1, 30.
51. Richard E. Bennett, "Mormons and Missourians: The Uneasy Truce," *The Midwest Review* 9 (spring 1987): 17.
52. Lewis Barney, Autobiography 1, 31. While it is not known exactly where in Missouri Barney spent the winter, many Mormons who traveled south into Missouri for provisions found work in Savannah, Weston, Westport (near Independence), and St. Joseph. Bennett, "Mormons and Missourians," 17. See also William Reynolds Terry, Autobiographical sketch (ca. 1858), 31–32, Church Archives; James Fackrell, Reminiscences [ca. 1850], 8–9, Church Archives; and Silas Hillman, Autobiography, 35, Harold B. Lee Library, Special Collections, Brigham Young University, Provo, Utah.
53. Daniel Tyler, *A Concise History of the Mormon Battalion, 1846–1847* (Glorieta, New Mexico: The Rio Grande Press, Inc., 1980), 212; Kate B. Carter, comp., *Treasures of Pioneer History*, 6 vols. (Salt Lake City: Daughters of Utah Pioneers, 1952–1957), 4:481; Preston, *Genealogy of the Barney Family*, 189.
54. Lewis Barney, Autobiography 1, 31.
55. Bennett, *Mormons at the Missouri*, 81.
56. Pratt, *Orson Pratt Journals*, 28 April 1846.
57. Christian, "Mormon Foreknowledge of the West," 11–26. See also Leonard J. Arrington, *Brigham Young: American Moses* (New York: Alfred A. Knopf, 1985), 123–124.
58. Doctrine and Covenants, Section 136:1. Besides confirming the structure of travel, one of the main messages of the revelation was that the Twelve Apostles with Young at the head would direct the move West. No other person, committee, or council had authority to do so. The effect, of course, was the elimination of George Miller, Lyman Wight, and even the Council of Fifty as contenders to direct the exodus. Bennett, "Finalizing Plans for the Trek West," 109–110.
59. Doctrine and Covenants, Section 136:18, 31.
60. Volunteers were solicited in late June and early July 1846 at Mt. Pisgah, a way station along the Mormon Trail across Iowa, for contributions of either means or

money or who would themselves volunteer for the pioneer expedition. Names of Volunteers and Donations for Pioneer Company, 1846 June 22–23 and July 1, Brigham Young, Papers, Federal and Local Government Files, Church Archives.

61. Lewis Barney, Autobiography 1, 31.

Chapter 9

1. "It Finally All Depends on God: A Conversation with Martin Marty," *Sunstone* 11, no. 2 (March 1987): 46.
2. Published works which describe the Mormon vanguard expedition to the Rocky Mountains include: Howard Egan, *Pioneering the West, 1846–1878: Major Howard Egan's Diary* (Richmond, Utah: Howard R. Egan Estate, 1917); William Clayton, *William Clayton's Journal* (Salt Lake City: The Deseret News, 1921), based on William Clayton, Diary 1847 Jan.–Dec., Church Archives; Erastus Snow, "Journey to Zion," *Utah Humanities Review* 2 (April, July 1948); Norton Jacob, *The Record of Norton Jacob*, C. Edward Jacob and Ruth S. Jacob, eds. (Salt Lake City: Stevens & Wallis, Inc., 1949), based on Norton Jacob, Reminiscence and Journal 1844 May–1852 Jan., Church Archives; Wallace Stegner, *The Gathering of Zion: The Story of the Mormon Trail* (New York: McGraw-Hill Book Company, 1971); Joseph E. Brown, *The Mormon Trek West* (Garden City, New York: Doubleday & Company Inc., 1980); Bennett, *We'll Find the Place;* and Thomas Bullock, *The Pioneer Camp of the Saints: The 1846 and 1847 Mormon Trail Journals of Thomas Bullock*, Will Bagley, ed. (Spokane, Washington: Arthur H. Clark Company, 1997), based on Thomas Bullock, Journals 1843–1849, Church Archives. Day-by-day summarizations of the journey are found in Hal Knight and Stanley B. Kimball, *111 Days to Zion* (Salt Lake City: Deseret Press, 1978; Big Moon Traders, 1997); and Andrew Jenson, *Day by Day with the Utah Pioneers: A Chronological Record of the Trek across the Plains* (Salt Lake City: Salt Lake Tribune, 1934).

   Merrill Mattes, noted bibliographer of the Oregon/California/Mormon Trails, judged Barney's rehearsal of the 1847 journey as a good account written in a "colloquial" style that "is warm and witty." Merrill J. Mattes, *Platte River Road Narratives: A Descriptive Bibliography of Travel over the Great Overland Route to Oregon, California, Utah, Colorado, Montana, and other Western States and Territories, 1812–1866* (Urbana: University of Illinois Press, 1988), 88.
3. Lewis Barney, Autobiography 1, 32.
4. Biographical sketches of the 148 are found in Jenson, *Latter-day Saints' Biographical Encyclopedia*, 4:693–725; and *Deseret News, 1997–98, Church Almanac* (Salt Lake City: Deseret News, 1996), 123–158. As late as 22 March 1847, it was contemplated that over 300 men would make the vanguard trek to Utah before the number was pared to 143, plus three women and two children. Bennett, "Finalizing Plans for the Trek West," 117.
5. One reason for the delay in departure was the anticipated arrival of Parley P. Pratt and John Taylor from England with money and equipment necessary for the trek. Bennett, "Finalizing Plans for the Trek West," 117–118.
6. Lewis Barney, Autobiography 1, 32.
7. Bennett, *We'll Find the Place*, 75. Norton Jacob, Lewis's senior by four years, identified the expedition as being composed of "18 High Priests, 80 Seventies [of which Barney was one], 8 Elders, 13 members, 8 of the Twelve, and 6 that do not belong to the Church." Jacob, *Record*, 53.
8. Clayton, *Intimate Chronicle*, 297.
9. The importance of domestic animals to nineteenth-century Americans, particularly those in transit, cannot be overstated. While pedestrian travel characterized

many if not most of the Latter-day Saint emigrants, even those who traveled in wagon trains, reliance upon livestock—horses, oxen, and traditional farm stock—was crucial to most endeavors. Audrey M. Godfrey, "No Small Miracle: The Movement of Domestic Animals across the Plains," *Nauvoo Journal* 9, no. 1 (spring 1997): 3–16.

10. John D. Unruh, Jr., *The Plains Across: The Overland Emigrants and the Trans-Mississippi West, 1840–1860* (Urbana: University of Illinois Press, 1979), 119.
11. Another significant reason they planned for a 1 March departure was to insure an arrival in the Great Basin by 1 June to plant crops for a fall harvest. Bennett, "Finalizing Plans for the Trek West," 102.
12. Not long into their journey on 4 May 1847, one of the company wrote that they "held a council and decided to continue on [the north] side of the Platte for the present as we wished to establish a road independent of the Gentile road for the accommodation of our families who should follow after." Charles Alfred Harper, *Diary of Charles Alfred Harper* (n.p.: n.p., 1971), 20, based on Charles Alfred Harper, Diary, 1847 Apr.–Aug., Church Archives.
13. Clayton, *Intimate Chronicle*, 298.
14. Lewis Barney, Autobiography 2, 37.
15. Lewis Barney, Autobiography 1, 32.
16. Ibid., 34–37; Journal of a member of Luke Johnson's Company of Ten, 21 April 1847, Church Archives; Horace K. Whitney, Diaries, 21, 27 April 1847, Church Archives. The loss of Barney's horse was recorded by a number of pioneer journalists for 27–28 April, including Norton Jacob, William Clayton, Amasa M. Lyman, Thomas Bullock, and Charles Harper.
17. Erastus Snow, "Journey to Zion," 113; Lewis Barney, Autobiography 1, 32.
18. Woodruff, *Journal* 3:171, 8 May 1847.
19. Levi Jackman, Journal, 1847–1849, 8–14 May, 11 June 1847, photocopy of MS, Church Archives.
20. Jackman, Journal, 8 May 1847.
21. Lewis Barney, Autobiography 1, 35.
22. Unruh, *Plains Across*, 119, 185.
23. Lewis Barney, Autobiography 1, 36; Bullock, *Journals*, 144.
24. Woodruff, *Journals*, 3:182, 23 May 1847; Clayton, *Intimate Chronicle*, 324–333.
25. Like the buffalo, many of the pioneers had never previously seen antelope. Levi Jackman described the unfamiliar animals as "something a medium between the deer and goat. They have hair like a deer and forked horns." Jackman, Journal, 3 May 1847.
26. Lewis Barney, Autobiography 1, 35.
27. Bullock, *Journals*, 159.
28. Jacob, *Record*, 54.
29. Lewis Barney, Autobiography 1, 36.
30. Ibid., 36–36a. Heber C. Kimball's diary entry for 10 June reads that Barney "killed an antelope and not being appointed a hunter, according to the remarks of some of the brethren, he had a right to divide his meat as he saw fit. He made me a present of a nice hind quarter which we took and cut up and salted ready for drying." "Pioneers Journal of Heber C. Kimball," *Utah Genealogical and Historical Magazine*, July 1940, 86. William Clayton on 10 June wrote, "Lewis Barney killed an antelope this afternoon which was distributed as he saw fit, inasmuch as he was not appointed a hunter." Clayton, *Journal*, 230. While Clayton's general practice was not to identify those who killed game, Barney's success prompted him to note that Barney also killed antelope on 22 and 23 June. Clayton, *Journal*, 257, 261.
31. Lewis Barney, Autobiography 1, 37.
32. Ibid., 37.
33. Jacob, *Record*, 59–60.

34. Lewis Barney, Autobiography 1, 38. Jacob said the canoes were twenty-three feet while Clayton said the craft was twenty-five feet in length. Jacob, *Record*, 59–60; Clayton, *Journal*, 239.
35. Lewis Barney, Autobiography 1, 38. See also Harper, *Diary*, 26.
36. Lewis Barney, Autobiography 1, 38; Clayton, *Journal*, 240–242. See also ferry accounts in Bullock, *Journals*, 356–357, showing Barney's tally.

    The ferry is located near the present-day restoration of Fort Caspar, located on the western outskirts of Casper, Wyoming. Kimball, *Historic Sites and Markers*, 82. For a description of Mormon ferries and the controversy over their locations on the North Platte see Robert A. Murray, "Trading Posts, Fort and Bridges of the Casper Area—Unraveling the Tangle on the Upper Platte," *Annals of Wyoming* 47, no. 1 (spring 1975): 4–30.
37. Wilford Woodruff reported on 17 June, "some of the emigrants report 1,000 wagons between Laramie & this place & there companies are arriving daily at the fording places." Woodruff, *Journals*, 3:206, 17 June 1847.
38. Bennett, *We'll Find the Place*, 199, fn. 41.
39. Lewis Barney, Autobiography 1, 38. Jacob reported himself being ill on 2 July. The following day Jacob said he was "baptized for the restoration of my health" and was later blessed by several of his companions, of whom one was Barney. Jacob, *Record*, 65.
40. Lewis Barney, Autobiography 1, 38. The group reached the Bear River on 10 July. The following day Jacob stated that it was John Norton who found "a fountain of petroleum or mineral tar." Jacob, *Record*, 67. Barney and Norton, both hunters, may have been hunting companions that day and found the tar pool together. The pool, or oil spring, became a noted curiosity on the trail and, still flowing, is located twelve miles south of Evanston, Wyoming. Kimball, *Historic Sites and Markers*, 94–95.
41. Clayton, *Journal*, 293.
42. Horace K. Whitney noted on July 14, "I have heard of but 4 antelopes being killed to-day, by the following men—Lewis Barney 2, Joseph Hancock, & Norton Jacobs." Whitney, Diaries, 14 July 1847.
43. Their course down Emigration Canyon was blazed by the Donner-Reed party the previous year.
44. Lewis Barney, Autobiography 1, 38–39.
45. Bennett, *We'll Find the Place*, 163–164.
46. Whitney, Diaries, 24 July 1847.
47. Woodruff, *Journal*, 3:235, 25 July 1847.
48. Jacob, *Record*, 70.
49. Lewis Barney, Autobiography 1, 40.
50. This gathering took place on Wednesday, 28 July. Jacob, *Record*, 72.
51. Lewis Barney, Autobiography 1, 39–40. Jacob recorded that William Vance differed with his associates, feeling "we should go farther, perhaps on the other side of the lake." Jacob, *Record*, 73.
52. Lewis Barney, Autobiography 1, 39–40. Even though Barney's recollection is given forty years after the event, his report of Brigham Young's language is very much like that of Jacob's contemporary account. Jacob, *Record*, 72–73.
53. Lewis Barney, Autobiography 1, 41.
54. Ibid., 42–44. Both Thomas Bullock and William Clayton noted Barney and Hancock's return on 28 July suggesting their return created some attention.
55. Lewis Barney, Autobiography 1, 44–45. Two weeks later, on Friday, 6 August, Lewis's role as a hunter did not end so favorably for his group. Jacob wrote: "Lewis Barney, one of the hunters that went back over the mountain last Tuesday, returned today without any meat, while the others went on towards Bear River. My ten is out of breadstuff, except [for] a little seed-corn, which we can grind on a hand-mill. Barney acted foolish in turning back without meat." Jacob, *Record*, 76.

56. Roberts, *Comprehensive History of the Church*, 3:287.
57. Lewis Barney, Autobiography 1, 40; Salt Lake Stake, Record of Members, 2, Church Archives.
58. Jacob, *Record*, 77.
59. Barney described of the effort to build the fort in Salt Lake City as being for, "protection against Indians that infested the country by thousands." They were, he said, "uncivilized, many of them showing signs of hostility." Lewis Barney, Autobiography 1, 45.

Chapter 10

1. Numbers for those entering the Salt Lake Valley in 1847 as well as those who wintered there are in dispute. The generalization presented here comes from Thomas Bullock's numbers ("a total of 2,095 for the year") listed in Roberts, *Comprehensive History of the Church*, 3:301; Eugene E. Campbell's, *Establishing Zion: The Mormon Church in the American West, 1847–1869* (Salt Lake City: Signature Books, 1988), 14, fn. 4; and "The Mormon Migration to Utah," in Richard D. Poll, et al., eds., *Utah's History* (Logan, Utah: Utah State University Press, 1989), 125. See also Andrew Jenson's emigration figures for 1847 in "Church Emigration Book, 1831–1847," Church Archives. Henry Smith Turner, a U.S. Army officer returning to the states from California in 1847 "passed the whole Mormon Emigration" and stated that "800 men—750 women—[and]1,556" children comprised the Great Basin–bound emigration. These numbers are nearly 50 percent more than those noted above. Turner left no information as to how he obtained these totals. Henry Smith Turner, *The Original Journals of Henry Smith Turner with Stephen Watts Kearny to New Mexico and California, 1846–1847*, Dwight L. Clarke, ed. (Norman, Oklahoma: University of Oklahoma Press, 1966), 133–134. Bullock, who "numbered the Men & families," which included children, shows Turner's figures are inflated. Bullock, *Journals*, 281.
2. Names of Pioneers, 1876 July 24, Brigham Young, Papers, General Office Files, Church Archives.
3. John Henry Evans and Minnie Egan Anderson, *Ezra T. Benson: Pioneer, Statesman, Saint* (Salt Lake City: Deseret News Press, 1947), 176.
4. Rosters of the ox teamsters and Young's group are found in Bullock, *Journals*, 258–259, 276–277.
5. Lewis Barney, Autobiography 1, 45. Jacob's and Bullock's lists of hunters identify eleven who composed the group. However, another man, Madison Welsh, may also have accompanied them, which could explain the dozen numbered by Barney. See Jacob, *Record*, 79, 17 August 1847; Bullock, *Journals*, 255, 11 August 1847.
6. Lewis Barney, Autobiography 1, 45. See also Jacob's mention of the sixty pounds of flour on 24 August 1847. Jacob, *Record*, 80.
7. Jacob, *Record*, 78.
8. Stegner, *Gathering of Zion*, 184.
9. Jacob, *Record*, 79, 16 August 1847.
10. Clayton, *Journal*, 347, 17 August 1847.
11. Bullock, *Journals*, 258–259; Whitney, Diaries, 17 August 1847.
12. Lewis Barney, Autobiography 1, 46–47. Jacob wrote that they forded the Green River on 23 August and that on 25 August they encountered "over a hundred Snake Indians, who gave us buffalo meat and were very friendly." Jacob, *Record*, 81.
13. Jacob, *Record*, 80.
14. Ibid., 81.

15. Whitney, Diaries, 30 August 1847. Bullock's account of their return describes isolated incidences of friction within Young's group. Bullock, *Journals*, 279, 293, 302, 311.
16. Jacob, *Record*, 82. Hancock eventually settled in Utah County where he died in 1893 at age 93 after years of traveling between the East and West Coasts.
17. Lewis Barney, Autobiography 1, 48. Jacob indicates in his diary that the decision to move on before stopping to obtain buffalo meat for the ox teamsters was made near Independence Rock on 4 September. Jacob, *Record*, 82.
18. Lewis Barney, Autobiography 1, 48. Jacob's 8 September account of the ox team's arrival reads: "About noon the head of our ox-team company arrived—four wagons led by Brother Wm. Clayton. . . . Two hours after, the main body passed by, did not stop to say 'how do you do', but moved on down the river! Towards night our hunters came in. Isaac Carpenter and L. Barney each killed an antelope." Jacob, *Record*, 83.

    Clayton, who chronicled the journey of the ox teamsters, described the meeting but gave no indication of hard feelings on the part of either group. Clayton, *Journal*, 360.
19. Lewis Barney, Autobiography 1, 49.
20. Bullock, *Journals*, 303, 309, 312, 314, 318.
21. Lewis Barney, Autobiography 1, 49. Jacob described the event in this way: "Friday, 10th [September 1847]—Moved on down the river 5 miles, then commenced winding our way over the Black Hills. Made 17-½ miles and camped on La Prele Creek. Beckstead killed a buffalo, and L. Barney another. A few miles after we started this morning, we saw a company of 6 or 7 men and 17 or 18 horses moving down on the other side of the river—supposed to be Indians." Jacob, *Record*, 84.
22. Lewis Barney, Autobiography 1, 49. Jacob's account reads: "Saturday, 11th—Early this morning Brethren Glines, N. Taylor, and Curtis arrived from the other camp and reported 17 or 18 horses stolen from them night before last, which are undoubtedly those we saw yesterday." Jacob, *Record*, 84.
23. Clayton, *Journal*, 362, 14 September 1847.
24. Ibid., 363; Jacob, *Record*, 84.
25. Lewis Barney, Autobiography 1, 50; Jacob, *Record*, 84.
26. Jacob, *Record*, 85.
27. Ibid., 85, 18 September 1847; Clayton, *Journal*, 363, 18 September 1847.
28. Clayton wrote that the camp arrived at Chimney Rock on Monday, 20 September where they paused until Friday, 24 September. Clayton, *Journal*, 364–365.
29. Lewis Barney, Autobiography 1, 50. See also Clayton, *Journal*, 363–364, 19 September 1847. In contrast to Barney's initial disappointment by not being allowed to hunt in the journey to the Salt Lake Valley, he was one of the most successful hunters on the return to Winter Quarters. Clayton, *Journal*, 361, 364, 368; Jacob, *Record*, 79–81, 83–86.
30. Lewis Barney, Autobiography 1, 50–51.
31. Ibid., 51.
32. Ibid., 52–53. Of this Clayton wrote, "During the day the brethren killed five cows and one bull which are considered sufficient to last the first division home. Clayton, *Journal*, 367.
33. Lewis Barney, Autobiography 1, 53–54. Jacob's diary also portrays the dissension that plagued the returning pioneers. See the entries on pages 79–84 in Jacob, *Record*, 16–18, 21–22, 29 August, 5 September. After another dispute, Clayton vented in his journal on Monday, 27 September:

    > It is plain and evident that there are several men who will find fault and deal out wholesale censure whatever is done, and for my part I

> shall remember John Pack, Thomas Cloward, Norton Jacobs and Joseph Hancock for some time to come. Such little, selfish, unmanly conduct as has been manifested by them, is rarely exhibited except by the meanest classes of society. A man who will openly and boldly steal is honorable when compared with some of their underhanded conduct. (Clayton, *Journal*, 367)

See also Stegner's summary of the difficulties and dissension in *Gathering of Zion*, 183–190.

34. Lewis Barney, Autobiography 1, 54. On 6 October 1847 Clayton wrote: "Some determined to go on a piece and amongst the rest, I felt more willing to go on than to tarry. Accordingly eleven wagons started, viz. Jackson Redding, William A. Empey, Lewis Barney, Roswel Stevens, Cummings, Joseph Hancock, H. W. Sanderson, John Pack, Thos. Cloward, Zebedee Coltrin and Norton Jacobs," joined by Clayton. Clayton, *Journal*, 369–370.
35. Lewis Barney, Autobiography 1, 54–55.
36. Ibid., 55.
37. Ibid., 56. See also Clayton, *Journal*, 370–371.
38. Lewis Barney, Autobiography 1, 56.
39. Clayton, *Journal*, 371, 8 October 1847.
40. Ibid., 371.
41. Lewis Barney, Autobiography 1, 56.
42. Whitney, Diaries, 11 October 1847.
43. Clayton, *Journal*, 372.
44. Bullock, *Journals*, 309, 312.
45. Lewis Barney, Autobiography 1, 57.
46. The old Presbyterian missionary station, which at the time was composed of a couple of double-log houses and six smaller single ones as well as corrals and two fenced in fields, was located near present-day Fullerton, Nebraska. Bennett, *We'll Find the Place*, 126.
47. Lewis Barney, Autobiography 1, 57. Clayton said that the Pawnees "show great fear of the Sioux." Thus when "some of the brethren gave them to understand that the Sioux were within five days of them. The chief immediately gave the word to the rest and in half an hour the squaws had loaded their corn on ponies and mules and then began to march towards the river." Clayton, *Journal*, 374, 16 October 1847.
48. Lewis Barney, Autobiography 1, 57–58.
49. Bullock, *Journal*, 318, 28 October 1847.
50. Lewis Barney, Autobiography 1, 58. Upon Brigham Young's approach to Winter Quarters, being one mile from the settlement, he called his company together and said:

> Brethren, I will say to the Pioneers, I wish you to receive my thanks for your kindness and willingness to obey orders; I am satisfied with you: you have done well. We have accomplished more than we expected. Out of one hundred forty-three men who started, some of them sick, all of them are well; not a man has died; we have not lost a horse, mule, or ox, but through carelessness; the blessings of the Lord have been with us. If the brethren are satisfied with me and the Twelve, please signify it. (which was unanimously done). I feel to bless you all in the name of the Lord God of Israel. You are dismissed to go to your own homes. (Smith, *History of the Church*, 7:616–618)

See also Bennett, *Mormons at the Missouri*, 165–166.

51. Lewis Barney, Autobiography 1, 58.

Chapter 11

1. Lewis Barney, Autobiography 1, 58.
2. Ibid.
3. Norma Baldwin Ricketts, *The Mormon Battalion: U.S. Army of the West, 1846–1848* (Logan, Utah: Utah State University Press, 1996), 8–9.
4. For a discussion of the division between the battalion and officers, non-Mormon and Mormon alike, see Larry D. Christiansen, "The Struggle for Power in the Mormon Battalion," *Dialogue: A Journal of Mormon Thought* 26, no. 4 (winter 1993): 51–69.
5. Arthur Barney, Journal, typescript, 6–7, Special Collections, Harold B. Lee Library, Brigham Young University, Provo, Utah. A humorous account of how Walter Barney dealt with another circumstance of near-starvation is found in Carter, *Treasures of Pioneer History*, 4:481.
6. Ricketts, *Mormon Battalion*, 10.
7. Samuel Thompson, Affidavit, 18 September 1879, and Walter Barney, General Affidavit, 20 June 1892, Selected Pension Application Files Relating to the Mormon Battalion, National Archives, Washington, D.C. Barney applied for a pension for this disability. This was followed by numerous applications for pension increases for the rest of the nineteenth and early twentieth centuries before his death at age 98 in 1917 in Monroe, Utah. Because each pension increase application required a doctor's examination, Walter's health status and disabilities are chronicled for the last forty years of his life in his lengthy pension application file. According to affidavits of associates and doctors' examinations, Walter thereafter was considered disabled for most of the rest of his life, never fully recovering from his injuries and illness.
8. Walter Barney, General Affidavit, 20 June 1892; Compiled Service Records of Volunteer Soldiers Who Served during the Mexican War in Mormon Organizations, National Archives, Washington, D.C.
9. Ricketts, *Mormon Battalion*, 169–171.
10. Walter Barney, General Affidavit, 20 June 1892.
11. Harriet May Bates, Biographical sketch of Joseph W. Bates, [n.d.], 2, Church Archives.
12. Ricketts, *Mormon Battalion*, 171, 197, 199.
13. Ibid., 283; Arthur Barney, Journal, 2.
14. Brigham Young, Papers, General Business Files, Gold Dust Accounts, Account Book, 1848–1849, Church Archives.
15. J. Marinus Jensen, *History of Provo, Utah* (Provo, Utah: by the author, 1924), 33, 35; Emma N. Huff, *Memories That Live: Utah County Centennial History* (Springville, Utah: Daughters of Utah Pioneers of Utah County, 1947), 116.
16. On 14 January 1848, Barney was in Kanesville, named after benefactor of the Saints, Thomas L. Kane. Barney, a seventy, was there in the now predominately Mormon community formerly and later called Council Bluffs to celebrate the "Seventies Jubilee" held in the Kanesville's log tabernacle. While there he signed a petition appealing to the federal government to open a post office in the town. Petition for post office near log tabernacle, Brigham Young, Papers, Administrative Papers, Church Archives.
17. Lewis Barney, Autobiography 1, 58–59.
18. Evan Molbourne Green, Papers [ca. 1848–1871], photocopy of MS, Church Archives.
19. Holmes, "The Missouri River Valley," 74–75.
20. *History of Harrison County, Iowa* (Chicago: National Publishing Company, 1891), 215.

21. Sally Young quoted in Joe H. Smith, *History of Harrison County, Iowa* (Des Moines, Iowa: Iowa Publishing Company, 1888), 120–121.
22. Cass Township was described as "an area of beautiful rolling prairie land amounting to twenty-three thousand and forty acres. . . . It is purely an agricultural section and as such is very valuable. The only native timber is found in the western part, chiefly in Six-mile Grove." *History of Harrison County* (1891), 215.
23. Smith, *History of Harrison County* (1888), 79–80; and Ibid., 71–72, 83, which describes Brown and Hawkins in this manner:

> It seems certain that Daniel Brown and family came with the Mormon exodus to Florence, Nebraska in the fall of 1846. Having trouble with Brigham Young, he soon left that branch of the Mormon church. He made a hunting tour over parts of this county in the autumn of 1846 and found what suited his fancy best for a home location, where the village of Calhoun was subsequently platted. . . . Upon July 10, 1847, the same year in which Daniel Brown effected settlement in April, came Uriah Hawkins and his family. They located on section 20, in Cass Township, and there the family have remained ever since.

24. "Among the first pieces of prairie land broken in the township was one on section 18. . . . It was done by Henry and Lewis Barney. . . . The first house built was the one erected in the summer of . . . 1848 by the Barney boys. They lived in tents while putting in their crops." *History of Harrison County* (1891), 72, 217–218. "When Mr. [Edward] Houghton came to the county there was no one living in Cass Township except John and Lewis Barney, Bryant and William Jolly and Uriah Hawkins." Ibid., 748.

    Henry Barney arrived in Six Mile Grove later than Lewis. Henry's first son, Alma, was born in Springfield, Illinois, on 14 July 1848. Because Henry apparently left Springfield, Illinois, for Utah in 1850, he may have moved to Six Mile Grove from Springfield in 1848 before returning to Springfield prior to his departure for Utah. Alma Barney, Brief History of the Life and Works of Alma Barney, 1, Church Archives.
25. Lewis Barney, Autobiography 1, 59.
26. Though Gail Holmes shows, in his map of the region, a village called Barney's Grove several miles from Six Mile Grove in Harrison County, it is probable that Six Mile Grove and Barney's Grove are the same location, the latter nomenclature being applied to the village toward the end of the Barneys' tenure in Iowa. The evidence for this conclusion comes by way of Uriah Hawkins being identified as residing in Six Mile Grove and Barney's Grove. Hawkins, who appears next to Lewis Barney in the 1850 census enumeration (in Six Mile Grove), is also identified in the *Frontier Guardian and Iowa Sentinel* as the organ's agent for Barney's Grove beginning on 2 October 1850. Gail Geo. Holmes, "A Prophet Who Followed, Fulfilled, and Magnified," 150, and Holmes, "The Missouri River Valley," in S. Kent Brown, Donald Q. Cannon and Richard H. Jackson, eds., *Historical Atlas of Mormonism* (New York: Simon & Schuster, 1994), 74–75; Journal History, 31 December 1851, 2–3.
27. The 1850 census of Pottawattamie County shows Charles Barney, with his family, living in proximity to his sons Luther and Benjamin and their families. Charles's family, on 12 November 1850, is identified as: Charles 61, Deborah 41, John 25, Harriett 16, Jefferson 14, William 9, and Sarah 5. Benjamin, Charles's oldest son from his second marriage, is 18 with his wife Caroline 24, and their two sons Benjamin 2 and Joseph ½ year. Luther's family consisted of himself 44, Lucinda 27, Ambrose 12, Charles 11, Lucien 9, Hyrum 7, Ebenezer 3, Elisha 1, and Luther ½ year. Seventh Census of the United States, 1850, National Archives, Washington, D.C.

Enumerated on 8 October 1850, "Louis," and Betsey Barney, 38 and 36 respectively, (they were actually both 42) are also listed in the 1850 census with their children Walter 12, Henry 10, and Joseph 7. Seventh Census, 1850. The disparity in the ages of everyone in the family suggests the information was supplied by someone outside the immediate family.

28. Lewis Barney, Autobiography 1, 59.
29. Horace H. McKenney, *Pioneer History of Harris Grove, 1851–1861* (n.p.: n.p., ca. 1925), 3.
30. Smith, *History of Harrison County* (1888), 79. With the Mormon evacuation of the county in 1852, legal title to land became the norm.
31. *History of Harrison County* (1891), 748.
32. The 1850 federal census identifies Lewis Barney as a carpenter.
33. There is some dispute regarding the time of Henry Barney's journey to Utah. Regarding the view that Henry arrived in Utah in 1849, William Adams, who had been working in Springfield, Illinois, since May 1848, wrote that in the spring of 1849, "Close to the first day of May, 1849, I started on my journey to Utah in company with Thomas Judd and family. Henry Barney and family, four wagons in all, we had a prosperous journey with no accidents." The caravan crossed Illinois and Iowa arriving at Kanesville about 1 June 1849. On July 7 Adams and his family joined the Andrew Perkins company of 100 wagons and went west, although he does not indicate whether Henry Barney continued with them or not. William Adams, Autobiography, 16–17, Church Archives. That Henry Barney arrived in Utah in 1849 is supported by the Utah territorial census for 1850 which identifies Henry as living in Provo, Utah, on 1 June 1850 along with his brother Walter. Utah Territory census schedules, 1850, 1860, 1870, Church Archives.

    The possibility that Henry arrived in Utah in 1850 comes from the Warren Foote Emigrating Journal stating that Henry Barney left the Missouri River Valley on 12 June 1850. He was assigned to the second division composed of ten people, two wagons, and twenty-two cattle. Four hundred seventy-six people comprised the company. Warren Foote Emigrating Journal, Church Archives.
34. Coates, "Refugees, Friends, and Foes," 77–78, 82.
35. Jenson, *Encyclopedic History of the Church*, 673.
36. Isaac Foster, Journal, 8 May 1849, typescript, Herbert S. Auerbach Collection, Department of Rare Books and Special Collections, Harvey S. Firestone Memorial Library, Princeton University, Princeton, New Jersey.
37. Winter Quarters Cemetery List, Church Archives.
38. Perkins and Gillen, Interview, 6, 10.
39. Early Mormon Activities in Indiana, 1830–1845, 2, 4, 9, 11, 23, 35, 48, Church Archives. For a broader view of the Tippetts family's experiences in the church prior to this time, see Alva Tippetts's brother Joseph's letter to Joseph Smith in April 1843. Joseph H. Tippetts to Joseph Smith, 2 April 1843, in Newel K. Whitney Collection, Special Collections, Harold B. Lee Library, Brigham Young University, Provo, Utah.
40. John Cook Bennett, *The History of the Saints, or an Expose of Joe Smith and the Mormons* (Boston: Leland & Whiting, 1842).
41. For a discussion of the genesis of plural marriage among the Saints, see Danel W. Bachman, "A Study of the Mormon Practice of Plural Marriage before the Death of Joseph Smith" (master's thesis, Purdue University, 1975). Lawrence Foster and Richard S. Van Wagoner also postulate the origins of Mormon polygamy. Foster, *Religion and Sexuality: The Shakers, the Mormons, and the Oneida Community* (Urbana, Illinois: University of Illinois Press, 1984), 123–180; Richard S. Van Wagoner, *Mormon Polygamy: A History* (Salt Lake City: Signature Books, 1989, 2nd

ed.), 1–72. Church practice of plural marriage was publicly announced in Salt Lake City, Utah Territory, in August 1852 by Mormon apostle Orson Pratt.

42. Nolan Barney, "Benjamin Franklin and Caroline (Beard) Barney: History of a Pioneer Family," *The Barney Family News* 42 (June 1989): 2–3.
43. Early Mormon Activities in Indiana, 4; 1850 Census for Pottawattamie County, Iowa.
44. Lewis Barney, Autobiography 1, 59.
45. The little girl's stepbrother Arthur wrote that Elizabeth and Alva Tippetts's daughter "lived to be about 25 years old and died at Monroe, Sevier Co., Utah." Arthur Barney, Journal, 5.
46. Lewis Barney, Autobiography 1, 59.
47. Preston, *Genealogy of the Barney Family*, 348.
48. Lewis Barney, Autobiography 1, 60. While the Mormons were away from the Nauvoo Temple, where sacred ordinances such as marriages and baptisms were authorized, religious ceremonies, such as baptisms, marriages, and sealings, continued to be performed while the Saints lived along the Missouri River. Bennett, *Mormons at the Missouri*, 188–190, 195–198.
49. The lack of Lewis's commentary on his domestic condition is one of the gnawing disappointments associated with his autobiographies, though the absence of information about family intimacy is consistent with most other nineteenth-century Latter-day Saint diarists and autobiographers.
50. *Frontier Guardian*, 14 November 1851.
51. Lewis Barney, Autobiography 1, 60.
52. *History of Harrison County* (1891), 217, 288.
53. *Frontier Guardian*, 14 November 1851.
54. Ezra T. Benson to Brigham Young, 13 May 1852, Kanesville, Iowa, Brigham Young, Papers, Incoming Correspondence, Church Archives.
55. Lewis Barney, Autobiography 1, 60.
56. *History of Harrison County* (1891), 287–289; Smith, *History of Harrison County* (1888), 194.
57. Lewis Barney, Autobiography 1, 60.
58. Ibid., 60–62.
59. Ibid., 62.
60. Journal History, 31 December 1852, supplement. There may be some incongruities in the numerical configurations of the families in this unofficial church record.
61. Luther's widow Lucinda Barney is found with her children in Benton County, Arkansas, in the 1860 census. A family account states that she died "near Camp Verde, Arizona," about 1882. Preston, *Genealogy of the Barney Family*, 346.
62. Emerine Barney and Benjamin Leland (also spelled Leyland) were married 8 April 1841 by James Carroll. Nauvoo Restoration Incorporation, Hancock Marriages, 40, Church Archives.
63. *Times and Seasons* 3, no. 9 (1 March 1842): 718.
64. Lyndon W. Cook, comp. *Nauvoo: Deaths and Marriages, 1839–1845* (Provo, Utah: Grandin Book Company, 1994), 110; Seventies Record, 3rd Quorum, 34–35; Patriarchal Blessings, Index; *Nauvoo Temple Register Endowment*, 318.
65. Seventh Census, 1850.
66. Edward S. White, *Past and Present of Shelby County, Iowa*, 2 vols. (Indianapolis: B. F. Brown and Company, Inc., 1915), 1:108–111, 214, 219, 369, 381.
67. *Saints' Herald* 25, no. 18 (15 September 1878): 287.
68. Unruh, *Plains Across*, 120.
69. Orson Hyde to Brigham Young, 27 May 1852, Kanesville, Iowa, Brigham Young, Papers, Incoming Correspondence. There were alternate routes across Nebraska taken by some Mormons, which may have prompted Hyde's inquiry. Stanley B.

Kimball, "The Mormon Trail Network in Nebraska, 1846–1848," in Allen and Welch, *Coming to Zion*, 127–139.

70. *Frontier Guardian*, 28 May 1852.
71. Ibid.
72. Unruh, *Plains Across*, 120.
73. *Frontier Guardian*, 28 May 1852.
74. Electa C. Briggs Williams, Autobiography, 1885, in Edward Stevenson, Collection 1849–1922, Church Archives.
75. Unruh, *Plains Across*, 185.
76. Jonathan S. Page, "Biography of Johnathon [*sic*] S. Page By Himself," typescript, Herbert S. Auerbach Collection, Department of Rare Books and Special Collections, Harvey S. Firestone Memorial Library, Princeton University Library, Princeton, New Jersey.
77. Ezra T. Benson to Brigham Young, 13 May 1852.
78. Mormon accounts of the 1852 emigration, contemporary and reminiscent, found in the Church Archives number about 100.
79. Thomas Margetts to Samuel W. Richards, 4 July 1852, Kanesville, Iowa, in the *Millennial Star* 14, no. 29 (11 September 1852): 461.
80. The roster for the group, later identified as the seventh emigrating company of 1852, identifies 304 travelers though the same source states 340 comprised the company. Perhaps the numbers were inadvertently transposed. Journal History, 31 December 1852 supplement, 41–49.

    The Barneys had known the Jolleys for several years. Bryant is one of those listed as having been one of the early settlers, along with Lewis Barney, in Cass Township, Harrison County, Iowa. *History of Harrison County* (1891), 748. The Barneys apparently had affection for Jolley as he had in 1848 baptized James Henry Barney, Lewis's son. High Priest Quorum General Records, 1901–1922, Millard Stake, Record of Members, Church Archives.

    The leadership of the travelers consisted of Jolley as captain, Barney and William R. Terry, Samuel Cotterall, J. Tedrow, and A. Winn as captains of five groups of ten family heads. Melvin L. Bashore, comp., "List of Officers in Pioneer Companies Which Crossed the Plains, 1847–1868" 1988, Church Archives.
81. Caroline Beard Barney quoted in Barney, "Benjamin Franklin and Caroline (Beard) Barney," 3.
82. George M. Brown, Diary, typescript, vol. 1, Church Archives.
83. Unruh, *Plains Across*, 185, 408–409.
84. George M. Brown, Diary.
85. Barney, "Benjamin Franklin and Caroline (Beard) Barney," 3.
86. Perkins and Gillen, Interview, 19.
87. Lewis Barney, Autobiography 1, 62.
88. See also Angelina Farley, Diary, 1850, Church Archives, and also the 1853 example in Lewis Dunbar Wilson, Autobiographical Sketch, typescript, 4, Church Archives.

    For a view of how overlanders on the Oregon Trail in 1852 handled discipline resulting from extreme circumstances see David J. Langum, "Pioneer Justice on the Overland Trails," *Western Historical Quarterly* 5, no. 4 (October 1974): 421–422.
89. Lewis Barney, Autobiography 1, 62. George M. Brown remembered the division occurring for more benign reasons. He wrote:

    > Some day's journey on the other side of the Fort Laramie we divided our company of 50 wagons into five companies of 10 wagons each and the captains of tens became captains of the respective companies, and we were to travel at a distance of two or three miles from each other; this we did in order to obtain better food for our cattle. George M. Brown, Diary.

Brown, ten years old at the time of the journey, failed to ascertain the cleavage between Jolley and others in the company, though he was apparently witness to Jolley and Barney's later confrontation.

90. Lewis Barney, Autobiography 1, 62.
91. Ibid., 62–63.
92. Ibid., 63. George M. Brown remembered, "One day a scene occurred which was both frightening and dangerous, but through the mercy and never-ceasing care of our Heavenly Father, resulted in no harm and at the same time it learned us a lesson." George M. Brown, Diary. In the typescript of Brown's diary the typist chose to leave out particulars of the encounter from the narrative, apparently feeling that the ugly scene reflected poorly on both men involved.
93. Lewis Barney, Autobiography 1, 64. Jolley's point of view in the matter is not extant. The only information supplied by his descendants about Jolley's journey to Utah in 1852 is that "no serious accidents happened on the journey although crossing the Platte River was a real challenge and at one time the wagon of Widow Shurtliff capsized, but happily no one was seriously hurt." Bryant Manning Jolley, *The Jolley Family Book: The Story of Henry Jolley and His Wife Francis Manning Jolley* (Provo, Utah: Brigham Young University Press, 1966), 314.
94. Lewis Barney, Autobiography 1, 65.
95. John Mack Faragher, *Women and Men on the Overland Trail* (New Haven: Yale University Press, 1979), 4.
96. Lewis Barney, Autobiography 1, 65. The Journal History confirms 12 September 1852 as the date of the arrival of Jolley's wagon train although no mention is made of the company's arrival in fragments. Journal History, 31 December 1852 supplement. William R. Terry, who was one of the original captains of ten, wrote that he "landed in the Valley of Salt Lake at one o'clock" on 9 September 1852, which was three days before Barney's company, suggesting that perhaps he was part of the initial fragmentation who pressed ahead. Terry, Autobiographical Sketch, 43.
97. *Millennial Star* 11, no. 22 (15 November 1849): 342.

Chapter 12

1. Much has been written about the Latter-day Saint community and the taming of the Great Basin interior through the mechanism of community and cooperation. See Ephraim Edward Ericksen, *The Psychological and Ethical Aspects of Mormon Group Life* (Chicago: University of Chicago, 1922; reprint, University of Utah, 1975); Milton R. Hunter, *Brigham Young the Colonizer* (Salt Lake City: Deseret News Press 1940; reprint, Peregrine Smith, Inc., 1973); Lowry Nelson, *The Mormon Village* (Salt Lake City: University of Utah Press, 1952); Leonard J. Arrington, *Great Basin Kingdom: An Economic History of the Latter-day Saints, 1830–1900* (Cambridge, Massachusetts: Harvard University Press, 1958); Joel Edward Ricks, *Forms and Methods of Early Mormon Settlement in Utah and the Surrounding Regions, 1847 to 1877* (Logan: Utah State University Press, 1964); Dean L. May, "The Making of Saints: The Mormon Town as a Setting for the Study of Cultural Change," *Utah Historical Quarterly* 45, no. 1 (winter 1977): 75–92; and Richard H. Jackson, ed., *The Mormon Role in the Settlement of the West* (Provo, Utah: Brigham Young University Press, 1978). See also Wayne L. Wahlquist, "A Review of Mormon Settlement Literature," *Utah Historical Quarterly* 45, no. 1 (winter 1977): 4–21.
2. Charles S. Peterson, "Imprint of Agricultural Systems on the Utah Landscape," in Jackson, ed., *The Mormon Role in the Settlement of the West*, 93; William Mulder, *Homeward to Zion: The Mormon Migration from Scandinavia* (Minneapolis:

University of Minnesota Press in cooperation with Brigham Young University Press, 1957, 2000), 192.

3. Peterson, "Imprint of Agricultural Systems," 91; Mulder, *Homeward to Zion*, 215.
4. Nelson, *The Mormon Village*, 4.
5. The earliest known property map of Salt Lake City, drawn by Thomas Bullock, dated 1847, and found in the Church Archives, shows no plot designated for Lewis Barney.

   Brigham Young wrote from "Great Salt Lake City" in the fall of 1848 to his associates who were still living in settlements on the Missouri River to say, "The city that we have laid out is already filled up, and we have many families that are present without an inheritance." Brigham Young to Orson Hyde, et al., 9 October 1848, Great Salt Lake City, *Frontier Guardian*, 7 February 1849.
6. Lewis Barney, Autobiography 1, 65. The Barneys stayed three days in Salt Lake City and then moved to Provo to Walter Barney's place. Carter, *Our Pioneer Heritage*, 10:316. The agricultural census of 1850 indicates that Walter had 10 improved and 60 unimproved acres in Provo valued at $300. He also had livestock valued at $1,225. (There were only six people in Utah County with a greater value of livestock than Walter at this time. It is likely his wealth was based upon his California goldfield ventures in 1848.) Henry in 1850 had 30 unimproved acres valued at $50 and livestock (horses and cows) worth $380. Utah Territory, Census Schedules, 1850–1860, 1870, Church Archives.
7. Registry of names of Persons Residing in the various wards, 1852, Brigham Young, Papers, Office Papers, Church Archives, hereafter Registry of names, 1852.
8. Historian's Office, Historical Record Book, 1843–1874, 164–166, Church Archives.
9. Provo Fifth Ward, Manuscript History, Church Archives. The ward was far enough away from Provo's center that settlers in this area, designated as the Provo fifth Ward, were evacuated in 1853 due to Indian troubles.
10. Lovisa Losee Barney quoted in Barney, "Benjamin Franklin and Caroline (Beard) Barney," 3.
11. Lewis Barney, Autobiography 1, 65. Lack of timber in Utah's valleys made adobe homes, generally one-level sun-baked clay or mud brick structures built around a lath frame, a favorite choice for dwellings, though log homes were the most common form of dwelling in the first years of Utah's settlement. See Richard H. Jackson, "The Use of Adobe in the Mormon Cultural Region," *Journal of Cultural Geography* 1 (1980): 82–87.

    It is safe to surmise that Lewis's two wives lived together in the adobe dwelling, though this arrangement later changed with the wives living separately in different communities. This latter arrangement seems to have been the most successful form of plural marriage in Utah. Stephanie Smith Goodson, "Plural Wives," in Claudia L. Bushman, ed., *Mormon Sisters* (Cambridge, Massachusetts: Emmeline Press Limited, 1976), 99–100.
12. Wayne Wahlquist, ed., *Atlas of Utah* (Provo, Utah: Weber State University and Brigham Young University Press, 1981), 55.
13. For an overview of early white settlement of Utah Valley see Richard Neitzel Holzapfel, *A History of Utah County* (Salt Lake City: Utah State Historical Society and Utah County Commission, 1999), 53–69.
14. Fray Angelico Chavez, trans., and Ted J. Warner, ed., *The Dominguez-Escalante Journal: Their Expedition through Colorado, Utah, Arizona, and New Mexico in 1776* (Provo, Utah: Brigham Young University Press, 1976), 59. The Catholic fathers' account of Utah Valley in September 1776 is found on pages 53–62.
15. Ibid., 57.
16. For an overview of the physiographic features and pre-Mormon history of Utah Valley see Holzapfel, *History of Utah County*, 1–11, 25–35.

17. For an overview of the Fort Utah battle and its lasting implications for white-Indian relations see John A. Peterson, *Utah's Black Hawk War* (Salt Lake City: University of Utah Press, 1998), 51–58. See also Howard A. Christy, "'What Virtue There Is in Stone' and other Pungent Talk on the Early Utah Frontier," *Utah Historical Quarterly* 59, no. 3 (summer 1991): 301–308; and Will Bagley, ed., *Frontiersman: Abner Blackburn's Narrative* (Salt Lake City: University of Utah Press, 1992), 151–157.
18. Holzapfel, *History of Utah County*, 40.
19. Jenson, *Encyclopedic History of the Church*, 683–684.
20. Holzapfel, *History of Utah County*, 39.
21. For varying views of Mormon attitudes toward Native Americans see Lawrence G. Coates, "Brigham Young and Mormon Indian Policies: The Formative Period, 1836–1851," *BYU Studies* 18, no. 3 (spring 1978): 428–452; Howard A. Christy, "Open Hand and Mailed Fist: Mormon-Indian Relations in Utah, 1847–1852," *Utah Historical Quarterly* 46, no. 2 (summer 1978): 216–235; Ronald W. Walker, "Toward a Reconstruction of Mormon and Indian Relations, 1847–1877," *BYU Studies* 29, no. 3 (fall 1989): 23–42; and Peterson, *Utah's Black Hawk War*.
22. Several factors figured into Mormon attitudes toward the land. Believing that the land was a gift from God, not the possession of any particular group of people, the mountains and vales of Utah were to be shared by the whites and Indians. Without federal regulation of land through a land office, no group of people could claim the territory exclusively. And, Brigham Young claimed Mormons never settled on Indian ground without permission. Walker, "Reconstruction of Mormon and Indian Relations," 35–36.
23. Richard H. Jackson, "The Mormon Indian Farms: An Attempt at Cultural Integration," in Jerry N. McDonald and Tony Lazewski, eds., *Geographical Perspectives on Native Americans: Topics and Resources* ([Los Angeles]: Association of American Geographers, 1976), 44.
24. Barney's family probably spent the winter of 1852–1853 in Provo despite secondary information stating they were in Palmyra/Spanish Fork before the end of 1852. See Spanish Fork Ward, Manuscript History, Church Archives; and Huff, comp., *Memories That Live*, 379. The Registry of names, 1852, shows the Barneys living within Provo and not in Palmyra/Spanish Fork. Lewis and Benjamin's absence in the 1852 registry may be explained by the winter's mill activity in Peteetneet Canyon.
25. Lewis Barney, Autobiography 1, 65. The Peteetneet Canyon site for a sawmill was looked upon favorably by others as well, creating competition among local citizens. Apostle George A. Smith, on 18 August 1852, "went up Peteetneet Kanyon to settle a dispute about a mill site." It is not known if the site in question concerned the Barneys' mill. George A. Smith, Papers, Journals, 18 August 1852, Church Archives.
26. Barney later sold this mill to Stephen Markham for $750. Markham's mill was "an upright saw, run by water." Carter, *Our Pioneer Heritage*, 14:286. See also Farozine Ellen Redd Bryner, "Lemuel Hardison Redd biographical sketch, 1956," typescript, 3–4, Church Archives.
27. Lewis Barney, Autobiography 1, 65.
28. Wards, first formed in Nauvoo, were usually composed of a few hundred members. The smaller "branches" served church members where the community and church were in a fledgling stage. Several wards and branches were attached to a "stake." The stake, made up of several wards or branches, was led by a president, the ward by a bishop, and branch by a president. In each case the presiding authority was a lay leader. Mormon practice is much the same today.

    Walter and Henry Barney are identified as being members of the Provo Third Ward as of 20 March 1851. Elias Hicks Blackburn, Notebook, 1851–1857, Church

Archives. By the end of 1852 Henry remained in the Third Ward while Walter moved to the Provo Fifth Ward described as consisting "of scattered settlers living on the river bottoms northeast of Provo." Provo Fifth Ward, Manuscript History; and Registry of names, 1852. The Registry of names, 1852, also indicates that Charles and John Barney became a part of the Fifth Ward upon their arrival in Provo.

29. George A. Smith, Papers, Journals, 5 August 1852.
30. Edward W. Tullidge, "History of Spanish Fork," *Tullidge's Quarterly Magazine* 3, nos. 2–3 (April, July 1884): 138; George A. Hicks, History of Spanish Fork, 1913, typescript, Special Collections, Harold B. Lee Library, Brigham Young University.
31. Jolley, *Jolley Family Book*, 314; Tullidge, "History of Spanish Fork," 138; Elisha Warner, *The History of Spanish Fork* (Spanish Fork, Utah: The Press Publishing Co., 1930), 34. The Registry of names, 1852, identified just over fifty family heads in Palmyra/Spanish Fork.
32. George A. Smith to Samuel W. Richards, 26 December 1852, in *Millennial Star* 15, no. 18 (30 April 1853): 286.
33. Chavez and Warner, *The Dominguez-Escalante Journal*, 53–54.
34. Brigham Young's office was built in 1852 and is presently located between the Lion and Beehive Houses in downtown Salt Lake City, though the latter two buildings were not built at the time Barney and his wives visited the president's office.
35. Endowment House Sealings and Endowment, Book A & A1, 1851–1854, Special Collections, Family History Library.
36. Deuteronomy 25:5–6. There is no record of the sealing of Elizabeth Beard Barney to her first husband, Alva, but Family History Library records indicate the children of Lewis and Elizabeth were sealed to Alva Tippetts. Family Group Sheets, Family History Library.
37. Hicks, History of Spanish Fork.
38. The Record of the Palmyra Branch, Church Archives. Adult males, the laity, composed the priesthood and had authority to perform both religious and nonreligious functions within the community.
39. Record of the Palmyra Branch.
40. Dale F. Beecher, "Colonizer of the West," in Black and Porter, *Lion of the Lord*, 180–183; Hunter, *Brigham Young the Colonizer*, 377; Wahlquist, *Atlas of Utah*, 90–91.
41. For an overview of education in early Utah see James B. Allen, "Everyday Life in Utah's Elementary Schools, 1847–1870," in Ronald W. Walker and Doris Dant, eds., *Nearly Everything Imaginable: The Everyday Life of Utah's Mormon Pioneers* (Provo, Utah: Brigham Young University Press, 1999), 359–385.
42. Hicks, History of Spanish Fork, 3. For other descriptions of the early history of Palmyra and Spanish Fork see William G. Hartley, *My Best for the Kingdom*, 255–263, 269–272.
43. Chavez and Warner, *The Dominguez-Escalante Journal*, 59.
44. In the first decades of Mormonism, when a church unit was organized—a branch or ward—it was also designated a stake. The stake would usually start with one ward. Thus, for Palmyra there was both a president, with spiritual responsibilities, representing the non-organized stake and a bishop, with temporal responsibilities, representing the ward. This arrangement was altered in Palmyra in March 1853 when George A. Smith chose Stephen Markham as bishop of the lower settlement. Spanish Fork, the upper settlement, was served by Bishop William Pace. Hartley, *My Best for the Kingdom*, 257–258, 260.
45. Provo Utah Central Stake, General Minutes, v. 9, 51, Church Archives. See also Record of the Palmyra Branch; Silas Hillman, Autobiography and journal [ca. 1866–1875], Church Archives. The record indicates that Lewis's father was present at his rebaptism. Before the year's end 54 percent of eligible Palmyrans were

either baptized initially or rebaptized. Presiding Bishopric, Statistical Reports, 1851–1869, 1877–1903, Church Archives, hereafter referred to as Presiding Bishopric, Statistical Reports.

46. Bushrod W. Wilson, Autobiography [ca. 1856], in Daughters of Utah Pioneers Collection, Church Archives.
47. Record of the Palmyra Branch. For a view of one man's discordant attitudes toward church dominance in Palmyra and Spanish Fork in the 1850s, see Davis Bitton, "'I'd Rather Have Some Roasting Ears': The Peregrinations of George Armstrong Hicks," *Utah Historical Quarterly* 68, no. 3 (summer 2000): 204–211.
48. Spanish Fork Ward, Manuscript History.
49. *Ingersoll's Century Annals of San Bernardino County [California], 1769 to 1904* (Los Angeles: Ingersoll, 1904), 668.
50. Family genealogical records state that Margaret married Joseph D. Gilbert in 1854, a New Yorker born in 1828, who was, as a youth, a practicing Latter-day Saint. In Nauvoo he received a patriarchal blessing in 1843. Patriarchal Blessings Index. Gilbert, the son of Mormon pioneer Truman Gilbert, appears in the 1852 Bishop's report living by his father in the Hobble Creek Ward in Utah Valley. Joseph D. and Margaret Matilda Gilbert are found in San Bernardino, California, in the 1860 federal census. They are not, however, among those listed as early Mormon settlers in San Bernardino. San Bernardino, Manuscript History, Church Archives. Still, the Gilberts are buried in the old Mormon pioneer cemetery in San Bernardino, Joseph dying in 1905 and Margaret following in 1915. A. Mikel Busby, comp., Marilyn Mills, ed., *San Bernardino Valley, 1847–1857: History & Tour, 150th Anniversary* (n.p.: Southern California Sesquicentennial Committee, 1997).
51. Edward Leo Lyman, *San Bernardino: The Rise and Fall of a California Community* (Salt Lake City: Signature Books, 1996), 371. While many of the Mormons who remained in San Bernardino became members of the RLDS Church, early membership records of that church do not indicate that the Gilberts became RLDS. An account of the demise and aftermath of the Mormon community in San Bernardino is found in Lyman, 371–431.

    The Gilberts apparently tried in 1864 to relocate to the eastern United States but the turmoil of the Civil War precluded their venture. *Ingersoll's Century Annals of San Bernardino County*, 668.
52. Spanish Fork Ward, Manuscript History; Hicks, "History of Spanish Fork," 8; Tullidge, History of Spanish Fork, 139.
53. Peterson, *Utah's Black Hawk War*, 29–30.
54. Details of the Ivie incident and subsequent killing of Keel are found in Peter Gottfredson, *History of Indian Depredations in Utah* (Salt Lake City: Skelton Publishing Co., 1919), 43–46. See also Don Carlos Johnson, *A Brief History of Springville, Utah* (Springville, Utah: William H. Gibson, 1900), and Luke William Gallup's account in "Sketches of my grandfather's life, from his history of his own life, 1920," 3, Church Archives.

    The man blamed for initiating Wakara's violent course, James Ivie, eventually settled in Scipio and during the Black Hawk War thirteen years later met a fate similar to the one he inflicted upon the Indian which started the Walker War. See Peterson, *Utah's Black Hawk War*, 269–270. Another view of Ivie's circumstances is found in Gottredson, *History of Indian Depredations in Utah*, 43–46.
55. The Palmyra/Spanish Fork militia was initially mustered on 30 April 1853 with Stephen Markham in command and Lieutenant Albert K. Thurber his adjutant. The unit was composed of five officers, three sergeants, four corporals, and twenty-seven privates. Hamilton Gardner, "The Utah Territorial Militia," 273–274, Church Archives. While the Barneys were not a part of this initial muster, by July Lewis was one of the town's defenders.

56. Peterson, *Utah's Black Hawk War*, 61.
57. Joseph Curtis, Reminiscences and diary, 1839–1881, 17 July 1853, Church Archives.
58. Conway B. Sonne, *World of Wakara* (San Antonio, Texas: The Naylor Company, 1962), 164.
59. Lewis Barney, Autobiography 1, 65. One of the more complete war accounts indicates that after Keel's death, "the assailants then rode on to Walker's camp and the entire band broke and fled up Peteetneet Canyon, firing on outlying settlers and seizing twenty-five head of cattle as they went." Howard A. Christy, "The Walker War: Defense and Conciliation as Strategy," *Utah Historical Quarterly* 47, no. 4 (fall 1979): 400–401. See also Warner, *The History of Spanish Fork*, 40, 42; Orson F. Whitney, *History of Utah*, 4 vols. (Salt Lake City: George Q. Cannon & Sons Co., 1892), 1:513–514; and Tullidge, "History of Spanish Fork," 156.
60. Lewis Barney, Autobiography 1, 65–66.
61. Ibid., 67. See also Arthur Barney, Journal, 11–12. Several accounts of the concern of the Utah Valley settlers over their fellow residents in Peteetneet Canyon describe efforts to rescue those attacked by the Indians. See Silas Hillman, Autobiography and Journal; "Journal and Diary of Albert King Thurber" in Kate B. Carter, comp., *Treasures of Pioneer History*, 6 vols. (Salt Lake City: Daughters of Utah Pioneers, 1952–1957): 3:293; and Verda McKee Kitchen, "Stephen Markham's History as Others Have Recorded It" (1982), 18, Church Archives.
62. Gottfredson, *Indian Depredations*, Supplement, 11. This does not count those killed in October 1853 in what has come to be called the Gunnison Massacre. See Christy, "Walker War," 417–418; and S. N. Carvalho, *Incidents of Travel and Adventure in the Far West; with Col. Frémont's Last Expedition* (New York: Derby & Jackson, 1857), 188–194. Lewis's brothers John and Benjamin participated in Utah County's defense during the Indian uprising. Indian Service Claims, 1861–1862, Brigham Young, Papers, Indian Claims, Church Archives.
63. Lewis Barney, Autobiography 1, 67.
64. Spanish Fork, Manuscript History. Despite the apparent safety of the Salt Lake Valley, in August 1853, it was decided by leaders in Salt Lake City to build a wall six miles in length and twelve feet high to surround and protect the city.
65. John W. Berry, Rank Roll, July 4th/55, Church Archives; Tullidge, "History of Spanish Fork," 139. Lewis Barney and his sons were remustered in July 1855 where Lewis was identified as having a rifle, a quarter pound of powder, a half pound of shot, and a powder horn. His sons Walter and Henry, while both enrolled, had no arms or ammunition.
66. Presiding Bishopric, Statistical Reports. The total of 339 in Palmyra on 6 April 1854 compared to the other Utah Valley communities with 1,609 in Provo, 887 in nearby Springville, 396 in Payson, 319 in Pleasant Grove, 264 in American Fork, and 161 in Cedar Valley.
67. Spanish Fork Ward, Manuscript History. For an overview of the Palmyra and Spanish Fork forts see Mary Henderson, History of Utah Forts, 1940, 73–78, Church Archives.
68. Jenson, "Fort Saint Luke," in *Encyclopedic History of the Church*, 256–257; Hicks, History of Spanish Fork.
69. Lewis Barney, Autobiography 1, 67–68. Despite his limited resources Barney continued his regular tithing contributions to the church. See the Account Book of Stephen Markham, Church Archives.

    Concerning sawmills in Utah, George A. Smith wrote on 20 March 1855 to the editor of *People's Journal* that "no colony [in the U.S.] has progressed with more equal and uniform rapidity [than Utah]. . . . It contains about 50,000 inhabitants who are almost exclusively members of the church. About one hundred saw Mills and forty grist Mills are in operation." Historian's Office, Letterpress Copybooks, vol. 1, 115–140, Church Archives.

70. Lewis Barney, Autobiography 1, 68. Elisha Warner wrote that after an infestation of grasshoppers in 1854 which came too late to damage the 1854 harvest, the following spring the next generation of grasshoppers hatched and "began to devour the sprouting crops. . . . Everything green was devoured by them, and the valley appeared as though scorched by fire." Warner, *History of Spanish Fork*, 46–47. One report indicated that 800 acres near Spanish Fork were stripped. Tullidge, "History of Spanish Fork," 142.

    For an overview of the grasshopper plague in Utah and Spanish Fork particularly see Davis Bitton and Linda P. Wilcox, "Pestiferous Ironclads: The Grasshopper Problem in Pioneer Utah," *Utah Historical Quarterly* 46, no. 4 (fall 1978); Arrington, *Great Basin Kingdom*, 148–156; and Hartley, *My Best for the Kingdom*, 274–276, 279–281.
71. Lewis Barney, Autobiography 1, 68.
72. Ibid., 71. Elisha Warner, writing about the Palmyra and Spanish Fork settlers in the aftermath of the grasshopper plague, said the "consideration and brotherly love the people manifested toward each other [made] the pages bright in retrospect." Warner, *History of Spanish Fork*, 48.
73. Tullidge, "History of Spanish Fork," 138.
74. The big field later became an element of contention between the entities.
75. Lewis Barney, Autobiography 1, 67; Spanish Fork Ward, Manuscript History; Tullidge, "History of Spanish Fork," 141; Hartley, *My Best for the Kingdom*, 273.
76. Record of the Palmyra Branch, 36–48. A report for 11 March 1855 states that the Palmyra Ward included "367 souls," made up of seven high priests, thirty-four seventies (of which Lewis Barney was one), twenty-seven elders, eighteen priests, fifteen teachers, two deacons, one hundred fifty-one not baptized, eighteen over eight and not baptized, ninety-five under eight, showing little change in Palmyra's population during 1855. Spanish Fork Ward, Manuscript History.
77. Brigham Young to Stephen Markham, 23 February 1856, Salt Lake City, Brigham Young Papers, Letterpress Copybooks, Church Archives.
78. Hartley, *My Best for the Kingdom*, 423.
79. Spanish Fork Ward, Manuscript History.
80. Lewis Barney, Autobiography 1, 69. For a description of the evolution of Spanish Fork from its Palmyra, Fort St. Luke, Upper and Lower Settlement antecedents see Hartley, *My Best for the Kingdom*, 255–260, 269–287.
81. Preston, *Genealogy of the Barney Family*, 347–348.
82. Brigham Young to John L. Butler, 29 May 1856, Salt Lake City, Brigham Young Papers, Letterpress Copybooks.

Chapter 13

1. Presiding Bishopric, Statistical Reports. For an overview of Spanish Fork through 1860 see Hartley, *My Best for the Kingdom*, 269–361.
2. Tullidge, "History of Spanish Fork," 300.
3. Lovisa Losee Barney quoted in Barney, "Benjamin Franklin and Caroline (Beard) Barney," 3.
4. Priscilla Merriman Evans, Autobiography, [ca. 1914], typescript, 41–42, Church Archives.
5. Jack McLaughlin, *Jefferson and Monticello: The Biography of a Builder* (New York: Henry Holt and Company, 1988), vii.
6. Mulder, *Homeward to Zion*, 215–216.
7. Beverly Beeton, "Teach Them to Till the Soil: An Experiment with Indian Farms, 1850–1862," *American Indian Quarterly* 3, no. 4 (winter 1977–78): 304.

8. Beeton, "Experiment with Indian Farms," 307. The other two farms were located at Twelve Mile Creek in Sanpete Valley and near Kanosh in Millard County. Ibid., 304–305. For an overview of the Spanish Fork Indian Farm and relations with Spanish Fork residents see Hartley, *My Best for the Kingdom*, 314–323, 328–329.
9. Wilford Woodruff to *St. Louis Luminary*, 30 May 1856, Historian's Office, Letterpress Copybook; Tullidge, "History of Spanish Fork," 142, 162; David L. Bigler, "Garland Hurt, the American Friend of the Utahs," *Utah Historical Quarterly* 62, no. 2 (spring 1994), 159; Hartley, *My Best for the Kingdom*, 314–316.
10. Evans, Autobiography, 42.
11. Ibid., 50.
12. Garland Hurt to J. M. Elliott, 4 October 1856, found in Walker, "Reconstruction of Mormon and Indian Relations," 35.
13. Lewis Barney, Autobiography 1, 71–72.
14. Ibid., 72. For a description of Grosepeen's status among the Utes, see Peterson, *Utah's Black Hawk War*, 60–62, 66. In contrast to the rancorous disposition of several of his Indian brethren, Grosepeen was known as a peacemaker. Ibid., 72.
15. Quoted in Barney, "Benjamin Franklin and Caroline (Beard) Barney," 3–4. A variation of the story is told by Lewis's granddaughter Edna Barney Perkins in Perkins and Gillin, Interview, 17. For other examples of Utah settlers intervening to save Indian children from being sold or killed see Brian Q. Cannon, "Adopted or Indentured, 1850–1870: Native Children in Mormon Households," in Walker and Dant, *Nearly Everything Imaginable*, 341–357; and Sondra Jones, *The Trial of Don Pedro Leon Lujan: The Attack against Indian Slavery and Mexican Traders in Utah* (Salt Lake City: University of Utah Press, 2000), 44–52.
16. Quoted in Barney, "Benjamin Franklin and Caroline (Beard) Barney," 3.
17. Warren Metcalf, "A Precarious Balance: The Northern Utes and the Black Hawk War," *Utah Historical Quarterly* 57, no. 1 (winter 1989): 28–29.
18. *Journal of Discourses*, 5:226, 13 September 1857.
19. Ibid., 4:52, 21 September 1856.
20. D. Michael Quinn, "The Practice of Rebaptism at Nauvoo," *BYU Studies* 18, no. 2 (winter 1978): 228.
21. Bennett, *We'll Find the Place*, 77–80.
22. Paul H. Peterson, "The Mormon Reformation of 1856–1857: The Rhetoric and the Reality," *Journal of Mormon History* 15 (1989): 74–76.
23. Lewis Barney, Autobiography 1, 73. For a treatment of the Reformation in Spanish Fork, see Hartley, *My Best for the Kingdom*, 297–302. A discussion of one man's negative view of the movement's effect in Spanish Fork is found in Bitton, "George Armstrong Hicks," 207–210, though Hicks stated that the most egregious of the Reformation's alleged abuses—blood atonement—was not present in Spanish Fork. Ibid., 209.

    For an overview of the Mormon Reformation among the Saints see Gustive O. Larson, "The Mormon Reformation," *Utah Historical Quarterly* 26 (January 1958): 45–63; and three works by Paul H. Peterson: "The Mormon Reformation" (Ph.D. Diss., Brigham Young University, 1981); "The Mormon Reformation of 1856–1857," 59–87; and "Brigham Young and the Mormon Reformation," in Black and Porter, *Lion of the Lord*, 244–261.
24. Peterson, "The Mormon Reformation of 1856–1857," 72–74. Late nineteenth-century church leaders acknowledged the excesses exhibited by some Mormons at this time who "exercised authority that was unjust and harmful," but underscored "the vast amount of good" that came from the retrenchment. Matthias F. Cowley, *Wilford Woodruff* (Salt Lake City: Deseret News, 1909, reprinted by Bookcraft, 1965), 375. See also Whitney, *History of Utah*, 1:565, and Roberts, *Comprehensive History of the Church*, 4:126–136.

25. Lewis Barney, Autobiography 1, 73. A Springville observer noted, "Some of the more impetuous became quite fanatic in their religious fervor. 'All who are not for us, are against us,' and 'It may be necessary to cleanse the platter,' were quotations frequently uttered by some whose zeal had run into fanaticism." Johnson, *A Brief History of Springville, Utah*, 45.
26. Peterson, "The Mormon Reformation of 1856–1857," 69.
27. Spanish Fork Ward, Manuscript History. The figure of 400 was an exaggeration, given that the following month only 439 were identified in the whole ward and children under eight were not baptized.
28. Lewis Barney, Autobiography 1, 73. The mechanism to ascertain the degree of reform necessary in the wards was an inquiry composed of about two dozen questions asked of each member including questions about personal belief, behavior, and hygiene. The usual procedure, with some local variation, was that after the home missionaries "catechized" the bishopric and the teachers (the equivalent of today's home teachers), the latter would in turn "catechize" and instruct the families for whom they had responsibility. Peterson, "The Mormon Reformation of 1856–1857," 69–71.
29. For an overview of the law of consecration and the economic features of nineteenth-century Mormonism see Leonard J. Arrington, Feramorz Y. Fox, and Dean L. May, *Building the City of God: Community and Cooperation among the Mormons* (Salt Lake City: Deseret Book Company, 1976), 15–40. Attempts at consecration were also employed in Nauvoo. Flanders, *Nauvoo*, 55. See also the 1842 Nauvoo consecration certificates, George Washington Thatcher Blair Collection, Church Archives.
30. Arrington, et al., *Building the City of God*, 77.
31. "Eleventh General Epistle of the Presidency of the Church of Jesus Christ of Latter-day Saints, to the Saints," 10 April 1854, in James R. Clark, ed., *Messages of the First Presidency of the Church of Jesus Christ of Latter-day Saints, 1833–1964*, 6 vols. (Salt Lake City: Bookcraft Inc., 1965), 2:139.
32. Arrington, et al., *Building the City of God*, 68.
33. Arrington, et al., approximate the level of participation in Utah County at about 60 percent in contrast to only 40 percent in the rest of the territory. Arrington, et al., *Building the City of God*, 66, 74.
34. The Tithing Office Ledger in the community indicates that Barney gave to the church $1,807 between 1853 and 1856 in the form of donations consistent with the barter economy: squash, wheat, corn, potatoes, eggs, butter, chickens, pork, cows, hay, wool, cloth, lumber, and labor. Palmyra Ward, Tithing Office Ledger, 1841–1857, 20, Church Archives.
35. Trustee in Trust, Consecration Deeds, 1854–1867, Book 2, 13, Church Archives; Utah County Records, Book H, 12–13, Utah County [Utah], Recorder's Office, Provo, Utah. The Provo Utah Central Stake, General Minutes, v. 9, 220, states that this consecration took place in 1858 rather than 1857, certainly the correct date. The sum of $742 suggests a reduction from his 1855 financial status when his assets totaled just over $1,300.

    Lewis's brothers were also consecrators: Benjamin F. in Palmyra, $481; John in Palmyra, $371; Henry in Harmony, $1,306; and Walter in Provo, $2,424. Trustee in Trust, Consecration Deeds, Book 1, 17, 21.
36. For an overview of consecration in Spanish Fork see Hartley, *My Best for the Kingdom*, 276–278.
37. Tullidge, "History of Spanish Fork," 142.
38. Lewis Barney, Autobiography 1, 69. Tullidge, "History of Spanish Fork," 143. Of note, this is the only civic office Barney ever held.
39. Further, as Lewis's brother Benjamin was initiated into the 50th Quorum of Seventy in Spanish Fork, Jolley administered the ordination. Seventies Quorum Records, Fiftieth Quorum, Genealogies, Church Archives. Jolley became bishop

of the Salem Ward (then Pondtown) about 1861. Bitton, "George Armstrong Hicks," 211; and Jenson, *Encyclopedic History of the Church*, 737.

40. For the Latter-day Saints' view of federal abuses leading to the expedition against the Saints see Roberts, *Comprehensive History of the Church*, 3:516–544, 4:198–238. The best overview of the so-called Mormon War remains Norman F. Furniss, *The Mormon Conflict, 1850–1859* (New Haven, Connecticut: Yale University Press, 1960). A balanced documentary of the conflict is LeRoy R. and Ann W. Hafen, eds., *The Utah Expedition, 1857–1858: A Documentary Account of the United States Military Movement under Colonel Albert Sidney Johnston and the Resistance by Brigham Young and the Mormon Nauvoo Legion* (Glendale, California: The Arthur H. Clark Company, 1958). A revisionist view to the material cited above is found in Richard D. Poll and William P. MacKinnon, "Causes of the Utah War Reconsidered," *Journal of Mormon History* 20, no. 2 (fall 1994): 16–44.
41. 8 December 1857, *Message from the President of the United States to the Two Houses of Congress, at the Commencement of the First Sessions of the Thirty-fifth Congress* (Washington: Congressional Globe Office, 1857), 11.
42. Poll and MacKinnon, "Causes of the Utah War Reconsidered," 20.
43. Ibid., 22, 25, 32–33.
44. Gardner, "Utah Territorial Militia," 305–306, 316–317, 327–328. For the military configuration of Spanish Fork and Utah County see also Hartley, *My Best for the Kingdom*, 310–312.
45. Tullidge, "History of Spanish Fork," 143.
46. Hafen and Hafen, *The Utah Expedition*, 58.
47. Johnston later died in 1862 as a Confederate general in the Battle of Shiloh. Furniss, *Mormon Conflict*, 98, 115, 215.
48. A description of Van Vliet's mission to the Mormon capital is found in Hafen and Hafen, *The Utah Expedition*, 35–55.
49. Lewis Barney, Autobiography 1, 76.
50. Ibid., 73–74; Spanish Fork Ward, General Minutes, vol. 2, Church Archives.
51. Lewis Barney, Autobiography 1, 74–75. Information about this activity is found in the Spanish Fork Ward, General Minutes.
52. Mormon estimations of the expedition marching toward them numbered as many as 13,000, including 4,600 soldiers, 3,200 government employees, and 4,930 contractors' employees not to mention the camp followers. Historian's Office Journal, 13 December 1858, Church Archives.
53. Gardner, "Utah Territorial Militia," 350–351, 354, 357, 388, 394–395; Hafen and Hafen, *Utah Expedition*, 30–34; Warner, *History of Spanish Fork*, 59. For the military perspective on the "Utah Expedition" see the "Journal of Capt. Albert Tracy, 1858–1860" *Utah Historical Quarterly* 13, nos. 1–4 (Jan., Apr., Jul., Oct. 1945): 58–67; Jesse Augustus Gove, *The Utah Expedition, 1857–1858: Letters of Capt. Jesse A. Gove* (Concord, New Hampshire: New Hampshire Historical Society, 1928); and concerning the army occupation of Utah see Harold D. Langley, ed., *To Utah with the Dragoons and Glimpses of Life in Arizona and California, 1858–1859* (Salt Lake City: University of Utah Press, 1974).
54. Evans, Autobiography, 48–49.
55. John Mott, Letters, 1858 and 1862, 20 June 1858, Spanish Fork City, Utah, Church Archives.
56. Furniss, *Mormon Conflict*, 133–134; Gardner, "Utah Territorial Militia," 357.
57. Lewis Barney, Autobiography 1, 76. A company of about eighty men, under the command of Albert K. Thurber, was enlisted from among the Spanish Fork settlers to serve in Echo Canyon. Barney was probably part of this unit. Warner, *Spanish Fork*, 59. See also William Byram Pace, Letters, 1857–1866, Church Archives.
58. Preston, *Genealogy of the Barney Family*, 347–348.

59. Lewis Barney, Autobiography 1, 76. William B. Pace, a commander over the Utah County militia, reported to church headquarters that on 30 October 1857 he "detailed Major [A. K.] Thurber [who was likely Lewis Barney's leader] and his command to build a heavy dam a few rods below the 11th crossing of Canyon Creek." They also constructed batteries and fortifications during the last week of October 1857. Journal History, 30 November 1857, 1–2.
60. Lewis Barney, Autobiography 1, 76. Reports were sent to Salt Lake City that over 1,500 cattle were captured and trailed down the canyon by Mormon defenders between 13 and 21 October 1857. Journal History, 13, 16, 21 October 1857.
61. John Pulsipher diary, quoted in Hafen and Hafen, *Utah Expedition*, 210.
62. Furniss, *Mormon Conflict*, 132–133.
63. Journal History, 26, 29 November 1857; Furniss, *Mormon Conflict*, 146.
64. John Pulsipher diary, quoted in Hafen and Hafen, *Utah Expedition*, 211.
65. Lewis Barney, Autobiography 1, 77–78.
66. Ibid., 78.
67. George A. Smith to John Lyman, 6 January 1858, Historian's Office, Letterpress Copybook, vol. 1, 507, Church Archives.
68. Richard D. Poll, "The Move South," *BYU Studies* 29, no. 4 (fall 1989): 75, 77–80, 83. Several hundred refugees never returned to their northern Utah homes but stayed in Utah County.
69. Tullidge, History of Spanish Fork, 144.
70. Gardner, "Utah Territorial Militia," 412–413.
71. Margaret W. Adams to Brother George [Webster?], 26–27 June 1858, Spanish Fork City, Utah, Church Archives.
72. Cost estimates of the "expedition" ranged from $14 million to $40 million for the government, draining the U.S. treasury, already depleted by the Financial Panic of 1857. Poll and MacKinnon, "Causes of the Utah War Reconsidered," 43.
73. Ibid., 43.

Chapter 14

1. Joan L. Severa, *Dressed for the Photographer: Ordinary Americans and Fashion, 1840–1900* (Kent, Ohio: Kent State University Press, 1995), 104–106, 115, 167; Johnson, *Brief History of Springville*, 30, 40–41.
2. Betsey Barney, silent on every other aspect of her life, was quoted in the *Deseret Evening News*, 1 February 1870, stating in a church meeting that she "was a believer in the patriarchal order of marriage [polygamy] and she felt to repudiate any attempt of men to infringe on the commands of God. . . . She prayed they might live faithfully so that they might encourage and assist their husbands and brothers in keeping the commands of God."

   Though Charles Barney was not a polygamist, he obviously had children who embraced the practice. (Some family genealogical materials include information stating that Charles married two other women plurally. This author has found nothing to substantiate the information and considers the claim dubious.) His wife Deborah is said to have told her daughter Sarah Jane, who became a plural wife, "that the Prophet Joseph told her personally about his revelation concerning the principle of polygamy, convincing her of its truthfulness." Erickson, "Life Sketch of Charles Barney," 6.
3. Ronald W. Walker's appraisal of Mormon-Indian attitudes, both from so-called traditional and revisionist perspectives, is important in considering the milieu in which the Black Hawk and other red-white conflicts occurred in Utah. See

Walker, "Toward a Reconstruction of Mormon and Indian Relations." See also Coates, "Brigham Young and Mormon Indian Policies; and Peterson, *Utah's Black Hawk War*.

4. See reports of Barney's public expressions about his religious belief at this time in Spanish Fork Ward, Genealogical and minutes book (1859–1869), 23 September 1860, Church Archives, and Seventies Quorums, 18th Quorum (1844–1975), 3 June 1860.
5. Lewis Barney, Autobiography 1, 81.
6. Henry Hamilton, Journals, Church Archives.
7. For example, William Jex, after his arrival in the community in the spring of 1858 lived successively in the old adobe fort, a dugout on a hillside, and a rental farm before finally taking "up a piece of land on the [Spanish Fork] river bottoms." He reported that after making his claim, his right to the land "was contested and a complaint was filed against me before the Bishop (Albert K. Thurber) who decided against me." An appeal to the Utah Stake high council reversed the decision and it was "decided that I had a perfect right to the land." William Jex, Autobiography [ca. 1921], typescript, 7–8, Church Archives.
8. Dimick B. Huntington, Journal, 1857–1859, 23, Church Archives.
9. Lewis Barney, Autobiography 1, 81.
10. Ibid., 82.
11. Historian Leonard J. Arrington says that the returns on the sale of lumber to the army amounted to $70 per thousand feet and that it was mostly a church enterprise. Arrington, *Great Basin Kingdom*, 198. See also Donald R. Moorman, with Gene A. Sessions, *Camp Floyd and the Mormons: The Utah War* (Salt Lake City: University of Utah Press, 1992), 57.
12. Lewis Barney, Autobiography 1, 81.
13. Holzapfel, *History of Utah County*, 87–92.
14. Lewis Barney, Autobiography 1, 81. The Mormons' good fortune is documented by George A. Smith:

> The advance of the Army of Utah into this Territory has been a regular windfall in favor of the Citizens by furnishing them a market for every article they have to spare. . . . Handsome sums have been realized by many individuals for fruit. Straw which has heretofore been useless, only as manure, sells to the Government at $20 per ton; and every article of forage or provision meets a ready cash sale; the lumbermen have had a golden harvest, furnishing lumber for building the quarters, hutting the Army and erecting storehouses. The adobe makers, masons, plasterers, carpenters and laborers are all getting their share of the shining gold. (George A. Smith to T.B.H. Stenhouse, 2 November 1858, Great Salt Lake City, Utah, Historian's Office, Letterpress Copybook, vol. 1)

See also Moorman, *Camp Floyd and the Mormons*, 56–58.

15. Arthur Barney, Journal, 13.
16. *Utah and the Mormons. Speech of Hon. John Cradlebaugh of Nevada on the Admission of Utah as a State Delivered in the House of Representatives, February 7, 1868* (Washington, D.C.: L. Towers & Co., 1863), 45–61, 65–66. See also Charles S. Peterson, "A Historical Analysis of Territorial Government in Utah under Alfred Cumming, 1857–1861" (master's thesis, Brigham Young University, 1958), 143–154.

For a brief but balanced view on the Potter-Parrish killings see Hubert Howe Bancroft, *History of Utah* (San Francisco: The History Company, 1890), 563–564 fn. See also Mary J. Chase Finley, *A History of Springville [Utah]*, (Springville, Utah: Art City Publishing, [ca. 1989]), 29–30, and David L. Bigler, *Forgotten Kingdom: The*

Mormon Theocracy in the American West, 1847–1896 (Spokane, Washington: Arthur H. Clark Company, 1998), 189–196.

17. Juanita Brooks infers that Lewis Barney's brother Henry may have been involved in the massacre by designating him as a receiver of booty from the murdered emigrants. Brooks, *The Mountain Meadows Massacre* (Norman, Oklahoma: University of Oklahoma Press, 1974), 151–152, 170. Henry moved to Harmony, Utah, apparently incident to a call to the Southern Indian Mission in the mid-1850s. There Henry became a member of the ward bishopric, served as a selectman, and developed a solid relationship with John D. Lee. Apparently because of his close association with Lee, Brooks implicates him in the killings. However, the $520 of booty she listed for 20 November 1857 is likely the money—$520 being the exact amount—he received from his service to the Indians reported on 4 August 1857. Brigham Young, Papers, Church Archives. Also, Henry Barney's name does not appear on the list by John D. Lee of fellow participants which Lee prepared for his defense during trial for the massacre. And in Charles Kelly's editing of John D. Lee's journal, Kelly notes Lee's meeting with several men on 11 May 1859 whom Lee cryptically refers to by initials and otherwise while he forthrightly mentions "Bro. Barney" without trying to mask his identity. Kelly suggests the cryptography is because the initials protect the identity of those who participated with Lee in the massacre. John D. Lee, *Journals of John D. Lee, 1846–1847 and 1859*, Charles Kelly, ed. (Salt Lake City: University of Utah Press, 1984), 204.
18. Non-Mormon superintendent of Indian affairs for Utah Territory, Jacob Forney, in his August 1859 report to his Washington superiors stated, "I fear, and I regret to say it, that with certain parties here there is a greater anxiety to connect Brigham Young and other church dignitaries with every criminal offense, than diligent endeavor to punish the actual perpetrators of the crime." Quoted in Whitney, *History of Utah*, 1:709–710.
19. Edward W. Tullidge, *History of Salt Lake City*, 2 vols. (Salt Lake City: Star Printing Company, 1886), 1:227. James Pace, one of the grand jurors, said, "In 1859 I was called as a Grand Juror to Provo, in the famous Cradlebaugh Court, and after being harangued there for near a month was discharged and returned to my own business at home." James Pace, Autobiographical sketch [ca. 1861], Church Archives.
20. Judiciary, Proceedings of Judge Cradlebaugh's Court, March–April 1859, Brigham Young, Papers, Administrative Papers, Church Archives. For an overview of Cradlebaugh's term in Utah see Bigler, *Forgotten Kingdom*, 189–196.
21. Furniss, *The Mormon Conflict*, 216–217.
22. Roberts, *Comprehensive History of the Church*, 4:507–509.
23. Journal History, 25 April 1859.
24. Quoted in Langley, *To Utah with the Dragoons*, 101.
25. The Church Historian's Office staff on 22 April 1859 reported "the rumors of one day," which included one church official in Salt Lake City being followed at night, a regiment of 1,000 on their way to Utah to punish local Indians who gave "their women the clap last year," a company from Arkansas and Missouri on their way to Iron County "to use up the folks there," three regiments from Camp Floyd marching on Salt Lake City after the confessions of Mormons "who had ropes put round their necks and hung until they made confession that the Mountain Meadow Massacre was perpetrated under orders of Gov. Young," fifty soldiers marching on Springville with warrants for perpetrators of the Parrish-Potter murders, and that Judge Cradlebaugh, with "3 or 400 dragoons started yesterday for Iron County to make arrests of the men charged with participating in the Mountain Meadow Massacre." Historian's Office Journal.
26. Journal History, 18–24 April 1859.
27. Lewis Barney, Autobiography 1, 81.

28. G[arland] Hurt to P. K. Dotson, 1 May 1859, Spanish Fork Indian Reservation, Adjunct Generals Office, Army Headquarters, War Department, Letters Received, 1859–1861, National Archives, Records of the War Department, U.S. Army Commands. War Department, Papers on Camp Floyd, Department of Utah, 1857–1861, vol. II, hereafter Adjunct Generals Office Records. Microfilm copy in Utah State Historical Society. I express my thanks to Polly Aird for referring me to this item.
29. G[arland] Hurt to [unidentified], 2 May 1859, Spanish Fork Indian Reservation, Adjunct Generals Office Records.
30. Lewis Barney, Autobiography 1, 81.
31. George Mayer, Reminiscence and diary, 1853 Jan.–1896 Apr., Church Archives.
32. Journal History, 27 April 1859.
33. Journal History, 14, 16 May 1859.
34. John Jacques to George Q. Cannon, 18 November 1859, Salt Lake City, Historian's Office, Letterpress Copybook, vol. 1. Others in Spanish Fork became discouraged. Thomas D. Evans wrote, "I became discouraged farming. I sold my farm and built a little store and went into the Mercantile business." Thomas D. Evans, Autobiography [n.d.], typescript, 11, Church Archives.
35. A report by Garland Hurt in March 1859 stated the population of Spanish Fork was nearly 2,000, though this figure is surely inflated. He also stated the town had one flouring mill and about 2,000 acres of land in cultivation. Garland Hurt to J. H. Simpson, 5 March 1859, Salt Lake City, Utah Territory, in J. H. Simpson, *Report of Explorations across the Great Basin of the Territory of Utah for a Direct Wagon-Route from Camp Floyd to Genoa, in Carson Valley in 1859* (Reno, Nevada: University of Nevada Press, 1983, first published in 1876), 453.
36. Simpson, *Report of Explorations across the Great Basin*, 453.
37. Hartley, *My Best for the Kingdom*, 345–346.
38. Lewis Barney, Autobiography 1, 81–82.
39. Barney's son Joseph Smith Barney was ordained a priest in the Spanish Fork Ward on 24 September 1859. Spanish Fork Ward, Aaronic Priesthood Minutes, Church Archives. Lewis Barney, writing from Spanish Fork on 3 June 1860, described the status of two quorum members to leaders of the Eighteenth Quorum of Seventies, of which he was a part, in Salt Lake City, Utah. Seventies Quorums, 18th Quorum, 1844–1975, Church Archives. Barney also bore his testimony at a church meeting in Spanish Fork on 23 September 1860. Spanish Fork Ward, Genealogical and minutes book, 1859–1869, Church Archives.

    Lewis's brothers John, Jeff, and Benjamin also stayed in the western part of Spanish Fork, eventually renamed Lake Shore, Benjamin until 1873 and John for the rest of his life. Barney, "Benjamin Franklin and Caroline (Beard) Barney," 4.
40. Springville Ward, Manuscript History, Church Archives; Jenson, *Encyclopedic History of the Church*, 830.
41. Johnson, *Brief History of Springville*, 40–41; Stout, *Diary*, 2:624, 690–694, 698; Roberts, *Comprehensive History of the Church*, 4:494–497.
42. Noah Packard, *A Synopsis of the Life and Travels of Noah Packard, Written by Himself* (Salt Lake City: n.p., ca. 1972), 1–14; Johnson, *Brief History of Springville*, 45.
43. Johnson, *Brief History of Springville*, 48–49, 54.
44. Journal History, 20 April 1859.
45. Ibid.; "Sketches of my grandfather's life," 8–9, Church Archives. Springville's population in 1860 numbered 1,357. Jenson, *Encyclopedic History of the Church*, 83. Garland Hurt's 1859 report to J. H. Simpson showed the community having "2 flouring-mills, 1 saw-mill, 1 shingle and lathing machine, and about 2,600 acres of land in cultivation." He also stated that "the tragical murder of Potter and the two

Parishes, in the spring of 1857, must ever cleave like bird-lime to its history." Simpson, *Report of Explorations Across the Great Basin*, 453.

46. Johnson, *Brief History of Springville*, 57–58.
47. Springville Ward, Manuscript History.
48. Ibid.; Johnson, *Brief History of Springville*, 57–59.
49. Lewis Barney, Autobiography 1, 82.
50. Preston, *Genealogy of the Barney Family*, 348.
51. David was born 10 September 1861. Monroe Ward, Record of Members, Church Archives.

Chapter 15

1. Seventies Quorum Records, Fiftieth Quorum, 10 March 1861; Doctrine and Covenants, Section 87:2, 6.
2. Maps of Utah roads and settlements, 1863, Church Archives. Toward the end of 1863 a road from Fairview north "over the Divide and far down Spanish Fork Creek" was nearly completed, making the transit from Utah Valley to Sanpete Valley more direct. "News from home," *Millennial Star* 25, no. 42 (17 October 1863): 667.
3. The 1860 census for Springtown shows Charles, Deborah, and William Barney, with $150 in real estate and $100 personal property. Also in Springtown were forty-one-year-old Walter Barney, his wife Susan, with their three children, having $300 in real estate and $600 personal property. Walter had twelve acres of improved land, horses, two cows, four oxen, three other cattle, twelve sheep, and two swine. It is not known what happened to Walter's wealth between 1850 and 1860 but it diminished considerably.

   Benjamin and Priscilla Barney had one child with eight improved acres, a farm valued at $60, two cows, and one ox worth $75. Lewis Barney and his family are not found in the 1860 Utah territorial census. Utah Territory, Census Schedules, 1850, 1860, 1870.
4. *History of Sanpete and Emery Counties, Utah* (Ogden, Utah: W. H. Lever, 1898), 11.
5. Ibid., 17, 20; Cindy Rice, "Spring City: A Look at a Nineteenth-Century Mormon Village," *Utah Historical Quarterly* 43, no. 3 (summer 1975); Jenson, *Encyclopedic History of the Church*, 826.
6. An exhaustive appraisal of Spring City beginnings is found in Michael Scott Raber, "Religious Polity and Local Production: The Origins of a Mormon Town" (Ph.D. diss., Yale University, 1978).

   For a brief overview of Springtown (Spring City) beginnings see Albert C. T. Antrei and Allen D. Roberts, A *History of Sanpete County [Utah]* (Salt Lake City: Utah State Historical Society and Sanpete County Commission, 1999), 403–410.
7. William Young Black, Letters, 1855–1874, Church Archives; Brigham Young to William Black, 12 July 1859, Great Salt Lake City, Utah, Brigham Young, Papers, Outgoing Correspondence.
8. Rice, "Spring City," 262.
9. "The Diary of Reddick N. Allred" in Carter, *Treasures of Pioneer History*, 5:348; Kaye C. Watson, *Life under the Horseshoe: A History of Spring City* (Spring City, Utah: Spring City Daughters of Utah Pioneers, 1987), 19.
10. "The Journal of Joseph Smith Black," in Carter, *Our Pioneer Heritage*, 10:316, states that Charles and his family moved to Springtown in 1859. Watson, *Life under the Horseshoe*, 265, provides a list of the 1859 settlers in Springtown but does not include Charles Barney.

11. Preston, *Genealogy of the Barney Family*, 353; Diary of Joseph Smith Black, typescript, 12–13, 35–36, Special Collections, Harold B. Lee Library, Brigham Young University, Provo, Utah.
12. William Black to Brigham Young, 10 February 1860, Springtown, Utah, Brigham Young, Papers, Incoming Correspondence, Church Archives.
13. Reddick N. Allred to Brigham Young, 4 September 1859, Nephi, Utah, Brigham Young, Papers, Incoming Correspondence.
14. William Black to Brigham Young, 7 February 1861, Springtown, Utah, Brigham Young, Papers, Incoming Correspondence.
15. Rice, "Spring City," 261–264.
16. While Lewis probably relocated to Springtown in late 1861 or early 1862, others of his immediate family apparently did not move until late 1862 or early 1863. Ward records for early 1863 describe James Henry and Joseph Smith Barney's initial affiliation with the Springtown Ward. Spring City Ward, Priesthood Minutes, 23 January, 28 February 1863, Church Archives. Also, Spanish Fork Ward priesthood minutes for 3 February 1863 state, "Recommends were voted to Walter T. and William H. [S.] Barney who had removed to Springtown, San Pete." Spanish Fork Ward, Aaronic Priesthood Minutes, Church Archives.
17. Lewis Barney, Autobiography 1, 83.
18. Raber, "Origins of a Mormon Town," 182. "Louis [Lewis] Barney built the first saw mill [in Spring City]. It was located where our power plant dam now stands. Sawdust signs still remain." Daughters of Utah Pioneers, Sanpete County Camp, *These . . . Our Fathers: A Centennial History of Sanpete County, 1849–1947* (Springville, Utah: Art City Publishing Co., 1947), 61.
19. Arthur Barney, Journal, 13–14.
20. Lewis Barney, Autobiography 1, 83–84.
21. Isaac Potter, Sketch, United States, Works Progress Administration, Collection, Utah State Historical Society; Ancestral File, Family History Library.
22. Joseph Garlic Shepherd, ca. 1930, quoted in Bliss Jarvis Brimley, "History of Moses Trader Shepherd," *Shepherd Family Organization Newsletter* (June 1978): 5.
23. "Journal and Diary of Albert King Thurber" in Carter, *Treasures of Pioneer History*, 3:303; Albert King Thurber, Diary, transcribed by Charles Kelly, 1952, Utah State Historical Society, Salt Lake City, Utah.
24. *Deseret News*, 8 April 1863.
25. *Deseret News*, 11 September 1867. See also "Journal and Diary of Albert King Thurber," 302–303. John Peterson describes Potter's collusion with Black Hawk's raiders and the circumstances of his death in *Utah's Black Hawk War*, 38, 205–207, 301, 326, 342–347.
26. With Lewis in his mid-fifties, on 8 November 1863 Elizabeth Barney bore a daughter, Sarah Emeline. Sarah Emeline's birth is recorded as having taken place in Spanish Fork, Utah, meaning that perhaps Elizabeth was living there or visiting with her sister Caroline, Benjamin's wife, still living in Spanish Fork. Monroe Ward, Record of Members.
27. Orson Hyde, *Speech of Elder Orson Hyde Delivered before the High Priests Quorum in Nauvoo, April 27th, 1845* (City of Joseph [Nauvoo], Illinois: John Taylor, 1845), 4.
28. Mulder, *Homeward to Zion*, 215.
29. William G. Hartley, "Common People: Church Activity during the Brigham Young Era," in Walker and Dant, *Nearly Everything Imaginable*, 252–254.
30. Thomas G. Alexander, *Mormonism in Transition: A History of the Latter-day Saints, 1890–1930* (Urbana, Illinois: University of Illinois Press, 1986), 108–109, 114; Ronald W. Walker, "'Going to Meeting' in Salt Lake City's Thirteenth Ward, 1849–1881: A Microanalysis," in Davis Bitton and Maureen Ursenbach Beecher, eds., *New Views of Mormon History: A Collection of Essays in Honor of Leonard J. Arrington* (Salt Lake City: University of Utah Press, 1987), 154.

31. John Wickliff Rigdon, son of former First Presidency member Sidney Rigdon, who visited Utah about 1865 before becoming a Mormon himself, wrote, "While I was at Utah I saw a great many things among the members of the Mormon church that I did not like. . . . They did not preach the Gospel when they went to church but would tell about drawing wood from the Kanyons, How to raise wheat & corn, not a word was said about the Gospel." John Wickliff Rigdon, Lecture on the early history of the Mormon Church, 1906, 84, Church Archives. (My thanks to Mark Ashurst-McGee for referring me to this item.) While Rigdon's generalization about the absence of preaching about Jesus' gospel is in error, given the preponderant evidence to the contrary, it does indicate that attention was paid to temporal matters in a religious context.
32. Spring City Ward, Priesthood Minutes.
33. The sole exception to this generalization is the call of Walter T. Barney to the Gila River in southern Arizona in the 1880s which will be discussed later.
34. "Letters Descriptive of President Young's Visit to the Southern Settlements," *Millennial Star* 25, no. 27 (4 July 1863): 421.
35. Lewis Barney, Autobiography 1, 85.
36. "From the Journal of Oluf Christian Larsen" in Carter, *Treasures of Pioneer History*, 6:204.
37. Sevier Stake, General Minutes, vol. 1, 13–15, Church Archives. The reconnaissance party, near present-day Gunnison, stumbled upon Barney Ward. Ward, a mountain man who had become a Mormon and who had been familiar with the region for about thirty years, encouraged them and gave a glittering report of the valley. Hafen, "Elijah Barney Ward," in LeRoy R. Hafen, ed., *The Mountain Men and the Fur Trade of the West*, 10 vols. (Glendale, California: Arthur H. Clark Company, 1969), 7:343–351.
38. Circleville Ward, Manuscript History, Church Archives.
39. Lewis Barney, Autobiography 1, 85–86.
40. "Journal of Oluf Christian Larsen," 6:204–205.
41. The Monroe Ward historical record states, "David Griffith and another arrived on the present site of Monroe, Feb. 20, 1864," suggesting Griffith was the first to settle the townsite. Monroe Ward, Manuscript History, Church Archives. In contrast, the Sevier Stake Manuscript History indicates that there was an enterprise of settlement at least a month before Allred's party scrutinized Sevier Valley and that Richfield was initially settled by Albert Lewis and eight or ten others on 6 January 1864. The record also states that Monroe was settled two days later on 8 January by Moses Gifford and Walter Jones with about twenty others. Sevier Stake, Manuscript History, Church Archives. The discrepancy of the precise time of the valley's settlement and of what was to become Monroe, Utah, will likely remain unresolved.
42. "Journal of Oluf Christian Larsen," 6:204–205.
43. Lewis Barney, Autobiography 1, 86.
44. "Journal of Oluf Christian Larsen," 6:204–205.
45. Lewis Barney, Autobiography 1, 86. "Among the first settlers of Monroe who located there in 1864 the following are remembered: . . . Walter and Lewis Barney, [and twenty-two others who were identified]. Most of these brethren had families with them. Perhaps as many as forty families spent the winter of 1864–1865 in Alma [Monroe]." Monroe Ward, Manuscript History.
46. Lewis Barney, Autobiography 1, 86. The first townsite, surveyed by Fox, extended four blocks north and south and three blocks east and west. The pioneers "drew lots" for their city blocks. Irvin L. Warnock, ed. and comp., *Thru the Years: Sevier County Centennial History* (Springville, Utah: Sevier County Centennial Committee, 1947), 226.
47. Lewis Barney, Autobiography 1, 86; Monroe Ward, Manuscript History; *Deseret News*, 15 June 1864.

48. Lewis Barney, Autobiography 1, 86–87. "These first settlers of Alma were very busy putting in crops and making other improvements in the spring and early part of the summer of 1864. That much being done a number of the settlers returned temporarily to their former homes." Monroe Ward, Manuscript History.
49. Ibid. Warnock, *Thru the Years*, 225.
50. Monroe Ward, Manuscript History.
51. Lewis Barney, Autobiography 1, 87.
52. Arthur Barney, Journal, 26.
53. Lewis Barney, Autobiography 1, 87.
54. The account of the first settlement of Circle Valley, found in the Church Archives, states that the first to gather to the area left their former residences in February–March 1864 and

> traveled through the Sevier country until they reached City Creek or the place where Junction now is located. There they stopped several days in camp while some of the brethren explored the surrounding country. They finally concluded to make their settlement in Circle Valley, as that locality seemed to possess the best facilities for a settlement. Wm. J. Allred was the appointed leader of the company. (Circleville Ward, Manuscript History)

55. Lewis Barney, Autobiography 1, 87. "Some of the settlers, after passing through the experiences of the spring and summer, got so discouraged in the fall that they left the settlement to return no more." Circleville Ward, Manuscript History.
56. Lewis Barney, Autobiography 1, 87–88.
57. Ibid., 88.
58. Index to the War of 1812 Pension Application Files, National Archives, Washington, D.C.; Nolan and Kaye Barney, "The Life of Charles Barney," 1980, typescript, in possession of author courtesy of Nolan Barney.
59. Lewis Barney, Autobiography 1, 88; Monroe Ward, Manuscript History; Orson Hyde to Brigham Young, 19 November 1865, Springtown, Utah, Brigham Young, Papers, Incoming Correspondence. Allred was called to a mission in Utah's Dixie.

Chapter 16

1. Gustive Larson estimates that there were less than 20,000 Native Americans in Utah "when white men made their first appearance." He uses University of Utah historian Andrew Neff's figure of 15,000 for 1861. Gustive O. Larson, *Outline History of Utah and the Mormons* (Salt Lake City: Deseret Book Company, 1965), 153. More recently geographer Klaus Gurgel has suggested that there were but 6,000 Indians in Utah at mid-century. Wahlquist, *Atlas of Utah*, 121.
2. The definitive discussion of the Black Hawk War is John A. Peterson's, *Utah's Black Hawk War*. Other treatments include Carlton Culmsee, *Utah's Black Hawk War* (Logan, Utah: Utah State University Press, 1973) and Gottfredson, *History of Indian Depredations in Utah.*
3. Peterson, *Utah's Black Hawk War*, 6.
4. Ibid., 2.
5. Ibid., 18–19.
6. Lewis Barney, Autobiography 1, 88. "Early in 1865 the settlers of Alma built a fort enclosing lot 1, or the southwest quarter of block 53. A corral for stock was built on the northeast quarter and a stockyard on the west half of the same block. This fort was built of log houses on the three sides while a rock wall, 10 feet high, was built on the east side. . . . The fort was built in nine days." Monroe Ward, Manuscript History.

7. Lewis Barney, Autobiography 1, 84.
8. Ibid., 84.
9. Peterson, *Utah's Black Hawk War*, 168–171.
10. Lewis Barney, Autobiography 1, 84–85.
11. Journal History, 13 September 1865.
12. Ibid.
13. "Journal of Oluf Christian Larson," 6:206, 212.
14. Linda King Newell, *A History of Piute County [Utah]* (Salt Lake City: Utah State Historical Society and Piute County Commission, 1999), 76.
15. "Journal of Oluf Christian Larsen," 6:212; Circleville Ward, Manuscript History; Gottfredson, *History of Indian Depredations*, 176–179; Peterson, *Utah's Black Hawk War*, 189–190; Newell, *History of Piute County*, 76–79.
16. Lewis Barney, Autobiography 1, 91.
17. Eliza M. Munson, "Questions concerning Black Hawk War Answered by Eliza M. Munson," Utah State Historical Society. My thanks to John A. Peterson for referring me to this source. See also Eliza Mariah Allred Munson, Autobiographical sketch, ca. 1930, Church Archives.
18. Circleville Ward, Manuscript History; Albert Winkler, "The Circleville Massacre: A Brutal Incident in Utah's Black Hawk War," *Utah Historical Quarterly* 55, no. 1 (winter 1987): 10; Newell, *History of Piute County*, 79. Arthur, Orson's half-brother of the same age, later wrote,

    > In the fall [a few years after Orson's death] there was a band of Indians come and camped near the sawmill [on Glenwood Mountain where Arthur had been working], they were on a buckskin hunt. There was one in the bunch known as the White Horse Chief [also known as Tamaritz], and it was reported that White Horse was the Indian that killed my brother Orson at Circleville during the Black Hawk War. I said that if I ever got the chance I would kill White Horse in revenge, although this was a long time after the war. So I went to the Indian's camp and made arrangements with the White Horse chief to go hunting with him next morning. But during the night it snowed about 6 inches of new snow. Next morning here comes my partner for the deer hunt, I was up against a hard proposition.

    Given that he could be tracked in the snow, Arthur decided against killing Tamaritz. "I never got a chance to go hunting with White Horse again," he said. "But White Horse chief ought to thank the Lord for sending the snow. I am sure thankful that our hunt terminated as it did, because that would have been murder in the first degree, as a peace treaty had been signed a long time before." Arthur Barney, Journal, 31–32. Tamaritz, the White Horse Chief, was, indeed, one of the hostiles involved in the Circleville Raid. Peterson, *Utah's Black Hawk War*, 189, 272–276.
19. Peterson, *Utah's Black Hawk War*, 190.
20. Lewis Barney, Autobiography 1, 88–89.
21. Ibid., 89.
22. George A. Smith, Papers, Journals, 25 March 1866.
23. Lewis Barney, Autobiography 1, 89–90.
24. Ibid., 90. Gottfredson, *History of Indian Depredations in Utah*, 193, presents a similar story with a little variation. See also the Monroe Ward, Manuscript History, and Wilford and Mildred Murdock, *Monroe, Utah: Its First One Hundred Years, 1864–1964* (Monroe, Utah: Monroe Centennial Committee and Monroe City, 1964), 16.
25. Lewis Barney, Autobiography 1, 90. "By the year, 1866, Indian trouble had become so serious that the people of Alma (Monroe) moved to Richfield for safety, alter-

nating a guard [at Alma], week by week, to watch the growing crops." Warnock, *Thru the Years*, 226.

26. Peterson, *Utah's Black Hawk War*, 247.
27. Reddick N. Allred to William Seely, 27 April 1866, in Andrew Madsen, Autobiographical sketch, ca. 1908, typescript, 24–25, Church Archives.
28. Peterson, *The Black Hawk War*, 245–246.
29. Allred to Seely, 27 April 1866.
30. "Journal of Oluf Christian Larsen," 6:213–214; Peterson, *The Black Hawk War*, 246. Newell, in *History of Piute County*, 91, suggests as many as twenty-five Indians were killed.
31. Peterson, *The Black Hawk War*, 247.
32. Winkler, "The Circleville Massacre," 4–21. See also Newell, *History of Piute County*, 82–87, where Newell identifies the Indians as Piutes.

    A family story by one of Walter T. Barney's grandchildren states that "while Walter Turner Barney was off guard for dinner some of the Indians began to revolt and the settlers had all the Indians killed when he got back." Florence Barney Frazier, "Life's History of my grandfather Walter Turner Barney," photocopy in possession of author. Another oral family story suggests that for revenge Lewis Barney was party to the Circleville Massacre. Circumstantially, however, Lewis could not have been there on the day of the killings due to his arrival in Alma at the same time the Indians were killed.
33. Lewis Barney, Autobiography 1, 90.
34. Sevier Stake, General Minutes, vol. 1, 1.
35. Lewis Barney, Autobiography 1, 90–91. "About 40 families were at that time living at Circleville. The vacation of the settlement took place June 20, 1866, most of them going north to Sevier and Sanpete counties, while a few crossed the mountains on the west to Beaver and other places leaving their fields of promising grain behind unharvested." Circleville Ward, Manuscript History.
36. Lewis Barney, Autobiography 1, 91.
37. Warnock, *Thru the Years*, 227.
38. Lewis Barney, Autobiography 1, 91. See also Watson, *Life under the Horseshoe*, 15.
39. Arthur Barney, Journal, 18–19.
40. Lewis Barney, Autobiography 1, 91.
41. Arthur Barney, Journal, 17–18.
42. John Wilson to George Swindle, 10 March 1868, Springville, Utah, in Sketch of George and Mary Magdalena Swindle, Church Archives; Murdock and Murdock, *Monroe, Utah*, 18; Warnock, *Thru the Years*, 227; Monroe Ward, Manuscript History; and Gottfredson, *Indian Depredations in Utah*, 279–284.
43. Lewis Barney, Autobiography 1, 91–92. Spring City Ward, Manuscript History, Church Archives, reported their "Crops [were] destroyed by grasshoppers." Salt Lake City was hit by the grasshoppers on 11 May 1868. See also Bitton and Wilcox, "Pestiferous Ironclads."
44. Lewis Barney, Autobiography 1, 92.
45. Orson Hyde to Brigham Young, 27 May 1868, Springtown, Utah, Brigham Young, Papers, Incoming Correspondence.
46. Stephen E. Ambrose, *Nothing Like It in the World: The Men Who Built the Transcontinental Railroad, 1863–1869* (New York: Simon & Schuster, 2000), 17.
47. Guelzo, *Abraham Lincoln*, 375.
48. Ambrose, *Nothing Like It in the World*, 279; John J. Stewart, "The Railroad Builder," in Black and Porter, *Lion of the Lord*, 263–264.
49. Sherman quoted in Charles Edgar Ames, *Pioneering the Union Pacific: A Reappraisal of the Builders of the Railroad* (New York: Appleton-Century-Crofts, 1969), 222.
50. Robert G. Athearn, *Union Pacific Country* (Chicago: Rand McNally & Company, 1971), 90; Ambrose, *Nothing Like It in the World*, 282–283.

51. Ibid., 283.
52. Ibid., 285; *Deseret News*, 27 May 1868; Athearn, *Union Pacific Country*, 90–91.
53. John W. Young to Brethren composing the construction Camp, 28 December 1869, John W. Young, Papers, Church Archives.
54. Peterson, *Utah's Black Hawk War*, 350.
55. Hyde to Young, 27 May 1868; *Deseret News*, 27 May 1868. Young, too, was concerned about the manpower needs for the railroad at the expense of the agrarian economy of the Saints. The emigration schedule for that season was calculated to get as many of the immigrants as possible in a position to assist the project. It did not hurt that an arrangement had been made that Mormon emigrants who hired on would receive free transportation from Omaha, Nebraska, to the Utah mountains. Athearn, *Union Pacific Country*, 91.
56. Lewis Barney, Autobiography 1, 92. Moses Gifford, a Missourian then living in Springtown, was born in 1833. Thirty-one-year-old George Robison, of Ephraim, was a Delaware native. Young John Zabriskie born in 1845 in Lee County, Iowa, just before the Mormon exodus to the West, was a nephew of Walter Barney. Arthur Barney's account of their railroad work significantly amplifies his father's story of the venture. Arthur Barney, Journal, 19–23.
57. Athearn, *Union Pacific Country*, 91. Stewart sets the figure at 3,000 Saints involved in the project. Stewart, "The Railroad Builder," 271.
58. Clarence A. Reeder, "The History of Utah's Railroads, 1869–1883," (Ph.D. diss., University of Utah, 1970), 32.
59. Lewis Barney, Autobiography 1, 92. Even Arthur found useful work: "As I was not old enough to work on the grade, father hired me out to pack water from the river upon the grade for the men to drink." Arthur Barney, Journal, 20.
60. *Deseret News*, 12 August 1868.
61. Lewis Barney, Autobiography 1, 92.
62. Ibid., 92–93. Arthur described his father's enterprise in producing railroad ties:

> Father took a contract to cut 1,600 ties for which he received a yoke of oxen. All we had to do was to cut these ties down and top them off at the top where the tree was big enough to make a tie. We paid for these oxen in 8 days. So we went farther up the canyon where the timber was larger, and father took a contract hewing square timber for bridges along the railroad. We worked scoring and hewing this bridge timber for a month. (Arthur Barney, Journal, 20–21)

63. Lewis Barney, Autobiography 1, 93; Perkins and Gillen, Interview, 8. Harriet Viola Barney, born 18 September 1867, was the eighth child born to Lewis and Elizabeth. Preston, *Genealogy of the Barney Family*, 348.
64. Lewis Barney, Autobiography 1, 93. Arthur Barney further writes, "Here we built a cabin and lived in dry canyon all winter gitting out ties and bridge timber. Father could average a dollar an hour working in the timber, but as I was only a boy I could make about 3 or 4 dollars a day." Arthur Barney, Journal, 21.

    Lewis, probably because he subcontracted his work, was one of the fortunate ones. Many of the Mormon workers that summer of 1868 were unpaid for their work until much later. The Union Pacific, running short on funds, reneged on payment to the Saints and Brigham Young's own advances to the workers were insufficient. Athearn, *Union Pacific Country*, 95.
65. Reeder, "History of Utah's Railroads," 42.
66. Ambrose, *Nothing Like It in the World*, 285–286; Athearn, *Union Pacific Country*, 94; Poll, et al., *Utah's History*, 219.
67. Lewis Barney, Autobiography 1, 93–94.
68. Ibid., 94.

69. Bancroft, *History of Utah*, 754; Reeder, "History of Utah's Railroads," 32–33.
70. Lewis Barney, Autobiography 1, 94.
71. Ibid.; Ninth Census of the United States, 1870, National Archives, Washington, D.C.
72. Ninth Census. Lewis was conspicuously absent from the 1870 Utah agricultural census in contrast to his brothers and sons whose holdings were all enumerated. Utah Territory, census schedules, 1850, 1860, 1870.
73. It was not until 1872 when U.S. troops were called in to quell hostile Indian activity that the last vestiges of the Black Hawk War were played out. Peterson, *Utah's Black Hawk War*, 367–369.

Chapter 17

1. James Henry Barney married Emily Tolton in Ephraim, Utah, on 4 March 1866. Lula Tolton Tanner, *That Their Children May Know: A Record of the Descendants of Edward Tolton* (n.p.: n.d.), 18; Preston, *Genealogy of the Barney Family*, 555. Joseph Smith Barney married Ormanda Azelia Rogers Oviatt on 4 November 1866. Preston, *Genealogy of the Barney Family*, 556. Evidence suggests that Lewis's three oldest sons made brief and unsuccessful efforts to relocate near their father in the 1860s and 1870s.
2. Leavitt Christensen, *Birth of Kanosh* (n.p.: J-Mart Publishing, ca. 1997), 19–21, 97–98.
3. Martha Sonntag Bradley, *A History of Beaver County [Utah]* (Salt Lake City: Utah State Historical Society and Beaver County Commission, 1999), 51–53, 77, 82–83, 91, 93.
4. Lyman and Newell, *A History of Millard County*, 17.
5. Chavez and Warner, *The Dominguez-Escalante Journal*, 67.
6. Edward A. Geary, *The Proper Edge of the Sky: The High Plateau Country of Utah* (Salt Lake City: University of Utah Press, 1992), 40.
7. Quoted in Geary, *Proper Edge of the Sky*, 36. George A. Smith, leading the southbound Iron Mission missionaries in January 1851, found an abandoned Indian village at Corn Creek where Kanosh is now located. He recorded "they had planted about 2 acres of corn, wheat, and beans, which from the stalks left on the ground, must have grown exceedingly fine. shows a very rich soil." He summarized that "this country is capable of sustaining a very extensive settlement." George A. Smith, Papers, Journal, 2 January 1851.
8. Lyman and Newell, *History of Millard County*, 37, 39, 114–115, 124. A fraction of the tribe later returned to their Corn Creek homeland.
9. A history of Kanosh, Utah, acknowledges both Lewis and Betsey as among the earliest residents of the settlement. Christensen, *Birth of Kanosh*, 1–3, 19–21, 97–98. See also Stella H. Day and Sebrina C. Ekins, *Milestones of Millard: 100 Years of Millard County* (Springville, Utah: Art City Publishing Co., 1951), 342–343.
10. During the 1860s James Henry was a "down and back" volunteer transporting Saints from the Missouri River Valley to Utah in both 1866 and 1867. Christensen, *Birth of Kanosh*, 97–98; Preston, *Genealogy of the Barney Family*, 555.
11. Sevier Stake, General Minutes, vol. 1, 2.
12. Lewis Barney, Autobiography 1, 94.
13. Arthur Barney, Journal, 23.
14. Lewis Barney, Autobiography 1, 94; Monroe Ward, Manuscript History.
15. Irvin L. Warnock and Lexia D. Warnock, comps. and eds., *Our Own Sevier: A Comprehensive, Centennial Volume, Sevier County, Utah, 1865–1965* (Richfield, Utah: Sevier County Commissioners, 1965), 4.

Jedediah Strong Smith in September 1826 was the first white man to identify his visit to the Sevier Valley, though he left little information about the area. Traveling southward to California after the mountain man rendezvous in northern Utah's Cache Valley, he entered Sevier Valley following it from north to south before exiting the valley to the west through Clear Creek Canyon. He called the Sevier River—"60 yds wide [of] muddy water"—the Ashley, to honor his friend, William Henry Ashley. Describing the valley's Indians as "rather above the midling size but in the mental scale lower than any I have yet seen," he stated their environ was a "valley being 6 or 8 miles wide and covered with Sedge and But little grass except along the river." Jedediah S. Smith, *The Southwest Expedition of Jedediah S. Smith: His Personal Account of the Journey to California, 1826–1827*, George R. Brooks, ed. (Lincoln, Nebraska: University of Nebraska Press, 1977), 48–50.

16. LeRoy R. and Ann W. Hafen, eds., *Old Spanish Trail, Santa Fe to Los Angeles: With Extracts from Contemporary Records and Including Diaries of Antonio Armijo and Orville Pratt* (Glendale, California: The Arthur H. Clarke Company, 1968), 341–342, 351–352.
17. William B. Smart and Donna T. Smart, eds., *Over the Rim: The Parley P. Pratt Exploring Expedition to Southern Utah, 1849–1850* (Logan, Utah: Utah State University Press, 1999), 47–55, 77; Rick J. Fish, "The Southern Utah Expedition of Parley P. Pratt, 1849–1850" (master's thesis, Brigham Young University, 1992), 64, 70–80.
18. *Deseret News*, 29 July 1872.
19. Monroe Ward, Manuscript History; Warnock and Warnock, *Our Own Sevier*, 330; *Deseret News*, 17 January 1872.
20. Sevier Stake, Manuscript History, Church Archives; Warnock and Warnock, *Our Own Sevier*, 369–270; Hunter, *Brigham Young the Colonizer*, 378–382.
21. Joseph Angell Young became the presiding ecclesiastical officer in Sevier Valley on 18 May 1872. When the Sevier Stake was organized on 24 May 1874 he was appointed stake president. Sevier Stake, Manuscript History.
22. Monroe Ward, Manuscript History. Of the function of Mormon Sunday Schools in Utah, "By the 1870s," writes William Hartley,

> two hundred Sunday Schools involved nearly fifteen thousand youth and adults. Sunday Schools created ward positions that Saints could be called to fill. For the first time, women and children participated directly in a Sabbath meeting as teachers and students, and many men became officers and teachers. Songs, prayers, scripture lessons, catechisms, and recitations were all part of the school. (Hartley, "Common People," 263)

On the revitalization of the Relief Society in Utah, Hartley has also written,

> For most LDS women, the Relief Society program was not reorganized until 1867, fully twenty years after the first Saints entered Utah. Therefore, for a full generation, women, most of whom did not attend sacrament meetings regularly, at best attended weeknight prayer meetings. For them, religion was concentrated on interactions at home and with neighbors rather than centered around formal, weekly church attendance. (Hartley, "Common People," 262)

23. Sevier Stake, Manuscript History.
24. *Deseret News*, 8 May 1872. See also 17 January, 5 July, 31 July, and 7 August 1872.
25. Arthur Barney, Journal, 23–24.
26. Arthur, now twenty, said that after his father departed, "there was nothing to do to occopy [*sic*] my time [so] I got into a little trouble." He and a chum tried their luck with the young ladies who returned to Alma that year. He and a girl who

worked "for an old danish lady" got carried away in animated conversation which "finely got to noisey" and "disturbed the old danish woman and out she come in her night clothes" and gave it to Arthur whom she mistook for the girl's previous suitor. Arthur supposed that when the former boyfriend came back she let him have it again even though he was innocent. Arthur Barney, Journal, 24–25.

27. Lewis Barney, Autobiography 1, 95; Arthur Barney, Journal, 24.
28. *Deseret News*, 17 January, 8 May, 17 July, and 21 August 1872.
29. Lewis Barney, Autobiography 1, 95. Making one's living from the earth was a complicated affair. Arthur Barney described the process of wheat retrieval:

> We got Uncle Ben to cut the wheat. In those days all grain was cut with a cradle, not the kind our mothers used for their babies, but a cradle made [for the] purpose to cut grain. They would take a cythe [*sic*] like you have seen them cut hay or brush; then they would make a frame to this snatch. [There] were four long crooked sticks fastened to this frame, and [you would] go out into a field of grain and start swinging the cradle. . . . The cradle leaves the grain in what we call a swath. Uncle Ben would make a swath, and father had an old wooden hand rake. he would rake the wheat up into bunches. I would follow up and tie these bunches into bundles. for a tie I took a handful of wheat and made a band around the bunch of wheat by twisting the heads together, then I would put this band around a bunch of wheat and draw the butt ends of this band, give it a twist and tuck the end of the band under the band, then you had a bundle. So you kept this up all day and when night comes if we have gone over two acres we have done a good days work. (Arthur Barney, Journal, 30)

30. The Diary of the City Council of Spring City, 1871–1886, Special Collections, Harold B. Lee Library, Brigham Young University. Barney's younger brother, William Street, who had emerged as one of the community leaders in Spring City, was later killed. Having been reappointed city assessor in the town on 5 April 1875, William was thrown from a horse just a month later and succumbed to his injuries. William's daughter, two-and-a-half-year-old Sarah Edna had passed away just three months previously. Charles's widow, Deborah, had been staying with her son William since the death of Charles ten years previously. The deaths had a particularly devastating effect on Lewis's in-laws who remained in Spring City. Tessie B. Pyper, comp., Spring City Cemetery Records, Family History Library; Diary of the City Council of Spring City, 1871–1886.
31. Arthur Barney, Journal, 26–27.
32. Charles S. Peterson, "'Book A—Levi Mathers Savage': The Look of Utah in 1873," *Utah Historical Quarterly* 41, no. 1 (winter 1973): 5–6; Poll, et al., *Utah's History*, 557, 687; Tenth Census of the United States, 1880, National Archives, Washington, D.C.
33. Sevier (Utah: County) Tax Assessment and Military Enlistment Records, 1873–1918, microfilm of MS, Church Archives, original MS in Sevier County, Recorder's Office, Richfield, Utah.
34. Incorporations, Sevier County, Recorder's Office, Richfield, Utah.
35. Kate B. Carter, ed., *An Enduring Legacy*, 12 vols. (Salt Lake City: Daughters of Utah Pioneers, 1982), 5:361; Murdock and Murdock, *Monroe, Utah*, 40.
36. Carter, *An Enduring Legacy*, 5:361.
37. Sevier Stake, General Minutes, 14 March 1874, vol. 1, 64.
38. Sevier Stake, General Minutes, 18 July 1874, vol. 1, 77 and 4 March 1876, vol. 1, 109; *Deseret News*, 11 March 1874; Murdock and Murdock, *Monroe, Utah*, 40. The *Deseret News* entry for 11 March 1874 identifies two teachers conducting the day

schools in Monroe, neither of whom were Barney, meaning he had by this time adopted the role of private educator which mostly characterized the rest of his teaching career.

39. Sevier Stake, General Minutes, 1 July 1875, vol. 1, 100.
40. Ibid., 23 October 1875, vol. 1, 105.
41. Sevier Stake, Manuscript History.
42. Charles S. Peterson, "The Limits of Learning in Pioneer Utah," *Journal of Mormon History* 10 (1983): 66–67.
43. Lewis Barney, Autobiography 1, 95; Sevier Stake, General Minutes, vol. 1, 16.
44. Sevier Stake, General Minutes, vol. 1, 31.
45. Lewis Barney, Autobiography 1, 95.
46. George Halliday to William B. Pace, August 1872, William Byram Pace, Collection, Church Archives.
47. Lewis Barney, Autobiography 1, 95. Johnson, in his early forties, was a Swedish convert to Mormonism. A Michael Johnson, though it is not demonstrable it is the Michael Johnson in question, while serving as a church missionary to Sweden, once laid his life on the line after being arrested in Stockholm and was eventually imprisoned in Malmo where he suffered due to his religious convictions. Upon his release he was banished to Copenhagen. Carter, *Heart Throbs of the West*, 2:310.
48. Utah Executive Record Books, 1850–1895, Book C, 584, Utah State Archives, Salt Lake City, Utah.
49. Corporations Register, Sevier County Recorder's Office, Richfield, Utah; Sevier Stake, Manuscript History, 8.
50. *Deseret News*, 14 January 1874.
51. Lewis Barney, Autobiography 1, 95–96. Barney described the result of the controversy:

    > The men not wishing to oppose their bishop very reluctantly went to work on the canal. After working 3 years, putting in 10,000 or 15,000 dollars, [and] finding it impractical, [the town] abandoned the work on the mammoth canal and went to work and enlarged the old canal which has so far [ca. 1880-1881] furnished a reasonable supply of water for all the land below it. (Lewis Barney, Autobiography 1, 96)

    Initially, the prospect of a municipal canal was used as a lure for potential settlers. *Deseret News*, 17 January, 1 May, and 5 July 1872
52. *Deseret News*, 14 January 1874.

Chapter 18

1. Arrington, et al., *Building the City of God* 136.
2. Ibid., 407–419.
3. Quoted in Arrington, *Great Basin Kingdom*, 323.
4. See also Acts 4:32–37, 4 Nephi 3 (Book of Mormon), and Moses 7:18 (Pearl of Great Price) for other scriptural precedents influencing the Latter-day Saints.
5. *Journal of Discourses*, 17:41, 43.
6. See Lyndon W. Cook, *Joseph Smith and the Law of Consecration* (Provo, Utah: Grandin Book Co., 1985).
7. Arrington, et al., *Building the City of God*, 136–143.
8. Arrrington, *Great Basin Kingdom*, 328.
9. Ibid., 328.
10. Richfield Ward, United Order Records, 1874–1881, 18 April 1874, 1, Church Archives.

11. Monroe Ward, Manuscript History; Richfield Ward, United Order Records.
12. Ibid., 33.
13. Lewis Barney, Autobiography 1, 96. A report to the *Deseret News* published 24 October 1874 stated that two-thirds of Monroe church members joined the United Order.
14. Monroe United Order, Minutes, 17 May 1874, Church Archives. In the United Orders' initial subscription, 174 Monroe residents joined, the Barneys being represented by James Henry, Mary, and Walter Barney. Richfield Ward, United Order Records, 35–38.
15. Monroe Ward, Historical Record, 21–24. Gifford, while remaining president of the Monroe Cooperative Mercantile Institution into 1875, had but a peripheral part to play in Monroe affairs thereafter. He and Michael Johnson were known thereafter as community dissenters. Apparently giving credence to Charles Darwin's claims regarding evolution popularized in 1859, when Gifford and Johnson moved south of town on Birch Creek the area became known thereafter as Monkeytown, playing on their apparent belief that man emerged from lesser mammals. Their dissent continued. In August 1877 Michael Johnson was the only candidate to oppose Sevier Stake president A. K. Thurber for the Utah territorial legislature. Thurber won 720 to 6. Monroe Ward, Historical Record; Nephi James Bates, Diary, 16 July 1879, Church Archives; Utah, Executive Record Books, 1850–1895, Book C, 183, Utah State Archives, Salt Lake City, Utah.
16. Lewis Barney, Autobiography 1, 97.
17. Sevier Stake, Manuscript History; Feramorz Y. Fox, "Experiment in Utopia: The United Order of Richfield, 1874–1877," *Utah Historical Quarterly* 32, no. 4 (fall 1964): 355–356; Arrington, et al., *Building the City of God*, 179. Not only was there reluctance to embrace the orders in some communities, there were even some at church headquarters who were less than enthusiastic about the new plan. Thomas G. Alexander, *Things in Heaven and Earth: The Life and Times of Wilford Woodruff, a Mormon Prophet* (Salt Lake City: Signature Books, 1993), 221–222.
18. Monroe Ward, Manuscript History. James Thompson Lisonbee was born 15 November 1829 in Pickens County, Alabama. He came to Utah in 1854, the year of his baptism into the Church of Jesus Christ. In 1871 he moved his family to Monroe. The following year they moved just north to Annabella. After a brief stay they moved back to Monroe. Mary Ellen and Zelaina Lisonbee, "A Brief History of the Life of James Thompson Lisonbee," Church Archives.
19. This is the population distribution for the 1880 census. The percentages were probably about the same for 1874. For contrast, in 1870 and 1880 the percentage of American-born in northern Utah's Cache Valley was 62. Dean L. May, "A Demographic Portrait of the Mormons, 1830–1980," in Thomas G. Alexander and Jessie L. Embry, eds., *After 150 Years: The Latter- day Saints in Sesquicentennial Perspective* (Midvale, Utah: Charles Redd Center for Western Studies, 1983), 59–60.
20. Sevier Stake, General Minutes, 19 April 1874, vol. 1, 72.
21. The absence of statistical data for 1874 requires generalizations based upon Monroe Ward statistical reports for 1877 through 1880 and the 1880 census. See the appraisal of Monroe in 1880 in the following chapter.
22. Monroe United Order, Minutes, 26 April 1874.
23. Lewis Barney, Autobiography 1, 97; Incorporations, Sevier County, Recorder's Office, Richfield, Utah.
24. Incorporations, Sevier County, Recorder's Office.
25. The community endeavor in Brigham City in northern Utah had been operating under apostle Lorenzo Snow's direction for several years with success, but the procedural particulars of their success were not codified and distributed.

26. See the community variation of United Order methods in Arrington, et al., *Building the City of God.*
27. Monroe United Order, Minutes, 29 April 1874.
28. Monroe Ward, Historial Record, 23 August 1874.
29. Ibid., 17 May 1874.
30. Arthur Barney, Journal, 33.
31. Monroe Ward, Historical Record, 3 August 1874.
32. Ibid., 13 September 1874.
33. Monroe United Order, Minutes, 21 September 1874, 8 October 1874.
34. Sevier Stake, General Minutes, 5 December 1874, vol. 1, 85.
35. Ibid., vol. 2, 56.
36. Monroe United Order, Minutes, 25 June 1874.
37. Monroe Ward, Historical Record, 26 July 1874.
38. Monroe United Order, Minutes, 23 September 1874, 9 November 1874.
39. Sevier Stake, General Minutes, Record Book A, 84, Church Archives.
40. Lewis Barney, Autobiography 1, 97.
41. Ibid.
42. Arrington, et al., *Building the City of God*, 186–187.
43. Monroe United Order, Minutes, 15 May 1874, 25 November 1874, 19 January 1875.
44. Arthur Barney, Journal, 33–34.
45. Monroe United Order, Minutes, 27 November 1874.
46. Lewis Barney, Autobiography 1, 97–98.
47. Ibid., 98. Of this move to Kanosh, Arthur wrote:

> At this time father and his sons Walter, Henry, Joseph and I decided to build a sawmill on fish creek, a tributary of clear creek which empties into the Sevier river just above Joetown [Joseph]. Clear creek canyon runs east and west, and heads at the head of three creeks which runs to Kanosh, which is in Millard county. . . . So we would all meet at the head of Fish creek where we were building this, the 3rd sawmill that father had built in Utah. . . . Part of the lumber from the mill went to Millard county, and part to Sevier county, after we got the mill built I quit it and left it to father and the other three sons. (Arthur Barney, Journal, 34)

The lumber enterprise for Lewis's sons was viable for several years. The gazetteer for 1879–1880 lists the "Barney Bros." as being lumber dealers in Kanosh. *Utah Directory and Gazetteer for 1879–80* (Salt Lake City: H. L. A. Culmer & Co., 1879), 362. Their productivity was such that even the canyon in which they worked acquired their name. In 1885 James V. Williams wrote that he and his sons obtained logs from "Barneys Canyon" to build their home. James Van Nostrand Williams, Reminiscences and diary, [ca. 1894]–1905, 85, Church Archives.

48. Monroe United Order, Minutes, 20 January 1875.
49. Ibid., 13 February 1875.
50. Lewis Barney, Autobiography 1, 98. The appraisals of consecrations for 8 October 1874 indicate that Lewis's contribution doubled the average consecration of the other fifty-seven subscribers. Only four others in the order consecrated more. Corporations Register, Sevier County, Recorder's Office.
51. Monroe United Order, Minutes, 26 February 1875. Barney's daughter Martha Ann divorced Robinson not long after this incident.
52. Monroe United Order, Minutes, 27 February 1875; Lewis Barney, Autobiography 1, 98–99.
53. Ibid., 99.

54. Ibid.
55. Monroe United Order, Minutes, 26 May 1875.
56. Sevier Stake, General Minutes, vol. 1, 94, 13 March 1875.
57. The definitive overview of the Godbeite movement in Utah is Ronald W. Walker, *Wayward Saints: The Godbeites and Brigham Young* (Urbana, Illinois: University of Illinois Press, 1998).
58. *Deseret News*, 1, 7 April 1875; 12 May 1875; 9 June 1875.
59. Monroe United Order, Minutes, 13 December 1875.
60. Ibid., 19 May 1875.
61. Arrington, et al., *Building the City of God*, 182, 188, 194.
62. Monroe United Order, Minutes, 24 May 1875.
63. Ibid., 7 June 1875; Lewis Barney, Autobiography 1, 99.
64. Monroe Ward, Historical Record, 216–225; Monroe Ward, Record of Members.
65. Monroe United Order, Minutes, 27 July 1875.
66. Arrington, et al., *Building the City of God*, 199.
67. Brigham Young to Albert K. Thurber and William Seegmiller, 13 October 1875, Brigham Young, Papers, Letterpress Copybooks, Church Archives.
68. Monroe United Order, Minutes, 88–94.
69. Within four months of being rejected by the order board, James T. Lisonbee was also released as Monroe Ward bishop. He was soon called to a Southern States mission at April general conference in 1876. He left his wife and six children for his mission to the American South on 30 May 1876. Serving zealously for eighteen months, he baptized thirty into the Church of Jesus Christ. But afflicted by chronic illness and believing his life in peril, with great difficulty he returned to Utah. When the Monroe Saints learned of his unfortunate circumstances, money was raised by ward members to provide means for his return. Lewis Barney was one of the forty-nine people who contributed nearly $100 for Lisonbee to return home. Enfeebled as he made his way westward, almost home, he made it to Springville, Utah. There he fell completely exhausted. He could go no farther. On 28 November 1877 in Springville, he was met by his wife and children, but even they could not rally his resources. There he died on 9 December 1877. He had stood his ground and, as valiantly as he could, given his all for the kingdom. See Monroe Ward, Manuscript History; Monroe Ward, Historical Record; James Thompson Lisonbee, Diary, Church Archives; and Garth N. Jones, *James Thompson Lisonbee's Missionary Labors: On the Sand Mountain of Northeastern Alabama and Northwestern Georgia, Beginnings of a New Gathering in the San Luis Valley of Colorado, 1876–1878* (Provo, Utah: Brigham Young University Press, 2000), 24–25, 63–70.

    Jones suggests that Lewis Barney was Lisonbee's "nemesis," primarily responsible for Lisonbee's demise in Monroe. But, as demonstrated in this discussion of the United Order, disfavor with Lisonbee and his United Order associates extended far beyond just Lewis Barney. Jones, *James Thompson Lisonbee*, 20–23, 63.
70. Quoted in Hartley, "Common People," 279–280.
71. Barney's meeting with Wells must have been on or about 9 September 1875 when Wells visited Richfield for a church conference. Journal History, 9 September 1875.
72. Monroe United Order, Minutes, 7 March 1876.
73. Ibid., 24 April 1876.
74. The Monroe United Order account book shows the transactions in Barney's name during his association with the order. See Monroe United Order, Account Book, Church Archives.
75. Monroe United Order, Minutes, 125, 128, 137, 140–141, 149.
76. Sevier Stake leaders "Met with [the] Board of Management of Monroe U.O. [on 21 March 1878] and deliberated & counseled as to the best mode of winding up its business and prepare for renewed effort in rolling on the work of God." Sevier Stake, General Minutes, 21 March 1878, vol. 1, 149.

77. Ibid., 25 November 1877, vol. 1, 140.
78. For an example of one who initially subscribed to Mormon teachings and culture only to later find contempt for the behavior of his coreligionists and their leaders, see Bitton, "George Armstrong Hicks," 196–222. Hicks later reversed his antagonism and returned to the Church of Jesus Christ in his last years.

Chapter 19

1. William G. Hartley, "The Priesthood Reorganization of 1877: Brigham Young's Last Achievement," *BYU Studies* 20, no. 1 (fall 1979).
2. Arrington, et al., *Building the City of God*, 154.
3. Sevier Stake, General Minutes, vol. 1, 149.
4. Brigham Young, Papers, Letterpress Copybooks, 20 January 1877; Sevier Stake, Manuscript History.
5. John Taylor, Orson Pratt, and Erastus and Lorenzo Snow, of the Quorum of Twelve Apostles arrived in Monroe on 25 April 1877. Each of them spoke to the theme of the United Order, encouraging the congregation in their participation of the same. *Deseret News*, 23 May 1877.
6. Lewis Barney, Autobiography 1, 99–100; *Deseret News*, 23 May 1877; Sevier Stake, General Minutes, 21 March 1878, vol. 1, 149.
7. Christian Henry Halvorsen, Diary, 1866–1879, 17 July 1877, Church Archives. Interestingly, Halvorsen, after going public with his complaint, wrote the following day that "I was notified that I was deliberated from the Order for having spoken against the leaders mismanagement in a public meeting." He no doubt felt satisfaction two weeks later on 1 August when he wrote, "I have heard that the Order is going to desolve next fall."
8. Lewis Barney, Autobiography 1, 100; Sevier Stake, General Minutes, vol. 1, 127–128. Harris's taxable assets in 1875 of $1,255 show him to be the third wealthiest man in Monroe. Sevier (Utah: County) Tax Assessment, 1873–1918. Harris had been appointed president of the Young Men's Mutual Improvement Association just prior to this on 18 April. *Deseret News*, 23 May 1877. Harris served as bishop of Monroe until his death in 1885.

   The installation of the new bishopric was made in conjunction with the church-wide priesthood reorganization implemented by Brigham Young just prior to his death, modernizing the organizational structure of the Church of Jesus Christ. The overall design of the stakes was also reconstituted at the same time. In the Sevier Stake, Franklin Spencer was chosen stake president with A. K. Thurber and William Seegmiller as counselors. Sevier Stake, Manuscript History. See Hartley, "The Priesthood Reorganization of 1877."
9. Lewis Barney, Autobiography 1, 100.
10. Sevier Stake, General Minutes, 15 July 1877, vol. 1, 129–130. The leaders considered were the stake presidency, high council, ward bishoprics, and stake and ward priesthood quorum presidencies. Of forty-seven of the fifty-five stake leaders whose ages are known, twenty-six were younger than forty years old, seven were in their forties, and eleven were in their fifties. Only three were older than sixty.
11. Clark, ed., *Messages of the First Presidency*, 2:284. See the Sevier Stake, General Minutes, vol. 1, at this time to see the implementation of the priesthood reorganization in Sevier Valley.
12. Lewis Barney, Autobiography 1, 100. The date of this appointment was 19 August 1877. Sevier Stake, General Minutes, vol. 1, 131. Describing the function of wards during this period, William Hartley has written, "The first ward callings were the bishoprics, including clerks, and then the acting teachers, but only a dozen or score of men served as acting teachers in a ward. Bishoprics and this corps of

teachers 'shouldered the ward's leadership and performed its labor.'" Hartley, "Common People," 261–262.

13. Presiding Bishopric, Statistical Report. "When Brigham Young died, gathered Zion included 104,000 Saints living in 240 wards. Wards averaged 81 families and 432 members per unit. But Salt Lake Stake's wards were larger than most, averaging 566 members. And wards in the Utah (Utah County) Stake were even larger, averaging 808 members." Hartley, "Common People," 250.
14. Sevier Stake, General Minutes, vol. 2, 178.
15. Hartley, "Common People," 267.
16. For tax purposes Barney's worth was appraised at $455, which included land worth $250, four cattle, a horse and mule, and two pigs. This contrasts with his 1875 appraisal of $200, understandably low because of his consecration to the order, which included land valued at $130 and a mule. Barney's taxable assets in 1877 of $455 exceeded the Sevier County average of $344 though in 1875 his paltry $200 was substantially less than the Monroe average of $338 and the Sevier County average of $312. (These figures for 1875 and 1877 do not include five in 1875 and sixteen in 1877, residents whose assets were valued over $1,500. These wealthy individuals were eliminated in the averages due to their inordinate weightiness in figuring averages. One, for example, was taxed for property worth over $7,000.) Barney's brothers' appraisals include: Walter, $354 (1873), $200 (1875), and $350 (1877); Benjamin, $215 and $435, for the latter two years only. James Henry Barney had property worth $276 in 1873, $190 in 1875, and $435 in 1877. Sevier (Utah County) Tax Assessment, 1873–1918.
17. Lewis Barney, Autobiography 1, 100.
18. Sevier Stake, General Minutes, 23 October 1875, vol. 1, 111.
19. In the early 1880s the Monroe school trustees, attempting to hire a seasoned educator to reinforce Mormon educational objectives, persuaded James V. Williams, who had been teaching in Utah since the 1860s, to teach Monroe's youth. Williams said that he was lured by the trustee's offer of "2 dollars a quarter for each scholar." But "after teaching 2 quarters the Trustees refused to pay [the] $42.25" owed him, forcing him into day work to make a living. Williams, Reminiscences and diary, 8 April 1880 [or 1881], 81. Perhaps because of Williams's bad experience, teachers for Monroe's children during the early 1880s were hard to retain. In early 1882 Eunice Stewart Harris, who later married Dennison L. Harris's son, attended to the needs of Monroe's children. Joyce Kinkead, ed., *A Schoolmarm All My Life: Personal Narratives from Frontier Utah* (Salt Lake City: Signature Books, 1996), 119.
20. Gwendolyn Jacobsen, *Memories of "Little Denmark": History of Elsinore and Brooklyn, Utah* (Richfield, Utah: Elsinore Literary Club, [n.d.]), 29, 77.
21. Lewis Barney, Autobiography 1, 101. While there were 200 children under the age of eight in Monroe in 1878, a system of regular day school in Monroe did not function. Noted Mormon educator Karl G. Maeser visited the settlement and reported, "School matters below par, but might be improved." Sevier Stake, General Minutes, vol. 2, 224; Sevier Stake, Manuscript History. On 19 August 1880, a correspondent from Monroe wrote to the *Deseret News* to say, "At present we have no school house but Miss Geneva Bean of Richfield is teaching school in the upper part of the U.O. granary and under the circumstances is doing remarkably well in giving the youth of this place a start for an education. We expect to take steps immediately to build a school house." Monroe Ward, Manuscript History.
22. Lewis Barney, Autobiography 1, 108–109.
23. Preston, *Genealogy of the Barney Family*, 348. Concerning William Edwards's death, his mother Elizabeth's granddaughter, Edna Briscoe Perkins, said that because of "Billy's" death near Christmas the boy's mother was thereafter unhappy during the holiday season. Perkins and Gillen, Interview, 18.

24. *Deseret News*, 20 March 1878.
25. Nephi James Bates, Reminiscences and diary, 28 June 1878.
26. *Deseret News*, 17 July 1878. "Chaplain Lewis Barney" opened this celebration with prayer.
27. Bates, Reminiscences and diary, 19 April 1879.
28. Bates said a continuing source of the problem were those who lived outside of Monroe on "the west side of the river." Not only was religion a point of division, but water usage and rights also mixed into the discord. Michael Johnson, "one of our worst enemies," was, according to Bates, one of the primary offenders. Bates, Reminiscences and diary, 1 May 1879, 16 July 1879.
29. Corporations Register, Sevier County, Recorder's Office; Monroe Ward, Manuscript History.
30. John Taylor's visit to Monroe, along with apostles Wilford Woodruff and Franklin D. Richards, occurred on 25 November 1881. According to Barney, Taylor sympathized with the Monroe Saints, telling them, "I understand you have had some trouble here in Monroe. You have had some losses in the Order through mismanagement and the want of experience and knowledge and wisdom to manage your business properly." "The most wise and skillfull businessmen frequently make mistakes and fail in their business arrangements. It requires more intelligence to manage the business of a community than of an individual," he told them. Indeed, "Many men cannot manage a wife and 2 or 3 children and a pig or two successfully." Lewis Barney, Autobiography 1, 107–108.
31. Lewis Barney is noted as having attended part of the jubilee celebration in Salt Lake City in 1880, though he said nothing of the event. *The Utah Pioneers: Celebration of the Entrance of the Pioneers into Great Salt Lake Valley* (Salt Lake City: *Deseret News*, 1880), 51.
32. The data supplied in this appraisal are based on church reports, Monroe's enumeration in the 1880 federal census, and geographer Lowell C. (Ben) Bennion's analysis of the census figures. My thanks to Ben Bennion for this information.
33. May, "Demographic Portrait of the Mormons," 51. Richfield, Utah, was also composed of 80 percent Latter-day Saints in the 1880 census.
34. Sevier Stake, Manuscript History, 2 November 1878; Murdock and Murdock, *Monroe, Utah*, 40, 44. In contrast to the tuition-financed common schools, the Presbyterian schools were held to be "free" schools paid for by denominational money from the east. There were upwards of 100 of them in Utah by 1885 to which as many as 5,000 Mormon children attended.
35. Davis Bitton and Linda Wilcox, "The Transformation of Utah's Agriculture, 1847–1900," in Thomas G. Alexander and John F. Bluth, eds., *The Twentieth Century American West: Contributions to an Understanding* (Midvale, Utah: Charles Redd Monographs in Western History, no. 12, Charles Redd Center for Western Studies, 1983), 57–83.

    While the overall LDS population in the Sevier Valley increased by about 170 percent between 1877 and 1881, Richfield, having one-fourth of the county populace, grew by but 7 percent and Monroe, with 16 percent of county numbers, grew by one-tenth. Monroe grew by 4 percent in 1881–1882 while the valley population dipped by almost 3 percent at the same time. Data based upon Presiding Bishopric, Statistical Reports. While the figures are LDS numbers, they probably reflect overall trends in the population.
36. Bitton and Wilcox, "Utah's Agriculture," 57, 73–74.
37. Tenth census of the United States, 1880; 1880 *Utah Gazetteer* quoted in Murdock and Murdock, *Monroe, Utah*, 53.
38. Arthur Barney, Journal, 36–40. Describing what probably occurred in the fall of 1879, Arthur, whose mother and siblings were with him, wrote, "We worked

fencing [in Salina Canyon] until late in the fall when we went back to Monroe to spend the winter, and to have a good time." "In 1880," he said, "I went to Frisco in Millard county, and put in that summer hauling charcoal from Summer's coal kilns to the smelter at Frisco, about 10 miles a haul, it took all day to make the trip . . . I worked until late in the fall, then I went home to Monroe for the winter." Arthur Barney, Journal, 36, 39–40.

39. Lewis Barney, Autobiography 1, 101–102.
40. Joseph Smith introduced the doctrine to the church in 1836: "Thus came the voice of the Lord unto me, saying: All who have died without a knowledge of this gospel, who would have received it if they had been permitted to tarry, shall be heirs of the celestial kingdom of God; Also all that shall die henceforth without a knowledge of it, who would have received it with all their hearts, shall be heirs of that kingdom." Doctrine and Covenants, Section 137:7–8.
41. Ibid., Section 128:15.
42. Pratt, *Autobiography of Parley P. Pratt*, 297.
43. St. George Temple, Baptisms for the Dead, Book I, 551–561, Family History Library.
44. Patriarchal Blessing Collection, Church Archives.
45. Lewis Barney, Autobiography 1, 102.
46. Ibid. The agricultural census of 1880 identifies Joseph Smith Barney in Kanosh with thirty improved acres, five acres in meadow, a farm valued at $800, with $100 in farm implements, $300 in livestock, and $50 in farm production. Walter T. Barney, also living in Kanosh, had thirty improved acres and five acres in meadow. The value of his farm was placed at $1,500 with $200 in farm implements, $600 in livestock, and $50 in farm production. James Henry apparently was not enumerated in the agricultural census nor was his father Lewis. United States Census Office, Tenth Census, Agriculture, Utah, 1880, Church Archives.
47. Lewis Barney, Autobiography 1, 102.
48. Ibid., 102–103. A summary from one of Barney's sermons at about this time demonstrates the nature of his belief and religious mindset. On the day he was appointed clerk of the seventies quorum in Monroe, 7 February 1882, the minutes (which he kept) state:

> I feel thankful that I am associated with this people that is considered so wicked and that there is so much evil spoken about. We are reproached in the eyes of the wicked. The Heathen may rage and the people iniagen [engage in] a vain thing. But they Can do nothing to hinder this kingdom from advancing, for the Lord holds the destinies of the armies of the nations in his hands. The Prophesies will all be full-filled. If they are then there will be armies gathered against us but we have nothing to fear but ourselves. If I can keep the commandments I have nothing to fear. (Record for the Seventies of Monroe Ward in the Sevier Stake of Zion, 41st Quorum, Seventies Quorum, Records)

49. Barney, describing an event in May 1881, noted a visit he had with "Father [William] McBride," from whom he received the patriarchal blessing the previous year. He said McBride

> called to see me and stayed over night. We enjoyed ourselves very agreeably reading and talking on the signs of the time and the present and future prospects and blessings promised the Latter-day Saints which was agreeable and encouraging, as the signs of the times showed plainly that the redemption of Israel was near at hand and that the hated and despised Mormons would soon be respected and honored by all that know them. (Lewis Barney, Autobiography 1, 103)

For a look at the roots of Mormon millenarianism see Grant Underwood, *The Millenarian World of Early Mormonism* (Urbana, Illinois: University of Illinois Press, 1993). For a view of its effects on another man in nineteenth-century Utah see James B. Allen, *Trials of Discipleship: The Story of William Clayton, a Mormon* (Urbana, Illinois: University of Illinois Press, 1987), 302–322.

50. The missionary role Lewis was ordained to in Nauvoo also played into his religious thinking. In the spring of 1881 he stated on 27 March, "We are required as seventy Apostles to prepare ourselves to promulage [the principles of the gospel] to the nation." Six weeks later on 8 May he said, "It is our duty to prepare and perfect ourselves in the ministry, that we may even go out to seal up the testimony to the nations of the earth." He "felt and do feel a desire to go and preach the Gospel and rid my garments of the blood of this generation. I feel that I would wish to open my mouth to witness that the God of Heaven has raised up his church upon the earth, because I know he has. I have a full testimony." His listeners heard him say, "I have been a Seventy for thirty-six years and if I do not have the privilege of going out [to the nations to preach], I will encourage my brethren at home." Record for the Seventies of Monroe Ward, 27 March, 8 May 1881.
51. Lewis Barney, Autobiography 1, 109. About this time Barney stated, "I then assisted to visit the Saints as a ward teacher. This being done, the teachers met together for the purpose of giving in their report to the bishop. After the reports were all given in, I was appointed head teacher of the Monroe Ward and elected to that office." Lewis Barney, Autobiography 1, 106.
52. Ibid., 109. The minutes of 7 February 1882 of the seventies meeting in Monroe, Utah reads, "Lewis Barney was then unanimously Chosen Clerk of the quorum And Accepted the appointment." Record for the Seventies of Monroe Ward, 7 February 1882, 15. The minutes for this particular meeting were kept by Lewis Barney. According to the minutes in the quorum record Barney kept minutes for the group on 7 February and 7 March 1882 only.
53. Lewis Barney, Autobiography 1, 107.
54. Ibid., 109.
55. Ibid., 103.
56. Arthur Barney, Journal, 40.
57. Lewis Barney, Autobiography 1, 103. The fact that the wedding celebration was held at Walter Jones's home may indicate the process of community healing was at work, despite differences that remained. Jones, once Moses Gifford's counselor in the Monroe Ward bishopric, had refrained from joining the United Order and was sufficiently estranged from Mormonism that his immediate family left the Church of Jesus Christ. See Karl C. Sandberg, "Getting Up a History of Monroe: The Long Shadow of the United Order," *Sunstone* 19, no. 4 (December 1996): 43.
58. Lewis Barney, Autobiography 1, 103.
59. Arthur Barney, 40–41. The D&RGW railroad was also known as the Sevier Valley Railroad. It was the intent of the D&RGW to intrude into the domain of the Union Pacific Railroad. The route

> emerged from Ogden and proceeded south to Nephi, then through Salt Creek Canyon, Sanpete and Sevier valleys to Salina. From Salina one branch went south through the most suitable pass to the drainage of the Colorado River and then southwest along the river to the Arizona border. A second branch was to fork east from Salina through Salina Pass and into Castle Valley, then by the most practical route to the Green River near the 39 degree parallel and continuing east from there to the Grand River. The route then followed the Grand to the Colorado border. The total distance was estimated at six hundred miles. (Reeder, "The History of Utah's Railroads," 373–375, 377)

See also Robert G. Athearn, "Utah and the Coming of the Denver and Rio Grande Railroad," *Utah Historical Quarterly* 27 (1959): 129–144.

60. The ledger accounts are found following the autobiographical account in Lewis Barney's Autobiography 1. See also Arthur Barney, Journal, 40–41.
61. Lewis Barney, Autobiography 1, 104–106. Barney recounted their work for Robbins in a letter to Arthur on 4 March 1882. "I know that you and Hyrum [Strong] was swindled out of four hundred and 30 dollars. Consequently you could not pay off the hands and they had to suffer loss. . . . We lost all we made there and have nothing to show for all the hard work that we have done on that side of the mountain." Lewis Barney to Arthur Barney, 4 March 1882, in Lewis Barney, Autobiography 1.
62. Nephi James Bates, Journal, 10 July 1882, Daughters of Utah Pioneers Collection, Church Archives.
63. Lewis Barney to Arthur Barney, 4 March 1882, in Lewis Barney, Autobiography 1.

Chapter 20

1. Arthur Barney, Journal, 3, 41.
2. Lewis Barney, Autobiography 1, 109.
3. Joel Hills Johnson, *A Voice from the Mountains: Life and Works of Joel Hills Johnson* (Mesa, Arizona: Lofgreen's Inc., 1982), 147–148; Jenson, *Encyclopedic History of the Church*, 376. Benjamin F. Johnson, younger brother of Joel, was "much pleased with the idea of colonizing" with his brothers in what he called "Rock Spring Valley." Johnson, *My Life's Review*, 241.
4. Johnson, *A Voice from the Mountains*, 163–164, 171, 173, 175, 187.
5. Perkins and Gillen, Interview, 4. For examples of others who searched at length for satisfaction on the Mormon frontier see Lorenzo Hill Hatch, *Lorenzo Hill Hatch Journal*, Ruth Savage Hilton, ed. (Provo, Utah: Brigham Young University Adult Education and Extension Services, 1958); Joseph Fish, *The Life and Times of Joseph Fish, Mormon Pioneer*, John H. Krenkel, ed. (Danville, Illinois: The Interstate Printers & Publishers, Inc., 1970); and Frank C. Robertson, *A Ram in the Thicket: The Story of a Roaming Homesteader Family on the Mormon Frontier* (Moscow, Idaho: University of Idaho Press, 1994, first published in 1950).
6. Newell, *History of Piute County*, 73–76.
7. Sevier Stake, General Minutes, vol. 1, 37–38.
8. *Deseret Evening News*, 2 February 1874; Sevier Stake, General Minutes, vol. 1, 39, 63; Pearson H. Corbett, *Jacob Hamblin: The Peacemaker* (Salt Lake City: Deseret Book Company, 1952), 343–357; and Newell, *History of Piute County*, 116–118, who reminds her readers that the McCarty brothers later joined up with Butch Cassidy's Wild Bunch.
9. Sevier Stake, General Minutes, vol. 1, 70, 77, 90, 98, 183–184; Sevier Stake, Manuscript History; Richfield Ward, United Order Records, 4; and Jenson, *Encyclopedic History of the Church*, 407.
10. Wesley R. Burr and Ruth J. Burr, *A History of the Burr Pioneers* (Salt Lake City: Charles and Sarah Burr Family Organization, 1995), 70.
11. Burrville Ward, Manuscript History, Church Archives.
12. Jenson, *Encyclopedic History of the Church*, 101, 407.
13. Tenth Census of the United States, 1880. A brief overview of the upper Grass Valley settlement is found in Newell, *History of Piute County*, 118–122.
14. Lewis Barney, Autobiography 1, 110, 112; Jenson, *Encyclopedic History of the Church*, 101.

15. Lewis Barney, Autobiography 1, 112. Most of the information about Barney's efforts to settle in Burrville are written in diary form rather than reminiscence which characterizes the bulk of his life writings.
16. Lewis Barney, Autobiography 1, 112–113.
17. Burrville Ward, Manuscript History.
18. Presiding Bishopric, Statistical Reports. The 1880 census identified 200 living in Burrville indicating that less than half the community was associated with the Church of Jesus Christ.
19. Lewis Barney, Autobiography 1, 113.
20. Barney filed on "40 acres of pasture land in Township 25, Section 29, Grass Valley." Lewis Barney, Autobiography 1, 111.
21. Ibid.
22. Ibid.
23. Burrville Ward, Sunday School Minutes, Book A, 1878–1893, 19, Church Archives; *Jubilee History of Latter-day Saint Sunday Schools, 1849–1899* (Salt Lake City: Deseret Sunday School Union, 1900), 351. Burrville's Ward Sunday School minutes during this period were also recorded by Barney.
24. Lewis Barney, Autobiography 1, 111.
25. Ibid., 113–115.
26. Ibid., 115.
27. Ibid., 115–117.
28. Ibid., 117–118.
29. Most of the temple work on this visit to the St. George Temple was accomplished for Elizabeth's deceased Beard and Almerode family members. St. George Temple, Endowments and Baptisms for the Dead, Family History Library.
30. Lewis Barney, Autobiography 1, 119.
31. Lewis Barney to Caroline Beard Barney, 23 May 1883, Burrville, Utah, in Lewis Barney, Autobiography 1. For information about the "Law of Adoption," in Mormon practice see Gordon Irving, "The Law of Adoption: One Phase of the Development of the Mormon Concept of Salvation, 1830–1900," *BYU Studies* 14, no. 3 (spring 1974): 291–314.
32. Lewis Barney, Autobiography 1, 119. Family sources indicate Henry Barney later died in a cave-in while digging a canal near Cannonville, Utah.
33. Lewis Barney to Caroline Beard Barney, 23 May 1883.
34. Burrville Ward, Manuscript History.
35. An "Elaborate Tables of Distances, Routes, Camping Places, etc." for travel between southern Utah and northern Arizona was popularized as early as 1876 in Utah. Barney and his family appear to have used the route recommended. "Arizona," *Salt Lake Daily Herald*, 30 March 1876.
36. See Peterson, *Take Up Your Mission*, 1–37.
37. Lewis Barney, BYU Typescript, 175–176.
38. Bob Thomas, "The Phantom of Willow Springs: A Trading Post Lost in Time beside an Old Wagon Road," *Arizona Highways* 73, no. 1 (January 1997): 16–19.
39. Lewis Barney, BYU Typescript, 176–177.
40. While briefly living in St. Thomas, Nevada, Henry Barney, Gibbons, and Curtis E. Bolton tackled the mighty Colorado River on a fishing expedition in April 1868. This was a year before John Wesley Powell made his famous exploration of the river which popularized to the rest of America the great intermountain drain to the Gulf of California. "Trip on the Colorado and Virgin Rivers," *Millennial Star* 30, no. 28 (11 July 1868): 435–437. Gibbons returned later in November 1868 and with Octavius D. Gass braved the Colorado again, this time running the river all the way to Yuma, Arizona. James H. McClintock, *Mormon Settlement in Arizona: A Record of Peaceful Conquest of the Desert* (Phoenix, Arizona: n.p., 1921), 125–126.

41. Lewis Barney, BYU Typescript, 177–178.
42. Ibid., 179–181.
43. *Do You Remember Luna: 100 Years of Pioneer History* (Albuquerque: The Luna Ward, 1983), 1–5; Luna Ward, Manuscript History, Church Archives; Jenson, *Encylopedic History of the Church*, 451, and the overview of the Church of Jesus Christ in New Mexico, Lyle K. Porter and Wilma H. Porter, *A History of the Church of Jesus Christ of Latter-day Saints in New Mexico, 1876–1989* (Albuquerque: the authors, 1997).
44. Jenson, *Encyclopedic History of the Church*, 66–69, 575–576.
45. Lewis Barney, BYU Typescript, 181–183.
46. Quoted in *Do You Remember Luna*, 8.
47. Lewis Barney, BYU Typescript, 183–184.
48. Ibid., 184–187.
49. Ibid., 188.
50. Irene Black, Ruth Mae Harris, and Lorraine Vance, *Circle of Sixteen: Family of Franklin Van Buren Barney and Lucy Ann Victoria Lindquist* (Orem, Utah: Likos Publishing, 1998). 23–24, 329–330; Franklin R. Barney, "The Walter Turner Barney Family," 1, typescript in possession of author; "Walter Turner Barney," *Mt. Graham Profiles: Graham County, Arizona, 1870–1977* (n.p.: Graham County Historical Society, n.d.); Preston, *Genealogy of the Barney Family*, 554–555.
51. *Arizona, the Grand Canyon State: A History of Arizona*, 2 vols. (Westminster, Colorado: Western States Historical Publishers Inc., 1975), 2:569.
52. Frank C. Lockwood, *Pioneer Days in Arizona: From the Spanish Occupation to Statehood* (New York: The Macmillan Company, 1932), 281–286.
53. James H. McClintock, *Arizona*, 3 vols. (Chicago: S. J. Clarke Publishing Co., 1916), 1:243–266; Malcolm L. Comeaux, *Arizona: A Geography* (Boulder, Colorado: Westview Press, 1981), 119.
54. Byrd Howell Granger, *Arizona Names: X Marks the Spot* (Tuscon, Arizona: The Falconer Pub. Co., 1983); *Arizona Star Weekly*, 27 October 1881; Jay J. Wagoner, *Arizona's Heritage* (Santa Barbara, California: Peregrine Smith, Inc., 1978), 187–189. For a background on the struggle of the Apache's in southeastern Arizona, see Marshall Trimble, *Arizona: A Panoramic History of a Frontier State* (New York: Doubleday & Co., 1977), 181–201.
55. Barney clearly used the first autobiography in the preparation of the second. Yet, what remains of the latter contains information not found in his previous effort. (A family story holds that the second autobiography was later torn apart by his daughter Martha Ann with sections then distributed to her children. Today only the document's first forty-page fragment survives.) The correspondence found in Barney's papers, incoming and outgoing, was copied into a letterbook.
56. Perkins and Gillen, Interview, 5.
57. Lewis Barney to Betsey Barney, 4 April 1886, in Lewis Barney, Papers, Correspondence, microfilm of MS, Church Archives.
58. A note, apparently written by a family member at the time the BYU Typescript was made, states: "David went back to gather some mares and colts he had not found when he and his mother left Bowie and his mother went back to help him through with them, at the request of Lewis Barney, David's father." Given Barney's statements to Martha Ann, there was more to the story than lost animals. Lewis Barney, BYU Typescript, 129a.
59. Perkins and Gillen, Interview, 18.
60. Lewis Barney, Papers, Diary, 14 July 1886.
61. Ibid., 14 July–13 August 1886.
62. Ibid., 8 September 1886.
63. W. L. Rusho, *Lee's Ferry: Desert River Crossing* (Salt Lake City: Tower Productions, 1998), 55.

64. Lewis Barney, Papers, Diary, 8 September 1886.
65. Ibid., 9–24 September 1886.
66. Lewis Barney to Arthur Barney, 26 September 1886, Burrville, Utah, Lewis Barney, Papers, Correspondence; Arthur Barney, Journal, 3.

Chapter 21

1. Frederick Jackson Turner, *The Frontier in American History* (New York: Henry Holt and Company, 1921), 1–2.
2. William Cronon, George Miles, and Jay Gitlin, "Becoming West: Toward a New Meaning for Western History," in Cronon, Miles, and Gitlin, *Under an Open Sky: Rethinking America's Western Past* (New York: W. W. Norton & Company, 1992), 3–27.
3. Turner, *Frontier in American History*, 3.
4. Price Ward, Record of Members, Church Archives; Hartley, "Common People," 270–271.
5. Thursey Jessen Reynolds, comp., *Centennial Echos from Carbon County* (n.p.: Carbon County Daughters of Utah Pioneers, 1948), 157, 164; Jenson, *Encyclopedic History of the Church*, 934; and Ronald G. Watt, *A History of Carbon County [Utah]* (Salt Lake City: Utah State Historical Society and Carbon County Commission, 1997), 24, 40, 43.
6. Watt, *History of Carbon County*, 77.
7. Reynolds, *Centennial Echos from Carbon County*, 156–167; Jenson, *Encyclopedic History of the Church*, 934.
8. Ibid., 167.
9. Deborah's obituary in the *Deseret News* described her death in Spring City, Utah: "She was a quiet and peaceable old lady, and died in full hope of a glorious resurrection." *Deseret News*, 3 October 1888.
10. Kanosh Ward, Relief Society Minutes, 6 January 1887, 144, Church Archives.
11. James Henry Barney to Lewis Barney, 2 March 1887, Kanosh, Utah, Lewis Barney, Papers, Correspondence.
12. James Henry Barney to Lewis Barney, 2 May 1887.
13. David Barney to Lewis Barney, 27 November 1887, Mancos, Colorado, Lewis Barney, Papers, Correspondence.
14. James Henry Barney to Lewis Barney, 26 April 1888, Kanosh, Utah; Lewis Barney to Betsey Barney, March or April 1889, Wellington, Utah, Lewis Barney, Papers, Correspondence.
15. Lewis Barney to B. F. Cummings, 11 April 1888, Wellington, Utah, Lewis Barney, Papers, Correspondence. This letter is David's reply to Arthur's favorable report of their father.
16. David Barney to Arthur Barney, 15 July 1888, Mancos, Colorado, Lewis Barney, Papers, Correspondence.
17. Barney was "ordained" by Seymour B. Young into Emery Stake's 101st Quorum of Seventies on 20 February 1888. Record of Ordination to Office of Seventy, Church Archives.
18. Betsey Barney to Lewis Barney, 24 February 1889, Kanosh, Utah, Lewis Barney, Papers, Correspondence.
19. B. F. Cummings to Lewis Barney, 11 April 1888, Salt Lake City, Utah, Lewis Barney, Papers, Correspondence.
20. David Barney to Lewis Barney, 7 March 1888, Mancos, Colorado, Lewis Barney, Papers, Correspondence. In June 1889 David also wrote to Lewis reminding his father that he was still interested in doing the work. David Barney to Lewis Barney, 10 June 1889.

21. Elizabeth Barney to Lewis Barney, 27 April 1888, Mancos, Colorado, Lewis Barney, Papers, Correspondence.
22. Betsey Barney to Lewis Barney, 24 February 1889, 16 March 1889, 7 April 1889, Kanosh, Utah, Lewis Barney, Papers, Correspondence.
23. On 2 July 1889 Barney served as proxy in the baptism for the dead of eighteen of Betsey's ancestors. Interestingly, he also was baptized for his deceased son Orson who was killed during the Black Hawk War in November 1865. That day Betsey was baptized for twenty-two of her female ancestors. On 16 July and 9 October Lewis and Betsey entered the temple again to perform vicarious baptisms for Barney, Turner, and Beard ancestors, Elizabeth's family. Betsey and Lewis's son James Henry and his wife Emily joined them in Manti in mid-October and performed work for James Henry's "relations in law," while Lewis performed ordinances for twenty of his ancestors, mostly born in the seventeenth century and who had lived in Rehoboth, Massachusetts. Manti Temple, Baptisms for the Dead, Book D, 244–245, 309–310, Family History Library.
24. Jenson, *Encyclopedic History of the Church*, 471–473.
25. Elizabeth Barney to Lewis Barney, 27 April 1888, Mancos, Colorado, Lewis Barney, Papers, Correspondence.
26. David Barney to Arthur Barney, 15 July 1888, Mancos, Colorado, Lewis Barney, Papers, Correspondence. See also Martha Ann and Tom Briscoe to Lewis Barney, 8 March 1890, Mancos, Colorado, Lewis Barney, Papers, Correspondence.
27. James Henry Barney to Lewis Barney, 29 June 1888, Kanosh, Utah, Lewis Barney, Papers, Correspondence.
28. David Barney to Lewis Barney, 10 June 1889, Mancos, Colorado, Lewis Barney, Papers, Correspondence.
29. Barney wrote David in September 1890 after David suggested by letter that he and his siblings, including Emeline and Albert, would visit their father the following year. "As far as Emeline, poor girl, I have but little hopes for her or that I shall ever see her again." Lewis Barney to David Barney, 21 September 1890, Manti, Utah, Lewis Barney, Papers, Correspondence. Family tradition also corroborates the family rift. It was reported by one family member that Emeline's husband Albert "wasn't very religious and didn't keep in very close touch with the family." This may have contributed to the family friction. Perkins and Gillen, Interview, 5.
30. Andrew Jenson, Prisoners for Conscience Sake, [ca. 1884–1892], Church Archives.
31. Van Wagoner, *Mormon Polygamy*, 119.
32. Lewis Barney to Azelia Barney, 14 June 1890, Manti, Utah, Lewis Barney, Papers, Correspondence.
33. Lewis Barney to John Barney, 7 June 1890, Manti, Utah, Lewis Barney, Papers, Correspondence.
34. Lewis Barney to John Barney, 26 June 1890, Manti, Utah, Lewis Barney, Papers, Correspondence. This communication, a plea to John to join him in Manti, describes his new living situation, "You will find me here in a log house west of the temple near the hill about three blocks from the temple."
35. David Barney to Lewis Barney, 14 September 1890, Mancos, Colorado, Lewis Barney, Papers, Correspondence.
36. Lewis Barney to David Barney, 21 September 1890, Manti, Utah, Lewis Barney, Papers, Correspondence. In July 1890 Lewis tried to obtain statements from Monrovians who knew of his losses during the Black Hawk War with hopes to "get something to help me live a little longer," by way of government reparations for losses incurred during Utah's Indian wars. Lewis Barney to Arthur Barney, 16 July 1890, Manti, Utah, Lewis Barney, Papers, Correspondence. The effort bore no

fruit. One contemporary source suggests Barney may have spent time ca. 1890 in Elsinore, Sevier County, Utah. Andrew Jenson, *The Historical Record* 9, nos. 7–12 (December 1890): 117.

37. For an overview of events leading to the abandonment of polygamy by the Latter-day Saints see James B. Allen and Glen M. Leonard, *The Story of the Latter-day Saints* (Salt Lake City: Deseret Book Company, 1976), 377–428; Edward Leo Lyman, *Political Deliverance: The Mormon Quest for Utah Statehood* (Urbana, Illinois: University of Illinois Press, 1986), 1–149; and B. Carmon Hardy, *Solemn Covenant: The Mormon Polygamous Passage* (Urbana, Illinois: University of Illinois Press, 1992), 39–166.

    For an overview of the implications of Mormon assimilation into the American mainstream and adjustments within the Church of Jesus Christ see Allen and Leonard, *Story of the Latter-day Saints*, 431–494; and Alexander, *Mormonism in Transition*, 1–59.

38. Manti Temple, Baptisms for the Dead, Book F, 338–341.
39. Ferron Ward records indicate the transferral of Joseph Smith Barney's LDS membership from Kanosh to Ferron occurred about 18 August 1890 though evidence indicates he retained ties to Kanosh to the mid-1890s. Ferron Ward, Record of Members, 41, Church Archives. Joseph S. Barney, though living in Ferron, died in 1917 in Salt Lake City during surgery.
40. Arthur Barney, Journal, 45. Arthur died in 1946 in Randlett, Utah.
41. Frederick H. Cabin, *The Land of the Cliff-Dwellers* (Boston: Appalachian Mountain Club, 1892), 99.
42. Ira S. Freeman, *A History of Montezuma County, Colorado* (Boulder, Colorado: Johnson Printing Company, 1958), 26–40, 119.
43. Andrew Jenson, *Deseret News*, 16 December 1893.
44. Jenson, *Encyclopedic History of the Church*, 469.
45. A dispute arose in the congregation during the absence of the branch president between his two counselors which divided the branch. Mancos Ward, Manuscript History, Church Archives; Fern D. Ellis, *Come Back to My Valley: Historical Remembrances of Mancos, Colorado* (Cortez, Colorado: Cortez Printers, 1976), 19–21. Another cause of dissension among the Mancos Saints may have originated in a rival group infiltrating the local Church of Jesus Christ near this time and drawing a number away from the congregation. William M. Packer, *Oscar and Ina Belle Geertsen: Family and Ancestors* (Provo, Utah: by the author, 1999), 130.
46. Presiding Bishopric, Statistical Reports. Other San Juan Stake wards were the Moab (Utah) with 153, Bluff (Utah) with 144, Monticello (Utah), and Burnham (New Mexico) with 68.
47. James Little, "Biography of William Rufus Rogers Stowell" (1893), typescript (1988), 81–82, Church Archives; Packer, *Oscar and Ina Belle Geertsen*, 130.
48. Jenson, *Deseret News*, 16 December 1893.
49. Quoted in Ellis, *Come Back to My Valley*, 23. Contemporary Native American influence in the area near Mancos diminished in the aftermath of the 1881 "Pinhook Draw Fight" near Moab, Utah, which affected the entire southwest Colorado and southeast Utah region. Rusty Solmon and Robert S. McPherson, "Cowboys, Indians, and Conflict: The Pinhook Draw Fight, 1881," *Utah Historical Quarterly* 69, no. 1 (winter 2001): 4–28.
50. Barney's church membership was transferred from the Price Ward on 20 June 1891 to the Mancos Ward. Price Ward, Record of Members; Mancos Ward, Record of Members.
51. Family Group Sheet, Family History Library.
52. Christensen, *Birth of Kanosh*, 91.
53. Barney to Clark and Johns, 24 April 1893.

54. Record of the Mancos Ward, Colorado, 1892–1902, Church Archives. Also, David Barney served as first counselor in the Mancos Ward Young Men's organization and as a ward teacher. Mancos Ward, Manuscript History.
55. *The Deseret Weekly*, 6 October 1894; Mancos Ward, Manuscript History.
56. Franklin Verner Briscoe, Interview, by Ronald O. Barney, 14 August 1976, Willow Flats, Idaho, typescript in possession of the author.
57. Record of the Mancos Ward, Colorado. Barney was buried in the Mormon cemetery, "sometimes called Webber Cemetery #1." The gravesite is "located 1½ miles south of Mancos on Webber Road #41 thence east ½ mile." It "was primarily used as a burial site for members of the LDS (Mormon) faith with the first burial in 1882." Barney and three of his grandchildren are buried there. Fern D. Ellis, "Cemeteries in Mancos," Family History Library. The present grave marker of recent placement indicating he died in 1895 is, of course, in error.
58. *Deseret News*, 19 November 1894.
59. Perkins and Gillen, Interview, 4.
60. Ibid., 6, 15–16.
61. Though the Denver and Rio Grande southern railway ran only three-quarters of a mile outside Mancos during Barney's stay there, the charge of ten cents per mile for passenger travel was considered extortionate. "Hence most of the people who visit Durango, which is forty miles distant by rail and only thirty miles by wagon road, generally travel in their old-fashioned way." Jenson, *The Deseret Weekly*, 16 December 1893.
62. Entry for 6 October 1881 in Woodruff, *Journal*, 8:57.

Bibliography

Printed Works

A Complete . . . American Atlas of North America and South America, etc., to the Year 1822. Philadelphia: H. C. Carey & I. Lea, 1823.

Adams, William Frederick, comp. *Commodore Joshua Barney*. Springfield, Massachusetts: Privately printed, 1912.

Ahlstrom, Sydney E. *A Religious History of the American People*. 2 vols. Garden City, New York: Image Books, 1975.

Alexander, Thomas G. *Mormonism in Transition: A History of the Latter-day Saints, 1890–1930*. Urbana, Illinois: University of Illinois Press, 1986.

———. *Things in Heaven and Earth: The Life and Times of Wilford Woodruff, a Mormon Prophet*. Salt Lake City: Signature Books, 1993.

Allen, James B. "Everyday Life in Utah's Elementary Schools, 1847–1870." In *Nearly Everything Imaginable: The Everyday Life of Utah's Mormon Pioneers*, edited by Ronald W. Walker and Doris Dant. Provo, Utah: Brigham Young University Press, 1999.

———. *Trials of Discipleship: The Story of William Clayton, a Mormon*. Urbana, Illinois: University of Illinois Press, 1987.

Allen, James B,. and Glen M. Leonard. *The Story of the Latter-day Saints*. Salt Lake City: Deseret Book Company, 1976.

Ambrose, Stephen E. *Nothing Like It in the World: The Men Who Built the Transcontinental Railroad, 1863–1869*. New York: Simon & Schuster, 2000.

Ames, Charles Edgar. *Pioneering the Union Pacific: A Reappraisal of the Builders of the Railroad*. New York: Appleton-Century-Crofts, 1969.

Angle, Paul M., comp. and ed. *Prairie State: Impressions of Illinois, 1673–1967, by Travelers and Other Observers*. Chicago: The University of Chicago Press, 1968.

Antrei, Albert C. T., and Allen D. Roberts. *A History of Sanpete County [Utah]*. Salt Lake City: Utah State Historical Society and Sanpete County Commission, 1999.

Arizona, the Grand Canyon State: A History of Arizona. 2 vols. Westminster, Colorado: Western States Historical Publishers Inc., 1975.

Arrington, Leonard J. *Brigham Young: American Moses*. New York: Alfred A. Knopf, 1985.

———. *From Quaker to Latter-day Saint: Bishop Edwin D. Woolley*. Salt Lake City: Deseret Book Company, 1976.

———. *Great Basin Kingdom: An Economic History of the Latter-day Saints, 1830–1900*. Cambridge, Massachusetts: Harvard University Press, 1958.

Arrington, Leonard J., Feramorz Y. Fox, and Dean L. May. *Building the City of God: Community and Cooperation among the Mormons*. Salt Lake City: Deseret Book Company, 1976.

Athearn, Robert G. *Union Pacific Country*. Chicago: Rand McNally & Company, 1971.

Backman, Milton V., Jr. "The Keys Are Right Here." In *Lion of the Lord: Essays on the Life and Service of Brigham Young*, edited by Susan Easton Black and Larry C. Porter. Salt Lake City, Utah: Deseret Book Company, 1995.

Bagley, Will. *Frontiersman: Abner Blackburn's Narrative*. Salt Lake City: University of Utah Press, 1992.

Bancroft, Hubert Howe. *History of Utah*. San Francisco, California: The History Company, 1890.

Barber, John W., and Henry Howe. *Historical Collections of the State of New York*. New York: S. Tuttle, 1841.

Barney, Mary, ed. *A Biographical Memoir of the Late Commodore Barney from Autobiographical Notes and Journals*. Boston: Gray and Bowen, 1832.

Bateman, Newton, et al., eds. *Historical Encyclopedia of Illinois and History of Hancock County*. 2 vols. Chicago: Munsell Publishing Company, 1921.

Bean, George Washington. *Autobiography of George W. Bean and His Family Records*. Compiled by Flora Diana Bean Horne. Salt Lake City: Utah Printing Company, 1945.

Beck, Lewis C. *A Gazetteer of the States of Illinois and Missouri*. Albany, New York: Charles R. and George Webster, 1823.

Beecher, Dale F. "Colonizer of the West." In *Lion of the Lord: Essays on the Life and Service of Brigham Young*, edited by Susan Easton Black and Larry C. Porter. Salt Lake City: Deseret Book Company, 1995.

Bell, Carol Willsey. *Ohio Genealogical Guide*. Youngstown, Ohio: Bell Books, 1990.

Bennett, John C. *The History of the Saints, or an Expose of Joe Smith and the Mormons*. Boston: Leland & Whiting, 1842.

Bennett, Richard E. "Finalizing Plans for the Trek West: Deliberations at Winter Quarters, 1846–1847." In *Coming to Zion*, edited by James B. Allen and John W. Welch. Provo, Utah: Brigham Young University Studies, 1997.

———. *Mormons at the Missouri, 1846–1852: "And Should We Die."* Norman, Oklahoma: University of Oklahoma Press, 1987.

———. *We'll Find the Place: The Mormon Exodus, 1846–1848*. Salt Lake City: Deseret Book Company, 1997.

Berry, Ellen T., and David A. Berry. *Early Ohio Settlers: Purchasers of Land in Southeastern Ohio, 1800–1840*. Baltimore: Genealogical Publishing Co., 1984, 1989.

Bigler, David L. *Forgotten Kingdom: The Mormon Theocracy in the American West, 1847–1896*. Spokane, Washington: Arthur H. Clark Company, 1998.

Billington, Ray Allen. *America's Frontier Heritage*. New York: Holt, Rinehart and Winston, 1966.

Bitton, Davis, and Linda P. Wilcox. "The Transformation of Utah's Agriculture, 1847–1900." In *The Twentieth Century American West: Contributions to an Understanding*, edited by Thomas G. Alexander and John F. Bluth. Midvale, Utah: Charles Redd Center for Western Studies, 1983.

Black, Irene, Ruth Mae Harris, and Lorraine Vance, comps. *Circle of Sixteen: Family of Franklin Van Buren Barney and Lucy Ann Victoria Lindquist*. Orem, Utah: Likes Publishing, 1998.

Black, Joseph Smith. "Diary of Joseph Smith Black." In *Our Pioneer Heritage*, compiled by Kate B. Carter. vol. 10. Salt Lake City: Daughters of Utah Pioneers, 1958–1977.

Bogue, Allen G. *From Prairie to Corn Belt: Farming on the Illinois and Iowa Prairies in the Nineteenth Century*. Chicago: Quadrangle Books, 1968.

Boyer-Reinstein, Julia, comp. *Town of Cheektowaga Historical Atlas*. Buffalo, New York: Buffalo & Erie County Public Library, Special Collections, 1953.

Bradley, Martha Sonntag. *A History of Beaver County [Utah]*. Salt Lake City: Utah State Historical Society and Beaver County Commission, 1999.

Brevet's Illinois Historical Markers and Sites. Sioux Falls, South Dakota: Brevet Press, Inc., 1976.

Brooks, Charles E. *Frontier Settlement and Market Revolution: The Holland Land Purchase*. Ithaca, New York: Cornell University Press, 1996.

Brooks, Juanita. *The Mountain Meadows Massacre*. Norman, Oklahoma: University of Oklahoma Press, 1974.

———. *On the Ragged Edge: The Life and Times of Dudley Leavitt*. Salt Lake City: Utah State Historical Society, 1973.

Brown, Benjamin. "Testimonies for the Truth." In *Gems for the Young Folks: Fourth Book of the Faith-Promoting Series*. Salt Lake City: Juvenile Instructor Office, 1881, reprint Bookcraft, 1968.

Brown, Joseph E. *The Mormon Trek West*. Garden City, New York: Doubleday & Company Inc., 1980.

Brown, S. Kent, Donald Q. Cannon, and Richard H. Jackson, eds. *Historical Atlas of Mormonism*. New York: Simon & Schuster, 1994.

Brown, Thomas D. *Journal of the Southern Indian Mission: Diary of Thomas D. Brown*. Edited by Juanita Brooks. Logan, Utah: Utah State University Press, 1972.

Bullock, Thomas. *The Pioneer Camp of the Saints: The 1846 and 1847 Mormon Trail Journals of Thomas Bullock*. Edited by Will Bagley. Spokane, Washington: Arthur H. Clark Company, 1997.

Burr, Wesley R., and Ruth J. Burr. *A History of the Burr Pioneers*. Salt Lake City: Charles and Sarah Burr Family Organization, 1995.

Busby, A. Mikel, comp., and Marilyn Mills, ed. *San Bernardino Valley, 1847–1857: History and Tour, 150th Anniversary*. N.p.: Southern California Sesquicentennial Committee, 1997.

Bushman, Richard L. *The Refinement of America: Persons, Houses, Cities*. New York: Vintage Books, 1993.

Cabin, Frederick H. *The Land of the Cliff-Dwellers*. Boston: Appalachian Mountain Club, 1892.

Campbell, Eugene E. *Establishing Zion: The Mormon Church in the American West, 1847–1869*. Salt Lake City: Signature Books, 1988.

———. "The Mormon Migrations to Utah." In *Utah's History*, edited by Richard Poll, et al. Provo, Utah: Brigham Young University Press, 1978.

Cannon, Brian Q. "Adopted or Indentured, 1850–1870: Native Children in Mormon Households." In *Nearly Everything Imaginable: The Everyday Life of Utah's Mormon Pioneers*, edited by Ronald W. Walker and Doris Dant. Provo, Utah: Brigham Young University Press, 1999.

Carey, H. C. *A Complete . . . American Atlas of North America and South America, etc., to the Year 1822*. Philadelphia: H. C. Carey & I. Lea, 1823.

Carr, Edward Hallett. *What Is History?* New York: Vintage Books, 1961.

Carr, Kay J. *Belleville, Ottawa, and Galesburg: Community and Democracy on the Illinois Frontier*. Carbondale, Illinois: Southern Illinois University Press, 1996.

Carter, Kate B., comp. *Heart Throbs of the West*. 12 vols. Salt Lake City: Daughters of Utah Pioneers, 1939–1951.

———. *Our Pioneer Heritage*. 20 vols. Salt Lake City: Daughters of Utah Pioneers, 1958–1977.

———. *Treasures of Pioneer History*. 6 vols. Salt Lake City: Daughters of Utah Pioneers, 1952–1957.

Cartwright, Peter. *Autobiography of Peter Cartwright: The Backwoods Preacher*. Edited by W. P. Strickland. New York: Carlton & Porter, 1856.

Carvalho, S. N. *Incidents of Travel and Adventure in the Far West; with Col. Frémont's Last Expedition*. New York: Derby & Jackson, 1857.

Chavez, Angelico, trans., and Ted J. Warner, ed. *The Dominguez-Escalante Journal: Their Expedition through Colorado, Utah, Arizona, and New Mexico in 1776*. Provo, Utah: Brigham Young University Press, 1976.

Chazanof, William. *Joseph Ellicott and the Holland Land Company: The Opening of Western New York*. Syracuse, New York: Syracuse University Press, 1970.

Christensen, Leavitt. *Birth of Kanosh*. N.p.: J-Mart Publishing, [ca. 1997].
Christian, Lewis Clark. "Mormon Foreknowledge of the West." In *Coming to Zion*, edited by James B. Allen and John W. Welch. Provo, Utah: Brigham Young University Press, 1997.
Clark, James R., ed. *Messages of the First Presidency of the Church of Jesus Christ of Latter-day Saints, 1833–1964*. 6 vols. Salt Lake City: Bookcraft, 1965.
Clayton, William. *An Intimate Chronicle: The Journals of William Clayton*. Edited by George D. Smith. Salt Lake City: Signature Books, 1995.
———. *William Clayton's Journal*. Salt Lake City: The Deseret News, 1921.
Coates, Lawrence G. "Refugees, Friends, and Foes: Mormons and Indians in Iowa and Nebraska." In *Coming to Zion*, edited by James B. Allen and John W. Welch. Provo, Utah: Brigham Young University Studies, 1997.
Comeaux, Malcolm L. *Arizona: A Geography*. Boulder, Colorado: Westview Press, 1981.
Cook, Lyndon W. *Joseph Smith and the Law of Consecration*. Provo, Utah: Grandin Book Co., 1985.
———. comp. *Nauvoo: Deaths and Marriages, 1839–1845*. Provo, Utah: Grandin Book Company, 1994.
Corbett, Pearson H. *Jacob Hamblin: The Peacemaker*. Salt Lake City: Deseret Book Company, 1952.
Cowley, Matthias F. *Wilford Woodruff*. Salt Lake City: Deseret News, 1909, reprint Bookcraft, 1965.
Cradlebaugh, John. *Utah and the Mormons. Speech of Hon. John Cradlebaugh of Nevada on the Admission of Utah as a State Delivered in the House of Representatives, February 7, 1868*. Washington, D.C.: L. Towers & Co., 1863.
Crawley, Peter. *A Descriptive Bibliography of the Mormon Church: Volume One, 1830–1847*. Provo, Utah: Religious Studies Center, Brigham Young University, 1997.
Cronon, William, George Miles, and Jay Gitlin. "Becoming West: Toward a New Meaning for Western History." In *Under an Open Sky: Rethinking America's Western Past*, edited by William Cronon, George Miles, and Jay Gitlin. New York: W. W. Norton & Company, 1992.
Culmsee, Carlton. *Utah's Black Hawk War*. Logan, Utah: Utah State University Press, 1973.
Daughters of Utah Pioneers. *Chronicles of Courage*. 9 vols. Salt Lake City: Daughters of Utah Pioneers, 1990–1998.
———. *An Enduring Legacy*. 12 vols. Salt Lake City: Daughters of Utah Pioneers, 1978–1989.
Daughters of Utah Pioneers, Sanpete County Camp. *These . . . Our Fathers: A Centennial History of Sanpete County, 1849–1947*. Springville, Utah: Art City Publishing Co., 1947.
Davis, James E. *Frontier America, 1800–1840: A Comparative Demographic Analysis of the Settlement Process*. Glendale, California: The Arthur H. Clark Company, 1977.
Day, Stella H., and Sebrina C. Ekins. *Milestones of Millard: 100 Years of Millard County [Utah]*. Springville, Utah: Art City Publishing Co., 1951.
Dewitt, Simeon. *A Map of the State of New York*. N.p.: n.p., 1804.
Dills, R. S. *History of Fayette County . . . Ohio*. Dayton, Ohio: Odell & Mayer, 1881.
The Doctrine and Covenants of the Church of Jesus Christ of Latter-day Saints. Salt Lake City: the Church of Jesus Christ of Latter-day Saints, 1981.
Donald, David Herbert. *Lincoln*. London: Jonathon Cape, 1995.
Doty, Lockwood R. *History of the Genesee Country (Western New York)*. 2 vols. Chicago: S. J. Clarke Publishing Company, 1925.
Downs, John P., and Fenwick Y. Hedley, eds. *History of Chautauqua County, New York and Its People*. 3 vols. Boston: American Historical Society, Inc., 1921.

Do You Remember Luna: 100 Years of Pioneer History. Albuquerque, New Mexico: The Luna Ward, 1983.

Egan, Howard. *Pioneering the West, 1846 to 1878: Major Howard Egan's Diary*. Richmond, Utah: Howard R. Egan Estate, 1917.

The 1850 Census of Illinois: Hancock County. Richland, Washington: Locust Grove Press, 1977.

Elliott, Isaac H. *Record of the Services of Illinois Soldiers in the Black Hawk War, 1831–1832, and in the Mexican War, 1846–1848*. Springfield, Illinois: Journal Company, 1902.

Ellis, David M., James A. Frost, Harold C. Syrett, and Harry J. Carman. *A History of New York State*. Ithaca, New York: Cornell University Press, 1967.

Ellis, Fern D. *Come Back to My Valley: Historical Remembrances of Mancos, Colorado*. Cortez, Colorado: Cortez Printers, 1976.

Ericksen, Ephraim Edward. *The Psychological and Ethical Aspects of Mormon Group Life*. Chicago: University of Chicago, 1922, reprint Salt Lake City: University of Utah, 1975.

Evans, John Henry, and Minnie Egan Anderson. *Ezra T. Benson: Pioneer, Statesman, Saint*. Salt Lake City: Deseret News Press, 1947.

Evans, Paul Demund. *The Holland Land Company*. Buffalo, New York: Buffalo Historical Society, 1924.

Faragher, John Mack. *Daniel Boone: The Life and Legend of an American Pioneer*. New York: Henry Holt and Company, 1992.

———. *Sugar Creek: Life on the Illinois Prairie*. New Haven, Connecticut: Yale University Press, 1986.

———. *Women and Men on the Overland Trail*. New Haven, Connecticut: Yale University Press, 1979.

Finley, Mary J. Chase. *A History of Springville [Utah]*. Springville, Utah: Art City Publishing, [ca. 1989].

Fish, Joseph. *The Life and Times of Joseph Fish, Mormon Pioneer*. Edited by John H. Krenkel. Danville, Illinois: The Interstate Printers & Publishers, Inc., 1970.

Flanders, Robert Bruce. *Nauvoo: Kingdom on the Mississippi*. Urbana, Illinois: University of Illinois Press, 1975.

Flint, Timothy. *The History and Geography of the Mississippi Valley*. Cincinnati: E. H. Flint and L. R. Linden, 1832.

Footner, Hulbert. *Sailor of Fortune: The Life and Adventures of Commodore Barney, U.S.N.* New York: Harper & Brothers, 1940.

Foster, Lawrence. *Religion and Sexuality: The Shakers, the Mormons, and the Oneida Community*. Urbana, Illinois: University of Illinois Press, 1984.

Frazer, Robert W. *Forts of the West: Military Forts and Presidios and Posts Commonly Called Forts West of the Mississippi River to 1898*. Norman, Oklahoma: University of Oklahoma Press, 1972.

Freeman, Ira S. *A History of Montezuma County, Colorado*. Boulder, Colorado: Johnson Printing Company, 1958.

French, J. H. *Gazetteer of the State of New York*. Syracuse, New York: R. Pearsall Smith, 1860.

Furniss, Norman F. *The Mormon Conflict, 1850–1859*. New Haven, Connecticut: Yale University Press, 1960.

Geary, Edward A. *The Proper Edge of the Sky: The High Plateau Country of Utah*. Salt Lake City: University of Utah Press, 1992.

Gems for the Young Folks: Fourth Book of the Faith-Promoting Series. Salt Lake City: Juvenile Instructor Office, 1881, reprint Bookcraft, 1968.

Givens, George W. *In Old Nauvoo: Everyday Life in the City of Joseph*. Salt Lake City: Deseret Book Company, 1990.

Goodson, Stephanie Smith. "Plural Wives." In *Mormon Sisters*, edited by Claudia L. Bushman. Cambridge, Massachusetts: Emmeline Press Limited, 1976.

Gottfredson, Peter. *History of Indian Depredations in Utah*. Salt Lake City: Skelton Publishing Co., 1919.

Gove, Jesse Augustus. *The Utah Expedition, 1857–1858: Letters of Capt. Jesse A. Gove*. Concord, New Hampshire: New Hampshire Historical Society, 1928.

Granger, Byrd Howell. *Arizona Names: X Marks the Spot*. Tuscon, Arizona: The Falconer Pub. Co., 1983.

Green, Emagene Veech. *And She Held Forth Her Hand: History and Genealogy of Mt. Pulaski, Illinois*. Lincoln, Illinois: n.p., 1961.

Gregg, Thomas. *A Descriptive, Statistical and Historical Chart of the County of Hancock [Illinois]*. Warsaw, Illinois: Thomas Gregg, 1846.

———. *History of Hancock County, Illinois*. Chicago: Chas. C. Chapman & Co., 1880.

Guelzo, Allen C. *Abraham Lincoln: Redeemer President*. Grand Rapids, Michigan: William B. Eerdman's Publishing Company, 1999.

Hafen, LeRoy R. "Elijah Barney Ward." In *The Mountain Men and the Fur Trade of the Far West*, edited by LeRoy R. Hafen. 10 vols. Glendale, California: Arthur H. Clark Company, 1969.

Hafen, LeRoy R., and Ann W. Hafen, eds. *Old Spanish Trail, Santa Fé to Los Angeles: With Extracts from Contemporary Records and Including Diaries of Antonio Armijo and Orville Pratt*. Glendale, California: Arthur H. Clark Company, 1968.

———. *The Utah Expedition, 1857–1858: A Documentary Account of the United States Military Movement under Colonel Albert Sidney Johnston and the Resistance by Brigham Young and the Mormon Nauvoo Legion*. Glendale, California: The Arthur H. Clark Co., 1958.

Hallwas, John E., and Roger D. Launius, eds. *Cultures in Conflict: A Documentary History of the Mormon War in Illinois*. Logan, Utah: Utah State University Press, 1995.

———. "Mormon Nauvoo from a Non-Mormon Perspective." In *Kingdom on the Mississippi Revisited: Nauvoo in Mormon History*, edited by Roger D. Launius and John E. Hallwas. Urbana, Illinois: University of Illinois Press, 1996.

Hamilton, Marshall. "From Assassination to Expulsion: Two Years of Distrust, Hostility, and Violence." In *Kingdom in the West Revisited: Nauvoo In Mormon History*, edited by John E. Hallwas and Roger D. Launius. Urbana, Illinois: University of Illinois Press, 1996.

Handbook of the Relief Society of the Church of Jesus Christ of Latter-day Saints. [Salt Lake City]: General Board of Relief Society, 1931.

Hardy, B. Carmon. *Solemn Covenant: The Mormon Polygamous Passage*. Urbana, Illinois: University of Illinois Press, 1992.

Harper, Charles Alfred. *The Diary of Charles Alfred Harper*. N.p.: n.p., 1971.

Hartley, William G. "Common People: Church Activity during the Brigham Young Era." In *Nearly Everything Imaginable: The Everyday Life of Utah's Mormon Pioneers*, edited by Ronald W. Walker and Doris Dant. Provo, Utah: Brigham Young University Press, 1999.

———. *My Best for the Kingdom: History and Autobiography of John Lowe Butler, A Mormon Frontiersman*. Salt Lake City: Aspen Books, 1993.

Hatch, Nathan O. *The Democratization of American Christianity*. New Haven, Connecticut: Yale University Press, 1989.

Hayes, Charles Wells. *The Diocese of Western New York: History and Recollections*. Rochester, New York: Scrantom, Wetmore & Co., 1904.

Heads of Families at the First Census of the United States Taken in the Year 1790, New York. Washington: Government Printing Office, 1908.

Helwig, Richard M., and Richard N. Helwig, eds. *Ohio Ghost Towns, No. 35, Knox County [Ohio]*. Sunbury, Ohio: The Center for Ghost Town Research in Ohio, 1995.

Herndon, William H. *Herndon's Life of Lincoln: The History and Personal Recollections of Abraham Lincoln as Originally Written by William H. Herndon and Jesse W. Weik*. Edited by Paul M. Angle. New York: De Capo Press, 1983.

Hill, Marvin S. *Quest for Refuge: The Mormon Flight from American Pluralism*. Salt Lake City: Signature Books, 1989.

Hill, N. N., Jr., comp. *History of Knox County, Ohio: Its Past and Present*. Mt. Vernon, Ohio: A. A. Graham & Co., 1881.

Hills, Gustavus. *Map of the City of Nauvoo*. New York: J. Childs, 1842.

Hilton, Ruth Savage, ed. *Lorenzo Hill Hatch Journal*. Provo, Utah: Brigham Young University Adult Education and Extension Services, 1958.

History of Crawford County, Arkansas: Press-Argus Centennial Edition. N.p.: n.p., ca. 1959.

History of Fayette County, Ohio 1984. Washington Court House, Ohio: Fayette County Genealogical Society, 1984.

History of Harrison County, Iowa. Chicago: National Publishing Company, 1891.

History of Henry County, Iowa. Dallas, Texas: N.p., 1982.

History of Logan County, Illinois: Its Past and Present. Chicago: Donnelly, Loyd & Co., 1878.

History of Sangamon County, Illinois. Chicago: Inter-state Publishing Company, 1881.

History of Sanpete and Emery Counties, Utah. Ogden, Utah: W. H. Lever, 1898.

Hoffman, Charles Fenno. "Galeno." In *Prairie State: Impression of Illinois, 1673–1967, by Travelers and Other Observers*. Compiled and edited by Paul M. Angle. Chicago: University of Chicago Press, 1968.

Hogan, Mervin B. *Mormon Involvement with Freemasonry on the Illinois and Iowa Frontier between 1840 and 1846*. Salt Lake City: N.p., 1983.

———. *The Two Joseph Smith's Masonic Experiences*. Salt Lake City: N.p., 1987.

Holmes, Gail Geo. "A Prophet Who Followed, Fulfilled, and Magnified." In *Lion of the Lord: Essays on the Life and Service of Brigham Young*, edited by Susan Easton Black and Larry C. Porter. Salt Lake City, Utah: Deseret Book Company, 1995.

Holzapfel, Richard Neitzel. *A History of Utah County [Utah]*. Salt Lake City: Utah State Historical Society and Utah County Commission, 1999.

Holzapfel, Richard Neitzel, and T. Jeffery Cottle. *Old Mormon Nauvoo and Southeastern Iowa*. Santa Ana, California: Fieldbrook Productions, Inc., 1991.

Howard, Robert P. *Illinois: A History of the Prairie State*. Grand Rapids, Michigan: William B. Eerdmans Publishing Company, 1972.

Howe, Henry. *Historical Collections of Ohio in Two Volumes*. Norwalk, Ohio: State of Ohio, 1898.

Huff, Emma N. *Memories That Live: Utah County [Utah] Centennial History*. Springville, Utah: Daughters of Utah Pioneers of Utah County, 1947.

Hughes, Richard T., ed. *The American Quest for the Primitive Church*. Urbana, Illinois: University of Illinois Press, 1988.

Hughes, Richard T., and C. Leonard Allen. *Illusions of Innocence: Protestant Primitivism in America, 1630–1875*. Chicago: University of Chicago Press, 1988.

Hunter, Milton R. *Brigham Young the Colonizer*. Santa Barbara, California: Peregrine Smith, Inc., 1973.

Hurt, R. Douglas. *The Ohio Frontier: Crucible of the Old Northwest, 1720–1830*. Bloomington, Indiana: Indiana University Press, 1996.

Hyde, Myrtle Stevens. *Orson Hyde: The Olive Branch of Israel*. Salt Lake City: Agreka Books, 2000.

Hyde, Orson. *Speech of Elder Orson Hyde Delivered before the High Priests Quorum in Nauvoo, April 27th, 1845*. City of Joseph [Nauvoo], Illinois: John Taylor, 1845.

Illinois: A Descriptive and Historical Guide. Chicago: A. C. McClurg & Co., 1939.

Illinois in 1837: a Sketch. Philadelphia: S. Augustus Mitchell, 1837.

Illustrated Historical Atlas of Erie Co., New York, from Actual Surveys and Records. New York: F. W. Beers & Co., 1880.

Illustrated Historical Atlas of Fayette County, Ohio. Philadelphia: L. H. Everts & Co., 1875.

Illustrated Historical Atlas of Hancock County, Illinois. Chicago: A. T. Andreas, 1874.

Ingersoll's Century Annals of San Bernardino County [California], 1769 to 1904. Los Angeles: Ingersoll, 1904.

Jackson, Richard H. "The Mormon Indian Farms: An Attempt at Cultural Integration." In *Geographical Perspectives on Native Americans: Topics and Resources*, edited by Jerry N. McDonald and Tony Lazewski. Los Angeles: Association of American Geographers, 1976.

———, ed. *The Mormon Role in the Settlement of the West*. Provo, Utah: Brigham Young University Press, 1978.

Jacob, Norton. *The Record of Norton Jacob*. Edited by Edward Jacob and Ruth S. Jacob. Salt Lake City: Stevens & Wallis, Inc., 1949.

Jacobsen, Gwendolyn. *Memories of "Little Denmark": History of Elsinore and Brooklyn, Utah*. Richfield, Utah: Elsinore Literary Club, n.d.

Jaynes, Peter H., ed. *Highlights of Henry County, Iowa History, 1833–1976*. Burlington, Iowa: Doran & Ward Lithographing Co., 1976.

Jensen, J. Marinus. *History of Provo, Utah*. Provo, Utah: J. Marinus Jensen, 1924.

Jenson, Andrew. *Day by Day with the Utah Pioneers: A Chronological Record of the Trek across the Plains*. Salt Lake City: Salt Lake Tribune, 1934.

———. *Encyclopedic History of the Church of Jesus Christ of Latter-day Saints*. Salt Lake City: Deseret News Publishing Co., 1941.

———. *Latter-day Saints' Biographical Encylopedia*. 4 vols. Salt Lake City: Andrew Jenson History Company/Andrew Jenson Memorial Association, 1901–1936.

Johnson, Benjamin Franklin. *My Life's Review*. Independence, Missouri: Zion's Printing & Publishing Co., 1947.

Johnson, Don Carlos. *A Brief History of Springville, Utah*. Springville, Utah: William H. Gibson, 1900.

Johnson, Joel Hills. *A Voice from the Mountains: Life and Works of Joel Hills Johnson*. Mesa, Arizona: Lofgreen's Inc., 1982.

Jolley, Bryant Manning. *The Jolley Family Book: The Story of Henry Jolley and His Wife Francis Manning Jolley*. Provo, Utah: Brigham Young University Press, 1966.

Jones, Garth N. *James Thompson Lisonbee's Missionary Labors: On the Sand Mountain of Northeastern Alabama and Northwestern Georgia, Beginnings of a New Gathering in the San Luis Valley of Colorado, 1876–1878*. Provo, Utah: Brigham Young University Press, 2000.

Jones, Sondra. *The Trial of Don Pedro Leon Lujan: The Attack against Indian Slavery and Mexican Traders in Utah*. Salt Lake City: University of Utah Press, 2000.

Journal of Discourses. 26 vols. Liverpool: S. W. Richards et al., 1853–1886.

Jubilee History of Latter-day Saint Sunday Schools, 1849–1899. Salt Lake City: Deseret Sunday School Union, 1900.

Kane, Thomas L. *The Mormons: A Discourse*. Philadelphia: King & Baird, 1850.

Kates, Frederick Ward, comp. *Patriot-Soldiers of 1775–1783: The Veterans of the War for American Independence of Chautauqua County, New York*. N.p.: Jamestown Chapter, National Society, Daughters of the American Revolution, 1981.

Kilner, Arthur R. *Greene County, Ohio: Births prior to 1869*. Bowie, Maryland: Heritage Books, Inc., 1988.

Kimball, Stanley B. *Heber C. Kimball: Mormon Patriarch and Pioneer*. Urbana, Illinois: University of Illinois Press, 1981.

———. *Historic Sites and Markers along the Mormon and Other Great Western Trails*. Urbana, Illinois: University of Illinois Press, 1988.

———. "The Mormon Trail Network in Nebraska, 1846–1848." In *Coming to Zion*, edited by James B. Allen and John W. Welch, Provo, Utah: Brigham Young University Studies, 1997.

Kinkead, Joyce, ed. *A Schoolmarm All My Life: Personal Narratives from Frontier Utah*. Salt Lake City: Signature Books, 1996.

Knight, Hal, and Stanley B. Kimball. *111 Days to Zion*. Salt Lake City: Deseret Press, 1978; Salt Lake City: Big Moon Traders, 1997.

Krenkel, John H., ed. *The Life and Times of Joseph Fish, Mormon Pioneer*. Danville, Illinois: The Interstate Printers & Publishers, Inc., 1970.

Langely, Harold D., ed. *To Utah with the Dragoons and Glimpses of Life in Arizona and California, 1858–1859*. Salt Lake City: University of Utah Press, 1974.

Larkin, Jack. *The Reshaping of Everyday Life, 1790–1840*. New York: Harper & Row Publishers, 1988.

Larsen, Oluf Christian. "From the Journal of Oluf Christian Larsen." In *Treasures of Pioneer History*, compiled by Kate B. Carter. 6 vols. Salt Lake City: Daughters of Utah Pioneers, 1952–1957.

Larson, Gustive O. *Outline History of Utah and the Mormons*. Salt Lake City: Deseret Book Company, 1965.

Launius, Roger D. *Joseph Smith III: Pragmatic Prophet*. Urbana, Illinois: University of Illinois Press, 1988.

Lee, John D. *Journals of John D. Lee, 1846–1847 and 1859*. Edited by Charles Kelly. Salt Lake City: University of Utah Press, 1984

———. *A Mormon Chronicle: The Diaries of John D. Lee, 1848–1876*. Edited by Robert Glass Cleland and Juanita Brooks. 2 vols. Salt Lake City: University of Utah Press, 1983.

LeSueur, Stephen C. *The 1838 Mormon War in Missouri*. Columbia, Missouri: University of Missouri Press, 1987.

Livsey, Karen E. *Western New York Land Transactions, 1804–1824: Extracted from the Archives of the Holland Land Company*. Baltimore: Genealogical Publishing Company, 1991.

Lockwood, Frank C. *Pioneer Days in Arizona: From the Spanish Occupation to Statehood*. New York: The Macmillan Company, 1932.

Lyman. Edward Leo. *Political Deliverance: The Mormon Quest for Utah Statehood*. Urbana, Illinois: University of Illinois Press, 1986.

———. *San Bernardino: The Rise and Fall of a California Community*. Salt Lake City: Signature Books, 1996.

Lyman, Edward Leo, and Linda King Newell. *A History of Millard County [Utah]*. Salt Lake City: Utah State Historical Society and Millard County Commission, 1999.

Marriage Records, Sangamon County, Illinois, 1821–1840. Springfield, Illinois: Sangamon County Genealogical Society of Illinois, n.d.

Martin, George A., ed. *Fences, Gates and Bridges: A Practical Manual*. New York: O. Judd Co., 1887.

Mattes, Merrill J. *Platte River Road Narratives: A Descriptive Bibliography of Travel over the Great Overland Route to Oregon, California, Utah, Colorado, Montana and Other Western States and Territories, 1812–1866*. Urbana, Illinois: University of Illinois Press, 1988.

May, Dean L. "A Demographic Portrait of Mormons, 1830–1980." In *After 150 Years: The Latter-day Saints in Sesquicentennial Perspective*, edited by Thomas G. Alexander and Jessie L. Embry. Midvale, Utah: Charles Redd Center for Western History, 1983.

McBeth, H. Leon. *The Baptist Heritage*. Nashville, Tennessee: Broadman Press, 1987.

McClintock, James H. *Arizona*. 3 vols. Chicago: S. J. Clarke Publishing Co., 1916.

———. *Mormon Settlement in Arizona: A Record of Peaceful Conquest of the Desert*. Phoenix, Arizona: N.p., 1921.

McKenney, Horace H. *Pioneer History of Harris Grove, 1851–1861*. N.p.: n.p., ca. 1925.
McLaughlin, Jack. *Jefferson and Monticello: The Biography of a Builder*. New York: Henry Holt and Company, 1988.
McLean County [Illinois] Marriage Records, 1831–1855. N.p.: Bloomington-Normal Genealogical Society, n.d.
McLellin, William E. *Journals of William E. McLellin, 1831–1836*. Edited by Jan Shipps and John W. Welch. Provo, Utah: Brigham Young University Studies and University of Illinois Press, 1994.
McPherson, James M., ed. *"To the Best of My Ability": The American Presidents*. New York: Dorling Kindersley Publishing, Inc., 2000.
Message from the President of the United States to the Two Houses of Congress, at the Commencement of the First Sessions of the Thirty-fifth Congress. Washington: Congressional Globe Office, 1857.
Miller, David E., and Della S. Miller. *Nauvoo: The City of Joseph*. Santa Barbara, California: Peregrine Smith, Inc., 1974.
Miller, Perry. "Errand into the Wilderness." In *Religion in America: A Reader,* edited by Jon Butler and Harry S. Stout. New York: Oxford University Press, 1998.
Morgan, Dale L. *The Great Salt Lake*. Albuquerque, New Mexico: University of New Mexico Press, 1973.
Moorman, Donald R., with Gene A. Sessions. *Camp Floyd and the Mormons: The Utah War*. Salt Lake City: University of Utah Press, 1992.
Mt. Graham Profiles: Graham County, Arizona, 1870–1977. N.p.: Graham County Historical Society, n.d.
Mulder, William. *Homeward to Zion: The Mormon Migration from Scandinavia*. Minneapolis: University of Minnesota Press in cooperation with Brigham Young University Press, 1957 and 2000.
Murdock, Wilford, and Mildred Murdock. *Monroe, Utah: Its First One Hundred Years, 1864–1964*. Monroe, Utah: Monroe Centennial Committee and Monroe City, 1964.
Nauvoo Temple Endowment Register, 10 December 1845 to 8 February 1846. Salt Lake City: N.p., 1974.
Nelson, Lowry. *The Mormon Village*. Salt Lake City: University of Utah Press, 1952.
Newell, Linda King. *A History of Piute County [Utah]*. Salt Lake City: Utah State Historical Society and Piute County Commission, 1999.
Newell, Linda King, and Valeen Tippetts Avery. *Mormon Enigma: Emma Hale Smith, Prophet's Wife, "Elect Lady," Polygamy's Foe, 1804–1879*. Garden City, New York: Doubleday & Company, 1984.
Norton, A. Banning. *History of Knox County, Ohio: From 1779 to 1862 Inclusive*. Columbus, Ohio: Richard Nevins, 1862.
Oaks, Dallin H., and Marvin S. Hill. *Carthage Conspiracy: The Trials of the Accused Assassins of Joseph Smith*. Urbana, Illinois: University of Illinois Press, 1979.
Oates, Stephen B. *With Malice toward None: A Life of Abraham Lincoln*. New York: HarperPerennial, 1994.
O'Callaghan, E. B. *The Documentary History of the State of New York*. 4 vols. Albany, New York: Weed, Parsons & Co., 1850.
Packard, Noah. *A Synopsis of the Life and Travels of Noah Packard, Written by Himself*. [Salt Lake City]: N.p., [ca. 1972].
Packer, William M. *Oscar and Ina Belle Geertsen: Family and Ancestors*. Provo, Utah: William M. Packer, 1999.
Paine, Ralph D. *Joshua Barney: A Forgotten Hero of Blue Water*. New York: The Century Co., 1924.
Pease, Theodore Calvin. *The Frontier State, 1818–1848*. Urbana, Illinois: University of Illinois Press, 1987.

———, ed. *Illinois Election Returns, 1818–1848*. Springfield, Illinois: Illinois State Historical Library, 1923.

Peck, John Mason. *A Gazetteer of Illinois, in Three Parts*. Jacksonville, Illinois: R. Goudy, 1834.

Peterson, Charles S. "Imprint of Agricultural Systems on the Utah Landscape." In *The Mormon Role in the Settlement of the West*, edited by Richard H. Jackson. Provo, Utah: Brigham Young University Press, 1978.

———. *Take Up Your Mission: Mormon Colonizing along the Little Colorado River, 1870–1900*. Tucson, Arizona: University of Arizona Press, 1973.

Peterson, John A. *Utah's Black Hawk War*. Salt Lake City: University of Utah Press, 1998.

Peterson, Merrill D. *Lincoln in American Memory*. New York: Oxford University Press, 1995.

Peterson, Paul H. "Brigham Young and the Mormon Reformation." In *Lion of the Lord: Essays on the Life and Service of Brigham Young*, edited by Susan Easton Black and Larry C. Porter. Salt Lake City, Utah: Deseret Book Company, 1995.

Poll, Richard, Thomas G. Alexander, Eugene E. Campbell, and David E. Miller, eds. *Utah's History*. Logan, Utah: Utah State University Press, 1989.

Porter, Lyle K., and Wilma H. Porter. *A History of the Church of Jesus Christ of Latter-day Saints in New Mexico, 1876–1989*. Albuquerque, New Mexico: Lyle K. and Wilma H. Porter, 1997.

Pratt, Orson. *The Orson Pratt Journals*. Edited by Elden J. Watson. Salt Lake City: Elden J. Watson, 1975.

Pratt, Parley P. *Autobiography of Parley P. Pratt*. Edited by Parley P. Pratt, Jr. Salt Lake City: Deseret Book Company, 1972.

Preston, Eugene Dimon. *Genealogy of the Barney Family in America*. Edited by William Clifford Barney. N.p.: The Barney Family Historical Association, 1990.

Prucha, Francis Paul. *The Sword of the Republic: The United States Army on the Frontier, 1783–1846*. New York: The Macmillan Company, 1969.

Putnam, Rufus. *Pioneer Record and Reminiscences of the Early Settlers and Settlement of Fayette County, Ohio*. Cincinnati: Applegate, Pounsford & Co., 1872.

Remini, Robert V. Andrew Jackson and the Course of American Democracy, 1833–1845. New York: Harper & Row, Publishers, 1984.

Reynolds, Thursey Jessen, comp. *Centennial Echos from Carbon County [Utah]*. N.p.: Carbon County Daughters of Utah Pioneers, 1948.

Ricketts, Norma Baldwin. *The Mormon Battalion: U.S. Army of the West, 1846–1848*. Logan, Utah: Utah State University Press, 1996.

Ricks, Joel Edward. *Forms and Methods of Early Mormon Settlement in Utah and the Surrounding Regions, 1847 to 1877*. Logan, Utah: Utah State University Press, 1964.

Roberts, B. H. *A Comprehensive History of the Church of Jesus Christ of Latter-day Saints, Century 1*. 6 vols. Provo, Utah: Brigham Young University Press, 1965.

———. *The Rise and Fall of Nauvoo*. Salt Lake City: Bookcraft, 1965.

Robertson, Frank C. *A Ram in the Thicket: The Story of a Roaming Homesteader Family on the Mormon Frontier*. Moscow, Idaho: University of Idaho Press, 1994.

Robinson, George F. *History of Greene County, Ohio*. Chicago: S. J. Clarke Publishing Co., 1902.

Rohrbough, Malcolm R. *The Trans-Appalachian Frontier*. New York: Oxford University Press, 1978.

Roster of Ohio Soldiers in the War of 1812. Baltimore: Genealogical Publishing Company, 1968.

Rusho, W. L. *Lee's Ferry: Desert River Crossing*. Salt Lake City: Tower Productions, 1998.

Sage, Leland L. *A History of Iowa*. Ames, Iowa: Iowa State University Press, 1974.

Schindler, Harold. *Orrin Porter Rockwell: Man of God, Son of Thunder*. Salt Lake City: University of Utah Press, 1966.

Schlesinger, Arthur M., Jr. *The Age of Jackson*. Boston: Little, Brown and Company, 1945.

Scioto Predestinarian Baptist Association, Minutes of the Seventy-Sixth Annual Session, Paint Creek Church, Fayette County, Ohio, August 13, 14, and 15, 1880. Mt. Sterling, Ohio: M. W. Schryver, 1880.

Severa, Joan L. *Dressed for the Photographer: Ordinary Americans and Fashion, 1840–1900*. Kent, Ohio: Kent State University Press, 1995.

Shi, David E. *In Search of the Simple Life: American Voices, Past and Present*. Layton, Utah: Gibbs M. Smith, Inc., 1986.

———. *The Simple Life: Plain Living and High Thinking in American Culture*. New York: Oxford University Press, 1986.

Shipps, Jan. "The Reality of the Restoration and the Restoration Ideal in the Mormon Tradition." In *The American Quest for the Primitive Church*, edited by Richard T. Hughes. Urbana, Illinois: University of Illinois Press, 1988.

Simpson, J. H. *Report of Explorations across the Great Basin of the Territory of Utah for a Direct Wagon-Route from Camp Floyd to Genoa, in Carson Valley in 1859*. Reno, Nevada: University of Nevada Press, 1983, first published in 1876.

Smart, William B., and Donna T. Smart, eds. *Over the Rim: The Parley P. Pratt Exploring Expedition to Southern Utah, 1849–1850*. Logan, Utah: Utah State University Press, 1999.

Smith, H. Perry, ed. *History of the City of Buffalo and Erie County*. Syracuse, New York: D. Mason & Co., 1894.

Smith, Jedediah S. *The Southwest Expedition of Jedediah S. Smith: His Personal Account of the Journey to California, 1826–1827*. Edited by George R. Brooks. Lincoln, Nebraska: University of Nebraska Press, 1977.

Smith, Joe H. *History of Harrison County, Iowa*. Des Moines, Iowa: Iowa Publishing Company, 1888.

Smith, Joseph, Jr. *History of the Church of Jesus Christ of Latter-day Saints: Period I: History of Joseph Smith, the Prophet*. Edited by B. H. Roberts, 2d ed., rev. 7 vols. Salt Lake City: Deseret Book Company, 1971.

Snow, Eliza Roxcy. *Personal Writings of Eliza Roxcy Snow*. Edited by Maureen Ursenbach Beecher. Salt Lake City: University of Utah Press, 1995.

Sonne, Conway B. *World of Wakara*. San Antonio, Texas: The Naylor Company, 1962.

Spencer, J. W. *Reminiscences of Pioneer Life in the Mississippi Valley*. Davenport, Iowa: Griggs, Watson, and Day, 1872; reprint in *The Early Days of Rock Island and Davenport: The Narratives of J. W. Spencer and J. M. Burrows*, edited by Milo Milton Quaife. Chicago: The Lakeside Press, 1942.

Stegner, Wallace. *The Gathering of Zion: The Story of the Mormon Trail*. New York: McGraw-Hill Book Company, 1971.

Stewart, John J. "The Railroad Builder." In *Lion of the Lord: Essays on the Life and Service of Brigham Young*, edited by Susan Easton Black and Larry C. Porter. Salt Lake City, Utah: Deseret Book Company, 1995.

Storke, Elliot G. *History of Cayuga County, New York, 1789–1878*. Syracuse, New York: D. Mason & Co., 1879.

Stout, Hosea. *On the Mormon Frontier: The Diary of Hosea Stout, 1844–1861*. Edited by Juanita Brooks. 2 vols. Salt Lake City: University of Utah Press, 1964.

Stringer, Lawrence B. *History of Logan County, Illinois*. 2 vols. Chicago: Pioneer Publishing Co., 1911.

Sweet, William Warren. *Religion on the American Frontier: The Baptists*. New York: Cooper Square Publishers, 1964.

Tanner, Lula Tolton. *That Their Children May Know: A Record of the Descendants of Edward Tolton*. N.p.: N.p., n.d.

Taylor, Alan. *William Cooper's Town: Power and Persuasion on the Frontier of the Early American Republic*. New York: Alfred A. Knopf, 1995.

Thompson, John H., ed. *Geography of New York State*. Syracuse, New York: Syracuse University Press, 1966.

Thurber, Albert K. "Journal and Diary of Albert King Thurber." In *Treasures of Pioneer History*, compiled by Kate B. Carter. Vol. 3. Salt Lake City: Daughters of Utah Pioneers, 1952–1957.

Town of Newstead, Founded 1823: Septquicentennial, 1832–1998. N.p.: N.p., [1998].

Trevelyan, George Macaulay. "Clio, a Muse." In *The Vital Past: Writings on the Uses of History*, edited by Stephen Vaughn. Athens, Georgia: University of Georgia Press, 1985.

Trimble, Marshall. *Arizona: A Panoramic History of a Frontier State*. New York: Doubleday & Co., 1977.

Tullidge, Edward W. *History of Salt Lake City*. 2 vols. Salt Lake City: Star Printing Company, 1886.

Turner, Frederick Jackson. *The Frontier in American History*. New York: Henry Holt and Company, 1921.

Turner, Henry Smith. *The Original Journals of Henry Smith Turner with Stephen Watts Kearny to New Mexico and California, 1846–1847*. Edited by Dwight L. Clarke. Norman, Oklahoma: University of Oklahoma Press, 1966.

Turner, O[rsamus]. *Pioneer History of the Holland Purchase of Western New York*. Buffalo, New York: Jewett, Thomas & Co., 1849.

Tuttle, Charles R., and Daniel S. Durrie. *An Illustrated History of the State of Iowa*. Chicago: Richard S. Peale and Company, 1876.

Tyler, Daniel. *A Concise History of the Mormon Battalion, 1846–1847*. Glorieta, New Mexico: The Rio Grande Press, Inc., 1980.

Under Dixie Sun: A History of Washington County [Utah]. Panguitch, Utah: Washington County Chapter Daughters of Utah Pioneers, 1950.

Underwood, Grant. *The Millenarian World of Early Mormonism*. Urbana, Illinois: University of Illinois Press, 1993.

Unruh, John D., Jr. *The Plains Across: The Overland Emigrants and the Trans-Mississippi West, 1840–1860*. Urbana, Illinois: University of Illinois Press, 1979.

Utah Directory and Gazetteer for 1879–1880. Salt Lake City: H. L. A. Culmer & Co., 1879.

Utah Pioneers: Celebration of the Entrance of the Pioneers into Great Salt Lake Valley. Salt Lake City: Deseret News, 1880.

Vanderhoof, E. W. *Historical Sketches of Western New York*. Buffalo, New York: The Mathews-Northrup Works, 1907, reprint 1972.

Van Wagoner, Richard S. *Mormon Polygamy: A History*. Salt Lake City: Signature Books, 1989.

Wagoner, Jay J. *Arizona's Heritage*. Santa Barbara, California: Peregrine Smith, Inc., 1978.

Wahlquist, Wayne, ed. *Atlas of Utah*. Provo, Utah: Weber State University and Brigham Young University Press, 1981.

Walker, Ronald W. "'Going to Meeting' in Salt Lake City's Thirteenth Ward, 1849–1881: A Microanalysis." In *New Views of Mormon History: A Collection of Essays in Honor of Leonard J. Arrington*, edited by Davis Bitton and Maureen Ursenbach Beecher. Salt Lake City: University of Utah Press, 1987.

———. *Wayward Saints: The Godbeites and Brigham Young*. Urbana, Illinois: University of Illinois Press, 1998.

Walker, Ronald W., and Doris Dant, eds. *Nearly Everything Imaginable: The Everyday Life of Utah's Mormon Pioneers*. Provo, Utah: Brigham Young University Press, 1999.

"Walter Turner Barney." In *Mt. Graham Profiles: Graham County, Arizona, 1870–1977*. Graham County Historical Society (n.d.).

Warner, Elisha. *The History of Spanish Fork [Utah]*. Spanish Fork, Utah: The Press Publishing Co., 1930.
Warnock, Irvin L., ed. and comp. *Thru the Years: Sevier County Centennial History*. Springville, Utah: Sevier County Centennial Committee, 1947.
Warnock, Irvin L., and Lexia D. Warnock, comps. and eds. *Our Own Sevier: A Comprehensive Centennial Volume, Sevier County, Utah, 1865–1965*. Richfield, Utah: Sevier County Commissioners, 1965.
Warren, Louis A. *Lincoln's Youth: Indiana Years, Seven to Twenty-one, 1816–1830*. New York: Appleton-Century-Crofts, Inc., 1959.
Watson, Kaye C. *Life under the Horseshoe: A History of Spring City*. Spring City, Utah: Spring City Daughters of Utah Pioneers, 1987.
Watt, Ronald G. *A History of Carbon County [Utah]*. Salt Lake City: Utah State Historical Society and Carbon County Commission, 1997.
Webb, Walter Prescott. *The Great Frontier*. Austin, Texas: University of Texas Press, 1964.
Weisenburger, Francis P. "The Passing of the Frontier, 1825–1850." In *The History of the State of Ohio*, edited by Carl Wittke. Vol. 3. Columbus, Ohio: Ohio State Archaeological and Historical Society, 1941.
Weller, Ethelyn. *A History of the Town of Newstead*. N.p.: Buffalo and Erie County Historical Society, 1971.
White, Edward S. *Past and Present of Shelby County, Iowa*. 2 vols. Indianapolis, Indiana: B. F. Brown and Company, Inc., 1915.
White, Sheryl Smith, comp. *David Dutton Yearsley and Mary Ann Hoopes*. N.p.: N.p., 1982.
White, Truman C. *Our County and Its People: A Descriptive Work on Erie County, New York*. 2 vols. N.p.: The Boston History Company, 1898.
Whitney, Ellen M., comp. and ed. *The Black Hawk War, 1831–1832*. Springfield, Illinois: Illinois State Historical Library, 1970.
Whitney, Orson F. *History of Utah*. 4 vols. Salt Lake City: George Q. Cannon & Sons Co., 1892.
Whittaker, David J., ed. *Mormon Americana: A Guide to Sources and Collections in the United States*. Provo, Utah: Brigham Young University Studies, 1995.
Willson, Marcius. *American History: Comprising Historical Sketches of the Indian Tribes*. New York: Ivison & Phinney, 1857.
Wilson, Douglas L. *Honor's Voice: The Transformation of Abraham Lincoln*. New York: Alfred A. Knopf, 1998.
Winn, Kenneth H. *Exiles in a Land of Liberty: Mormons in America, 1830–1846*. Chapel Hill, North Carolina: University of North Carolina Press, 1989.
Woodruff, Wilford. *Wilford Woodruff's Journal, 1833–1898, Typescript*. 9 vols. Edited by Scott G. Kenny. Midvale, Utah: Signature Books, 1983–1985.
Wycoff, William. *The Developer's Frontier: The Making of the Western New York Landscape*. New Haven, Connecticut: Yale University Press, 1988.

Periodicals

Allen, James B. "To the Saints in England: Impressions of a Mormon Immigrant." *BYU Studies* 18, no. 3 (spring 1978).
Athearn, Robert G. "Utah and the Coming of the Denver and Rio Grande Railroad." *Utah Historical Quarterly* 27 (1959).
Barney, Nolan. "Benjamin Franklin and Caroline (Beard) Barney: History of a Pioneer Family." *The Barney Family News* 42 (June 1989).
Barney, Ronald O. "'A Man You Could Not Help Likeing': Joseph Smith and Nauvoo, Illinois, Portrayed in a Letter by Susannah and George W. Taggart." *BYU Studies* 40, no. 2 (2001).

Bartlinski, James. "Commodore Joshua Barney: Joshua Barney's Naval Career during the American Revolution, 1775–1784." *The Barney Family News* 84, 85 (winter 1999–2000, spring 2000).

Beeton, Beverly. "Teach Them to Till the Soil: An Experiment with Indian Farms, 1850–1862." *American Indian Quarterly* 3, no. 4 (winter 1977–1978).

Bennett, Richard E. "Mormons and Missourians: The Uneasy Truce." *Midwest Review* 9 (spring 1987).

Bigler, David L. "Garland Hurt, the American Friend of the Utahs." *Utah Historical Quarterly* 62, no. 2 (spring 1994).

Bishop, M. Guy. "What Has Become of Our Fathers?: Baptism for the Dead at Nauvoo." *Dialogue: A Journal of Mormon Thought* 23, no. 2 (summer 1990).

Bitton, Davis. "'I'd Rather Have Some Roasting Ears': The Peregrinations of George Armstrong Hicks." *Utah Historical Quarterly* 68, no. 3 (summer 2000).

———. "The Sovereignty of God in John Calvin and Brigham Young." *Sunstone* 5, no. 5 (September–October 1980).

Bitton, Davis, and Linda P. Wilcox. "Pestiferous Ironclads: The Grasshopper Problem in Pioneer Utah." *Utah Historical Quarterly* 46, no. 4 (fall 1978).

Black, Susan Easton. "Do We Know How Many Latter-day Saints Died between 1846 and 1860 in the Migration to the Salt Lake Valley?" *Ensign* 28, no. 7 (July 1998).

———. "How Large Was the Population of Nauvoo." *BYU Studies* 35, no. 2 (1995).

Bushman, Richard L. "The Historians and Mormon Nauvoo." *Dialogue: A Journal of Mormon Thought* 5, no. 1 (spring 1970).

Christiansen, Larry D. "The Struggle for Power in the Mormon Battalion." *Dialogue: A Journal of Mormon Thought* 26, no. 4 (winter 1993).

Christy, Howard A. "Open Hand and Mailed Fist: Mormon-Indian Relations in Utah, 1847–1852." *Utah Historical Quarterly* 46, no. 2 (summer 1978).

———. "The Walker War: Defense and Conciliation as Strategy." *Utah Historical Quarterly* 47, no. 1 (fall 1979).

———. "'What Virtue There Is in Stone' and other Pungent Talk on the Early Utah Frontier." *Utah Historical Quarterly* 59, no. 3 (summer 1991).

Coates, Lawrence G. "Brigham Young and Mormon Indian Policies: The Formative Period, 1836–1851." *BYU Studies* 18, no. 3 (spring 1978).

Dye, Nancy Schrom, and Daniel Blake Smith. "Mother Love and Infant Death, 1750–1920." *Journal of American History* 73, no. 2 (September 1986).

Ehat, Andrew F. "It Seems Like Heaven Began on Earth: Joseph Smith and the Constitution of the Kingdom of God." *BYU Studies* 20, no. 3 (spring 1980).

"Faith of the Church of Christ in these Last Days." *The Evening and the Morning Star* 2, no. 23 (August 1834) and *Messenger and Advocate* 2, no. 12 (September 1836).

Flanders, Robert Bruce. "The Kingdom of God in Illinois: Politics in Utopia." *Dialogue: A Journal of Mormon Thought* 5, no. 1 (spring 1970).

Fox, Feramorz Y. "Experiment in Utopia: The United Order of Richfield, 1874–1877." *Utah Historical Quarterly* 32, no. 4 (fall 1964).

Gentry, Leland H. "The Mormon Way Stations: Garden Grove and Mt. Pisgah." *BYU Studies* 21, no. 4 (fall 1981).

Godfrey, Audrey M. "No Small Miracle: The Movement of Domestic Animals across the Plains." *Nauvoo Journal* 9, no. 1 (spring 1997).

Godfrey, Kenneth W. "Joseph Smith and the Masons." *Journal of the Illinois State Historical Society* 64, no. 1 (spring 1971).

———. "The Nauvoo Neighborhood: A Little Philadelphia or a Unique City Set upon a Hill." *Journal of Mormon History* 11 (1984).

Hartley, William G. "'Almost Too Intolerable a Burthen': The Winter Exodus from Missouri." *Journal of Mormon History* 18, no. 2 (fall 1992).

———. "Mormons and Early Iowa History (1838–1858): Eight Distinct Connections" *Annals of Iowa* 59, no. 3 (summer 2000): 217–260.
———. "The Pioneer Trek: Nauvoo to Winter Quarters." *Ensign* 27, no. 6 (June 1997).
———. "The Priesthood Reorganization of 1877: Brigham Young's Last Achievement." *BYU Studies* 20, no. 1 (fall 1979).
Hill, Marvin S. "Quest for Refuge: An Hypothesis as to the Social Origins and Nature of the Mormon Political Kingdom." *Journal of Mormon History* 2 (1975).
———. "The Shaping of the Mormon Mind in New England and New York." *BYU Studies* 9, no. 3 (spring 1969).
Irving, Gordon I. "The Law of Adoption: One Phase of the Development of the Mormon Concept of Salvation, 1830–1900." *BYU Studies* 14, no. 3 (spring 1974).
Jackson, Richard H. "The Use of Adobe in the Mormon Cultural Region." *Journal of Cultural Geography* 1 (1980).
Jenson, Andrew. *Historical Record*. 9, nos. 7–12 (December 1890).
Jessee, Dean C. "Brigham Young's Family." *BYU Studies* 18, no. 3 (spring 1978).
Jorgensen, Lynn Watkins, et al. "The Mantle of the Prophet Joseph Passes to Brother Brigham: A Collective Spiritual Witness." *BYU Studies* 36, no. 4 (1996–1997).
Ketchum, Richard M. "Memory as History." *American Heritage* 42, no. 7 (November 1991).
Kimball, Heber C. "Pioneer Journal of Heber C. Kimball." *Utah Genealogical and Historical Magazine* (July 1940).
Kimball, Stanley B. "The Iowa Trek of 1846." *Ensign* 2, no. 6 (June 1972).
———. "The Mormon Trail Network in Iowa, 1838–1863: A New Look." *BYU Studies* 21, no. 4 (fall 1981).
———. "Nauvoo West: The Mormons of the Iowa Shore." *BYU Studies* 8, no. 2 (winter 1978).
Langum, David J. "Pioneer Justice on the Overland Trails." *Western Historical Quarterly* 5, no. 4 (October 1974).
Larson, Gustive O. "The Mormon Reformation." *Utah Historical Quarterly* 26 (January 1958).
"Letters Descriptive of President Young's Visit to the Southern Settlements" *Latter-day Saints' Millennial Star* 25, no. 27 (4 July 1863).
Lyon, T. Edgar. "The Current Restoration in Nauvoo, Illinios." *Dialogue: A Journal of Mormon Thought* 5, no. 1 (spring 1970).
Margetts, Thomas, to Samuel W. Richards, 4 July 1852, Kanesville, Iowa. *Latter-day Saints' Millennial Star* 14, no. 29 (11 September 1852).
Marty, Martin. "It Finally All Depends on God: A Conversation with Martin Marty." *Sunstone* 11, no. 2 (March 1987).
Metcalf, Warren. "A Precarious Balance: The Northern Utes and the Black Hawk War." *Utah Historical Quarterly* 57, no. 1 (winter 1989).
Moore, R. Laurence. "What Children Did Not Learn in School: The Intellectual Quickening of Young Americans in the Nineteenth Century." *Church History: Studies in Christianity and Culture* 68, no. 1 (March 1999).
Murray, Robert A. "Trading Posts, Fort and Bridges of the Casper Area—Unraveling the Tangle on the Upper Platte." *Annals of Wyoming* 47, no. 1 (spring 1975).
Peterson, Charles S. "'Book A—Levi Mathers Savage': The Look of Utah in 1873." *Utah Historical Quarterly* 41, no. 1 (winter 1973).
———. "The Limits of Learning in Pioneer Utah." *Journal of Mormon History* 10 (1983).
Peterson, Paul H. "The Mormon Reformation of 1856–1857: The Rhetoric and the Reality." *Journal of Mormon History* 15 (1989).
Pitcavage, Mark. "'Burthened in Defense of our Rights': Opposition to Military Service in Ohio during the War of 1812." *Ohio History* 104 (summer–autumn 1995).

Poll, Richard D. "The Move South." *BYU Studies* 29, no. 4 (fall 1989).
Poll, Richard D., and William P. MacKinnon. "Causes of the Utah War Reconsidered." *Journal of Mormon History* 20, no. 2 (fall 1994).
Quinn, D. Michael. "The Mormon Succession Crisis of 1844." *BYU Studies* 16, no. 2 (winter 1976).
———. "The Practice of Rebaptism at Nauvoo." *BYU Studies* 18, no. 2 (winter 1978).
Rice, Cindy. "Spring City: A Look at a Nineteenth-Century Mormon Village." *Utah Historical Quarterly* 43, no. 3 (summer 1975).
Salmon, Rusty and Robert S. McPherson. "Cowboys, Indians, and Conflict: The Pinhook Draw Fight, 1881." *Utah Historical Quarterly* 69, no. 1 (winter 2001).
Sandberg, Karl C. "Getting Up a History of Monroe: The Long Shadow of the United Order." *Sunstone* 19, no. 4 (December 1996).
Saum, Lewis O. "Providence in the Popular Mind of Pre–Civil War America." *Indiana Magazine of History* 72 (December 1976).
Shepherd, Joseph Garlic. In "History of Moses Trader Shepherd," Bliss Jarvis Brimley. *Shepherd Family Organization Newsletter* (June 1978): 5.
"Sketches of the Mormon Era" *Gregg's Dollar Monthly and Old Settler's Memorial* 1, no. 6 (October 1873) reprinted in *Annals of Iowa* 12, no. 8 (April 1921).
Smith, George A., to Samuel W. Richards, 26 December 1852. *Latter-day Saints' Millennial Star* 15, no. 8 (30 April 1853).
Smith, James E. "Frontier Nauvoo: Building a Picture from Statistics." *Ensign* 9, no. 9 (September 1979).
Snow, Erastus. "Journey to Zion (An Original Journal, Part I)." *Utah Humanities Review* 2, no. 2 (April 1948).
Thomas, Bob. "The Phantom of Willow Springs: A Trading Post Lost in Time beside an Old Wagon Road." *Arizona Highways* 73, no. 1 (January 1997).
Tracy, Albert. "Journal of Capt. Albert Tracy, 1858–1860." *Utah Historical Quarterly* 13, nos. 1–4 (January–October 1945).
Tullidge, Edward W. "History of Spanish Fork." *Tullidge's Quarterly Magazine* 3, nos. 2–3 (April–July 1884).
Walker, Ronald W. "The Challenge and Craft of Mormon Biography." *BYU Studies* 22, no. 2 (spring 1982).
———. "Toward a Reconstruction of Mormon and Indian Relations, 1847–1877." *BYU Studies* 29, no. 3 (fall 1989).
Webb, Robert. "The Baptist Church at Lincoln's New Salem." *The Primitive Baptist Library Quarterly* 7, no. 3 (January–March 1995).
Winkler, Albert. "The Circleville Massacre: A Brutal Incident in Utah's Black Hawk War." *Utah Historical Quarterly* 55, no. 1 (winter 1987).
Yeoman, Walter. "Sketch of Elder Yeoman." *Messenger of Peace* 51, no. 10 (15 May 1925).
Yorgason, Laurence M. "Preview on a Study of the Social and Geographical Origins of Early Mormon Converts, 1830–1845." *BYU Studies* 10, no. 3 (spring 1970).
Youngberg, Florence C. "A Heritage of Strength, Love and Endurance." *Pioneer* 35, no. 6 (November–December 1988).

Newspapers

Arizona Star Weekly
Deseret Evening News
Deseret News
Deseret Weekly
Frontier Guardian and Iowa Sentinel

Illinois Intelligencer
Iowa Territorial Gazette and Advertizer
Ohio Register
Mormon Tribune
Nauvoo Expositor
Nauvoo Neighbor
Salt Lake Herald
Salt Lake Tribune
Sangamo Journal
Spectator
Times and Seasons
Warsaw Signal

Manuscripts

Baptist Church of Jesus Christ at Lake Fork, Minutes. Primitive Baptist Library, Carthage, Illinois.

Barney, Arthur. Journal. Typescript. Harold B. Lee Library, Special Collections, Brigham Young University, Provo, Utah.

Barney, Franklin R. The Walter Turner Barney Family. Copy in possession of author.

Barney, Lewis. Lecture on the Exodus of the Latter-day Saints from the United States to the Rocky Mountains, 14 July 1888. Copy in possession of author.

———. Letter to Andrew Jenson, 21 April 1890, Kanosh, Utah. Copy in possession of author.

———. Letter to Clark and Johns, 24 April 1893, Mancos, Colorado. Copy in possession of author.

Barney, Nolan. "Deborah Riffle Street Barney," 1992. Copy in possession of author.

Barney, Nolan, and Kaye Barney. "The Life of Charles Barney," 1980. Copy in possession of author.

Barney, Ronald O. "Barney Origins in America: Puritans and Yankees in the New World, 1630–1800." Typescript in possession of the author.

Black, Joseph Smith. Diary of Joseph Smith Black. Typescript. Harold B. Lee Library, Special Collections, Brigham Young University, Provo, Utah.

Blair, W. W. Journal. Archives, Community of Christ, Independence, Missouri.

Boyer-Reinstein, Julia, comp. Town of Cheektowaga Historical Atlas. Buffalo and Erie County Public Library, Special Collections, Buffalo, New York.

Butler, Charles. Papers. Library of Congress, Washington, D.C.

"A Complete Record of the Sales of Lands within the County of Fayette and State of Ohio, 1820–1828." Ohio Historical Society, Columbus, Ohio.

Diary of the City Council of Spring City, 1871–1886. Harold B. Lee Library, Special Collections, Brigham Young University, Provo, Utah.

Early Reorganization Minutes. Archives, Community of Christ, Independence, Missouri.

Ellis, John M. Letter to Matthias Bruen, 29 December 1825, Kaskaskia, Illinois. American Home Missionary Society, Papers, Incoming Correspondence. Microfilm, Church Archives.

———. Letter to Absalom Peters, 23 May 1826, 10 January 1827, Springfield, Illinois. American Home Missionary Society, Papers, Incoming Correspondence. Microfilm, Church Archives.

Emslie, Peter. A Deed Atlas of the County of Erie, N.Y., showing the Dimensions of Lots and Subdivisions of lots as they were originally conveyed by the Holland Land

Company . . . compiled from the Holland Land Company's Deed Books &c. Buffalo and Erie County Historical Society, Buffalo, New York.
Erickson, Rhoda Black. Sixth Generation: Continuation of the Descendants of Jacob Barney, 1634. Copy in possession of author.
Foster, Isaac. Journal. Typescript. Herbert S. Auerbach Collection, Department of Rare Books and Special Collections, Harvey S. Firestone Memorial Library, Princeton University, Princeton, New Jersey.
Frazier, Florence Barney. "Life's History of My Grandfather Walter Turner Barney." Copy in possession of author.
Goodell, Joel. Letter to Rev. [Horace] Hooker, 12 May 1831, Liberty, Missouri. Papers, Missionary Society of Connecticut. Microfilm, Western Reserve Historical Society, Cleveland, Ohio.
Hicks, George A. History of Spanish Fork, 1913. Harold B. Lee Library, Special Collections, Brigham Young University, Provo, Utah.
Hillman, Silas. Autobiography. Harold B. Lee Library, Special Collections, Brigham Young University.
Howe, Eldridge G. Letter to Absalom Peters, 23 May 1826, Springfield, Illinois. American Home Missionary Society, Papers, Incoming Correspondence. Microfilm, Church Archives.
———. Letter to Matthias Bruen, 11 February 1826, Springfield, Illinois. American Home Missionary Society, Papers, Incoming Correspondence. Microfilm, Church Archives.
Hyde, Myrtle S. "Kanesville Places: A Preliminary Study," September 1990. Copy in possession of author.
Knight, Elijah. Early Recollections of Western New York, 1885. Typescript. Newstead Historical Society, Akron, New York.
Loomis, Chester. Charles A. Loomis, Correspondence, 1821–1839. Rare and Manuscript Collections, Carl A. Kroch Library, Cornell University, Ithaca, New York.
Munson, Eliza M. Questions Concerning Black Hawk War Answered by Eliza M. Munson. Utah State Historical Society, Salt Lake City, Utah.
Nuttall, L. John. Diary. Typescript. Harold B. Lee Library, Special Collections, Brigham Young University, Provo, Utah.
Page, Jonathan S. "Biography of Johnathon S. Page." Typescript. Herbert S. Auerbach Collection, Department of Rare Books and Special Collections, Harvey S. Firestone Memorial Library, Princeton University, Princeton, New Jersey.
Parker, Barnes. Letter to Lewis and Henry Barney, 8 May 1876, 21 September 1877, Austin, Texas. Photocopy in possession of author.
Pratt, Louisa Black. Historical Notes on Charles Barney, her grandfather. Typescript in possession of author.
Thurber, Albert King. Diary, transcribed by Charles Kelly, 1952. Utah State Historical Society, Salt Lake City, Utah.
Tippets, Joseph H., to Joseph Smith, 2 April 1843. Newel K. Whitney Collection, Special Collections, Harold B. Lee Library, Brigham Young University, Provo, Utah.

Church Records and Manuscripts

(Church Archives, unless noted otherwise. All materials owned by the Church of Jesus Christ are used with permission.)

Adams, Margaret W. Letter to George [Webster], 26–27 June 1858, Spanish Fork, Utah.

Adams, William. Autobiography.
Allred, Reddick N. Letter to William Seeley, 27 April 1866.
Backenstos, J. B. J. B. Backenstos's List of Carthage Greys and Warsaw Independents Involved in Joseph and Hyrum Smith's Murders.
Barney, Alma. Brief History of the Life of Alma Barney.
Barney, Lewis. Letter to John Taylor, 19 October 1879, Monroe, Utah. John Taylor, Papers, Incoming Correspondence.
———. Papers, 1886–1888. Microfilm.
———. Reminiscence and Diary, 1878–1882. [Autobiography 1].
———. Reminiscence, [ca. 1886]. [Autobiography 2].
Bashore, Melvin L., comp. "List of Officers in Pioneer Companies Which Crossed the Plains, 1847–1868," 1988.
Bates, Harriet May. Biographical Sketch of Joseph W. Bates, [n.d.].
Bates, Nephi James. Journal. Daughters of Utah Pioneers Collection.
———. Reminiscences and Diary.
Benson, Ezra T. Letter to Brigham Young, 13 May 1852, Kanesville, Iowa. Brigham Young, Papers, Incoming Correspondence.
Berry, John W. Rank Roll, July 4th/55.
Bigler, Henry W. Journal, 1846–1899.
Black, William. Letter to Brigham Young, 10 February 1860, Springtown, Utah. Brigham Young, Papers, Incoming Correspondence.
———. Letter to Brigham Young, 7 February 1861, Springtown, Utah. Brigham Young, Papers, Incoming Correspondence.
Black, William Young. Letters, 1855–1874.
Blackburn, Elias Hicks. Notebook, 1851–1857.
Blair, George Washington Thatcher. Collection.
Bleak, James. Annals of the Southern Utah Mission.
Brigham Young's Daily Transactions in Gold Dust. Brigham Young, Papers.
Brown, George M. Diary.
Bryner, Farozine Ellen Redd. Lemuel Hardison Redd Biographical Sketch, 1956.
Bullock, Thomas. Journals. 1843–1849.
Burrville Ward. Manuscript History.
———. Sunday School, Minutes.
Church Emigration Book, 1831–1847.
Circleville Ward. Manuscript History.
Clayton, William. Diary 1847 Jan.–Dec.
Coltrin, Zebedee. Journal, 1832.
Curtis, Joseph. Reminiscences and Diary, 1839–1881.
Early Mormon Activities in Indiana, 1830–1845.
Elders Licences, Nauvoo, Illinois.
Ellis, Fern D. Cemeteries in Mancos [Colorado]. Family History Library.
Endowment House. Sealings and Endowments, 1851–1854. Special Collections, Family History Library.
Evans, Priscilla Merriman. Autobiography, [ca. 1914].
Evans, Thomas D. Autobiography, [n.d.]. Typescript.
Fackrell, James. Reminiscences, [ca. 1850].
Farley, Angelina. Diary.
Ferron Ward. Record of Members.
First Presidency. Office Papers of L. John Nuttall, ca. 1875–1905.
Gardner, Hamilton. The Utah Territorial Militia.
Green, Evan Molbourne. Papers, [ca. 1848–1871].
Halliday, George. Letter to William B. Pace, August 1872. William Byram Pace Collection.

Halvorsen, Christian Henry. Diary.
Hamilton, Henry. Journals.
Henderson, Mary. History of Utah Forts, 1940.
Hillman, Silas. Autobiography and Journal, [ca. 1866–1875].
Historian's Office.Historical Record Book, 1843–1874.
———. Journal.
———. Letterpress Copybooks.
Hogan, Mervin B., comp. Record of Nauvoo Lodge Petitions.
Huntington, Dimick B. Journal, 1857–1859.
Hyde, Orson. Letter to Brigham Young, 27 May 1852, Kanesville, Iowa. Brigham Young, Papers, Incoming Correspondence.
———. Letter to Brigham Young, 19 November 1865, Springtown, Utah. Brigham Young, Papers, Incoming Correspondence.
———. Letter to Brigham Young, 27 May 1868, Springtown, Utah. Brigham Young, Papers, Incoming Correspondence.
———. Letter to Mary Hyde, 27 August 1869, Springtown, Utah. Romania Jeannette Hyde Woolley Collection.
Indian Service Claims, 1861–1862. Brigham Young, Papers, Indian Claims.
Jackman, Levi. Journal, 1847–1849.
———. Sketch of Life, 1851.
Jacob, Norton. Reminiscence and Journal 1844 May–1852. Jan.
Jenson, Andrew. Prisoners for Conscience Sake, [ca. 1884–1892].
Jex, William. Autobiography, [ca. 1921].
Journal History of the Church of Jesus Christ of Latter-day Saints, 1830–.
Journal of a Member of Luke Johnson's Company of Ten.
Judiciary, Proceedings of Judge Cradlebaugh's Court, Mar.–Apr. 1859. Brigham Young, Papers, Administrative Papers.
Kanosh Ward. Record of Members.
———. Relief Society, Minutes.
Kitchen, Verda McKee. Stephen Markham's History as Others Have Recorded It, 1982.
Lisonbee, James Thompson. Diary.
Lisonbee, Mary Ellen and Zelaina Lisonbee. A Brief History of the Life of James Thompson Lisonbee.
Little, James. Biography of William Rufus Rogers Stowell (1893). Typescript (1988).
Logan County, Illinois. Cemetery Inscriptions. Family History Library.
Lucas, Samuel D. Letter to Gov. Lilburn Boggs, 4 October 1838, Boonville, Missouri. Photocopy.
Luna Ward. Manuscript History.
Lyman, Amasa. Journals.
Madsen, Andrew. Autobiographical Sketch, ca. 1908.
Mancos Ward. Manuscript History.
———. Record of Members.
———. Record of the Mancos Ward, Colorado, 1892–1902.
Manti Temple. Baptisms for the Dead. Family History Library.
Martin, Moses. Journals, 1834.
Mayer, George. Reminiscence and Diary, 1853–1896.
Meeks, Priddy. Autobiography and Reminiscence. Typescript.
Millard Stake. High Priest Quorum, General Records.
Monroe Ward. General Minutes.
———. Historical Record.
———. Manuscript History.
———. Record of Members.
———. United Order, Minutes.

Mormon Battalion Subscription Lists, August 1846. Brigham Young, Papers, Administrative Papers.
Mott, John. Letters, 1858 and 1862.
Munson, Eliza Mariah Allred. Autobiographical Sketch, [ca. 1930].
Murdock, John. Autobiography, [ca. 1859–1867].
Names of Committee Selected by Council to Move Families, Goods, into Nauvoo. Brigham Young, Papers, Administrative Papers.
Names of Pioneers, 1876 July 24. Brigham Young, Papers, General Office Files.
Names of Volunteers and Donations for Pioneer Company, 1846. Brigham Young, Papers, Administrative Papers.
Nauvoo Masonic Lodge. Account Book.
Nauvoo Restoration Incorporated. Land Records, Rowena Miller, comp.
Nauvoo Temple. Baptisms for the Dead. Family History Library.
———. Endowment Register, Family History Library.
———. Recorder's Ledger, Book A.
Pace, James. Autobiographical Sketch, [ca. 1861].
Pace, William Byram. Letters, 1857–1866.
Palmer, James. Reminiscences, ca. 1884–1898.
Palmyra Ward. Record of the Palmyra Branch.
———. Tithing Office Ledger, 1841–1857.
Partridge, Edward. Diary.
Patriarchal Blessings.
Petition for Post Office near Log Tabernacle. Brigham Young, Papers.
Pratt, Orson. Journals, 1833–1836.
Presiding Bishopric. Statistical Reports, 1851–1869, 1877–1903.
Price Ward. Record of Members.
Provo Fifth Ward. Manuscript History.
Provo Utah Central Stake. General Minutes.
Pyper, Tessie P., comp. Spring City Cemetery Records. Family History Library.
Record of Ordination to the Office of Seventy.
Registry of Names of Persons Residing in the Various Wards, &c., as p. Bishop's Reports, December 28th, A.D. 1852. Brigham Young, Papers.
Richfield Ward. United Order Records, 1874–1881.
Rigdon, John Wickliff. Lecture on the Early History of the Mormon Church, 1906.
Salt Lake Stake. Record of Members.
San Bernardino, Manuscript History.
Seventies Quorum Records. Fiftieth Quorum, Genealogies.
———. 41st Quorum, Monroe Ward.
———. Record for the Seventies of Monroe Ward.
———. Records of the 18th Quorum.
———. 32nd Quorum.
Sevier Stake. General Minutes.
———. Manuscript History.
Sketches of My Grandfather's Life [Luke William Gallup], from His History of His Own Life, 1920.
Smith, George A. Letter to John Lyman, 6 January 1858. Historian's Office, Letterpress Copybooks.
———. Papers, Journals.
Smith, John. Letter to George A. Smith, 7 January 1841, Ambrosia, Iowa. George A. Smith, Papers, Incoming Correspondence.
———. Papers, 1832–1854, Journals.
Smith, Joseph. Daybook B.
———. Daybook C. Microfilm.

Spanish Fork Ward. Aaronic Priesthood Minutes.
———. Genealogical and Minutes Book (1859–1869).
———. General Minutes.
———. Manuscript History.
Spring City Ward. Manuscript History.
———. Priesthood Minutes.
Springville Ward. Manuscript History.
St. George Temple. Baptisms for the Dead. Family History Library.
———. Endowments and Baptisms for the Dead. Family History Library.
St. Thomas Ward. Miscellaneous Records, 1865–1882, Census of St. Thomas.
———. Record of Members.
Terry, Williams Reynolds. Autobiographical Sketch, [ca. 1858].
Thomas, Marilyn Wright and Hazelmae Taylor Temple. "1835 Tax List, Sangamon County, Illinois." Family History Library.
Tithing Accounts. Daybooks B, C, Nauvoo, Illinois.
Tolton, Edward. Letter to A. M. Musser, 7 June 1867.
Trustee in Trust. Consecration Deeds, 1854–1867.
Warren Foote. Emigrating Company. Journal.
Whitney, Horace K. Diaries.
Wilcox, Linus L. Letter to Ellsworth Burr, 2 August 1840, La Harpe, Illinois. Typescript.
Williams, Electa C. Autobiography, 1885. Edward Stevenson, Collection, 1849–1922.
Williams, James Van Nostrand. Reminiscences and Diary, [ca. 1894]–1905.
Wilson, Bushrod W. Autobiography [ca. 1856], in Daughters of Utah Pioneers, Collection.
Wilson, John. Letter to George Swindle, 10 March 1868, Springville, Utah. Sketch of George and Mary Magdalena Swindle.
Wilson, Lewis Dunbar. Autobiographical Sketch.
Winter Quarters Cemetery List.
Young, Brigham. Papers.
Young, Brigham. Letter to John Lowe Butler, 29 May 1856, Salt Lake City. Brigham Young, Papers, Letterpress Copybooks.
———. Letter to Stephen Markham, 23 February 1856, Salt Lake City. Brigham Young, Papers, Letterpress Copybooks.
———. Letter to Albert K. Thurber and William Seegmiller, 13 October 1875. Brigham Young, Letterpress Copybooks.
Young, John W. Letter to Brethren Composing the Construction Camp, 28 December 1869. John W. Young, Papers.
Young, Mary Ann Angell. Letter to Brigham Young, 15 April 1841, Nauvoo, Illinois. Brigham Young, Papers, Family Correspondence.

Government Records

Arkansas. State Auditor. County Tax Records, 1829–1869, Crawford County, 2. Microfilm, Family History Library.
Fayette County, Ohio. Grantee Index to Deeds, A–D, 1810–1913. Microfilm, Family History Library.
———. Marriages, Book A, 1810–1830. Microfilm, Family History Library.
———. Tax Record, vol. 424 (1819), vol. 430 (1825). Microfilm, Family History Library.
Hancock County, Illinois. Assessor's Office. Books of Assessment, 1840, 1842, 1850. Church Archives.

———. Bond and Mortgage, Book 1, 2. Hancock County Courthouse, Carthage, Illinois.
———. Deed Book K, O. Hancock County Courthouse, Carthage, Illinois.
Henry County, Iowa. Land Deed, Books A, B. Henry County Courthouse, Mt. Pleasant, Iowa.
———. Original Entries Record [Patents]. Henry County Courthouse, Mt. Pleasant, Iowa.
Illinois. Election Returns, Index. State of Illinois, Archives Division, Springfield, Illinois.
———. Executive Record, 1818–1832, Index. State of Illinois, Archives Division, Springfield, Illinois.
———. Lists of Land Subject to Taxation in Various Counties, 1823–1838, State of Illinois, Archives Division, Springfield, Illinois.
———. Public Domain Land Tract Record Listing. State of Illinois, Archives Division, Springfield, Illinois.
Knox County, Ohio. Deed Book, A–F, 1809–1814. Mt. Vernon, Ohio. Microfilm, Family History Library.
———. Tax Record. Mt. Vernon, Ohio. Microfilm, Family History Library.
Sangamon County, Illinois. Sangamon/Logan Counties, Documents. Illinois State Historical Society, Springfield, Illinois.
Sevier County, Utah. Corporations Register. Sevier County Recorder's Office, Richfield, Utah.
———. Incorporations. Sevier County Recorder's Office, Richfield, Utah.
———. Tax Assessment and Military Enlistment Records, 1873–1918. Sevier County Recorder's Office, Richfield, Utah. Microfilm, LDS Church Archives.
State of Utah. Executive Record Books, 1850–1895. Utah State Archives, Salt Lake City, Utah.
United States. Application for Service Pension, Mexican War. National Archives, Washington, D.C.
———. Application for Service Pension, War of 1812. National Archives, Washington, D.C.
———. Compiled Service Records of Volunteer Soldiers Who Served during the Mexican War in Mormon Organizations. National Archives, Washington, D.C.
———. Eighth Census of the United States, 1860. National Archives, Washington, D.C.
———. Fifth Census of the United States, 1830. National Archives, Washington, D.C.
———. First Census of the United States, 1790. National Archives, Washington, D.C.
———. Fourth Census of the United States, 1820. National Archives, Washington, D.C.
———. Index to War of 1812 Pension Application Files. National Archives, Washington, D.C.
———. Ninth Census of the United States, 1870. National Archives, Washington, D.C.
———. Revolutionary War Pension and Bounty Land Warrant Application Files. National Archives, Washington, D.C.
———. Second Census of the United States, 1800. National Archives, Washington, D.C.
———. Seventh Census of the United States, 1850. National Archives, Washington, D.C.
———. Sixth Census of the United States, 1840. National Archives, Washington, D.C.

———. Tenth Census of the United States, 1880. National Archives, Washington, D.C.
———. Third Census of the United States, 1810. National Archives, Washington, D.C.
———. War Department, Papers on Camp Floyd, Department of Utah, 1857–1861. National Archives, Washington, D.C. Microfilm, Utah State Historical Society, Salt Lake City, Utah.
———. Works Progress Administration. Collection. Utah State Historical Society, Salt Lake City, Utah.
———. Works Progress Administration. Historical Records Survey. *Inventory of the County Archives of Ohio, No. 42, Knox County (Mr. Vernon) I, 1939*. Columbus, Ohio.
Utah County, Utah. Utah County Records, Book H. Utah County Recorder's Office, Provo, Utah.
Utah Territory. Census Schedules, 1850, 1860, 1870. Church Archives.

Interviews

Briscoe, Franklin Verner. Interview by Ronald O. Barney, 14 August 1976, Willow Flats, Idaho. Typescript in possession of author.
Perkins, Edna Briscoe and Elda Barney Gillen. Interview by Raymond G. Briscoe, ca. 1978. Typescript in possession of author.

Theses and Dissertations

Bachman, Danel W. "A Study of the Mormon Practice of Plural Marriage before the Death of Joseph Smith." Master's thesis, Purdue University, 1975.
Baglier, Janet Dorothy. "The Niagara Frontier: Society and Economy in Western New York and Upper Canada, 1794–1854." Ph.D. diss., State University of New York, Buffalo, 1993.
Ellsworth, S. George. "A History of Mormon Missions in the United States and Canada, 1830–1860." Ph.D. diss., University of California, 1951.
Fish, Rick J. "The Southern Utah Expedition of Parley P. Pratt, 1849–1850." Master's thesis, Brigham Young University, 1992.
Peterson, Charles S. "A Historical Analysis of Territorial Government in Utah under Alfred Cumming, 1857–1861." Master's thesis, Brigham Young University, 1958.
Peterson, Paul H. "The Mormon Reformation." Ph.D. diss., Brigham Young University, 1981.
Raber, Michael Scott. "Religious Polity and Local Production: The Origins of Mormon Town." Ph.D. diss., Yale University, 1978.
Reeder, Clarence A. "The History of Utah's Railroads, 1869–1883." Ph.D. diss., University of Utah, 1970.

Index